PERSONAL GROWTH AND BEHAVIOR 82/83

Nathaniel Jackson, *Editor*
El Camino College

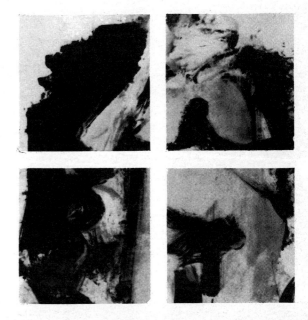

Cover Painting:
NATIONAL MUSEUM OF AMERICAN ART, Smithsonian Institution:
Willem De Kooning, WOMAN VIII, 1961, Gift of S.C. Johnson and Son, Inc.

ANNUAL EDITIONS

The Dushkin Publishing Group, Inc. Sluice Dock, Guilford, Ct. 06437

Volumes in the Annual Editions Series

● Indicates currently available

Fourth Edition

Manufactured by George Banta Company, Menasha, Wisconsin, 54952

Library of Congress Cataloging in Publication Data
Main entry under title:
Annual editions: Personal growth and behavior.
    1. Personality—Periodicals. 2. Adjustment (Psychology)—Periodicals. I. Title: Personal growth and behavior.
155.2' 05   75-20757
ISBN 0-87967-386-9

CONTENTS

1

Becoming a Person: Seeking Self-Identity

2

Sex Roles and Sex Differences

3

Determinants of Behavior: Motivation, Environment, and Physiology

4

Problems
Influencing
Personal Growth

5

Relating
to Others

6

Dynamics of Maladjustment: The Individual and Society

7

Enhancing Human Adjustment: Learning to Cope Effectively

TOPIC GUIDE

This topic guide can be used to correlate each of the articles in *Personal Growth and Behavior 82/83* to one or more of the topics normally covered by textbooks used in personal growth and behavior courses. Each article corresponds to a given topic area according to whether it deals with the subject in a primary or secondary fashion. These correlations are intended for use as a general study guide and do not necessarily define the total coverage of any given article.

TOPIC AREA	TREATED AS A PRIMARY ISSUE IN:	TREATED AS A SECONDARY ISSUE IN:
Aggression	6. What We Know and Don't Know About Sex Differences 8. How Nursery Schools Teach Girls to Shut Up 10. The Psychological Pressures on the American Male	7. Males and Females 14. The American Compulsion to Win
Aging	21. The Age of Melancholy 25. Living Longer	12. Breaking Out of the Lockstep 14. The American Compulsion to Win 22. When Husband and Wife Disagree About Sex 32. The Masked Generation
Behavior Control	7. Males and Females 8. How Nursery Schools Teach Girls to Shut Up 10. The Psychological Pressures on the American Male 15. Changing Channels 16. The Promise of Biological Psychiatry 32. The Masked Generation 38. Prisoners of Fear	12. Breaking Out of the Lockstep 14. The American Compulsion to Win 22. When Husband and Wife Disagree About Sex
Family Life	26. When Mommy Goes to Work . . . 27. The Father of the Child	22. When Husband and Wife Disagree About Sex 30. Coupling, Marriage and Growth
Learning	4. Does Personality Really Change After 20? 8. How Nursery Schools Teach Girls to Shut Up 32. The Masked Generation 42. Psychological Hardiness	2. Erik Erikson's Eight Ages of Man 44. You Are What You Do 45. Examine Yourself, and Find Your Future
Motivation	13. New Psychology 14. The American Compulsion to Win 15. Changing Channels	8. How Nursery Schools Teach Girls to Shut Up 12. Breaking Out of the Lockstep 17. The Puzzle of Obesity
Psychobiology	4. Does Personality Really Change After 20? 7. Males and Females 16. The Promise of Biological Psychiatry	17. The Puzzle of Obesity 18. Mental Patterns of Disease 25. Living Longer 39. New Light on Schizophrenia
Psychology and Society	10. The Psychological Pressures on the American Male 12. Breaking Out of the Lockstep 32. The Masked Generation 35. On Being Sane in Insane Places 36. A Darkness at Noon 37. Boredom 40. Tracking the Causes of Madness 41. Health as Transcendence of Environment	3. Adolescent Americans 7. Males and Females 8. How Nursery Schools Teach Girls to Shut Up 11. Androgyny 14. The American Compulsion to Win 25. Living Longer 33. The Good a Good Friend Can Do 42. Psychological Hardiness

TOPIC AREA	TREATED AS A PRIMARY ISSUE IN:	TREATED AS A SECONDARY ISSUE IN:
Relating to Others	22. When Husband and Wife Disagree About Sex 28. Disclosing Oneself to Others 29. Loneliness 30. Coupling, Marriage and Growth 31. The Sexual Balance of Power 33. The Good a Good Friend Can Do 44. You Are What You Do 45. Examine Yourself, and Find Your Future	4. Does Personality Really Change After 20? 15. Changing Channels 16. The Promise of Biological Psychiatry 26. When Mommy Goes to Work . . . 27. The Father of the Child
Self-Concept	1. What It Means to Become a Person 3. Adolescent Americans 5. Becoming One's Own Man 12. Breaking Out of the Lockstep 29. Loneliness 34. R.D. Laing 44. You Are What You Do 45. Examine Yourself, and Find Your Future	9. The More Sorrowful Sex 10. The Psychological Pressures on the American Male 11. Androgyny 17. The Puzzle of Obesity 38. Prisoners of Fear
Stress	12. Breaking Out of the Lockstep 20. That Helpless Feeling 42. Psychological Hardiness 46. Fired!	19. Anxiety 22. When Husband and Wife Disagree About Sex 23. "Old" Is Not a Four-Letter Word 24. Facing Up to Death 32. The Masked Generation
Therapy	16. The Promise of Biological Psychiatry 22. When Husband and Wife Disagree About Sex 43. Shopping for the Right Therapy	32. The Masked Generation 33. The Good a Good Friend Can Do 38. Prisoners of Fear 40. Tracking the Causes of Madness 45. Examine Yourself, and Find Your Future

PREFACE

Behavior is a dynamic process influenced by factors of heredity and environment. The individual is constantly modifying his or her behavior according to the challenges encountered in daily living. The purpose of this anthology is to provide a survey of how the so-called "normal" personality relates to other individuals and to stress.

Annual Editions: Personal Growth and Behavior 82/83 is about people. It describes ways in which people behave with one another and explains how they react to common situations. It is intended to offer an overview of the different approaches taken in the field of psychology to illuminate human behavior. The articles collected here reflect both the current interests of people working actively in the field as well as some classic viewpoints. Each article has been carefully reviewed by the editor, the Annual Editions staff, and members of the advisory board listed in the front of this book.

We feel that *Annual Editions: Personal Growth and Behavior 82/83* is one of the most useful and current collections available for the student of introductory psychology or personal adjustment. The articles focus on personal development as a dynamic process of growth and behavior. It is kept up-to-date through annual revision, which depends on feedback and suggestions from the people who use it. Please take the time to return the post-paid article rating form on the last page of this book with your comments.

Nathaniel Jackson,
Editor

Becoming a Person: Seeking Self-Identity

1

From infancy through old age people face the continuous challenge, pain, and reward of self-discovery and change. Everyone shares the problems of developing a sense of identity. Psychologists have identified certain recognizable stages in this process of personal growth, and this section deals with these stages.

The infant's concerns—nourishment, comfort, protection—are primarily biological. But the quality of care a child receives at this time can seriously affect later emotional maturity. When the infant reaches toddlerhood, dependency, while still great, is modified by a growing sense of autonomy. By the time a child enters school, his or her world has enlarged beyond the home to encompass the growing influence of peers and social institutions.

Adolescence marks the transition from childhood to adulthood. It is a time of dramatic and often dismaying physical and emotional changes, each of which is experienced with intense heightened self-consciousness. During this time the intellect stretches far beyond experience, often providing a radically different way of looking at things. It is not surprising that self-identity may be elusive at this stage, given conflict with family and peers, academic pressures, increasing sexual activity, and perhaps experimentation with alcohol and drugs. The adolescent is no stranger to anxiety.

Maturity implies more than age. It might be defined as that state in which the individual acts more than he or she is acted upon. It involves the ability to make moral as well as empirical judgments. Choices are made; goals set. This stage of development is often defined largely by family and work.

The years of maturity are characterized by growth in career and family. Middle age, generally conceived as beginning in the mid- to late forties, may be characterized as self-assessing and consolidating. Successes and failures are tallied with an increasing sense of urgency, as career mobility often levels off and the family is no longer the dynamic entity it once was. On the positive side, the individual may come to feel an increasing confidence in his or her abilities, which is reflected in a feeling of authority.

Old age is generally a time of reflection. It is a time to draw enjoyment from past achievements or perhaps despair from failures. The challenges of this period may include a decline in overall health, deaths of friends and spouses, and retirement—all demanding some of the most difficult adjustments of a lifetime.

No doors are closed between the stages of life outlined here. The process of becoming a person occurs in a constant state of flux, and is in many ways circular. What are some of the similarities in each stage of growth? To what extent does the mature individual reflect his or her childhood, and how does rearing influence the child?

What It Means to Become
A Person

CARL R. ROGERS

Carl R. Rogers, psychologist and psychotherapist, is famous for his client-centered approach to personality and psychotherapy.

A frequently-raised question is: "What problems do people bring to you and other counselors at the Counseling Center?" I always feel baffled by this question. One reply is that they bring every kind of problem one can imagine, and quite a number that I believe no one would imagine. There is the student concerned about failing in college; the housewife disturbed about her marriage; the individual who feels he is teetering on the edge of a complete breakdown or psychosis; the responsible professional man who spends much of his time in sexual fantasies and functions inefficiently in his work; the brilliant student, at the top of his class, who is paralyzed by the conviction that he is hopelessly and helplessly inadequate; the parent who is distressed by his child's behavior; the popular girl who finds herself unaccountably overtaken by sharp spells of black depression; the woman who fears that life and love are passing her by, and that her good graduate record is a poor recompense; the man who has become convinced that powerful and sinister forces are plotting against him;—I could go on and on with the many different and unique problems which people bring to us. They run the gamut of life's experiences. Yet there is no satisfaction in giving this type of catalog, for, as counselor, I know that the problem as stated in the first interview will not be the problem as seen in the second or third hour, and by the tenth interview it will be a still different problem or series of problems. You can see why I feel baffled as to how to answer this simple question.

I have however come to believe that in spite of this bewildering horizontal multiplicity, and the layer upon layer of vertical complexity, there is a simple answer. As I follow the experience of many clients in the therapeutic relationship which we endeavor to create for them, it seems to me that each one has the same problem. Below the level of the problem situation about which the individual is complaining—behind the trouble with studies, or wife, or employer, or with his own uncontrollable or bizarre behavior, or with his frightening feelings, lies one central search. It seems to me that at bottom each person as asking: "Who am I, *really?* How can I get in touch with this real self, underlying all my surface behavior? How can I become myself?"

THE PROCESS OF BECOMING

Getting Behind the Mask

Let me try to explain what I mean when I say that it appears that the goal the individual most wishes to achieve, the end which he knowingly and unknowingly pursues, is to become himself.

When a person comes to me, troubled by his unique combination of difficulties, I have found it most worth while to try to create a relationship with him in which he is safe and free. It is my purpose to understand the way he feels in his own inner world, to accept him as he is, to create an atmosphere of freedom in which he can move in his thinking and feeling and being, in any direction he desires. How does he use this freedom?

It is my experience that he uses it to become more and more himself. He begins to drop the false fronts, or the masks, or the roles, with which he has faced life. He appears to be trying to discover something more basic, something more truly himself. At first he lays aside masks which he is to some degree aware of using. One young woman describes in a counseling interview one of the masks she has been using, and how uncertain she is whether underneath this appeasing, ingratiating front there is any real self with convictions.

> I was thinking about this business of standards. I somehow developed a sort of knack, I guess, of—well—a habit—of trying to make people feel at ease around me, or to make things go along smoothly. There always had to be some appeaser around, being sorta the oil that soothed the waters. At a small meeting, or a little party, or something—I could help things go along nicely and appear to be having a good time. And sometimes I'd surprise myself by arguing against what I really thought when I saw that the person in charge would be quite unhappy about it if I didn't. In other words I just wasn't ever—I mean, I didn't find myself ever being set and definite about things. Now the reason why I did it probably was I'd been doing it around home so much. I just didn't stand up for my own convictions, until I don't know whether I have any convictions to stand up for. I haven't been really honestly being myself, or actually knowing what my real self is, and I've been just playing a sort of false role.

You can, in this excerpt, see her examining the mask she has been using, recognizing her dissatisfaction with it, and wondering how to get to the real self underneath, if such a self exists.

In this attempt to discover his own self, the client typically uses the therapeutic relationship to explore, to examine the various aspects of his own experience, to recognize and face up to the deep contradictions which he often discovers. He learns how much of his behavior, even how much of the feeling he experiences, is not real, is not something which flows from the genuine reactions of his organism, but is a facade, a front, behind which he has been hiding. He discovers how much of his life is guided by what he thinks he *should* be, not by what he is. Often he discovers that he exists only in response to the demands of others, that he seems to have no self of his own, that he is only trying to think, and feel,

From lectures delivered at Oberlin College under auspices of Her Wellie Heldt Lecture Fund. Copyright © Board of Trustees of Oberlin College, 1954.

and behave in the way that others believe he *ought* to think, and feel, and behave.

In this connection I have been astonished to find how accurately the Danish philosopher, Soren Kierkegaard, pictured the dilemma of the individual more than a century ago, with keen psychological insight. He points out that the most common despair is to be in despair at not choosing, or willing, to be one's self; but that the deepest form of despair is to choose "to be another than himself." On the other hand "to will to be that self which one truly is, is indeed the opposite of despair," and this choice is the deepest responsibility of man. As I read some of his writings I almost feel that he must have listened in on the statements made by our clients as they search and explore for the reality of self—often a painful and troubling search.

This exploration becomes even more disturbing when they find themselves involved in removing the false faces which they had not known were false faces. They begin to engage in the frightening task of exploring the turbulent and sometimes violent feelings within themselves. To remove a mask which you had thought was part of your real self can be a deeply disturbing experience, yet when there is freedom to think and feel and be, the individual moves toward such a goal. A few statements from a person who had completed a series of psychotherapeutic interviews, will illustrate this. She uses many metaphors as she tells how she struggled to get to the core of herself.

> As I look at it now, I was peeling off layer after layer of defenses, I'd build them up, try them, and then discard them when you remained the same. I didn't know what was at the bottom and I was very much afraid to find out, but I *had* to keep on trying. At first I felt there was *nothing* within me—just a great emptiness where I needed and wanted a solid core. Then I began to feel that I was facing a solid brick wall, too high to get over and too thick to go through. One day the wall became translucent, rather than solid. After this, the wall seemed to disappear, but beyond it I discovered a dam holding back violent, churning waters. I felt as if I were holding back the force of these waters and if I opened even a tiny hole I and all about me would be destroyed in the ensuing torrent of feelings represented by the water. Finally I could stand the strain no longer and I let go. All I did, actually, was to succumb to complete and utter self-pity, then hate, then love. After this experience, I felt as if I had leaped a brink and was safely on the other side, though still tottering a bit on the edge. I don't know what I was searching for or where I was going, but I felt then, as I have always felt whenever I really lived, that I was moving forward.

I believe this represents rather well the feelings of many an individual that if the false front, the wall, the dam, is not maintained, then everything will be swept away in the violence of the feelings that he discovers pent-up in his private world. Yet it also illustrates the compelling necessity which the individual feels to search for and become himself. It also begins to indicate the way in which the individual determines the reality in himself—that when he fully experiences the feelings which at an organic level he *is*, as this client experienced her self-pity, hatred, and love, then he feels an assurance that he is being a part of his real self.

The Experiencing of Feeling

I would like to say something more about this experiencing of feeling. It is really the discovery of unknown elements of self. The phenomenon I am trying to describe is something which I think is quite difficult to get across in any meaningful way. In our daily lives there are a thousand and one reasons for not letting ourselves experience our attitudes fully, reasons from our past and from the present, reasons that reside within the social situation. It seems too dangerous, too potentially damaging, to experience them freely and fully. But in the safety and freedom of the therapeutic relationship, they can be experienced fully, clear to the limit of what they are. They can be and are experienced in a fashion that I like to think of as a "pure culture," so that for the moment the person

is his fear, or he *is* his anger, or he *is* his tenderness, or whatever.

Perhaps again I can indicate that somewhat better by giving an example from a client that will indicate and convey something of what I mean. This comes from the recording of the thirty-first interview with this woman. She has talked several times of a recurrent feeling which troubles her and which she can't quite pin down and define. Is it a feeling that developed because she practically had no relationship with her parents? Is it a guilty feeling? She is not quite sure, and she ends this kind of talk with this statement:

> Client: And I have the feeling that it isn't guilt. (Pause: she weeps) So . . . course I mean, I can't verbalize it yet. It's just being *terribly hurt!*
>
> Therapist: M-hm. It isn't guilt except in the sense of being very much wounded somehow.
>
> C: (Weeping) It's . . . you know, often I've been guilty of it myself, but in later years, when I've heard parents . . . say to their children, "stop crying," I've had a feeling, as though, well, why should they tell them to stop crying? They feel sorry for themselves, and who can feel more adequately sorry for himself than a child. Well, that is sort of what . . . I mean, as-as though I thought that they should let him cry. And . . . feel sorry for him too, maybe. In a . . . rather objective kind of way. Well, that's . . . that's something of the kind of thing I've been experiencing. I mean, now . . . just right now.
>
> T: That catches a little more of the flavor of the feeling, that it's almost as if you're really weeping for yourself. . . .
>
> C: And then of course, I've come to . . . to see and to feel that over this . . . see, I've covered it up. (Weeps) I've covered it up with so much *bitterness*, which in turn I've had to cover up. (Weeps) *That's* what I want to get rid of! I almost don't *care* if I hurt.
>
> T: (Gently) You feel that here at the basis of it as you experienced it, is a feeling of real tears for yourself. But that you *can't* show, mustn't show, so that's been covered by bitterness that you don't like, that you'd like to be rid of. You almost feel you'd rather absorb the hurt than to . . . than to feel the bitterness. (Pause) And what you seem to be saying quite strongly is, I do *hurt*, and I've tried to cover it up.
>
> C: I didn't *know* it.
>
> T: M-hm. Like a new discovery really.
>
> C: (Speaking at the same time) I never really did know. It's almost a physical thing. It's . . . it's sort of as though I were looking within myself at all kinds of . . . nerve endings and-and bits of-of . . . things that have been sort of mashed. (Weeping)
>
> T: As though some of the most delicate aspects of you—physically almost —have been crushed or hurt.
>
> C: Yes. And you know, I do get the feeling, oh, you poor thing. (Pause)
>
> T: Just can't help but feel very deeply sorry for the person that is you.

I hope that perhaps this excerpt conveys a little bit of the thing I have been talking about, the experiencing of a feeling all the way to the limit. She was feeling herself as though she were nothing but hurt at that moment, nothing but sorrow for her crushed self. It is not only hurt and sorrow that are experienced in this all-out kind of fashion. It may be jealousy, or destructive anger, or deep desire, or confidence and pride, or sensitive tenderness, or shuddering fear, or outgoing love. It may be any of the emotions of which man is capable.

What I have gradually learned from experiences such as this is that the individual in such a moment is coming to *be* what he *is*. When a person has, throughout therapy, experienced in this fashion all the emotions which organismically arise in him, and has experienced them in this knowing and open manner, then he has experienced *himself*, in all the richness that exists within himself. He has become what he is.

The Discovery of Self in Experience

Let us pursue a bit further this question of what it means to become one's self. It is a most perplexing question and again I will try to take from a statement by a client, written between interviews, a suggestion of an answer. She tells how the various facades by which she has been living have somehow crumpled and collapsed, bringing a feeling of confusion, but also a feeling of relief.

1. BECOMING A PERSON

She continues:

> You know, it seems as if all the energy that went into holding the arbitrary pattern together was quite unnecessary—a waste. You think you have to make the pattern yourself; but there are so many pieces, and it's so hard to see where they fit. Sometimes you put them in the wrong place, and the more pieces not fitted, the more effort it takes to hold them in place, until at last you are so tired that even that awful confusion is better than holding on any longer. Then you discover that left to themselves the jumbled pieces fall quite naturally into their own places, and a living pattern emerges without any effort at all on your part. Your job is just to discover it, and in the course of that, you will find yourself. You must even let your own experience tell you its own meaning; the minute *you* tell it what it means, you are at war with yourself.

Let me see if I can take her poetic expression and translate it into the meaning it has for me. I believe she is saying that to be herself means to find the pattern, the underlying order, which exists in the ceaselessly changing flow of her experience. Rather than to try to hold her experience into the form of a mask, or to make it be a form or structure that it is not, being herself means to discover the unity and harmony which exists in her own actual feelings and reactions. It means that the real self is something which is comfortably discovered *in* one's experience, not something imposed *upon* it.

Through giving excerpts from the statements of these clients, I have been trying to suggest what happens in the warmth and understanding of a facilitating relationship with a therapist. It seems that gradually, painfully, the individual explores what is behind the masks he presents to the world, and even behind the masks with which he has been deceiving himself. Deeply and often vividly he experiences the various elements of himself which have been hidden within. Thus to an increasing degree he becomes himself—not a facade of conformity to others, nor a cynical denial of all feeling, nor a front of intellectual rationality, but a living, breathing, feeling, fluctuating process—in short, he becomes a person.

The Person Who Emerges

I imagine that some of you are asking: "But what *kind* of a person does he become? It isn't enough to say that he drops the facades. What kind of person lies underneath?" Since one of the most obvious facts is that each individual tends to become a separate and distinct and unique person, the answer is not easy. However I would like to point out some of the characteristic trends which I see. No one person would fully exemplify these characteristics, no one person fully achieves the description I will give, but I do see certain generalizations which can be drawn, based upon living a therapeutic relationship with many clients.

Openness to Experience

First of all I would say that in this process the individual becomes more open to his experience. This is a phrase which has come to have a great deal of meaning to me. It is the opposite of defensiveness. Psychological research has shown the way in which sensory evidence, if it runs contrary to the pattern of organization of the self, tends to be distorted in awareness. In other words we cannot see all that our senses report, but only the things which fit the picture we have.

Now in a safe relationship of the sort I have described, this defensiveness, or rigidity, tends to be replaced by an increasing openness to experience. The individual becomes more openly aware of his own feelings and attitudes as they exist in him at an organic level. He also becomes more aware of reality as it exists outside of himself, instead of perceiving it in preconceived categories. He sees that not all trees are green, not all men are stern fathers, not all women are rejecting, not all failure experiences prove that he is no good, and the like. He is able to take in the evidence in a new situation, *as it is*, rather than distorting it to fit a pattern which he already holds. As you might expect, this increasing ability to be open to experience makes him far more realistic in dealing with new people, new situations, new problems. It means that his beliefs are not rigid, that he can tolerate ambiguity. He can receive much conflicting evidence without forcing closure upon the situation. This openness of awareness to what exists at *this moment* in *this situation* is, I believe, an important element in the description of the person who emerges from therapy.

Perhaps I can give this concept a more vivid meaning if I illustrate it from a recorded interview. A young professional man reports in the forty-eighth interview the way in which he has become more open to some of his bodily sensations, as well as other feelings.

> Client: It doesn't seem to me that it would be possible for anybody to relate all the changes that I feel. But I certainly have felt recently that I have more respect for, more objectivity toward, my physical makeup. I mean I don't expect too much of myself. This is how it works out. It feels to me that in the past I used to fight a certain tiredness that I felt after supper. Well, now I feel pretty sure that I really *am* tired—that I am not making myself tired—that I am just physiologically lower. It seemed that I was just constantly criticizing my tiredness.
>
> Therapist: So you can let yourself *be* tired, instead of feeling along with it a kind of criticism of it.
>
> C: Yes, that I shouldn't be tired or something. And it seems in a way to be pretty profound that I can just not fight this tiredness, and along with it goes a real feeling that being tired isn't such an awful thing. I think I can also kind of pick up a thread here of why I should be that way in the way my father is and the way he looks at some of these things. For instance, say that I was sick, and I would report this, and it would seem that overtly he would want to do something about it but he would also communicate, "Oh, my gosh, more trouble." You know, something like that.
>
> T: As though there were something quite annoying really about being physically ill.
>
> C: Yeah, I am sure that my father has the same disrespect for his own physiology that I have had. Now last summer I twisted my back, I wrenched it, I heard it snap and everything. There was real pain there all the time at first, real sharp. And I had the doctor look at it and he said it wasn't serious, it should heal by itself as long as I didn't bend too much. Well this was months ago—and I have been noticing recently that—hell, this is real pain and it's still there—and it's not my fault.
>
> T: It doesn't prove something bad about you—
>
> C: No—and one of the reasons I seem to get more tired than I should maybe is because of this constant strain and so—I have already made an appointment with one of the doctors at the hospital that he would look at it and take an X-ray or something. In a way I guess you could say that I am just more accurately or objectively sensitive to this kind of thing. I can say with certainty that this has also spread to what I eat and how much I eat. And this is really a profound change, and of course my relationship with my wife and the two children is—well, you just wouldn't recognize it if you could see me inside—as you have—I mean—there just doesn't seem to be anything more wonderful than really and genuinely—really *feeling* love for your own children and at the same time receiving it. I don't know how to put this. We have such an increased respect—both of us—for Judy and we've noticed just—as we participated in this—we have noticed such a tremendous change in her—it seems to be a pretty deep kind of thing.
>
> T: It seems to me you are saying that you can listen more accurately to yourself. If your body says its tired, you listen to it and believe it, instead of criticizing it; if it's in pain, you can listen to that; if the feeling is really loving your wife or children, you can *feel* that, and it seems to show up in the differences in them too.

Here, in a relatively minor but symbolically important excerpt, can be seen much of what I have been trying to say about openness to experience. Formerly he could not freely feel pain or illness, because being ill meant being unacceptable. Neither could he feel tenderness and love for his child, because such feelings meant being weak, and he had to maintain his facade of being strong and masculine. But now he can be genuinely open to the experiences of his organism—he can be tired when he is tired, he can feel pain when his organism is in pain, he can freely experience the love he feels for his daughter, and he can also feel and express annoyance toward her, as he goes on to say in the next portion of the interview. He can fully live the experiences of his total organism, rather than shutting them out of awareness.

Trust in One's Organism

A second characteristic of the persons who emerge from therapy is that the person increasingly discovers that his own organism is trustworthy, that it is a suitable instrument for discovering the most satisfying behavior in each immediate situation.

If this seems strange, let me try to state it more fully. Perhaps it will help to understand my description if you think of the individual as faced with some existential choice: "Shall I go home to my family during vacation, or strike out on my own?" "Shall I drink this third cocktail which is being offered?" "Is this the person whom I would like to have as my partner in love and in life?" Thinking of such situations, what seems to be true of the person who emerges from the therapeutic process? To the extent that this person is open to all of his experience, he has access to all of the available data in the situation on which to base his behavior. He has knowledge of his own feelings and impulses, which are often complex and contradictory. He is freely able to sense the social demands, from the relatively rigid social "laws" to the desires of friends and family. He has access to his memories of similar situations, and the consequences of different behaviors in those situations. He has a relatively accurate perception of this existential situation in all of its complexity. He is better able to permit his total organism, his conscious thought participating, to consider, weigh, and balance each stimulus, need, and demand, and its relative weight and intensity. Out of this complex weighing and balancing he is able to discover that course of action which seems to come closest to satisfying all his needs in the situation, long-range as well as immediate needs.

In such a weighing and balancing of all of the components of a given life choice, his organism would not by any means be infallible. Mistaken choices might be made. But because he tends to be open to his experience, there is a greater and more immediate awareness of unsatisfying consequences, a quicker correction of choices which are in error.

It may help to realize that in most of us the defects which interfere with this weighing and balancing are that we include things which are not a part of our experience, and exclude elements which are. Thus an individual may persist in the concept that "I can handle liquor," when openness to his past experience would indicate that this is scarcely correct. Or a young woman may see only the good qualities of her prospective mate, where an openness to experience would indicate that he possesses faults as well.

In general, then, it appears to be true that when a client is open to his experience, he comes to find his organism more trustworthy. He feels less fear of the emotional reactions which he has. There is a gradual growth of trust in, and even affection for, the complex, rich, varied assortment of feelings and tendencies which exist in him at the organic level. Consciousness, instead of being the watchman over a dangerous and unpredictable lot of impulses, of which few can be permitted to see the light of day, becomes the comfortable inhabitant of a society of impulses and feelings and thoughts, which are discovered to be very satisfactorily self-governing when not fearfully guarded.

An Internal Locus of Evaluation

Another trend which is evident in this process of becoming a person relates to the source or locus of choices and decisions, of evaluative judgments. The individual increasingly comes to feel that this locus of evaluation lies within himself. Less and less does he look to others for approval or disapproval; for standards to live by; for decisions and choices. He recognizes that it rests within himself to choose; that the only question which matters is: "Am I living in a way which is deeply satisfying to me, and which truly expresses me?" This I think is perhaps *the* most important question for the creative individual.

Perhaps it will help if I give an illustration. I would like to give a brief portion of a recorded interview with a young woman, a graduate student, who had come for counseling help. She was initially very much disturbed about many problems, and had been contemplating suicide. During the interviews one of the feelings she discovered was her great desire to be dependent, just to let someone else take over the direction of her life. She was very critical of those who had not given her enough guidance. She talked about one after another of her professors, feeling bitterly that none of them had taught her anything with deep meaning. Gradually she began to realize that part of the difficulty was the fact that she had taken no initiative in *participating* in these classes. Then comes the portion I wish to quote.

I think you will find that this excerpt gives you some indication of what it means in experience to accept the locus of evaluation as being within oneself. Here then is the quotation from one of the later interviews with this young woman as she has begun to realize that perhaps she is partly responsible for the deficiencies in her own education.

Client: Well now, I wonder if I've been going around doing that, getting smatterings of things, and not getting hold, not really getting down to things.

Therapist: Maybe you've been getting just spoonfuls here and there rather than really digging in somewhere rather deeply.

C: M-hm. That's why I say—(slowly and very thoughtfully) well, with that sort of a foundation, well, it's really up to *me*. I mean, it seems to be really apparent to me that I *can't depend on someone else* to give me an education. (very softly) I'll really have to get it myself.

T: It really begins to come home—there's only one person that can educate you—a realization that perhaps nobody else *can give* you an education.

C: M-hm. (long pause—while she sits thinking) I have all the symptoms of fright. (laughs softly).

T: Fright? That this is a scary thing, is that what you mean?

C: M-hm. (very long pause—obviously struggling with feelings in herself).

T: Do you want to say any more about what you mean by that? That it really does give you the symptoms of fright?

C: (laughs) I, uh—I don't know whether I quite know. I mean—well, it really seems like I'm cut loose (pause), and it seems that I'm very—I don't know—in a vulnerable position, but I, uh, I brought this up and it, uh, somehow it almost came out without my saying it. It seems to be—it's something I let out.

T: Hardly a part of you.

C: Well, I felt surprised.

T: As though: "Well for goodness sake, did I say that?" (both chuckle).

C: Really, I don't think I've had that feeling before. I've—uh, well, this really feels like I'm saying something that, uh, *is* a part of me really. (pause) Or, uh, (quite perplexed) it feels like I sort of have, uh, I don't know. I have a feeling of *strength*, and yet, I have a feeling of—realizing it's so sort of fearful, of fright.

T: That is, do you mean that saying something of that sort gives you at the same time a feeling of, of strength in saying it, and yet at the same time a frightened feeling of *what* you have said, is that it?

C: M-hm. I am feeling that. For instance, I'm feeling it internally now—a sort of surging up, or force. As if that's something really big and strong. And yet, uh, well at first it was almost a physical feeling of just being out alone, and sort of cut off from a—support I had been carrying around.

T: You feel that it's something deep and strong, and surging forth, and at the same time, you just feel as though you'd cut yourself loose from any support when you say it.

C: M-hm Maybe that's—I don't know—it's a disturbance of a kind of pattern I've been carrying around, I think.

1. BECOMING A PERSON

T: It sort of shakes a rather significant pattern, jars it loose.

C: M-hm. (pause, then cautiously, but with conviction) I, I think—I don't know, but I have the feeling that then I am going to begin to *do* more things that I know I should do. . . . There are so many things that I need to do. It seems in so many avenues of my living I have to work out new ways of behaving, but—maybe—I can see myself doing a little better in some things.

I hope that this illustration gives some sense of the strength which is experienced in being a unique person, responsible for oneself, and also the uneasiness that accompanies this assumption of responsibility.

Willingness to be a Process

I should like to point out one final characteristic of these individuals as they strive to discover and become themselves. It is that the individual seems to become more content to be a process than a product. When he enters the therapeutic relationship, the client is likely to wish to achieve some fixed state; he wants to reach the point where his problems are solved, or where he is effective in his work, or where his marriage is satisfactory. He tends, in the freedom of the therapeutic relationship, to drop such fixed goals, and to accept a more satisfying realization that he is not a fixed entity, but a process of becoming.

One client, at the conclusion of therapy, says in rather puzzled fashion: "I haven't finished the job of integrating and reorganizing myself, but that's only confusing, not discouraging, now that I realize this is a continuing process. . . . It is exciting, sometimes upsetting, but deeply encouraging to feel yourself in action, apparently knowing where you are going even though you don't always consciously know what that is." One can see here both the expression of trust in the organism, which I have mentioned, and also the realization of self as a process.

Here is another statement of this same element of fluidity of existential living. "This whole train of experiencing, and the meanings that I have thus far discovered in it, seem to have launched me on a process which is both fascinating and at times a little frightening. It seems to mean letting my experience carry me on, in a direction which appears to be forward, toward goals that I can but dimly define, as I try to understand at least the current mean-

ing of that experience. The sensation is that of floating with a complex stream of experience, with the fascinating possibility of trying to comprehend its ever-changing complexity." Here again is a personal description of what it seems like to accept oneself as a stream of becoming, not a finished product. It means that a person is a fluid process, not a fixed and static entity; a flowing river of change, not a block of solid material; a continually changing constellation of potentialities, not a fixed quantity of traits.

CONCLUSION

I have tried to tell you what has seemed to occur in the lives of people with whom I have had the privilege of being in a relationship as they struggled toward becoming themselves. I have endeavored to describe, as accurately as I can, the meanings which seem to be involved in this process of becoming a person. I am sure that I do not see it clearly or completely, since I keep changing in my comprehension and understanding of it. I hope you will accept it as a current and tentative picture, not as something final.

One reason for stressing the tentative nature of what I have said is that I wish to make it clear that I am *not* saying: "This is what you should become; here is the goal for you." Rather, I am saying that these are some of the meanings I see in the experiences that my clients and I have shared. Perhaps this picture of the experience of others may illuminate or give more meaning to some of your own experiences.

I have pointed out that the individual appears to have a strong desire to become himself; that given a favorable psychological climate he drops the defensive masks with which he has faced life, and begins to discover and to experience the stranger who lives behind these masks—the hidden parts of himself. I have pictured some of the attributes of the person who emerges—the tendency to be more open to all elements of his organic experience; the growth of trust in one's organism as an instrument of sensitive living; the acceptance of the fearsome responsibility of being a unique person; and finally the sense of living in one's life as a participant in a fluid, ongoing process, continually discovering new aspects of one's self in the flow of experience. These are some of the things which seem to me to be involved in becoming a person.

Erik Erikson's Eight Ages Of Man
One man in his time plays many psychosocial parts

David Elkind

DAVID ELKIND *is professor of psychology and psychiatry at the University of Rochester.*

At a recent faculty reception I happened to join a small group in which a young mother was talking about her "identity crisis." She and her husband, she said, had decided not to have any more children and she was depressed at the thought of being past the child-bearing stage. It was as if, she continued, she had been robbed of some part of herself and now needed to find a new function to replace the old one.

When I remarked that her story sounded like a case history from a book by Erik Erikson, she replied, "Who's Erikson?" It is a reflection on the intellectual modesty and literary decorum of Erik H. Erikson, psychoanalyst and professor of developmental psychology at Harvard, that so few of the many people who today talk about the "identity crisis" know anthing of the man who pointed out its pervasiveness as a problem in contemporary society two decades ago.

Erikson has, however, contributed more to social science than his delineation of identity problems in modern man. His descriptions of the stages of the life cycle, for example, have advanced psychoanalytic theory to the point where it can now describe the development of the healthy personality on its own terms and not merely as the opposite of a sick one. Likewise, Erikson's emphasis upon the problems unique to adolescents and adults living in today's society has helped to rectify the one-sided emphasis on childhood as the beginning and end of personality development.

Finally, in his biographical studies, such as "Young Man Luther" and "Gandhi's Truth" (which has just won a National Book Award in philosophy and religion), Erikson emphasizes the inherent strengths of the human personality by showing how individuals can use their neurotic symptoms and conflicts for creative and constructive social purposes while healing themselves in the process.

It is important to emphasize that Erikson's contributions are genuine advances in psychoanalysis in the sense that Erikson accepts and builds upon many of the basic tenets of Freudian theory. In this regard, Erikson differs from Freud's early co-workers such as Jung and Adler who, when they broke with Freud, rejected his theories and substituted their own.

Likewise, Erikson also differs from the so-called neo-Freudians such as Horney, Kardiner and Sullivan who (mistakenly, as it turned out) assumed that Freudian theory had nothing to say about man's relation to reality and to his culture. While it is true that Freud emphasized, even mythologized, sexuality, he did so to counteract the rigid sexual taboos of his time, which, at that point in history, were frequently the cause of neuroses. In his later writings, however, Freud began to concern himself with the executive agency of the personality, namely the ego, which is also the repository of the individual's attitudes and concepts about himself and his world.

It is with the psychosocial development of the ego that Erikson's observations and theoretical constructions are primarily concerned. Erikson has thus been able to introduce innovations into psychoanalytic theory without either rejecting or ignoring Freud's monumental contribution.

The man who has accomplished this notable feat is a handsome Dane, whose white hair, mustache, resonant accent and gentle manner are reminiscent of actors like Jean Hersholt and Paul Muni. Although he is warm and outgoing with friends, Erikson is a rather shy man who is uncomfortable in the spotlight of public recognition. This trait, together with his ethical reservations about making public even disguised case material, may help to account for Erikson's reluctance to publish his observations and conceptions (his first book appeared in 1950, when he was 48).

In recent years this reluctance to publish has diminished and he has been appearing in print at an increasing pace. Since 1960 he has published three books, "Insight and Responsibility," "Identity: Youth and Crisis" and "Gandhi's Truth," as well as editing a fourth, "Youth: Change ·and Challenge." Despite the accolades and recognition these books have won for him, both in America and abroad, Erikson is still surprised at the popular interest they have generated and is a little troubled about the possibility of being misunderstood and misinterpreted. While he would prefer that his books spoke for themselves and that he was left out of the picture, he has had to accede to popular demand for more information about himself and his work.

The course of Erikson's professional career has been as diverse as it has been unconventional. He was born in Frankfurt, Germany, in 1902 of Danish parents. Not long after his birth his father died, and his mother later married the pediatrician who had cured her son of a childhood illness. Erikson's stepfather urged him to become a physician, but the boy declined and became an artist instead—an artist who did portraits of children. Erikson says of his post-adolescent years, "I was an artist then, which in Europe is a euphemism for a young man with some talent and nowhere to go." During this period he settled in Vienna and worked as a tutor in a family friendly with Freud's. He met Freud on informal occasions when the families went on outings together.

These encounters may have been the impetus to accept a teaching appointment at an American school in Vienna founded by Dorothy Burlingham and directed by Peter Blos (both now well known on the American psychiatric scene). During these years (the late nineteen-twenties) he also undertook and completed psychoanalytic training with Anna Freud and August Aichhorn. Even at the outset of his career, Erikson gave evidence of the breadth of his interests and activities by being trained and certified as a Montessori teacher. Not surprisingly, in view of that training, Erikson's first articles dealt with psychoanalysis and education.

It was while in Vienna that Erikson met and married Joan Mowat Serson, an American artist of Canadian descent. They came to America in 1933, when Erikson was invited to practice and teach in Boston. Erikson was, in fact, one of the first if not the first child-analyst in the Boston area. During the next two decades he held clinical and academic appointments at Harvard, Yale and Berkeley. In 1951 he joined a group of psychiatrists and psychologists who moved to Stockbridge, Mass., to start a new program at the Austen Riggs Center, a private residential treatment center for disturbed young people. Erikson remained at Riggs until 1961, when he was appointed professor of human development and lecturer on psychiatry at Harvard. Throughout his career he has always held two or three appointments simultaneously and has traveled extensively.

Perhaps because he had been an artist first, Erikson has never been a conventional psychoanalyst. When he was treating children, for example, he always insisted on visiting his young patients' homes and on having dinner with the families. Likewise in the nineteen-thirties, when anthropological investigation was described to him by his friends Scudder McKeel, Alfred Kroeber and Margaret Mead, he decided to do field work on an Indian reservation. "When I realized that Sioux is the name which we [in Europe] pronounced "See us" and which for us was *the* American Indian, I could not resist." Erikson thus antedated the anthropologists who swept over the Indian reservations in the post-Depression years. (So numerous were the field workers at that time that the stock joke was that an Indian family could be defined as a mother, a father, children and an anthropologist.)

Erikson did field work not only with the Oglala Sioux of Pine Ridge, S. D. (the tribe that slew Custer and was in turn slaughtered at the Battle of Wounded Knee), but also with the salmon-fishing Yurok of Northern California. His reports on these experiences revealed his special gift for sensing and entering into the world views and modes of thinking of cultures other than his own.

It was while he was working with the Indians that Erikson began to note syndromes which he could not explain within the confines of traditional psychoanalytic theory. Central to many an adult Indian's emotional problems seemed to be his sense of uprootedness and lack of continuity between his present life-style and that portrayed in tribal history. Not only did the Indian sense a break with the past, but he could not identify with a future requiring assimilation of the white culture's values. The problems faced by such men, Erikson recognized, had to do with the ego and with culture and only incidentally with sexual drives.

The impressions Erikson gained on the reservations were reinforced during World War II when he worked at a veterans' rehabilitation center at Mount Zion Hospital in San Francisco. Many of the soldiers he and his colleagues saw seemed not to fit the traditional "shell shock" or "malingerer" cases of World War I. Rather, it seemed to Erikson that many of these men had lost the sense of who and what they were. They were having trouble reconciling their activities, attitudes and feelings as soldiers with the activities, attitudes and feelings they had known before the war. Accordingly, while these men may well have had difficulties with repressed or conflicted drives, their main problem seemed to be, as Erikson came to speak of it at the time, "identity confusion."

It was almost a decade before Erikson set forth the implications of his clinical observations in "Childhood and Society." In that book, the summation and integration of 15 years of research, he made three major contributions to the study of the human ego. He posited (1) that, side by side with the stages of psychosexual development described by Freud (the oral, anal, phallic, genital, Oedipal and pubertal), were psychosocial stages of ego development, in which the individual had to establish new basic orientations to himself and his social world; (2) that personality development continued throughout the whole life cycle; and (3) that each stage had a positive *as well* as a negative component.

Much about these contributions—and about Erikson's way of thinking—can be understood by looking at his scheme of life stages. Erikson identifies eight stages in the human life cycle, in each of which a new dimension of "social interaction" becomes possible—that is, a new dimension in a person's interaction with himself, and with his social environment.

TRUST vs. MISTRUST

The first stage corresponds to the oral stage in classical psychoanalytic theory and usually extends through the first year of life. In Erikson's view, the new dimension of social interaction that emerges during this period involves basic *trust* at the one extreme, and *mistrust* at the other. The degree to which the child comes to trust the world, other people and himself depends to a considerable extent upon the quality of the care that he receives. The infant whose needs are met when they arise, whose discomforts are quickly removed, who is cuddled, fondled, played with and talked to, develops a sense of the world as a safe place to be and of people as helpful and dependable. When, however, the care is inconsistent, inadequate and rejecting, it fosters a basic mistrust, an attitude of fear and suspicion on the part of the infant toward the world in general and people in particular that will carry through to later stages of development.

It should be said at this point that the problem of basic trust-versus-mistrust (as is true for all the later dimensions) is not resolved once and for all during the first year of life; it arises again at each successive stage of development. There is both hope and danger in this. The child who enters school with a sense of mistrust may come to trust a particular teacher who has taken the trouble to make herself trustworthy; with this second chance, he overcomes his early mistrust. On the other hand, the child who comes through infancy with a vital sense of trust can still have his sense of mistrust activated at a later stage if, say, his parents are divorced and separated under acrimonious circumstances.

This point was brought home to me in a very direct way by a 4-year-old patient I saw in a court clinic. He was being seen at the court clinic because his adoptive parents, who had had him for six months, now wanted to give him back to the agency. They claimed that he was cold and unloving, took things and could not be trusted. He was indeed a cold and apathetic boy, but with good reason. About a year after his illegitimate birth, he was taken away from his mother, who had a drinking problem, and was shunted back and forth among several foster homes. Initially he had tried to relate to the persons in the foster homes, but the relationships never had a chance to develop becuase he was moved at just the wrong times. In the end he gave up trying to reach out to others, because the inevitable separations hurt too much.

Like the burned child who dreads the flame, this emotionally burned child shunned the pain of emotional involvement. He had trusted his mother, but now he trusted no one. Only years of devoted care and patience could now undo the damage that had been done to this child's sense of trust.

AUTONOMY vs. DOUBT

Stage Two spans the second and third years of life, the period which Freudian theory calls the anal stage. Erikson sees here the emergence of *autonomy*. This autonomy dimension builds upon the child's new motor and mental abilities. At this stage the child can not only walk but also climb, open and close, drop, push and pull, hold and let go. The child takes pride in these new accomplishments and wants to do everything himself, whether it be pulling the wrapper off a piece of candy, selecting the vitamin out of the bottle or flushing the toilet. If parents recognize the young child's need to do what he is capable of doing at his own pace and in his own time, then he develops a sense that he is able to control his muscles, his impulses, himself and, not insignificantly, his environment—the sense of autonomy.

When, however, his caretakers are impatient and do for him what he is capable of doing himself, they reinforce a sense of shame and doubt. To be sure, every parent has rushed a child at times and children are hardy enough to endure such lapses. It is only when caretaking is consistently overprotective and criticism of "accidents" (whether these be wetting, soiling, spilling or breaking things) is harsh and unthinking that the child develops an excessive sense of shame with respect to other people and an excessive sense of doubt about own abilities to control his world and himself.

If the child leaves this stage with less autonomy than shame or doubt, he will be handicapped in his attempts to achieve autonomy in adolescence and adulthood. Contrariwise, the child who moves through this stage with his sense of autonomy buoyantly outbalancing his feelings of shame and doubt is well prepared to be autonomous at later phases in the life cycle. Again, however, the balance of autonomy to shame and doubt

set up during this period can be changed in either positive or negative directions by later events.

It might be well to note, in addition, that too much autonomy can be as harmful as too little. I have in mind a patient of 7 who had a heart condition. He had learned very quickly how terrified his parents were of any signs in him of cardiac difficulty. With the psychological acuity given to children, he soon ruled the household. The family could not go shopping, or for a drive, or on a holiday if he did not approve. On those rare occasions when the parents had had enough and defied him, he would get angry and his purple hue and gagging would frighten them into submission.

Actually, this boy was frightened of this power (as all children would be) and was really eager to give it up. When the parents and the boy came to realize this, and to recognize that a little shame and doubt were a healthy counterpoise to an inflated sense of autonomy, the three of them could once again assume their normal roles.

INITIATIVE vs. GUILT

In this stage (the genital stage of classical psychoanalysis) the child, age 4 to 5, is pretty much master of his body and can ride a tricycle, run, cut and hit. He can thus initiate motor activities of various sorts on his own and no longer merely responds to or imitates the actions of other children. The same holds true for his language and fantasy activities. Accordingly, Erikson argues that the social dimension that appears at this stage has *initiative* at one of its poles and *guilt* at the other.

Whether the child will leave this stage with his sense of initiative far outbalancing his sense of guilt depends to a considerable extent upon how parents respond to his self-initiated activities. Children who are given much freedom and opportunity to initiate motor play such as running, bike riding, sliding, skating, tussling and wrestling have their sense of initiative reinforced. Initiative is also reinforced when parents answer their children's questions (intellectual initiative) and do not deride or inhibit fantasy or play activity. On the other hand, if the child is made to feel that his motor activity is bad, that his questions are a nuisance and that his play is silly and stupid, then he may develop a sense of guilt over self-initiated activities in general that will persist through later life stages.

INDUSTRY vs. INFERIORITY

Stage Four is the age period from 6 to 11, the elementary school years (described by classical psychoanalysis as the *latency phase*). It is a time during which the child's love for the parent of the opposite sex and rivalry with the same sexed parent (elements in the so-called family romance) are quiescent. It is also a period during which the child becomes capable of deductive reasoning, and of playing and learning by rules. It is not until this period, for example, that children can really play marbles, checkers and other "take turn" games that require obedience to rules. Erikson argues that the psychosocial dimension that emerges during this period has a sense of *industry* at one extreme and a sense of *inferiority* at the other.

1. BECOMING A PERSON

The term industry nicely captures a dominant theme of this period during which the concern with how things are made, how they work and what they do predominates. It is the Robinson Crusoe age in the sense that the enthusiasm and minute detail with which Crusoe describes his activities appeals to the child's own budding sense of industry. When children are encouraged in their efforts to make, do, or build practical things (whether it be to construct creepy crawlers, tree houses, or airplane models—or to cook, bake or sew), are allowed to finish their products, and are praised and rewarded for the results, then the sense of industry is enhanced. But parents who see their children's efforts at making and doing as "mischief," and as simply "making a mess," help to encourage in children a sense of inferiority.

During these elementary-school years, however, the child's world includes more than the home. Now social institutions other than the family come to play a central role in the developmental crisis of the individual. (Here Erikson introduced still another advance in psychoanalytic theory, which heretofore concerned itself only with the effects of the parents' behavior upon the child's development.)

A child's school experiences affect his industry-inferiority balance. The child, for example, with an I.Q. of 80 to 90 has a particularly traumatic school experience, even when his sense of industry is rewarded and encouraged at home. He is "too bright" to be in special classes, but "too slow" to compete with children of average ability. Consequently he experiences constant failures in his academic efforts that reinforces a sense of inferiority.

On the other hand, the child who had his sense of industry derogated at home can have it revitalized at school through the offices of a sensitive and committed teacher. Whether the child develops a sense of industry or inferiority, therefore, no longer depends solely on the caretaking efforts of the parents but on the actions and offices of other adults as well.

IDENTITY vs. ROLE CONFUSION

When the child moves into adolescence (Stage Five— roughly the ages 12-18), he encounters, according to traditional psychoanalytic theory, a reawakening of the family-romance problem of early childhood. His means of resolving the problem is to seek and find a romantic partner of his own generation. While Erikson does not deny this aspect of adolescence, he points out that there are other problems as well. The adolescent matures mentally as well as physio- logically and, in addition to the new feelings, sensations and desires he experiences as a result of changes in his body, he develops a multitude of new ways of looking at and thinking about the world. Among other things, those in adolescence can now think about other people's thinking and wonder about what other people think of them. They can also conceive of ideal families, religions and societies which they then compare with the imperfect families, religions and societies of their own experience. Finally, adolescents become capable of constructing theories and philosophies designed to bring all the varied and conflicting aspects of society into a working, harmonious and peaceful whole. The adolescent, in a word, is an impatient idealist who believes that it is as easy to realize an ideal as it is to imagine it.

Erikson believes that the new interpersonal dimension which emerges during this period has to do with a sense of *ego identity* at the positive end and a sense of *role confusion* at the negative end. That is to say, given the adolescent's newfound integrative abilities, his task is to bring together all of the things he has learned about himself as a son, student, athlete, friend, Scout, newspaper boy, and so on, and integrate these different images of himself into a whole that makes sense and that shows continuity with the past while preparing for the future. To the extent that the young person succeeds in this endeavor, he arrives at a sense of psychosocial identity, a sense of who he is, where he has been and where he is going.

In contrast to the earlier stages, where parents play a more or less direct role in the determination of the result of the developmental crises, the influence of parents during this stage is much more indirect. If the young person reaches adolescence with, thanks to his parents, a vital sense of trust, autonomy, initiative and industry, then his chances of arriving at a meaningful sense of ego identity are much enhanced. The reverse, of course, holds true for the young person who enters adolescence with considerable mistrust, shame, doubt, guilt and inferiority. Preparation for a successful adolescence, and the attainment of an integrated psychosocial identity must, therefore, begin in the cradle.

Over and above what the individual brings with him from his childhood, the attainment of a sense of personal identity depends upon the social milieu in which he or she grows up. For example, in a society where women are to some extent second-class citizens, it may be harder for females to arrive at a sense of psychosocial identity. Likewise at times, such as the present, when rapid social and technological change breaks down many traditional values, it may be more difficult for young people to find continuity between what they learned and experienced as children and what they learn and experience as adolescents. At such times young people often seek causes that give their lives meaning and direction. The activism of the current generation of young people may well stem, in part at least, from this search.

When the young person cannot attain a sense of personal identity, either because of an unfortunate childhood or difficult social circumstances, he shows a certain amount of *role confusion*—a sense of not knowing what he is, where he belongs or whom he belongs to. Such confusion is a frequent symptom in delinquent young people. Promiscuous adolescent girls, for example, often seem to have a fragmented sense of ego identity. Some young people seek a "negative identity," an identity opposite to the one prescribed for them by their family and friends. Having an identity as a "delinquent," or as a "hippie," or even as an "acid head," may sometimes be preferable to having no identity at all.

In some cases young people do not seek a negative identity so much as they have it thrust upon them. I remember another court case in which the defendant was an attractive 16-year- old girl who had been found "tricking it" in a trailer located just outside the grounds of an Air Force base. From about the age of 12, her mother had encouraged her to dress seductively and to go out with boys. When she returned from dates, her sexually frustrated mother demanded a kiss-by-kiss, caress- by-caress description of the evening's activities. After the mother had vicariously satisfied her sexual needs, she proceeded to call her daughter a "whore" and a "dirty tramp."

As the girl told me, "Hell, I have the name, so I might as well play the role."

Failure to establish a clear sense of personal identity at adolescence does not guarantee perpetual failure. And the person who attains a working sense of ego identity in adolescence will of necessity encounter challenges and threats to that identity as he moves through life. Erikson, perhaps more than any other personality theorist, has emphasized that life is constant change and that confronting problems at one stage in life is not a guarantee against the reappearance of these problems at later stages, or against the finding of new solutions to them.

INTIMACY vs. ISOLATION

Stage Six in the life cycle is young adulthood; roughly the period of courtship and early family life that extends from late adolescence till early middle age. For this stage, and the stages described hereafter, classical psychoanalysis has nothing new or major to say. For Erikson, however, the previous attainment of a sense of personal identity and the engagement in productive work that marks this period gives rise to a new interpersonal dimension of *intimacy* at the one extreme and *isolation* at the other.

When Erikson speaks of intimacy he means much more than love-making alone; he means the ability to share with and care about another person without fear of losing oneself in the process. In the case of intimacy, as in the case of identity, success or failure no longer depends directly upon the parents but only indirectly as they have contributed to the individual's success or failure at the earlier stages. Here, too, as in the case of identity, social conditions may help or hinder the establishment of a sense of intimacy. Likewise, intimacy need not involve sexuality; it includes the relationship between friends. Soldiers who have served together under the most dangerous circumstances often develop a sense of commitment to one another that exemplifies intimacy in its broadest sense. If a sense of intimacy is not established with friends or a marriage partner, the result, in Erikson's view, is a sense of isolation—of being alone without anyone to share with or care for.

GENERATIVITY vs. SELF-ABSORPTION

This stage—middle age—brings with it what Erikson speaks of as either *generativity or self-absorption,* and stagnation. What Erikson means by generativity is that the person begins to be concerned with others beyond his immediate family, with future generations and the nature of the society and world in which those generations will live. Generativity does not reside only in parents; it can be found in any individual who actively concerns himself with the welfare of young people and with making the world a better place for them to live and to work.

Those who fail to establish a sense of generativity fall into a state of self-absorption in which their personal needs and comforts are of predominant concern. A fictional case of self-absorption is Dickens's Scrooge in "A Christmas Carol." In his one-sided concern with money and in his disregard for the interests and welfare of his young employee, Bob Cratchit, Scrooge exemplifies the self-absorbed, embittered (the two often go together) old man. Dickens also illustrated, however, what Erikson points out: namely, that unhappy solutions to life's crises are not irreversible. Scrooge, at the end of the tale, manifested both a sense of generativity and of intimacy which he had not experienced before.

INTEGRITY vs. DESPAIR

Stage Eight in the Eriksonian scheme corresponds roughly to the period when the individual's major efforts are nearing completion and when there is time for reflection—and for the enjoyment of grandchildren, if any. The psychosocial dimension that comes into prominence now has *integrity* on one hand and *despair* on the other.

The sense of integrity arises from the individual's ability to look back on his life with satisfaction. At the other extreme is the individual who looks back upon his life as a series of missed opportunities and missed directions; now in the twilight years he realizes that it is too late to start again. For such a person the inevitable result is a sense of despair at what might have been.

These, then, are the major stages in the life cycle as described by Erikson. Their presentation, for one thing, frees the clinician to treat adult emotional problems as failures (in part at least) to solve genuinely adult personality crises and not, as heretofore, as mere residuals of infantile frustrations and conflicts. This view of personality growth, moreover, takes some of the onus off parents and takes account of the role which society and the person himself play in the formation of an individual personality. Finally, Erikson has offered hope for us all by demonstrating that each phase of growth has its strengths as well as its weaknesses and that failures at one stage of development can be rectified by successes at later stages.

The reason that these ideas, which sound so agreeable to "common sense," are in fact so revolutionary has a lot to do with the state of psychoanalysis in America. As formulated by Freud, psychoanalysis encompassed a theory of personality development, a method of studying the human mind and, finally, procedures for treating troubled and unhappy people. Freud viewed this system as a scientific one, open to revision as new facts and observations accumulated.

The system was, however, so vehemently attacked that Freud's followers were constantly in the position of having to defend Freud's views. Perhaps because of this situation, Freud's system became, in the hands of some of his followers and defenders, a dogma upon which all theoretical innovation, clinical observation and therapeutic practice had to be grounded. That this attitude persists is evidenced in the recent remark by a psychoanalyst that he believed psychotic patients could not be treated by psychoanalysis because "Freud said so." Such attitudes, in which Freud's authority rather than observation and data is the basis of deciding what is true and what is false, has contributed to the disrepute in which psychoanalysis is widely held today.

Erik Erikson has broken out of this scholasticism and has had the courage to say that Freud's discoveries and practices were the start and not the end of the study and treatment of the human personality. In addition to advocating the modifications of psychoanalytic theory outlined above, Erikson has also suggested modifications in therapeutic practice, particularly in the treatment of young patients. "Young people in severe trouble are not fit for the couch," he writes. "They want to face you, and they want you to face them, not a facsimile of a parent, or wearing the mask of a professional helper, but as a kind of over-all individual a young person can live with or despair of."

Erikson has had the boldness to remark on some of the negative effects that distorted notions of psychoanalysis have had on society at large. Psychoanalysis, he says, has contributed to a widespread fatalism—"even as we were trying to devise, with scientific determinism, a therapy for the few, we were led to promote an ethical disease among the many."

Perhaps Erikson's innovations in psychoanalytic theory are best exemplified in his psycho-historical writings, in which he combines psychoanalytic insight with a true historical imagination. After the publication of "Childhood and Society," Erikson undertook the application of his scheme of the human life cycle to the study of historical persons. He wrote a series of brilliant essays on men as varied as Maxim Gorky, George Bernard Shaw and Freud himself. These studies were not narrow case histories but rather reflected Erikson's remarkable grasp of Europe's social and political history, as well as of its literature. (His mastery of American folklore, history and literature is equally remarkable.)

While Erikson's major biographical studies were yet to come, these early essays already revealed his unique psycho-history method. For one thing, Erikson always chose men whose lives fascinated him in one way or another, perhaps because of some conscious or unconscious affinity with them. Erikson thus had a sense of community with his subjects which he adroitly used (he calls it *disciplined subjectivity)* to take his subject's point of view and to experience the world as that person might.

Secondly, Erikson chose to elaborate a particular crisis or episode in the individual's life which seemed to crystallize a life-theme that united the activities of his past and gave direction to his activities for the future. Then, much as an artist might, Erikson proceeded to fill in the background of the episode and add social and historical perspective. In a very real sense Erikson's biographical sketches are like paintings which direct the viewer's gaze from a focal point of attention to background and back again, so that one's appreciation of the focal area is enriched by having pursued the picture in its entirety.

This method was given its first major test in Erikson's study of "Young Man Luther." Originally, Erikson planned only a brief study of Luther, but "Luther proved too bulky a man to be merely a chapter in a book." Erikson's involvement with Luther dated from his youth, when, as a wandering artist, he happened to hear the Lord's Prayer in Luther's German. "Never knowingly having heard it, I had the experience, as seldom before or after, of a wholeness captured in a few simple words, of poetry fusing the esthetic and the moral; those who have suddenly 'heard' the Gettysburg Address will know what I mean."

Erikson's interest in Luther may have had other roots as well. In some ways, Luther's unhappiness with the papal intermediaries of Christianity resembled on a grand scale Erikson's own dissatisfaction with the intermediaries of Freud's system. In both cases some of the intermediaries had so distorted the original teachings that what was being preached in the name of the master came close to being the opposite of what he had himself proclaimed. While it is not possible to describe Erikson's treatment of Luther here, one can get some feeling for Erikson's brand of historical analysis from his sketch of Luther:

"Luther was a very troubled and a very gifted young man who had to create his own cause on which to focus his fidelity in the Roman Catholic world as it was then.... He first became a monk and tried to solve his scruples by being an exceptionally good monk. But even his superiors thought that he tried much too hard. He felt himself to be such a sinner that he began to lose faith in the charity of God and his superiors told him, 'Look, God doesn't hate you, you hate God or else you would trust Him to accept your prayers.' But I would like to make it clear that someone like Luther becomes a historical person only because he also has an acute understanding of historical actuality and knows how to 'speak to the condition' of his times. Only then do inner struggles become representative of those of a large number of vigorous and sincere young people—and begin to interest some troublemakers and hangers-on."

After Erikson's study of "Young Man Luther" (1958), he turned his attention to "middle-aged" Gandhi. As did Luther, Gandhi evoked for Erikson childhood memories. Gandhi led his first nonviolent protest in India in 1918 on behalf of some mill workers, and Erikson, then a young man of 16, had read glowing accounts of the event. Almost a half a century later Erikson was invited to Ahmedabad, an industrial city in western India, to give a seminar on the human life cycle. Erikson discovered that Ahmedabad was the city in which Gandhi had led the demonstration about which Erikson had read as a youth. Indeed, Erikson's host was none other than Ambalal Sarabahai, the benevolent industrialist who had been Gandhi's host—as well as antagonist—in the 1918 wage dispute. Throughout his stay in Ahmedabad, Erikson continued to encounter people and places that were related to Gandhi's initial experiments with nonviolent techniques.

The more Erikson learned about the event at Ahmedabad, the more intrigued he became with its pivotal importance in Gandhi's career. It seemed to be the historical moment upon which all the earlier events of Gandhi's life converged and from which diverged all of his later endeavors. So captured was Erikson by the event at Ahmedabad, that he returned the following year to research a book on Gandhi in which the event would serve as a fulcrum.

At least part of Erikson's interest in Gandhi may have stemmed from certain parallels in their lives. The 1918 event marked Gandhi's emergence as a national political leader. He was 48 at the time, and had become involved reluctantly, not so much out of a need for power or fame as out of a genuine conviction that something had to be done about the disintegration of Indian culture. Coincidentally, Erikson's book "Childhood and Society," appeared in 1950 when Erikson was 48, and it is that book which brought him national prominence in the mental health field. Like Gandhi, too, Erikson reluctantly did what he felt he had to do (namely, publish his observations and conclusions) for the benefit of his

Erikson in a seminar at his Stockbridge, Mass., home.

"Young analysts are today proclaiming a 'new freedom' to see Freud in historical perspective, which reflects the Eriksonian view that one can recognize Freud's greatness without bowing to conceptual precedent."

ailing profession and for the patients treated by its practitioners. So while Erikson's affinity with Luther seemed to derive from comparable professional identity crises, his affinity for Gandhi appears to derive from a parallel crisis of generativity. A passage from "Gandhi's Truth" (from a chapter wherein Erikson addresses himself directly to his subject) helps to convey Erikson's feeling for his subject.

"So far, I have followed you through the loneliness of your childhood and through the experiments and the scruples of your youth. I have affirmed my belief in your ceaseless endeavor to perfect yourself as a man who came to feel that he was the only one available to reverse India's fate. You experimented with what to you were debilitating temptations and you did gain vigor and agility from your victories over yourself. Your identity could be no less than that of universal man, although you had to become an Indian—and one close to the masses—first."

The following passage speaks to Erikson's belief in the general significance of Gandhi's efforts:

"We have seen in Gandhi's development the strong attraction of one of those more inclusive identities: that of an enlightened citizen of the British Empire. In proving himself willing neither to abandon vital ties to his native tradition nor to sacrifice lightly a Western education which eventually contributed to his ability to help defeat British hegemony—in

all of these seeming contradictions Gandhi showed himself on intimate terms with the actualities of his era. For in all parts of the world, the struggle now is for *the anticipatory development of more inclusive identities* . . . I submit then, that Gandhi, in his immense intuition for historical actuality and his capacity to assume leadership in 'truth in action,' may have created a ritualization through which men, equipped with both realism and strength, can face each other with mutual confidence."

There is now more and more teaching of Erikson's concepts in psychiatry, psychology, education and social work in America and in other parts of the world. His description of the stages of the life cycle are summarized in major textbooks in all of these fields and clinicians are increasingly looking at their cases in Eriksonian terms.

Research investigators have, however, found Erikson's formulations somewhat difficult to test. This is not surprising, inasmuch as Erikson's conceptions, like Freud's, take into account the infinite complexity of the human personality. Current research methodologies are, by and large, still not able to deal with these complexities at their own level, and distortions are inevitable when such concepts as "identity" come to be defined in terms of responses to a questionnaire.

Likewise, although Erikson's life-stages have an intuitive "rightness" about them, not everyone agrees with his formulations. Douvan and Adelson in their book, "The Adolescent Experience," argue that while his identity theory may hold true for boys, it doesn't for girls. This argument is based on findings which suggest that girls postpone identity consolidation until after marriage (and intimacy) have been established. Such postponement occurs, says Douvan and Adelson, because a woman's identity is partially defined by the identity of the man whom she marries. This view does not really contradict Erikson's, since he recognizes that later events, such as marriage, can help to resolve both current and past developmental crises. For the woman, but not for the man, the problems of identity and intimacy may be solved concurrently.

Objections to Erikson's formulations have come from other directions as well. Robert W. White, Erikson's good friend and colleague at Harvard, has a long standing (and warm-hearted) debate with Erikson over his life-stages. White believes that his own theory of "competence motivation," a theory which has received wide recognition, can account for the phenomena of ego development much more economically than can Erikson's stages. Erikson has, however, little interest in debating the validity of the stages he has described. As an artist he recognizes that there are many different ways to view one and the same phenomenon and that a perspective that is congenial to one person will be repugnant to another. He offers his stage-wise description of the life cycle for those who find such perspectives congenial and not as a world view that everyone should adopt.

It is this lack of dogmatism and sensitivity to the diversity and complexity of the human personality which help to account for the growing recognition of Erikson's contribution within as well as without the helping professions. Indeed, his psycho-historical investigations have originated a whole new field of study which has caught the interest of historians and political scientists alike. (It has also intrigued his wife, Joan, who has published pieces on Eleanor Roosevelt and who has a book on Saint Francis in press.) A recent issue of Daedalus, the journal for the American Academy of Arts and Sciences, was entirely devoted to psycho-historical and psycho-political investigations of creative leaders by authors from diverse disciplines who have been stimulated by Erikson's work.

Now in his 68th year, Erikson maintains the pattern of multiple activities and appointments which has characterized his entire career. He spends the fall in Cambridge, Mass., where he teaches a large course on "the human life cycle" for Harvard seniors. The spring semester is spent at his home in Stockbridge, Mass., where he participates in case conferences and staff seminars at the Austen Riggs Center. His summers are spent on Cape Cod. Although Erikson's major commitment these days is to his psycho-historical investigation, he is embarking on a study of preschool children's play constructions in different settings and countries, a follow-up of some research he conducted with preadolescents more than a quarter-century ago. He is also planning to review other early observations in the light of contemporary change. In his approach to his work, Erikson appears neither drawn nor driven, but rather to be following an inner schedule as natural as the life cycle itself.

Although Erikson, during his decade of college teaching, has not seen any patients or taught at psychoanalytic institutes, he maintains his dedication to psychoanalysis and views his psycho-historical investigations as an applied branch of that discipline. While some older analysts continue to ignore Erikson's work, there is increasing evidence (including a recent poll of psychiatrists and psychoanalysts) that he is having a rejuvenating influence upon a discipline which many regard as dead or dying. Young analysts are today proclaiming a "new freedom" to see Freud in historical perspective—which reflects the Eriksonian view that one can recognize Freud's greatness without bowing to conceptual precedent.

Accordingly, the reports of the demise of psychoanalysis may have been somewhat premature. In the work of Erik Erikson, at any rate, psychoanalysis lives and continues to beget life.

Freud's "Ages of Man"

Erik Erikson's definition of the "eight ages of man" is a work of synthesis and insight by a psychoanalytically trained and worldly mind. Sigmund Freud's description of human phases stems from his epic psychological discoveries and centers almost exclusively on the early years of life. A brief summary of the phases posited by Freud:

Oral stage—roughly the first year of life, the period during which the mouth region provides the greatest sensual satisfaction. Some derivative behavioral traits which may be seen at this time are *incorporativeness* (first six months of life) and *aggressiveness* (second six months of life).

Anal stage—roughly the second and third years of life. During this period the site of greatest sensual pleasure shifts to the anal and urethral areas. Derivative behavioral traits are *retentiveness* and *expulsiveness*.

Phallic stage—roughly the third and fourth years of life. The site of greatest sensual pleasure during this stage is the genital region. Behavior traits derived from this period include *intrusiveness* (male) and *receptiveness* (female).

Oedipal stage—roughly the fourth and fifth years of life. At this stage the young person takes the parent of the opposite sex as the object or provider of sensual satisfaction and regards the same-sexed parent as a rival. (The "family romance.") Behavior traits originating in this period are *seductiveness* and *competitiveness*.

Latency stage—roughly the years from age 6 to 11. The child resolves the Oedipus conflict by identifying with the parent of the opposite sex and by so doing satisfies sensual needs vicariously. Behavior traits developed during this period include *conscience* (or the internalization of parental moral and ethical demands).

Puberty stage—roughly 11 to 14. During this period there is an integration and subordination of oral, anal and phallic sensuality to an overriding and unitary genital *sexuality*. The genital sexuality of puberty has another young person of the opposite sex as its object, and discharge (at least for boys) as its aim. Derivative behavior traits (associated with the control and regulation of genital sexuality) are *intellectualization* and *estheticism*.

—D.E.

Adolescent Americans

Medical problems for this population are a mix of injury,
disease, anxiety, rapid growth and social ills

Mary Grace Kovar

*Mary Grace Kovar is chief of the Analytical Coordination
Branch, Division of Analysis, at the National Center for Health
Statistics in the Department of Health, Education and Welfare,
Washington, D.C. She has been the coordinator of* HEALTH
UNITED STATES *(the DHEW Secretary's report to the Congress
on the health of the nation) since its inception, and is author of
the chapter on children and youth in the 1978 volume.*

This is a good time to take stock of the health and
health-related behavior of adolescents in America.
With the baby boom behind us, the number of children becoming teenagers is decreasing each year.
For that reason alone, the number of adolescents
having babies, using illegal drugs, smoking and
drinking, and dying from accidents and violence will
decline. But it's time we listened to them to learn
how to help them.

What are they like? How do they feel? What are
they doing? As John Knowles has said, "By the time
they are sixteen, society says that they shall have
cars, drink beer, smoke, eat junk at drive-ins, and
have a go at fornication." But what are the facts of
their day-to-day lives? Let's look at some of the information about twelve-to-seventeen-year-olds from
national surveys and scholarly studies. Much of what
is reported here is based on data from the National
Center for Health Statistics and other components
of the Public Health Service such as the Alcohol,
Drug Abuse and Mental Health Administration and
the Center for Disease Control; from the National
Institute of Education, the Bureau of the Census,
and from studies by specialists in certain aspects of
adolescent behavior, including Melvin Zelnick and
John Kantner at Johns Hopkins, and other colleagues at universities and centers.

While some data—the number of births and
deaths, the number of people, the number of cases
of venereal disease—have been routinely collected
for many years, there were few surveys or studies
about the health or health-related behavior of
adolescents until about ten years ago. Thus we have
trouble comparing adolescents today with their parents when they were the same age, but we can look
at some of the changes that have taken place in the
past few years.

What we learn is that adolescents in general are
a healthy group. Their needs for traditional medical
care are—or should be—modest. The diseases of
early childhood are behind them and chronic conditions don't usually become a problem until later in
life. When asked why they don't see a doctor, most
teenagers say they are "Healthy. Don't need one."
And the statisticians confirm that they are largely
right, but not completely.

In a recent survey of twelve-to-seventeen-year-
olds who underwent physical examinations, the data
revealed certain problems: One adolescent out of
twenty had a significant cardiovascular condition.
Of these, about 45 percent showed signs of mur-
murs; thirteen percent suffered from hypertension.
Even in adolescence, blood-pressure readings
warned of future problems.

When doctors looked at such things as hearing,
sight, and dental problems, they were surprised to
learn that while five percent reported having trouble hearing, only one percent showed any impaired
hearing. Slightly more than forty percent of those
surveyed were unable to see well enough to read at
the 20/20 level at the standard distance without correction; only about a third wore corrective lenses.
Even so, nearly a third of those who wore glasses
failed to reach the 20/20 level with their glasses.

1. BECOMING A PERSON

About two-thirds of the adolescents examined needed dental care; more than half had decayed teeth. The teenage nemesis, acne, had struck two-thirds of the study group, although few suffered from severe cases.

Records kept by doctors and hospitals reveal that just over half of all adolescents surveyed had visited a private physician during the course of the year. About a fifth of these visits were for examinations or observation. One-quarter of the diagnoses made were sore throats, colds or other respiratory conditions; another third named skin problems, infections and parasitic ailments, and diseases of the nervous system.

Very few teenagers are hospitalized in any year—only about six percent. While disease plays a relatively minor role, injury looms large. About sixteen percent of all visits made by adolescents to physicians and nearly a quarter of all of the days spent in hospitals were because of injuries. Among the boys, fully one-third of the days spent in the hospital can be attributed to injury. When hospital admission is caused by disease, the most common ailments are digestive, respiratory or mental in nature. Childbirth accounts for one-fifth of the days that adolescent girls spend in hospitals.

Only six out of every ten thousand teenagers died in 1976, seventy percent as a result of motor vehicle accidents and violence. The leading disease resulting in death was cancer (just over eight percent of the deaths), followed by diseases of the circulatory system (less than five percent).

Twilight Zone

From this evidence we gather that many of the special problems teenagers face are not, strictly speaking, medical. But the fact that they aren't sick does not mean that they do not suffer from health problems in a broader sense. Their uneven growth and development, their ignorance of what is happening to them physically as well as emotionally, their experience of being in the twilight zone—neither child nor adult—and their behavior (which can lead ultimately to serious medical difficulties, including lifelong social limitations, physical disability or even premature death) all point to the teenage years as a critical period.

The Health Examination Survey in the late nineteen-sixties of youths twelve through seventeen years of age confirmed a good many things we already knew, and surprised us with other facts. The teenage "growth spurt" alters body tissue at a rate unparalleled at any other time except the immediate postneonatal period. Surely unsettling for many, it is complicated by the wide variation among different adolescents. Girls, for example, at the onset of adolescence, are taller and heavier than boys. Their peak rate of growth comes about a year and a half before boys'. Girls, on average, also begin their adolescent growth spurt earlier than boys. In early adolescence we also find a wide variation in height (especially among boys), and in the weight of both sexes during middle adolescence. The growth spurt does not come upon all boys and girls at the same time—nor does sexual maturation.

No wonder that just about half of all boys asked preferred to be taller and nearly half the girls reported that they wished they were thinner.

In general, adolescents thought of themselves as being in poorer health than their parents rated them. Despite that fact, adolescents were less likely to report the presence of health problems, and much less likely than their parents to say that a doctor should be consulted if specific problems arose.

In contrast, the adolescents were much more likely to report some degree of nervousness than their parents. But when asked if they would want to see a doctor about nervousness, more than forty percent of the adolescents said no.

Alcohol and Drugs

According to high-school kids, beer, wine and marijuana are widely available at school. Almost half of those surveyed said they could easily get marijuana at school, and nearly forty percent said the same of alcohol. Senior-high-school students were about twice as likely as junior-high students to report ready availability. There is no question that adolescents today are more likely to use marijuana, tobacco and alcohol than were the adolescents of a few years ago.

Use of alcohol and tobacco appears to have increased until the mid-1970's; since then, the use of these "traditional" substances seems to have remained relatively constant. In 1977 over half of all adolescents had tasted alcohol; about a third had had a drink within the month. Somewhat fewer smoked tobacco, with almost half reporting they had tasted it, but less than a quarter having smoked within the month. Both drinking and smoking are more common among older adolescents. About half of the sixteen-to-seventeen-year-olds had had a drink within the month; about a third had smoked.

Use of marijuana, which was much rarer than tobacco usage in the early 1970's, had increased and continues climbing, especially among the older adolescents. The surveys show that in 1974, ten percent of the sixteen-to-seventeen-year-olds had smoked marijuana in the month before the interview, yet only three years later, in 1977, nearly thirty percent of the kids that age had smoked marijuana within the month.

The majority of adolescents in the United States today have tried one or more of these substances at least once by the time they finish high school. More than ninety percent of the 1977 high-school graduating class had tried alcohol and more than three-quarters of them had smoked cigarettes. As for psychoactive drugs, it turns out that nearly a quarter of the class of 1977 had experimented with stimulants, and almost twenty percent with tranquilizers or sedatives not prescribed by a doctor.

Nearly two-thirds of the graduating class of 1977 had tried one or more illicit drugs. And the proportion of seniors who have tried illicit drugs has been steadily mounting because of the appreciable rise in marijuana use. While just under half of the class of 1975 had tried marijuana, two years later the figure had climbed nearly ten percent. In the same period no change was reported in the use of other illicit drugs. But more than a third had tried hallucinogens, inhalants, opiates or cocaine.

Having tried a substance does not indicate abuse; nor does it mean that youngsters continue to use it regularly. One measure of abuse is daily or near daily use in the past thirty days. Almost thirty percent of the seniors reported that they smoked cigarettes daily, six percent reported daily use of alcohol, and almost ten percent reported daily use of marijuana.

The daily use of marijuana by high-school seniors is mounting somewhat more rapidly among boys than girls. If past patterns hold, boys' using a substance more and then girls' taking it up, many more children are likely to turn to daily use of marijuana. There is also some indication of increasing use of cocaine among young adults, which could spread to the adolescents.

Sexual Activity

Few children attain sexual maturity before age twelve, and few are not sexually mature by eighteen. We know that adolescent girls are more likely to engage in sexual activity than formerly, but we don't know whether this is also true for boys of the same age. Some of the adverse consequences of sex—unwanted pregnancy and childbearing—are obviously more damaging to girls, but both sexes can acquire venereal disease and suffer the emotional consequences of all these possible outcomes.

Larger numbers of unmarried adolescent girls have had sexual intercourse and they are having their first experiences at younger ages than in the past. Figures from 1971 show that more than a quarter of unmarried seventeen-year-olds reported that they had had sexual intercourse at least once. Five years later, by 1976, it was just over forty percent. These girls also may have had more than one sexual partner. And fifteen-year-old girls are likely to have engaged in sexual activity. In 1971, fourteen percent reported having had intercourse at least

once; by 1976 it was eighteen percent. While fifteen-year-old black girls are more sexually active than white girls of the same age, over five years the increase among white girls has been far greater.

Teenage Pregnancies

If everything else (birth control, abortion) had remained the same, the substantial increase in sex would have meant an increase in unwanted pregnancies and childbirth. Instead, teenage birth rates have been declining steadily since 1972, when almost 237,000 births were reported among fifteen-to-seventeen-year-old girls, or nearly forty per thousand. Four years later, with 215,000, the rate fell to about thirty-five per thousand. The birth rate is still high among black adolescents. In 1976, there were slightly more than eighty live births per thousand in the fifteen-to-seventeen age group. But the decrease from 1970 is quite dramatic—in that year black girls gave birth to more than one hundred babies per thousand.

Of most concern is the number of babies born to girls who are not yet fifteen themselves—almost twelve thousand in 1976. While this is a very small number—four-tenths of a percent of all births—these young mothers are barely out of childhood themselves. Obviously they are neither physiologically prepared for pregnancy (with the known physical risk to the child) nor are they psychologically or economically ready to be parents.

The increased risk of low birth weight may be the single most important medical aspect of adolescent pregnancy. Studies show that a baby weighing 2,500 grams or less at birth is nearly twenty times as likely to die the first year of life as the child of higher birth weight. Low birth weight is also associated with various difficulties later on in life, especially neurological ones. Low-birth-weight babies face greater risks of becoming deaf and blind.

Certainly the age at which a young woman has her first child is critical, for the younger she is, the greater the damage to her future. Often the age at which a young girl gives birth to her first child determines her economic welfare. If she has not completed high school, her chances of graduating are very small. Failure to graduate from high school severely limits her, since employment may be difficult to find and, if found, the job is likely to be at low pay with little chance for promotion.

Teenage mothers are more likely to suffer from poverty and welfare dependency. Nearly half of all payments from the Aid to Families with Dependent Children program went to households with women who were teenagers when they bore their first child. These teenage mothers and their children pay a heavy price.

The current decline in birth rates among teenagers in the face of increased sexual activity is due to adolescent girls' using contraception more than ever before, and to the greater availability of abortions. In the five years from 1971 to 1976, adolescent girls reported a dramatic increase in contraceptive use, including using the most effective methods with more regularity. Still, in 1976, only about a third of the adolescent girls who had had intercourse used contraception the first time.

Sexually transmitted diseases cannot be prevented by reliance on the pill or an intrauterine device. Gonorrhea is the most common of the sexually transmitted diseases. By the mid-seventies it had reached epidemic proportions. In 1975, fifteen-to-nineteen-year-olds reported nearly thirteen cases per thousand—three times the incidence in 1955. Fortunately, rates seem to have stabilized in the past few years, but there is no guarantee that they will not rise again.

What's It All About?

Is there a way to tie all the health-related things that teenagers do in one neat package? Do we know what to do about their drug use, their unprotected sexual intercourse and their alienation from conventional medical care? What do we know and what don't we know?

What we now know is that the use of alcohol, tobacco, and marijuana is widespread among adolescents, regardless of their economic or social status or where they live. The use of these substances is far more common when someone else in their family smokes or drinks. And when it comes to abuse, it seems that the family plays an important role.

We know that adolescent girls are engaging more and more in sexual activity. We know, too, that sexual activity is not restricted to any social or economic class. But we don't know very much about how the other members of the families behave sexually and we know practically nothing about boys' sexual activity. Nor do we know enough about why some teenage couples use contraception effectively and others don't.

As might be expected, health and economic status go hand in hand. Adolescents from poor families are in poorer health than those in families with more money. They are sick more often, they (and their parents) perceive themselves as being in poorer health, and their eyes, ears and teeth are more likely to be defective or uncared-for. Children who receive no medical care or poor medical care early in life suffer the ill effects as teenagers. Adolescents and younger children from low-income families are less likely to be treated by private physicians and less likely to receive dental care.

For most adolescents, these years are a physically healthy period during which they test a wide variety of different ways of behaving. Teenagers are faced with few—but often conflicting—guidelines. This is especially so in a period of rapid and uneven physical and social change. No wonder adolescents suffer from anxiety.

What needs to be done? Surely, we must acknowledge that coping with changing behavior is critically important. But we must not neglect medical care. If we focus exclusively on one aspect of an adolescent's life—sex, drugs, mental health or medical problems—and ignore the others, we will fail to meet their multiple needs.

DOES PERSONALITY REALLY CHANGE AFTER 20?

ZICK RUBIN

Zick Rubin, who says he hasn't changed much in recent years, is Louis and Frances Salvage Professor of Social Psychology at Brandeis University and a contributing editor of *Psychology Today*. He is the coauthor (with the late Elton B. McNeil) of *The Psychology of Being Human*, Third Edition, an introductory psychology textbook that has been published by Harper & Row.

I n most of us," William James wrote in 1887, "by the age of 30, the character has set like plaster, and will never soften again." Though our bodies may be bent by the years and our opinions changed by the times, there is a basic core of self—a personality—that remains basically unchanged.

This doctrine of personality stability has been accepted psychological dogma for most of the past century. The dogma holds that the plaster of character sets by one's early 20s, if not even sooner than that.

Within the past decade, however, this traditional view has come to have an almost archaic flavor. The rallying cry of the 1970s has been people's virtually limitless capacity for change—not only in childhood but through the span of life. Examples of apparent transformation are highly publicized: Jerry Rubin enters the 1970s as a screaming, war-painted Yippie and emerges as a sedate Wall Street analyst wearing a suit and tie. Richard Alpert, an ambitious assistant professor of psychology at Harvard, tunes into drugs, heads for India, and returns as Baba Ram Dass, a long-bearded mystic in a flowing white robe who teaches people to "be here now." And Richard Raskind, a successful ophthalmol-

ogist, goes into the hospital and comes out as Renée Richards, a tall, well-muscled athlete on the women's tennis circuit.

Even for those of us who hold on to our original appearance (more or less) and gender, "change" and "growth" are now the bywords. The theme was seized upon by scores of organizations formed to help people change, from Weight Watchers to est. It was captured—and advanced—by Gail Sheehy's phenomenally successful book *Passages*, which emphasized people's continuing openness to change throughout the course of adulthood. At the same time, serious work in psychology was coming along—building on earlier theories of Carl Jung and Erik Erikson—to buttress the belief that adults keep on developing. Yale's Daniel Levinson, who provided much of Sheehy's intellectual inspiration, described, in *The Seasons of a Man's Life*, an adult life structure that is marked by periods of self-examination and transition. Psychiatrist Roger Gould, in *Transformations*, wrote of reshapings of the self during the early and middle adult years, "away from stagnation and claustrophobic suffocation toward vitality and an expanded sense of inner freedom."

The view that personality keeps changing throughout life has picked up so many adherents recently that it has practically become the new dogma. Quantitative studies have been offered to document the possibility of personality change in adulthood, whether as a consequence of getting married, changing jobs, or seeing one's children leave home. In a new volume entitled *Constancy and Change in Human Development*, two of the day's most influential behavioral scientists, sociologist Orville G. Brim, Jr., and psychologist Jerome Kagan, challenge the defenders of personality

stability to back up their doctrine with hard evidence. "The burden of proof," Brim and Kagan write, "is being shifted to the larger group, who adhere to the traditional doctrine of constancy, from the minority who suggest that it is a premise requiring evaluation."

And now we get to the newest act in the battle of the dogmas. Those who uphold the doctrine of personality stability have accepted the challenge. In the past few years they have assembled the strongest evidence yet available for the truth of their position—evidence suggesting that on several central dimensions of personality, including the ones that make up our basic social and emotional style, we are in fact astoundingly stable throughout the course of adult life.

The 'Litter-ature' on Personality

Until recently there was little firm evidence for the stability of personality, despite the idea's intuitive appeal. Instead, most studies showed little predictability from earlier to later times of life—or even, for that matter, from one situation to another within the same time period—thus suggesting an essential lack of consistency in people's personalities. Indeed, many researchers began to question whether it made sense to speak of "personality" at all.

But whereas the lack of predictability was welcomed by advocates of the doctrine of change through the life span, the defenders of stability have another explanation for it: most of the studies are lousy. Referring derisively to the "litter-ature" on personality, Berkeley psychologist Jack Block estimates that "perhaps 90 percent of the studies are methodologically inadcquate, without conceptual implication, and even foolish."

Block is right. Studies of personality have been marked by an abundance of untested measures (anyone can make up a new "scale" in an afternoon), small samples, and scatter-gun strategies ("Let's throw it into the computer and get some correlations"). Careful longitudinal studies, in which the same people are followed over the years, have been scarce. The conclusion that people are not predictable, then, may be a reflection not of human nature but of the haphazard methods used to study it.

Block's own research, in contrast, has amply demonstrated that people *are* predictable. Over the past 20 years Block has been analyzing extensive personality reports on several hundred Berkeley and Oakland residents that were first obtained in the 1930s, when the subjects were in junior high school. Researchers at Berkeley's Institute of Human Development followed up on the students when the subjects were in their late teens, again when they were in their mid-30s, and again in the late 1960s, when the subjects were all in their mid-40s.

The data archive is immense, including everything from attitude checklists filled out by the subjects to transcripts of interviews with the subjects, their parents, teachers, and spouses, with different sets of material gathered at each of the four time periods.

To reduce all the data to manageable proportions, Block began by assembling separate files of the information collected for each subject at each time period. Clinical psychologists were assigned to immerse themselves in individual dossiers and then to make a summary rating of the subject's personality by sorting a set of statements (for instance, "Has social poise and presence," and "Is self-defeating") into piles that indicated how representative the statement was of the subject. The assessments by the different raters (usually three for each dossier) were found to agree with one another to a significant degree, and they were averaged to form an overall description of the subject at that age. To avoid potential bias, the materials for each subject were carefully segregated by age level; all comments that

referred to the person at an earlier age were removed from the file. No psychologist rated the materials for the same subject at more than one time period.

Using this painstaking methodology, Block found a striking pattern of stability. In his most recent report, published earlier this year, he reported that on virtually every one of the 90 rating scales employed, there was a statistically significant correlation between subjects' ratings when they were in junior high school and their ratings 30 to 35 years later, when they were in their 40s. The most self-defeating adolescents were the most self-defeating adults; cheerful teenagers were cheerful 40-year-olds; those whose moods fluctuated when they were in junior high school were still experiencing mood swings in midlife.

'Still Stable After All These Years'

Even more striking evidence for the stability of personality, extending the time frame beyond middle age to late adulthood, comes from the work of Paul T. Costa, Jr., and Robert R. McCrae, both psychologists at the Gerontology Research Center of the National Institute on Aging in Baltimore. Costa and McCrae have tracked people's scores over time on standardized self-report personality scales, including the Sixteen Personality Factor Questionnaire and the Guilford-Zimmerman Temperament Survey, on which people are asked to decide whether or not each of several hundred statements describes them accurately. (Three sample items: "I would prefer to have an office of my own, not sharing it with another person." "Often I get angry with people too quickly." "Some people seem to ignore or avoid me, although I don't know why.")

Costa and McCrae combined subjects' responses on individual items to produce scale scores for each subject on such overall dimensions as extraversion and neuroticism, as well as on more specific traits, such as gregariousness, assertiveness, anxiety, and depression. By correlating over time the scores of subjects tested on two or three occasions—separated by six, 10, or 12 years—they obtained estimates of personality stability. The Baltimore

researchers have analyzed data from two large longitudinal studies, the Normative Aging Study conducted by the Veterans Administration in Boston and the Baltimore Longitudinal Study of Aging. In the Boston study, more than 400 men, ranging in age from 25 to 82, filled out a test battery in the mid-1960s and then completed a similar battery 10 years later, in the mid-1970s. In the Baltimore study, more than 200 men between the ages of 20 and 76 completed test batteries three times, separated by six-year intervals. Less extensive analyses, still unpublished, of the test scores of women in the Baltimore study point to a similar pattern of stability.

In both studies, Costa and McCrae found extremely high correlations, which indicated that the ordering of subjects on a particular dimension on one occasion was being maintained to a large degree a decade or more later. Contrary to what might have been predicted, young and middle-aged subjects turned out to be just as unchanging as old subjects were.

"The assertive 19-year-old is the assertive 40-year-old is the assertive 80-year-old," declares Costa, extrapolating from his and McCrae's results, which covered shorter time spans. For the title of a persuasive new paper reporting their results, Costa and McCrae rewrote a Paul Simon song title, proclaiming that their subjects were "Still Stable After All These Years."

Other recent studies have added to the accumulating evidence for personality stability throughout the life span. Gloria Leon and her coworkers at the University of Minnesota analyzed the scores on the Minnesota Multiphasic Personality Inventory (MMPI) of 71 men who were tested in 1947, when they were about 50 years old, and again in 1977, when they were close to 80. They found significant correlations on all 13 of the MMPI scales, with the highest correlation over the 30-year period on the scale of "Social Introversion." Costa and McCrae, too, found the highest degrees of stability, ranging from .70 to .84, on measures of introversion-extraversion, which assess gregariousness, warmth, and assertiveness. And Paul Mussen and his colleagues at Berkeley, analyzing interviewers' ratings of 53 women who were seen at ages 30 and 70, found significant correlations on such aspects of introversion-extraversion as talkativeness, excitability, and cheerfulness.

Although character may be most fixed in the domain of introversion-extraversion, Costa and McCrae found almost as much constancy in the domain of "neuroticism," which includes such specific traits as depression, anxiety, hostility, and impulsiveness. Neurotics are likely to be complainers throughout life. They may complain about different things as they get older—for example, worries about love in early adulthood, a "midlife crisis" at about age 40, health problems in late adulthood—but they are still complaining. The less neurotic person reacts to the same events with greater equanimity. Although there is less extensive evidence for its stability, Costa and McCrae also believe that there is an enduring trait of "openness to experience," including such facets as openness to feelings, ideas, and values.

Another recent longitudinal study of personality, conducted by University of Minnesota sociologist Jeylan Mortimer and her coworkers, looked at the self-ratings of 368 University of Michigan men who were tested in 1962–63, when they were freshmen, in 1966–67, when they were seniors, and in 1976, when they were about 30. At each point the subjects rated themselves on various characteristics, such as relaxed, strong, warm, and different. The ratings were later collapsed into overall scores for well-being, competence, sociability, and unconventionality. On each of these dimensions, Mortimer found a pattern of persistence rather than one of change. Mortimer's analysis of the data also suggested that life experiences such as the nature of one's work had an impact on personality. But the clearest message of her research is, in her own words, "very high stability."

Is *Everybody* Changing?

The high correlations between assessments made over time indicate that people in a given group keep the same rank order on the traits being measured, even as they traverse long stretches of life. But maybe *everyone* changes as he or she gets older. If, for example, everyone turns inward to

about the same extent in the latter part of life, the correlations—representing people's *relative* standing—on measures of introversion could still be very high, thus painting a misleading picture of stability. And, indeed, psychologist Bernice Neugarten concluded as recently as five years ago that there was a general tendency for people to become more introverted in the second half of life. Even that conclusion has been called into question, however. The recent longitudinal studies have found only slight increases in introversion as people get older, changes so small that Costa and McCrae consider them to be of little practical significance.

Specifically, longitudinal studies have shown slight drops over the course of adulthood in people's levels of excitement seeking, activity, hostility, and impulsiveness. The Baltimore researchers find no such changes in average levels of gregariousness, warmth, assertiveness, depression, or anxiety. Costa summarizes the pattern of changes as "a mellowing—but the person isn't so mellowed that you can't recognize him." Even as this mellowing occurs, moreover, people's relative ordering remains much the same—on the average, everyone drops the same few standard points. Thus, an "impulsive" 25-year-old may be a bit less impulsive by the time he or she is 70 but is still likely to be more impulsive than his or her agemates.

The new evidence of personality stability has been far too strong for the advocates of change to discount. Even in the heart of changeland, in Brim and Kagan's *Constancy and Change in Human Development*, psychologists Howard Moss and Elizabeth Susman review the research and conclude that there is strong evidence for the continuity of personality.

People Who Get Stuck

The new evidence has not put the controversy over personality stability and change to rest, however. If anything, it has sharpened it. Although he praises the new research, Orville Brim is not convinced by it that adults are fundamentally unchanging. He points out that the high correlations signify strong associations between measures, but not total constancy. For example, a .70 correlation between

scores obtained at two different times means that half of the variation (.70 squared, or .49) between people's later scores can be predicted from their earlier scores. The apostles of stability focus on this predictability, which is all the more striking because of the imperfect reliability of the measures employed. But the prophets of change, like Brim, prefer to dwell on the half of the variability that cannot be predicted, which they take as evidence of change.

Thus, Costa and McCrae look at the evidence they have assembled, marvel at the stability that it indicates, and call upon researchers to explain it: to what extent may the persistence of traits bespeak inherited biological predispositions, enduring influences from early childhood, or patterns of social roles and expectations that people get locked into? And at what age does the plaster of character in fact begin to set? Brim looks at the same evidence, acknowledges the degree of stability that it indicates, and then calls upon researchers to explain why some people in the sample are changing. "When you focus on stability," he says, "you're looking at the dregs—the people who have gotten stuck. You want to look at how a person grows and changes, not at how a person stays the same."

Brim, who is a president of the Foundation for Child Development in New York, also emphasizes that only certain aspects of personality—most clearly, aspects of social and emotional style, such as introversion-extraversion, depression, and anxiety—have been shown to be relatively stable. Brim himself is more interested in other parts of personality, such as people's self-esteem, sense of control over their lives, and ultimate values. These are the elements of character that Brim believes undergo the most important changes over the course of life. "Properties like gregariousness don't interest me," he admits; he does not view such traits as central to the fulfillment of human possibilities.

If Brim is not interested in some of the personality testers' results, Daniel Levinson is even less interested. In his view, paper-and-pencil measures like those used by Costa and McCrae are trivial, reflecting, at best, peripheral aspects of life. (Indeed, critics suggest that such research indicates only that people are stable in the way they fill out personality scales.) Levinson sees the whole enterprise of "rigorous" studies of personality stability as another instance of psychologists' rushing in to measure whatever they have measures for before they have clarified the important issues. "I think most psychologists and sociologists don't have the faintest idea what adulthood is about," he says.

Levinson's own work at the Yale School of Medicine (see "Growing Up with the Dream," *Psychology Today,* January 1978) has centered on the adult's evolving life structure—the way in which a person's social circumstances, including work and family ties, and inner feelings and aspirations fit together in an overall picture. Through intensive interviews of a small sample of men in the middle years of life—he is now conducting a parallel study of women—Levinson has come to view adult development as marked by an alternating sequence of relatively stable "structure-building" periods and periods of transition. He has paid special attention to the transition that occurs at about the age of 40. Although this midlife transition may be either smooth or abrupt, the person who emerges from it is always different from the one who entered it.

The midlife transition provides an important opportunity for personal growth. For example, not until we are past 40, Levinson believes, can we take a "universal" view of ourselves and the world rising above the limited perspective of our own background to appreciate the fullest meaning of life. "I don't think anyone can write tragedy—real tragedy—before the age of 40," Levinson declares.

Disagreement Over Methods

As a student of biography, Levinson does not hesitate to take a biographical view of the controversy at hand. "To Paul Costa," he suggests in an understanding tone, "the most important underlying issue is probably the specific issue of personality stability or change. I think the question of *development* is really not important to him personally. But he's barely getting to 40, so he has time." Levinson himself began his research on adult development when he was 46, as part of a way of understanding the changes

he had undergone in the previous decade. He is now 60.

Costa, for his part, thinks that Levinson's clinical approach to research, based on probing interviews with small numbers of people, lacks the rigor needed to establish anything conclusively. "It's only 40 people, for crying out loud!" he exclaims. And Costa doesn't view his own age (he is 38) or that of his colleague McCrae (who is 32) as relevant to the questions under discussion.

Jack Block, who is also a hardheaded quantitative researcher— and, for the record, is fully 57 years old— shares Costa's view of Levinson's method. "The interviews pass through the mind of Dan Levinson and a few other people," Block grumbles, "and he writes it down." Block regards Levinson as a good psychologist who should be putting forth his work as speculation, and not as research.

As this byplay suggests, some of the disagreement between the upholders of stability and the champions of change is methodological. Those who argue for the persistence of traits tend to offer rigorous personality-test evidence, while those who emphasize the potential for change often offer more qualitative, clinical descriptions. The psychometricians scoff at the clinical reports as unreliable, while the clinicians dismiss the psychometric data as trivial. This summary oversimplifies the situation, though, because some of the strongest believers in change, like Brim, put a premium on statistical, rather than clinical, evidence.

When pressed, people on both sides of the debate agree that personality is characterized by *both* stability and change. But they argue about the probabilities assigned to different outcomes. Thus, Costa maintains that "the assertive 19-year-old is the assertive 40-year-old is the assertive 80-year-old...*unless something happens to change it.*" The events that would be likely to change deeply ingrained patterns would have to be pretty dramatic ones. As an example, Costa says that he would not be surprised to see big personality changes in the Americans who were held hostage in Iran.

From Brim's standpoint, in contrast, people's personalities—and especially their feelings of mastery, con-

trol, and self-esteem—will keep changing through the course of life... *unless they get stuck.* As an example, he notes that a coal miner who spends 10 hours a day for 50 years down the shaft may have little opportunity for psychological growth. Brim believes that psychologists should try to help people get out of such ruts of stability. And he urges researchers to look more closely at the ways in which life events—not only the predictable ones, such as getting married or retiring, but also the unpredictable ones, such as being fired or experiencing a religious conversion—may alter adult personality.

At bottom, it seems, the debate is not so much methodological as ideological, reflecting fundamental differences of opinion about what is most important in the human experience. Costa and McCrae emphasize the value of personality constancy over time as a central ingredient of a stable sense of identity. "If personality were not stable," they write, "our ability to make wise choices about our future lives would be severely limited." We must know what we are like—and what we will continue to be like—if we are to make intelligent choices, whether of careers, spouses, or friends. Costa and McCrae view the maintenance of a stable personality in the face of the vicissitudes of life as a vital human accomplishment.

Brim, however, views the potential for growth as the hallmark of humanity. "The person is a dynamic organism," he says, "constantly striving to master its environment and to become something more than it is." He adds, with a sense of purpose in his voice, "I see psychology in the service of liberation, not constraint."

Indeed, Brim suspects that we are now in the midst of "a revolution in human development," from a traditional pattern of continuity toward greater discontinuity throughout the life span. Medical technology (plastic surgery and sex-change surgery, for example), techniques of behavior modification, and the social supports for change provided by thousands of groups "from TA to TM, from AA to Zen" are all part of this revolution. Most important, people are trying, perhaps for the first time in history, to change *themselves.*

Some social critics, prominent

among them Christopher Lasch in *The Culture of Narcissism*, have decried the emphasis on self-improvement as a manifestation of the "Me" generation's excessive preoccupation with self. In Brim's view, these critics miss the point. "Most of the concern with oneself going on in this country," he declares, "is not people being selfish, but rather trying to be better, trying to be something more than they are now." If Brim is right in his reading of contemporary culture, future studies of personality that track people through the 1970s and into the 1980s may well show less stability and more change than the existing studies have shown.

The Tension in Each of Us

In the last analysis, the tension between stability and change is found not only in academic debates but also in each of us. As Brim and Kagan write, "There is, on the one hand, a powerful drive to maintain the sense of one's identity, a sense of continuity that allays fears of changing too fast or of being changed against one's will by outside forces. . . . On the other hand, each person is, by nature, a purposeful, striving organism with a desire to be more than he or she is now. From making simple new year's resolutions to undergoing transsexual operations, everyone is trying to become something that he or she is not, but hopes to be."

A full picture of adult personality development would inevitably reflect this tension between sameness and transformation. Some aspects of personality, such as a tendency to be reclusive or outgoing, calm or anxious, may typically be more stable than other aspects, such as a sense of mastery over the environment. Nevertheless, it must be recognized that each of us reflects, over time, both stability and change. As a result, observers can look at a person as he or she goes through a particular stretch of life and see either stability or change or—if the observer looks closely enough—both.

For example, most people would look at Richard Alpert, the hard-driving psychology professor of the early 1960s, and Ram Dass, the bearded, free-flowing guru of the 1970s, and see that totally different persons are here now. But Harvard psychologist David McClelland, who knew Alpert well, spent time with the Indian holy man and said to himself, "It's the same old Dick!"—still as charming, as concerned with inner experience, and as power-oriented as ever. And Jerry Rubin can view his own transformation from Yippie to Wall Streeter in a way that recognizes the underlying continuity: "Finding out who I really was was done in typical Jerry Rubin way. I tried everything, jumped around like crazy with boundless energy and curiosity." If we look closely enough, even Richard Raskind and Renée Richards will be found to have a great deal in common.

Whether a person stays much the same or makes sharp breaks with the past may depend in large measure on his or her own ideas about what is possible and about what is valuable. Psychological research on adult development can itself have a major impact on these ideas by calling attention to what is "normal" and by suggesting what is desirable. Now that researchers have established beyond reasonable doubt that there is often considerable stability in adult personality, they may be able to move on to a clearer understanding of how we can grow and change, even as we remain the same people we always were. It may be, for example, that if we are to make significant changes in ourselves, without losing our sense of identity, it is necessary for some aspects of our personality to remain stable. "I'm different now," we can say, "but it's still me."

As Jack Block puts it, in his characteristically judicious style: "Amidst change and transformation, there is an essential coherence to personality development."

For further information read:

Block, Jack, "Some Enduring and Consequential Structures of Personality" in A.I. Rabin et al. eds., *Further Explorations in Personality*, Wiley-Interscience, 1981, $24.50.

Brim, Orville G., Jr., and Jerome Kagan, eds., *Constancy and Change in Human Development*, Harvard University Press, 1980, $27.50.

Costa, Paul T., Jr., and Robert R. McCrae, "Still Stable After All These Years: Personality as a Key to Some Issues in Adulthood and Old Age," in Paul B. Baltes and Orville G. Brim, Jr., eds., *Life-span Development and Behavior* Vol. 3, Academic Press, 1980, $35.

Levinson, Daniel J., et al., *The Seasons of a Man's Life*, Alfred A. Knopf, 1978, $10.95; paper; Ballantine Books, 1979, $5.95.

Becoming One's Own Man

Adult life, a new study argues, is a series of crises. The most crucial begins when men reach their mid-thirties

DANIEL J. LEVINSON

The following article is adapted from the newly published book The Seasons of a Man's Life,* by professor of psychology Daniel J. Levinson and four colleagues at Yale University. It is based on the results of an exhaustive study of forty men — executives, academic biologists, novelists, and hourly wage earners — conducted over a period of years.

Levinson's team studied its subjects with the primary aim of creating "a developmental perspective on adulthood in men." As the work progressed, the researchers came to reject the common notion of adulthood as a fixed and unchanging state in favor of the concept of the life process as a sequence of seasons — periods or stages within the total life cycle. Moreover, as a man progresses from one season to the next, he almost invariably goes through a sequence of transitions: in early adulthood, in mid-life, and again in the later years. Each of these transitions produces predictable crises and patterns of behavior. Perhaps the most crucial of these begins in the mid-thirties, as men outgrow dependence in an effort to become their own men.

The effort to be more fully one's own person — to be more independent and self-sufficient and less subject to the control of others — is found at many ages. We see it, for example, in the two-year-old stubbornly insisting on his rights and trying to maintain his own initiative in a world that seems forever to be constraining him. In the Early-Adult Transition, the adolescent-becoming-adult has a special concern for his own independence as he struggles to pull away more completely from parents and from the pre-adult self that is still so strongly tied to them.

This issue takes a new form, and a central place, in the end phase of Settling Down. This phase, Becoming One's Own Man, extends from about thirty-six or thirty-seven to forty or forty-one. It represents the culmination of Settling Down and, more broadly, the peaking of early adulthood and the first stirrings of what lies beyond.

A man's primary developmental tasks in Becoming One's Own Man are to accomplish the goals of Settling Down, to advance sufficiently on his ladder, to become a senior member of his enterprise, to speak more clearly with his own voice, to have a greater measure of authority, and to be less dependent (internally as well as externally) on other individuals and institutions in his life.

There is a built-in dilemma here. On the one hand, a man wants to be more independent, more true to himself and less vulnerable to pressures and blandishments from others. On the other hand, he seeks affirmation in society. Speaking with his own voice is important, even if no one listens — but he especially wants to be heard and respected and given the rewards that are his due. The wish for independence leads him to do what he alone considers most essential, regardless of consequences; the wish for affirmation makes him sensitive to the responses of others and susceptible to their influence.

The developmental tasks of Becoming One's Own Man — carrying through the Settling Down enterprise, becoming more senior and expert, and getting affirmed by society — assume primary importance during the late thirties. A man is likely to be rather sensitive, even touchy, about anything in the environment or in himself that interferes with these aims. Since the successful outcome of this period is not assured, he often feels that he has not accomplished enough and that he is not sufficiently his own man. He may have a sense of being held back, of being oppressed by others and restrained by his own conflicts and inhibitions.

External circumstances during these years are frequently restrictive and damaging to self-esteem. Organizations often operate so rigidly or corruptly that an individual places his career in jeopardy if he is very forthright or eager to take the ball and run. It is generally safer to avoid controversy and be a loyal member of the "team" and not to speak too loudly with one's own voice. As a man advances, he comes in closer contact with senior men who have their territories to maintain and protect. Their interest in him often contains a subtle mixture of support and intimidation. He receives a double message: "Be a good boy and you'll go far," together with, "Make trouble and you're dead."

The difficulties of this period have important internal sources as well. The wish for affirmation and advancement makes a man especially vulnerable to social pressure. A man who has prided himself on his ability to act autonomously realizes now that he is not as independent as he had thought. In crucial situations he has been too eager to please, too sensitive to criticism, too conforming to speak and act on the basis of his own convictions. He wants to be his own man, but he also wants desperately to be understood and appreciated, to have his talents affirmed, to succeed in his enterprise.

But the difficulty goes deeper than this. Becoming One's Own Man represents a peaking in the aspirations of early adulthood. A man wants to become a "senior" adult, to realize the fruits of the labors of the past fifteen or twenty years, to accomplish goals that will provide a base for his life in the years to come. The urgency of the desire for manhood, however, brings about a resurgence of the little boy in the adult.

It is not necessarily a sign of pathology or impaired development in early adulthood that many boyish qualities operate with great force. Indeed, the intensification of the boy-man conflict is a step forward. It creates the possibility of resolving the conflict at a higher level.

During this period, however, the intensified conflict becomes an inner source of difficulty. The adult self desires to fulfill certain values, to be a productive member of society, and to bear as best he can the responsibilities that this demands. The boyish self contributes to this effort in many ways with his imagination, energy, and idealism, his sense of adventure and wonderment. However, the boyish self is also a source of opposition and discontent. He wants to attain great heights through magical omnipotence rather than the sweat of his brow. He wants things to go effortlessly his way, without having to consider the conflicting needs or requirements of others. When sufficient recognition is not forthcoming, the little boy feels totally deprived and humiliated. When a boss or other authority is restrictive or imposing, it is the little boy who feels utterly helpless and intimidated. The boyish self becomes the ingratiating sycophant, the ever agreeable "nice guy" or the impulsive, self-defeating rebel—but not the persevering worker or the leader who uses his authority for constructive, humane ends. It is the little boy inside the man who transforms the ordinary mortals with whom he is involved—bosses, wives, mentors, colleagues—into tyrants, corrupters, villainous rivals, seducers, and witches.

There is always some mixture of reality and distortion in these experiences. To some degree the persons and institutions in a man's life *are* tyrannical, corrupting, and exploitative. He often finds it hard to sort things out. During this time he frequently vacillates between the extremes of depressive self-blame (when he feels absolutely inept, impotent, and lacking in inner resources) and paranoid rage (when he blames an evil or uncaring world for suppressing or ignoring his enormous talents and virtues). When these internal conflicts and external stresses are at their height, it is difficult indeed to maintain one's good judgment and initiative.

During the period of Becoming One's Own Man, relationships with mentors who have helped in earlier development are likely to be especially stormy and vulnerable. The termination of a close tie with a mentor is often a mutually painful, tortuous process. A man in his late thirties is not only giving up his current mentor, he is outgrowing the readiness to be the protégé of any older person. He must reject the mentoring relationship not because it is intrinsically harmful but because it has served its purpose. It has helped him to make a basic developmental advance, but in Becoming One's Own Man, a new task arises: a man must move toward becoming a senior adult and full peer of his former mentors, teachers, and bosses. He himself must become a men-

tor, father, constructive authority, and noncompetitive friend of other adults. This developmental achievement is the essence of adulthood. If a man is to assume responsibility for others and for himself during middle adulthood, he must attain his "seniority."

The little boy still desperately wants the mentor to be a good father in the most childish sense—a father who will make him special, will endow him with magical powers, and will not require him to compete or prove himself in relation to would-be rivals. It is also the little boy who anxiously makes the mentor into a bad father—a depriving, dictatorial authority who has no real love and merely uses him for his own needs. The relationship is made untenable by the yearning for the good father, the anxiety over the bad father, and the projection of both these internal figures onto the mentor, who is then caught in a bind.

One of the novelists in our study, Allen Perry, presented us with a vivid example of a significant mentor relationship. At forty-four, he recalls the story as if it had happened yesterday. In his early twenties, after college and military service, Perry went to New York with the single aim of becoming a writer. He took an extension course taught by Calvin Randall, who was then an editor at a leading publishing house. They immediately formed a close bond:

Randall gave me tremendous support and encouragement. I was very close to this man—enormously, deeply committed to him, in fact. He had a wonderful quality, but I later realized that this quality was good only if you were young, and once you became a man yourself it almost became a matter of competition.

But the break occurred some years later, when Perry was thirty-five. He had just completed his second novel and taken it to his mentor. By this time Randall was editor in chief and a nationally known figure, "due partly to his connection with my work." It took him two weeks to get around to the manuscript. And, when they finally met, it was a great disappointment:

I realized that he wasn't interested in my work so much as in his own career. If there was ever a person who demonstrated the sad effects of the sin of hubris, it's him. He really lost touch with his protégés, myself included. I'd come to discuss a manuscript and he'd spend two or three hours describing his great publishing plans. When he moved to another firm, he asked me to shift with him. If the relationship had remained as it was, I wouldn't have hesitated. Instead, I decided to give him up. I still remember distinctly the letter I wrote him almost ten

years ago. These are close to the actual words: "To go with you now, even including the fact that I admire you so much, would be an admission that you are absolutely essential to my development, when, in fact, you must be aware that this is not true. It's no insult to you, your credentials or your talent, but it would have been demeaning to my integrity as a writer." I learned later from someone who was there that he burst into tears when he read the letter. He was hurt for a long time and felt that I had betrayed him. For me, however, it was an act of liberation. I realize now that thirty-five is really a very vulnerable period. Breaking with Calvin Randall was just the beginning of some liberating process.

Allen Perry's bitterness did not destroy his attachment to Randall. His son, born at the time of the break, was named after the mentor. The relationship is now amicable but reserved—perhaps as good as it can be:

I'm very thankful at this moment that we've patched it all up. I'm a grown man, you know, and not his boy. I have an excellent editor now. We are friendly, but it's not the kind of passionate relationship I had with Randall. I don't think I'll ever have that again, or want it. Now it's my turn to give that help to others, though I'll never have Calvin's interest or skill at it.

Men rarely have mentors after about forty. A man may have valued relationships with family, friends, counselors, and co-workers, but the mentor relationship in its full, early-adult form is rare. It is surrendered, with other things, as part of Becoming One's Own Man. One result is a greater ability and interest in being a mentor to others.

The Settling Down period is the culmination of early adulthood, the time for a man to realize the hopes of his youth. What are the various ways of going through this period, and what are its outcomes? Ignoring those men whose lives remained unstable and in a state of flux throughout the Settling Down period, we distinguished four ways of establishing a second adult life structure and Becoming One's Own Man. There is nothing absolute about these categories; they are simply a convenient means of describing variations. However, everyone we studied went through one or another of these sequences.

The first and most common pattern—fifty-five percent of the men we studied fell within it—we defined as advancement within a stable life structure. Here, life proceeds more or less according to expectations. During the early Settling Down phase, a man makes his primary commitments, defines an enterprise, and gradually enriches and elaborates the initial life structure. He may experience a

1. BECOMING A PERSON

good deal of hardship and suffering, but the stresses are manageable and the satisfactions outweigh the difficulties.

The final goal of advancement in this sequence is often defined concretely in terms of a key event that in the man's mind symbolizes true success. This event carries the ultimate message of his affirmation by society. The young writer does not want to write just another book; he wants to make a quantum leap in his writing. The academic biologist aspires to become a full professor, to achieve seniority in his university and discipline, to make a major breakthrough in his research, or, if truth be told, to win the Nobel Prize. The executive knows by thirty-five that he must reach a certain level by forty; otherwise, he will be unable to advance further. The worker, too, seeks a higher job grade or a supervisory position. He may obtain a union position, such as shop steward, that carries another form of seniority. Or he may define his goals less in terms of occupation and more in terms of family, leisure, or community.

Whatever their goals, these men form a life structure early in the Settling Down period and maintain it throughout. Important changes may occur—in place and kind of residence, job, income, life-style, family pattern—but these represent advancements, enrichments, or difficulties within the existing framework and not a change in the basic structure.

Around forty, these men reach the top rung of their Settling Down ladder and attain goals that represent the culmination of years of striving. Reaching this level is not the end of the story. The successes of this period bring a man into a new and different world. He is now a newcomer entering a "senior" world. In the process of establishing himself, he has joined an establishment. It bears the responsibility for many people—whether in industry, the university, writing/publishing, trade unions, the extended family. He starts afresh in this world, and if he remains in it, his life structure will evolve in unanticipated ways over the course of middle adulthood.

About twenty percent of our men fall into a pattern of serious failure or decline within a stable life structure. Some of them fail in gross and obvious ways during the course of Settling Down. Others achieve a good deal of external success but fail in certain crucial respects that make the entire enterprise pointless in their own eyes.

None of the hourly workers found it possible to make a significant advance in job level during their late thirties. A few were reconciled to this and found other ways—through their unions, families, or community life—to gain a sense of progress and seniority.

Equivalent kinds of failure in Settling Down were found in three of our ten executives. All three had with great effort achieved positions in middle management by their mid-thirties. They started the phase of Becoming One's Own Man with great hopes for advancement, and failure came to them as a bitter disappointment.

Other middle managers received occasional promotions and were able to remain in the company without too great humiliation. By the late thirties, however, they had reached their ceilings: not only would they fail in their goals but their sense of direction and their possibilities for the future were undermined. The structure of management in industry is pyramidal, with only one position in top management for every fifteen or twenty in middle management. Since the culture of management places a great value on upward mobility, most middle managers are doomed to personal failure, ranging in degree from moderate to devastating.

A similar pyramid exists—although with different characteristics—in our universities. The outcome of that competition can be as devastating as in industry. Some of the faculty members we studied at a first-rate university were told in their late thirties that they would not be promoted to tenured professorships and would have to leave the following year. This is more the rule than the exception in such universities: the majority of younger faculty members, like middle managers in industry, do not gain senior positions. Most of them go to other universities, at various academic levels and salaries. In each case the change represents both advancement and a kind of demotion. It is accompanied by the most contradictory self-evaluation and feelings.

The third and most volatile response to this period can best be defined as breaking out: trying for a new life structure. Often the conflicts that are generated undermine and destroy marriage or career; sometimes the result is a sense of alienation from every aspect of a man's world.

Such a response is perhaps the most dramatic example of the late thirties as a time of crisis. Just when one is most eager to become his own man and to fulfill his adult aspirations, he feels that there is something fundamentally wrong. Having made his bed (marital, occupational, or whatever), he cannot continue to lie in it. Yet to change is to tear the fabric of his life, to destroy much that he has built over the last ten or fifteen years. As he struggles to make the fateful decision—to break out or to stay put—he is likely to be moody, uncommunicative, alternately resentful of others and critical of himself.

The difficulty lies partly in the actuality of his life. This man's life structure is indeed flawed. It does not permit him to live out crucially important aspects of the self, and it requires him to be someone he can no longer accept. But the flaws have existed, and have been tolerated, for some time. They become intolerable now because the tasks of Becoming One's Own Man are so urgent: it is essential to pursue the dream, to be a person of independence and integrity, to be more fully a man, to be less enslaved by the little boy in himself who desperately needs to be cared for and who is victimized by his inner ties to powerful, exploitative adults.

The process of breaking out may go on in marriage and other relationships with women. As a man struggles with the little boy in himself, he struggles as well with the maternal figures in himself and his wife. He experiences his wife largely in maternal terms: at best, a good mother benignly nurturing her flock and managing the family life; at worst, a destructive witch or selfish bitch, using both her strength and her weakness to keep him in line and prevent him from becoming what he truly wants to be.

As he sees it, his wife cannot hear what he is trying to tell her, nor can she appreciate his need for greater measures of both autonomy and intimate sharing. From her point of view, he is unaccountably upset, full of strong but inchoate grievances, suddenly critical of her and of the life they have labored so long to achieve, yet unable to tell her what he now wants. It is difficult to sort out the various elements in this situation: both husband and wife have been involved in creating the relationship, and both will have a part in determining its outcome.

The result may be separation and divorce, but there are other outcomes as well. A period of open warfare or silent conflict may end in a kind of cold-war truce in which a poor marriage is endured because of various external and internal constraints. In some cases the couple are able to change themselves and their lives and make their marriage more satisfactory than before.

This sequence highlights the difficulties and potential costs of forming a badly flawed life structure at the start of the Settling Down period. As a man starts the phase of Becoming One's Own Man, the flaws become less tolerable and he is faced with a terrible dilemma. If he remains in this structure there is the danger that he will be unable to become his own man. On the other hand, he has already made major commitments within the early Settling Down structure and changing them may be hurtful to family, coworkers, and others who depend on him. Breaking out of this structure is a tough undertaking, indeed.

If a man tries to terminate his occupation or his marriage, it will take several years to carry through the process of separation. The first occupation and marriage/family will continue to hold a significant place in his life, though they will have new meanings and a new place in the structure. The breaking out may be dramatized by a single decisive act, a marker event such as moving out of the home or quitting a job or going to another part of the country. But the process of breaking away began earlier and will go on for much longer than is usually recognized. The process of breaking in—making new choices and building a new life—is also time-consuming. A man may remarry soon after leaving his first wife, but it will take several years to establish a new marriage (and, often, a new family). If he makes a change in occupation, he will go through a period of transition as he leaves one occupational world and gradually enters the next.

Finally, and this is the hardest blow of all, before a man who breaks out at thirty-seven can create a new life structure in which to realize his early adult aspirations, he enters the Mid-life Transition at forty or forty-one. Now all of his aspirations and illusions come into question. We found that every man who attempted a major life change in the late thirties, as part of Becoming One's Own Man, went through a period of considerable instability and flux lasting eight to ten years. It is not possible to establish a new structure until the Mid-life Transition ends and a new stable period, Entering Middle Adulthood, begins in the mid-forties.

Are the costs of undertaking such extreme changes greater or less than the gains? Should a highly flawed Settling Down structure be dismantled, or should a man stay put and try to repair or endure it? There are no simple answers here. The problem is that the key choices a man makes in forming his life structure at the start of Settling Down are very hard to modify. A highly flawed structure will be extremely costly in any case, whether he stays put or breaks out. Part of the diffi-

culty is that a man in this predicament cannot predict the costs and gains of any course of action. Small wonder, then, if he feels overwhelmed by the negative prospects of either choice: staying put may lead to a kind of living death (or suicide); breaking out may be destructive to his loved ones and not bring the better life he craves.

The fourth basic pattern we have identified as advancement that produces a change in life structure. A man receives a promotion or a drastic increase in income. At first glance the increase seems to be a great boon, an opportunity to live better and do things that he has long wanted to do. But this gain propels him into a new world in which he has new roles and relationships. It activates new aspects of the self while providing little room for the expression of other, formerly important aspects. In short, it leads to a change in his life structure. The advancement is a mixed blessing, and it may turn out to be a curse.

This sequence is well represented by an executive, Roger Mohn. After getting his engineering degree, he returned to his hometown and took a job in a large manufacturing firm, where he has worked ever since. At twenty-four, he got married and began a life that had great stability until his mid-thirties. During this time he worked in a shop that made special products. He found the work interesting, and he had little desire for advancement. By his early thirties Mohn was the head of the shop and traveled around the country developing and testing new products. He and his wife bought a home in a modest middle-class neighborhood. Their two children were born when he was thirty-one and thirty-five. This time—in the early Settling Down period—was the high point of his adult life. He loved his work and devoted long hours to it.

When Mohn was thirty-seven the company rewarded him with a middle-management position as purchasing manager. Unable to refuse this advancement, he entered a new occupation and a new world. The promotion was a first step in

changing his life structure. He gave up the leadership of the small production-centered world he loved and took on managerial functions in an impersonal, competitive world that lay beyond his earlier ken. Although he enjoyed it less, he was excited by the challenge and did well. As he turned forty, he was offered a senior position as manager of manufacturing, with responsibility for four hundred people and an annual budget of $9 million.

From thirty-seven to forty, Roger Mohn succeeded occupationally beyond his most extravagant dreams. But the advancement changed the character of his life. It eliminated what had been the central element of his earlier life structure: the metal shop and his distinctive role within it. It introduced a major new element: an executive position for which he lacked experience and motivation and for which he was given minimal training. The new job tripled his income and placed him among colleagues at work whose class level was markedly above his. It enabled him—or forced him—to move out of the lower middle class in which he had been firmly rooted by his family of origin and his own commitments. In brief, Roger Mohn's promotions during the phase of Becoming One's Own Man, from thirty-seven to forty, took him off the ladder he had earlier chosen. The new ladder permitted much greater external success but was beyond his primary aspirations and alien to his primary cultural world. He overreached himself. The years from forty-one to forty-five were the low point of his life.

These are the possibilities—and the tragedies—of the Settling Down period. The basic character of this period is the same for all men. It stems from the major developmental tasks and issues confronting us all. At the same time, men work on these tasks in myriad ways, and there are infinite variations in the individual life course. Whatever its course and outcome, this period comes to an end at around forty as new developmental tasks gain primacy and a new period begins

Sex Roles and Sex Differences

Sex is determined by biology. Sexual identity, or the way we *perceive* our sexuality, is far more complicated. Until recently the prevalent view was that sex roles are primarily learned, that we are born psychosexually neutral. Lately, however, researchers have produced evidence that biological predisposition to maleness or femaleness is inborn. This inborn bias provides the standard against which environmental forces are experienced, considered, and internalized. From this point of view, rearing and other environmental factors reinforce rather than define.

The question of sexual differences raises political as well as psychological controversy. Many beliefs about differences between men and women are the result of cultural stereotyping. Empirical evidence is often unavailable or subject to conflicting interpretation.

Some stereotypes seem to be supported by evidence: males *are* more aggressive, females more verbal. Other stereotypes crumble under investigation: females are *not* more social, males more analytical. Still other stereotypes resist confirmation or denial. But the myths continue because those who believe in them see only that which confirms their beliefs.

Some sex differences are apparently real, then, and an explanation may lie in the way male and female brains are organized. Further, it may be that these organizational differences are inherited. Research into biochemical differences and the brain's sensorimotor processes has documented certain areas of competency by sex, for example: men have better daylight vision, women better night vision; men have faster reaction time and excel in spatial skills; women are more sensitive to touch and excel in verbal skills and fine motor coordination. One implication of this research is that boys and girls, since they *learn* differently, might each learn more effectively if *taught* differently.

In some ways men and women appear to suffer differently, also. Many researchers have concluded that women are more vulnerable to depression than men. On the other hand, women are more likely to seek help for their problems while men have been conditioned not to. Suppression of so-called "feminine" traits, such as dependency and passivity, make men more prone to sexual anxiety than women.

Such sexual pressures undoubtedly have contributed to the trend toward androgyny that blossomed in the 1960s, out of which strode the unisex sensibility manifested from fashion through science fiction. Purely speaking, androgyny is that which removes gender and sexual preference from most areas of human behavior.

We have witnessed in the last decade a constriction of traditional sex roles, but not many people would call for androgyny as an answer to the problems of sex differences. Men and women are different. What is important is that the differences be equally valued. Consider the following questions while reading this section. What factors contribute to sexual identity? How do sexual stereotypes interfere with personal growth? Is true androgyny possible given the hormonal differences and the effect they have on behavior?

31

WHAT WE KNOW AND DON'T KNOW ABOUT SEX DIFFERENCES

Myth, Reality and Shades of Gray

Eleanor Emmons Maccoby and Carol Nagy Jacklin

Eleanor Emmons Maccoby is professor of psychology and Chairman of the Department of Psychology at Stanford University. She is well-known for her work in many areas of developmental child psychology, including attachment in early childhood, and the development of sex differences. Maccoby has been a fellow at the Center for Advanced Study in the Behavioral Sciences, and is a past president of the American Psychological Association's Division of Developmental Psychology. Currently she is President of the Western Psychological Association, and was elected a Fellow of the American Academy of Arts and Sciences in 1974.

Carol Nagy Jacklin received her M.A. in psychology in 1961 from the University of Connecticut and her Ph.D. in 1972 from Brown University. In 1971-72 she worked with Professor Maccoby as an NIH postdoctoral fellow. Since 1972 she has been a research associate at Stanford University. Jacklin's interests are in the development of sex differences and infant learning and perception.

In a dispassionate look at all the evidence, two researchers lay the state of our psychological knowledge out flat. Yes, girls differ from boys, but...

The physical differences between men and women are obvious and universal. The psychological differences are not. Yet people hold strong beliefs about sex differences, even when those beliefs fail to find any scientific support.

Some popular views of sex differences are captured in a scene from the Rodgers and Hammerstein musical, *Carousel.* A young man discovers he is to be a father. He rhapsodizes about the kind of son he expects to have. The boy will be tall and tough as a tree, and no one will dare to boss him around. It will be all right for his mother to teach him manners, but she mustn't make a sissy out of him. The boy will be good at wrestling, and able to herd cattle, run a riverboat, drive spikes.

Then the prospective father realizes, with a start, that the child may be a girl. The music moves to a gentle theme. She will have ribbons in her hair. She will be sweet and petite, just like her mother, and suitors will flock around her. There's a comic relief from sentimentally, when the expectant father brags that she'll be half again as bright as girls are meant to be. But then he returns to the main theme: his daughter will need to be protected.

The lyrics in this scene reflect some common cultural stereotypes. There are also some less well-known stereotypes in the social science literature on sex differences. We believe there is a great deal of myth in both the popular and scientific views about male-female differences. There is also some substance.

In order to find out which generalizations are justified and which are not, we spent three years compiling, reviewing and interpreting a very large body of research—over 2,000 books and articles—on the sex differences in motivation, social behavior, and intellectual ability. We examined negative as well as positive evidence. At the end of our exhaustive and exhausting search, we were able to determine which beliefs about sex differences are supported by evidence, which beliefs have no support, and which are still in slightly discordant note, introduced for adequately tested.

First, the myths:

From preschool to early adolescence, the sexes are very similar in their verbal abilities. But at about age 11, they begin to diverge.

MYTH ONE:
Girls are
more "social"
than boys.

There is no evidence that girls are more likely than boys to be concerned with people, as opposed to impersonal objects or abstract ideas. The two sexes are equally interested in social stimuli (e. g., human faces and voices), and are equally proficient at learning by imitating models. They are equally responsive to social rewards, such as praise from others, and neither sex consistently learns better for this form of reward than for other forms.

In childhood, girls are no more dependent than boys on their caretakers, and boys are no more willing than girls to remain alone. Girls do not spend more time with playmates; the opposite is true, at least at certain ages. The two sexes appear to be equally adept at understanding the emotional reactions and needs of others, although measures of this ability have been narrow.

Any differences that do exist in the sociability of the two sexes are more of kind than of degree. Boys are highly oriented toward a peer group and congregate in larger groups; girls associate in pairs or small groups of children their own age, and may be somewhat more oriented toward adults, although the evidence on this is weak.

MYTH TWO:
Girls are
more suggestible
than boys.

Boys are as likely as girls to imitate other people spontaneously. The two sexes are equally susceptible to persuasive communications, and in face-to-face situations where there is social pressure to conform to a group judgment about an ambiguous situation, there are usually no sex differences in susceptibility. When there are, girls are somewhat more likely to adapt their own judgments to those of the group, although some studies find the reverse. Boys, on the other hand, appear to be more likely to accept peer group values when these conflict with their own.

MYTH THREE:
Girls have
lower self-esteem
than boys.

Boys and girls are very similar in overall self-satisfaction and self-confidence throughout childhood and adolescence. (The information on childhood is meager, but what there is indicates no sex difference.) The sexes do differ in the areas in which they report greatest self-confidence. Girls rate themselves higher in the area of social competence, while boys more often see themselves as strong, powerful, dominant, potent.

Through most of the school years, boys and girls are equally likely to believe they can influence their own fate, as opposed to falling victim to chance. During the college years (not earlier or later), men have a greater sense of control over their destiny, and are more optimistic in predicting their own performance on a variety of school-related tasks. However, this does not imply a generally lower level of self-esteem among women of this age.

MYTH FOUR:
Girls lack
motivation to
achieve.

In the pioneering studies of achievement motivation, girls were more likely to report imagery about achievement when asked to make up stories to describe ambiguous pictures, as long as the instructions did not stress either competition or social comparison. Boys need to be challenged by appeals to their ego or competitive feelings, for their achievement imagery to reach the level of girls. Although boys' achievement motivation does appear to be more responsive to competition arousal, that does not imply that they have a higher level of achievement motivation in general. In fact, when researchers observe behavior that denotes a motive to achieve, they find no sex differences or find girls to be superior.

MYTH FIVE:
Girls are better
at rote learning
and simple
repetitive tasks.
Boys are better
at high-level
tasks that require
them to inhibit
previously learned
responses.

Neither sex is more susceptible to simple conditioning, in which stimuli become connected with responses in what is assumed to be a rather automatic

Male superiority on visual-spatial tasks is not found in childhood, but appears fairly consistently in adolescence and adulthood.

process. Neither sex excels in rote-learning tasks, such as learning to associate one word with another. Boys and girls are equally proficient at tasks that call on them to inhibit various responses, e.g., discrimination of certain items from others, a task requiring the subject to avoid attending or responding to irrelevant cues.

Boys are somewhat more impulsive during the preschool years, but after that the sexes do not differ in ability to wait for a delayed reward or inhibit early, incorrect responses, or on other measures of impulsivity.

MYTH SIX:
Boys are
more "analytic"
than girls.

The sexes do not differ on tests of cognitive style that measure one's ability to analyze, i.e., the ability to respond to a particular aspect of a situation without being influenced by the context, or restructure the elements of a problem in order to achieve a solution. Boys and girls are equally likely to repond to contextual aspects of a situation that are irrelevant to the task at hand. Boys are superior only on problems that require visual discrimination or manipulation of objects set in a larger context; this superiority seems to be accounted for by spatial ability, which we discuss below, and does not imply a general analytic superiority.

MYTH SEVEN:
Girls are
more affected
by heredity,
boys by
environment.

Male identical twins are intellectually more alike than female identical twins, but the two sexes resemble their parents to the same degree. Boys are more vulnerable to damage by a variety of harmful agents in the environment both before and after birth, but this does not mean that they are more affected by environmental influences in general.

The two sexes learn with equal facility in a wide variety of situations. If learning is the primary means by which the environment affects us, then the two sexes are equivalent in this regard.

MYTH EIGHT:
Girls are
"auditory," boys
"visual."

Male and female infants do not seem to respond differently to sounds. At most ages, boys and girls are equally adept at discriminating speech sounds. There is no sex difference in memory for sounds previously heard.

No study shows a sex difference among newborns in time spent looking at visual stimuli. During the first year of life, neither sex emerges clearly as more responsive to what they see. From infancy to adulthood, the sexes exhibit a similar degree of interest in visual stimuli. They also seem to be alike in ability to discriminate among objects, identify shapes, estimate distances, and perform on a variety of other tests of visual perception.

Our examination of the social science literature also revealed some sex differences that are fairly well-established:

DIFFERENCE ONE:
Males
are more
aggressive than
females.

A sex difference in aggression has been observed in all cultures in which aggressive behavior has been observed. Boys are more aggressive physically and verbally. They engage in mock-fighting and aggressive fantasies as well as direct forms of aggression more frequently than girls. The sex difference manifests itself as soon as social play begins, at age two or two and a half. From an early age, the primary victims of male aggression are other males not females.

Although both sexes become less aggressive with age, boys and men remain more aggressive through the college years. Little information is available for older adults.

DIFFERENCE TWO:
Girls have
greater
verbal ability
than boys.

Girls' verbal abilities probably mature somewhat more rapidly in early life, although a number of recent studies find no sex differences. During the period from

It is true that boys and men are more aggressive, but this does not mean that females are the passive victims of aggression.

preschool to early adolescence, the sexes are very similar in their verbal abilities. But at about age 11, they begin to diverge; female superiority increases through high school, and possibly beyond. Girls score higher on tasks that involve understanding and producing language, and on "high-level" verbal tasks (analogies, comprehension of difficult written material, creative writing) as well as "lower-level" measures (such as fluency and spelling).

DIFFERENCE THREE:
Boys excel in visual-spatial ability.

Visual-spatial ability involves the visual perception of figures or objects in space and how they are related to each other. One visual-spatial test has the subject inspect a three-dimensional pile of blocks, and estimate the number of surfaces visible from a perspective different than his own. Another has him look at a figure, then select one from a set of four that matches the original if rotated in a plane. Male superiority on visual-spatial tasks is not found in childhood, but appears fairly consistently in adolescence and adulthood, and increases through the high school years. The sex differences are approximately equal on analytic tasks (those that require separation of an element from its background) and nonanalytic ones.

DIFFERENCE FOUR:
Boys excel in mathematical ability.

The two sexes are similar in their early acquisition of quantitative concepts and their mastery of arithmetic in grade school. Beginning at about age 12 or 13, however, boys' mathematical skills increase faster than girls'. The greater rate of improvement does not seem to be entirely due to the fact that boys take more math courses, although the question has not been extensively studied.

The magnitude of the sex difference varies depending on the study, and is probably not as great as the difference in spatial ability. Both visual-spatial and verbal processes are sometimes involved in solving math problems; some problems can be solved in either way, while others cannot, a fact that may help to explain why the size of the sex difference varies from one study to another.

On some questions, we found ambiguous findings or too little evidence on which to base conclusions. These questions are still open to further research.

QUESTION ONE:
Are there differences in tactile sensitivity?

Most studies of tactile sensitivity in infancy or ability to perceive by touch at later ages do not show sex differences. When differences are found, girls are more sensitive, but since this finding is rare, we cannot be confident that it is meaningful. Most studies in which the results are analyzed by sex deal with new borns, more work is needed with other ages.

QUESTION TWO:
Are there differences in fear, timidity and anxiety?

Studies that involve direct observation of fearful behavior usually do not find sex differences. But teacher ratings and self reports usually reveal girls as more timid or more anxious. The problem with self reports is that we do not know whether the results reflect real differences, or only differences in people's willingness to report anxiety.

Since the very willingness to assert that one is afraid may lead to fearful behavior, the problem may turn out to be unimportant. But it would be desirable to have measures other than self-reports, which now contribute most of the data from early school age on.

QUESTION THREE:
Is one sex more active than the other?

Sex differences in activity level do not appear in infancy. They begin to show up when children reach the age of social play. Some studies find that during the preschool years, boys tend to be more active, but many studies do not find a sex difference. This discrepancy may be partially traceable to the kind of situation in which measurements are made. Boys appear to be especially stimulated to bursts of high activity when other boys are present. But the exact way in which the situation controls activity level remains to be established.

Activity level is also affected by motivational states—fear, anger, curiosity—and therefore is of limited usefulness in identifying stable individual or group differences. We need more detailed observations of the vigor and quality of children's play.

QUESTION FOUR:
Is one sex more competitive than the other?

Some studies find boys to be more competitive than girls, but many find the sexes to be similar in this regard. Almost all the research on competition has involved situations in which competition is maladaptive. For example, two people might be asked to play the prisoner's dilemma game, in which they have to choose between competitive strategies that are attractive to the individual in the short run, and cooperative strategies that maximize both players' gains in the long run. In such situations, the sexes are equally cooperative.

In settings where competitiveness produces greater individual rewards, males might be more competitive than females, but this is a guess based on common-sense considerations, such as the male interest in competitive sports, and not on research in controlled settings. The age of the subject and the identity of the opponent no doubt make a difference too; there is evidence that young women hesitate to compete against their boyfriends.

QUESTION FIVE:
Is one sex more dominant than the other?

Dominance appears to be more of an issue in boys' groups than in girls' groups. Boys make more attempts to dominate each other than do girls. They also more often attempt to dominate adults.

But the dominance relations between the sexes are complex. In childhood, the segregation of play groups by sex means that neither sex frequently tries to dominate the other; there is little opportunity. When experimental situations bring the two sexes together, it is not clear whether one sex is more successful in influencing the behavior of the other. In mixed adult groups or pairs, formal leadership tends to go to the males in the early stages of an interaction, but the longer the relationship lasts, the more equal influence becomes.

QUESTION SIX:
Is one sex more compliant than the other?

During childhood, girls tend to be more obedient to the commands and directions of adults. But this compliance does not carry over into relationships with peers. Boys are especially concerned with maintaining their status in their peer group, and therefore are probably more vulnerable than girls to pressures and challenges from that group, although this has not been well-established. It is not clear that in adult interactions, one sex is consistently more willing to comply with the wishes of the other.

QUESTION SEVEN:
Are nurturance and "maternal" behavior more typical of one sex?

There is very little information about the tendencies of boys and girls to be nurturant or helpful toward younger children or animals. Cross-cultural work does indicate that girls between six and 10 are more often seen behaving nurturantly in our own society, the rare studies that report nurturant behavior involve observation of free play among nursery-school children. These studies do not find sex differences, but the setting usually does not include children who are much younger than the subjects being observed. It may be that the presence of younger children would elicit sex differences in nurturant behavior.

Very little information exists on how adult men respond to infants and children, so we can't say whether adult females are more disposed to behave maternally than adult males are to behave paternally. But if there is a sex difference, it does not generalize to a greater female tendency to behave altruistically. Studies of people's willingness to help others in distress have sometimes found men to be more helpful, sometimes women, depending on the identity of the person needing help and the kind of help that is required. Overall, the sexes seem similar in degree of altruism.

QUESTION EIGHT:
Are females more passive than males?

The answer is complex, but for the most part negative. The two sexes are highly alike in their willingness to explore a novel environment, when they both have freedom to do so. Both sexes are highly responsive to social situations of all kinds, and although some individuals tend to withdraw from social interaction and simply watch from the sidelines, they are as likely to be male as female.

We said earlier that girls are more likely to comply with adult demands, but compliance can take an active form, running errands and performing services for others are active processes. Young boys seem more prone than girls to put out energy in bursts of strenuous physical activity, but the girls are not sitting idly by while the boys act, they are simply playing more quietly. Their play is fully as organized and planned, possibly more so. When girls play, they actively impose their own design upon their surroundings as much as boys do.

It is true that boys and men are more aggressive, but this does not mean that females are the passive victims of aggression—they do not yield or withdraw in the face of aggression any more frequently than males do, at least during the phases of childhood that have been observed. We have already noted the curious fact that while males are more dominant, females are not

especially submissive, at least not to boys and girls their own age. In sum, the term "passive" does not accurately describe the most common female personality attributes.

We must conclude from our survey of all the data that many popular beliefs about the psychological characteristics of the two sexes have little or no basis in fact. Yet people continue to believe, for example, that girls are more "social" than boys, or are more suggestible than boys, ignoring the fact that careful observation and measurement show no sex differences.

The explanation may be that people's attention is selective. It is well-documented that whenever a member of a group behaves the way an observer expects him to, the observer notes the fact, and his prior belief is confirmed and strengthened. But when a member of the group behaves in a way that is not consistent with the observer's expectations, the behavior is likely to go unnoticed, so the observer's prior belief remains intact.

This probably happens continually when those with entrenched ideas about sex differences observe male and female behavior. As a result, myths live on that would otherwise rightfully die out under the impact of negative evidence.

Males and females and what you may not know about them

THE POTENTIAL DIFFERENCE between men and women begins with the assembly of a new set of chromosomes at conception, when one pair is coded either XX for females or XY for males. The difference a Y chromosome makes becomes physiologically explicit about six to seven weeks later. What else chromosome and hormone patterns do to set males and females apart—in behavior as well as body—is more problematic.

Most scientists believe both nature and nurture are responsible for sex differences. Some stress the striking degree of similarity between the sexes and the way this resemblance has grown through the ages.

Yet men and women *are* different, and these differences emerge in the realms of education, child rearing, sports, the military, the marketplace and the workplace, triggering some of the hottest social controversies of our day.

How, exactly, are they unalike? Here's what scientists know—and would like to know—about this engrossing topic.

Bigger boys, more mature girls

At birth, boys are on average half an inch longer and five ounces or so heavier than girls. They remain slightly larger throughout most of childhood. Newborn girls are about four to six weeks more advanced than boys in skeletal development, according to a leading expert on growth, Dr. J.M. Tanner of the University of London. Certain other organ systems are also more mature in female infants. Girls continue to mature more rapidly; according to some researchers they generally walk, talk and become toilet trained sooner than boys. Girls get their permanent teeth earlier and reach puberty about two years before boys do. They also have their adolescent growth spurt earlier, making them temporarily taller than boys.

But men end up longer-legged and about five inches taller. The average American woman between age 35 and 44 is 5 feet 4 inches tall and weighs 152 pounds; the average man in the same age group is 5 feet 9 inches and weighs 179.

After puberty, males and females differ significantly in heart, lungs, blood, bone, muscle and fat. Boys develop larger hearts and lungs, more red blood cells and more hemoglobin. Their skeletons broaden at the shoulders; they put on muscle and develop a greater capacity than females for neutralizing the chemical by-products of muscular exercises.

The female skeleton at puberty broadens at the hips, and the female body builds up an energy reserve of fat—both changes in preparation for possible childbearing. Young adult males average about 50% muscle and 16% fat, females about 40% muscle and 25% fat.

More muscle is one reason why men tend to be better adapted for heavy physical work than women. Male and female muscle fibers are not very different in strength; however, men have more of them relative to their size.

The other key to physical performance is aerobic power, the maximum amount of oxygen an individual can get into the body and to the cells. Boys and girls start out about equal in this respect, but a Swedish study showed that after puberty women's aerobic maximums averaged about 80% to 85% of men's on the basis of weight. Under conditioning programs, however, women can narrow the gap in aerobic power and muscular strength. For example, sedentary college men in one study had 22% more aerobic power than sedentary college women before both went through an eight-week training program; men had only 8% more after.

Men and women differ most in muscular strength of the upper body, and they are most nearly equal in strength of legs and abdominal muscles. After seven weeks of Army basic training, women demonstrated, pound for pound, 84% as much strength as men in the abdominal muscles and 79% in the legs but only 70% in the upper body. Army physical training standards reflect the recognition of sex differences in strength. Young women must do at least 16 push-ups, for instance, but young men must do at least 40.

Both men and women athletes enjoy advantages related to their gender. Women gain balance and agility from their lower center of gravity. Men, with more muscle mass, more aerobic capacity, greater upper body strength and longer bones, can in general throw harder, jump farther and run faster.

The running and swimming speed gaps, however, have been narrowing in recent decades—men are only about 10% faster in current world records. In long-distance swims a woman's narrower shoulders, lighter body and insulating, buoyant body fat are a plus. The English Channel swimming record is held by a woman.

The vulnerable male

In life as in sports, the physiological advantage of women is most apparent over the long haul. On average, American women live nearly eight years longer than men. Some researchers say that three-quarters of this sex difference can be explained by learned behavior that has been encouraged or condoned more for men than for women, especially smoking and the excessive competitiveness, aggressiveness, hostility and impatience often lumped together as "coronary prone" behavior.

Other investigators emphasize biological and genetic explanations for the male's greater vulnerability, which begins, in fact, at conception. Although at least 120 boys are conceived for every 100 girls, male rates of spontaneous abortions and stillbirths are so much higher that at birth the ratio is 105 to 100.

More male than female babies are born malformed; more die at childbirth, in the first week and year of life, and in every year thereafter. Men suffer from higher rates of chronic conditions that are leading causes of death. By the time the male and female survivors are old enough to have children, their numbers are about equal. By age 65 there are seven surviving men for every ten women.

Why should males be more fragile than females? Physiological maturity may be a factor. Girls, after all, are more mature in the womb and are born with a four- to six-week head start to help them weather the risks of infancy.

The endocrine system may hold a clue, too. Dr. Estelle Ramey and her colleagues at Georgetown University theorize that the male hormone testosterone has a gradually damaging effect on the cardiovascular system.

Another source of vulnerability is the difference in the sex chromosome pattern: XX for females, XY for males. The genes that govern the presence or absence of dozens of genetic diseases and disorders are carried on X chromosomes. Females with a defective gene on one X chromosome are likely to have a protective, healthy, matching gene on the other X. Males don't have a second X, so chances are that with one bad gene they will manifest—not just carry—such X-linked disorders as hemophilia and some kinds of muscular dystrophy.

The genetic shield of women doesn't end there. According to Dr. David T. Purtilo and Dr. John L. Sullivan of the University of Massachusetts Medical School, research indicates women have extra disease-fighting genes, twice as many as men carry on their sex chromosomes. Not surprisingly, the recovery rate of women from most diseases is better than that of men.

The vulnerable female

The immunological advantage of females is a double-edged sword, Purtilo and Sullivan point out. It's good for fighting disease, but it also predisposes women to form antibodies against their own system, as in lupus erythematosus, a connective tissue disorder that strikes nine females for every male.

Women appear to be sick more frequently than men, and no one is certain of all the reasons. Data analyzed by University of Michigan demographer Dr. Lois M. Verbrugge shows women have more episodes of acute respiratory and gastrointestinal problems and higher rates of chronic conditions, such as arthritis, anemia, diabetes, hypertension and some forms of heart disease. They are also more poorly nourished and have poorer vision. On the other hand, females tend to have better teeth and better hearing than men.

In terms of absence from work, the two health profiles almost balance out: an average of 4.9 workdays a year lost by men, 5.7 lost by women.

The way we act

Mental illness strikes the sexes rather evenhandedly, with two exceptions. Men are more subject to personality disorders, including antisocial behavior and drug or alcohol abuse. Women seem more vulnerable to anxiety and depression—not just the everyday blues but also clinical depression, a mood disturbance severe enough to impair functioning.

In the case of depression, researchers are following tangled clues, biological as well as psychological and social. One difference they have uncovered is that marriage protects men from mental illness but increases the risk for women.

Research on sex differences in social behavior, learning, motivation and perception is extensive. Yet after scrutinizing hundreds of studies, Dr. Eleanor Maccoby and Dr. Carol Jacklin, Stanford University psychologists, found the evidence insufficient or too ambiguous to answer a number of key questions. For instance, they couldn't say with confidence whether females are more fearful, timid and anxious than males; whether males are more competitive; whether females are really more disposed to be nurturant or motherly.

What Maccoby and Jacklin could report in 1974 in *The Psychology of Sex Differences* (published by Stanford University Press) was that on most psychological measures males and females are more alike than different. They uncovered no proof that girls are more interested in social, boys in nonsocial stimulation. Studies indicated that the sexes persist on tasks to a similar degree, follow a similar course in the development of moral reasoning, and are about equally helpful and altruistic. Nevertheless, the researchers noted ways in which development varies.

▶ Boys tend to obey their parents less than girls do.

▶ Up to about age 18 months the incidence of angry outbursts triggered by frustration is similar in boys and girls. After that, such outbursts decrease quickly for girls but not for boys. One study found nursery school boys and girls crying with equal frequency but usually for different reasons: the girls because of physical injury, the boys because an object or adult wouldn't do what they wished.

▶ From as early as age 2 to 2½, males are more aggressive—readier to fight and more willing to hurt another person physically or verbally. This difference in aggression is the most solidly established sex difference in social behavior. Maccoby and Jacklin believe that although aggression is learned, there is a biological basis for boys' greater ease, on average, in absorbing the lesson.

▶ Neither sex appears to be more oriented toward people, but girls tend to stick together in pairs or small groups and to like their playmates. Boys congregate in larger groups, and liking or not liking each other seems secondary to the activity at hand.

▶ Maccoby and Jacklin found little reliable evidence that boys are consistently more active than girls, but beginning in the preschool years "boys appear to be especially stimulated to bursts of high activity by the presence of other boys." Boys also make many more attempts to dominate each other than girls do in their groups, possibly because large groups may need a pecking order more than small ones do. Boys tend to overestimate their status in their peer group more often than girls do.

▶ Girls generally get better grades than boys throughout their school years yet tend to underestimate their intellectual abilities more than boys. By the time they reach college, young women have less confidence in their ability to perform assigned tasks well.

Although they found no sex difference in overall intelligence, Maccoby and Jacklin found "fairly well established" evidence of some differences related to learning. On average, girls from age 11 on do better on tests of verbal skills, from spelling to understanding difficult passages and writing creatively. (Recent findings from the National Assessment of Educational Progress confirm this conclusion, with girls scoring three to four percentage points higher than male peers on reading tasks, as much as ten to 20 points higher on writing skills.)

Girls are also less vulnerable to language disturbances: Three to four times more boys than girls stutter; three to ten times more boys suffer reading disabilities.

From adolescence on, males outperform females on visual-spatial tasks—visualizing shapes and mentally moving or rotating them. (However, a number of recent research studies, including two with a national sample, have not found this sex difference.)

Sex and the teaching of math

On the average, the sexes are intellectual specialists. Females tend to outperform men in verbal skills; males in general are better at math.

Lately, the mathematics gap has become a hot topic. According to Dr. Elizabeth Fennema of the University of Wisconsin, it should be. Lack of verbal skills doesn't seem to stand in the way of men's success, she says, but lack of math skills keeps women from doing a number of things, particularly from qualifying for well-paid jobs in science, engineering and technology.

Actually, the lack of language skills undoubtedly does hold some men back. But serious language deficiencies show up early in the school years, and the need to do something about them has been well accepted. As measured by the Scholastic Aptitude Test (SAT) verbal scores of high school seniors, college-bound boys eventually catch up to the girls. Since 1972 boys have even outperformed girls slightly.

The math disparity, on the other hand, doesn't show up until adolescence and has no similar tradition of remediation. Recent research has defined the discrepancy more precisely. In a national sample of 13-year-olds and of 12th-graders the younger girls did as well as their male counterparts on algebra and word problems and did better by five percentage points on computation. By senior year, boys and girls who had taken the same math courses achieved about the same in algebra and computation, but the boys outperformed the girls by six to 12 percentage points on word problems.

On the math section of the SAT, young men averaged 491 out of 800 possible points in 1980; young women averaged 443. Women are not absent from the higher-scoring SAT takers, just outnumbered—10% of the females and 20% of the males score 600 or above.

Could there be some innate factor that primes men for superior math performance? If so, its identity is still unknown. Some researchers, thinking spatial visualization might be the key, have been searching for evidence of inborn spatial superiority. But that theory seems less convincing than it once did. In any event, no sex difference has been found in some recent tests of spatial visualization.

Another group of researchers used to believe that girls scored lower simply because they took fewer math courses. That argument, too, seems less persuasive these days. Fennema believes a more promising clue lies in the specific kind of math problem that tends to trouble girls more than boys. This stumbling block is the nonroutine problem that calls for putting math knowledge together on your own in a fresh way.

Why the difference? "Somewhere along the way we are not allowing girls to develop independence of thought in learning," Fennema warns. Yet the difference isn't inevitable. Some junior high classes do a good job of developing mathematical skills among both sexes. The University of Wisconsin researcher is trying to find out why.

Dr. Patricia Casserly of the Educational Testing Service has also been looking closely at individual math classrooms to see what elicits high performance. Out of about 100 high school advanced calculus classes in which boys and girls performed equally well and both achieved above the national average on standardized tests, she chose 20 classes with varied and modest family backgrounds. The key to the students' success turned out to be good instruction from teachers who had a degree in mathematics, science or engineering rather than in education. These teachers treated both boys and girls as "partners in a quest." They got across the idea that "all mathematicians have problems if they go far enough; it's O.K. to struggle," a particularly encouraging message for bright girls who are used to doing everything easily and well and face their first real challenge in math class.

EQUALS, a University of California project to promote women's participation in mathematics, has published an informative handbook containing a how-to section on the teaching of problem solving and a collection of engrossing problem-solving activities. For a copy of the 134-page handbook, write to Lawrence Hall of Science, University of California, Berkeley, Cal. 94720, Attn.: EQUALS. Enclose a $5 check or money order payable to Regents, University of California.

▶ On average, boys do better than girls in math beginning about age 12 or 13 (see the box at left).

Are brains alike?

Now an intriguing new question arouses controversy. Do men and women act differently because their brains are different?

Primarily on the basis of work with lower animals, some respected researchers speculate that prenatal sex hormones program pathways in the brain and central nervous system, laying down predispositions for certain kinds of behavior.

As Dr. John Money, director of the Psychohormonal Research Unit at the Johns Hopkins Medical Institutions, explains it, "... the irreducible difference between the sexes is that men impregnate, and women menstruate, gestate and lactate." Other than these biological functions, the sexes share all behaviors; only the prevalence of the behavior "or the ease with which it is elicited can be labeled masculine or feminine," Money writes. Parental care is a case in point: "... regardless of species, males or females can be parental, but the threshold for the release of parental care when the helpless young demand it is different, the mother being more immediately responsive."

A number of investigators are trying to relate left and right hemisphere brain organization to female verbal ability and male math and spatial ability. This research builds on the assumption that in most right-handed individuals, the left brain dominates verbal and sequential thought, and the right brain is more critical for the performance of spatial and other nonverbal tasks. Some studies suggest that women are more likely to use both sides of the brain for language, whereas men have a tendency to process it exclusively on the left, theoretically leaving the right hemisphere unimpeded for solving spatial problems.

However, Stanford psychologist Dr. Diane McGuinness and neuroscientist Dr. Karl Pribram point out a flaw in the theory: Some right hemisphere specialties, such as recognizing faces, are tasks in which women excel. They theorize that priming by

Can you solve this problem?

When the National Assessment of Educational Progress gave the following problem to a sample of 2,200 17-year-olds, 46% of the boys but only 39% of the girls were able to answer correctly in the 88 seconds allotted. Problems of this sort require not only basic computation but also use of various reasoning skills; some researchers attribute the different success rates to failure of the schools to encourage such skills in girls to the extent that they are encouraged in boys.

Juan's mother has three five-dollar rolls of dimes and two ten-dollar rolls of quarters to use for Juan's school lunch.

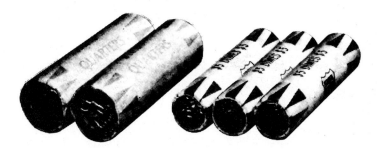

If Juan takes exactly 45 cents to school every day for his lunch, which of the following statements is true?

  A. *He uses all of the quarters before all of the dimes.*
  B. *He uses all of the dimes before all of the quarters.*
  C. *He spends all of both coins at the same time.*
  D. *I don't know.*

ANSWER: B

prenatal hormones produces greater visual acuity in males and greater sensitivity to loudness and speech sounds in females. They also think it's possible that the difference in muscular competence (men do better with their large muscles and women excel in fine muscle and finger dexterity) reinforces the difference in sensory biases and leads to major differences in behavior and personality. McGuinness and Pribram point to the "manipulative" male who enjoys "the challenge of coming to grips with the physical environment" and the "communicative" female with "a strong interest in people and social situations."

Biology and culture

Even the most biologically oriented researchers warn that the human product is unpredictable because human beings, individually and in groups, are more susceptible than any

other animal to learning and to being influenced by the impact of the social environment. Male and female Eskimos score the same on spatial tests. British boys often score better than girls on verbal tests. Is it their cultures that make the difference?

Then, too, a culture may assign roles with or without regard for innate qualifications. Although men in general are clearly better adapted than women for strenuous physical labor, there are societies in which women carry all the heavy burdens.

What is the most useful knowledge to be gleaned from all the research thus far? It may be this: As individuals, we are not predestined, bound or limited by the fact of gender. The only inevitable differences between the sexes are the few irreducible distinctions—the ones you knew about all along.

HOW NURSERY SCHOOLS TEACH GIRLS TO SHUT UP

Nursery-school teachers are much more likely
to react to a boy's behavior, bad or good, than to a girl's.
By rewarding boys for aggression and girls for passivity,
they mold behavior that will cause both sexes pain later.

Lisa A. Serbin and K. Daniel O'Leary

Lisa A. Serbin teaches psychology at the Binghamton campus of the State University of New York, where she is also codirector of the Butternut Hill Preschool. The school serves as a laboratory to develop and evaluate programs for cognitive and psychological growth. The goal, Serbin emphasizes, is growth for all the children, male and female.

K. Daniel O'Leary, a practicing clinical psychologist, is professor of psychology and coordinator of the Child Psychological Clinic at SUNY, Stony Brook. He got his Ph.D. at the University of Illinois in 1967. O'Leary wrote *Classroom Management: The Successful Use of Behavior Modification* with Susan O'Leary, and *Behavior Therapy: Application and Outcome* with Terence Wilson.

As NURSERY-SCHOOL CHILDREN busily mold clay, their teachers are molding behavior. Unwittingly, teachers foster an environment where children learn that boys are aggressive and able to solve problems, while girls are submissive and passive. The clay impressions are transient, but the behavioral ones last into adulthood and present us with people of both sexes who have developed only parts of their psychological and intellectual capabilities.

There has been constant conjecture about when and how sex-role stereotypes develop. We looked into 15 preschool classrooms and found that teachers act and react in quite different ways to boys and to girls. They subtly encourage the very behavioral patterns that will later become painful for children of both sexes.

John was a five-year-old bully. When someone didn't follow his directions or give him the toy he wanted, John lost his temper. He pushed, shoved, shouted, and threw things. When we first watched John in his classroom, he was playing peacefully with another boy at building a Tinker-Toy tower.

Then John asked the other child for a piece of material the boy was using. When he was refused, John began to tear the tower apart. The other boy protested, and John raised his hand threateningly. The other children across the room instantly sang out in chorus: "Teacher, John's hitting!" Mrs. Jones looked over and ordered John to stop. She strode across the room, pulled John away, and spent the next two minutes telling him why he shouldn't hit people. Five minutes later, John was hitting another classmate.

This brief scene shows how a teacher can reinforce exactly the behavior that's causing a problem. For John, as for many children, being disruptive is an effective means of getting a far larger dose of attention than good behavior can bring. Children get attention for good behavior about as often as Congressmen get mail in praise of their activities, so it's not surprising that most children (and some Congressmen) become adept at attracting attention by bad-boy tactics.

Our classroom observations showed that disruption is far more likely to get attention for a John than it is for a Jane. Teachers responded over three times as often to males as to females who hit or broke things, and the boys usually got a loud public reprimand. When teachers did respond to girls, they most often delivered a brief, soft rebuke that others couldn't hear.

How to Cure a Bully. Bullies like John are made, not born. We taught his teacher how to get rid of the problem very simply: we explained that she was to ignore his aggressive acts, except to prevent the victim from being harmed. We suggested that instead she concentrate on the child John was attacking, by saying something warm like, "I am very sorry you got hurt. Let me get a nice game for you to play with." When children learn that they will be ignored for their misbehavior, they stop it almost immediately. John ceased bullying.

Teachers were not usually aware that they reacted differently to aggression from boys and girls. One teacher suggested that the behavior of boys is harder to ignore because "boys hit harder."

It's Tough to Nip Sexism in the Bud

The opponents of sexism have assumed, not illogically, that making people aware of their prejudices will cure them. Now an elaborate social-psychological study of schoolchildren cautions that teaching sexual equality is neither easy nor predictable. On this subject, girls learn their lessons more readily than boys.

Harvard psychologist Marcia Guttentag and a research team set up an ambitious program they thought would nip sexism in the bud. They developed a six-week curriculum in three large, ethnically diverse school districts in the Boston area, working with over 1,000 children in three age groups: kindergarten (age five), fifth grade (10), and ninth grade (14). The children read stories, saw films, acted out plays, and worked on special projects, all designed to raise their young consciousnesses.

The new curriculum concentrated on three types of stereotypes—work, family, and personality—and aimed to make the children more flexible in their assumptions about the sexes. Women,

they learned, can do any job men do, and men can have fun doing things around the house with their families. Both sexes, they learned, should share desirable personality traits—men can be sensitive and warm and women assertive and competent.

Guttentag trained the teachers with behavior-modification techniques, so that they would not act according to the unconscious bias that O'Leary and Serbin found. And, recognizing the power of the peer group at any age, she talked to the kids about how friends influence their ideas and actions.

The researchers knew from tests they gave before the program began that by age five, most of the children were ripe old sexists. The majority were thoroughly convinced by television and their playmates that boys are strong and fine and can do all sorts of interesting jobs, but that girls are weak and silly and best kept at home. Children of all social classes and economic backgrounds held these stereotypes, and it didn't matter whether their mothers worked outside the home or not.

The children in every grade thought they knew exactly which jobs were for men and which for women; the boys had the more restricted opinion of what jobs were open to women. Everyone thought they knew which personality traits were "masculine" and which "feminine." But, like adults, they weren't as quick to apply these stereotypes to themselves. When they described their own personalities, both sexes picked admirable qualities that they would otherwise associate with either males or females, e.g., strong, obedient, good-looking. Finally, like adults, the kids were more likely to view the opposite sex in stereotypic terms than their own.

The efforts to broaden the children's views of sex roles did not work quite as the researchers had planned. To their surprise, fifth-grade boys with working mothers, and ninth-grade boys with working and nonworking mothers, became notably more stereotyped in their views of women and more rigid and outspoken about "woman's place" after the six-week program. It didn't matter whether their mothers were waitresses

(continued on next page)

If teachers really do perceive hitting by boys as potentially more dangerous to other children, it's easy to understand why they're reluctant to ignore the act, but it's ironic that their attention aggravates the problem.

In contrast to the aggression and disruptive behavior typical of boys, girls usually rely on dependency or withdrawal to get adult attention. Feminists have strongly criticized television, educational media and the schools for training girls to be passive and dependent. Television usually depicts women in subservient roles, and the very books from which a child learns to read show girls as unaggressive and dependent. Our observations confirm that these same stereotypes are being encouraged in the classroom. So children of either sex simply use the sex-typed tactic that fits adult prejudice.

We found that teachers were more likely to react to girls when they were within arm's reach, either literally or figuratively clinging to the teachers' skirts (all the teachers we observed were women). Sheila, for example, was so

frequently underfoot that Mrs. Cox constantly stumbled over her. Sheila was a bright, attractive child who asked many interesting questions, but she refused to play with the other children. Except for her extreme dependency, Sheila's development was normal for her age.

In an attempt to deal with the problem and give her more self-confidence, Mrs. Cox talked with Sheila frequently, and often touched her affectionately. When she saw Sheila playing alone, Mrs. Cox would go over and encourage her to join the other youngsters. Despite considerable effort, this attention produced no change in Sheila's behavior.

The school director then asked Mrs. Cox to look at or speak to Sheila only when she was with other children. For several days, Sheila clung even more tenaciously to her teacher's skirt, but after a week she ventured out to join the other children. Two weeks later, her extreme dependency had vanished.

Girls Learn to Cling. The pattern of teachers giving attention to nearby, dependent girls repeated itself time and

time again. When boys were near, the teacher would praise them and then give them directions to do things on their own. By contrast, she would praise and assist the girls but *not* send them off to work by themselves.

In our study, we sent trained observers into 15 classrooms to record behavior by using a well-defined set of criteria. We identified 13 specific types of teacher response to seven categories of the children's behavior. An observer watched for any of the 91 possible interactions during a 20-second period, then recorded results for 10 seconds. We did the classroom studies in half-hour units. Where we report differences in the teachers' reactions to boys and girls, statistical tests have shown that the differences we observed were far greater than what would be expected by chance alone.

Teachers, we found, actually teach boys more than they teach girls. Many studies show that there are sex differences in important cognitive skills. Boys, on the average, tend to have better analytic problem-solving abilities, to be or doctors; peer-group pressures at school outweighed the example the boys got at home. The boys' ambivalence about sex-role equality was often reflected in projective tests. For instance, one 10-year-old began a story about a picture of a female mechanic working on a car:

". . . She fixes the car good and she's been asking for a raise for a long time. Since she did a good job . . . he is going to give her a big raise. She thought that was great. When he gave her an extra bonus, she got to go home and cook a meal because her father was at work where he was a chef in a pizza place."

But then his uncertainties about working women took over:

"But when she went home, the boss found a mistake. There was a hole in a gasoline part and it cost him a whole lot of money. But he decided that he wouldn't take off the raise because she did a good job on all the other parts. When he shut the trunk the whole car fell apart. And then he got ferocious and called her up and said, 'You are fired.' The end."

If many of the boys remained traditional, many of the girls turned into fledgling feminists as a result of the new curriculum. From five to 14, they were consistently more ready than the boys to accept the ideas that women can enter a wide variety of jobs, and combine work and family. The ninth-grade girls were the most responsive to the intervention program, and showed the greatest attitude change; their self-esteem increased and they no longer felt that personal attractiveness was the sole route to success. Their male peers, by contrast, expressed their traditional opinions more freely. In only one ninth-grade class, taught by a strong and enthusiastic teacher, did boys join girls in shifting to more egalitarian views.

Guttentag's work reminds us that lessons about liberation are not enough to change attitudes and behavior. School programs do some good, and some teachers do even better. Indeed, the teachers' enthusiasm and extensive use of the curriculum materials were strongly related to the children's new attitudes. But kids pick up what they see around them far more than what adults tell them. What kids see is that men have more power, and that you can have things your way with power. They see men in a greater variety of jobs, and they see that mom is the main person who takes care of them. Those observations don't make them sexist, simply realistic. To change the observations, we would have to change the reality.

So I think it was unduly hopeful of the researchers to expect that six weeks' exposure to a vision of sex-role equality would outweigh the immediate benefits of the familiar division of labor. It's tough to persuade boys to give up the comforts of having mom at home to gain something so abstract as a flexible personality. Few children and not many adults are willing to let go of what they know for an uncertain, if well-intentioned, promise.

The researchers are optimistic about their work, concluding that school programs can be effective in shaping sex-role attitudes. To them, the glass is half full. What concerns me about the results of the study is that it increased the distance between the boys and the girls; the girls became less stereotyped about sex roles but the boys held tenaciously to the traditional views. This line of male resistance and mis-understanding is exactly what many adults who believe in sexual equality are facing. The glass is still half empty.

—Carol Tavris

---

better at spatial reasoning and to have higher mathematical abilities than girls. Girls, on the other hand, have better reading and other verbal skills [see "What We Know and Don't Know About Sex Differences," *pt*, December 1974].

These academic abilities may be nurtured, or nullified, by the classroom guardians. Parents make a major contribution to the shaping of social behavior, and there's evidence that they act differently toward boys and girls as early as the first few months of life. Fathers and mothers both turn boy infants out toward the world and push them; little girls more often get hugged up close, face to face. Children learn their academic skills, however, largely in the classroom, where boys learn to do one thing and girls learn to do another.

All 15 of the teachers gave more attention to boys who kept their noses to the academic grindstone. They got both physical and verbal rewards. Boys also received more directions from the teacher, and were twice as likely as the girls to get individual instructions on how to do things. Whether the directions were delivered by word or by demonstration, they made the boys much more capable of fending for themselves. **Boys Learn to Do.** In one classroom, the children were making party baskets. When the time came to staple the paper handles in place, the teacher worked with each child individually. She showed the boys how to use the stapler by holding the handle in place while the child stapled it. On the girls' turns, however, if the child didn't spontaneously staple the handle herself, the teacher took the basket, stapled it, and handed it back.

On another occasion, a teacher was showing a small group of three-year-olds how the same quantity of water can be poured to fill several different containers of varying heights and widths. Three children, Michael, Patty and Daniel, sat nearby, obviously fascinated by the activity, which demonstrates the "conversation" concept that marks a major milestone in a child's development.

The teacher let Michael try to pour the water himself, explaining how water can change shape without changing amount. Patty asked if she could try and was told to wait her turn. The teacher gave Daniel a chance to pour the water, and then put the materials away! Despite another request, Patty never got her turn. She never received the individual instruction the boys got in manipulating the materials.

There is ample evidence, from other studies, of the clear relationship between problem-solving ability and the amount of instruction and direction a child receives. So the superiority of boys over girls in spatial and analytic reasoning is at least partially a result of the way each sex learns to manipulate the environment—learning that begins in nursery school with boys who staple and pour, and girls who must sit passively by and watch.

It could be argued, of course, that boys require more instruction than girls, either because they are less well coordinated or because girls are more likely to acquire skills by watching others and therefore do not need as much individual instruction. Even if this is the case, however, boys and girls are still receiving a strikingly different amount of a type of adult attention that is important in the development of problem-solving ability. Boys are shown how lawn mowers and erector sets work, and they wind up with better spatial and analytic skills. Girls are encouraged to stay by their mothers and teachers, where they talk and read. It's the girls who rate higher in verbal and reading ability.

We found one exception to the general pattern. When the class engaged in an explicitly feminine, sex-typed activity such as cooking, the teachers did tend to pay more attention to the girls.

Even so, they still offered brief conversation, praise and assistance, while the boys got detailed instructions.

Malignant Neglect. With this sole exception, then, we found that in nursery-school classrooms teachers are much less likely to react to a girl's behavior, whether appropriate or not, than to a boy's. The girls' actions have considerably less effect on their environment, at least in terms of adult reaction, than do the actions of boys. Coupled with portrayals of the ineffectual female on television and in books, benign neglect in the classroom rapidly becomes malignant.

The cure, of course, does not lie in reversing the situation so that boys become dependent and girls disruptive. Nor does it lie entirely with teachers, who are only one link in an important chain of events. Children of both sexes should learn to be neither too disruptive nor too dependent, and teachers need to be aware of how they can either perpetuate or prevent these qualities, depending on their actions.

We feel that the differential treatment of boys and girls limits the freedom of both sexes to develop psychologically and intellectually. Later psychological problems, as well as differences in academic and on-the-job achievements, may be the price we all pay for preschool inequities. We agree with Sandra Bem [see "Androgyny Vs. the Tight Little Lives of Fluffy Women and Chesty Men," *pt*, September] that people need access to the entire spectrum of human behavior in order to cope with the complexity of our current world. That access can be guaranteed to the molders of clay only by the molders of children.

For more information read:

Maccoby, E.E. and C.N. Jacklin. *The Psychology of Sex Differences.* Stanford University, 1974, $18.95.

O'Leary, K.D., K.F. Kaufman, R.E. Kass and R.S. Drabman. "The Effects of Loud and Soft Reprimands on the Behavior of Disruptive Students" in *Exceptional Children*, Vol. 37, pp. 145-155, 1970.

Serbin, L.A., K.D. O'Leary, R.N. Kent and I.J. Tonick. "A Comparison of Teacher Response to the Preacademic and Problem Behavior of Boys and Girls" in *Child Development*, Vol. 44, pp. 796-804, 1973.

Hess, R.D. and V.C. Shipman. "Early Experience and the Socialization of Cognitive Modes in Children" in *Child Development*, Vol. 36, pp. 869-886, 1965.

THE MORE SORROWFUL SEX

Anywhere from two to five times as many women as men are likely to be diagnosed as depressed. The reasons are largely cultural—having to do with what "being feminine" requires, says a researcher who has investigated the sexually lopsided numbers. The problem may be reaching epidemic proportions.

Maggie Scarf

Maggie Scarf is a science writer who specializes in psychology and psychiatry. She is the author of *Body, Mind, Behavior* (New Republic Books, 1976) and the recipient of three national awards from the American Psychology Foundation. With the aid of an Alicia Patterson Foundation Fellowship, she has been studying depression in women over the various stages of the life cycle.

Do numbers lie? If not, the evidence is clear and overwhelming: females from adolescence onward—and throughout every phase of the life cycle—are far more vulnerable to depression than are males.

It turns up in virtually every study, carried out anywhere and everywhere. And while the figures may vary from one investigation to the next, the general trend is always the same. More women are in treatment for depression, in every institution—inpatient and outpatient—across the country, in state and county facilities, in community mental-health centers. And when the figures are adjusted for age, or phase of life, or socioeconomic circumstances, the outcome is still the same.

For every male diagnosed as suffering from depression, the head count is anywhere from two to six times as many females. The statistics show variation according to who is doing the counting, what the criteria are, the geographic location, and so forth. But the numbers are never equal.

As one might expect, the consistent disparity—those sexually lopsided statistics—has presented itself as a puzzle to experts of every theoretical hue and stripe. And there have been numerous efforts, on the part of psychiatrists, psychologists, epidemiologists (those who study patterns of illness in the population at large), sociologists, and others, to explain what remains a most peculiar phenomenon. Why, after all, should one sex be more vulnerable to depressive disorder than the other? It is, in a way, as strange as the idea of one sex getting flu, or measles, or appendicitis, or some other illness, far more frequently than the other. Some people insist, in fact, that it's not true: the statistical findings are erroneous, they say, because of certain biases in the counting.

That is "the-numbers-do-lie" point of view. According to that view, the unequal figures—and the fact that so many more women are in treatment for some form of depression—bears witness only to the eagerness of doctors and psychotherapists to *label* women. That is, the distressed person who happens to be female will get one particular dog tag—"depression"—hung around her neck with undue alacrity. But women are not in actuality, some experts have insisted, one whit more depressed than males.

So runs the argument made by Phyllis Chesler in her book *Women and Madness*. Psychologist Chesler contends that women tend to get diagnosed—that is, *called*—"depressed," or "disturbed," or "crazy," or "mad" with somewhat sinister readiness. Such psychiatric putdowns are, she maintains, nothing more than a covert societal mechanism, a means for punishing women who do not adjust to and accept their "femininity" under terms laid down by the male-dominated mental-health Establishment (which represents the community at large). The woman who fails to accept her female role, along with its attendant inferior social status, isn't "behaving," and she gets socked with a psychiatric diagnosis. The diagnosis itself, in the view of Chesler and others, is a handy "medical" and scientifically respectable device for keeping women in their place.

Could this explain those strange statistics? Might the high rates of depression among women be just a social phantasmagoria—a "scientific finding" related to nothing more than the biases of psychotherapists and clinicians? Are females actually no more melancholy, afflicted, anxious, troubled, depressed than males—but simply seen as being so?

Chesler's views have a certain compelling quality—especially since those depression statistics are disturbing, and one would like to explain (since one can't simply wish) them away. But I am among those who believe that her argument, as well as the empirical evidence she amasses in support of it, is probably largely false. I have not, after four years of studying the problem of women and depression in a wide variety of clinical settings, actually encountered anyone whom I suspected to be suffering from a disorder that could be called "psychiatric labeling."

The women whom I have come to know well or only slightly, whom I've talked to at length or just a little, whom I've seen just once or several times over periods of months—were all suffering. They were in pain, and in need of help; there just was no question about it.

Debra Thierry, for example, at age 22, had an image of herself as something superfluous in the human world. She told me during one of our interviews that she felt as if she were "litter." She was, she said, like a piece of drifting newspaper, "something that's just floating around, being blown around the sidewalk, underfoot, you know, being kicked aside. . . ." She was excess matter in the universe, unwanted and without value. Such feelings, and the diagnosis of the state she was in, have nothing at all to do with "psychiatric stigmatization."

Neither did the diagnosis ("depressive neurosis") of Kay Ellenberger, the slender, dark-haired wife of a successful Pittsburgh lawyer. I interviewed Kay at Western Psychiatric Institute and Clinic of the University of Pittsburgh Medical School, where she was an inpatient. She told me that she'd come home after successfully playing in a tennis tournament, and suddenly felt "as if the bottom were dropping out of my life, and that I was a nothing. That I'd promised to do too many things I didn't care about for too many people I didn't give a damn about. I was on all these committees, and running like crazy; but it was stupid and meaningless. And I wanted out—to quit trying—to be dead."

"The women whom I've come to know were in pain. They weren't suffering from 'psychiatric labeling.'"

While her children were at school, she had emptied the medicine cabinet and swallowed everything in sight. Could one imagine, even for a moment, that her suffering wasn't "real"—that her extreme misery, her psychological hurting, weren't actually there?

Or that a patient like 43-year-old Muriel Clough, who kept saying that she was "struggling to liberate" herself, was the victim of antifeminine bias? I came to know Muriel well during the six weeks that she spent at the Dartmouth-Hitchcock Mental Health Center. She was struggling to liberate herself, assuredly, but she kept saying that her marriage was much better and her relationship with her husband was "much more intimate" during those times when she was completely *down* and at the nadir of the depression. I could go on and on, but make the same point: these women, none of them, were victims of a "conspiracy" of the male-dominated mental-health Establishment.

One may argue that the experiences of a single investigator who is studying the problem in some of this nation's most advanced psychiatric facilities can't pretend to anything like Chesler's systematic and data-supported overview of the treatment women receive in the entire mental-health-care system. And I will acknowledge at once that mine is a close-up look, the account of where I've gone and what I've seen, of the kinds of things that happened in the types of places that I happened to go to—which is surely open to charges of particularities, quirkiness, biases of every kind.

But so are Chesler's statistics—or, at least, her interpretation of them. Most epidemiologists consider *Women and Madness* a political and polemical tract that bears no resemblance to anything that could be called "scientific" or "objective." The late Marcia Guttentag, who directed a nationwide study of what many consider to be an "epidemic" of depression among women, made a careful study of the same statistical data that Chesler used. Chesler's figures were found to be based on *absolutes*—that is, on simple head counts of female and male patients in county and state psychiatric facilities. Because she found so many more women of age 65 and over in those mental institutions, Chesler concluded that antifeminine bias was rampant among the (mostly male) psychiatric Establishment; and that women were being railroaded, via the "diagnosing" track, into geriatric careers as mental patients.

But what Chesler did not do was adjust those figures for age. If there are more women of age 65 and over in mental institutions, it is because there are more women of that age in the population as a whole. Women live longer. In fact, given the larger number of women of that age in the overall population, there were years, so the Guttentag study group found, when women were underrepresented in psychiatric hospitals. Chesler's claim, that old women are tossed into mental institutions that are actually custodial homes, was simply not found to be substantiated.

Indeed, as one worker on the Guttentag project (officially entitled "The Women in Mental Health Project at Harvard") told me, there were years when *men*, in proportion to their numbers in the population, were overrepresented in mental institutions, as a group. Men are, furthermore, far more likely to be committed to institutions against their will. Male diagnoses very frequently involve problems with other people—alcoholism, aggressive acting-out of psychological problems, and so on—and they are often brought in by the police and sent via the courts to institutions.

Women, on the other hand, tend to receive the more "passive" diagnoses: they become depressed, or perhaps schizophrenic, but they don't usually hurt anyone. For that reason, women are more commonly brought in for treatment by their friends or families, and they are committed *voluntarily.*

Each sex does, intriguingly, appear to take the lead in specific types of psychiatric disturbance. Men, as a group, show far higher rates of alcoholism, drug disorders, and behavior disorders of childhood and adolescence—in short, the more action-oriented, disruptive-to-others kinds of difficulty. Where women are concerned, there is one single category in which they hog the diagnostic stage to an almost preposterous degree. And that is, of course, depression.

The Guttentag group came away from their analysis of the mental-health statistics with a sense that the finding of so much more depression among women was discomfiting but real. Not only was there the excess of treated depressions: moreover, there also seemed to be vast numbers of women who were depressed for various reasons, and who had many of the clear-cut symptoms of depression, but who were walking around, not realizing that they "had" anything, and therefore not seeking treatment.

There could, nevertheless, be a very different sort of a kink in those statistics on women and depression. The fact is that in order to be diagnosed as "suffering from depression," you have to go to a doctor in the first place, and women just plain do go to see their doctors more often. Not only do they consult doctors with a demonstrably greater frequency, but they do so about many more minor kinds of problems and of disabilities.

The difference in what researchers call "health-care-seeking behaviors" springs into being, apparently, sometime just around puberty. Before puberty, as Mitchell Balter, a psychologist at the National Institute of Mental Health, told me, girls and boys see physicians with roughly the same frequency. The younger males may, in fact, take a slight lead in number of visits. But *after* puberty, the picture shifts rapidly: there is a sharp increase on the part of the girls, and a decrease for boys. And the changed pattern—women seeing their doctors more often—will persist throughout adult life.

Going to the doctor seems to be, in essence, a particularly "feminine" way of coping with stress, and of dealing with a variety of difficulties and distresses. Sixty percent of all patient

---

"Vast numbers of women had clear-cut symptoms of depression, but were walking around without realizing it."

---

visits are female-patient visits.

If, furthermore, the patient is not only freely expressive about her sorrows, sadnesses, and life disappointments, but has a few physical symptoms to boot, she may readily be diagnosed as suffering from a depression. She may be given medications—either tranquilizers or antidepressants—to help her weather her current difficulties. The use of medically prescribed mood-altering drugs is a very widespread phenomenon, and the majority of those using them (70 percent in toto) are women. According to NIMH's Balter, a study completed in 1972 indicated that some 23 percent of women between the ages of 18 and 29 (nearly one-fourth the entire age group) had taken some psychotropic medication during the preceding year. Among men of the same age, only 6 percent had done so, and they had used less potent types of medication.

After age 30, the males' use of mood-changing drugs increased: it doubled to 12 percent in the years between 30 and 44. But among females, there was also a steep rise: from 23 percent to a hefty 32 percent. Roughly one-third of all women in this age-group (30 to 44) were using prescription drugs to treat their moods. The psychotropic medications were, for the most part, being prescribed by internists and family practitioners (85 percent of those who said they used mood-altering drugs reported that they had never seen a psychiatrist).

The classic chicken-and-the-egg phenomenon could certainly account for varying rates of male and female patients "in treatment for depression." For, when the numbers of such patients are counted, women—if they go to doctors more often—would obviously be diagnosed and medicated with greater frequency, and therefore have a larger representation.

Many men with the same minor symptoms (as well as the same degree of distress and unhappiness) might never go to their doctors at all. And if a man *did* consult his physician with, for example, a digestive complaint, he would be far less inclined to discuss any emotional components of what would be viewed as a physical problem. Undoubtedly, the same symptoms in a male and female may be seen, by a clinician, as reflecting different underlying problems. Is that antifeminine bias? Or an awareness, on the part of doctors, that women show a much higher rate of depression? Again, the questions and answers are circular.

In any event, the male patient's sex-appropriate behavior will dictate more stoicism, less free expression of sadnesses and weaknesses, and less owning-up to physical and mental difficulties. Men are far more reluctant to take on, even on a transitory basis, the "sick role." It is too inconsistent with standard cultural ideals of independence, autonomy, masculinity.

Men and women may, in other words, be *feeling* in much the same dysphoric, unhappy, anxious, depressed ways but *behaving* very differently. Women may be assuming the culturally "available" sick-and-dependent role when they are stressed, while men fail to seek medical attention. The exorbitant number of depressed women could be a statistical red herring: men and women might be equally depressed, but men may not be counted as "cases" because they have never gone in for treatment.

But that just isn't the case. For, **powerful evidence from so-called community studies indicates that women really are more depressed than men—irrespective of who does, or who doesn't, go to the doctor.**

What are community studies? Just that: studies of the community at large. What is involved is the selection of a random sample of respondents that is representative of the larger population; and the careful and systematic interviewing of those people in their homes.

If the study happens to be an assessment of psychiatric symptoms in the members of the community, then the research interviewer will fill out a comprehensive questionnaire that covers many aspects of psychological functioning. For instance, to elicit information about the possible existence of a depressive disorder, the interviewer might initially ask: "Did you ever have a period that lasted at least one week when you were bothered by feeling depressed, sad, blue, hopeless, down in the dumps, that you just didn't care anymore, or worried about a lot of things that could happen? What about feeling irritable or easily annoyed?"

If the respondent's replies happen to be in the affirmative, then other questions will follow. Those would touch upon sudden changes in appetite, in sleeping patterns, in energy levels, in interest in customary activities, in sexual functioning. And there would be queries about "feeling guilty," "worthless," or "down on oneself," as well as about problems in concentrating and making decisions, and even in thinking. There would be questions about thoughts of dying and/or suicide.

Myrna M. Weissman, director of the Yale Depression Unit and an epidemiologist by training, has just completed a community study of representative samples of the population in New Haven, Connecticut. Weissman told me that her survey, like all others that have been done, has uncovered the same phenomenon: an almost frightening amount of depression among women respondents. "Regardless of who is or who isn't going to the doctor—and a number of depressed women who were interviewed were *not* in treatment—women are far more depressed than are men."

Much of the female depression discovered in the community study did, she continued, include milder forms of disturbance. "When you get out in the community, and talk to people in their homes, you draw in the somewhat less severe cases, too. Because, you see, for a person to get into psychiatric treatment he or she has to be in pain and be really hurting. Getting help takes energy, and it can be expensive; and some feel it's still a bit of a stigma. And so what our nets take in are people who are doing some suffering, but who aren't in such torment that they can't say, 'Oh well, I can live with it, and besides, what's the

---

"Being female means (frequently) never being encouraged to become a self-sufficient person."

---

use.' They're mildly symptomatic, maybe more transiently symptomatic. But they don't feel bad enough—or maybe don't know enough—to go for help."

In terms of overall volume—sheer numbers of women who are depressed—Weissman is one among a number of experts who have spoken of what seems to be a steady rise in the course of the past decade. Her own research on suicide attempts among females indicates a similar surge upward, primarily among younger women. "This has been well

documented in several countries over the past 10 years," she said. "And, while all suicide attempters may not be depressed, I would say that most of them are."

As rates of depression among women have increased, the age at which they come to clinics for treatment has been inching downward. "Right now," observed Weissman, "the typical person who comes to the Yale Depression Unit is a woman, and she is under the age of 35." This age-shift downward (in the earlier years of this century, the typical depressed patient was described as someone in his 40s or older) may be due to the fact that women who might have come in later in their lives are now appearing earlier, and with far less serious symptoms. "Or," she continued, "it may be due to the fact that help is more available and getting treatment is more acceptable." "Or," Weissman smiled, shrugging slightly, "it may be because the treatments—both drug and psychotherapeutic—are themselves so radically improved."

Weissman, in collaboration with Gerald Klerman of the Alcohol, Drug Abuse and Mental Health Administration (ADAMHA), has written what is considered a classic paper on the topic of women and depression. Reviewing all possible "explanations" for the sexually tilted statistics, they concluded that the figures represent the real situation, and that the findings are true.

Women simply *are* more depressed, in the aggregate, than are men, in the aggregate. The next question is: why?

As one might imagine, theoretical "answers" to that question abound. It would be impossible to review every one of them here. Let me say only that the most obvious sort of solution to the riddle, "female hormones," does not really stand up under close and systematic scrutiny. Endocrines may affect mood, in various ways and at particular times; but they don't really provide reasons for the huge differential in overall male and female rates of depressive illness. Let us therefore turn instead to some of the likelier explanations that have thus far been offered.

One has to do with a trait considered "normally feminine"—meaning, more prominent among females—and that is dependency. Girls and

women are expected in our culture to show higher dependency needs than boys and men do. That is simply one aspect of the designated sex role, and both males and females are being taught their lines from the moment of birth onward. Psychological experiments, for instance, have demonstrated that parents hold new babies differently: an infant in a pink blanket, *believed* to be a girl, will be held and cuddled much more than a newborn who is wrapped in blue.

As the psychologist Judith Bardwick has written: "The dependency, passivity, tears, and affection-seeking normal to both sexes in younger children are defined as feminine in older children, and girls can remain dependent and infantile longer. . . . This has a very pervasive and significant effect: unless something intervenes, the girl will continue to have throughout womanhood a great need for approval from others. Her behavior will be guided by the fear of rejection or loss of love. An independent sense of self with a resulting sense of self-esteem can only evolve when the individual, alone, sets out to attain goals and, with reasonable frequency, achieves them."

This independent sense of self, notes Bardwick (in *Psychology of Women: A Study of Biocultural Conflicts*), is rarely achieved among females. More often, the young girl learns to appraise her worth as a function of the appraisals of others, to value herself insofar as she *is* valued. Being female means (frequently) never being encouraged to become a self-sufficient individual. And girls receive many instructions on that aspect of femininity throughout the long apprenticeship of childhood.

Now it may well be, theorizes Bardwick, that the greater dependency shown by girls and women is not merely due to the powerful acculturating forces that move them in this direction: there may be inborn, biologically based behavioral tendencies of that kind that come into play as well. But in any case, the lack of an *inner* impulse to break away from the dependent relations of early childhood—and the manifest assumption, on everyone's part, that she will not do so—fosters a situation in which the girl, and later, woman, gives her highest priorities to pleasing others, to being attractive to others, to being cared for, and to caring for others.

"An independent sense of self," Bardwick writes, "can only occur when one has many experiences in which he is responsible while he cannot completely depend upon his original sources of love and support." (By switching to the pronoun "he" in this sentence, Bardwick seems to underscore the notion that a person who *does* develop this sort of independence is unlikely to be a "she.") The overall point, however, is that women receive ferocious training in a direction that leads away from thinking, "What do I want?" and toward "What do *they* want or need of me?"

Being successful then translates to being successful in meeting the expectations of others: pleasure has much to do with the act of pleasing. This readily leads to a situation in which good feelings about the self— that is, self-esteem—become dependent upon the esteem of those around one. Feelings of emotional well-being, a sense of one's worthfulness as a person, are hostage to the moods, attitudes, and approval of others (or, maybe, to one critically important other person). One is likable/lov-

---

"The depressed woman has lost something she vitally depended on. More often than not, it is a love bond."

---

able/significant only to the extent that one is liked/loved/significant to someone else. It follows, then, that in times of interpersonal drought— when sources of emotional supply are unusually low, or not there—the "normally feminine, normally dependent" woman may experience her inner world as emptied of what is good and meaningful to her. The props of her self-regard, if they've been held in place primarily by feedback from the environment, may simply begin to crumble and fall down. Under the circumstances, a woman may become far too harsh in her assessment of herself and of her

worth and usefulness as a human being. She may feel helpless about her life circumstances, and hopelessly ineffectual in terms of her capacity for mastering or changing them. She may, in a word, become depressed.

This is, I suspect, the point at which "normal feminine dependency" becomes transformed into something that can be viewed as pathological—into a clinical depressive illness, involving a very well-recognized cluster of psychological and biological symptoms. The depressed woman is someone who has lost. She has lost "something" upon which she vitally depended. The tone is of something profoundly significant having been taken away, of some crucial life's territory having been surrendered. And what I have seen emerge, with an almost amazing regularity, is that the "loss" in question is the loss of a crucially important and often self-defining emotional relationship.

Despite the complex, varying, dizzyingly diverse matters and difficulties that any person *could* potentially become depressed about, there appeared to be one kind of a loss—more than any other—that had triggered a depressive episode in the women that I interviewed. And that was the loss of a love bond.

Depressions, when they "happen" in women, happen in one kind of context with the greatest of frequency. That context is the loss of emotional relatedness: "attachments" are the critical variable. Some writers have speculated that a much greater investment in one's love attachments might simply go along with culturally transmitted sex-role expectations correlated with "being feminine." Women are not only supposed to be more dependent, but also to be warmer, more expressive, more eager to relate on a personal level, and so forth. Because of intensive and early "femininity training," they might show a greater propensity to put more of themselves into—and therefore to risk more in—a few powerfully important relationships.

To fail in those relationships is, then, equated with "failing in everything." To slip there can mean a headlong slide downward into desperation and misery. It is around such "losses of love" that the depressive clouds tend to gather and to darken: impor-

tant figures leaving or dying; the inability to establish a meaningful bond; being forced, by a natural transition in life, to relinquish an important love tie; a marriage that is ruptured, threatening to rupture, or simply growing progressively distant; the splintering of a love affair or recognition that it is not going to endure. These are among the most common "causes" of female depression.

Men do not appear to become depressed, with this near-predictable regularity, over the rupture, or threatened rupture, of emotional bonds. Again, this could have much to do with role expectations about what "being masculine" involves: independence, action, aggressiveness, and a high motivation toward competing, winning, achieving. For men, the more usual depressive motifs involve work issues, status, and success problems—difficulties in "making it" out there, in the world at large.

Such issues can, of course, be upsetting to women as well, but they don't touch upon the same tender, raw nerve ending of concern. Likewise, this isn't meant to suggest that men don't ever become severely depressed over the loss of a love attachment. But certain core concerns do seem to set the stage for a serious depression in the male and in the female—and in the two sexes, those core concerns are often somewhat different.

And the experience of *being depressed* may be qualitatively different in some important respects for men and for women. One recent survey of college students carried out at Yale University by psychologists Eve Chevron, Donald M. Quinlan, and Sidney J. Blatt found that depressed females suffered "significantly higher levels of . . . experiences of loneliness, helplessness, dependency, and the need for external sources of security." But for the males questioned in the study, the depressive issues had much more to do with "self-criticism and the failure to live up to expectations."

Some experts have gone so far as to hypothesize that a greater sensitivity to fluctuations in a woman's love attachments is bred into the human female genotype because, in the primitive environment in which our species evolved, "loving and protective mother" could be equated with "helpless infant's survival." The mother who fell in love with her baby, and remained emotionally "bound," would stay close by the infant, protecting him or her from being taken as prey. This view has it that the female's high valuation of her emotional attachments was a behavioral tendency that was "selected for" during evolutionary prehistory—because it is a human survival mechanism. And, obviously, those girl babies whose mothers behaved in those ways would have lived to reproduce and pass the same tendencies along to their own female children!

Males and females may, in fact, be marching to somewhat different kinds of inner music. (Or to notes that are similar, but arrangements that are not at all the same.) It is possible that, as Harvard psychologist Jerome Kagan has suggested, the two sexes are "sensitized to different aspects of experience and gratified by different profiles of events."

Everyone does, clearly, keep his or her interior scorecard, a running self-assessment and estimate that continuously monitors the question "How am I doing?" The suggestion raised here is that, in terms of what is "most satisfying" and "most disturbing," males and females do that self-grading somewhat differently.

And for women, whose tendency may be to do their self-rating in terms of the health of their emotional attachments, much more—a far greater amount of "self"—will be at risk in their loving connections. The enhanced vulnerability to depression might be traceable, in fact, to the higher psychic investments being made in that vitally important and crucial business of loving. It could have much to do, as well, with the sort of social climate that we all inhabit nowadays—one not noted, I fear, for the permanence of security-giving emotional attachments.

To be depressed is to be in a state of emotional paralysis, to dare nothing, to try nothing, to freeze. The painfulness of it, that noxious state of helplessness and inferiority, is real—as real as any form of physical pain. Like physical pain, it will often demand a person's complete attention. How often I've spoken with women who seemed preoccupied and distracted; whose energies were being totally absorbed in the effort to retain some equilibrium in their lives. That hurting, like physical hurting, could dominate consciousness with its urgency, its demands. Some women, when I talked with them, were finding it impossible to see beyond the suffering of the moment. Others, less seriously depressed, found it possible to "get out of it for awhile" when life presented some pleasant diversion; but only in the knowledge that they'd be returning home to where the pain was, to the wounded self.

The depressed person *is* wounded, though the injury can't be seen or lo-cated. The person is "changed," diminished; usually he or she has experienced a morbid drop in confidence. Guilt, anxiety, irritability, hostility: those are common ingredients, found in variable proportions, in the depressive stew. It is, experientially, a fairly horrible mixture. And the person suffering from depression, filled with this feast of dysphoric feeling, usually becomes far less able to cope in the outer world, less able to be flexible and to negotiate.

The depressed person must, moreover, operate with less-than-normal energies and capacities. And because there is that true diminution in adaptability, the person's dealings with the environment tend to become off-the-mark, erratic, and often genuinely self-defeating. "Feeling bad," then, has plenty of consequences. The person suffering from depression is, at best, either pedaling-in-place in life, or losing valuable ground.

And the "depressed person" is very liable to be a woman. According to Robert M. A. Hirschfeld, chief of the depression section at the National Institute of Mental Health, survey data indicates that one in every five Americans has at least moderate depressive symptomatology. We are talking, then, about a group of people on the order of 40 million—and two-thirds of that group are women! It is, as Hirschfeld acknowledged, a public-health problem of almost staggering proportions.

The Psychological Pressures on the American Male

by Herb Goldberg

The women's liberation movement has made it clear, even to the dullest observer, that the female in our society is a victim. In many cases she is a victim of the chauvinistic male who has kept her locked in a servile role, "thinged" her by treating her as a household and sex object and in myriad other ways denied her important decision-making power relating to her social mobility, her body and her freedom to express and experience herself.

It is woman's inherent strength and survival sense which motivates her to liberate herself. But why does the male remain pathetically quiet and passive on his own behalf? In his own way, he too is a victim in a society which has saddled him with destructive role contradictions and conflicts. In fact, I believe that it is virtually impossible, because of these conflicts, for him to live a life which is emotionally authentic and socially satisfying.

Maybe his plight eludes him because his struggle is more subtle and the chances for the remedy by social and legislative change are far more remote. Male enslavement in our society is deeply rooted in psychological discontinuities and in contradictions between his early emotional and social experiences as a boy and the demands which the culture and society place upon him as an adult. His liberation therefore has to spring out of his individual consciousness. It must come from his *attitude towards himself* through an awakening to, and a working out of, these psychological binds and life-exhausting pressures under which he is forced to live.

Male psychological difficulties in our culture are rooted in the nature of the early parent-son relationship. In our society, it is the female who is principally responsible for the physical and emotional upbringing of children in the critical first five years of life. The father is traditionally away from home working during the day, and when he is home in the evening he is often tired and distracted. His involvement with his children is all too often perfunctory and primarily confined to weekends. Or he may be totally absent during these early years because of military service, traveling jobs or as a result of divorce, in which case the woman is almost always given custody of the children. The male child therefore learns from the earliest years that it is the female who controls his most profound needs and experiences.

Then, suddenly, when he nears school age it becomes imperative for the male to shift his identification 180 degrees and to act and express himself in a totally masculine way. The female child never undergoes such an abrupt transition. She can happily and comfortably maintain her early identification with a mother who continues to guide her and serve as a model. Clearly, however, the deep-rooted identification with the female is a powerful psychological component of every male as well, and yet society pressures the boy to repress this critical, very real aspect of himself.

This conflict sets the foundation for a critical psychological vulnerability. On the one hand, it becomes a source of anxious defensiveness in the male personality which shows up eventually in his exaggerated need to maintain a masculine image. It also inhibits him from experiencing and expressing his passive and dependent sides, which we are culturally conditioned to think of as feminine, without a heavy burden of guilt. No wonder men are prone to psychophysiological disorders such as ulcers and heart attacks.

Many males find it impossible to allow themselves to relax, do nothing, be cared for and indulge themselves in passive dependent behaviors, even when their emotional and physical health and needs call for it. For example, men frequently feel threatened by and uncomfortable about being sick in our society. They tend to ignore early symptoms of illness, and when they are undeniably sick, they resist staying in bed for long periods of time, even when it's necessary for recuperation. It may well be that this inability to express passivity is an important factor in the relatively shorter life span of the male.

A counterpart to this may be seen in the fact that in the private practices of psychotherapists there are many more women than men among the clientele. The superficial conclusion often drawn is that women are more unstable or have more emotional problems than men. However, in reality it may simply be a reflection of the male resistance to dependency, to self-exposure and to the expression of his emotional self. Consequently, most males would not seek out help until they encountered a severe, immobilizing crisis.

The above-described discontinuities also make the male more prone to sexual anxiety. For many men, sexual involvement becomes a never-ending round of self-reassurance and proving, or they withdraw from it into an obsession with work. Each sexual encounter becomes a test of their masculinity, as they often become involved in a continual need to perform and prove themselves potent.

If they fail, they accuse themselves of being inadequate, not real men, and sometimes even of being latent or actual homosexuals. Here even nature is no friend of the male. A frigid female can continue to perform sexually and even hide the fact of her frigidity if she so chooses. Psychologically, frigidity and impotency are equivalent syndromes. However, the social response to frigidity has traditionally been, at worst, an accepting one, and at times it has even been regarded as a legitimate resistance to masculine insensitivity. The impotent male, on the other hand, is held responsible for his own inadequacy and is left feeling demeaned and humiliated by it. He must lie there and bathe in his agony and self-hate.

The intense masculine anxiety towards the feminine component within himself shows up in his attitudes toward touching other men. The social response to women holding or kissing each other is generally a casual and accepting one. But touching between males is acceptable at best only if it is acted out in a very brief and limited way.

Though there is clearly more psychological rationalization for male homosexual behavior in our society by virtue of the strong underlying female identification, the cultural response to this behavior is again significantly less sympathetic than it is towards the female. The stereotypical cultural image of the male homosexual has until recently been one of a bathroom-lurking pervert who preys on little boys. Furthermore, the typical heterosexual male reaction to male homosexuals is often one of revulsion, and occasionally violence, to the point where "straight" males have made sport of beating up homosexuals. No such reaction is commonly seen among females towards lesbianism. Once again, the strong need to repress the feminine component in himself seems to push the male toward behaving in defensive, "masculine," overcompensatory ways.

A more commonly recognized result of the male's fear of his feminine side is seen in his resistance to open and spontaneous emotional expression. Crying or behaving in frightened ways are examples of emotions tolerated readily in the female. But a man who cries easily and often would be looked upon by most as being unstable, infantile or neurotic. Picture for a moment the reaction a man would receive if he burst into tears on a regular basis over frustrations at his place of employment. Picture, then, the response the female receives for similar behavior. The female can generally repair matters in the ladies' room. More often than not, the male ends up in a therapist's office trying to find out what went wrong.

As a boy, the male is discouraged from playing with girls. Playing house, cooking, playing with dolls and similarly domestically oriented games are not masculine and are therefore discouraged. Parents worry when they see this behavior in their sons. They often begin to envision an incipient homosexual and frantically try to divert the boy's attention toward "masculine" activities such as sports. Consequently, when he has grown up and married, he has had too few appropriate learning experiences as a boy which would allow him to find comfortable mutual play activities with females. Once married, however, many men tend to feel guilty and anxious if they continue to indulge in playful activities primarily with other males. They come to feel obligated to include their wives in their activities and to find a place in hers.

I see a principle cause here as the male's inability to honestly and guiltlessly say to his wife, "No, I don't want to spend all or most of my free time with you because I really don't get that much pleasure from it." As an aside, there are few more pathetic sights in our society, in my opinion, than that of a man trotting after his wife on a weekend or vacation and doing an endless succession of "her things" such as shopping and eating out. During these activities, it is not uncommon to see the man's head turning like a swivel looking at each female as she walks by, feeling guilty about it and trying to hide and deny this response from his wife when he is confronted by it. His distracted looking at other women may be as much an expression of his underlying boredom and resentment as it is a sexual response. At least partially, it is a form of passive aggression which says, "I may be too guilty to tell you I don't want to be here doing this with you, but I'll be damned if either of us will have a good time."

Eventually, his resentment may begin to express itself as a refusal to go out and then progress into disengagement as he stays glued to the TV weekends watching sporting events and drinking beer.

The feminist movement has dramatized the fact that the woman is treated as an object, specifically a sex object. The counterpart male reaction is, however, generally overlooked; it is one which is equally dehumanizing. That is, the male is a status symbol whose attractiveness is measured by his earning capacity, the status of his profession or job and the amount of his power. Equally as fearful as a woman's loss of desirability and attractiveness through age, therefore, is the man's dread of losing his job, his income, failing in competition with peers or being usurped by younger men who are brighter and more up to date. All of these anxieties are intensely wearing and destructive, because for most males in our society, ego and attractiveness are tied in with work status and earning capacity. Just as women are learning to say "to hell with it" to their roles as housekeepers and mothers, so must men in an age of "future shock" and automation learn to untie their self-image from earning power and employment status.

Finally, women have been rightfully and legitimately demanding the privilege of control over their bodies, specifically demanding the right of decision regarding abortions. It is surprising that the same men who support this goal for women fail to recognize its male equivalent in their own condition. Specifically, I am speaking of military duty. The acceptance of military duty as a given fact of life has built into it a significantly greater potential loss of control over one's body than denial of the right of abortion. By accepting his military role without right of decision, he has in effect said that the society can control the decision-making power over his right to live. The woman in our society is not faced with any such equivalent situation.

It is a phenomenon worthy of exploring that the male in our culture—whose psychological life is a nest of conflicts, discontinuities, guilt, contradictions and critical vulnerabilities—has not actively begun to liberate himself.

ANDROGYNY

Andrew Kopkind

You see them in shopping malls and Manhattan boutiques, in locker rooms and ladies' lounges, in school rooms, factories, kitchens, bedrooms, on television and in the movies. They wear pants suits and leisure suits, jeans and caftans, blow-dry haircuts, herbal perfumes; they are rock singers who twirl their hips, coeds who dig the Alaskan pipeline, a football tackle who crochets, a Brownie in the Little League, a President-elect who broadcasts love and compassion and weeps at the news of his election. They practice the many ways of androgyny, but they rarely recognize its profound novelty. They are—we are—skirting the edge of a revolution in sexual consciousness so radical that it could make the disruptions of the last decade seem like tantrums in a sandbox.

Androgyny—literally, man-woman—is as old as prehistoric myth and as new as next fall's fashions. It is as banal as unisex hairdos and as basic as human equality, as pop as David Bowie and as cultivated as Virginia Woolf. It stretches from Bloomsbury to Bloomingdale's. Its expressions are the many mixtures of manners, styles and values assigned by custom—or law—to only one or the other sex: dominance, breadwinning, decisiveness to males; dependence, child rearing, tenderness to females. Convention calls it a sin, or a joke, to reassign those roles; both comedy and religion contain plenty of cautionary tales on the subject. But androgyny implies not a mere exchange or reversal of the roles, but liberation from them, the removal of the stereotypes of sex, an escape from the jailhouse of gender.

"Behavior should have no gender," Stanford psychologist Sandra Bem insists. What people do for a living, what they wear, how they express themselves or how they confront the everyday world has nothing to do with their sex types. That, at least, is the androgynous ideal. If true androgynes evolve from this heavily stereotyped society, they will be tender and dominant, dependent and decisive, ambitious and nurturing according to their human temperament, not their gender.

But for most people, the reality of manners and morals in our sex-polarized civilization is so far from that ideal plane that it is hard to see how it will be reached, what is pushing us there—and why it should be an ideal in the first place.

Simply to sense the androgynous current that runs beneath the surface of ordinary events is difficult enough. The heads that bob up seem only tenuously connected: Mick Jagger, Patti Smith, Twyla Tharp, Lauren Hutton, Cary Grant; tuxedoed women in *Vogue;* families that share a hair dryer in TV commercials; middle-aged couples in matching acrylic leisure/pants suits; fathers minding the kids while mothers go to the office. They all partake of an androgynous sensibility that was almost unknown a generation ago. Some people *look* androgynous: they incorporate masculine and feminine body characteristics and mannerisms in a hybrid whole. Others *behave* androgynously: they work, play or act in ways not completely "appropriate" to their gender. And still others *feel* androgynous: their emotions do not correspond to the list of acceptable passions assigned to their sex.

There is no uniform scale yet in use that measures the development of an androgynous personality (although Sandra Bem is working on the problem: she believes healthy sexual adjustment should be plotted against androgynous perfection, not masculine/feminine polarity). Nor is there a way to chart the movement toward androgyny in the society at large. But almost everyone has impressions that something peculiar is happening to sex roles. By and large, role changing is still a joke or a sin. But one morning, not too far in the future, the critical mass of Americans may wake up and realize that androgyny is on its way—and all hell will break loose.

The trend began decades ago, but between the death of Victoria and the dawn of Aquarius androgyny was confined to hothouse environments of intellectuals, actors, musicians and other freaks. It hardly moved out of Bloomsbury, Greenwich Village or the Hollywood Hills.

Then the marshaled forces of the sexual revolution in the late 1960s propelled androgyny out of its bohemian closets and into Middle American family rooms. The bottom line of feminism and gay liberation has been the obliteration of socially defined roles. Women no longer have to look, act or feel the way men's fantasies dictate. Homosexuals can be free of the emotional straitjackets tailored by heterosexual demands. In back of those battlelines, others removed from the struggles have the opportunity—and the impetus—to summon up those parts of themselves that were always restrained by propriety.

In the beginning the muse of androgyny created denim, unstyled and impersonal, then washed, crushed, crimped and flared—but preeminently the unisex texture. Soon men and women were sharing work boots, hiking boots, Frye boots, clogs, Adidas sneakers, Earth Shoes; jogging suits, snowmobile suits, jumpsuits, silk shirts, beads and bracelets, pendants and necklaces, turquoise rings, perfumes.

"Men's scents used to be a joke," Annette Green of New York's Fragrance Foundation reports. "Hai Karate advertised with grunts. And then Aramis came along and it took the male perfume market seriously." And no wonder. American men last year spent $208 million on cologne, an increase of 18 percent over the previous year. According to *Beauty Fashion* magazine, "the sound barrier of masculinity has been smashed and the blue-collar worker does not consider it 'faggish' to use the heavier colognes."

The androgynous sensibility invaded high fashion: Gernreich and Courreges added a dimension of spacey, sexy masculinity to feminine frills. Cardin began tailoring men's clothes to emphasize sleek figures and forms. Men and women could now wear their new suits with the same style of turtleneck sweater—and a piece of jewelry if they chose. The Marlboro dude became the Winston androgyne, showing off his gold good-luck charm hanging deep in his cleavage, his blowdry hair immobile in strong wind or calm.

The imported flotsam and jetsam of the Third World made its way from hippie head shops and college-town bazaars to fashionable unisex boutiques. Most of it was well-suited for androgynous wear: who knew whether maharajas or maharanis wore a particular style of shirt or piece of jewelry; who cared whether a camel driver or his wife fancied sheepskin jackets. At home any sex could play the import game.

Better than the Third World as a spring of unisex styles was Outer Space. If sex-typed fashions could be altered on the road from Morocco, they were ready-to-wear from Krypton. Androgyny is a prevailing theme in futurist and other-worldly literature: men and women in sci-fi movies set centuries ahead in time are often identically clothed, ornamented—and conveniently bald, whether because of evolution or advanced barbering. Space is the great sex leveler. Technology and convenience, at least, demand that Soviet male and female cosmonauts wear unisex clothing, perform the same tasks and treat each other as equals. It might somehow be awkward for a cosmonaut man to hold the space hatch open for a cosmonaut woman on their way down the stairs to a new planet.

Space and science fiction allow a different kind of escape from mundane sex roles. Two of the most androgynous rock stars—David Bowie and Elton John—have futurist personae: Bowie has been, on different occasions, Ziggy Stardust (a man from Mars) and the Man Who Fell to Earth. John plays as Captain Fantastic and sings in "Rocket Man," one of his early hits, "I'm not the man they think I am at home/Oh!no, no, no/I'm a rocket man." And the most twisted androgynous fantasy of all is Alice Cooper, who transcends sex roles altogether with the force of corruption and mockery.

The politics of pure androgyny has always had significant historical support, while under social attack. Philosophers and psychologists have maintained that each human has "masculine" and "feminine" characteristics, but society channels individuals into that category in which behavior matches sexual appearance. The other half—the unused complement of traits—is then lost, forgotten or repressed, often with dire results for the person's psyche or soul.

Aristophanes, Plato's character in *The Symposium*, formulated the famous allegory of three original sexes—male, female and hermaphrodite—split into halves by Zeus; each half has spent the succeeding aeons searching for its mate to regain completion (as homosexual man, lesbian female and heterosexual). Hinduism, Buddhism and Zoroastrainism all contain visions of Creation that postulate androgynous beings cleaved into single, incomplete sexes. Freud and Jung saw evidence of continuing conflict between masculine and feminine instincts, or unconscious memories in the individual. Contemporary psychotherapists often encourage patients to awaken their submerged "other" selves to achieve healthy wholeness. In therapy, if not in life, men are supposed to cry and solicit affection, women are helped to express anger and assert their independence. D.H. Lawrence—by turns an egregious male chauvinist and prophet of androgyny—saw in "The Rainbow" the evolution of a feminine principle that would renew the world spoiled by men. Proust, Artaud, Cocteau, Apollinaire—there is a hidden literary history of androgyny that only now can be understood in a social context.

But the doctors—of the church, of philosophy, of medicine and literature—have not always been helpful. They customarily confuse androgynous behavior with sexual preference or with gender identity. Their confusion has become common fallacy, so that many people mistake androgyny for bisexuality or homosexuality or neuter sexuality—or with hermaphroditism or transsexuality. It is none of the above. Androgyny is the principle that *unties* gender and sexual orientation from human activity. Androgynous people can be male or female, heterosexual or homosexual. They can be as sexually hot as Jagger or Dietrich or as cool as Bowie or Audrey Hepburn. They move toward an existence in which those aspects of sexuality do not confine their behavior.

As for sexual preference, Sandra Bem argues that it is utterly irrelevant "to anything other than the individual's own love or pleasure," and should be ignored as a social fact, no more or less interesting than the color of one's eyes or the length of fingernails. Roles of emotion or behavior based on sex, she continues, are not only absurd but destructive of human health and happiness; to be poured into a masculine or feminine mold makes both men and women unable to cope with the complexities of life.

In a series of devilishly clever experiments, in which subjects chose simple tasks or performed certain actions, Bem saw that the most highly "polarized" men and women neither enjoyed themselves nor performed effectively. In one test, in which subjects were supposed to interact with a tiny kitten, the "super-feminine" women could not deal with the nurturing task, while the more androgynous women handled the situation best. Bem and her colleagues have a long way to go to flesh out their pioneering studies. But they seem to have discovered that traditional sex roles constrict both men and women and impair their power to fulfill themselves in work and play.

But if orientation and roles are irrelevant and absurd, gender clearly is not. "Even if people were all to become psychologically androgynous, the world would continue to consist of two sexes, male and female would continue to be one of the first and most basic dichotomies that young children would learn and no one would grow up ignorant of or even indifferent to his or her gender," Bem writes. The point is that even gender has limited relevance: it does not demand inevitable roles. Women can be comfortable with their female bodies, but they do not have to bear or raise children—unless they want to. Men can be secure in their masculine physiques, but they do not have to chase girls, play basketball, father families or join the career rat race—unless it pleases

them to do so. Such decisions can be left to individual personality and inclination.

Finally, it does not really matter whether traits of temperament are inherited or acquired, or even if they are in some ways attached to gender. Perhaps there are evolved "feminine" or "masculine" qualities—or perhaps they are arbitrarily assigned, like "masculine" and "feminine" rhymes, or "male" and "female" plugs and sockets. Not to worry: one follows or ignores the logic of one's instincts or wishes—not what social convention determines them to require. "Androgyny," Columbia Professor Carolyn Heilbrun writes, "seeks to liberate the individual from the confines of the appropriate."

Definitions are necessary and distinctions are required precisely because androgyny is so ill-considered in our culture. We cannot describe it in our "dead language," as Adrienne Rich says scornfully, because our concepts and the words that signify them are tied to sex-role stereotypes. An aboriginal Eskimo who never left the North Pole could describe a world without snow only in terms of snow. We sexual aborigines can describe a world without sex roles only in terms of sex roles.

Alexandra Kaplan and Joan Bean, whose compilation of recent research papers on androgyny (*Beyond Sex-Role Stereotypes*) marks the beginning of a new approach to sexual psychology, contend that androgynous people have always existed, but until now they have been "invisible" to social scientists—and almost everyone else except the odd poet or the chroniclers of the bizarre. So there is no readily available vocabulary to describe the "hybrid" androgynous qualities that are being born: the trait between dominance and dependence, synthesizing tender and competitive, or combining assertive and nurturing.

If a man steps out of his assigned roles he is denigrated as a "sissy." If a woman oversteps hers, she is chastised as "mannish." More than most men, who have the power to set the language as well as the roles of social games, women and homosexuals have always known the perils of exceeding propriety. Even after a decade of women's liberation, females who dress, behave or work in previously "masculine" territory are conspicuous, isolated and subtly or blatantly condemned (often with patronizing praise). In the same way, gay men who inhabit the "feminine" category of man-loving are pushed into grotesque expressions of all the other qualities in that sex role: they are called "queens" and they act out that assigned part with mincing manners, campy styles and drag. If society says that a woman in a "man's job" is mannish, she will act that way; if it says gays are "sissies," they will ultimately act out their own parodies.

Not only homosexuals are deformed by such type-casting. Men of whatever sexual orientation who exhibit tenderness or shyness, or who easily express their feelings, are usually treated with contempt or condescension. One of the saddest examples of the genre was Adlai Stevenson, whose sensitive, slightly vulnerable wit was widely deprecated in Washington as evidence of his lack of guts, vigor, clout—in short, "balls." Lyndon Johnson despised him for it: "Why, he has to sit down to pee," Johnson once said of Stevenson. So much for the popularity of androgynous qualities.

Senator Muskie's well-known outburst of emotion in New Hampshire during his 1972 presidential primary campaign probably cost him the Democratic nomination. And this year, Jimmy Carter's lack of "decisiveness," his rhetoric of "compassion" and his soft-spoken manners surely diminished his popularity in those constituencies least responsive to those slightly androgynous qualities. Not for nothing did Carter slip in the polls as his personality became more familiar. Americans expect their presidents to be high up on the index of masculinity (self-reliant, defends own beliefs, independent, assertive, strong personality, competitive, individualistic, etc.) and nowhere near the items on the femininity list (yielding, shy, gullible, soft-spoken, compassionate, childlike, eager to soothe hurt feelings, etc.).

Early in the primaries a particularly astute though unliberated aunt of a friend of mine saw Carter on television and decided some "presidential" dimension of masculinity was missing. "*Faigele!*" she pronounced in her Bronx Yiddish idiom—"Fairy!" and walked away from the TV. Her idiom had no other word for what she saw.

Carter is hardly a sexual ideologue's vision of an androgyne, nor did Muskie or Stevenson come close to that idea. Beneath their thinnish skins beat macho hearts. But it's obvious that, more than many political leaders, they moved slightly centerward from the polar masculine stereotype. Kennedy spoke of vigor and strength, Carter conveyed compassion and love. No matter how real or disingenuous either candidate's rhetoric may have been, the identity they projected was strikingly different. One writer on sexual topics recently mused that Carter's victory was an important sign of a changing national consciousness, and that perhaps an androgyne could someday be president of the United States.

The President-elect is presumably no *faigele,* despite Aunt Frieda's suspicions, nor are most of the men who are beginning to acquire androgynous manners. But a sex-stereotyped society can imagine no other category for androgynous men except a sexual one. Similarly, most of the women who wear "man's style" clothes, sport unisex tastes and invade masculine precincts of work or study are not lesbians. Yet custom gives androgynous women pejorative labels and locks them in a sexual role. Even an acquisition of high fashion does not always help: the classiest models are called "Vogue dykes," an epithet that manages to combine the joke

and the sin of androgyny. The most glaring irony of all is that in a more androgynous world it would not be necessary, or even intelligent, to make any distinctions or disclaimers of sexual orientation in relation to behavior.

But in the sex-typed world there is clearly a connection between homosexual and feminist *culture* and androgynous *styles.* Gays in large measure make up the androgynous vanguard; feminists are both theoreticians and practitioners of androgyny. Sexual outcasts (it makes no difference whether self or society does the casting) are able to invent new roles because they are not allowed to maintain the old ones. Self-reliant, assertive women have to develop their own feminist culture: the dominant society will not let them back into the world of wallflowers and housewives on their own terms. Gay men who have been consigned to the "sissy" world of emotional self-consciousness cannot travel back to the land of passionless masculinity and cold rationality. But their new makeshift culture contains the available models for later androgynous styles.

The preeminent example of an androgynous community in the early years of the century, way before the recent liberation movements were born, was the Bloomsbury set, the informal but internally cohesive group of English writers, critics, artists and floating intellectuals who hung on in a slightly unfashionable section of London during and after the First World War. At its center was Virginia Woolf, her husband Leonard, sister Vanessa Bell and brother-in-law Clive Bell, the biographer Lytton Strachey, the economist John Maynard Keynes and the critic Roger Fry. On the periphery, but very much revered, was the novelist E.M. Forster.

The artistic and intellectual output of Bloomsbury was prodigious. But, most of all, it was a unique model of a civilized community based on equality. The members recognized the basis of their civilization: "The equality of the sexes, the outer manifestation of the equality of the masculine and feminine impulses, are essential to civilization," Carolyn Heilbrun writes of Bloomsbury in her trenchant study *Toward a Recognition of Androgny.* Virginia Woolf was convinced that she and her world were approaching androgyny, although she feared that the ideal would explode as it neared reality; perfection and completion could not exist in imperfect, fragmented surroundings. She saw a signal of androgyny in a single, silent falling leaf, "pointing to a force in things which one has overlooked."

Many of the Bloomsbury setters were homosexual or bisexual, and the byways of "inappropriate" sexuality were always very much in their hearts and minds. There were famous romantic triangles and quadrangles, scandalous ruptures of ceremony, hilarious practical jokes. Lytton Strachey appeared before the tribunal trying him for conscientious objection to military service wearing earrings, shoulder-length hair, an outlandish robe, and carrying an air pillow, which he blew up before the judges. He said it was necessary for his hemorrhoids. When asked what action he would take if a German soldier attempted to rape his sister, he replied impishly, "I should try to interpose my body." The Bloomsbury biographer, David Gadd, calls Strachey's response "a memorable reply whose monstrous ambiguity was fully appreciated by Lytton's three sisters," who were in the courtroom. But despite the famous japes, a premium was placed on the conquest of the vices of the old social order; jealousy, competitiveness, vindictiveness. Because of the sexual orientation of many in the group, its self-proclaimed androgyny has always been confused with the preferences of the members. But the truth of the situation was the other way around: the members' extraordinary sexual orientation gave them both perspective and motivation to explore innovative, androgynous relationships.

Bloomsbury gives historic context and some intellectual nuances to the new androgyny, but not much more. When you look for androgyny today you are apt to find it in much less transcendantal places. Former Los Angeles Ram Rosey Greer crochets his own pretty things and sings a pop song, "It's All Right to Cry," but he owes little of his sensibility to Lytton Strachey. It is seen in fleeting glimpses: Minnesota Viking Fran Tarkenton sending a touchdown pass to teammate Sammy White, and the two of them celebrating the event by holding hands as they walk back down the field—not in the old back-slapping jock gesture but in a manner that two schoolgirls would have used.

On the screen it is the androgynous Fred Astaire in *That's Entertainment, II*, soft-shoeing alongside the heavily masculine Gene Kelly—still charming and still macho after all these years. Or Garbo, Dietrich or Katherine Hepburn, in almost any of their old roles—but especially opposite leading men with an androgynous bent: Grant, for example, not Gable.

In fact, there's so much androgynous manhood around that some new Hollywood stars are making a buck on the backlash. Sylvester Stallone, writer and hero of *Rocky*, told the *New York Times'* Judy Klemesrud, "I don't think that even Women's Lib wants all men to become limp-wristed librarians. I don't know what's happening to men these days. There's a trend towards a sleek, subdued sophistication and a lack of participation in sports. In discos, men and women look almost alike, and if you were a little bleary-eyed, you'd get them mixed up. I think it's wrong . . . . There doesn't seem to be enough real men to go around."

Bloomsbury had indicated that in its origins androgyny would flower in the upper registers of social class and intellect, and that it would be carried along on a politically progressive, countercultural movement. Those connections still hold. Androgyny in the seventies has been limited to the educated middle class and the radical counterculture. You look for androgynous styles in *Vogue* and Bloomingdale's, not

McCall's and Penny's. Economic status and social registry somehow give people the security to discard the anchors of sex roles.

Androgyny in the twentieth century may have begun in England, but it is hardly surprising that it is blooming in America. There are both particular and general forces contributing to its forward motion. The economic necessity for women to work—and its social acceptance—has made the old roles of housewifery, and the emotions that go with them, absurd and often dysfunctional. Simply to break through conventional feminine roles is to move towards an androgynous synthesis.

But beyond that, the constellation of brand-new needs, demands and desires in "postindustrial" America has brought across-the-board changes in consciousness. For instance, the transformation of the nature of work from farm and factory to "services" has propelled many young men out of traditional "masculine" work roles and the emotional haberdashery suited to those jobs. Their new roles often let them share family roles formerly consigned to women. The men do not automatically become androgynous, but they are not so securely tied to the masculine pole any more.

Along the leading edge of change, the vectors point toward equality—in the political economy as well as the political culture. If the coming issue in government is redistribution of wealth, the issue in human relationships is the redistribution of power. It is equality not for its own sake, not because it is self-evident or endowed by the Creator, but because the next stages of social evolution cannot function well without it. The sage political economist Robert Heilbroner wrote recently that the gross inequalities of American capitalism will destroy it. In the same way, gross inequalities in communities and families will destroy them. Alexandra Kaplan and Joan Bean see androgyny growing as the structure of the acquisitive society weakens. "A society that supports androgyny would probably not be based on capitalistic consumerism, which is a direct outgrowth of the competitive, achievement-oriented values of the male model. Flexibility in sex-role norms seems to be more related to a social-welfare economy," they say.

Gloria Steinem noted recently that hard and fast distinctions between the sexes always accompany stages of imperial expansion in a society—those times when men think it necessary to keep women semislaves, in order to bear and rear offspring for the expanding nation. As we near a no-growth, resource-short, shrinking political economy in America, she continues, the polarized patriarchy will begin to break up.

In time, evolutionary changes may follow the economic ones. If women are less necessary as sexual objects and men as sexual subjects, their physical characteristics could be transformed. Gone would be the classic Rubenesque female, two-thirds breasts and hips; gone too the stallionoid male, the walking phallic symbol. There need be no dimunition of sexual activity or pleasure. In fact, psychologists find that sexual fulfillment is increased as partners move toward an androgynous center. One writer told me, "Men and women who keep to the myth of their sex type stay separated even when they're together. They are afraid of each other, always aware of the differences. They may extol those differences, but the important ones aren't in their sex attributes but in their humanity. Androgyny doesn't mean a race of sexless androids, but a wider variety of sexual possibilities than exists now."

The convulsions that will accompany the collapse of the old sexual culture will make most recent political events seem puny by comparison. In fact, they may have already begun. A great deal of nonsense will be loosed upon the world, as freed men and women scramble for new standards of behavior and anchors of being. People will mistake transient excesses for final accountings, bemoan the leveling of differences, extol the former virtues. Those with vested interests in polarized roles will predict the direst consequences of androgyny. They will not only be men. Or women. Renee Richards, the transsexual, sees only calamity arising as the familiar signposts fall.

"If someone can be sex-tied," she sighs, "there's so much less anxiety. I mean, I'd rather have pink rooms for girls and blue for boys. How can you tell who's who in a yellow room?"

Determinants of Behavior: Motivation, Environment, and Physiology

Behavior is a complex puzzle on which psychologists, sociologists, and biologists have long been working. None has produced a definitive explanation but each has contributed to a greater understanding of the subject.

Behaviorists take the view that all we can know about people is what they do—their behavior. Nothing is inferred. The tools of behavior modification according to this theory are reward and punishment. Freud's psychoanalytic theory, on the other hand, defines determinants of behavior in terms of repressed sexual and aggressive instincts. Behavior is modified through analysis.

Humanistic psychology developed as a reaction against these approaches, charging them with not fully explaining all of man's dimensions. The "new psychology" takes a holistic view of man, using a wide variety of techniques including encounter, gestalt, meditation, and biofeedback.

Biologists research behavior from the physiological point of view. One of the earliest theories of motivation concerns the concept of instinct. An instinct may be defined as an inborn biological force that predisposes one to behave in a certain manner. A more recent theory considers that mental imbalance and in a wider sense human behavior is biological in nature and can be altered by drugs. This may be the beginning of a better understanding of why certain types of behavior occur in the first place.

Sociobiology seeks to establish a genetic basis for social behavior. Applying Darwin's reasoning to social behavior, this controversial theory posits that human nature is genetically determined, the result of evolution, and that qualities like altruism, gratitude, sympathy, and moralism are rooted in gene selfishness. Although sociobiology is short on hard proof, it has excited much interest for its promise in unifying the study of behavior, encompassing as it does animal life from fruit flies to man.

Psychobiologists are presenting evidence that behavior is in large part physiologically programmed. Studies in the origin of violence have uncovered demonstrable links between sensory stimulation in infants and proper development of the pleasure centers of the brain.

Characteristics as diverse as creativity and obesity may also be the result of biological programming. Comparisons of creative people with "average" people have shown consistently different brain wave patterns, leading psychobiologists to conclude creativity may be the result not of inspiration or imagination but of the right alpha waves. Similarly, obesity too seems to be biologically programmed into some individuals.

The different approaches to behavior research indicate the complexity of the subject. What empirical evidence does each view offer to support its claims? What are the practical applications of each approach?

Breaking Out Of The Lockstep

Fred Best

Fred Best is currently directing a special evaluation of work sharing programs for the California Employment Development Department. Previously he held positions with the National Commission for Employment Policy, the U.S. Department of Commerce, the U.S. Department of Health, Education and Welfare, and the U.S. Department of Labor. Dr. Best holds an MBA from the University of California at Berkeley and a Ph.D. in sociology from the University of Massachusetts at Amherst. This article is adapted from his most recent book, Flexible Life Scheduling, *published by Praeger.*

HAVE you ever felt like you were on a treadmill going directly from school to work to retirement with no stops along the way? Have you ever wished you could arrange your life differently, to include more vacation-time or time for further education or travel? Have you ever felt that your time increasingly wasn't yours, but belonged to somebody else? Well, you're not alone.

The fact is, for most people in our society the activities of education, work, and leisure are arranged in a "linear life plan." Stated simply, this means that most of us march in linear fashion through school in youth, to forty consecutive years of work or child-rearing in mid-life, to retirement in old age. While this pattern had healthy features in the past, today it seems to be stifling the vibrancy and productivity of our lives and our society. Indeed, there are increasing indications that we need more flexibility in the ways we schedule the days, weeks, and years of our lives.

In human terms, there are countless individual problems stemming from the inflexibility of today's linear life pattern. To cite a few examples:

☐ In Detroit there is a 25-year-old assembly-line worker who left school without getting his high school diploma. Today he would like to finish high school and try college, but his job allows no opportunity to work part time or take a leave of absence to resume his education.

☐ In San Francisco, a city planner in her early thirties has just become pregnant. Ideally, she would like to take a year off, then work two-thirds time for a few years before reimmersing herself in her career. Unfortunately, the penalties to her advancement would be tremendous, and opportunities for reduced worktime in her current job are nonexistent. As a result, she will struggle with fourteen-hour days between her job and child-rearing, contributing less than she would like to both.

☐ In the Texas town of Killeen, a man in his late forties has worked at the local meat-packing plant for more than twenty consecutive years. He has the savings and desire to take a year off to travel around the country, but will lose his job if he does so.

☐ In New York City, a black woman has been unemployed for more than a year, and wonders why worktime can't be reduced in order to create more jobs.

☐ In Salt Lake City, a 66-year-old man finds himself bored with retirement, but unable to find work.

The stories are countless: persons trapped unwillingly inside – or outside – the lockstep flow from school to work to retirement. (If you answered "Yes" to one of the questions at the beginning, you might add your own story.) Together, these stories add up to a growing human demand for more flexible life patterns.

There are also signs that the way we distribute education, work, and leisure over total lifespans is draining away the productive potential and financial solvency of our society. This can be seen in the problem of overeducation, which is preparing more and more people for a limited number of high-quality jobs. Another problem is the frequent shortage of jobs in the last several decades, with unemployment locking *out* of the lockstep many who wanted to be *in*. Both of these problems lead to an enormous waste of human potential and extraordinary expense for the society that must pay for this waste. Finally, the competition for work has pushed older people into increasingly earlier retirement, creating years of non-income-earning time which can lead to poverty among the elderly and is already threatening to bankrupt the Social Security system. Clearly, we need

From *The Wharton Magazine,* Winter 1980-81. Adapted from the author's book, FLEXIBLE LIFE SCHEDULING: BREAKING THE EDUCATION-WORK-RETIREMENT LOCKSTEP (Praeger Special Studies, New York, 1980).

to re-think our approach to education, work, and leisure.

My basic proposition is that changes in societal conditions are making more flexible timing of education, work, and leisure not only desirable but very possible. The century-long trend of increasing years for school in youth and early retirement in old age seems to be coming to an end; in fact, the proportion of non-worktime at the extremes of the life cycle may actually be reduced in coming years in favor of more time for leisure and learning during the middle of life. Further still, there is cause to speculate that any increases of nonworktime during mid-life will not come in a monolithic form, such as a standard reduction of the workweek, but rather in a myriad of forms ranging from increased part-time employment to extended sabbaticals.

What basis do I have for forecasting these departures from the past? The answer to this question lies in numerous social trends that are attenuating and even reversing the forces that gave rise to the linear life plan.

First of all, there are signs that even the seemingly unchanging nature of life- and family-cycle dynamics is undergoing transformation. To be sure, the stages of youth, adulthood, and old age will not disappear. However, people are living longer nowadays, and this is expanding the time frame for distributing education, work, and leisure over a lifetime. In 1900, when the average life expectancy at age 20 was 42 years (to age 62), the notion of obtaining all of one's schooling in youth to prepare for adulthood was a sound idea. Today's life expectancy at 20 is about 55 years (to age 75), so the idea of recurrent education throughout longer lifespans is both reasonable and increasingly common.

ALSO, until recently the financial responsibility for dependents during mid-life required men to pursue continuous employment in order to fulfill their roles as "breadwinners," and this required women to forgo or minimize employment in order to care for children or elderly relatives. Today, family units are generally separated from older relatives, couples are having fewer children, and women are seeking career involvements outside the home. As a result, husbands and wives are beginning to share housekeeping and income responsibilities in ways that may allow and require more flexible life schedules.

Again, the increasing life expectancy and better health of older people is altering the very definitions of "old age" and "retirement." Between 1940 and 1975, the life expectancy for persons aged 65 increased from 12.8 to 16.0 years. Thus, failure to work in some fashion during the later stages of life may produce severe financial hardships over the increasing number of non-income-earning years, and growing numbers of older persons may both prefer and be able to work well beyond current retirement ages. Further, the projected costs of funding future retirement pensions for an increasingly larger elderly population raises questions about whether tomorrow's workers should work past age sixty-five.

In addition to these changes, the competition for jobs which once fostered the linear life plan may ironically help bring about its demise in the coming decades. In the past, social policies and individual decisions that prolonged years of schooling during youth and retirement in old age worked in part as a kind of "work sharing" that improved mid-life employment opportunities by reducing the size of the labor force. Today, there is declining benefit to be gained from further expansion of schooling in youth or earlier retirement, and consequently a growing desire for more work opportunities among the young and old. If we cannot create an adequate number of jobs in some other way, we may find it desirable to reduce worktime in mid-life in order to spread employment among a larger number of persons.

This idea of work reductions in mid-life becomes particularly pertinent in view of the increasing labor force participation of women. Current trends show that two out of every three new entrants into the labor force are women. This growing pursuit of paid work on the part of women is causing rapid growth of the working or job-seeking population and thus intensifying the unemployment problem. One solution is the possibility of sharing work between the sexes as well as among age groups, particularly if increased family income from married women workers encourages men to forgo income-earning worktime in exchange for more time off the job.

The last major force giving rise to new life patterns concerns changing attitudes toward work and leisure. Numerous studies have indicated that Americans are willing to forgo some earnings in order to have more free time. These studies and other workplace experiments show that these new preferences are not ideal dreams of how the world might be under perfect conditions but rather responses to hard economic trade-off choices in which earnings are sacrificed to reduce or change worktime arrangements. These studies reveal that preferences for alternative worktimes vary tremendously – in fact, available data show the emergence of a whole variety of institutional reforms concerning both worktime and life scheduling.

GIVEN these social trends, there are two different approaches to be taken with regard to changes in worktime. One concerns the rescheduling of *existing* worktime in order to maximize the personal utility of an individual's free time. The other concerns the *reduction* of worktime, or actually working less – an option that has always looked attractive but until now was not economically or institutionally feasible.

How might *existing* worktime be rescheduled over weeks, months, and years? The average American worker in 1978 had about two weeks vacation, plus five holidays, and worked about 39 hours a week for 49 weeks every year – totaling about 1,900 hours of work per year. In weekly terms, this amount of worktime might be rescheduled so that the average person would work four 10-hour days, three and a half 11-hour days, or three 13-hour days with respective weekends of three to four days' length. In monthly terms it might be possible to work three 52-hour five- or six-day workweeks and then take off one week out of every four. Similarly, two concentrated work periods of eight consecutive 10-hour days would allow two extended periods of seven days away from work during the average month.

The workyear presents even wider possibilities. Existing worktime could be rescheduled so that individuals could work forty-four 45-hour workweeks and have eight weeks' paid vacation every year, or work forty 50-hour workweeks with twelve weeks' annual vacation. Along a similar line, someone might work 50-

3. DETERMINANTS OF BEHAVIOR

hour workweeks for half the year and 30-hour workweeks for the other half.

This rescheduling of existing worktime is already going on in many workplaces across the country. However, there are indications that more far-reaching changes are to come. Indeed, many people may actually find themselves working less than 1,900 hours a year.

A cautious bit of speculation is called for at this point. If economic growth in the United States averages around 3.3 percent a year during the next two and a half decades, the average American worker is likely to be willing and able to forfeit about 25 percent of that growth in exchange for more free time. Further, if the GNP is going up but workers are working fewer hours, then more workers must be hired to take up the slack. Here we have a partial solution to the unemployment problem, since companies can hire more employees with the money they save by giving their employees more free time instead of raises. Many of these new employees would be highly capable or have the potential to become so, and thus everyone would benefit.

For the average worker, additional free time gained in lieu of prospective pay increases could mean a decline of total yearly worktime from the 1,900 hours mentioned earlier to about 1,818 hours in 1985, and to something like 1,700 hours by the year 2000. If these speculations are correct, increased free time by 1985 could take the form of a 37-hour workweek, two weeks' additional yearly paid vacation, paid sabbaticals of 3.7 months every seven years, or retirement at age 63. By the year 2000, additional free time could take the form of a 35-hour workweek, five weeks' additional yearly vacation, nine-month sabbaticals, or retirement at age 61. Of course, such increases in free time would most likely come as a combination of these forms.

The question is, which forms are likely to be the most popular? First of all, it is unlikely, given current social trends, that more free time would take the form of earlier retirement. Second, extra free time would probably be used only marginally to increase the amount of schooling during early life. Most likely, we would expect a small portion of added free time to come in the form of shorter workweeks, and a large portion to come in extended periods away from work, such as longer vacations, holidays, and sabbaticals.

If there is individual flexibility in determining the amount and scheduling of

worktime, patterns could vary significantly according to a person's sex and life-cycle stage. For example, people in early child-rearing years, particularly women, might prefer shorter workweeks and moderate vacations. On the other hand, people in pre-, late-, and post-child-rearing stages of life would likely tend toward longer vacations and sabbatical-like leaves from work. Taking into consideration the 3.3 percent growth rate and 25 percent trade-off rate noted above, an individual life-cycle plan in the year 2000 might resemble the following:

Student Years: Part-time work and extended time for education and leisure.

Single and Non-Offspring Years: Longer workweeks of 45 to 50 hours with annual vacations ranging from eight to fourteen weeks and some sabbaticals.

Early Child-Rearing Years: Shorter workweeks of 25 to 40 hours with moderate annual vacations of two to four weeks.

Late and Post-Child-Rearing Years: Moderate to long workweeks of 40 to 45 hours with long annual vacations of five to eight weeks and extended sabbatical leaves.

Old Age: Short to moderate workweeks of 25 to 40 hours and long vacations and sabbatical leaves.

Of course, there have always been individuals who have found ways even within the existing system to alter the scheduling of their lives. For example, there is the well-known case of Dr. John Coleman, former president of Haverford College, who took a sabbatical from the ivy-covered walls of academe to work as a farmhand, ditchdigger, and at other odd jobs in order to test his conviction that school sheltered students and faculty from much of real life. In addition, newspapers from time to time carry stories about successful corporate executives who leave high-paying positions in order to tour the world or set up an apple farm in Virginia. There are numerous reports of military officers who retire on pensions at age 40, take a year off, then start lucrative second careers. Other more daring efforts at mid-life career changes are familiar to all of us, as are people who voluntarily work part-time or take extra leaves of absence at their own expense for "minisabbaticals" every year. Then there are the

somewhat shady reports of those who have used prolonged unemployment insurance or disability benefits to finance personal sabbaticals. Thus, a fair number of individuals have taken it upon themselves to use their wits and the resources available to them to forge life schedules that match their needs and aspirations. However, these pioneer efforts at alternative life patterns are often highly costly to the individual, occasionally illegal, and certainly still a rarity.

Getting From Here to There

While our society can sustain a certain number of life-scheduling mavericks, any broadly based movement toward more flexible lives will require major adjustments of our principal social institutions. However, the list of problems that must be overcome if work organizations are to allow more life-scheduling flexibility seems overwhelming. Indeed, practical administrators would rightly express grave reservations about the feasibility of such changes.

Foremost among these reservations would be the problems of coordination and communication created by individualized work schedules. Tasks that depend upon cooperation among many workers could become more difficult with employees working a variety of daily, weekly, or yearly schedules. Predictability would decline, continuity of effort could become erratic, and the simple arrangement of a meeting could become a major ordeal. Many organizational functions that are now mechanical could become cumbersome and costly.

OF particular concern to employers would be the matter of fringe benefits and other fixed labor costs. The amount of money spent on the fringe benefits of workers is frequently fixed by virtue of employment rather than hours worked, and so would cost more for employees working less than "full time." To further complicate matters, individual worktime reductions, accompanied by an increase in the total number of workers, would often cause increases in worker-related taxes paid by employers. Any adjustment of such increased labor costs by pro-rating or other devices would likely be more complex and expensive than current standardized systems. Also, established and simple guidelines for determining retirement benefits would become cumbersome. Without a doubt, greater worklife flexibility would increase organizational costs by requiring more supervisory effort, more intricate record-keeping, and new ways of assessing the performance and accountability of employees.

In addition, personnel problems could result from conflicts caused by less standardized procedures concerning seniority rights, and worker morale could be damaged through a loss of personal influence within organizations. There is also the danger that flexible worklives might facilitate the loss of trained employees, and possibly trade secrets, to competitors. Obviously, someone who has six months off may use that time to freelance for the competition, or to go job-hunting. Finally, there are fears that departures from standardized work hours would vastly complicate collective bargaining agreements and invite union hostilities. All in all, those concerned with the practical problems of administering work organizations are apt to view work-scheduling flexibility with a jaundiced eye, seeing increased costs of operation and lowered productivity.

Of course, more flexible work patterns could also have positive impacts on work organizations. For instance, increased worklife flexibility could actually boost productivity in some cases. Several studies have indicated that worktime reforms improved employee morale, reduced absenteeism and counterproductive activities, and frequently increased worker output. Also, increased free time adjusted to individual needs provides employees with opportunities for retraining to prevent skill obsolescence and for personal renewal as a palliative for exhaustion and job boredom. If that Texan who worked twenty years at the meat-packing plant could take a year's sabbatical to travel, wouldn't he be more productive (and happier) when he returned?

In addition, one of the problems mentioned earlier – that of possibly losing employees to competitors–could turn out to have a positive side. Opportunities for leaves of absence and other increases of free time might allow nonproductive or "dead-ended" workers to find new and more suitable jobs to the benefit of themselves *and* their old organizations. It is also possible that firm tax burdens for unemployment and welfare services might be lowered in some instances.

In fact, there are many times when an organization's *in*-flexibility can work counter to productivity. Take the case of Don and Jeff. Don was the general manager of a small radio station, Jeff his program director. They both had worked there several years, and felt burned out by the pressures of their jobs; so they decided they'd like to hire a new program director and then share the general manager's job, each one having six months on and six months off. Both knew the operation intimately, both were equally qualified, and both were willing to earn half a salary in exchange for six months off to study and travel. The response of their superiors? Decidedly negative. The end result? Don and Jeff both left within a year for other jobs, and the radio station lost two talented and qualified workers.

Diversity of Skills

Contrary to most expectations, thoughtfully developed work scheduling innovations can enhance organizational performance. The diversity of skills among a firm's personnel could be increased by hiring a greater and more heterogenous number of workers at shorter work hours. In some cases, work scheduling flexibility could increase an organization's adaptability to emergencies and fluctuations of business, as well as reduce the need for prime overtime pay rates. Finally, worktime reforms are likely to be increasingly prized by employees as fringe benefits that can in some cases become acceptable substitutes for pay raises, and can also provide the firm with an effective asset in recruiting quality personnel.

T is important to keep in mind that the adaptability of work organizations to more flexible approaches will vary tremendously because of individual constraints and options. The product type, size, structure, and stability of an organization are important considerations. For example, organizations concerned with continuous, year-round mass production might prefer an arrangement with a workweek of three days at twelve hours a day, so that an even production level can be maintained. On the other hand, an organization with seasonal or batch production might want a schedule with extended vacations or a "six-month-on, six-month-

off" arrangement, so that workers are gone when things are slow. Similarly, small firms face different constraints than large corporations – although fewer people means less difficulty in time and record-keeping, each person then becomes correspondingly more crucial to the production process and hence absence is more inconvenient. Finally, the level of capital investment and the nature of technologies will influence organizational flexibility, as will the ways in which employees are organized and supervised. However, it seems that the benefits to be gained by flexible worklife scheduling make the effort of solving these problems well worthwhile.

The Worktimes, They Are A-Changin'

Now that we've looked at some of the pros and cons to flexible worklife scheduling, the question arises, "Have any firms actually solved any of these problems and implemented some of these reforms?" The answer is definitely yes–in fact, there appears to be a deluge of worktime experiments taking place right now, both nationally and internationally. These innovations are tampering with every aspect of worktime from the hours of the workday to the total worklife. They bear testimony to the likelihood that we are not moving toward some monolithic worktime reduction such as a "standard 35-hour workweek," but rather toward a wide variety of reforms and innovations that will be combined to increase overall worklife flexibility.

In the area of rescheduling of *existing* worktime, one of the most heralded types of worktime reform has been flexitime. (See "Flexitime: The Supervisors' Verdict" in the Summer 1980 issue.) Flexitime began during the mid-1960's in Europe and made its American debut in the early 1970's. Since that time, the practice has evolved from a novelty to a common idea that appears to be spreading rapidly within both the public and the private sector.

Flexitime allows employees to arrive for work and depart at any time during the day as long as they are in attendance during specified "core hours," such as 10 a.m. to 3 p.m., and work a full workday. While there are no overall figures on the incidence of flexitime, it has been estimated that 13 percent of all firms and 6 percent of all employees within the United States were participating in flexitime programs in 1977.

In the "big picture" of lifetime scheduling, daily flexitime does not offer the promise of altering overall life patterns. However, the emergence and rapid assimilation of this idea has accomplished a great deal in the way of provoking thought about other forms of work-scheduling flexibility. It has also demonstrated to employers that departure from the standard "8-hour-a-day work-week" need not cause organizational anarchy. Indeed, the notion of flexitime has proven itself so manageable that some firms are beginning to experiment with the notions of "flexiweeks" and "flexi-months."

ORKWEEK innovations in the United States first attracted popular attention with the wave of experiments involving the "compressed workweek" that surfaced around 1970. The major thrust here was the "four-day, forty-hour workweek" in which employees continued to work forty hours a week, but put in ten hours a day in order to gain three-day weekends. While this innovation was originally hailed as a "revolution in worktime," its growth seems to have leveled off in the late 1970's. However, as in the case of flexitime, attention given to the compressed workweek seems to have paved the way for a number of work scheduling experiments. For example, there have been reports of three or three-and-a-half day workweeks with work-days lasting eleven or thirteen hours. One recent reform initiated with union cooperation at Du Pont created a system of rotation between regular and night shifts in which employees work four twelve-hour days between two-day weekends and receive seven days' extended leave a month. This plan has been in operation since 1974 and is considered an "all around success" because it provides workers with free time they can use

and allows plants to maintain continuous 24-hour operation.

Perhaps the most impressive move toward flexible worklives has been the development of "flexiyear contracts" by a number of private firms in Europe. The general idea of this innovation is that employer and employee meet together once a year to negotiate an overall work time agreement for the next year. Such negotiations have opened the possibility of novel arrangements such as six months on and six months off, part-time work for part of the year (such as summer when children are home), and all manner of other options. It is claimed that such yearly negotiations improve worker morale and productivity and allow employers to plan a number of worktime arrangements that creatively meet the needs of both firm and workers.

One of the major thrusts in the *reduction* of worktime has been a growing interest in part-time work. Not only did the portion of the work force employed in "voluntary" part-time work increase from 10.6 to 18.7 percent between 1954 and 1977, but there has been a growing movement to remove the stigma of a "second-rate" job from part-time employment. Until recently, most part-time jobs were low-paying, tended to entail menial tasks, offered virtually nothing in the way of security or fringe benefits, and presented little opportunity for career advancement. Today, a growing coalition of women, youths, and older workers is advocating the creation of "permanent part-time jobs" offering fringe benefits such as health insurance and the potential for career advancement.

Another growing worktime reform that is somewhat akin to part-time employment is "job splitting." As in the example of Don and Jeff, this innovation entails the performance of one full-time job by two or more people. The idea first made its appearance in California during the mid-1960's and although there are no figures on the incidence of job splitting, numerous accounts suggest that the practice has grown and spread across the country. This particular reform seems applicable to many occupations; for example, there have been reports of two or more people successfully sharing positions such as high school principal, city planner, college professor, secretarial receptionist, and many other types of work. Pauline Kael and Penelope Gilliatt used

to share the job of movie reviewer at the *New Yorker*, six months on and six months off. Perhaps the most remarkable case has been the sharing of the foreign minister's position in the country of Liechtenstein. There is no question that "job splitting" requires special effort and unusual cooperation by participants, but when the match of employees is appropriate, employers have found that this practice can offer numerous unexpected benefits.

ART-TIME work and job-splitting are two new and fast-growing ways of increasing free time and decreasing unemployment. However, since the mid-1940's, most of the gains in free time during the "work years of life" have come in the form of longer vacations and paid days off. Indeed, extended vacations have become an increasingly frequent goal of collective bargaining efforts, and vacations of over six weeks' length are becoming increasingly common. The recent initiative of the United Auto Workers to bargain for successive stages of paid days off with the ultimate goal of obtaining a four-day, 32-hour workweek is a case in point. Such movement toward days off indicates renewed interest on the part of organized labor toward using bargaining influence to gain free time.

Unions have frequently been against flexible scheduling because they see it as undermining hard-won rights such as overtime pay and job security provisions, and possibly fragmenting worker solidarity needed for effective bargaining. However, various workplace experiments have indicated that unions and workers have a lot to gain from some of these reforms. For example, one workplace innovation has been the so-called "cafeteria benefit plan," in which individual employees can choose between several options such as a pay raise, additional life insurance, or added vacation. Unions have been reserved about such cafeteria plans in the past, but are now finding that such approaches can facilitate member solidarity by allowing the development of a dollar-value bargaining agenda rather than internal conflicts over the priority given to life insurance as opposed to more time off.

This idea of allowing individual employees the choice of forgoing income for more free time within the context of the workmonth and the workyear has been successful in several places. A much-heralded program, set up by Santa Clara County in California, allows employees the choice of voluntarily forgoing 5 percent of their annual income for ten and a half days' added vacation (the level of pay is reduced proportionally for all work and vacation days), 10 percent for twenty-one days, and as much as 20 percent for forty-two days off. During the first year of operation, some 17 percent of all county employees requested one of these options. Participation in subsequent years has declined because of increased work loads and resistance of mid-level supervisors, but these voluntary trade-off options have become a permanent program supported by the public employee unions and top county management.

Other local governments are developing programs similar to the one in Santa Clara County. One of the most notable of these is a voluntary three-month leave of absence program in which lawyers employed by a number of California counties are allowed to exchange 25 percent of their annual earnings for a three-month leave each year. This program has been judged a success because it allows attorneys to recover from their stressful work during the rest of the year, and has provided funds for the hiring of additional lawyers.

Voluntary trade-off programs of a less dramatic nature have also been developed within the private sector. For example, the New York Telephone and Telegraph Company allows telephone operators to take one day off each week without pay if the arrangement is made in advance. Personnel officials for the company report that most operators tend to request the day-off option.

Finally, the idea of sabbaticals has been extended beyond the academic environment in recent years. Despite some criticisms, the well-known United Steelworkers sabbatical negotiated in 1963 was renewed in 1974 and is still firmly intact. This program allows up to thirteen weeks' paid vacation every four years for senior workers. Sabbatical leaves of up to one year have been implemented among a small number of firms. For example, the Rolm Corporation in California provides a one-year leave with pay to employees who have worked six continuous years with the firm. Additionally, a number of major corporations have initiated programs allowing their executives one- to two-year "sabbaticals" for approved public service projects.

These and other innovations provide evidence that the adaptability of work organizations to flexible worklives is still largely untapped. Certainly, there are problems to overcome and trade-offs to be made. However, new technologies are being developed that allow worktime innovations that might have been impossible a few years ago. For example, the rise of flexitime has stimulated the production of new time-keeping devices that allow supervisors an efficient and uncostly means of overseeing employee worktime. Similarly, a number of large corporations are beginning to realize that their vast computing facilities can be applied to the task of staggering employee work schedules and adjusting fringe benefits to variations in individual worktime arrangements.

While the task of adjusting to widespread worktime flexibility is certainly not to be underestimated, it is also important that it not be viewed as impossible. There is no law written by the hand of God that the standard workweek must be 40 hours and that employees will have two-week vacations each year. Different types of organizations and occupations will certainly confront different obstacles to increased flexibility, but there is good reason to believe that a great deal can be done to increase the options available to all of us.

There is a story concerning a certain Mr. Creech, who allegedly wrote in the margin of his painstaking translation of Lucretius, "Memo: When I have finished my book, I must kill myself." He reportedly carried out his resolution, a testimony to the beliefs of a past age which assumed life without work to be meaningless. Values and lifestyles have changed greatly since the dour Mr. Creech wrote his dismal memo. Nonetheless, most industrial nations must still be viewed as "work societies." Despite the advances of technology, work still remains the essential and focal activity of human life. Yet it is sad that we have come to view our lives primarily in terms of preparing for work, performance at work, and finally deliverance from work. It is even more saddening from the standpoint of human fulfillment and growth that learning, working, and leisure should be unduly cramped into segregated compartments of life.

I maintain that it is near idiocy to believe that youth is solely for school, middle age for applying what we learned in youth, and old age for a denial of either of these vitalizing opportunities. Actually, the learning process continues to our last days. The world changes constantly around us, and different stages of life impose new lessons every bit as vital as the "basics" we learned in childhood. Increasingly, it appears that those who do not confront work in youth are ill-prepared – despite the best of educations – for the demands and opportunities of mid-life; and those who flee their jobs in their early sixties are all too often stranded upon an island of empty time from which there are no bridges to return. Finally, leisure seems to have become at once our most precious and most wasted commodity. If anything, our free time should represent the potential to renew and rebuild our spirits, and to pull the fabric of our lives together in a way that balances the meaning of our learnings, the purposes that drive us to work, and the personal pleasures that do much to make these efforts worthwhile. All too often, "leisure" is forced upon us in ways we cannot appreciate, or made unduly harried by the pressures of mid-life.

More flexible life patterns could loosen the time binds that too often prevent the natural flow of human activities, as well as nurture and renew our spirits through opportunities to actualize personal dreams. Of course, many life changes and dreams can be attained *within* the realm of work. However, others require time away from the job. We all have a deeply felt yearning for what we might have been and may yet become – a desire to more freely explore things like playing the guitar, writing a book, building a house, or raising a child. Such dreams take time, and one promise of more flexible life patterns is that each individual might arrange the time of his life in ways that help turn some of those dreams into reality.

3. DETERMINANTS OF BEHAVIOR

Suggested Reading

ALLAN COHEN AND HERMAN GADON, Alternative Work Schedules: Integrating Individual and Organizational Needs, *Addison-Wesley, 1978. A treatise dealing with organizational constraints and options concerning alternative work patterns.*

JANET ZOLLINGER GIELE, *"Changing Sex Roles and Family Structure,"* Social Policy, January-February 1979. *An insightful discussion of changing sex and family roles, with particular attention given to the likely growth in demand for more flexible worktime conditions.*

HAROLD SHEPPARD AND SARA RIX, The Graying of Working America, *The Free Press, 1977. An excellent data-based discussion of older populations now and in the future, with particular attention given to the problem of financing pension programs for the large post-World War II "baby boom" generation.*

DYCKMAN W. VERMILYE, ED., Relating Work and Education, *Jossey-Bass Publishers, 1977. An anthology dealing with many issues of the emerging relationships between education and work.*

WILLARD WIRTZ AND THE NATIONAL MANPOWER INSTITUTE, The Boundless Resource, *New Republic Book Company, 1975. A major volume on the topic of life scheduling flexibility written by a consortium of policy makers and scholars working under the leadership of former Secretary of Labor Willard Wirtz.*

WORKTIME AND EMPLOYMENT, *Special Report No. 28, October 1978. (Available on request from the National Commission for Employment Policy, 1522 K Street, Suite 300, Washington, D.C. 20005.)*

New Psychology: New Image of Man

BY ELEANOR HOOVER

John Brodie, the articulate former quarterback for the San Francisco 49ers, reports an ecstatic interlude when "time stood still" while he was dropping back to throw a pass . . .

A young man working his way through medical school by drumming in a jazz band reports many years later, that in all his drumming he had three peaks when he suddenly felt like a great drummer and his performance was perfect . . .

Experience—any experience—once was ignored in psychology as "unscientific." Particularly these, which the late psychologist Abraham Maslow called "peak experiences."

They are vivid moments when things fall into place, one's vision is clear and life is meaningful.

They happen, it was thought, only to artists, poets, mystics or saints. But Maslow found they also happen to the healthiest, most creative and happy people.

Now a new study indicates they are "widespread, almost commonplace in American society today." Nobody talks about them "because somehow they seem odd, illogical—inexplicable," says the Rev. Andrew M. Greeley, the sociologist who conducted the study for the National Research Opinion Center.

It seems that such moments are linked to feelings of self-fulfillment, creativity, achievement—or simple at-one-with-the-universe reverie. Apparently, they can happen to anyone. Interest in them is part of something loosely called the "new psychology."

"The core of the new psychology," says Hugh Redmond of Johnston College at the University of Redlands, "is based on a new image or vision of man—on what he is and what he can do."

If the new psychology needs a label, "humanistic" probably fits best.

What humanistic psychology has triggered is a growing interest in expanding man's awareness—to enhance creativity, health, learning, problem solving and to produce what one brain researcher calls "intrinsically rewarding ecstatic experiences."

Much of what is happening is still outside the ivied halls of the academy. But not for long.

The curriculum committee of Harvard University recently approved an undergraduate course in altered states of consciousness.

"Students," one professor says, "are coming into the colleges and demanding that these experiences be recognized."

Humanistic psychology grew out of opposition to the major expressions of traditional psychology—mainly Skinnerean behaviorism and Freudian psychoanalysis.

"For as long as I can remember—until now—if it didn't have pink eyes, a long tail and a twitchy nose and run in a maze, it wasn't psychology," an older psychologist says.

It has been called everything from a "post-Freudian revolution" to a "brain revolution" and "a revolution in consciousness."

If such terms seem to overstate the case for humanistic psychology (and they do to many), they are not strong enough for a few who, in the words of one observer, see it as nothing short of "a Reformation slouching to meet its Luther at a yet undiscovered cathedral door."

Taken as a whole, humanistic psychology consists of a loose but important network of approaches, disciplines, techniques, and areas of mind and brain research which see man from all sides—wholly different from the view we are used to.

Its main aspects, which tend to overlap, are these:

—Where once man was seen as merely a bundle of responses to stimuli, moldable in any direction, there is a focus on individuality, the person and the intrinsic complexity, richness and power of mind and consciousness.

—Where once mind and body were split, there is a "coming together," a regard for wholeness and the way the mind affects the body and the body affects the mind. This "holistic" approach can be found today in education, medicine and sports as well as psychology.

—Where thought, logic and rationality were once dominant, there is more recognition of emotions as well as "spiritual" feelings. The goal is to be a whole person who is a harmonious blend of all his parts.

—Where once "objectivity" meant banishing subjective experience from science, it is now being allowed back in. The belief of humanistic psychologists is that there is no basic contradiction and that a new science can be built which also includes the observer's experience.

—Where once man was seen as blindly buffeted by instinctual forces such as the id. superego and ego, there is a new belief in man's built-in capacity for growth, self-transcendence or self-actualization.

3. DETERMINANTS OF BEHAVIOR

—Where once, under the old Freudian "medical model," Man was seen as either "sick" or "well," he is now seen as having a natural ability to make changes in himself rather quickly, once he sees what needs to be done. "The basic idea is," says James Fadiman of Stanford, "that you are capable of being more than you are and you know how to do it."

—Where once Man was seen as a more or less static or "fixed" system, there is a new interest in "energy flow" and "energy fields"—in Eastern meditation and yoga, seen as a means of releasing energy. A new polarity therapy is based on this idea of energy and the "natural ability of the body to balance itself."

—Where once the idea of will and willpower was so loaded with guilt and repression that generations rebelled against it, there is a renewed interest in the will and in responsibility for self as a positive, natural and liberating force.

—Where once purpose or meaning were seen as "religious," each is finding its way back into psychology. This recognition of a "spiritual dimension" to man is a major change. Esalen's founder, Mike Murphy, calls this "the cutting edge—the psychology of the future."

Humanistic psychology began with the work of Abraham Maslow more than 20 years ago, grew and expanded in the Human Potential Movement for about 10 years, and became a full-fledged "psychology" only two years ago.

That was when humanistic psychology was accepted by the American Psychological Assn. as its newest and 32nd branch—along with experimental, physiological, clinical, educational, child and other such venerables, some of which go back almost 65 years.

To some unregenerate members of the Assn. for Humanistic Psychology—remembering its bitter turbulent history as a "third force" movement—recognition by the American Psychological Assn. may be "death by victory." They are proud, but they hope their "joyous movement" will not be diverted.

(That there were tensions between the two groups is understandable. The American Psychological Assn. is made up largely of psychologists with university affiliations. Many Assn. for Humanistic Psychology members work outside the academy—many as therapists—or in university departments other than psychology. Lacking university support, they developed much of the new psychology at "growth centers" around the country like Esalen at Big Sur.)

To understand humanistic psychology, there must be an understanding of classical behaviorism and Freudian psychoanalysis—the two traditional psychologies to which Maslow's work, humanistic psychology and the Human Potential Movement stand more or less opposed.

A main point at issue is the notion of an "inner man."

Behaviorism (which, since its founding, has evolved into Skinnerean behaviorism, from B. F. Skinner of Harvard, its most famous spokesman) takes the view that all we can know or scientifically study about an organism is what it does, how it behaves—hence the name behaviorism. Its tools are stimulus-response and reward-punishment, and its body of knowledge is called learning theory.

The experimental schema is simple. A hungry rat is put in a maze. Hunger is its stimulus. Reward is a food pellet at the end of the maze. To get the food, the rat must learn, for example, to overcome obstacles put in his way.

How the rat behaves—what it does and how it learns—is what is important to classical behaviorists. Nothing more. And nothing further is inferred. The rat model is, of course, an analogy to human behavior.

A therapy based on this system—behavior modification—is well thought-of by most psychologists. At least it isn't often challenged. It has had good success in reducing obesity, phobias, and in helping cases of autism—a disorder in which a child remains regressed at early stages of development.

Behavior modification assumes that disorders, habits, ills—whatever one wishes to call them—are learned, and can be changed by methods worked out in the labs. That is, undesired behavior can be stopped through punishment and desired behavior increased through reward.

Another name for this is operant conditioning, which, simply put by one therapist is, "people do what they are rewarded for doing." As Skinner told a Reed College symposium on "Behavior Control" two weeks ago, "inner man is an illusion."

The humanists deplore this view and all else in psychology that fragmentizes and reduces.

Freudianism is more concerned with what goes on inside the individual. In fact, it sees man as buffeted by internal unconscious urges and the battlefield of instinctual drives like the id. ego and superego, with "neurosis" (a term less used today) the almost inevitable result.

Psychoanalysis, of course, was the "sole" time-honored way of alleviating such complaints until the newer, freewheeling humanistic-oriented "therapies" came along.

But sexual repression was a pressing problem in Freud's day. It is less so now. And nowhere did Freud have much to say about what has become one of today's most pressing problems—a sense of meaninglessness in life.

Freud's was a pessimistic view. He once wrote to a friend, "I have always confined myself to the ground floor and basement of the edifice called Man." Aldous Huxley once said he should have said the basement-basement.

If Freud is the basement, the humanists see themselves as the attic or penthouse. Rollo May, a founder of the Assn. for Humanistic Psychology, sounded the clarion call at the beginning of the movement.

"We represent the New Underground in psychology," he said. "I see a crucially important value for the (association) if we are able to find and be the kind of psychology that speaks out of the being of man, rather than out of techniques."

May thinks psychology owes Freud a debt of gratitude for bringing "repressed hostilities, irrational urges" and other "dark" areas of the unconscious out into the open. But he feels Freud's system left out too much that is human.

He warns the behaviorists they run the risk of creating a totally mechanical society. The title of Skinner's latest book. "Beyond Freedom and Dignity," suggests just that to most humanists. The Skinnerian reply is that Man's "freedom" is illusory and leaves him abandoned to uncontrollable forces in his environment.

This issue has political overtones. The battle continues.

Maslow was the first major American psychologist to postulate that man is an evolutionary creature whose higher nature is just as "instinctoid" (his word) as his lower nature . . . and to see problems, difficulties and "sickness" arising when this upward-evolution—this need for "self-actualization"—is blocked.

"This higher nature," Maslow said, "includes the need for meaningful work, for responsibility, for creativeness, for being fair and just, for doing what is worthwhile and for preferring to do it well."

Peak experiences are way stations along the path of this upward evolution—way stations that are both necessary and desirable. Maslow believed.

"Maslow's importance," explains British author-psychologist Wilson, "is that he places these experiences of transcendence at the core of his psychology. Peak experiences are moments of meaning which enhance our self-image and stimulate our will.

" . . . As the meaning pours in, you ask yourself, 'Why doesn't this happen all the time?' . . . and the answer is obvious: 'Because I allow the will to become passive and the senses close up. If I want more meaning then I must force my senses wide open by an increased effort of the will . . .' "

One of those with reservations about peak experience is Sam Keen of the Assn. for Humanistic Psychology. He favors a more "Zen, homogenized way of living . . . Some neurotics reach the point where they need peak experience all the time."

"We can't assume our own experiences are always correct either," says Stanford's Fadiman.

"By that I mean that my gut feelings may be no more accurate than my intellectual feelings. I've made as many mistakes being led by my gut or my gonads as by my mind. That's where a lot of encounter got stuck."

Humanistic psychology is already way ahead of any simple definitions. Its adherents—or, at least, its avantgarde—say that man, as we usually think of him, is far too narrow a concept.

The language of the humanists now takes on a "spiritual," almost mystical tone—something unheard and unheard-of in scientific circles before.

But then the humanists have been outrageous right along. Once after Maslow had delivered a paper at an American Psychological Assn. meeting, a famous psychologist rushed at him shouting, "Maslow—you are an evil man—you want to destroy psychology."

Ironically, Maslow went on to become the association's president a few years later.

What is different today is that humanistic ranks—although small—include so many well credentialed and influential scientists that they can no longer be dismissed as merely "misguided," "misled," "unscientific"—or, least of all, "kooky."

Nor can these new ideas be credited to the "squishy California atmosphere" or California's "tolerance for peculiar life-styles" as some writers do. They seem to be everywhere.

Anyone who remembers the flashy, flamboyant Human Potential Movement of a few years back may have trouble reconciling it with humanistic psychology's newfound respectability.

The Human Potential Movement (which was to blend with, and finally become indistinguishable from, the Assn. for Humanistic Psychology) was born out of the cultural upheaval of the 60s.

Affluence, the sexual revolution, the campus revolt, changing life styles, women's liberation, drugs, the flower children, television, more leisure and rising middle-class expectations all played a part. For whatever reason, thousands of people found their lives somehow flat and self-limiting.

Much earlier, after World War II, the GI Bill of Rights had brought thousands of ex-GIs onto the campuses where, with the newfound existential wisdom of war, many went into clinical psychology.

"Until then, the practice of psychotherapy had been limited almost exclusively to professionals having an MD degree—owing to the accidental historical fact that Freud just happened to be an MD himself. No other reason," says Dr. Tom Greening, a humanistic therapist.

With the flood of clinical psychologists into the market-place, psychotherapy ceased to be the monopoly of the MDs and the luxury solely of the rich. It unleashed a floodgate of self-exploration, self-examination and self-awareness.

Much of this had begun before Maslow and the humanists appeared on the scene. Astrology, I Ching, Tarot cards, esoteric religions and meditation were flourishing.

And encounter—that crucible of honest, bruising group plain talk, where people "can drop their masks and express true feelings"—was on everyone's lips if not in their living rooms.

"What happened," says Fadiman, the Stanford psychologist, "is we learned that being 'well-bred' meant dying slowly. 'Well-bred' in the sense of suppressing our real feelings. What has finally come across is that emotional honesty is necessary for mental health."

He adds, "And there were an awful lot of dead people walking around."

Encounter was big business. Corporations like TRW had major programs aimed at "sensitizing" employes, believing this resulted in more productive work. (Now some of them offer yoga classes at lunch.)

By the end of the 60s, National Training Laboratories could claim that more than half the presidents of the 500 largest U.S. corporations had exposed themselves to group experience. Encounter finally filtered down to churches, schools, police departments, the Army—and around the world.

At the same time, Esalen was deep in its far-out forays in self-exploration. Some called it "freaky audacity and a willingness to try anything that stretches the self."

Whatever it was, it met a a real need of the time (and still does: there are Esalen-like growth centers now in Scotland, London, Amsterdam, Munich, Paris, the Costa del Sol in Spain, and Japan.)

Esalen and humanistic psychology met officially when Murphy, Esalen's founder, had a first, "chance" meeting with Maslow who "just happened" to be lost in the hills above Big Sur one day in the early '60s—a story Murphy tells which is positively eerie in coincidence.

But nowhere else could one glimpse the real "cutting edge" of change as readily as at Assn. for Humanistic Psychology conventions.

Its members tended to greet each other with bear hugs, lie around on convention floors and create culture shock at famous hotels by skinny-dipping in the early hours of the morning.

They danced to bongo drums by the pool, held workshops on "play" where they romped and cavorted like children, and practiced what they preached—a celebration of life.

("The battle to maintain a balance between the theoretical and the experiential still rages," says one member today.)

This freewheelingness cost them some of their most eminent members some years ago. After an episode where students pitched a tent in the lobby of the elegant Fairmont Hotel in San Francisco to protest high room rates, Rollo May, Gardner Murphy and some others resigned.

But May rejoined two years later with a simple statement:

"Somewhere, there has got to be a psychology that includes poetry, art, a movement toward social justice and that will help me understand myself—and nowhere does it exist—even beginningly—outside the (association)."

Packed seminars and workshops introduced professionals, and the lay public who attended in large number, to the latest developments in techniques for self-discovery: aikido, gestalt, rolfing, autogenic training, bioenergetics, transactional analysis, sensory and body awareness, Zen meditation, Tibetan Buddhism, sensual massage, transpersonal workshops, biofeedback, psychosynthesis and much more.

Many seminal ideas and subjects got their first airing at Assn. for Humanistic Psychology forums, among them the now famous seminar on "Should a Professional Therapist Go to Bed with His Patient if Mutually Attracted?"

"It was an attempt," explains Eleanor Criswell, a California State College, Sonoma, psychology professor, "to bring certain things out in the open that are well known in the profession but seldom talked about. Actually, it was more or less engineered by a psychiatrist who had written a book on the subject which was being released that day.

"Many of our people—among them Albert Ellis, the famous sexologist, and onetime firebrand—argued against the practice, warning that it could interfere with people getting well, totally disrupt the therapeutic situation and easily be exploitive on the part of the therapist."

Members of the audience—some women—wanted to know if the therapist would, with equal impartiality, sleep with an old and homely female patient or say, a male patient "who needed it."

"The press went wild," continues Criswell. "It was in every magazine and newspaper . . . People were aghast. But the next year, at their meeting in Hawaii, the American Psychological Assn. held a seminar on the same subject and it wasn't mentioned anywhere in the media."

This point about the trend-setting capacities of the Assn. for Humanistic Psychology is well taken. For years, since its founding in 1962, it has always held its convention in the same city as the American Psychological Assn.—only a few days before or after, so that psychologists who wished to attend both meetings could do so conveniently.

It was always a study in contrasts. The button-down academicians would file in, university-style, with decorum, and listen to formal papers formally delivered at a lecture.

"But," said one observer, "it was clear that, with each successive year, more and more of their colleagues turned up bearded and braless, and some even enrolled in the 'touchie-feelie' seminars run by that 'wild bunch'—the Assn. for Humanistic Psychology."

Now the "movement" seems to be settling down, its youthful exuberance curbed, if not peaked. At last year's Assn. for Humanistic Psychology convention in New Orleans, observers noted fewer "thrill seekers," fewer crowds and a growing trend toward the transcendental—and a mystical language.

Humanistic psychology is working a change in the traditional academic fare long taught to psychology students in the universities.

Words like love, consciousness, values, meaning and purpose are creeping back into the textbooks. For a long time, the only chapter on love was to be found in a standard text by Harry Harlow—and that was on love between primates.

Now human love comes under scrutiny. So do trust, altruism, self-esteem. One of psychology's leading learning theorists, Ernest R. Hilgard, is studying hypnosis at Stanford.

While animal experimentation is not necessarily on the wane, Claremont College Graduate School phased out its rat laboratory—in deference to new priorities.

Courses in the new psychology, including parapsychology, are turning up on campuses in all parts of the country. Experimental Johnston College at the University of Redlands bases an entire four-year course around new transpersonal psychology—which combines the humanistic with the "spiritual." Students use encounter at the beginning of each semester to decide on their course of study.

At Northern Illinois University, psychologist-educator Thomas Roberts uses an imagery technique much used in the new psychology called "fantasy journey" to instruct electric shop teacher trainees. He asks students to relax and begins, softly:

"Now imagine you are an electron in a wire . . . you are hopping, swirling, leaping, brushing around with other electrons, all pushing and bumping against each other—rapidly, heatedly . . . now you are outside the wire, feel the force, the pull and intensity of the electronic field . . . now take a trip down an electric coil itself, feel yourself sliding, bumping, interwinning with other electrons in the rush of forces . . ."—and it goes on.

"Its been very successful," Roberts says, "because people learn better when they have the experience of something."

Symbolic visualization, twilight images and directed daydreams are being used in classrooms, mind-dynamic and creativity workshops, the newer "spiritual" disciplines (once called "therapies") like transpersonal psychology and psychosynthesis, and memory and hypnosis courses.

For centuries, of course, they have been part of many ancient systems of Eastern meditation, notably Tibetan Buddhism—all of which are attracting growing numbers of people in the West, particularly among students of the new psychology.

Psychology has always had an identity crisis.

As an outgrowth of philosophy and wanting to earn its spurs as a "real" science, a young psychology needed the security of imitating medicine and physics.

From medicine, it took the sickness model and studied pathology.

From early physics, it took the mechanistic idea of studying the parts and not the whole.

It chopped behavior into segments like reaction time and worked with worms, rats, dogs and apes that could be managed and controlled.

The results were often criticized—in the profession and out.

Ten years ago, writer-critic Gerald Sykes called psychology "a raw ungainly science" and declared:

"We know less about ourselves than about any other portion of society, and our lack of self-knowledge is now our most acute social problem . . . I would like to know what the psychologists have done to help us."

Now, the debate between the "new" psychology and the "old" raises the same basic questions: What is science, what is psychology and what should it be studying? Most crucial—what is man?

Neuropsychologist Robert Ornstein, author of the bestselling "Psychology of Consciousness," threw out this battle cry to a UCLA audience last year:

"Somehow, academic psychology got diverted from the study of the most interesting areas and into the most trivial. It was a terrible mistake but this kind of meeting marks the end of that kind of diversion. We're here to turn the mainstream of psychology back to the time when methods and techniques were devoted to the study of real phenomena such as mind and how people experience the world to the fullest."

Donald Hebb, though, speaking at a recent American Psychological Assn. convention in Montreal on "What Psychology Is All About," assailed misguided people "who want us to deal directly with the mystery of existence now. Some of this is simply antiscience . . . which we needn't bother with here. When someone thinks a science can be run that way, there is much to be said. Subjective science? There isn't such a thing."

Can psychology, in fact, be humanistic and scientific at the same time? A growing number of professionals are saying yes.

But since, in the "new psychology," man is being redefined, it may require a redefinition of scientific method.

The scientific method has always demanded "objectivity" (that the experimenter see impartially what is there), verifiability (that the experiments can be repeated by others) and predictability.

At issue, of course, is "objectivity." Humanistic psychologists demand that this term be reexamined and that the subjective be let back in—where they believe it has always been anyway.

They say that overwhelming evidence shows that we "choose" what we see or perceive as surely as we choose our words or a new pair of shoes.

What the humanists call for is a new science of ordinary and extraordinary subjective experience.

And, they say, it isn't so extraordinary after all—hypnosis has been studied scientifically for a century and a half.

Charles Tart of Davis proposes a new method. He calls it "specific state science." In it, scientists do research by entering into the research area themselves.

Instead of remaining outside and "objective," they go into states like meditation, hypnosis, sensory deprivation and other altered states of consciousness.

Then their collected reports can be tested against one another to verify the validity of the knowledge obtained.

This, he says, is not really different from the way science now works with normal consciousness to achieve consensus on certain observable data.

Tart's point is that all knowledge is basically experiential.

This is the belief of John Lilly—the MD-biophysicist, neurophysiologist-psychoanalyst who did the famous work with dolphins. He sees it as the best tradition of an older science. He quotes British biologist J.B.S. Haldane's advice to his students: "You will not understand what is necessary in the way of scientific control unless you are the first subject in your experiment."

In what is surely the most remarkable and little known scientific meeting of its kind in the world, a diverse group of psychologists, medical doctors, holy men, physicists, philosophers and anthropologists from everywhere converge on Council Grove, Kan., once a year for a special conference.

It is cosponsored by the Assn. for Humanistic Psychology and the Menninger Foundation.

Its purpose? The study of experience involving an expansion or extension of consciousness beyond the usual ego boundaries and the limitation of time and space. It is by invitation only.

Some psychologists still feel that such areas as altered states of consciousness are off limits, off base and too far out.

But to Andrew Weil, MD, author of "The Natural Mind," the desire to alter consciousness periodically is an innate, normal drive comparable to hunger or the sex drive. He believes it is visible in 3- and 4-year-olds when they whirl themselves into dizziness or squeeze each other around the chest until they lost their breath.

Some evidence for this seems to come from research on a part of the brain called the limbic system. Sensations which range from mild pleasure to intense joy or euphoria come from electrical stimulation of the limbic.

James Olds has found that hungry rats will give up on getting food if they have to cross an electric grid containing 60 microamperes of electricity, but to obtain this brain stimulation, they will cross grids charged with 450 microamperes.

To the behaviorists, the humanists are fuzzy-minded, romantic and unscientific—and are leading us to disaster with the "carrot" of freedom and no controls. Some behaviorists say they are the true humanists.

To the humanists, behaviorists, by and large, are scripting a "Clockwork Orange" future for mankind. Some admire behavior modification therapy and would like to see it adapted to humanistic goals—but (and it is a big but) with the control coming from the person himself.

Fortunately, the humanists overall show a talent for the self-awareness they preach.

Psychologist Richard Farson, for example, cautions that "peak experiences" may only have meaning in terms of valleys. "The fact that we can't always sustain such moments shouldn't make them invalid. We must learn to appreciate them while they last. Art and education also make life better—but, by the same token, make it more complicated and difficult. But then, everything we value tends to make life more difficult."

In "Power and Innocence," Rollo May once wrote: "The Human Potential Movement has fallen heir to the form of innocence prevalent in America, namely that we grow toward greater and greater moral perfection." He means, he explains, that the darker side of Man must be faced too, and sensitivity developed to both.

"A sense of wonder . . . ," Maslow has said of happy, creative people, "like that of an unspoiled child . . ."

The children's story, "The Wizard of Oz," tells how the Tin Woodman, the Cowardly Lion and the Scarecrow already have what they traveled so far to ask from the wizard—brains, courage and a heart. All the wizard could do for them was to make them aware that they already owned what they wanted so badly.

The Terms and Concepts

Here is a glossary of terms and concepts associated with the "new psychology:"

Altered states of consciousness—Defined by Hugh Redmond of Johnston College as ". . . no more than any state or experience that we have which is significantly different from the 'normal' way we experience ourselves or reality—as in meditation or the hypnagogic state which is when we are between dreaming and waking."

Therapy—An unpopular term among many humanistic psychologists who seek to "demmystify" the process. They believe that the medical model—the usual "sick-well" dichotomy—is distorting: that most people are not "patients" in the traditional sense but are in need of the releasing of self-actualizing potentialities; that the therapist should be open, honest and self-disclosing rather than "removed" as in the classic psychoanalytic mode.

Esalen—The original "growth center" on the rocky, coastal hills of Big Sur, where in experiential seminars, workshops, classes and "happenings," the Human Potential Movement began. It cautions that some of its programs may be "risky" to some people and that "no one come whose interest is 'cure.' " It explores trends in education, religion, philosophy and the physical and behavioral sciences which emphasize potentialities and values of human existence.

Aikido—An ancient Japanese martial art involving *ki* or the universal flow of energy which is inhibited by tension, conflict or competition. The idea is to remain centered, balanced and "in harmony with the laws of nature" in the face of attack or any attempt to throw you off balance.

Rolfing—A rigorous deep massage and manipulation of the body aimed at realigning the body structure so as to release excessive, long built-up tensions. The assumption is that one's body mirrors one's emotional past and that rolfing is the way to greater physical and emotional freedom and balance. Ten individual sessions are usually required. Also known as structural integration.

Gestalt—An existential, nonanalytic form of therapy developed by Fritz and Laura Perls and perfected at Esalen. The focus is on what IS rather than might have been, was, should be, could be, etc. The endless "why-because" games are avoided and emphasis is on choice and growth. A favorite technique involves a person being in the "hot seat" while the leader and others in the group make you act out who you are.

Autogenic feedback training—A Western method for learning to control such body functions as heartbeat and temperature. Alyce and Elmer Green of Menninger Clinic have adapted a system first developed by German psychoanalyst Johannes Schultz, which uses words and phrases to quiet the mind and turn it inward. They combine it with biofeedback to enhance awareness.

Human Potential Movement—A spontaneous middle-class cultural movement begun in the early '60s largely in California, which shares with humanistic psychology the revolt against "dehumanizing" instituions and practices believed to lead to flat, narrow, self-limiting lives, both professionally and otherwise. Emphasis is on seeing man as a whole being—a blend of body, mind, emotions and even spirit—and on tapping inherent built-in capacities for growth and development through a wide variety of sensory-awareness, encounter and other techniques.

Encounter—The ground rules for this group process is that participants be open and honest, avoid theorizing and instead talk about their feelings. The object is to explore interpersonal relations. Derived from several sources, it was a mainstay of Esalen for many years where it now includes techniques and ideas from gestalt, sensory awareness, bioenergetics, massage and structural integration.

Bioenergetics—The theory is that when people are hung up in the head, they are emotionally musclebound as well. This is another technique, like rolfing, which attempts to break those blocks and allow repressed emotions to rise into consciousness, according to Alexander Lowen, its founder.

Sensory awareness—Yet another method developed at Esalen for climinating the tyranny of the head, it includes relaxation verbal and nonverbal communication, sensory encounter, meditation, massage plus some yoga and zen.

Yoga—An ancient method of tuning in to both body and mind at the same time, of achieving deep relaxation, of toning muscles and inner organs, and as a means to higher self-realization in "cosmic consciousness." It has many forms which emphasize different things—Hatha, raja, bhakti and juana.

Zen—A classic, meditative practice which emphasizes no-mind and is an ancient gateway to deep inner-consciousness. One suspends thoughts and concentrates on breathing. Usually involves zazen—meditative sitting in the lotus position. One sect uses koans—ancient riddles ("What is the sound of one hand clapping?") intended to "trick" the mind into new thoughts and perceptions.

Biofeedback—A process by which you are wired to machines which allow you to see and monitor the continual responses of your heart, skin, blood pressure or brain waves and thus learn to consciously control them. An important byproduct is relaxation.

Transpersonal psychology—The avant-grade of humanistic psychology. What used to be suggested by "spiritual" or "transcendental" but something new. A nonreligious focus on what Abraham Maslow called "the farthest reaches" of the person; a questing for meaning and purpose which transcends individual differences. Sometimes called the "fourth psychology (the other three being behavioristic, psychoanalytic and humanistic.)

Psychosynthesis—The "farthest reaches" of transpersonal which begins with a synthesis of body-mind-emotions. A rich, electic blend of esoteric disciplines, exercises, imagery, movement, self-identification, creativity, gestalt, meditation, training of the will, symbolic art work, journal-keeping, ideal models and development of intuition. Developed by the late Italian humanistic psychoanalyst, Roberto Assagioli, and growing fast.

Massage—Not thought of as a "service" to be performed but as a "caring" relationship between two people. First consideration is given to the feelings and sensory relationship between both partners and then to technique.

Tibetan Buddhism—After Chinese troops invaded their homeland a decade ago, 4,000 lamas fled mountainous Tibet taking their eclectic religion (it incorporates all forms of Buddhism) around the world. The Vajrayana the oldest and most sophisticated sect which has a center in Berkeley—believes that enlightenment comes from stripping away false values from the "perfection" which lies beneath—a very humanistic and transpersonal view.

Parapsychology—That branch of psychology dealing with those psychic effects and experiences that appear to fall outside the scope of physical law such as ESP, telepathy and psychokinesis. First explored in the '30s by J. B. Rhine of Duke University and recognized two years ago by the National Assn. for the Advancement of Science as a legitimate area of inquiry.

The American Compulsion to Win

Or, How to Strike Out Early Forever

Dr. Thomas Tutko
and William Bruns

Dr. Thomas Tutko is a professor of psychology at San Jose State and codirector of the Institute for the Study of Athletic Motivation, the most prominent sports psychological testing center in the U.S.

William Bruns was sports editor for *Life* and now works as a free-lance writer in Los Angeles.

If left to their own devices, most youngsters take up a sport just to be with their friends and to have fun. They don't start out putting the emphasis on winning that parents and coaches do. Their greatest achievement is simply to belong, to be a member of a team or a club. The second biggest thing in their life is to make a contribution—to play, not to sit on the bench. Belonging and contributing are normal needs, which can be fulfilled by all of us. But they are being subverted at the childhood level by a gilt-edged emphasis on winning and competition.

I feel that competition is a learned phenomenon, that people are not *born* with a motivation to win or to be competitive. We inherit a potential for a degree of activity, and we all have the instinct to survive. But the will to win comes through training and the influences of one's family and environment. As the song in *South Pacific* says, "you've got to be carefully taught." The song is talking about prejudice, but it's the same thing. From a very early age we are bombarded by direct, indirect, subtle, behavioral, and verbal messages to the effect that the important thing in life is to be a winner—and the earlier the better. If you want to be a successful high school athlete you must specialize, and specialize early. . . .

It's interesting to note that children often have a different perspective of what sports are about. When they play tennis, for example, and adults aren't around to ask "Who's winning?" the idea is to keep the ball going back and forth, even if it bounces two or three times or goes off the court. That's the thrill; not to slam the ball down the opponent's throat. Unfortunately, the adults soon come along and start insisting that the youngsters "play by the rules"; that is, play to win.

"How can they have fun," we reason, "if they don't play to win? If there's not a situation created where one side wins and the other loses?" At a Little League meeting one night, an obviously uptight father interpreted what I was saying as "Let's not have the kids compete." Was that my philosophy? Because his feeling was that "Competition is life."

I agreed that learning to compete obviously has merit, since one finds himself competing most of his life, either with others or within himself. But I pointed out that adults share a common misconception: that children will not compete unless adults are around to take over and show them how. But children are competing all the time—in school, at home, among their friends, on the playground. Given free time, they love to get into some kind of activity; they do it naturally. If a group of adults were to take eighteen youngsters who liked to play baseball out on the field, and were to hang around just to answer questions about technique, the youngsters would soon choose up teams and they sure as hell would compete. They would work out a balance in the teams and adjust to any imbalance naturally. They wouldn't have uniforms and nobody would be keeping statistics, but everybody would play the entire game and they would all have fun. What's equally important, it would be a growth experience; they would be doing it themselves rather than having the adults run the show. . . .

Most children in this country, when they reach the age of five or six, can generally find an organized sport waiting for them at the nearest playground, recreation center, gym, skating rink, or swimming pool. This American compulsion to organize everything for our young athletes reflects a growing belief by many parents that the earlier you learn a sport—the earlier you learn to *compete*—the better your chances are of becoming a professional or an Olympic hero. If, that is, you haven't been burned out, injured, or eliminated along the way. Once again we have applied an adult model to a growing child. We continue to raise our expectations of children while lowering the age at which they can compete. We fail to make the critical distinction between learning a sport in a fun, low-key situation and having to compete to win in that sport at a very early age. It's not *when* you start your child in sports that counts; it's what your goals are. If you are starting your five-year-old in ice hockey because you dream that he'll one day play for the Montreal Canadiens (even if you don't admit it to anybody), then your behavior is destructive. On the other hand, early involvement in sports can be a healthy outlet for the child who has sensitive, patient parents and coaches. . . .

. . . Enlightened coaches maintain that the following guidelines should serve for those parents and coaches who are dealing with very young, beginning athletes: (1) keep it fun, for the child as well as the adults; (2) be agonizingly patient; (3) reward effort, not performance, unless the performance deserves it; and (4) remember that the aim is simply to introduce the child to a sport in a noncompetitive environment where he can learn the fundamentals without the pressure of executing them in front of a critical audience.

Fierce competition should be the last step in the development of young athletes. They should first learn the skills of the sport, the give-and-take of participation, the enjoyment of being active. Children are naturally inquisitive; they want to know how to play a game and how to improve. As they gain confidence they will seek out competition at their own level.

Alas, the reverse is true for many youngsters. They are thrown into competitive sports before they have sufficient confidence and a proper grasp of the fundamentals. Adults are so anxious to test the skills of young athletes, and so worried that children will grow bored with sports unless they "play for keeps," that they try to build the roof of the house before they have the foundation. They put Fenwick in a situation where he must learn to perform a skill under pressure before he is comfortable with the sport. He may still be overcoming his fears of getting hit by a baseball, making a head-on tackle, or falling on the ice at full speed, when suddenly he also has to win. His coach wants to win. His parents want to see their boy win. The child who just wants to learn how to pick up a ground ball and throw it correctly to first base is confounded by the fact that he has to throw out the runner and kill a rally. Not only that, he stands to be accused of not listening or not trying if he goofs up. If he continues to fail, he may be relegated to the bench.

Anyone who has ever taken up a sport knows the frustration—almost impossibility—of trying to pick up a skill while being under pressure to perform that skill. But we expect this of our children all the time. The average person might feel very differently if he himself were once thrust into a pressure situation while being evaluated by his peers and his superiors. For example, how would a mechanic feel if he were suddenly shown a totally new type of engine, given a box of tools, and told to repair the engine while a gallery consisting of his neighbors, friends, and opponents from a competing garage cheered or booed, depending on how he fared with the engine?

The assumption in childhood sports seems to be that if children don't learn to compete early, they're not going to be able to compete later in life. Defenders of this ethic argue that man is competing from the day he is born, and that the rewards in society—good grades, a good job, even finding the right mate—go to the competitor, the person who knows how to win. Where better to learn to compete than in the gym or on the athletic field? A clinching argument, these people feel, is that there is just as much pressure on a youngster when he is taking a math test as when he's up at bat. "What's the difference?" they ask.

My rebuttal is that the athletic pressures are far more severe. When a youngster fails the math test, he's all alone; the teacher may be the only one who knows his real score. Nobody really gives a damn about his test, except maybe his parents. And they don't say, "Boy, on question four, you really understood your math!" But place this youngster on the basketball court and let him miss two free throws with the score tied late in the game: he knows it, his opponents know it, his coach knows it, his teammates know it, and the spectators know it. The poor youngster has nowhere to turn for support. . . .

[Or] we have some poor little ten-year-old who comes to the plate with the bases loaded in the last inning. The bat's heavier than he is, he's afraid he'll get hurt by the ball, he doesn't even know if he'll hit it—he's just praying for a walk. Yet everybody is evaluating him. Not only that, we tell him this is for his own good; it is building character! No wonder he has a distorted perception of sports—and adults.

I strongly believe that when we force competition prior to the child's capability of handling the pressures involved—and without the proper support and encouragement—the long-term detriments will outweigh any supposed benefits. The years between eight and twelve are a vital identifying period, a

time when children are trying to find themselves, in a psychological sense. They are trying to determine their capabilities and their limitations; they want to learn to deal with certain problems and to handle them effectively; they are in the process of trying to relate to other people and trying to discover their own worth, to be of value; it's a period of building confidence and taking on an attitude about themselves.

Children use play during this period as one way of growing up, of "trying out" life, on their own level, at their own pace, among their peers. Play is necessary for their development and should have a serious place in society. Instead, adults have taken over children's play, as if to say that unstructured, unorganized, sandlot games are no longer possible or important in today's society, especially in the suburbs and small cities. If we continue to plunge children too quickly into a grown-up world and cheat them out of the opportunity to prepare for life in a low-key, low-pressure fashion, we can expect a generation of adults to emerge who are totally alienated from competitive sports.

Gale E. Mikles, chairman of Michigan State University's athletic education department, is among those who feel that America is going overboard in the push for competitive sports, especially with six- and seven-year-olds. A former college wrestling coach, Mikles says, "The competitive spirit comes too soon now for most children to handle, tearing down basic values taught at home and destroying valuable young friendships. What organized sport really does with kids is to break down their own individuality and train them to fit into a system. It does not help to develop their own personality." Bill Harper, a philosophy professor and director of intramural sports at Emporia State, Kansas, contends that competitive sports thwart playfulness. "What do coaches from the Little League up say when they want to praise a player?" he asks. "They say he is a hard worker. Any time you have games in which the participants have less control than the organizers about how they play, who they play, when they play, then it is not really play. Kids get started in sports because they are playful, but they get caught in a system where they are playing for other rewards."

By imposing a competitive ethic fashioned by adults, we may be damaging the child's growing-up process. We interfere with a positive development by telling the child that he's not any good in

a particular area and by placing great emphasis on that lack of ability. If he continues to be criticized, or rides the bench every season, or always plays on a losing team with a coach who stresses that winning is the most important thing, he may start to take on the identity of a loser—"Ah, I'm no good." If children can't learn to enjoy themselves outside the confines of winning, if they are led to believe they are failures if they don't succeed, then what values are sports imparting?

Let's take the example of a youngster participating in Little League. He's led to believe that this artificially induced area has some value in the real world, perhaps that it is even a very vital part of life. If he doesn't do particularly well or his team doesn't win or he has a difficult time learning the skills, he may develop a sense that he's a failure. If he continues to try his best in a sport but continues to lose—in an environment where the stress is on winning—he may even begin to feel rejected by his coaches and parents. They may try to hide their disappointment, but you don't fool too many children. This feeling of rejection may begin to interfere with other areas of life, such as social interaction and schoolwork. Instead of athletics helping him develop in other areas, they can actually destroy areas that might be more vital in later life.

By introducing competition too early, by having screening devices, by picking All-Star teams, by handing out trophies and keeping league standings, by emphasizing batting averages and touchdown passes—by many subtle means—we remind the young athlete of whether or not he's a "winner." The trouble with placing an overriding importance on league championships and trophies is that these are unrealistic goals for all but a handful of people. When you start giving out trophies, you differentiate children; unless you give everyone the same kind of trophy, you're telling the loser, "You're different from the winner." But children know who the better ball players are. They're aware of where they stand and how good they are in comparison with their peers. To give out trophies simply accentuates this difference. It makes the youngster who doesn't have talent feel even less capable, and it gives a distorted perspective to the youngster who gets the higher trophy—not to mention his parents, who can display it on the mantel as evidence that they are raising a hell of an athlete, and must therefore be a hell of a set of parents.

CHANGING CHANNELS/ How TV Shapes American Minds

Television is more than just a little fun and entertainment. It's a whole environment, and what it does bears an unpleasant resemblance to behavior modification—on a mass scale.

ROSE K. GOLDSEN

Rose K. Goldsen, PhD, is professor of sociology at Cornell University. This article is adapted from her book, *The Show and Tell Machine,* published by The Dial Press.

The television day in most of the United States begins between six and seven in the morning and ends an hour or two after midnight. Visual and aural materials to fill these hours are selected by station managers who command the nation's only licensed transmission facilities. Whatever they approve for broadcast is assured certain access to the eyes and ears of a citizenry whose custom is to set up a television receiver in the home's intimate environment and keep it activated an average of almost seven hours a day.

Since the managers of the major commercial stations choose to deliver virtually the same programs and schedule them at the same times of day, the images and sounds that issue simultaneously from the nation's most powerful transmitters are almost identical. They coalesce into a kind of cloud that settles over the country coast to coast, a cloud of visual and aural symbols creating the new kind of total environment in which Americans must now learn to live, to think and to feel.

The general population does not usually recognize the airwaves as a coast-to-coast highway with direct access to 71 million homes. Nor does the public usually notice how television's massive contribution to the environment we make and share with one another drastically alters the public culture. However, it is quite customary to accept the TV set as "the new member of the family."

This new member of the family is an electronic machine, but it still acts like any other family member. Sometimes it commands attention, sometimes it yields it to others. The images coming through its screen and the sounds coming through its loudspeaker join the rest of the family at mealtimes and bedtimes, at times for working and for relaxing, when visitors come or when the family is alone. Like any other family member, the machine alters the traffic patterns in the home, changes the rhythms of the day, the very atmosphere of the places it enters. It introduces its own views of the world, its own definitions of reality, its own myths and symbolic forms.

The business end of the broadcasting enterprise is supported by advertisers eager to use the machine as a showcase to exhibit their wares inside the home, yet in a context of their own choosing. Thus, commercials introduce every program, interrupt every program and separate each program from the one that follows. They are skillfully crafted little dramas, rarely lasting longer than 60 seconds, often 30 seconds, sometimes 20, even 10. Their rhythm sets up a more rapid counterpoint to the slower movement of television's programmed "dayparts": sign-on time, morning news, local time, daytime TV, fringe time, evening news, access time, prime time and late-night shows. (In just such a fashion did the medieval day ebb and flow with its dayparts, each of which also bore a special name: prime, terce, sext, none and vespers.)

Commercials, familiar to Americans since radio days, have become so much a part of American life that by now the public pays them only glancing attention. It is quite common to accept them as often irritating, sometimes offensive, occasionally amusing but, on the whole, tolerable interruptions to the programs. However, to advertisers and broadcasters it's the other way around: programs are important only as envelopes into which they can conveniently tuck commercials during about 22 percent of the broadcast day.

Through this casual, ubiquitous and repeated exposure, commercials visit effortlessly upon the entire population—from the youngest child to the eldest graybeard—an awareness of companies, brand names, products, services, and selected attitudes and values to go with them, that in an earlier day would have required hours spent poring over images and text in disciplined and concentrated study of every mail-order catalog in the country. In the same effortless way, families get to know shows, commercials and the stars who move back and forth between them better than they know their own cousins, aunts, uncles, grandparents and godparents.

Television programs are made and booked to capture attention and hold it until the commercial comes along. Although the broadcasting business likes to kid audiences into thinking of themselves as the customers of television, audiences are in fact the product television offers for sale. Programs corral them so they can be counted off and sold to advertisers by the head.

Sometimes television watchers are likened to voters, the audience presumably "voting" by changing channels or turning off the set. Such "voting" for programs, however, occurs in a system that disenfranchises minorities who have no way to place their own candidates on any ballot, nor channels to mobilize public support so that they might become majorities. Without such institutionalized procedures, even the most widespread discontent can find no orderly ways to become an effective policymaking force. In their absence, the main recourse is the negative power of boycott—in this case, a simultaneous blackout of millions of television screens.

In the political sphere, such arrangements would be called plebiscite, general strike or insurrection. A political system offering only these alternatives for making the public will known is usually called totalitarian. We do not yet have a similarly familiar term for our television system. Oligopoly has been suggested, and it is indeed suitable to describe the economic arrangements that exist in television. It is unpleasant to the ear, however, and not so widely understood. When this country was founded and none of these terms was in current use, the term *established*—as in *established religion*—described a system that offered the populace an ideology hammered away at so insistently and backed by the weight of public authority.

Television programs face a continuing dilemma. To hold an audience they must evoke human feelings, stir human emotions, engage human passions. Yet, as soon as viewers find their intellectual curiosity awakened, as soon as they allow themselves to be gripped by fear or anxiety, love or hate, terror or revulsion or rage, as soon as they are on the way to being overcome by laughter or engulfed by tears, the program delivers them to the commercials. Reactions that have been engaged are disengaged. Under an avalanche of repetition and a constant barrage of interruptions, emotions the programs might have called into being have no chance to develop. All are aborted virtually at the moment of conception.

Television programs resolve the dilemma quite simply: they give up any pretense of trying to awaken absorbing interest or achieve true dramatic depths. Thus, most of the programs offered on American television are the electronic equivalent of materials appearing in the pulp magazines or near-pulps, in the mass-produced paperbacks, comic books and tabloids available at any newsstand. Indeed, these are the sources from which many television programs were originally derived. Other programs reverse the cycle, reappearing on newsstands in print versions sold by syndicating companies or the syndicating arm of the production company that initially turned them out. These syndicating businesses circulate, recirculate and recycle television shows.

People in the television business admit quite frankly. that the programs aim principally to attract attention and amass audiences without asking for the investment of self demanded by drama—or by any discourse, for that matter—which takes itself and its audience seriously. "We're a medicine show," they say, and, in fact, it has become quite acceptable to treat the airwaves as if they were an invisible midway.

Even the format of news programs is designed to package commercials conveniently, at the expense of the context needed to make sense out of the events reported. Within the tight confines of the evening news, about two dozen topics are touched upon in as many minutes, so that scenes of war or peace efforts, famine and pestilence, football and baseball games, beauty pageants and moon landings, punctuated by Dow-Jones closing stock market averages and the weather, jostle up against one another indiscriminately. The stage is set in such a way that any interest or feeling that may have been aroused by one of these presentations is likely to be extinguished by the next one following hard on its heels, or by the commercials.

Television watchers quickly learn to vary the amount of attention they pay to the machine, diminishing it when the commercials come on, increasing it for the program. No matter what the set is bringing into the home, however, it rarely gets undivided attention. Exceptions occur—usually such historic on-camera firsts as assassinations and ensuing state funerals, the first moon landings, the first broadcast congressional hearings on organized crime, the Watergate hearings, presidential impeachment panel and the like. Such broadcasts are good for several replays before they, too, fade into the background, commanding no more attention than any other rerun.

Television's images and sounds, designed for the mundane familiarity of the home environment, fit themselves in and around its daily routines, a pleasant and comfortable accompaniment to them. Daytime serials are made to accompany housewives as they iron or do household chores. Saturday morning cartoons accompany children at play in front of the set or mesmerized by it. A social group watches a news broadcast or a crime show, and the programs weave themselves effortlessly around the conversation and the banter. If the doorbell buzzes or the telephone rings, it's the easiest thing in the world to withdraw attention from the set in favor of the visitor at the door or the caller on the line.

Ninety-nine percent of American homes have at least one TV set. In 40 percent, there are two or more. Frequently one of the machines is set up in the bedroom. Children climb into bed with their parents and all watch together in pleasant, cozy relaxation. When a child is ailing, the set keeps him or her company in the sickroom. It joins lovemaking as couples cuddle up together and watch the screen. Some people place a TV set in the bathroom: it is relaxing to lie in the warm bathwater, letting muscle tension drain away, half-watching the familiar images on the screen, half-listening to the familiar sounds.

The standardized format of television demands divided attention: now the program, now the commercials. Viewers bestow divided attention: the set and the home, the home and the set. Even if someone watching alone should find something in the program more than mildly stirring, attention is distracted by familiar house noises as the furnace clicks on or off, an elevator groans to a stop, the dog whines fitfully in his sleep, the logs in the fireplace crackle and snap. And then the commercial comes along, the watcher turns away, gets a beverage from the refrigerator, a sandwich and returns, refreshed and relaxed, to the sounds and the images appearing on the screen.

Reciprocal inhibition is a technical term describing this way of reacting with divided attention. It is often deliberately taught in psychological laboratories and consulting rooms as a technique for bringing about systematic desensitization. It can be done with electric shock; it can be done with images. The procedure using images and fantasy materials to extinguish emotions and excise feelings is called imaginal desensitization. The steps that "cure" strong feelings through imaginal desensitization are these:

1. The person (called a "subject") views familiar images in a comfortable, nonthreatening, reassuring situation. No emotional arousal is noted.

2. Certain images known to arouse subject's emotional reactions are introduced. With arousal, relaxation ceases.

3. Viewing is interrupted, viewer turns away.

4. A respite period of 30 to 60 seconds is introduced during which the scene shifts. Subject resumes relaxation, often helped by eating or drinking something.

5. As emotions subside, viewing of the same familiar images is resumed.

6. The cycle is repeated.

Imaginal desensitization is effective in whittling away at emotions until a person can remain relaxed, undisturbed and unmoved even while watching scenes that had originally raised gravest concern, acutest distress or most painful anxiety. Those who practice the technique claim that the resultant emotionless state becomes generalized so that when a person trained in imaginal desensitization comes upon scenes in real life that are the same or similar to those seen over and over again as imaginary dramas, he or she can even then continue to remain detached and unmoved by them.

In the desensitization laboratory, as in home viewing, the atmosphere is pleasant, familiar, unthreatening, predictable, legitimate. There is no room here for passion and emotion, no room for panic, disgust, revulsion, horror. Desensitization sessions discourage such intense feelings in favor of the nice sensations that go with relaxation, unguarded acceptance, comfort and reassurance. Desensitization sessions chase away even quieter emotions: no room here for dislike, not even for mild rejection. As soon as any disturbing emotion begins to be felt, viewing is interrupted to allow relaxation and placidity to take over. The pacing of the session, the security of the situation and predictability of events enable the viewer to hold back strong feelings. The more placid feelings then have a chance to move in and attach themselves to the very images and symbols that formerly called forth such intense emotions.

The technical term for this process is positive reinforcement. Through desensitization and positive reinforcement, the viewer learns the new associations and unlearns the old—a systematic mode of emotional education and reeducation.

Dramatizations are effective aides to emotional reeducation: psychodrama, sociodrama, role taking, role reversals. They provide opportunities for rehearsal and repetition, allowing new associations to entrench themselves more securely as old ones are shed. They are effective not only for those who take the roles, but also for those who look on. The social reinforcement brought about by group sharing validates the legitimacy of accepting the new associations. Such emotional reeducation in socially shared situations, particularly with dramatic aids, is called consciousness raising.

Systematic imaginal desensitization chips away at feelings and emotions people's pasts have taught them

Who Runs the Show?

Like national parks, offshore oil and other public patrimonies, the airwaves belong to the people of the United States. This public entrusts their use to station owners and managers who agree to transmit over them only materials that serve "the public interest, convenience and necessity." The agreement is binding on station licensees; networks are affected only indirectly in their role as owners and operators (each owns five TV stations). Station licenses are renewable every three years and may be withdrawn for cause.

The Federal Communications Commission (FCC) is the government agency Congress established in 1934 when the Communications Act was passed. The act as amended still states the rules franchise holders are legally bound to adhere to. The seven commissioners of the FCC are supposed to keep broadcasters honest by making certain they meet their statutory obligations, including the one about "the public interest, convenience and necessity." With very rare exceptions, the FCC has consistently withheld judgment on whether any program content or format or programming practice affects the public interest, convenience and necessity either positively or negatively. Not once has a television station's license to broadcast been withdrawn on these grounds, or renewal been denied. Nor has the FCC ever ruled on whether an industry organized around the studied manipulation of attention for the sake of selling it to advertisers well serves the public interest.

The principal restrictions on the content or duration of any materials going over the air are those that broadcasters voluntarily agree to impose on themselves. The notable exception to this is a congressional statute that bans advertisement of certain carcinogens over the public airwaves.

The broadcasting industry's own trade and lobbying association is the National Association of Broadcasters. This association has set up a Code Authority that NAB members are invited to join. Those who do, solemnly pledge to abide by certain rules, among them to limit the amount of time dedicated to commercials.

Assuming compliance with this code, stations that volunteer to take the pledge (about two-thirds of the membership) fill 26.6 percent of daytime broadcast hours with extraneous interruptions, 20 percent of afterschool hours and 15.8 percent of Saturday morning and primetime evening hours. A station on the air from six in the morning till two the following morning (at least 70 percent of all commercial stations are in this category) would fill, at that rate, about five hours a day with such extraneous materials. This estimate does not include time devoted to eulogies and closeup shots of products embedded in shows as if they were merely part of the fun.

Commercial stations account for all except perhaps 15 percent of broadcast hours. Most of them are linked to one of three major broadcasting systems: the American Broadcasting Companies, CBS Inc. and the National Broadcasting Company (ABC, CBS and NBC). These corporations own and operate all affiliated stations in New York, Los Angeles and Chicago. They own and operate additional affiliates in six other important metropolitan areas: ABC in San Francisco and Detroit, CBS in Philadelphia and St. Louis and NBC in Cleveland and Washington, D.C. Through their owned and operated stations alone they gain access to 33 percent of the nation's television homes. Coast-to-coast affiliates that, in effect, rent their facilities to these networks some 12 hours a day, guarantee them further direct and simultaneous access to the rest of the nation's television homes. Each network owns and operates seven AM and seven FM radio stations and also provides network feeds to coast-to-coast radio affiliates, as well.

(continued on the following page)

All three networks are engaged in other enterprises that are not, strictly speaking, in the broadcasting business but are intimately linked with it. NBC is owned by the RCA Corporation, one of the 20 largest, most powerful companies in the world. It is a leader in global communications, color television receivers, consumer electronics and defense electronics. RCA's consumer electronic division makes color and black-and-white TV sets, records and stereo tapes. In the electronic components field, RCA manufactures color TV picture tubes, discrete semiconductors, integrated circuits, and broadcasting and communications equipment. A wide variety of electronic equipment and systems is made for military and space programs under federal contracts. RCA's Global Communications Division is an international communications common carrier operating system of satellite, cable and radio channels. Its Alaskan and American units are important operations.

RCA owns and operates the world's leading vehicle-renting and leasing corporation, Hertz. Its publishing interests include Random House and all its subsidiaries. Its food interests include Banquet Foods (frozen and prepared items) and Oriel Foods (food distribution). It owns a carpet company, Coronet Industries, and until recently, a computer business. RCA has begun to produce, distribute and promote video games, and as of September 1977 it will market a home video cassette recorder-player.

CBS Inc. (formerly the Columbia Broadcasting System) is also engaged in consumer activities, publishing, record and music businesses. The CBS Records group consists of the company's domestic and foreign recording industry operations. Columbia House is responsible for the Columbia record and tape clubs and produces handcraft kits, hobby craft tools (Exacto) and other craft products. The musical instruments division manufactures and markets musical instruments and accessories, including Steinway pianos and Fender guitars and amplifiers, among others. The retail stores division sells stereo components and phonograph records and tapes through retail outlets. The toys division includes Wonder Products and Creative Playthings, manufacturing and retail outlets. CBS publishing interests include the publishing company of Holt, Rinehart and Winston and its subsidiaries, and BFA Educational Media (audiovisual and print materials for elementary and high school markets). It also owns Fawcett Publications, Inc., which publishes *Woman's Day, Mechanix Illustrated*, more than 30 special-interest magazines and Crest and Gold Medal paperback books. CBS also owns the Popular Library line of mass-market paperbacks. W.B. Saunders, publisher of books in health and sciences, is owned by CBS, along with five proprietary schools catering to students preparing for paramedical careers.

ABC (formerly American Broadcasting-Paramount Theaters) has maintained its interest in motion picture enterprises, operating about 100 movie screens in theaters and drive-ins throughout the country. ABC is engaged in producing and distributing phonograph records; ABC Records, its wholly owned subsidiary, produces records under several dozen different labels. ABC's publishing division includes W. Schwann, Inc., *High Fidelity, Modern Photography* and numerous satellite publications, besides farm journals, specialty magazines and religious works. ABC also owns the Wallace-Homestead Book Publishing Company. Other enterprises include theme parks and scenic attractions, such as the Historic Towne of Smithville near Atlantic City, Silver Springs and Weeki Wachee Spring, near Ocala and Tampa, Florida. Having moved ahead of the other two networks in TV popularity for the first time in its history in 1977, the corporation is considering further acquisitions with the accompanying increase in revenues.

to attach to images, symbols, relationships, events. Repeated and routinized reinforcement shows them, as old emotional ties are extinguished, how to reattach their feelings to new ones. Consciousness is raised through rehearsal in imagination of dramatic role-playing socially shared. In the clinical situation, these procedures are called behavior modification. The parallel to the broadcast materials TV brings into the home and the circumstances under which people admit them is exact.

Therapists engaged in behavior modification claim that it takes between 10 and 30 sessions to wipe out even the most deeply rooted associations. They claim that imaginal desensitization breaks associative links as strong as those binding alcoholics to alcohol and homosexuals to same-sex partners. They claim rates of cure that exceed those reported for psychoanalysis, depth psychology, hypnosis, many group techniques and procedures of psychological counseling. The cure rates reported for imaginal desensitization accompanied by consciousness raising are even more impressive, since, in the clinical situation, the images viewers are asked to watch have not been captured on videotape or preserved on film. They are not projected on a screen or viewed on a television monitor. The images viewed in imaginal desensitization sessions are those a person conjures up in his own imagination: they exist nowhere except in the mind's eye.

Suppose these subjects had been viewing real dramatic productions, skillfully mounted, enacted by experienced actors and actresses delivering clever dialog, aided by elaborate sound effects and carefully orchestrated mood music. Would they have unlearned their deeply rooted emotional associations even more quickly? Would they have learned to reattach them elsewhere and then would that "deconditioning" and "reconditioning" have engaged even deeper levels of their personalities? Would the result have been even more lasting? And what if they had spent their formative years viewing those scenes, not just 10 to 30 relatively brief sessions in a consulting room?

The answers to these questions are evident to any student of culture, even the rankest amateur. Procedures and practices that modern behavior therapists and patients carry out in treatment sessions are private versions of those all cultures carry out publicly, particularly in socially shared spectacles. Such events are not designed deliberately to "cure" this or that individual's painful feelings and replace them with pleasanter ones; yet they do something essentially similar for the social group as a whole. Since human feelings have a certain promiscuous quality—they can attach themselves to virtually anything—every culture must cultivate the feelings of its own members, routing them frequently and periodically so that most people will be likely to make and maintain the proper associations. Public spectacles signal to all which feelings are appropriate and which are inappropriate under given conditions—however the particular group defines "appropriate" and "inappropriate." Repetition and social sharing validate the definitions.

It is an ancient insight, not just a newly discovered principle of contemporary psychology, that access to human feelings is through human imaginations. Myth and story, drama and art, music and poetry, play and games and dance and ritual all touch imaginations and form imaginations—the very terrain in which human minds develop. Socrates warned that stories shape the minds of children. Martin Heidegger, a contemporary philosopher, asks, "What is called thinking?" and answers, thinking is metaphor, minds are made by poesy. *Mind: An Essay on Human Feeling* is the title of Susanne K. Langer's seminal work on the nature of human thought. At the beginning of the 18th century, essayist Andrew Fletcher saw the potential political power residing in control of symbols that capture imaginations through song and story. "If a man were permitted to make all the ballads," wrote Fletcher, "he need not care who should make the laws of a nation."

Those who are unwilling to pay attention to history or acknowledge any wisdom in the collective conscience can turn to literally tons of contemporary research reports in the social sciences that document how easy it is to get people to attach, detach and reattach their feelings and emotions as a consequence of the associations that dramatizations, films and even still photographs and passing discourse have released in the imagination. It's especially easy to channel the emotions of children this way, and they can be cured even of their terrors after watching the briefest dramatizations.

Some of this research is kept under lock and key, available only to those who have hired researchers to conduct the investigations on behalf of their companies, products and ideologies. Much of it, however, is available in professional journals serving the subfield of public opinion, spun off by the academic disciplines of sociology and psychology, then picked up by students of political science, child development, education, journalism, communications and so on. To trace the intellectual origins of this kind of scholarship would lead us far back into time. A list of those who have written the classic works of the present century and have set its particular style would include Walter Lippmann and Harold D. Lasswell, along with Harwood L. Childs, Carl I. Hovland, Robert K. Merton, Paul F. Lazarsfeld and Samuel A. Stouffer.

The power to dominate a culture's symbol-producing apparatus is the power to create the ambience that forms human consciousness. It is a power we see exercised daily by the television business as its airborne midway penetrates virtually every home with the most massive continuing spectacle on record. Wittingly and unwittingly this business and its client industries set the stage for a never-ending performance stripping away emotional associations that centuries of cultural experience have linked to patterns of behavior, institutional forms, attitudes and values that many cultures and subcultures revere and need to keep vigorous if they are to survive. The daily consciousness-raising sessions transmitted by television demonstrate incessantly the narrow range of alternatives selected by a handful of people as eminently worthy of attention and collective celebration. The scale is so vast, the images and sounds so insistent, the support system so interpenetrating, that few families can pit their own authority against the authority of the show-and-tell machine. They are drowned out by this emissary in every home of powerful communications empires that span the globe.

The unanticipated outcome is that the United States enjoys the dubious distinction of having allowed the television business to score a first in human history: the first undertaking in mass behavior modification by coast-to-coast and intercontinental electronic hookup.

THE PROMISE OF
BIOLOGICAL PSYCHIATRY

PAUL H. WENDER
AND DONALD F. KLEIN

Paul H. Wender is professor of psychiatry at the University of Utah College of Medicine. His research interests include the origins of schizophrenia, genetics and behavior, and minimal brain dysfunction in children and adults. A former president of the Psychiatric Research Society, Wender serves as a consultant to five journals, among them *Psychiatry* and *Psychiatry Research*. His work on the adoption studies, involving Danish and American adults, earned him a first prize for research from the American Psychiatric Association in 1974.

Donald F. Klein is professor of psychiatry at the Columbia University College of Physicians and Surgeons. Although he has a small consulting practice, Klein essentially works full time in research and research administration. He is director of research at the New York State Psychiatric Institute, an attending psychiatrist at Presbyterian Hospital in New York, and president-elect of the American College of Neuropsychopharmacology. Among the many other positions he has held are chairman of the Clinical Psychopharmocology Review Group of the National Institute of Mental Health (NIMH) and president of the American Psychopathological Association. The article by Klein and Wender is published by Farrar, Straus, & Giroux: *Mind, Mood, and Medicine: A Guide to the New Biological Psychiatry.*

In facing the puzzle of mental illness, psychiatric savants of the first half of the twentieth century believed that Freudian theory would provide the answers. However, in the second half of the century, scientific research has uncovered evidence that biological malfunctions are central to mental illness and that much of the by now entrenched psychodynamic theory is irrelevant or even misleading. Ironically, the biological discoveries might have pleased Freud, who repeatedly emphasized the constitutional predispositions that many of his intellectual descendants forgot.

We now know that even some disorders believed to be "neurotic" are biologically based—and that drugs offer the closest thing to a long-term cure. For example, some patients who suffer from agoraphobia—panic attacks—have found that their symptoms have not been cured by lengthy psychoanalysis or behavior therapy but may virtually disappear after they take a new medication. In addition, a form of biological depression that we call "vital depression" is frequently misdiagnosed as having a purely psychological basis—sometimes tragically so, since a large fraction of the 30,000 suicides a year in the United States are probably committed by people with vital depressions, which can often be controlled or reversed by medication.

The tremendous increase in pharmacological preparations capable of helping people with emotional disorders has forced us to rethink what the bases might be for those disorders. At the same time, solid information on the inheritance of emotional disorders has become available through a new methodology: the study of children whose parents suffer from those illnesses but who are raised in adoptive homes.

The public is largely unaware that different sorts of emotional illnesses are now responsive to specific medications, and, unfortunately, many doctors are similarly unaware. Many psychologists and psychiatrists acknowledge that biology may play a role in severe and uncommon forms of psychiatric illness. But the great majority seem to believe that, aside from the 1 percent or so who suffer from schizophrenia or the roughly 5 percent who have a major mood disorder such as manic-depressive illness, most are psychological in origin.

Recent studies challenge that view. For example, adoption studies have shown that for each schizophrenic, there may be 3 to 10 times as many people who have a milder form of the disorder that is genetically—and therefore biologically—related to the most severe forms of the illness. If these findings are confirmed, it would mean that somewhere between 2 and 8 percent of Americans have a lifelong form of personality disorder that is genetically produced. This finding is extremely important and not widely known.

Current data also indicate that genetic factors play a role in the major mood disorders, which may occur in as many as 15 to 20 percent of the population in their lifetime. They are also implicated in a family of disorders we call the "Unnamed Quartet," which includes some forms of alcoholism, "antisocial personality" (the current euphemism for sociopaths and psychopaths), hyperactivity in children, and a complaint among women known as Briquet's syndrome, which is often termed hysteria.

The new biological psychiatry does not simplistically deny the contributing role of psychological factors in the complaints that prompt people to seek help. It recognizes that certain forms of psychological experience may precipitate (or "cause") psychiatric disorders in those who are biologically predisposed to them. Also, some psychological problems develop as secondary effects of biologically produced illnesses and may remain even after those illnesses have been cured. Most important, a number of psychiatric disorders may occur as "phenocopies," that is, they may resemble biological mental illness but actually arise from maladaptation and mislearning—which in turn may be related to family and cultural indoctrination. To further obscure the picture, the demoralizing effects of bad marriages, urban anomie, economic deprivation, and other social disruptions are often misdiagnosed as illness.

Part of the current chaos in psychiatry comes from a failure to identify and separate the discrete biological, psychological, and reality factors that can result in human misery. This chaos leads not just to theoretical arguments but also to frequent failure to provide the correct remedy for the correct patient. We believe that the sophisticated armamentarium of drugs now available makes possible effective treatment of a wide range of symptoms that are biologically based. Further, we feel that psychiatrists, particularly the younger ones trained in universities that emphasize biological treatment, are able to diagnose those disorders. Psychologists and social workers rarely have that training.

To those who say drugs treat only symptoms and do not eliminate basic problems, we reply that the new medications seem to relieve symptoms by normalizing some deep abnormality that is closely related to underlying causes. If drugs do not necessarily provide a permanent cure, neither does psychotherapy, in most cases.

The Coming of Specific Drugs

Until the 1940s, there were no specific psychiatric drugs. Bromides, barbiturates, and opiates were known to sedate disturbed patients but did not reverse the symptoms of severe mental illnesses such as the schizophrenias or manic-depressive psychoses. They did ameliorate anxiety, but only at the cost of fogging the minds of the recipients, who had to decide between being unhappy and being intoxicated. In the 1950s, the first specific drug appeared: chlorpromazine (trade name Thorazine). It was synthesized when an antihistamine chemical relative was found to sedate surgical patients. However, clinical observations showed that this drug did much more than simply calm certain schizophrenic patients; it removed their peculiar disorganizing symptoms.

Coauthor Donald Klein recalls the stunning impact of the discovery on clinical work in the early 1950s. Klein was in charge of a ward of psychotic World War I veterans who had been hospitalized for more than 30 years, had not responded to a wide variety of therapies, and, for the most part, sat quietly, staring blankly at walls. After receiving a supply of chlorpromazine for experimental use, Klein and his colleagues timidly placed some of the patients on extremely small doses, with little expectation of change. Some weeks later one of them came up to Klein and said, "Doc, when am I getting out of here?" The man did not know where he was or what had happened during the past 30 years; a modern Rip Van Winkle, he knew nothing of the Great Depression, World War II, the atomic bomb, or jet travel. Shortly thereafter, another patient showed the same awakening. The patients' outlook had changed unbelievably, and so had Klein's.

Large-scale, controlled studies rapidly confirmed the beneficial effects of Thorazine and other chemically related antipsychotic drugs such as Stelazine and Prolixin. These studies differed entirely from what had been called research in most previous psychiatric and psychological investigations. In this new approach, patients were studied who met specific diagnostic criteria; they were randomly treated either with active medicine or an inactive placebo. Further, neither patient nor physician knew what the patient was receiving, so that the effects of biases and expectancies would be greatly reduced. The double-blind technique employed is now standard operating procedure in medicine, but was not in the 1950s.

Chlorpromazine not only worked dramatically but its effect was also scientifically demonstrable in the experiments. Its discovery played a major role in the release of thousands of chronic mental patients across the country. (The desirability of that policy is now being reconsidered. Thirty years of experience with these drugs have documented both their efficacy and their limitations. Many patients do not respond completely to them and still require extensive social support, although their hallucinations and delusions are under control.)

The development of the antipsychotic agents was paralleled by the discovery of the usefulness of lithium in mania and the two families of antidepressants—the tricyclic and monoamine oxidase inhibitors—which alleviated the symptoms of the most severely depressed patients. The drugs are best known under the trade names Elavil, Tofranil, and Nardil.

Both the antidepressants and the antipsychotics could, in many instances, completely reverse a patient's symptoms. And, unlike the better known minor tranquilizers, such as Valium and Librium, they produced no pleasant psychological effect in a normal person (but may be experienced as noxious). Most important, they were not addicting. Although the antipsychotic and antidepressant drugs were first used in treating major psychiatric illnesses, they have more recently proved beneficial in dealing with less devastating but still handicapping symptoms—for example, agoraphobia.

Take the case of a woman we'll call Mary J., a 23-year-old unmarried buyer for a department store who was stricken by a series of panic attacks. She would suddenly be overcome by dizziness, a pounding heart, and an inability to catch her breath while walking down the street or riding on public transportation. Several specialists could not detect any physical reason for the attacks. The vague diagnosis was usually "nerves" or "a virus." The prescription: Valium and rest.

As the panics continued, bringing with them daily chronic anticipatory anxiety, Mary J. abandoned subways and buses in favor of taxis, and sat in the back at the theater or at church, primed for a quick escape. After spending more and more time simply staying at home with her parents, finally giving up her job, she decided to seek a psychoanalyst.

On the analyst's couch, Mary J. free-associated and recounted her dreams. Eventually, she began to suspect that the panics might be related to a love affair. Six weeks before the attacks started, she had been quite upset: her lover had moved to another city. The analyst closed in on that possibility with penetrating questions. Had her sexual adjustment been guilt-free after she had begun the affair? Didn't her fear of being out on the street reflect her unconscious doubts about her sexual self-control—that is, her fear of identification as a streetwalker? Didn't her clinging dependence on her family show her fear of adulthood and her unconscious desire to substitute her father for other men?

For four years Mary J. reworked such baroque structures while her illness waxed and waned. The panic-free months restored her confidence but were invariably followed by relapses. The analyst interpreted the relapses as resistance—a flight from insight into primitive impulses.

Ultimately, depletion of the family's financial resources, combined with growing disillusionment, encouraged her to switch to a new, short, inexpensive form of treatment: behavior therapy. The patient engaged in relaxation exercises and visits to public places that were designed to "desensitize" her to the fearful stimuli gradually. For a while she exper-

DRUGS VERSUS PSYCHOTHERAPY: THE PAYOFF MATRIX

Medication is the best treatment for some psychiatric illnesses. But how can sufferers know whether or not they have one of those illnesses?

Correct diagnosis is obviously essential for anyone seeking help. In general, a patient is more likely to receive a correct diagnosis and recommendation for treatment from a physician—a psychiatrist—than from a psychologist or social worker. We say *more likely* because many psychiatrists have not been sufficiently trained in either systematic diagnosis or biological psychiatry; they may regard drugs as applicable only to the most seriously disturbed patients. A clinic that offers diagnostic screening by psychiatrists and a staff that includes psychologists and social workers is often in a good position to prescribe sound alternative treatments.

The best clinics are affiliated with departments of psychiatry at schools of medicine, which will provide referrals. A research clinic is often the best place to contact expert psychopharmacologists. Two examples are the Depression and Anxiety Evaluation Service of the Columbia University Department of Psychiatry (under the supervision of Donald Klein) and the Mood Disorder Clinic in Salt Lake City (directed by Paul Wender).

Because of the variety of possible diagnoses and treatments, a patient should attempt the difficult task of questioning a physician about his or her approach to therapy. The patient should explore the psychiatrist's theoretical background, therapeutic plan, and manner of conducting the treatment and evaluating the results. Once in therapy, the response to treatment provides a partial clue to the correctness of the diagnosis. Rapid amelioration of a long-standing condition after taking drugs would seem to confirm both the diagnosis and the benefits of the medication. However, there is a certain amount of trial and error in drug prescription, and it is not unusual for patients to respond to the second or third medication prescribed rather than to the first.

Failure to respond to all known biological treatments does not necessarily mean that the patient's problems are strictly psychological. It may simply mean that useful biological treatments have yet to be developed for his or her symptoms.

Analogously, failure to respond to psychotherapy does not necessarily mean that one's problems are biological, since the failure may stem from differences in people's ability to change entrenched ways, or possibly, from a mismatch between patient and treatment (or patient and therapist).

Should drug treatment or psychotherapy be tried first? That sort of question has been often discussed in game theory; it involves what is called the "payoff matrix," which evaluates the advantages and disadvantages of four possible options:

1. The patient has a biological illness and receives only drug treatment.
2. The patient has a biological illness and receives only psychotherapy.
3. The patient does not have a biological illness and receives only drug treatment.
4. The patient does not have a biological illness and receives only psychotherapy.

What are the relative costs in time, money, and personal hazards? Drug treatment is specific, not time-consuming, and cheap; it can be evaluated in four to six weeks.

If the patient has a biological illness and is treated with drugs (option 1), he receives the optimal treatment. If he does not have a biological illness and is treated only with drugs (option 3), he will receive an inappropriate treatment, but that will be determined cheaply and fairly rapidly. If he has a biological illness and receives only psychotherapy (option 2), he may waste considerable time and money. If he does not have a biological illness, psychotherapy will be an appropriate treatment (option 4).

Another major question concerns patients in category three, who do not have a biological illness but receive drug treatment. Treatment with the major psychiatric drugs is not entirely safe, but it is safer than treatment with many commonly used agents, such as penicillin. All drugs produce side effects—occasionally, fatal ones. The risks of the major psychiatric drugs used in therapeutic amounts with the recommended precautions are low, probably much lower than the risk of anesthesia in routine surgery.

—P. H. W. & D. F. K.

ienced relief, but her progress ended abruptly with a chain of panic attacks in quick succession.

Mary J. and her parents were thrown into despair, seeing nothing ahead but a grim invalidism. However, a year later she was living alone in an apartment in the city, working at her old job, and looking forward to possible marriage. She had volunteered to take part in an experiment in control of phobias that required her to take an antidepressant medication. The drug blocked her panic attacks. Supportive psychotherapy helped her to control her anticipatory anxiety and allowed her to resume normal activities. Mary J. stopped taking the medication after six months, and her phobic symptoms have not returned. Strikingly, controlled studies show that antidepressants are regularly effective in illnesses like hers.

The Right Drug for the Right Patient

By the first decade of this century, psychiatrists had described two major families of psychiatric illness: the disorders of mood and the schizophrenias. They had also hinted at the existence of a third group, the "psychopathies."

The mood disorders include a loose collection of depressed emotional states (sadness, demoralization, grief) and exaggerated euphoria or mania. Depression, the most common mental disorder, may arise from biological malfunction, realistic losses, or maladaptation. How can vital depression be distinguished from the other kinds?

To us, there are two central features: a particular abnormal mood and certain physiological changes. Vital depressives exhibit a marked loss of interest in life—an overall inability to experience pleasure which has been described as "painful anesthesia." Many will deny they are depressed, and, since the word is ordinarily used to mean sad or in a state of grief, they are correct. In addition, vital depressions are accompanied by alterations in physiological functioning, including a kind of insomnia, energy changes during the day, fatigue, inability to concentrate, decreased appetite, and loss of sexual interest.

For instance, Harry M., a lawyer in his 50s, had been in group and individ-

ual therapy for two years because of increasingly severe depression and thoughts of suicide. Despite professional success, a satisfying marriage, and well-adjusted children, he had little self-esteem and thought himself a failure. Unlike his brothers, he was an inept athlete and socially uneasy, although, like his mother, he displayed considerable aptitude as an artist. His father had singled him out for particularly low regard. The group members had pointed out his distorted self-perception and its relation to his family experience, but he had not improved.

Unfortunately, either because of or in spite of his therapy, Harry M.'s depression increased. In the past year, he had begun to awaken at 3 or 4 A.M., tossing sleeplessly until the alarm rang. Both at work and at home he had become fearful, irascible, and suicidally preoccupied. His sex drive had vanished, he had lost weight, and he no longer enjoyed painting.

After reluctantly agreeing to a trial of antidepressant medication, Harry M. found that within a few days his sleep patterns had returned to normal. As the dosage was increased, his appetite and his interest in sex returned. In three or four weeks' time, his major complaints disappeared. He no longer thought of suicide; he enjoyed his family, his work, and painting.

Most surprisingly, with the continuation of medication his lifelong low self-esteem began to disappear. Without becoming either manic or even high, he enjoyed a psychological well-being he had never before experienced. When the medication was stopped after nine months, his depressive symptoms did not immediately return, but gradually his feelings of self-esteem and well-being disappeared. It was apparent to both his psychiatrist and Harry M. that his serious illness, his chronically depressed mood, his lifelong chronic feelings of low self-esteem had biological origins, and he began to take medication on a maintenance basis. Intermittent attempts to discontinue the medication resulted in a return to the premedicated state. Although it had been possible to explain his low self-esteem and social discomfort psychologically, the response of both to medication indicated they were manifestations of a biological abnormality.

Unlike Harry's case, other depres-

sions, often misleadingly called neurotic depressions, usually occur in the context of distressing life events or chronic maladaptation and do not seem to be associated with any physiological alteration. Nor do they respond to the usual antidepressant medication or electroconvulsive treatment.

Two additional examples of disturbances that are biologically based are known as emotionally unstable character disorder and hysteroid dysphoria. The first, common in adolescence, consists of short periods of tense, empty, self-isolating unhappiness alternating with periods of impulsiveness, low frustration tolerance, rejection of rules, and demand for immediate gratification. Lithium has had a suitable stabilizing effect on such rapid mood oscillations. Hysteroid dysphoria, found most often in women, is characterized by histrionic, applause-seeking behavior and repetitive, sudden, severe depressions in response to rejection, especially in romantic situations. There is developing evidence that one class of antidepressant has a stabilizing effect on this disorder.

The group of disorders we refer to as the Unnamed Quartet often show up in members of the same family. Researchers, particularly at Washington University in St. Louis, have documented the tendency of certain psychiatric disorders to run in families. They have determined that close relatives of hyperactive children, some kinds of alcoholics, people with antisocial personalities, and women with Briquet's syndrome are more likely than average to have the same disorder or one of the other three disorders in the Quartet. (Women with Briquet's syndrome suffer recurrent and perplexing pains and other symptoms, which occur from head to toe, involve multiple organ systems, and usually instigate much unsuccessful medical intervention.)

For example, studies of the relatives of incarcerated women with antisocial personalities reveal an increased frequency of alcoholism and antisocial personality among their brothers and fathers, and of Briquet's syndrome among their mothers. Obviously, such familial association could be the product of either heredity or environment. Such studies cannot discriminate between those cases. However, the adoption studies can.

The effectiveness of medication in childhood hyperactivity is well known—although, by ignoring systematic observations, some dispute the existence of this disorder or claim that it is the product of healthy children rebelling against repressive schools. The adoption studies support the hypothesis that some forms of the disorder are genetic. Controlled trials of drugs such as the amphetamines and methylphenidate (Ritalin) have shown that these medications produce substantial benefit; they not only calm patients but enable them to focus their attention as well.

It is fairly evident that most psychotherapeutic techniques are of exceedingly little value in treatment of Briquet's syndrome, alcoholism, and antisocial personality. And there is only sketchy evidence that medication may be useful in some forms of these problems—perhaps in adult "hyperactivity." This is unfortunate because the social costs of alcoholism and antisocial personality are immense.

The remaining major category of biologically produced mental disorders is that of the schizophrenias. They include disturbances that most people associate with the terms "mad" and "insane," which at times involve hallucinations and delusions, disorganized thought, peculiar movements, flat or inappropriate emotional responses, and withdrawal into unreality. The acute forms, which may be biologically different from the chronic form, occur in people who previously were relatively healthy and are often triggered by loss or disappointment. Chronic schizophrenia often occurs in people who are deviant as children—socially inept, isolated, withdrawn, or rebellious. Among the relatives of patients with schizophrenia, a high proportion show a spectrum of odd characteristics that are not always labeled as mental illness but seem to be muted forms of schizophrenic symptoms, variously called schizoid, borderline schizophrenic, and "schizotypal." These people can be extremely shy and unsociable, cold and distant, sensitive and poetic, or militant and fanatic. Many are often misidentified as neurotic.

That genetic factors play an important role in the causation of the schizophrenias and the borderline schizophrenias is shown by the adoption studies. That there are actual neurological changes in schizophrenia is not as well known. One study of preadolescent children who were the offspring of schizophrenics showed that approximately half (the number expected to develop schizophrenia or borderline schizophrenia) had neurological signs, such as changed reflexes, that disappeared with age. Follow-up studies will show whether these neurologically impaired children become the psychiatrically impaired ones.

More direct evidence is provided by recent X-ray studies of the brain with the CAT scanner, which enables radiologists to visualize the exact size and location of the normally occurring ventricles (fluid-filled portions) of the brain. Studies of schizophrenics have shown that a substantial proportion of them have enlarged ventricles, a typical sign of neurological disease; the more severe their brain changes are, the greater the degree of social isolation they suffer prior to the onset of the manifest illness, and the less they respond to antipsychotic medication. These findings imply that brain changes may antedate the psychosis. Further, the irreversibility of some schizophrenic illness may be due to brain damage.

The Adoption Studies

In each of the types of psychiatric disorder, the same or similar disorders occur with increased frequency among blood relatives. Further, the closer the relationship, the more probable it is that the relative will have the same illness. This is hardly absolute proof that the disorders are inherited. Many psychiatrists argue that the disorder is psychological and might be spread by "contagion" or by exposure of a child to a pathological parent.

Biological psychiatrists attempted to deal with this objection by studying identical and fraternal twins. Identical (monozygotic) twins, who come from a single egg cell, are believed to possess exactly the same genes and to be carbon copies of each other, while fraternal (dizygotic) twins are no more closely related genetically than any pair of siblings. Genetic researchers

hypothesized that if schizophrenia were entirely genetic, monozygotic twins should be "concordant" in all instances: that is, if one twin were schizophrenic, the other should be, too—100 percent of the time. Among dizygotic twins, the probability of one being schizophrenic when the other was should be no greater than the probability for two siblings: 5 percent to 10 percent.

Twin research showed that in monozygotic pairs, if one twin had schizophrenia, then the other twin was concordant (that is, had either schizophrenia or a schizoid personality) in about 40 percent to 80 percent of instances. The psychologically oriented psychiatrists regarded that as strong evidence for the role of psychological factors in producing schizophrenia. Since all pairs were not concordant, they reasoned that environment must have a role in determining whether a person with a predisposition to the disease will, in fact, develop it. Actually, all the research did was teach us something about twinning.

That not all monozygotic twins develop schizophrenia is a puzzling genetic phenomenon, but not an entirely unfamiliar one. Similar percentages of twins with congenital medical difficulties like hair lip and juvenile diabetes are not concordant for such abnormalities.

In the mid-1960s, a new strategy for resolving the nature/nurture issue was invented: adoption studies. Adoption makes it possible to separate the effects of nature and nurture because it separates the influence of biological parents (who provide the genes) from the influence of the adopting parents (who provide the psychological environment). The notion of studying children of psychiatrically disturbed parents who are brought up by others occurred almost simultaneously to Leonard Heston in Oregon and to Seymour Kety, David Rosenthal, and Paul Wender at the National Institute of Mental Health.

In a series of studies, Heston, Kety, Wender, and Rosenthal studied the psychiatric status of American and Danish adults born of schizophrenic parents but adopted in infancy. They were compared with adults whose biological parents were not known to be schizophrenic and who had been adopted at an early age by parents in ostensibly good psychological health. Each patient was examined by a psychiatrist who knew nothing of family background. An analysis of the diagnoses showed that adopted children born of schizophrenic parents and reared from infancy by nonschizophrenic adoptive parents are more likely to be schizophrenic than are children of the same age and sex born to and reared by nonschizophrenics. In general, 10 percent to 20 percent of the children of schizophrenics who were raised by adoptive parents developed schizophrenia or borderline schizophrenia. (If both parents were schizophrenic the figure was closer to 45 percent). Significantly fewer of the adopted children of nonschizophrenics did so. Clearly, *some* forms of schizophrenia have a genetic component.

The adoption studies also found that children of schizophrenics who were reared by their ill parents did not show a greater rate of illness than children of schizophrenics reared by normal parents. Finally, children born to normal parents and placed by a regrettable (but scientifically fortunate) error of an adoption agency with schizophrenic parents did not show a greater rate of schizophrenia than adopted dren born to and raised by normal parents. Thus the idea of a phenocopy for schizophrenia that is caused by one's upbringing was challenged by this research.

The adoption data, here greatly condensed, are so striking that they make some of the recent popular antipsychiatry viewpoints seem absurd. For example, it is difficult to see how Thomas Szasz can include schizophrenia as an example of his "myth of mental illness" when the myth has a genetic component. Further, R. D. Laing's position—that psychosis is the response to destructive family conditions—can be true only if we conclude that psychosis is the response of normal people to destructive family conditions to which they have never been exposed.

The success of the adoption technique in separating nature and nurture in schizophrenia rapidly led to its use with other categories of psychiatric illness. Research into the inheritance patterns of vital depression is in an early stage, but a recent study completed in Belgium showed that the biological parents of adopted children with the manic-depressive form of mood disorder had a greater frequency of the same illness than did the biological parents of normal adopted children. (The adopting parents of manic-depressive children had no more mood difficulties than the adopting parents of normal children.) This somewhat different adoption strategy also showed the operation of heredity.

Among the Unnamed Quartet, all except Briquet's syndrome have been investigated in adoption studies. These studies strongly suggest that the three other sets of symptoms in the group have a genetic component. For example, in one study, the rate of alcoholism was four times as great among adopted children whose biological fathers were alcoholic as among those whose biological fathers were not.

Lastly, the adoption technique has been applied to criminality. Obviously, "criminality" itself cannot be genetic. What *may* be genetic are certain characteristics—such as impulsivity, egocentricity, and lack of empathy—which may predispose an individual to criminal behavior. These personality characteristics are frequently found among so-called antisocial personalities.

Investigators in Denmark and Sweden employed the adoption strategy to investigate the possible contribution of genetic factors to criminality. In one study, they found that adopted children whose biological fathers had committed a criminal offense roughly comparable to a U.S. felony were more likely to exhibit criminal behavior than adopted children whose fathers had no criminal record; that tendency was further amplified if the adoptive father had a criminal record. This last finding indicates the dovetailing of biological and psychosocial factors. In another study, the operation of genetic factors in criminality was not evident except when the biological parents were alcoholic as well as criminal. We are not arguing that criminality is solely biological, but rather that in some criminals biological components may play a role.

Thus the adoption studies have documented the presence of genetic factors in all three major categories of psychiatric illness. They have also demonstrated that the minor forms of these disorders are often genetically related to the severe forms.

The Emerging Biology of the Mind

Of prime importance for some theories of biological psychiatry are recent discoveries that help to explain how nerve impulses may be transmitted in the brain. When one of the 10 trillion brain cells that govern sensing, thinking, moving, and feeling is stimulated, an electrical impulse travels along a cell extension called an axone, releasing a small packet of chemicals known as neurotransmitters, which either stimulate or inhibit the cells they contact. Because certain transmitters occur in specific parts of the brain, malfunctions of those brain areas might be related to underactivity or overactivity of particular systems of neurotransmitters. Presumably, faulty transmission of many kinds could, by increasing or decreasing the activity of specific portions of the brain, be implicated in mental illness. The antipsychotic and antidepressant drugs may very well operate by influencing particular neurotransmitters.

The evidence is in bits and pieces that must be put together like a jigsaw puzzle. Contradictory results require frequent revisions of tentative theories, but the skeletal structure is highly persuasive—especially in the areas of depression and psychosis. In vital depression, evidence from a variety of sources indicates that a decreased effect of particular neurotransmitters (the biogenic amines) may produce depression, while an excessive effect may produce an excited or manic state. These data coalesce with earlier discoveries that animals receiving electrical stimulation of parts of the brain that tend to contain high concentrations of biogenic amines seem to experience greater pleasure (as do a few humans whose brains have been similarly stimulated). Depleting the nerve cells of biogenic amines decreases the responses of the animals to such stimulation.

Further hints that chemical processes may be at work in the schizophrenias come from the disorder known as amphetamine psychosis—a chronic overdose disturbance in "speed freaks," which so closely resembles paranoid schizophrenia that urine tests are necessary to discriminate between the two. Animal research indicates that amphetamines increase activity of nerve cells that use the neurotransmitter dopamine; antipsychotic drugs interfere with the action of dopamine and block the symptoms of amphetamine psychosis.

We have alluded to but not spelled out the special features of the major psychiatric drugs. Most people's experience with licit psychoactive drugs is confined to alcohol, the barbiturates, and the minor tranquilizers. All of these drugs nonspecifically decrease arousal and anxiety at the cost of producing a certain amount of dulling (which is far less in the case of Valium and Librium than with the older sedatives). In addition, their action is similar on disturbed and nondisturbed people. Highly anxious subjects are made more calm; calm people are put to sleep.

The major psychiatric drugs are entirely different. When they are effective, they normalize a severe derangement. Antipsychotics, sometimes called "major tranquilizers," reduce the excitement seen in some schizophrenias and in manic patients, but also improve incoherence, withdrawal, and confusion, which do not seem to be the kind of symptoms that should respond to "sedation." Further, when given to normal people who are anxious because of approaching examinations or divorces, antipsychotics will produce an individual who is as anxious and unhappy as before, but who now has useless side effects. The major antidepressants may relieve the symptoms of vital depression—and some other disorders—but do not make normal people happier.

The greatest testimony to a drug's nonabusability is the total indifference with which the younger generation of "street users" regards it. They have vindicated the judgment of an elderly volunteer morphine addict to whom Klein administered a dose of Thorazine when it was first released. The man remarked: "I don't know what this crap is, Doc, but it won't sell on the street."

That the emphasis on medication in treatment of psychiatric illness is consistent with accepted practice in other branches of medicine may be best illustrated by an analogy. Heart failure often occurs after repeated episodes of coronary thrombosis in which cardiac

muscles die. As the muscle mass decreases, the heart is unable to pump vigorously enough and the kidneys are unable to rid the body of excess salt and water. As a result, fluid accumulates, requiring even greater force (which the heart cannot muster) and aggravating the "heart failure."

There are two medical approaches, which are usually combined. One prescribes chemicals that enable the kidneys to rid the body of excess salt and water, and the other prescribes drugs, such as digitalis, that allow the heart muscle to pump more forcefully. The second approach strikes closest to the "underlying cause" and remedies a defect closer to the source (which is arteriosclerosis, the closing of nutrient-carrying blood vessels). Often, the best that physicians can do is to strike the problem near its source but not eliminate it.

Those who emphasize the curative value of psychotherapy have produced no scientific evidence of cure, although improvement does seem to occur. There is much evidence that psychotherapy works by countering the demoralizing effects of being ill. From this viewpoint, it is psychotherapy that is superficial, symptomatic treatment when it is applied to an illness with a major biological component. For example, pernicious anemia is treated with injected Vitamin B-12 rather than by correction of the malabsorption problems of the gut; diabetes is treated with insulin rather than by correction of pancreatic malfunction. In both instances treatment must be given indefinitely, as is often the case in psychiatry. Medicine accepts the fact that it rarely has one-shot cures. Schizophrenics and depressives who require maintenance medication are analogous to diabetics who must reconcile themselves to a lifetime regimen of insulin treatment.

This is not to say that the major psychiatric drugs are perfect. Long-term high-dosage treatment with antipsychotics may produce a neurological syndrome that can be irreversible if the drugs are not stopped promptly. Lithium may produce frequent urination when it has been used for several months. The use of lithium for periods of up to 20 years is unassociated with serious illness from kidney disease; there are minor anatomical changes of no functional importance.

The long-term effects (more than 10 years) of the antidepressant drugs have never been systematically studied. Their probable safety over relatively long periods of time must be weighed against the very real known risk of suicide in the case of the hopeless, depressed person.

Nonbiological Causes of Unhappiness

In our own practice, we attempt to determine the relative roles played by reality, maladaptation, and mental illness in causing the patient's complaint. Reality factors can be divided into roughly five types:

☐ Catastrophe—such as death, accident, desertion—in which the psychiatrist can be of help only by offering support or by assisting the patient in gaining perspective on the event.

☐ Interpersonal and preferential reality—such as an unsatisfying marriage or job. Frequently, patients turn to long-term psychotherapy in cases of this kind, when a more effective approach would simply be to encourage them to face reality and attempt to modify it.

☐ Developmental reality—changes associated with the life cycle, for instance, with adolescence, early marriage and parenthood, midlife crises, and old age. Here, too, patients often mistakenly turn to long-term psychotherapy when what is needed is support and perspective.

☐ Personal limitations. Sunday painters who seek world recognition or natural athletes who dutifully try to conform to parental expectations of an academic career may become chronically miserable when they cannot attain unreasonable goals. Therapy may focus on recognition and acceptance of limitations. Despite their good intentions, "growth therapies" that promise conversion of all ugly ducklings into swans can produce exacerbated pain through inevitable disappointment.

☐ Social reality—for example, the loneliness and sense of dislocation that sometimes mark the move from rural to urban environments, or the anxiety, depression, and demoralization that can accompany chronic social deprivation. Psychiatry has inherited many of these problems, but no long training or arcane theory is needed to diagnose the unhappiness that results from suburban isolation, bureaucratic stultification, or malnutrition and racial prejudice. Social reform and concrete aid are needed.

The second major psychological source of unhappiness—maladaptation—may arise from family indoctrination or the jarring aspects of the surrounding culture. In at least one respect we agree completely with Freudian theory: mislearning in the form of sexually repressive attitudes inculcated in the child can be a major source of severe unhappiness. Other kinds of familial or cultural attitudes that may produce later conflict are fierce competitiveness, exaggerated submissiveness, and fear of intimacy. Familial or cultural training can also produce maladaptation if it is incompatible with psychological temperament—a situation reminiscent of Munro Leaf's story of Ferdinand the Bull: he became desperately unhappy when he was trained to be aggressive; all he wanted to do was smell the flowers. Problems of maladaptation and mislearning sometimes respond to psychotherapy. When psychotherapy *is* effective, the advantages of any specific technique may stem from its mesh with the patient's belief system rather than from any inherent healing qualities of the technique itself.

Drug Therapy: A Blow to Human Vanity?

As the research evidence regarding the effectiveness of drug therapy has become more compelling, psychologists, social workers, and pastoral counselors have found themselves in an uncomfortable position, since their training and their professional societies have not emphasized advances in systematic diagnosis, neurochemistry, and psychopharmacology. Those psychologists, social workers, and pastoral counselors who have recognized the possible role of biological components in a great range of mental illnesses—and many of them have resisted such recognition—have had to come to terms with both their training gaps and their legal status, which prevent them from prescribing biological treatments. Inevitably, rationalization, motivated perception, and the pocketbook are likely to play a part in the ardent defense of the nonbiological position by some of the

therapists who are not physicians. An unfortunate aspect of that position is that many psychologists and social workers are not adequately trained to distinguish patients with biological disorders, although a few special training programs are beginning to try to remedy this deficiency.

But the most unfortunate aspect of the current situation is that there is enough psychotherapeutic work available for *all* therapists. Patients with biological disorders who have been successfully treated medically often need psychological treatment, and the large segment of the patient population that is unhappy because of unrealistic expectations can be optimally helped only by psychological techniques. Cooperation, not competition, would be in the patients' and therapists' best interest.

The lay public's resistance to medical treatment of psychiatric disorders comes from several directions. First, the middle and upper classes are suffering from cultural lag. Nurtured on psychoanalysis and sustained by the promises of Gestalt therapy, transactional analysis, primal scream, and other therapies, they still believe that psychotherapy is the treatment of choice and that treatment with medication is inferior.

A second source of resistance to the new information can best be understood philosophically. Historians have described three major blows to human vanity. The first came from Copernicus, who posited that the earth went around the sun and not the sun around the earth. Thus our planet was not, by God's designation, the hub of the universe. The second blow came from Darwin, who argued that we were descended from apelike creatures and not from Adam and Eve. (Or, in Mark Twain's words, that we were a little lower than the angels and a little higher than the French.) The third blow came from Freud, who argued against our feelings of autonomy. We were not fully in control of our behavior but were, to varying degrees, controlled by the unconscious. Unlike Copernicus and Darwin, Freud offered us a sop. If we underwent psychoanalysis, we might become aware of the unconscious determinants of our behavior and thus learn to control them, to some extent.

The biological theory of mental ill-

ness is a fourth blow. It implies that sometimes one cannot *by oneself* control moods and behavior psychologically, which is contrary to many theological and philosophical positions—and to a few psychotherapeutic ones such as Szasz's—which hold that we are completely responsible for our feelings and acts. But we have been presented with evidence that in many circumstances one *can't* control oneself. One must sometimes give up the effort to control—or recognize that one has already involuntarily abdicated control—and those who want to believe in free will or pure psychological determinism find this very hard to accept.

A third source of resistance is that most people tend to regard medications as concealing or suppressing the symptoms of a disorder rather than as attacking the impairment. For example, one typically depressed patient, who accepted antidepressant medication only after considerable resistance, recovered dramatically and then returned to the psychiatrist, saying, "Now, let's get into psychotherapy, *really* get to the bottom of this problem and solve it once and for all." To the therapist, the patient's statement was ironic; there is no systematic evidence that psychotherapy does get to the root of a biological depression.

We think that the antipsychotics, the antidepressants, and lithium are not "masking" the symptoms of an illness; nor are they directly correcting the "underlying cause." They are relieving the symptoms by normalizing some deep malfunctioning closely related to the underlying causes. They are not second-class therapy. They are the best therapies we have now.

To those who may feel we are vastly oversimplifying, we respond that we do not mean to deny the complexity, subtlety, and richness of the sources of human behavior. On the contrary, we believe that by recognizing the biological components of mental illness and their appropriate treatments, we can free more people to make the fullest use possible of their psychological resources.

THE PUZZLE OF OBESITY

Don't blame fat on greed or sloth.
It takes heredity, psychology, and environment
to accomplish the feat.

JUDITH RODIN

Judith Rodin *is an associate professor of psychology at Yale University, where she continues to study obesity as well as the psychology and physiology of aging. Rodin received her Ph.D. in social psychology from Columbia University in 1970 and then studied neurobiology at the University of California at Irvine. Rodin's imaginative interdisciplinary work has won her many honors, including the American Psychological Association's 1977 Early Career Award for outstanding scientific contribution. She serves on several governmental and professional committees concerned with the problem and treatment of obesity, and has published dozens of research articles in the field.*

The wages of gluttony is fat. None of the other six deadly sins is as difficult to hide, and the punishment of added pounds continually reminds the sinner of his transgression. Yet obesity does not have as lengthy a past as, say, lust or greed. For most of human history the problem has been how to get more food, not how to eat less, and much of the world's population still needs to gain weight. But in the West, millions of people want to lose it and cannot—at least not for long.

There rests the irony of obesity: Almost any fat person can lose pounds but few can keep them off. This stubborn fact feeds a whole weight-reducing industry of gadgets and gimmicks, to say nothing of making many overweight people feel miserable. Popular explanations are that the obese person is either a weak-willed glutton or a love-starved neurotic; the one overeats because he is greedy, the other overeats as emotional compensation.

Both explanations are wrong for most overweight people. I have reviewed over 100 studies on the psychology and physiology of eating—laboratory and field studies, self-reports and observations—and conducted many studies of my own. I find that it is not that overweight people eat more than their leaner friends, but that they eat in different ways and under more circumstances. Further, I find that the factors once thought to cause obesity—lethargy, self-hatred, low metabolism—are instead the results of being obese.

Fat, one of the basic constituents of body tissue, is an admirable result of evolution. It allows for compact storage of energy reserves, cushions the body against bumps and blows, provides insulation, and in moderate amounts promotes sex appeal by providing attractive curves in the proper places. Fat molecules are well adapted to the energy needs of the body, for they help balance the input of food and the output of energy. The question is how that balance is broken to cause excessive fat storage.

Many obese people believe the answer is physical: They say their glands, or their large bones, or their genes force them to be fat. But only 5 percent of all cases of obesity are caused primarily by medical problems such as endocrine malfunction, brain damage, or hereditary diseases. The other 95 percent, including some 500-pounders, have no apparent medical problem. The failure to find medical explanations has generated new theories that regard obesity as the breakdown of a normal process instead of as a special illness.

Two points of view about the origins of human obesity have emerged recently. One holds that obesity is "learned" from cultural standards, ethnic values, and the use of food for social, instead of nutritive, purposes. The other view proposes that some individuals are biologically programmed to be fat. (Clearly, both views assume that the environment must provide an overabundance of food before a disposition to obesity, whether genetic or learned, can be expressed.) In my opinion these views are not mutually exclusive. Obesity is not a single disorder but a set of syndromes. Two problems need to be distinguished: What factors maintain fat and keep people from being able to reduce, and what causes obesity in the first place.

1 What keeps people fat

Our metabolic machinery is set up in such a way that the fatter we are, the fatter we are primed to become. This unfortunate state occurs, first, because the larger a fat cell gets, the greater its capacity to store fat and become still larger; second, overweight people tend to have higher baseline levels of insulin than people of normal weight. This condition, called hyperinsulinemia, enhances fat storage because it accelerates the entry of sugar into the fat cell and speeds the conversion of sugar into fat. It also increases a person's hunger pangs and food consumption. Obese people also release more insulin after a meal than thin people do, which in turn may cause them to eat more.

Insulin production is further affected by eating habits. Food eaten rapidly or in one or two large meals makes insulin turn sugar to fat faster than the same amount of food eaten in small portions; and a meal high in carbohydrates and calories produces more insulin than a meal consisting of proteins.

Metabolic changes thus maintain obesity by increasing the body's fat-producing and fat-storage capacities, but these changes are a result of overeating and not its cause. Ethan Sims and his colleagues demonstrated this point in a study conducted at a Vermont state prison. Normal-weight volunteers were paid to eat two or three times their normal daily caloric intake. The men gained an average of 26 percent over their initial lean weight, some of them with great difficulty, and they were kept at this new weight for several months. With few exceptions, when the men overate, their mass of fatty tissue increased and endocrine and metabolic changes occurred like those observed in the obese. From this study and others that support it, we can conclude that most overweight people initially had normal metabolism, but overeating and gaining weight threw their systems out of kilter.

A second explanation of obesity assumes that inactivity is the culprit. Jean Mayer has documented the popular assumption that obese people are less active than slender ones. Using time-lapse photography to observe girls during sports activities at summer camps, he found that the obese children were less active than the lean ones. When swimming, for instance, the obese girls preferred to float at the shallow end of the pool, while the lean girls swam energetically at the deep end. Obese adults also tend to be inactive. Anna-Marie Chirico and Albert Stunkard attached pedometers to normal-weight and obese men and women who were matched by occupation, a fat baker and a thin baker, for example. The normal-weight adults, on the average, walked significantly farther than the obese.

Most people conclude from such studies that laziness breeds plumpness, but actually it may be the other way around. Obesity makes physical activity more difficult and probably less pleasurable than normal weight does and may encourage people to be sedentary. With less exercise, overweight people burn fewer calories and lower their metabolic rates.

I believe that laziness alone will not make a person obese—unless he also eats a good deal more than he has previously. We recently followed 100 obesity outpatients for one year after they had lost weight. Over 70 percent of them became more active and energetic, and this was not the result of differences in basal metabolism. Inactivity may be a consequence of obesity or only a small contributing factor to it, although it is clearly important in a person's staying overweight.

Unhappiness is a third force that keeps a fat person fat. My studies leave me more impressed than ever with the profound psychological consequences of being overweight and of the social stigma attached to it. The pathologies associated with obesity in Western society are probably more often social than medical. Fat people often feel ashamed of their supposed lack of self-control, and studies have shown that people tend to dislike obese individuals and discriminate against them. Where Twiggy and Cher are the ideal images of health and beauty, even the somewhat plump may feel like outcasts.

Many psychotherapists hold that unhappiness and other emotional states are prime causes of obesity, that persistent overeating comes from unresolved psychological conflicts, or that overeating is a substitute for other satisfactions. A more enlightened outlook, but one consistent with this attitude, regards the fat person as the victim of unconscious forces that trap him in a repetitive, self-destructive pattern. These conclusions come primarily from clinical case studies, which chronicle a long list of the obese person's woes: anxiety, alienation, low self-regard, mistrust, behavioral immaturity, and hypochondria. No wonder that, with labels like these, fat people prefer apple pie to an analyst. But clinical studies can be misleading.

The fault in most psychiatric explanations of obesity is that no single personality type characterizes all obese people. Some people with extreme eating disorders—the massively obese or those who suffer from anorexia nervosa, a condition in which people almost starve themselves to death—undoubtedly have severe psychological disturbances. But they are a minority. Research based on random samples rather than on clinical case studies (which get a biased group of people who choose therapy) finds that most overweight people are psychologically normal. Some are neurotic, unloved, or psychotic, but so are some thin people. In cultures in which the ideal figure is slightly overweight, obesity and mental illness are unrelated. In the United States, obesity is correlated with mental problems only among women of the upper and middle classes, where pressure to reduce is intense.

Clinicians, I believe, have simply failed to distinguish psychological factors in the development of obesity from those that are created by being obese. Fat people in a thin society are bound to feel distressed. Moreover, reducing itself creates emotional conflicts. Numerous studies find that dieting makes some people depressed, anxious, or apathetic; other dieters may actually have psychotic episodes. Clinicians interpret these results to mean that fat people need to stay fat to preserve their distorted self-images or that eating keeps their psychological defenses intact; but, again, I think the weight problem precedes the psychological one.

Intestinal bypass operations have provided a unique opportunity to study the psychological consequences of fast weight loss. George Bray and I found that patients who undergo this operation, which short-circuits two thirds of the intestine, eat less and lose much of their desire for sweet foods. Weight loss is substantial, relatively permanent, and stabilizes after one or two years. (Obese people who lose the same amount of weight as bypass patients, by dieting, do not lose their craving for sweets. This extraordinary finding tells us that something about the intestine itself — perhaps the amount of absorptive surface or the number of sugar receptors in the intestinal wall — probably influences a person's desire for food and perception of sweet tastes.)

Bypass surgery is potentially dangerous, so people who are accepted for the operation are extremely heavy, from 250 to more than 500 pounds. If anyone has a "fat self-image," these patients do.

Charles Solow, Peter Silberfarb, and Katherine Swift found that after bypass surgery, patients felt happier, had higher self-esteem, worked better, and made more friends — in direct proportion to the number of pounds lost. The cloud of depression lifted. These findings fail to support the view that obese people do not lose weight, or feel bad if they do, because they have a low self-concept or because fat is a defense mechanism. As weight goes down, self-esteem goes up. So much for the "obese personality."

Once people gain weight, they usually try to diet, but these efforts have unfortunate consequences. Active dieting not only makes the dieter unhappy at the prospect of giving up favorite foods for life, it actually increases the chances of overeating, as C. Peter Herman and Deborah Mack discovered. They found, through a simple questionnaire, that almost everyone — fat, thin, or chubby — can be classified into two types: those who consciously restrain their eating and those who do not. They also showed that conscious restraint is fragile, vulnerable to outside influences that make the dieter eat.

Herman and Mack put casual and controlled eaters in a situation that required them to drink one or two large milkshakes, or none. Then the volunteers were encouraged to eat as much ice cream as they wanted. When restrained eaters were required to finish two large milkshakes, they subsequently ate more ice cream than if they had drunk no milkshakes or only one. Once they

decided they had already overeaten, they gave up their restraint on food with that "what the hell" reaction familiar to so many people. But those who generally did not worry about what they ate behaved in the opposite fashion. The more milkshake they drank, the less ice cream they later ate.

Overeating is not the only thing that weakens conscious vigilance — so does drinking liquor or being entertained and distracted. This is why many people nibble so much at cocktail parties — drinks, flirtations, and conversations conspire to defeat their best intentions.

From these studies, I suggest that overweight people are caught in a bind. Their hyperinsulinemia and enlarged fat cells prime their metabolic apparatus to make and store fat. Their obesity increases their physical inactivity, which further lowers metabolism and energy expenditure. They need fewer calories to maintain high levels of body weight. And they are unhappy because of social pressure and discrimination. Finally, and most frustrating, their obesity produces numerous attempts to diet — and such efforts can make them more likely to overeat. But if all these factors are largely consequences of obesity, what causes obesity in the first place?

2 What makes people fat

For generations, people have observed that fat parents tend to have fat children. It is an accurate observation. As a study by Ramsdell Gurney showed, when both parents were stout, 75 percent of their children were also; when both parents were lean, only 9 percent of their children were fat. When one parent was overweight, so were 41 percent of the children.

This finding may indicate that genetic factors influence obesity — or it may just mean that heavy parents overfeed their children. Although human obesity is not caused by a single gene for "fat," new evidence suggests that genetic factors do influence human obesity. Genes affect not only total body fat but also the rela-

tive amounts of fat in abdominal and subcutaneous body tissue and its distribution on the body and limbs.

The quantity of fat the body is capable of storing is determined by the number of fat cells and their average size. Some researchers believe that the number of fat cells is genetically fixed. Others think that cell number is determined by early nutrition. Many bottle-fed babies drink more formula than they need because of the mothers' notions of how much infants should eat; such overfeeding stimulates the development of fat cells. I think both factors are involved.

Good evidence that a disposition to obesity is set in early childhood, between birth and the age of two, comes from Jerome Knittle. This critical period, he believes, determines the number of fat cells a person will have throughout life. By age two, obese children have more and larger fat cells than children of standard weight. After age two, weight loss in obese children does nothing to alter the number of fat cells; the size of the cells gets smaller, but not their number. Many obese children tend to become obese adults because they have a permanent excess of fat-making machinery that can never be lost by dieting.

Studies of identical twins allow researchers to disentangle the role of genetic and environmental factors. Horatio Newman and his colleagues found that among 50 pairs of identical twins reared together, the average difference in body weight in each pair was four pounds; only one pair differed in body weight by more than 12 pounds. Among 19 pairs of identical twins reared separately, the average difference in body weight was about 10 pounds, and five pairs were more than 12 pounds apart. The environment, therefore, can control or encourage obesity in individuals, whether or not they have a genetic tendency to be fat.

One such environmental factor is a person's social class, as Stunkard clearly documented. His analysis of a 1960 survey of a cross section of the people living in midtown Manhattan found that the lower a person's socioeconomic status and that of his parents, the greater the likelihood of

The prevalence of obesity is much greater among lower income groups than among the wealthy. When Albert Stunkard compared the socioeconomic level of nearly 1,000 obese people with the socioeconomic level of their parents, the relationship was striking, and it suggests a strong environmental role in the onset of overweight.

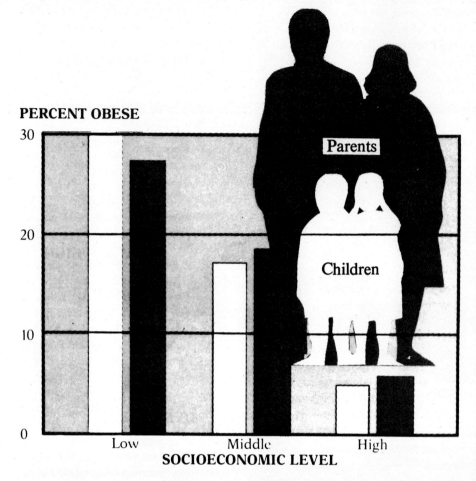

PERCENT OBESE

SOCIOECONOMIC LEVEL

obesity. Stunkard showed that social class can actually be a cause of obesity, because the study took into consideration the income and education not only of all the participants, but also of their parents when the participants were children. It is unlikely that a person's current obesity could have influenced his parents' social class—therefore, the strong correlation tells us that parents' social class must contribute to a person's chances of becoming obese.

Also, Stunkard found, the longer a person's family had been in this country, the less likely he or she was to be obese. Presumably, the younger generations adopt the slim American ideal and modify their parents' diet of pasta, kasha, dumplings, or potato pancakes.

The signs and signals of food that surround us constantly in this abundant society have even more immediate influences on eating habits than do family and class. The sight or aroma of a favorite food or the realization that a regular mealtime has arrived often makes people want to eat even when they do not feel hungry. Everyone occasionally overeats in the presence of tempting food and good company, but many overweight people are highly, sometimes uncontrollably, responsive to the sight and smell of food. They can't say no. Finding the reason plagues researchers and victims alike. During the last several years, my students and I have been concentrating on the role of a per-

son's responsiveness to food in the origins and maintenance of obesity.

In a series of studies conducted a decade ago, Stanley Schachter, Larry Gross, and Richard Nisbett reported that their overweight students were excessively influenced in their desire to eat by the taste, smell, and sight of good food. Similarly, Lee Ross found that obese people ate twice as many cashews when bright lights were focused on the nuts as when the lights were dimmed. People of normal weight ate about the same number of cashews, regardless of how well they could see them. I too did an experiment that showed that when overweight people listened to a mouth-watering description of culinary marvels, they ate far more when they had the chance than normal-weight people did.

O verweight people also tend to eat more when they are excited, distressed, or amused. Cynthia White showed overweight and normal-weight students four film segments at four different sessions. Three

films aroused various emotions: a distressing film about subincision (a ritual slitting of the penis); a funny film, Charlie Chaplin in *The Tramp;* and a sexually arousing stag film. The fourth film, a travelogue about India, bored its audience.

After viewing the films, participants went into another room for a new task—to evaluate, and eat, different kinds of crackers. White found that the obese ate significantly more food after viewing any of the arousing films than after seeing the travelogue. But persons of normal weight ate the same amount of food regardless of which film they had seen. The obese do eat more when they are emotionally excited, no matter what the emotion.

And emotions are more easily aroused in obese people than in people of normal weight. Donald Elman, Stanley Schachter, and I tested Columbia University undergraduates; half of the subjects were obese, half were of normal weight. They listened to one of two kinds of tapes: emotionally disturb-

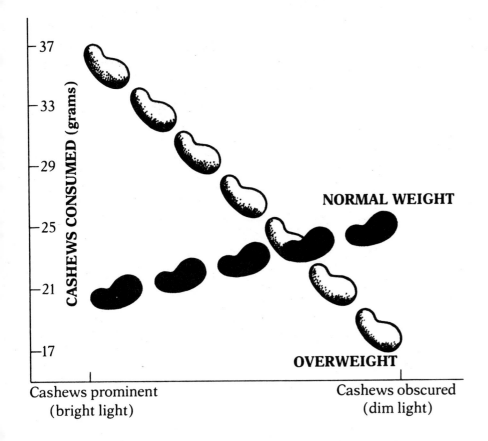

CASHEWS CONSUMED (grams)

37
33
29
25
21
17

NORMAL WEIGHT

OVERWEIGHT

Cashews prominent
(bright light)

Cashews obscured
(dim light)

A study by Lee Ross demonstrates the vulnerability of overweight people to prominent displays of food. Normal-weight people ate about the same number of nuts whether the nuts were under a bright light or obscured in dim light, but overweight people ate many more nuts when the light drew their attention to them.

ing stories that detailed either the bombing of Hiroshima or the person's own hypothetical death of leukemia, or emotionally neutral stories about rain or seashells. The obese students who heard the neutral tapes were not emotionally aroused, but those who heard the emotional tapes were far more upset than were the others.

We reasoned that if the obese are more reactive and emotional than are normal-weight people, the threat or experience of pain would be more disturbing to them. In order to test this supposition, we asked obese and slender men to master a complex, 20-step maze with four possible paths at each step.

After explaining that we were studying the effects of reward and punishment on learning, we asked each student to go through the maze three times without making an error. Most students received either a severe or a mild shock after each mistake; a control group got no shock at all. The shock dramatically disrupted the learning ability of obese men but had no such effect on students of normal weight:

Number of errors made with

	No shock	Low shock	High shock
Normal-weight	228.7	163.4	198.1
Obese	189.9	228.8	286.5

I wish to stress that everyone responds to external cues to some extent. But some people are more responsive than others—and some of them go on to become overweight. Indeed, many fat people are highly responsive to a wide variety of stimuli around them, not just to food, and overeating is one aspect of this tendency. They respond rapidly to complex stimuli; they have good memories for words connected with food and other topics; they tend to be easily distracted from their work.

The experiments suggest that the obese have a heightened sensitivity to many external stimuli. But is the complementary pattern true, that they have a lessened sensitivity to internal signals? Perhaps overweight people rely on outside cues because they cannot read their own physiological states correctly.

This is a common hypothesis, but it is

unsupported. It is simply not true that people get fat because they cannot interpret hunger pangs, low blood sugar, and other physiological signals that tell them when they are hungry. Normal-weight people are no better than fat people at listening to many of their internal messages. Among human beings, food intake is not determined by gastric hunger contractions; the stomach does not always tell us what it wants. In fact, most people are pretty bad at knowing how many calories they have consumed or how much food their bodies need; they use quantity of food, thickness of milkshake, time of day, and social ritual to decide whether and how much to eat. The reason seems to be that, as the human brain has become more developed, the neocortex—and its gift of conscious decision-making—overrides the primitive brain centers, which control eating in lower animals. The irony is that this very advance in brain power makes us more vulnerable to overeating, because conscious control of eating is so easily disrupted.

To explore further the dependence of overweight people on external cues, I studied the perception of time, which, like the desire for food, has both biological and psychological components. When I asked obese people to judge the passage of time while sitting quietly in a dark room with no outside stimulation, their estimates of a 15-minute interval were highly varied and inaccurate relative to the estimates of normal-weight people.

Next I reasoned that external events and signals that mark the passage of time would improve the accuracy of an obese person's estimate of time. What better markers than events that bore a person or whet his interest? In my experiment, one group of heavy and one group of normal-weight students listened to a funny tape selection by comedian David Frye from *Richard Nixon, Superstar*, and one group in each category listened to a boring passage from a geography textbook.

Although the fat and normal-weight groups agreed in their judgments of how interesting or boring the 15-minute tapes were, their assessments of time differed. The obese judged the interval to be longer than normal-weight students did when the tape was boring, and somewhat shorter when the tape was funny.

What does time have to do with food? If more time seems to elapse for the obese when they are bored, and if the passage of time is a powerful cue for eating (as Schachter and Gross found), overweight people should eat sooner when they are bored than when they are doing something that absorbs them. Any activity that affects perceived passage of time should affect how much an obese person eats.

This hypothesis was borne out. Fat people eat more frequently when they are bored than normal-weight people, but they eat less frequently when they are involved in absorbing work. The implication for weight watchers is clear.

Most of the early work on obesity and responsiveness came from college-age middle- and upper-class white students who were moderately overweight (15 to 40 percent above standard). Recently my colleagues and I expanded the range of people tested. We now have data from hundreds of individuals who vary from slightly overweight to massively obese. We went to summer camps for girls—some for average weight, some for overweight—so we could reach young children and teenagers. We interviewed people in obesity clinics and in self-help therapy groups, which gave us more range in the age of people studied (up to 60), in ethnicity (blacks, Mexicans, and Chinese), and in educational background (from grade school on).

The results are enigmatic. For one thing, in every weight group, thin to fat, there were some people who were highly responsive to food cues and some who were not. But on the average, across all categories, classes, and weight levels, the moderately overweight people were the most susceptible to the sight and smell of food—more than people of normal weight and even more than many of the truly obese. Indeed, some of the heaviest people—who weighed as much as 400 pounds—were no more responsive to food cues than people of normal weight.

This startling range emphasizes the complexity of obesity. External responsiveness may lead to overeating and weight gain, but the *degree* of obesity is influenced and perpetuated by many things, including genetic predisposition, number of fat cells, and the changes in metabolism and psychological state that result from overeating. Unhappily, it is still not known just which individuals will become plump and which will become truly obese.

Richard Nisbett, who believes obesity is biologically determined, thinks that responsiveness to outside cues results from dieting. Fat people on diets, he says, are literally starving; no wonder they pay so much attention to food. They are chronically below what Nisbett calls their "biological set point," the weight they were born to have, and all hungry creatures pay close attention to signs of food around them. Nisbett's evidence shows that some of the physiological and behavioral responses of overweight animals are comparable to those of hungry slender people.

I disagree with Nisbett. I think that external responsiveness is a major cause of overweight, not the other way around. Joyce Slochower and I observed what happened at an eight-week summer camp for normal-weight girls. It was a land of milk and honey, chocolate bars and ice cream, a teenager's heaven. The girls who were hyperresponsive to all kinds of external cues (as determined in a pretest at the beginning of the summer) gained the most weight; activity level and emotional adjustment had nothing to do with who gained weight.

Further, people who get fat in adolescence and adulthood do not change their reactions to food—even if they become thin again. In a study of women in a reducing club, I found that losing weight did not reliably change the women's degree of responsiveness to delicious food. Hot-fudge sundaes set their mouths watering when the women were heavy, and also when they were thinner. The same was true for girls at summer weight-loss camps and for adult dieters in clinics and self-help groups. The attraction of delicious food neither increases (as Nisbett would predict) nor decreases with weight loss. Overweight people may be hungry all the time, although I doubt this, but that does not account for their vulnerability to good food. In fact, most overweight people—in hundreds and hundreds of cases that we have observed—report that they never feel hungry.

Perhaps the difference between normal-weight and overweight people has to do with long-term regulatory mechanisms. Those who maintain a normal weight may occasionally gain a few pounds when they are in a food-rich world, such as a Caribbean cruise ship provides, but they are able to cut back periodically to stay in shape. Those who go on to become considerably overweight, or obese, have lost this regulatory ability. Slochower and I found support for this idea in our summer-camp study. Among the girls who began the summer already overweight, 86 percent reached their highest weight during the last week—they gained steadily throughout the summer. But among normal-weight girls who gained, 70 percent reached their peak before the eighth week and then began to lose. Possibly the novelty of the camp and its lavish supply of food was wearing off; possibly each girl's long-term regulatory system was taking over. That system could be biological, psychological, or both.

These converging lines of evidence show that most people who are extremely responsive to external cues gradually gain weight, especially if there is a lot of food around.

One intriguing question is whether this heightened responsiveness actually can make a person hungrier, both physiologically and psychologically. I have already mentioned that overeating changes metabolism and endocrine responses, which work to maintain fat.

In our laboratory, we showed that responsiveness to external cues itself causes the same metabolic changes, particularly the secretion of insulin. An overweight, externally responsive person could literally be "turned on" by a piece of chocolate cake — that is, secrete more insulin at the thought or sight of the cake, actually feel hungry, eat the cake, and store the food as fat.

A second way that external cues have a direct physiological effect is that they energize the person to notice and desire food. The reverse is also true: Increased physiological arousal makes a person more responsive to powerful cues from the environment, which in turn evokes the proper action. Arousal increases the likelihood that the most available, or the most dominant, or the most reinforcing response is the one chosen. For most overweight people, but also for many normal-weight people, the dominant response is to eat. Stress or anxiety can lead to overeating, but so can other emotions, and so can nonemotional stimulants — such as caffeine. Those morning coffee breaks may create a genuine hunger for coffeecake.

The problem is to discover how the responsiveness of fat people to food cues and other outside stimuli develops. One possibility is that an early environment in which food is both scarce and unpredictable encourages children to depend on external cues to regulate eating. When food appears at erratic intervals, a person would be wise to eat whenever possible, regardless of internal needs. If this pattern is established early enough, it may last through life.

One experiment that supports this argument comes from Larry Gross, who tested the role of early nutritional experience on the later eating habits of rats. Some of his infant rats could eat freely whenever they wanted to, some ate once a day, and some were fed at random intervals that varied from eight to 48 hours. Gross found that the latter group of rats became the most responsive to variations in the taste and caloric density of their diets. After three months, the rats were allowed to eat when they chose, but even with plenty of good food around them all the time, the formerly deprived rats were still the most responsive to variations in diet. Like the obese, Gross's deprived rats were always interested in food, whether they were hungry or not. Like the obese, when food was freely available, the rats overate and grew fat.

The analogies to human beings are tantalizing. We might expect that in societies where food is normally scarce, a large proportion of the population would behave like Gross's rats. Because most human societies once lived under unpredictable conditions with a scarcity of food, the physiological mechanisms that assured overeating in the presence of abundant food once may have been adaptive. A mechanism that makes an aroused organism attend and respond to important stimuli — a snarling dog, a luscious peach, a crying infant — has obvious biological benefits.

Under conditions of abundance, the same mechanisms that once saved our lives threaten to endanger our survival by making us obese. The old adage had the truth backwards: Inside every thin man is a fat man who will escape if given half a chance.

The onset and degree of overweight are determined by a combination of genetic, psychological, and environmental events. As we grow up, our culture, ethnicity, nutritional customs, and parents' income and values determine many of our eating habits and food preferences. Both a heightened responsiveness to food cues and a high number of fat cells in the body may develop during early childhood, predisposing a person to overweight and causing high rates of recidivism in reducing programs.

So far, the most reliable deterrent to obesity is the realization that a fat, bouncing baby may well grow into a fat, lethargic adult. An ounce of prevention, in this case, is worth pounds of cure.

For further information:

Bray, G. A. "The Overweight Patient." *Advances in Internal Medicine*, ed. G. H. Stollerman. Year Book Medical Publishers, Vol. 21, 1976.

Cahnman, W. J. "The Stigma of Obesity." *Sociological Quarterly*, Vol. 9, 1968, pp. 283-299.

Knittle, J. L. and J. Hirsch. "Effect of Early Nutrition on the Development of Rat Epididymal Fat Pads: Cellularity and Metabolism." *Journal of Clinical Investigation*, Vol. 47, 1968, pp. 2091-2098.

Rodin, J. "Obesity: Why the Losing Battle?" Master lecture series on Brain and Behavior Relationships, American Psychological Association, 1977.

Rodin, J. and J. Slochower. "Externality in the Nonobese: The Effects of Environmental Responsiveness on Weight." *Journal of Personality and Social Psychology*, Vol. 33, 1976, pp. 338-344.

Schachter, S. and J. Rodin. *Obese Humans and Rats.* Halsted Press, 1974.

Stunkard, A. J. *The Pain of Obesity.* Bull Publishing Co., 1976.

Mental Patterns of Disease

JOAN AREHART-TREICHEL

The type of person you are may tell you more than just how you handle your social relationships. Some medical researchers are now finding evidence that, for some of us, it can predict what kind of disease we're likely to get. Small comfort unless we can find out early enough to change our ways.

Joan Arehart-Treichel is medical editor of *Science News* in Washington, D.C.

There is increasing evidence that certain personality types are prone to specific physical diseases or impairments—heart attacks, cancer, arthritis, ulcers, asthma and others. The personalities of three real people are described below. Try to predict the health risks inherent in each of their personalities.

Melinda B of San Diego, California, has been secretary to a bank vice-president for 14 years. The vice-president has keen admiration for her quiet efficiency, willingness to work overtime and dedication to the job even when she is sick. He is concerned, however, that Melinda is a loner who keeps her emotions bottled up inside her. He's right. Melinda has feelings of isolation and tendencies toward emotional repression that go back to her childhood. Her parents died when she was five, and she was raised by a possessive uncle who refused to let her marry the one man she loved.

Wally R of Nashville, Tennessee, is a devoted husband, father and a hard-working gas station manager. He dotes on activity and adventure. When he's not scrubbing the station driveway or fixing the roof of his house, he's off bass fishing or quail hunting. Wally's family and friends think of him as a happy, bustling fellow who also has a tendency to be clumsy. Wally is forever falling off a ladder, hitting his thumb with a hammer or tripping over a hose.

Robert G is one of the busiest gynecologists in Scarsdale, New York. Before he gets out of bed in the morning, he dictates patient histories and correspondence. He often reads his medical journals while shaving or eating breakfast. He regularly puts in a 15-hour day and boasts to both colleagues and friends that he has the largest gynecologic caseload on the East Coast. Much of his limited time away from the office is also taken up with professional matters—running the county medical society and building a new medical arts building. Both his colleagues and his family describe him as aggressive, time urgent, competitive and, of course, eminently successful.

Doctors who have studied the link between personality traits and susceptibility to certain diseases or physical impairments would predict cancer for Melinda, a fatal accident for Wally and a heart attack for Robert.

In fact, Melinda did die from pancreatic cancer two years ago. And Wally did die 11 months ago on a fishing trip. His motorboat hit a submerged root and tossed him out of the boat. He was knocked unconscious and, not having a lifejacket on, he drowned. Fortunately, Robert is not dead yet, and if he's smart, he'll set about immediately altering his heart attack-prone behavior.

The link between personality and disease susceptibility is nothing new; it goes back centuries. Hippocrates, the father of Western medicine, was interested in the link between psyche and soma. However, modern medicine dating from the 17th century on has given psychosomatic medicine short shrift, paying more attention to how the mind or body works independently than to how they hook up and function as a unit. Psychiatrists think "it's all in the mind"; nephrologists, that "it's all in the kidneys"; proctologists, that "it's all up the rectum." Or as Philip Pinkerton, M.D., of Liverpool, England, puts it more politely in the *British Medical Journal:* "The psychosomatic approach is by no means universally endorsed by the medical profession. The conservative doctor views it with mistrust, believing that psychology bears little relevance to 'real disease.'" John W. Mason, M.D., a psychoendocrinologist with the Walter Reed Army Medical Center in Washington, D.C., agrees: "We must face the fact that the psychosomatic approach has not yet had the sweeping revolutionary impact on medicine of which it appears capable."

During the past several decades, however, some intrepid doctors have been trying to put Humpty Dumpty back together again. And one of the most striking findings to emerge from their research is that certain personality traits can predispose people to certain physical illnesses.

Probably the toughest evidence to date indicating that personality can do a person in concerns the link between so-called Type A personality and heart attacks. The bulk of the research in this area has been conducted by two San Francisco cardiologists, Meyer Friedman, M.D., and Ray H. Rosenman, M.D. These two physicians have spent 15 years associating the aggressive, time urgent, competitive, highly successful person (Type A) with the occurence of heart attacks; and his or her counterpart, the more relaxed, easygoing Type B person with the lack of them. Friedman and Rosenman's evidence is impressive not only because they have spent a long time collecting it, but because it consists of both retrospective and prospective studies. In other words, they first spent time looking back into the personalities of men who had already had heart attacks.

And when they found striking similarities in their personalities, they then studied the personalities of men who had not yet had heart attacks—and successfully predicted which men would.

One of the most noticeable characteristics of the Type A personality, the San Francisco cardiologists have found, is the inability to derive real satisfaction from achievements. That type of person is more interested in the number of achievements he racks up (seeing 160 patients a day, playing eight sets of tennis or selling 60 insurance policies).

Another interesting aspect they've found is that women as well as men span Type A and B personalities. Historically, men have been far more susceptible to heart attacks than have women, at least up until the onset of menopause. So many physicians assumed that sex hormones offer women protection against heart attacks. During the past couple of years, however, heart attacks among younger women have soured at an alarming rate. Some investigators attribute this rise to an increase of smoking among women. But some others concede that the rise might also be due to women competing more in the marketplace. As more and more women assume professional responsibilities, it will be interesting to see whether female heart attacks increase commensurately.

Still another link between personality and disease susceptibility that has been building during the past few years concerns the lonely, emotionally repressed individual and a vulnerability to cancer. An outstanding researcher in this area is Caroline Thomas, M.D., of the Johns Hopkins University School of Medicine. And Thomas's study is especially impressive because it is exclusively prospective.

From 1947 to 1964, Thomas studied 17 successive classes of students at the Johns Hopkins Medical School. The students were checked out for heartbeat rate, cholesterol level in the blood and reactions to cold, exercise and other stresses. If they had diseases, the diseases were noted. The causes of death for their parents, grandparents, uncles and aunts were recorded. The students filled in detailed questionnaires about their early childhood, schooling, family life, diet, medication, hobbies, emotional outlook, aims, as well as habits such as smoking or drinking. They were given Rorschach and figure-drawing tests to reveal such characteristics as aggression, passivity, anxiety, hostility and depressive trends.

By the middle of the 1960s, then, Thomas had exhaustive prospective data on 1,337 subjects, and all but six of the subjects have kept in touch with her as they have moved from early adulthood into middle age. So far, 15 of the subjects have suffered heart attacks, 46 have gotten cancer and 16 have committed suicide. Thomas has looked back on the personality information that she had for these victims to see whether certain traits might have predicted the causes of death and found that indeed they might have.

She found, as had Friedman and Rosenman, that the attack victims had been high-gear persons. She found that the suicide victims had not been close to their parents in childhood, and even as young people had been especially sensitive to stress, reacting to it with irritability and an urge to get away from it all. And the cancer victims were low-gear persons, seldom prey to outbursts of emotions. They had had feelings of isolation and unhappiness dating back to childhood.

"We did not make up any hypotheses beforehand about cancer patients," Thomas explains. "I had selected them as a comparison group for the suicides, thinking that the cancer victims have solid, demonstrable physical illnesses." When the

different personality types were analyzed, Dr. Thomas says, "it turned out, however, that cancer victims were much more like the suicide victims than they were like the heart attack victims."

Claus and Marjorie Bahnson, a husband and wife psychology team at the Eastern Pennsylvania Psychiatric Institute in Philadelphia, have described both the heart attack personality and the cancer personality with their own retrospective studies. Says Claus Bahnson: "The heart attack personality vents his frustrations, irritations, anxieties and other negative emotions outwardly by bellowing, cursing or what have you. The cancer personality takes the same negative emotions out inwardly, that is, he internalizes them."

Another striking aspect of the cancer personality, the Bahnsons have found, is that he believes his mental and bodily strength to be greater than that of other people. Says Claus Bahnson: "They are master builders and independent people who operate on their own motivations." Or as Marjorie Bahnson puts it: "The heart attack personality feels that he is under greater stress than are other people, even when this is not true. The cancer personality may be under greater stress than other people, but he will say, 'Everything is fine.' "

The ego strength of the cancer personality, in fact, is further buttressd by the Bahnsons' findings that cancer personalities tend to have fewer psychiatric disturbances than do the mentally ill. "The cancer personality," Claus Bahnson declares, "has accepted social restrictions more than has the heart attack personality. He is religious, committed, good—perhaps too good for his own health."

The heart attack personality, on the other hand, seems to be without religious beliefs. Or as Friedman and Rosenman report: "We cannot say positively that the increase in the Type A behavior pattern has been directly influenced by the continuing loss of religious faith and other sustaining myths and rituals. We can declare, however, with considerable certainty, that we have rarely encountered this behavior pattern in any person whose religious and patriotic beliefs take precedence over his preoccupation with the accumulation of 'numbers' or the acquisition of personal power."

The Bahnsons have asked cancer patients to describe their childhoods, and they sound similar to those of Thomas's cancer victims—lonely, unhappy, lacking in communication with their parents. If there were any two adjectives the patients had for their parents, they were "unloving" and "cold." If the absence of parental warmth leaves a child susceptible to cancer, then perhaps the loss of one's parents has the same effect. The Bahnsons are now undertaking an epidemiological study with the Western German Research Institute in Heidelberg to find out. They want to determine whether the 1.8 million German children who lost their parents during World War II are now experiencing, as 40 and 50 year-olds, more incidences of cancer than Germans of comparable age who did not lose their parents during the war.

Sarah J of Cleveland, Ohio, was brought up in a well-to-do family. Her mother was warm and loving, but her father was cold and strict. He made it clear that he believed women to be inferior to men. He sent Sarah's brother to the university, but not Sarah. Then the depression hit. Sarah was on her own in the world, resentful that she had been denied the education that her brother had frittered away. Some years later Sarah married, had her own family and threw herself into her roles with zest. She was a super wife, mother and housekeeper but made it apparent to her husband and children that she would much rather be out of the house holding down a professionally challenging position. When her family encouraged her to seek a position, however, she said, "Oh, who would want to hire me? My education is limited; I have no skills." Then came the time for her children to go away to college; Sarah no longer had a challenge. Just about that time, she had to undergo a serious operation that left her physically exhausted and depressed. Shortly thereafter, she came down with the rheumatoid arthritis that she has to this day. It causes her intense pain and some crippling.

Sarah, by all accounts, is a rheumatoid arthritis personality, according to various studies that have been conducted in recent years. Four out of five rheumatoid arthritis victims are women, and for good reason—the disease appears to arise in those frustrated by the traditional female sex role. The evidence that has accumulated shows that rheumatoid arthritis victims tend to be frustrated over unfulfilled ambitions primarily because they have feelings of inadequacy harking back to their childhood. Their feelings of inadequacy have arisen because they had strict parents who did not encourage them to strike out on their own and achieve. Because of these frustrations, rheumatoid arthritis victims often funnel their need for recognition outside the home into being exceptional housekeepers and mothers. They are self-sacrificing, orderly, punctual, tidy perfectionists.

One of the best studies underscoring the rheumatoid arthritis personality as a stifled, frustrated woman was undertaken several years ago by Dr. Franz Alexander and his colleagues. Nine psychoanalyst judges reviewed personality information on 83 patients with rheumatoid arthritis, asthma, ulcers, hypertension or other disease. The judges were significantly more successful in picking out the rheumatoid arthritis victims on the basis of their personalities than they were with the other disease victims. They correctly picked the rheumatoid arthritis patients two out of three times. It will be interesting to see, as more and more women seek professional fulfillment, whether the incidences of rheumatoid arthritis among women drop.

Gastrointestinal ulcers is still another physical illness that seems to occur in persons with a particular personality. Evidence for this personality basis, as for rheumatoid arthritis, has been accumulating from numerous studies for some years now. Back in 1957, for instance, Herbert Weiner, M.D., of the Albert Einstein College of Medicine in New York City did a fascinating study on the personality underlying ulcer susceptibility. He evaluated 2,073 army inductees for psychological characteristics and measured the levels of pepsinogen in their blood. (Pepsinogen is secreted by the stomach lining and oversecretion of it has been strongly linked with peptic ulcers.) He found a strong correlation between high levels of pepsinogen in the blood and certain psychological characteristics. He then predicted which of the men would get peptic ulcers during basic training on the basis of both pepsinogen levels and the corresponding psychological profile. Nine men developed ulcers. Weiner had predicted seven of the nine.

The major characteristics that Dr. Weiner found in the ulcer personality are intense needs that are principally "oral" in nature and that are exhibited in terms of wishing to be fed, to lean on others, to seek close bodily contact with others. When attempts to fulfill these needs fail, the victim becomes angry, but he does not express his anger because he is afraid he will lose further that which he desires. The nonulcer personalities, Dr. Weiner found, were, in contrast, less dependent, more narcissistic and freer in expressing their anger.

Weiner's findings are similar to those of William J. Grace, M.D., Stewart Wolf, M.D., and Harold G. Wolff, M.D., who analyzed 19 patients who had been plagued by ulcerative colitis for six months to 24 years. Psychiatric interviews exposed these characteristics: overdependence on parents, which reflected itself in a need to please other people. One patient said, "I can't stand having anybody mad at me."

Other characteristics of the ulcer personality that have emerged from these and other studies are tendencies to be tidy, prim, mild, mannerly, conscientious, punctual and inhibited. People with such personalities are also thin-skinned, alert to real or imagined assaults from the world. They fear rejection and thus make few advances to other people; however, they form strong attachments, usually toward older persons, whom they often end up marrying. The male ulcer patients tend to marry wives who are mother substitutes.

Still another illness that seems to arise from parental interactions in early childhood is asthma. But unlike cancer, which seems to stem from a lonely, unhappy childhood; rheumatoid arthritis, which seems to strike persons having overly strict parents; and unlike ulcers, which seem to develop in individuals who are overly dependent on Mother; asthma's origin is not so clear-cut. Some evidence suggests that it too strikes those who are overly dependent on their parents. Other evidence, however, suggests that it assails those whose parents are not concerned enough about them. Two case histories cited by Pinkerton in the *British Medical Journal* illustrate both theories.

James, age 10, is a mild asthmatic whose breathing is virtually unimpaired; yet he goes to the doctor often and frequently misses school. He is an only child, born after three abortions, and is said to have been a weakling as a baby. When he first developed asthma at age four, both parents became acutely concerned and stayed up nights with him.

John, age nine, on the other hand, has been asthmatic since infancy and still spends a lot of time in the hospital. John's father was away from home for long periods when the boy was younger. The father is as intolerant of illness in others as he is in himself and constantly exorts the boy to do away with his medicine. John's mother has a better understanding of the problem but is unable to influence her husband. There is now a two-year-old sister who is asthma-free and clearly the father's favorite. As a result, John resents his asthma and tries to suppress symptoms and medication when he really needs it.

James, Pinkerton concludes, illustrates the asthma personality that arises from having overly protective parents. John, he says, illustrates the asthma personality caused by parents who don't evidence enough concern.

If the asthma personality is hard to pin down, the migraine personality is even more diffuse. Wolff studied 46 migraine sufferers and found that nine-tenths of them were "unusually ambitious and preoccupied with achievement and success." But this was an Anglo-American study. German studies show a link between hysteria, depression and migraines. For example, Gerhard S. Barolin, M.D., of the University Nerve Clinic in Vienna studied 450 migraine sufferers over a decade and found that many of them were prone to hysteria and depression. But then some French studies depict the migraine victim as a bon vivant— a happy-go-lucky type who likes to dine and make love.

Are there national differences among migraine victims? "I doubt it," Barolin replies. "More likely these are different interpretations of very 'soft' data."

Soft data, yes, that is the weak link in all the studies tying certain personalities with certain diseases. Thoughts, emotions and behavior are incredibly complex and even tougher to link up with specific physiological events in the body. "There is no shortage of data relating disease to psychosocial factors," Walter Reed's Mason admits. "The shortage is in the mediating mechanisms."

Still, investigators are making progress in this direction. Friedman and Rosenman, for example, have hard-core evidence that Type A behavior leads to a marked rise of cholesterol in the blood—a major risk factor in heart disease. In a pilot study, the Bahnsons have found a strong correlation between depression in psychiatric patients and lowered immune competence. Since the immune system is known to play a major role in warding off cancer, this finding could help explain why people with lonely, unhappy childhoods might be more prone to cancer.

Emotions have also been found to act on the brain's hypothalamus, and the hypothalamus links directly with the autonomic nervous system that controls chemical secretions in the gastrointestinal tract. So it is quite possible that if an ulcer personality is upset, an emotional disturbance will signal the hypothalamus, the autonomic nervous system and, in turn, gastric secretions in the stomach; and too much gastric secretion will set an ulcer into motion. Neal E. Miller, M.D., of Rockefeller University has also found that chronic fear increases gastric secretions in the stomachs of rats and gives them ulcers.

Numerous questions, of course, remain to be answered. How might the same personality trait, say fastidiousness, lead to ulcers in some people, yet to rheumatoid arthritis in others? Why don't all people with the same personality traits end up with the same diseases? Surely other factors must also enter the picture—such as sex, age, weight, certain stressful events—that trigger the disease or genetic predisposition to it. The cancer personality, for example, might not get a tumor unless he has also inherited a defective immune system. The rheumatoid arthritis personality would probably not develop that disease unless some event in her life deprived her of her usual outlets for personal fulfillment. Perhaps the ulcer personality would not develop an ulcer unless he had also inherited an overly active stomach.

Even with this constellation of factors to be considered, though, the link between personality and disease susceptibility is becoming even more compelling. This is the admission of physicians who are in the vanguard, and they are attempting to impress this fact on their less astute (or less open-minded) colleagues. For instance, Irvine H. Page, M.D., editor of the medical publication with the world's largest circulation, *Modern Medicine*, recently admonished his physician readers: "The sensible physician will recognize and evaluate personality types in relation to other risk factors."

ANXIETY

Anxiety is closely related to the action of two natural chemicals in the brain; drugs that relieve anxiety may also make people unable to cope with change or adversity.

JEFFREY A. GRAY

Jeffrey A. Gray *is lecturer in psychology in the Department of Experimental Psychology, University of Oxford, and since 1965 has been a Fellow of University College, Oxford. His Ph.D. in psychology is from the University of London, and he has been a Travelling Fellow for the United Kingdom Medical Research Council and a guest investigator at The Rockefeller University in New York City. Gray is the author of* The Psychology of Fear and Stress *and* Elements of a Two-Process Theory of Learning *and is the editor of* Pavlov's Typology.

Many people suffer from some form of extreme anxiety. Some experience sporadic attacks of panic for no apparent reason, others go around in a state of continual apprehension. Still others are afflicted with phobias, that is, persistent, excessive fears of objects or situations that most people would not consider significant sources of danger. The most common and crippling of these conditions is agoraphobia. A person with this phobia fears to go outside and may remain housebound for years. There is an important, if less obvious, element of anxiety in the obsessive-compulsive neurosis, in which a person feels a compulsive urge to perform some apparently unnecessary ritual, such as the repeated washing of perfectly clean hands. If the ritual is prevented, there is a great surge of anxiety. It is difficult to assess the number of people who suffer from these conditions. Many do not bother to consult a doctor, even though they are as severely affected as others who do. It has been estimated that there are four million phobics in Britain alone. If we add to these conditions the extremely

common reactive depression, in which anxiety is a prominent symptom, the number would be greatly swelled.

The usual way of controlling anxiety is with drugs, which cure none of the conditions described but that do help patients manage their anxiety. The drug with the longest pedigree—though it is usually prescribed by the patient, not the physician—is alcohol. These days a physician is more likely to prescribe one of the benzodiazepines, for example, Librium (chlordiazepoxide) or Valium (diazepam). Before these tranquilizers were developed in the 1950s, the medical profession relied chiefly on various barbiturates, such as Amytal (sodium amobarbital). The choice among these drugs is to a large extent arbitrary, although safety and convenience appear to favor the benzodiazepines. Experiments with animals show that all these drugs have similar effects on behavior. Collectively they are known as minor tranquilizers or antianxiety drugs, and their use in Western society is widespread and growing.

All of these drugs appear to relieve anxiety, but there has been no understanding of how they work. Patients who take them say they are no longer beset with anxiety. With the help of the drugs, they are able to work, to sleep, and to go places they had feared to visit. But the effect of the drugs on the human body—especially on the nervous system—has been unknown. Any drug powerful enough to have such profound effects on emotions and behavior may also have other, unnoticed physiological effects that alter behavior in additional ways

that neither the patient nor the doctor connects with the drug.

Because the problem seemed serious, we embarked on a series of studies to identify the precise effects of the drugs on the brain. We succeeded in isolating those effects, and in the process found that reliance on the drugs can have two serious consequences: When people lose their disabling anxieties they may also be losing their ability to cope with changes in their lives; what is more, the tranquilizers may make them likely to give up when faced with difficulties.

Alcohol and Amytal were the first antianxiety drugs to come under laboratory scrutiny. In the late 1930s Neal Miller used the drugs with rats, and Jules Masserman used them with cats to study the psychological nature of anxiety. In the 1960s investigators began to look at drugs like Librium and Valium. By now there has been an enormous number of studies on the behavioral effects of all these drugs in a wide variety of species ranging from goldfish to chimpanzees. From these experiments it is clear that the behavioral effects of the antianxiety drugs are similar, no matter which drug is used or which species is studied. This similarity encourages the belief that, in the case of antianxiety drugs, it is possible to use studies of laboratory animals to predict the reactions of human beings. Since all species react similarly, it also suggests that the drugs act on a part of the brain that developed early in evolution. If so, anxiety is ancient and probably predates human beings.

Because these drugs are prescribed to lessen anxiety, they should make an animal less worried about danger. This prediction is easy to test. Suppose that we first train a rat to run down an alley for food and then begin to shock the animal each time it enters the box that contains its reward. When punished in this way, a sober animal soon learns to stop running to the box. But an animal injected with Amytal, Librium, or alcohol continues to go to the food despite the painful shock.

This phenomenon closely resembles the "Dutch courage" shown by soldiers who take a nip of whiskey before battle. Miller first reported Dutch courage in rats, and Masserman first reported it in cats; the experiments have since been repeated sufficiently often and in a sufficient variety of ways for it to be clear that Dutch courage is as universal a phenomenon in animals as it is in human beings. It is not absurd to suppose that animals experience an emotional state similar to human anxiety and that they respond in similar ways to treatment with antianxiety drugs.

Dutch courage is not due to a loss in the ability to feel pain, because drugged animals will flinch or jump at the same intensity of electric shock as sober ones. Nor do the drugs reduce aggressive behavior produced by painful sensations. If two rats are caged together and their feet are given painful shocks, they at once start fighting. Such fighting is not reduced— and may even be increased—by antianxiety drugs. It will of course surprise no one that alcohol does not reduce the aggressive response to a blow in the face, while it does reduce the fear of such a blow. But it is disturbing that this conclusion also applies to the other tranquilizers handed out so liberally by physicians. Margaret Lynch, Janet Lindsay, and Christopher Ounsted, working in a children's hospital in Oxford, have suggested that the recent spate of battered-baby cases may be due in part to this same pair of effects— reduced fear of the consequences of one's actions with no loss of aggression—in a parent chronically maintained on a drug like Librium or Valium.

The Dutch-courage experiment shows that it is difficult for an animal in-jected with an antianxiety drug to behave appropriately in anticipation of shock, but that behavior directly produced by shock (flinching, fighting) continues in the drugged animal. From this we might conclude that the antianxiety drugs dull the expectation of pain, but not pain itself. This is part of the truth, but not the whole of it. For if an animal can avoid a shock by doing something (running down the alley or jumping a barrier, for example), its behavior is unimpaired by the drugs. It is only when the avoidance of shock depends on *not* doing something (as in the Dutch-courage experiment) that the animal's behavior is altered by these drugs. Antianxiety drugs specifically prevent the animal from withholding an action that it has learned will bring pain. One might say the drugs make animals more impulsive.

This finding can in principle account for many of the effects of antianxiety drugs on human social behavior. As Miller remarked about alcohol, this drug "has a perplexing variety of effects, making some aggressive, others amorous, some tearful, and others talkative." If we suppose that after drinking alcohol or taking Librium or Amytal people behave in ways that were previously restrained by fear of the consequences, all these effects can be attributed to a single effect—the reduction of fear.

The experiments I have described so far have all depended on the use of painful stimuli, such as electric shocks. Yet it is comparatively rare for human fears to focus on impending pain (the dentist's chair is probably the most common exception to this rule). How, then, can we account for anxiety in the absence of threatened pain? Some fears, almost certainly, are innate and reflect ancient dangers to the survival of our species (the widespread fear of snakes is the most obvious example of this). But the majority require a more complex explanation, and one has emerged from research by Abram Amsel, who studied what happens when an animal fails to get an expected reward.

This situation arises when, after an animal has been rewarded with food or water for, say, pressing a lever, it presses the lever again and nothing happens. The effects of the omitted reward are clearly emotional. The animal becomes visibly disturbed (it may, for example, try to bite the experimenter or attack another animal) and shows in a variety of ways that it finds the experience of nonreward highly unpleasant. Animals that fail to get expected rewards and animals that have received painful shocks behave in very similar ways; for example, both become aggressive.

One effect of nonreward is that the animal eventually stops doing whatever once brought it the reward. But if the animal is first injected with one of the antianxiety drugs, it finds it much harder to give up this behavior (just as it finds it harder to give up punished behavior). In an experiment by Miller and his associates, rats were trained to run in an alley for a food reward. After this habit was well established, the food was removed from the goal box. Rats injected with Amytal and placed in the alley kept running to the empty goal box much longer than did undrugged rats. They acted, in other words, as though they found their failure to be rewarded less of a deterrent than do sober animals.

This kind of finding helps us understand why the antianxiety drugs have such pervasive and powerful effects on human behavior. These drugs apparently do more than release behavior that is normally restrained by fear of pain; they also release behavior that is restrained by fear of failure, frustration, and disappointment. And there are few of us who do not harbor such fears, at least to some degree.

More complicated experiments show that, just as in the case of painful stimuli, antianxiety drugs do not lessen the impact of failure once the animal experiences it; instead, the drugged animal behaves as though it is less concerned by the possibility that it *might* fail to get a reward. As an illustration of this point, consider the way an animal behaves when a reward is unpredictable, sometimes present and sometimes absent. Rats trained to run down an alley for food that is only sometimes in the goal box come to run faster than rats trained to expect a reward at the end of every trip. Amsel has shown that the extra speed shown by rats that cannot depend on their reward reflects the in-

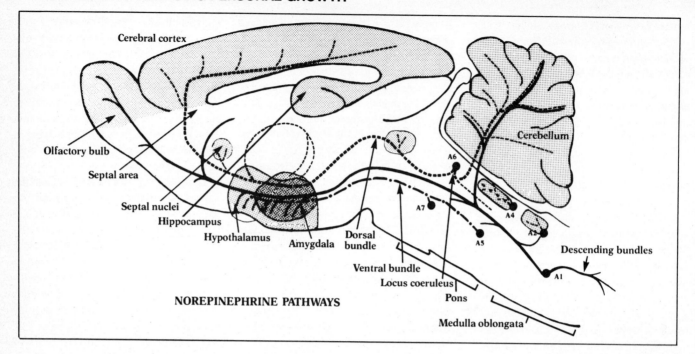

Cerebral cortex

Cerebellum

Olfactory bulb

Septal area

Septal nuclei

Hippocampus

Hypothalamus Amygdala

Dorsal bundle

Ventral bundle

Locus coeruleus

Pons

Descending bundles

A6

A7

A4

A5

A2

A1

NOREPINEPHRINE PATHWAYS

Medulla oblongata

This map of a rat brain shows the long nerve fibers that transmit norepinephrine. The fibers extend from nerve cells clustered near the cerebellum (A1 through A7). Antianxiety drugs apparently interfere with the transmission of norepinephrine, which concentrates in the shaded areas, from neurons in the locus coeruleus (A6) to those in the hippocampus and septal areas.

creased emotional excitement that is generated by the possibility of disappointment. Notice that the rats run faster *before* they reach the goal box and discover whether they have been rewarded. As shown both in our laboratory and by other researchers, antianxiety drugs block this effect of anticipated nonreward. Under the influence of Amytal or Librium, rats rewarded intermittently run no faster than rats that are always rewarded. They "keep their cool" when faced with possible failure.

But let us now change the experimental situation slightly by adding a second alley to the first and rewarding the rats in both goal boxes, giving them unpredictable rewards in the first alley and continual rewards in the second. Amsel and Jacqueline Roussel have shown that, in such a double runway, rats run faster in the second alley after they have found the first goal box empty than after they have found food there. This again

reflects the emotional excitement generated by nonreward; but now the rats run faster *after* they have experienced failure. Under these conditions, rats injected with antianxiety drugs run just as fast as undrugged rats. Evidently these agents dampen the emotional excitement generated by the threat of failure, but not the excitement generated by failure itself. One might expect the antianxiety drugs to help a student during the period between taking an exam and hearing the results, but not necessarily to help him come to terms with a failing mark.

The behavioral effects of the antianxiety drugs, as we have considered them so far, seem therapeutic. Under certain circumstances it could be valuable to care less about the threat of punishment or the possibility of failure. But our picture of these drugs would be incomplete if we omitted two negative features of their action.

The first of these is that the antianxiety drugs lessen an animal's ability to notice change in its environment and to respond to new events. Brendan McGonigle, for example, trained rats to discriminate between black and white doors, rewarding them with food when they ran through the right door. He then changed the pattern on the doors so the rats could solve the problem either by continuing to use the black-white cue or by using a new cue—horizontal or vertical stripes. Finally, he removed the black-white cue and left only the stripes. Drugged rats learned the original black-white discrimination just as well as sober ones, but they failed to notice the significance of the added stripes; in the final stage of the experiment, their performance broke down. This failure to notice significant changes in one's environment may be a factor in the increased likelihood of accidents that occurs after taking antianxiety drugs. Traffic accidents under the influence of alcohol are the most dramatic example of this.

The second negative aspect of the antianxiety drugs is that they prevent animals from learning to persist when faced with an adverse and unpredictable environment. If we train two groups of rats to run in an alley, giving one group rewards part of the time and the other rewards at the end of every run, and then stop the rewards altogether, the two groups behave differently. Although both groups eventually stop running to the empty goal box, the group that was rewarded only part of the time keeps running to the empty box much longer than the group that had learned to expect food on every trip. As argued by Amsel, this persistence results from the rats' development of tolerance for frustration. Robert Brown and Alan Wagner have shown that this tolerance for frustration even applies to electric shock: Rats trained with partial rewards and then shocked for entering the goal box continue to enter the box long after rats trained always to expect rewards have given up. The converse is also true. An animal that receives gradually increasing intensities of shock together with rewards will develop a tolerance for electric shock. If such rats are then put back in the alley and neither shocked nor rewarded, they continue running to the empty goal box longer than rats that were never shocked. It is probable that this persistence in the face of nonreward or shock is but one aspect of a general tolerance for stress that results when an animal is repeatedly exposed to unpleasant or painful events, a process Miller has called "toughening up."

But Joram Feldon and I have shown that this persistence never develops if the rats are trained with partial reward while under the influence of Amytal or Librium. And Nicola Davis and I have shown that Librium can block the development of tolerance for electric shock. Thus the antianxiety drugs prevent animals from "toughening up," from learning to persist in the face of adversity. There is clearly a moral here that every physician should bear in mind. The best way to help a failing marriage, for example, might not be to drug the partners, but to let them adapt to each other.

The various behavioral effects of the drugs I have described fit together nicely if the animal has what I have proposed as a "behavioral inhibition system." According to my hypothesis, activity in this system underlies the emotion of anxiety and is counteracted by the antianxiety drugs. The system is activated by three kinds of input: signals of impending punishment, signals of impending nonreward, and novel events. And the system produces three kinds of output: inhibition of behavior (as in the Dutch-courage experiment), increased emotional excitement or "arousal," and increased attention to novel events.

The behavioral inhibition system serves the animal by suppressing behavior that has become maladaptive while the animal scans its environment for new ways to meet an immediate challenge. But under conditions in which there is no better alternative than the old behavior, the behavioral inhibition system develops the animal's necessary added persistence.

If the behavioral inhibition system exists, it must be in the brain. A first clue to *where* in the brain comes from cases of brain damage (lesions) that result in behavior similar to that caused by antianxiety drugs. If the drugs act by impairing the function of a particular brain region, then destruction of that region should produce effects on behavior similar to those produced by these drugs. Two brain structures seem likely sites for the action of antianxiety drugs: the septal area and the hippocampus. We have recently completed a review of the numerous reports of the behavioral effects of lesions in these areas. Two key findings emerge. First, in the great majority of cases, lesions in both areas have strikingly similar effects; second, whenever the effects of the lesions do resemble each other, the direction of the behavioral change produced by the lesions is the same as that produced by the antianxiety drugs.

Faced with this pattern of data, the first question to ask is: Why do the behavioral effects of the two lesions resemble each other so closely? There is a ready answer. The septal area and the hippocampus are closely interrelated, both anatomically and physiologically. Cells in the medial septal area send their fibers to the hippocampus; conversely, one of the major direct projections of the hippocampus is to the lateral septal area. The hippocampus normally emits a pattern of high-voltage, rhythmic, slow brain waves ranging from about 4 to 12 cycles per second (hertz) known as the hippocampal theta rhythm. The function of this rhythm is a matter of considerable dispute, but it is well established that the rhythm is controlled by cells located in the medial septal area. Thus lesions in the septal area destroy both a major input to the hippocampus and a major output from it, as well as radically altering hippocampal electrical activity by permanently abolishing the theta rhythm.

It is natural to suppose, therefore, that the septal area and the hippocampus form part of a single functional "septo-hippocampal system." In 1970 I proposed that the antianxiety drugs alter behavior by acting on this system, and in particular, that they in some way impair septal control of the hippocampal theta rhythm.

A more precise hypothesis arose out of some simple experiments in which Gordon Ball and I recorded hippocampal electrical activity in an undrugged rat's brain while the animal, which was free-moving but connected to the recording apparatus by cable, ran in an alley for a water reward. We found that the rat displayed a theta rhythm throughout the experiment, but that the frequency of the hippocampal waves varied according to what it was doing or what was happening to it. When the animal drank, it produced low frequencies of theta (below about 7 hertz). When it was running down the alley toward the goal box, the animal produced high theta frequencies (above about 8.5 hertz). When the rat discovered an empty goal box, the omission of reward produced an intermediate frequency that, in a group of rats, averaged 7.7 hertz. This same frequency appeared when the rat explored a new environment.

Because of these findings, we had to give up the hypothesis that the antianxiety drugs impair general septal control of hippocampal theta. For if they did, the drugs would impair an animal's ability to approach a reward or to consume food or water, and they do not. Both running toward a water reward and drinking the water are accompanied by theta rhythm, the former at high frequencies, the latter at low. Our hypothesis necessarily became that antianxiety drugs impair septal control of hippocampal theta only in a small frequency band centered on 7.7 hertz (the frequency we had observed in response to nonreward and novelty, which we knew were affected by the drugs).

To test this prediction, we implanted a stimulating electrode in the medial septal area of each rat and a recording electrode in its hippocampus. We could now "drive" their hippocampal theta rhythm artificially, imposing any frequency we liked on the rhythm by delivering short pulses of electricity to the septal area. When we plotted the

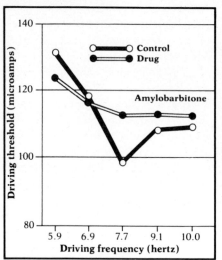

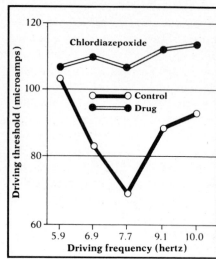

threshold current required to drive the theta rhythm in this way as a function of stimulation frequency, we obtained a characteristic curve—the theta-driving curve—that has a minimum threshold at exactly 7.7 hertz. Every one of a range of antianxiety drugs we have tested eliminates this minimum in the theta-driving curve by selectively increasing the threshold at 7.7 hertz. This result is a striking confirmation of our prediction. Further confirmation that the theta rhythm at 7.7 hertz is related to anxiety came from experiments in which we drove this rhythm by electrical stimulation of the septal area and changed the rat's behavior in ways exactly opposite to the changes produced by the antianxiety drugs. (Perhaps we have discovered a way of making animals more anxious.)

Given these findings, we wondered how the antianxiety drugs perform this peculiar trick of selectively increasing the threshold at 7.7 hertz. In an effort to throw more light on this question, Neil McNaughton, David James, and I tried to mimic the effect of the antianxiety drugs on the theta-driving curve by using drugs with better-understood effects on chemicals in the brain.

The brain consists of millions of discrete elements (nerve cells, or neurons) connected in incredibly complex patterns. The small gap between neurons, which is their point of connection, is known as the synapse. Transmission of messages across the synapse is accomplished by a chemical (a neurotransmitter) that, when released by one neuron, triggers electrochemical activity

in the next. A number of different chemicals are thought to perform this function in different parts of the brain. Pharmacologists have succeeded in synthesizing a number of drugs that can affect the action of neurotransmitters, and using some of them we investigated the possible role of neurotransmitters in the action of the antianxiety drugs.

Two of these neurotransmitters belong to a chemical family known as the monoamines: norepinephrine and serotonin. When we blocked the brain's synthesis of norepinephrine, the theta-driving curve showed a rise in the threshold at 7.7 hertz; this is precisely what happens when an animal takes antianxiety drugs. Blocking the synthesis of serotonin produced a mirror image of this effect. It lowered thresholds at every frequency except 7.7 hertz. Thus the normal shape of the theta-driving curve depends on the joint functioning of neural systems that use norepinephrine and serotonin to transmit messages across the synapse.

These results clearly pointed to a neural input using norepinephrine as its neurotransmitter to the hippocampus, the septal area, or both as the place where antianxiety drugs act on the brain. Such an input was not hard to find, for it had been described a decade before by a group of Swedish neuroanatomists using a technique known as fluorescence histochemistry. This process causes nerve fibers that contain norepinephrine to fluoresce brightly under the microscope. When they mapped a rat's brain with this technique, they found a

particular cluster of cell bodies, called the locus coeruleus, in the lower part of the brain. The cluster gives off long norepinephrine-containing fibers that travel to both the hippocampus and the septal area, as well as to other parts of the brain. These fibers ascend the brain in the dorsal noradrenergic bundle. This bundle of fibers, then, seemed the most likely site of the antianxiety drugs' action on the theta-driving curve.

To test this assumption Peter Kelly, Neil McNaughton, and I used a poison, 6-hydroxydopamine, that affects only fibers containing norepinephrine. By injecting this poison into the dorsal noradrenergic bundle, we destroyed this fiber tract with minimal damage to other neural systems. The lesion we created reduced the amount of hippocampal norepinephrine to only 3 percent of its normal level. If our hypothesis was right, it should also have removed the 7.7 hertz minimum from the theta-driving curve, as do the antianxiety drugs. This is what we found.

If these electrophysiological observations have anything to do with the behavioral effects of the antianxiety drugs, then our destruction of the dorsal noradrenergic bundle should also have changed behavior in the same manner as the drugs did. Animals whose brains have been so injured should not learn to persist in the face of adversity. Trained to run in the alley for food but rewarded only part of the time, they should stop running to the goal box soon after all rewards are withdrawn. When Susan Owen, Michael Boarder, Marianne

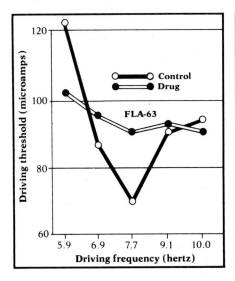

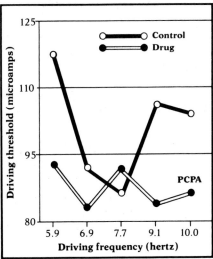

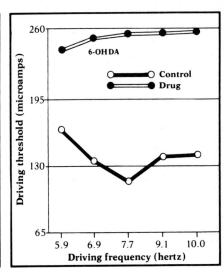

Researchers can deduce how and where antianxiety drugs work by experimenting with the brain's chemical messengers, norepinephrine and serotonin. Blocking the synthesis of norepinephrine with FLA-63 increases the minimum threshold of the theta-driving curve at 7.7 hertz; this is what happens when an animal takes an antianxiety drug. In contrast, blocking the synthesis of serotonin with p-chlorophenylalanine (PCPA) lowers thresholds at every frequency except 7.7 hertz. The site of the drugs' effect was found by using 6-hydroxydopamine (6-OHDA), which destroys fibers containing norepinephrine in the dorsal bundle and thereby removes the 7.7 hertz minimum.

Fillenz, and I tested rats under these conditions, the results were clear-cut. The rats did not persist but gave up as soon as did undamaged rats that had been rewarded each time they ran in the alley. In other experiments, we investigated reactions to novelty in the lesioned animals. These too were abolished, as they are by the antianxiety drugs.

These data point to the dorsal noradrenergic bundle, and particularly to its connections with the septo-hippocampal system, as the place where antianxiety drugs have an important effect. Looking at the results of other research strengthens our conclusions. Kjell Fuxe's group in Sweden has shown that stress increases activity in neurons containing norepinephrine that are found in the higher parts of the brain, and that all major antianxiety drugs can eliminate this increased activity. Jay Weiss has demonstrated that levels of norepinephrine drop in the brains of rats exposed to

intense shock or cold, as though the neural systems concerned are unable to keep up with the demands made on them. As repeated exposure leads animals to develop tolerance for these stresses, the levels of norepinephrine rise. Weiss has shown that Miller's toughening-up process, which follows repeated exposure to unpleasant events, is the result of an increased capacity in the animal's brain to synthesize norepinephrine so that it is better able to cope with excessive demand for the neurotransmitter.

Systems that use norepinephrine, then, are involved in the way the animal responds to a variety of stressful events (nonreward, novelty, shock, cold). But there is also evidence that suggests an important role for systems that use serotonin as the neurotransmitter. The pathways in the brain that carry serotonin follow much the same course as those that carry norepinephrine, and

they too connect extensively with the septal area and the hippocampus. As we have seen, the normal shape of the theta-driving curve depends on the joint functioning of neurons that contain the two neurotransmitters. Fuxe's group has shown that stress increases the activity of neurons that contain serotonin and that this increase is counteracted by the antianxiety drugs — exactly the same pattern reported by his group for neurons that contain norepinephrine. Finally, Larry Stein in Philadelphia, as well as Nicholas Tye and Susan Iversen in Cambridge, England, have presented evidence implicating serotonin in animals' responses to punishment and in the behavioral effects of Valium and Librium. It seems likely that anxiety involves increased activity among neurons in the higher parts of the brain that contain both neurotransmitters, and that the connections of these kinds of neurons with the septo-hippocampal system play a particularly important role.

This excursion into the neuropsychology of anxiety in rats can give us important insights into the understanding of anxiety in human beings. The first concerns the connection between anxiety and depression. The two states are so close that psychiatrists often have great difficulty distinguishing between them.

4. PROBLEMS INFLUENCING PERSONAL GROWTH

If we ask what gives rise to depression, we find an interesting answer: loss (of a loved one, a job, status, and so on). "Loss" may easily be translated into "removal of an accustomed source of reward," and this, as we have seen, acts on behavior much as punishment does and probably by means of the same physiological mechanisms. Thus it is possible that anxiety and depression are merely different names for the same fundamental state. The terms simply distinguish between the circumstances that have precipitated it: events associated with danger in the case of anxiety, events associated with the loss of reward in the case of depression. This inference is strengthened by the fact that the monoamines (norepinephrine and serotonin) have been implicated in depression as well as in anxiety.

Our increased understanding of anxiety may also help us to discover why certain people are particularly likely to display this emotion. It is known that individuals who suffer from phobias, anxiety states, reactive depression, etc., do not constitute a random sample of the population, but have enduring personality traits that both precede and outlast their illness. In the light of the experiments described in this article, I suggest that their predisposition toward anxiety and depression may consist in a high sensitivity to threats of danger or loss.

Finally, we have gained some insight into the costs and benefits of the antianxiety drugs themselves. These agents are valuable because they can reduce the emotional and behavioral effects of anticipated punishment, failure, frustration, and disappointment. But their value demands a price. Part of this price lies in the very therapeutic effects for which we value these drugs. A person who fails to give up behavior that is repeatedly punished may be courageous or inflexible, depending on the circumstances and on one's value judgments. But two other effects of the antianxiety drugs are more obviously harmful. They reduce a person's capacity to react to changes in the environment; and, what is most important, they keep a person from developing persistence in the face of unpredictable adversity. Since unpredictable adversity is one of the most predictable ingredients of life, this effect may make the price of the antianxiety drugs too high.

For further information:

Gray, J. A. "Drug Effects on Fear and Frustration: Possible Limbic Site of Action of Minor Tranquilizers." *Handbook of Psychopharmacology*, Vol. 8, ed. by Leslie L. Iversen, Susan D. Iversen, and Solomon H. Snyder. Plenum Publishing Corp., 1977.

Gray, J. A. "The Neuropsychology of Anxiety." The 1977 Myers Lecture. *British Journal of Psychology* (in press).

Mason, S. T., and Susan D. Iversen. "Learning in the Absence of Forebrain Noradrenaline." *Nature*, Vol. 258, 1975, pp. 422-424.

Stein, Larry, C. D. Wise, and Barry D. Berger. "Antianxiety Action of Benzodiazepines: Decrease in Activity of Serotonin Neurons in the Punishment System." *The Benzodiazepines*, ed. by S. Garattini, E. Mussini, and L. O. Randall. Raven Press, 1973.

Weiss, J. M., H. I. Glazer, L. A. Pohorecky, John Brick, and N. E. Miller. "Effects of Chronic Exposure to Stressors on Avoidance-Escape Behavior and on Brain Norepinephrine." *Psychosomatic Medicine*, Vol. 37, 1975, pp. 522-534.

That Helpless Feeling:
The Dangers of Stress

"...Feelings of helplessness can lead to more than just disease: loss of control in one's life can end in loss of life itself..."

Douglas Colligan

In 1957 Dr. Curt Richter, a Johns Hopkins psychologist, drowned two wild rats. He dropped Rat One into a tank of warm water, and since rats are generally pretty good swimmers, it lasted for about 60 hours before finally becoming exhausted and drowning. With Rat Two he tried something different. Before releasing it in the water, he held it in his hand until it stopped struggling. Once he dropped it into the tank, it splashed around for a few minutes, then passively sank to the bottom. Richter claims that Rat Two had despaired of escape even before it got wet, and, in effect, died of helplessness. In the eighteen years that have passed since those rats drowned, an impressive pile of evidence has accumulated showing that there's a little of Rat Two in each of us.

mong the first scientists to have stumbled on this fact is a group at the University of Rochester School of Medicine and Dentistry. One of them is Dr. Robert Ader, professor of psychiatry and psychology, who, in a series of animal experiments, pioneered much of the group's research by studying how factors such as helplessness affected diseases ranging from diabetes to cancer. A level-headed, objective researcher, Dr. Ader told me: "I'd say that a feeling of helplessness would be one of the psychological factors which could precipitate disease." Conditions are optimal for a physical breakdown, he explained, when there is (1) a biological predisposition, (2) a stress that is perceived as a stress, and (3) an inability to cope with this stress. He says that in a healthy individual there is a balance or harmony among these forces, but that where there is a very high biological predisposition to a particular disease, it takes very little stress to upset this internal harmony and precipitate the disease. From this it follows that someone less biologically vulnerable would need a much larger dose of stress before developing the same disease.

In one of the more dramatic demonstrations of Ader's principle of balance, Dr. William A. Greene, a member of the Rochester group and a professor of medicine and psychiatry, conducted a twelve-year study which consisted of weekly interviews with a woman stricken with leukemia. Greene noted that the leukemia surfaced about the time the woman was told her first husband, suffering from tuberculosis, was given just one more year to live. At the beginning of the study she told Greene she wanted to live only until her son, then ten years old, had grown up and settled. Over the years, changes in the woman's disease were noted, such as an increase in the number of her white blood cells just before Dr. Greene's annual summer vacation. On another occasion, when the woman was faced with the imminent collapse of her second marriage and the added stress of menopause, there was what he described as a "major acceleration of the leukemic process." Finally, when the woman's son left home for the service, she suffered a major relapse and had to be hospitalized intermittently over the next four years. Shortly after her son returned home, engaged to be married, the woman died.

In a paper ominously titled "Giving Up as a Final Common Pathway to Changes in Health," Dr. Arthur Schmale, a member of the Rochester group and an associate professor of medicine, reports on five studies based on tape-recorded interviews with 240 hospitalized and institutionalized patients and their families. The patients' problems ranged from infectious diseases and malignant tumors to a variety of psychiatric disabilities, and, according to the report, 80 per cent of these cases had experienced "an actual, a threatened, or a symbolic loss of a highly valued form of gratification, with feelings of either helplessness or hopelessness." This "giving up complex," as he described it, preceded these people's admission to the hospital and was brought on by a number of life changes such as getting fired, getting a promotion, being retired, or the death of someone close.

The idea that disease can be influenced by psychological factors is not a new one. Peptic ulcers, hypertension, hyperthyroidism, rheumatoid arthritis, ulcerative colitis, neurodermatitis, and asthma have long been called "psychosomatic." But now it would seem that any distinction between psychosomatic and nonpsychosomatic disease is completely arbitrary. Outside of the Rochester group, one of the firm believers in this theory is Dr. Samuel Silverman, associate clinical professor of psychiatry at the Harvard Medical School, who seems to enjoy making the flat statement, "I think all diseases have emotional factors."

During his more than twenty years as a psychoanalyst, Silverman noted that prior to becoming physically ill, his patients shared certain common factors which he believes can be used to predict the onset and the nature of the

"…Weiss discovered that rats he had rendered helpless had a depleted supply of the fight-or-flight secretion, norepinephrine…"

illness. Important elements he found were predisposition to a sickness because of heredity or prior illness, and the patient's ability to discharge severe tensions through normal or abnormal psychological outlets. If a psychological manifestation of distress, such as guilt or rage, suddenly disappears, the trouble usually surfaces again at the body's weakest point, the target organ. Finally, he adds to these indicators the concept of somatic identification—when a person develops an ailment similar to one suffered by a relative or friend.

In his book *How Will You Feel Tomorrow?* Silverman tells of a number of instances when he was able to predict a patient's illness; but what may be his most famous case of forecasting occurred last September, shortly after President Ford pardoned former President Nixon. A *Time* reporter had asked Silverman for his opinion of Nixon's future health in light of the presidential pardon. Silverman responded, "I thought it was very threatening to his life."

Because Nixon kept such a tight rein on his emotions, Silverman guessed that post-Watergate pressures would cause a physical, not emotional, breakdown. He decided the trouble would surface in Nixon's legs, because of previous phlebitis attacks and foot and knee injuries, and in the lungs, because of prior bouts of pneumonia. He also foresaw the potentially lethal complication of a clot traveling between the two areas. "Two days later he threw an embolism, and I became a prophet," he told a *Medical World News* reporter.

Intense feelings of helplessness can lead to more than mere physical disease: loss of control in one's life can end in loss of life itself—sometimes by accelerating an existing disease process, sometimes by sudden heart attacks.

Probably the most striking example of what Dr. Martin Seligman, associate

professor of psychology at the University of Pennsylvania, calls "psychogenic, sudden, and mysterious death" from helplessness is a story told him by Major F. Harold Kushner, an army medical officer who was held by the Vietcong for five and a half years. Among the prisoners in Kushner's POW camp was a tough young marine, 24 years old, who had already survived two years of prison-camp life in relatively good health. Part of the reason for this, it seemed to Kushner, was that the camp commander had promised to release the man if he cooperated. Since this had been done before with others, the marine turned into a model POW and the leader of the camp's thought-reform group. As time passed he gradually realized that his captors had lied to him. When the full realization of this took hold he became a zombie. He refused to do all work, rejected all offers of food and encouragement, and simply lay on his cot sucking his thumb. In a matter of weeks he was dead. Considering that the man had enjoyed relatively good physical health, Seligman feels that a strictly medical explanation of his decline into death isn't adequate. A more suitable explanation, he says, is that the psychological shock of discovering that all his actions were futile, or wasted, destroyed any motivation to stay alive any longer. "Hope of release sustained him," Seligman writes. "When he gave up hope, when he believed that all his efforts had failed and would continue to fail, he died."

In a thorough catalog of such grim events, Dr. George Engel of the Rochester group collected a file of 170 cases of sudden death that occurred over a six-year period. Engel broke down the reasons for the deaths into eight causal categories. Of these, five categories involved helplessness in one form or another: the death or threatened loss of a loved one, acute grief, mourning or anniversary of mourning, and finally, loss of stature and self-esteem. Engel's files include stories that illustrate this: the twelve-year-old girl who dropped dead on hearing of the death of her older brother; an 88-year-old man who died immediately after receiving the news of his daughter's death; and the sudden death of another man during an anniversary concert in memory of his wife. Engel found that the common element in all

these cases of sudden death was a tremendously intense emotion coupled with feelings of helplessness.

But why is it that some people succumb to helplessness, while other survive? The behavioral viewpoint holds that we learn to be helpless; the biochemical theory maintains that the body's hormonal system gets bent out of shape by stress.

On the behavioral side, Martin Seligman believes the answer lies in what he describes as the personality's "dance of development" which begins in infancy and continues through old age. Learning to cope is a matter of practice, according to Seligman, and the less successful a person has been in coping in his life, the more he's going to believe himself helpless. The longer this continues, the more dangerous it becomes, not only mentally, but physically.

Seligman's theory that helplessness is something learned began to take shape about ten years ago when he was doing stress tests on dogs. The animals were suspended in hammocks and periodically given shocks they could not escape. Seligman found that when he took the same animals and gave them another shock test in a device called a shuttle box—a container half-electrified, half-insulated—the dogs made no attempt to escape the shocks but simply lay down on the electrified gridwork and whimpered. In a comparison study Seligman found that an unshocked dog had no trouble in figuring out how to move over to the safe side of the shuttle box. On the basis of experiments like these, he defines helplessness as "the perception of uncontrollability."

Something similar, Seligman believes, happens in humans. He and others have been able to test out his theory, on people, using techniques such as blasts of loud, inescapable noise to produce an experimental state of helplessness. The procedure is to take two groups of people, usually college students ("The white rat and the college sophomore are the most widely used subjects of psychological experiments," he says), and put them in a situation where they are exposed to periodic blasts of loud noise. Members of one group eventually discover they can stop the noise by pressing a button. The other group is exposed to the same noise, but is given no controlling device.

These groups then take a second test, which also includes blasts of noise which each group can shut off simply by moving a hand from one side of a shuttle-box device to another. Seligman found that those who had already learned to turn off the noise were also successful in this experiment; those who had been exposed to inescapable noise did nothing. "If you ask them why they're not doing anything," Seligman says, "they'll say something like, 'Because I learned there was nothing that I could do.' In fact, in one study 60 per cent of the people tested said that."

r. Jay Weiss is convinced a better explanation lies hidden in the body's complicated biochemistry. At Rockefeller University's laboratory of physiological psychology, he's examining the relationship between helplessness and the chemical balance of catecholamines, a volatile group of secretions that have a tremendous influence as neurotransmitters, chemical messengers between nerve cells in the brain and the sympathetic nervous system. Some researchers believe these catecholamines can be a major cause of psychiatric illnesses when they are thrown out of balance. Weiss has concentrated on one catecholamine in particular, norepinephrine. Experimenting with rats, he found that those placed under stressful conditions they couldn't control became severely depleted of norepinephrine. Testing the helpless animals in an experiment similar to Seligman's shuttle-box test, he found that the rats did not avoid the shock, but simply sat there and suffered, just like Seligman's helpless dogs. The reason they did this, Weiss maintains, was not because they had learned it was futile to try, but because they were so lacking in

norepinephrine that they could not organize themselves well enough to react.

Weiss remains unimpressed by Seligman's hypothesis. "Personally, I believe the evidence is very scant," he says, and points to the fact that he has been able to explain a number of cases of learned helplessness with his norepinephrine theory—officially known as the "motor activation deficit" hypothesis. In one case he gave rats a cold-water dunking which he says diminishes their supply of norepinephrine but does not cause helplessness. They responded to a learning situation in the same way Seligman's helpless dogs had, but Weiss believes the rats' helplessness is best defined as "lack of control," as opposed to Seligman's phrase, "perception of uncontrollability." In another test, Weiss injected a rat with a chemical that blocked the norepinephrine from depleting and again ran the rat through helplessness conditioning using uncontrollable shock. It had little trouble coping in a subsequent learning experiment. And, to show that the reason rats can't cope with major problems is because they don't have enough norepinephrine, and not because they've learned it's no use to cope, he gave rats that had been subjected to uncontrollable stress a learning situation that required very little physical movement. The rats were put in a shock apparatus where they could switch off the shock by simply poking their noses through a hole. Weiss found that helpless rats had no trouble learning this.

Do these findings mean we should start lining up for our norepinephrine shots? "That paper," Weiss said, gesturing toward a summary of his test findings, "I can guarantee you will someday be modified. It can't be that simple. But the point is, we can go a long way with that."

Despite disagreements between Seligman and Weiss, three basic points recur in their pronouncements on helplessness: it is a powerful psychological force; it has both behavioral and biochemical factors; and how much damage it does depends on the individual's ability to cope with it.

As yet, no one has been able to say more objectively than these two men why an intangible event outside the body is translated into physical damage within. As a general explanation, Engel says that once the realization comes that all control has been lost, animals and men first struggle to reestablish control, then become totally passive, or give up. This alternating method of coping can be repeated over and over again, and the longer it goes on, Engel says, the more an individual's

health will deteriorate. For some, however, it's the struggling reaction which has a greater corrosive effect on the body's health. In others, it's the passive, or the parasympathetic, phase that is the more dangerous one.

According to Seligman, the parasympathetic phase of reaction may also explain some of those cases of sudden death medically attributed to heart failure. In a parasympathetic reaction, important bodily functions such as the heartbeat are tremendously depressed or slowed down. In connection with this, Seligman points to one finding Curt Richter made in an autopsy on one of his helpless, drowned rats: the animal's heart was engorged with its own blood, indicating that its pulse had been depressed to a lethal level.

n the meantime, the Rochester group is continuing its now twenty-year-long search for the reason the mind turns on the body. "We know something about physiological and biological changes," George Engel told me, "but no one knows what role they play, if any, in susceptibility to disease." Even though there are gaps in what researchers know about the mechanisms of helplessness, they do know some of its most common causes. In his survey of hospitalized patients Dr. Schmale found grief to be one of the most common reasons for the "giving up complex," and in his catalog of sudden deaths Dr. Engel found that a huge portion of them happened to grief-stricken individuals. A famous study often mentioned in this context is entitled "Broken Heart," done by a group of British researchers studying the mortality rate of 4,500 widowers within six months of their wives' deaths. Compared with other men the same age, the widowers studied had a mortality rate that was 40 per cent higher.

Another fairly common source of helplessness these days is unemployment. "Deprive a man of work and you may remove his most meaningful source of instrumental control," says Seligman. "In our society your work is your identification. Take that away from many people and you remove the most important thing in their lives."

4. PROBLEMS INFLUENCING PERSONAL GROWTH

One of the few studies done on the unhealthy effects of losing a job was conducted about ten years ago by Dr. Sidney Cobb, now professor of community health and psychiatry at Brown University, who studied 100 men laid off from a Detroit auto plant. He monitored their health over a two-year period that began six weeks before the layoff; at the end of his study he found that the suicide rate among the men was 30 times the average rate; there were three cases of ulcers, eight cases of arthritis, five of hypertension requiring hospitalization, two of labile high blood pressure, six of severe depression, one of alcoholism, three of alopecia (hair falling out), and one of gout. He also noted that three of the men's wives had been hospitalized for peptic ulcers, extremely rare among women. "The point is," he says, "this also took its toll on the family."

And if grief or joblessness doesn't get to you, old age will. As a group, the elderly probably are exposed to more helplessness-producing situations than just about any other segment of society. Often prematurely retired and shuttled away to convalescent homes for their family's convenience, the elderly frequently have few real choices in their lives. "We are a nation that deprives old persons of control over their lives," Seligman says. "We kill them."

As just one example of this, he refers to an obscure doctoral dissertation in which the researchers interviewed 55 women, average age 82, who were about to enter a nursing home. When asked how much freedom of choice they felt they had, 38 of the group said they had some, while 17 said they had no other choice. At the end of their first ten weeks in the home only one of the 38 had died, while 16 of the choiceless were dead.

Only now are doctors, psychologists, and psychiatrists beginning to react to these discoveries about what the mind can do to the body.

In view of the health threat of helplessness, Seligman thinks it's not a bad idea to have a bimonthly checkup during the first year following a life crisis. A useful tool in this context, he says, might be the Holmes-Rahe Social Readjustment Rating Scale. This is a shopping list of 43 of the most common stressful life events that seem to play a part in the disease process. It was developed after years of interviews, testing, and retesting by Dr. Thomas H. Holmes, professor of psychology and behavioral sciences at the University of Washington School of Medicine, and it was further refined with the help of Captain Richard H. Rahe, head of the stress medicine division at the Naval Health Research Center in San Diego. Holmes and Rahe give each life event a number rating in "life-change units" on a relative scale of one to 100. The top score of 100 is reserved for the death of a spouse, 47 is for getting fired, and a low of 11 points is for minor violations of the law. In one test of the scale Holmes found that of those who scored over 300 points within one year, 86 per cent had experienced some serious health change, while of those who scored between 150 and 300 points in the same length of time, only 48 per cent had experienced similar health changes.

When calculating whether one has exceeded the 300 mark, it should be borne in mind that the total life-change units can encompass a year of major personal disasters or a mix of minor and major disruptions—both good and bad. Such a year might look like this: you just bought a $60,000 co-op (mortgage over $10,000: 31 life-change units); your father is laid up with a heart attack (change in health of family member: 44); as a result of really brilliant moves in your career (outstanding personal achievement: 28), your income takes a tremendous jump (change in financial state: 38); in the meantime, your marriage is falling apart (change in number of arguments with spouse: 35), your sex life has evaporated (sex difficulties: 39), and you and your spouse decide on a trial separation: 65; you move out (change in residence: 20) to a cockroach-infested studio (change in living conditions: 25); separation ends in divorce: 73; and your car gets towed away from in front of the courthouse (minor violation of the law: 11). The total score: 409. The prognosis: not good.

Dr. Schmale feels such a scale, used

as an interview technique, could alert a doctor to a patient's candidacy for illness. He points out that all but two of the life changes listed (marriage and pregnancy) that rate a score of 39 or above cover crises which involve some severe disruption or deprivation—basic conditions for the giving-up complex.

Research is moving toward the point where awareness of the helplessness factor can be a valuable tool in determining the prognosis of a disease. In one study, Dr. Schmale interviewed 51 women who were being given tests for cervical cancer because of some "suspicious" cells found in the course of routine Pap tests. Schmale's interviews revealed that 18 of the women had experienced some recent deep personal loss and, as a result, were engulfed by feelings of hopelessness. None of the other 33 showed any signs of such feelings. Schmale and his co-investigator predicted that the 18 deeply troubled women would be more prone to cancer. And the results showed that while only 8 of the 33 had cancer, 11 of the 18 who had experienced hopelessness did.

An increasing number of studies like this are constantly raising two very important points: that being unable to cope is very dangerous, both mentally and physically, and that disease is no longer the simple medical concept it once was. As Ader remarks: "The germ theory simply can't account for why people get sick, because if it could— I don't know how big your office is, but if somebody gets the flu, then I don't understand why everybody doesn't get it." Research in these areas by Weiss, Seligman, and the Rochester group continues to unearth information about the shadowy and often volatile relationship between the mind and the body, but we must wait for the definitive answer to why some of us, like Rat Two, are unequal to the task of swimming for our lives.

THE AGE OF MELANCHOLY

There are growing signs that melancholy—ranging from ordinary
sadness to severe depression—is the most common psychological complaint
of our times. On the following pages, the nation's highest-ranking
mental-health officer ponders the evidence, while other
authorities explore social and biological forces contributing to the
malaise, the roots of the depressive personality, and the startling
numbers that show women are much more likely to suffer than men.

Gerald L. Klerman

Gerald L. Klerman, M.D., is administrator of
the federal Alcohol, Drug Abuse, and Mental
Health Administration. This article has been
adapted from a paper presented at the conference "Vulnerable Youth: Hope, Despair,
and Renewal," sponsored by the University
of Chicago's Student Mental Health Clinic
and Department of Psychiatry in April of
1978. The conference papers, edited by
Miriam Elson and John F. Kramer, will be
published by University of Chicago Press.

It is the pastime of some writers, historians, and psychiatrists to divide life into various "Ages." One very successful instance of this labeling was the 1947 poem by W. H. Auden, "The Age of Anxiety," which seemed to capture a syndrome that was widespread in the population. Many people, particularly psychiatrist Robert Lifton, related that anxiety to man's awareness of the power to destroy our entire species by nuclear means.

Auden's poem has had tremendous intellectual and even clinical impact. It inspired a symphony by Leonard Bernstein and a ballet by Jerome Robbins, both called "The Age of Anxiety." By focusing public attention on anxiety, it may have also contributed to the development of new drugs (like tranquilizers) and new psychothera-

peutic techniques (like biofeedback and desensitization) for coping with the symptoms.

In the mid-60s, a series of papers began to speculate that anxiety was giving way to depression and despair as dominant moods in modern man. Whereas the middle decades of this century were labeled an Age of Anxiety, there are indications that the later decades will be considered an Age of Melancholy.

How good is the evidence indicating an actual increase in epidemiologic rates of depression? Some is valid and some is not. For instance, more articles about depression are written now than ever before. There is an increase in the prescription of antidepressant drugs, yet there is also an increase in use of antianxiety drugs. A slight increase in the diagnosis of depression is seen in nationwide data. But the fact that more people are being diagnosed as depressed—in general hospitals, community mental-health centers, and clinic settings— may be an artifact of the greater attention given to the problem and of extensions in insurance coverage. For the record, it is nicer to call someone depressed than schizophrenic or paranoid.

Excellent data worldwide indicate a rise in suicide attempts, although

not necessarily deaths. In the United States, the suicide-attempt rate has increased dramatically, almost tenfold, and mostly among young adults. Women have higher rates than men do, with the highest prevalence under age 30. The most common technique is pill ingestion, perhaps a tribute to our new technology.

Other findings, less well documented, also show that the median age of depressed patients is dropping. The textbooks written before World War I concentrated, in their discussion of depressions, on "involutional melancholia" (a disorder of the middle years), and found the median age to be in the 40s and 50s. A study examining the discharge records at the Massachusetts Mental Health Center found that immediately after World War II the median age of patients was in the 40s, and the most common diagnosis was involutional melancholia. But in three recent studies in the United States, the median age of patients admitted to depression research studies was in the early 30s.

The depressive phenomenon is well known throughout the history of Western civilization. There are excellent descriptions in the Bible, particularly of Saul's depression, which was

From *Psychology Today*, April 1979. Reprinted by permission of the author.

115

treated by David with some success. Clinical descriptions also appear in Egyptian, Greek, and Roman literature, in which a modern clinician has no difficulty in recognizing the symptoms of depression. It is hard to find an equally good description of schizophrenia in ancient literature, although many hallucinatory states are described.

Writers in at least two periods of Western European literature paid increased attention to depression. Most notable was the interest in depression of Elizabethan writers in the 16th century; later came the emotional outpourings of the Romantics, particularly the German, French, and Russian writers. More recently, a number of influential literary figures—Samuel Beckett, Walker Percy, A. Alvarez, Sylvia Plath—have portrayed themes of alienation, despair, and depression.

To what extent literature reflects epidemiologic trends, nobody knows. It is easy to believe that we have moved into an Age of Melancholy, preceded by an Age of Anxiety. The Age of Melancholy is a period when rising expectations, generated after World War II, have come up against the harsh realities of population explosion and doomsday prophecies—such as those of the Club of Rome and other seers of the future. A situation that may psychologically predispose individuals to depression is a gap between expectations and actuality. We experience feelings of despair perhaps not so much when a situation is bad, but when we have given up hope.

In addition to looking at depression clinically and developmentally, it is useful to step back a bit and consider depression as an evolutionary phenomenon for our species, and for most mammalian species. Emotional states like depression, anxiety, fear, and anger have a function in the lives of organisms, including human organisms, in that they promote adaptation of the organism to the environment. That idea was first enunciated by Darwin in his book *The Expression of the Emotions in Man and Animals:* not only are morphologic structures adapted by natural selection, he proposed, but there is also an evolutionary selective sequence to emotional states, which he called "mental and expressive capacities."

Darwin described in great detail his observations of emotional expression in lower animals, as well as in primates and humans, and showed by drawings that in monkeys and humans, the same facial muscles are involved in the expression of anger, fear, and sadness. Many of Darwin's ideas and observations lay dormant until after World War II, when a remarkable upsurge of interest and study in the biology of behavior occurred. For example, the field popularly known as ethology has emerged, in which zoologists like Konrad Lorenz and Niko Tinbergen observe animal behavior under natural conditions.

Harry F. Harlow, William T. McKinney, and their colleagues have gone one step further from natural observations and experimentally induced various emotional states. By separating rhesus monkey offspring from their mothers or from their peers, the researchers induced certain psychopathologic states—most prominently depression—in the babies. The baby monkey is first separated from the mother. The two can see each other through a cage, but they cannot touch each other. That may seem like a cruel thing to do, but human beings sometimes do the equivalent inadvertently.

In Harlow's model, there is a two-stage sequence to the emotional response of the monkeys. The first stage of behavioral response, as described by the authors, is that of protest. An increase in motor activity occurs, as well as an increase in vocalization, and the animals run around the cage and pound on the window separating them from their mothers, as though they are seeking to reestablish contact. If there were close-up films of the monkeys' faces, we would see expressions that we would register empathically as anguish and fearfulness, maybe even anxiety. In the second stage—which the investigators call the despair stage—the parties give up, the infant huddles in the corner, the mother turns away and her face begins to droop. All motor activity is reduced. Again, the facial expressions are empathically identifiable as despair to most human observers. Jane Goodall reports similar observations in chimpanzees separated from one another. There are even death reactions among some chimps she has studied in the African setting.

In a series of studies based upon dogs, psychologists John Paul Scott and John L. Fuller showed that the most reliable index of a dog's reaction to separation was the high-pitched wail. They studied the various effects of drugs on that form of vocalization, and the only drugs they found that reduced the dog's wail were the imipramine medications, which are used for their antidepressant effect upon human beings. Such drugs as the barbiturates and thorazine had no effect on the high-pitched wail, until the drugs actually put the animal to sleep. The vocalization of the dog is related to the degree of separation, as anyone who has left a dog in an automobile while shopping knows. The vocalization is an indirect form of evidence that there are biochemical and physiologic mechanisms built into mammals that react to the disruption of the attachment bonds.

Though the capacity to become depressed seems not to be an exclusively human one, it has been part of our evolutionary heritage and has played a biologically adaptive function. It performs what psychiatrist George L. Engel called a "signal" function, by alerting the social group, particularly the parental or mothering group, that one of its precious offspring is in some danger. That function is based in part on two facts

> ## "Attachment bonds have been essential to the survival and development of our species."

about mammalian species in general, and primates in particular: first, we produce very few offspring compared with fish or insects; and, second, our offspring are born biologically immature and truly helpless.

Many of us as adults may feel, at times, that we are helpless and we need to be taken care of, but we are for the most part capable of biological survival. That assurance is not true of human infants or other mammalian infants. In order for the species to have survived as long as we have, mechanisms had to develop to nurture and protect helpless offspring.

One general thesis that can be drawn from these data is that the affective state of depression is a specific response to the disruption of attachment bonds. Attachment bonds have been useful, even essential, to the survival and development of our species. They are served by a psychobiological apparatus developed through the centuries that we have inherited from our mammalian ancestors, particularly the primates. One interesting aspect of the apparatus is that we resist with great biological force any disruption of attachments. We do not give up our bonding without great psychological and physiological anguish. One index of the strength of our attachments is the effect of bereavement on our physical and emotional health.

Data from a study in England and Wales of more than 4,000 widowed men indicate that widowers have mortality rates over and above age-matched male peers for the first year of being widowed. During the first four to six months, a widower's death rate increases by more than 140 percent, compared with men of the same age and social class. After that period, the ratio returns to some degree of normality, but it does not become totally normal for one year. There are other indices that the loss of a mate, or other bereavement, has a powerful impact. People with previous histories of alcoholism increase their drinking. There is a general increase in ingestive behaviors, in pill-taking of various sorts, and in cigarette smoking. Humans react vigorously, with the total body, to the disruption of attachment bonding.

Now, what is the clinical significance? How do those manifestations of separation relate to the phenomena that may be seen in clinical work? In a large project in New Haven, Connecticut, we attempted to investigate some of the effects of disruptions of attachment bonding on human beings by looking at 185 clinically depressed individuals who met certain research criteria. We had the good fortune of being able to compare the patients with 185 normals selected in a household survey and matched for age, sex, and social class.

Both samples were interviewed for the presence or absence of various types of life stress—in the six to 12 months prior to the onset of symptoms in the case of patients and, in the case of the normals, the six to 12 months prior to the actual interviews. We used a modification of a common technique involving a checklist of various kinds of life events that are considered to be stressful, such as death, separation, and divorce. Supposedly positive events, such as Christmas and taking a vacation, were also included. From that list of over 60 items, we extracted several events and grouped them according to a rather simple distinction between "exits and entrances." Some events represent the exits or disappearances of people from the social field, such as death, separation, divorce, or a son going into the army, whereas others represent entrances of people into the life space, or interpersonal space, of the individual.

When patients and controls were compared, there was no statistically significant difference between them regarding entrances, but there was a very dramatic difference with regard to exits. The depressives had experienced far more episodes of loss and separation, in one form or another.

How does the evidence on the effects of life stresses relate to the kinds of phenomena that we deal with clinically in the cases of young adults? Eriksonian concepts of developmental stages are pertinent here. Young individuals in our society, in particular, are involved in a number of developmental tasks, the most important of which includes leaving the parental home and establishing independence. As part of modern life, we place a high value on independence. This goes against a certain amount of our biological heritage. As I have already indicated, we do not give up our attachment bonds easily; we do so at an emotional and physiologic cost. Yet, in a modern industrial society such as ours, we move from one place to another—for school, for a job, and from that job to another. We send our children to summer camp, to pajama parties, on weekend trips.

In other words, we purposely train our children to anticipate the disruption of attachment bonding and to be

able to cope with the uncomfortable sense of separation and anxiety it brings. Anybody who has worked at a summer camp has seen the frequent mood of anxiety among the children or even the counselors. I have read accounts of the military during the Civil War, and the most common neurological diagnosis in the Union camps was something called nostalgia. There is a brilliant set of descriptions of the emotional reactions, particularly in periods of nostalgia, in young enlisted men entering the camps. From those accounts came physician George Beard's 1880 description of "neurasthenia," with its fatigue, weakness, and sense of despair—symptoms that we would see now as a reaction to separation.

> "Compared to others, depressives experience far more episodes of loss or separation—of exits over entrances."

We expect our young today to move out, to leave the attachment of the primary family. In fact, if they stay too long with the primary family, we consider them dependent and as not moving along properly in the developmental cycle. More important, we see separation as an opportunity for growth and development. In the Eriksonian scheme, the outcome is the achievement of the capacity for intimacy, in order to create new forms of attachment bonding, especially with members of the opposite sex. With new attachments come a commitment to some sense of enduring responsibility and a capacity to share in emotional give-and-take.

I would propose that the sharp separation of old and new attachment bonding is a relatively new experience in the history of our species. Most of the social support systems on which our forebears relied until recently have emphasized some degree of stability and continuity.

The three most common social support systems have been the family, the church, and the immediate neighborhood. Ever since the introduction of urban life, we have relied upon those three social support systems as buttresses against disruptive emotional states, including depression, fear, and anger. It is a characteristic of the present time that all three of those social support systems are in various degrees of disarray.

Many people talk about the changes in the family, the extent to which the family seems to exist only at Thanksgiving, funerals, or other ritualistic occasions. The nuclear family is the subject of a good deal of criticism. People even claim that it is about to be done away with, given the high divorce rate. I do not hold with the conventional wisdom. If divorce is an actual illness, its cure seems to be the remarriage of the partners. People may not like marriage, but they seem to seek it out with a certain repetitive compulsion.

The church—organized religion—has played two important roles as a social support system. It attempted to provide cognitive meaning to life, and consolation during periods of despair, particularly those associated with death and other mysteries of existence. Second, the church was until recently the main system for the delivery of social services. We have now secularized the process with social-service agencies, child-guidance clinics, family services, and so on.

For most Americans, the church no longer provides cognitive meaning or a support system. However, the fact that many of today's youths are seeking alternative religious groups indicates that there are limits to which people in general, and the young in particular, can exist without some kind of a social support system. As for continuity and support from a community of neighbors, in an era marked by personal mobility and urban change, the neighborhood that has remained intact for 25 years is considered so rare as to merit a news story.

The theory that all or most depression can be explained as a reaction to loss or separation is a tempting one. Many theorists and textbook writers have emphasized one aspect or another of those phenomena as a necessary condition to understanding depression, whether as a normal mood, as a symptom, or as a syndrome. However, I think it is more important to recognize that there are limits to that theory of depression.

First of all, loss and separation are not the antecedent events in all clinical depressions. In the group of depressives from the New Haven study mentioned previously, we could find a history of discernible loss or separation only in about 25 percent of the patients who were clinically depressed, although there was a predominance of exits or entrances with the group. Of course, 25 percent is far higher than the 5 to 10 percent incidence found for normal controls. From the point of view of causation, loss and separation are important factors; they increase the relative risk of certain populations to depression, but they cannot be regarded as universal. Some people have attempted to extend the point and talk about unconscious loss or symbolic loss. While that approach has some utility, I think it blurs what is an important fact: only in about a quarter of adult cases do we find a clear precipitating event that falls in the category of loss or separation. Second, not all individuals who are exposed to loss, separation, or disruption of attachment bonds become depressed. Most individuals do cope with things like going to college, being drafted, or going to summer camp. Most even cope with so profound a disruption as the death of a parent or a child. There have been some very good studies of individuals in the bereavement situation. Evidence from those studies indicates that the majority of individuals who are widowed and bereaved do go through a period of emotional distress, with increased susceptibility to physical illness and increased use of the health-care system. However, by the end of one year, about 85 percent of them are back to normal.

In the third place, loss, separation, and disruption are not specific to depression. By that I mean that they have been described as the precipitating events for a wide variety of clinical conditions, not only psychiatric but also medical, such as coronary artery disease, peptic ulcer, rheumatoid arthritis, and automobile accidents.

Loss, separation, and disruption of attachment bonding thus seem to result in a general propensity for illness, perhaps more so for depression; but on the evidence, their influence is not conclusive. I believe that environmental stress, particularly loss or separation or disruption of bonding, cannot explain the clinical phenomena by itself. One must look to other aspects of the life of the individual or the social support systems available to give an explanation, let alone a prediction, of the individuals who adapt and the others who do not. Some of those factors may be genetic; others may be early life experiences in which the individual became sensitive to loss, a major theme in clinical theory. Another possible factor is any circumstance that lowers the self-esteem of the individual. Still other factors mentioned in the literature are changes in the social support system, the absence of the extended family, and the inability to make friends or develop group supports.

Peter M. Lewinsohn, a behaviorist, defines one of the propensities to depression as the absence of a social repertoire: one of the things that characterizes normal people, he says, is the capacity to elicit from those around us the positive social reinforcements that are necessary for building self-esteem. He speculates that the depressed individual is lacking in that set of social skills—per-

> "In modern life,
> the main forces that
> initiate depression
> are threats to
> the sense of self."

haps because of some failure in early development or social learning.

While the accelerated pace of loss and separation in modern life may not alone explain the seeming surge in depressive disorders, it seems to provide a climate in which such disorders are likely to proliferate. As we mature from the state of actual biological helplessness of our infancy, we become less dependent for biological survival upon our attachments, particularly those to parents. Attachments to human beings acquire a new function in our adaptation. They are not as important as they have been in the biological past of our species for survival, but they become important for our sense of self-worth, for our identity, and for the meaning and value we give to ourselves.

It is a thesis of many who have studied those phenomena that the biological function of depressive feelings changes as the maturity of the organism unfolds. Yet the psycho-physiological and biological apparatus that we have inherited through the millennia has not been modified. We still resist with great protest any disruption of our attachment bonding. What has changed are the stimuli, the environmental circumstances that initiate or terminate those profound reactions. In modern life, the main forces that initiate depressive responses are more often threats to the psychosocial integrity of the individual—to the sense of self, which is enhanced by our attachment to work, family, friends, and community— than to our physical well-being and survival.

For further information, read:

Klerman, G. L. and J. E. Izen. "The Effects of Bereavement and Grief on Physical Health and General Well-Being," Advances in Psychosomatic Medicine, Vol. 9, 1977.

Goodall, Jane. In the Shadow of Man, Houghton Mifflin, 1971, out of print.

Lorenz, K. and P. Leyhausen. Motivation of Human and Animal Behavior: An Ethological View, Van Nostrand Reinhold, 1973, $18.95, paper, $7.95.

Scott, J. P., J. M. Stewart, and V. J. De Ghett. In Separation and Depression: Clinical and Research Aspects, J. P. Scott and E. C. Senay, eds., American Association for the Advancement of Science, 1973, $19.95.

WHEN HUSBAND AND WIFE DISAGREE ABOUT SEX

William H. Masters & Virginia E. Johnson

WILLIAM MASTERS *and* VIRGINIA JOHNSON *are codirectors of the Reproductive Biology Research Foundation in St. Louis. They pioneered a new kind of psychotherapy when in 1958 they began clinical treatment of sexually dysfunctional men and women.*

Even in an exemplary marriage, differences in temperament mean that at times a husband and wife will find themselves emotionally at odds. With or without words, one may signal a wish to make love and the other either ignores the signal or counters it, saying, in effect, "I'm not in the mood." Often the refusal is tempered—not now, not here, not that way.

No matter how the response is phrased, as outright refusal or conditional acceptance, it puts an emotional discrepancy into sharp focus. The feelings of the husband and wife are in conflict. The real issue isn't making love; it's feeling loved. Although the wife may never say it, she is thinking: "If he loved me, he wouldn't insist." And the husband thinks: "If she loved me, she wouldn't refuse."

The emotional stakes are high, a fact underscored by the bitterness and hurt feelings that quarrels over sexual differences often generate. Differences can be successfully negotiated, but the process will be simpler if husband and wife share fundamental convictions about sex.

Success becomes more problematical for the couple with a basic disagreement, particularly if one holds conventional views toward sex and the other takes an unconventional approach. Should the wife accommodate her husband and accept the traditional female role, for instance, or is she equally free to express desire and initiate sex? Must intercourse be reserved for a customary time and place, or can it be enjoyed whenever and wherever the mood dictates?

Obviously, if a man and wife hold opposing views on such questions, they will have difficulty compromising. But even in those marriages in which husbands and wives are essentially of the same mind, conflicting feelings about intercourse on any given occasion are the rule rather than the exception.

How such conflicts are handled is crucial in establishing the atmosphere of a marriage. A negative approach creates defensiveness and resentment on the part of one or both partners, undermining their relationship. A positive approach leads to openness and trust. The difficulty, of course, lies in understanding the differences between the two approaches and implementing that understanding.

Negative approaches to sexual conflicts are characterized by fear, hopelessness or ignorance. Fear, for instance, impels some couples to minimize their dissatisfactions. If they are just patient enough, they tell themselves, the problem will go away. Other couples may acknowledge the problem but become defensive about it, each partner seeking reassurance in the belief that "it's not my fault."

In its most paralyzing form, fear expresses itself by the denial that any problem exists, or by refusal to face the problem even after it has become apparent.

In one case, a couple came for treatment because the wife had never experienced orgasm. It soon became evident that the husband had problems of his own. He was often impotent but saw himself as a virile male who, because of fatigue or too much to drink, would on rare occasions be uninterested in sex. It was his wife, he insisted, who could not function sexually; he himself did very well, thank you.

His wife confirmed his description of the situation. Although she must have been aware of his failures, she saw his impotence as her fault and agreed with him that the problem was hers alone.

No effort was made to persuade husband or wife that they both might be deceiving themselves. Instead, the husband was told during one counseling session that when he and his wife had intercourse that night, he was to permit his wife to assume the superior position. He was given those instructions with full awareness that this variation, which ran contrary to his picture of himself as the dominant male, would put him under considerable tension and thus make it unlikely that he could perform satisfactorily.

The following day he reported that he had failed to have an erection, and he quickly explained that this happened because he had eaten too much at dinner. He was told that his failure had been anticipated, that it resulted from emotional stress and that his inability to perform was, for him and under those circumstances, natural. He was reassured that this did not demean him as a man or prove that he was sexually incompetent. It did, however, demonstrate two things: that under stress he reacted as a human being and that he was subject to occasional impotence.

Once his fear of being something less than a man could be recognized for what it was—an adolescent image of the male as a sexual athlete—he was relieved of the need to deny the existence of his problem and could concentrate on learning to cope with emotional tensions. The more confident he became, the more certainly his body asserted itself—and the more readily his wife responded. She had been as much a victim of his tensions as he was. Once she was released from the fear the she was the cause of their sexual unhappiness, she was free to let a sense of physical pleasure rise to the surface of awareness and culminate naturally in orgasm.

Some couples make no attempt to deny the existence of a sexual conflict—on the contrary, they may fight openly about it—but they proceed to handle matters in ways that are just as self-defeating. One wife endured almost total frustration for years, furious with her husband because, as she saw it, "he didn't know how to do it right." Nevertheless, she continued to engage in sex whenever he made a request. "I feel used," she admitted, "but I also feel that I'm doing my duty. He supports me and the children, and if this is what he wants, that's what I do."

Over the years her anger intensified, and her husband, who genuinely regretted his inability to be more sexually effective, became increasingly impotent. Once in a while, however, he got back at his wife without being fully aware of what he was doing. On occasions when it was clear that she did not want to have intercourse but grimly agreed to it anyway, he found himself able to prolong his performance almost indefinitely.

Some couples use stereotypes to explain away all their difficulties. If a husband and wife cannot agree on how often to have sex, the wife can reassure herself that it is all her husband's fault because, as everyone knows, "the more you give a man the more he wants." And her husband can remain confident that his wife's lack of enthusiasm is no reflection on him because, as everyone knows, "most women really don't have much interest in sex." Such false stereotypes help countless couples suppress anxiety and avoid the underlying source of their discontent. With this kind of sedation some marriages can struggle along for years.

One other ill-advised approach should be mentioned. A couple may acknowledge to each other that their sexual relationship is far from perfect and both agree to do whatever they can to increase their pleasure. Unity of purpose starts them in the right direction—but they immediately take a wrong turn. They pull sex out of context; that is, they consider the physical act a skill to be practiced and improved, like dancing or tennis. But sexual intercourse is not just a skill to be mastered or a game to be played. To reduce sex to a physical exchange is to strip it of richness and subtlety and, even more important, ultimately to rob it of all emotional value. Less pleasure, not more, is the almost certain outcome.

As a hypothetical example, consider the husband who decides that his wife's inability to have more than one orgasm is an indication that she still isn't totally free in the acceptance of the pleasures of her body. Since she is both curious and suggestible, she thinks it a good idea when he suggests that she use a vibrator as a means of going into training, as it were, for bigger and better and more frequent orgasms.

Incorporated in this decision are two errors. The first involves pulling sex out of context. The fact that the husband wants his wife to experiment with a mechanical device symbolizes what the two of them are doing to their sexual relationship. Instead of seeing it as an extension of their marriage, reflecting how they feel about themselves and each other, they are turning it into a performance.

This means that the wife cannot relax and enjoy her sexual feelings because she will be straining for more than one orgasm.

The second error is that the husband is acting as the authority for his wife. Her concurrence does not alter the fact that he is using male standards and male attitudes as guidelines for female sexual behavior, something no man should presume to do. Even if he happens to guess right, what he is doing is wrong—because his wife then comes to conclusions on the basis of her husband's reasons, not her own, and the damage to her self-confidence can be incalcuable.

Exactly the same situation prevails when a wife tells a husband what he is thinking or feeling. Where sex is concerned, *each partner must accept the other as the final authority on his or her own feelings*. In affirming that principle, a man and woman have taken the first step toward achieving sexual harmony in marriage. They are telling each other that they accept without question the fact that they are individuals, separate but not separated, different but not dissimilar, and that their happiness must flow both from the delight they find in their differences and the security they derive from their similarities.

This is not a conviction easily attained, especially for young men and women. In growing up, the emphasis was never on what they shared. On the contrary, considerable emotion was invested in sharpening the sense of difference between male and female, and in using that difference as a way of defining themselves sexually. If girls like to talk, then a boy's taciturnity is an assertion that he is a male. If boys like to compete, then a girl's cooperativeness marks her as female. Each sex defined itself by deliberately choosing *not* to think or feel or behave like the other.

With such a heritage, it is no simple matter for a married couple to overcome the prejudices of the past and to understand that the differences between them are essentially no more and no less than the differences between any two individuals. As long as a man and woman use those differences as a way of separating themselves to prove that they are male and female, conflicts will remain threatening. But for men and women who accept conflict as an opportunity for growth, much depends on whether they have developed an adequate system of communication.

Suppose a husband wishes intercourse four times a week while his wife welcomes it just twice. Arithmetic suggests a compromise of three times a week. But the idea is, of course, ludicrous. The husband will still feel frustrated, the wife may feel imposed upon, and neither one will have learned anything about the other's feelings. If that were not enough, there remains the final incongruity: The real difference between them has nothing to do with numbers. Frequency is almost never the true issue.

Had this couple been able to communicate with each other, their goal would not have been to determine how many times to make love each week but to discover, if possible, their true feelings on the matter. The husband might have felt that he was failing to excite his wife or that he was in need of more care and warmth than usual. His wife might have felt oppressed by financial pressures, or unhappy because she had put on weight, or preoccupied by her new job.

Even if they fully unburdened their feelings, they would still have to deal with the fact that the husband's sexual needs were, at least for the present, greater than those of his wife. But the problem would not be that of taking or demanding versus not giving or submitting—it would be that of finding the best way to express care and concern for each other and to meet the needs of whichever partner was under the greater emotional strain.

This kind of communication is not easy, but it can be achieved by any couple willing to make the effort and to abide by two principles. The first calls for *neutrality*, the second for *mutuality*.

Neutrality requires both husband and wife to assume that past sexual discord will not necessarily repeat itself in the future, because each partner will try to change. Each credits the other with good intentions and the will to act on those intentions. Each accepts full responsibility for what he or she does—or fails to do—in making the effort to act differently. And each accepts responsibility for functioning sexually and does not hold the other accountable for the body's responses. If a man and woman are to have a good physical relationship, each must strive to be *responsive* to the other, not *responsible* for the other.

The second principle, mutuality, requires all sexual messages between two people, whether conveyed by words or actions, by tone of voice or touch of fingertips, to be exchanged in the spirit of having a common cause. Mutuality means two people united in an effort to discover what is best for both. In attempting to reconcile differences, they must avoid what lawyers call "adversary proceedings," in which each tries to prove that he is right and his opponent is wrong.

By contrast, mutuality calls for both partners to accept the idea that no conflict involving sex can be resolved on an either/or basis. If sexual disagreements are habitually settled in favor of one partner's wishes at the expense of the other's, the ultimate penalty will be paid by both. Suppressed resentment or unhappiness tends to short-circuit sexual feelings, and desire goes dead. This was described by a man who had come for therapy with his wife,

after 15 years of marriage. For more than 13 of those years, the wife had never been orgasmic but had tolerated perfunctory acts of intercourse. Then she read a book that convinced her that she had a right to expect full satisfaction. She became increasingly unhappy, however, as her efforts to reach a climax proved unsuccessful. Her husband, too, became unhappy. He also began losing his ability to have an erection or, if he achieved one, to maintain it.

"She *should* want an orgasm," he said, "and if she could have it, so much the better. But after a while this one desire dominated the sex act. My desires and everything else became subordinate, so what was there in sex for me to look forward to? In other words, sex became sexless."

It would be simple to say that his wife had made him impotent. But that would be just another instance of making one partner (in this case, the wife) responsible for the other partner's inability to function sexually.

Her real failure lay in not being responsive to her husband's emotional state. His failure lay in not signaling his growing dismay. Their distress was the consequence of failure to approach their problem in a neutral, nonfault-finding way, and their failure to be motivated by mutual concern.

This couple had accumulated frustrations and hurt feelings over the years, piling them up like bricks to build a wall of anger until eventually they lost sight of each other. Given their particular life histories, and especially the wife's severe emotional deprivation during childhood and adolescence, there was little they themselves could do unassisted, and they were wise to choose therapy. But suppose, in a comparable situation, neither partner had had a crippling childhood, and suppose, too, that they had been married only a few years. What might they have done to forestall a sexual crisis?

They could have talked. A husband and wife who find themselves troubled by sexual frustration are going to have to say so. Each must disclose his true feelings: I think, I feel, I wish, I need, I'm afraid—clear, candid statements that relieve one partner of having to guess, usually wrongly, what the other is experiencing. Both must resist the temptation to interpret each other: you think, you feel, you want, you need, you're afraid—opinions which, no matter how accurate, put the other on the defensive and set the stage for conflict.

Such honest communication is not simple. Cultural inhibitions, internalized over the years, do not disappear overnight. In the same way that men and women conceal their naked bodies because they have been taught to do so—and, more important, because they are afraid they may be physically unattractive—they also conceal their sexual feelings because they are afraid those feelings may be emotionally unappealing to their partners.

In addition, they may be reticent because they lack a comfortable vocabulary. Clinical words can prove chilling and vulgar words can prove disruptive in the kind of talks that take place, not during sexual encounters but in times of emotional communion, when a man and woman are struggling to be reflective and truthful.

Talking is certainly not the only way of communicating about sex and it is not necessarily the best way; words can mislead as well as illuminate. Nevertheless, for most people most of the time talking is indispensable, and the fact that the line goes dead when sex is the subject means that a considerable amount of important information remains shrouded in silence.

Assuming, however, that each partner sees the situation through the other's eyes, the next step is to negotiate the differences that threaten to deprive them of gratification. Negotiating differences, however, is not a matter of bargaining or setting terms. Negotiate, in these circumstances, reflects its definition as meaning "to move through, around or over in a satisfactory way," as in dancing. And the purpose of negotiation is conciliation. Business negotiations end with a conditional contract that states, in effect, "If and when you do X, I will do Y." Sexual negotiations end with a trusting commitment that states, in effect, "I will do my best to do X because I know you will do your best to do Y."

If such expressions of willingness to change are to be more than empty promises, they must be translated into reciprocal action. Generally speaking, it is not enough for just one person to make the effort. Under those circumstances, what may seem to be passive acceptance of change on the other's part is actually disguised passive resistance.

A husband and wife, for instance, can agree that she has been much more eager for sex than he has and that, without intending to, she has made him more resistant than he would otherwise be. He says that if she makes an effort to restrain her expression of desire, he will take the initiative more frequently. Each understands the other's feelings; both express a determination to change.

Soon, however, it becomes evident that while the wife is holding to her promise, the husband's response is less than impressive. From the wife's point of view, intercourse occurs with frustrating infrequency. Again they resolve to do better; and once again the husband's actions fail to match his intentions. Plainly, his avowed wish to improve his sexual relationship with his wife is not a truthful representation of his deepest feelings. For reasons he himself may not understand, he is not actively committed to conciliation. He is, in reality, resisting it.

The commitment requires each partner to try—and to keep on trying. It is the effort itself that means so much, even when success is not immediately achieved. But simple tenacity of purpose is not the entire answer. The outcome hinges to a considerable degree on how failure is handled. What a man and woman need of each other is the security that comes from knowing that occasional failures will not be used against them—they will not be ridiculed,

scolded or punished. On the contrary, the failures will be not his or hers but *theirs*.

A brief illustration concerns a man whose physical motions during intercourse are not to the wife's satisfaction. Because he moves too rapidly and forcefully, in a rhythm not in harmony with her own, she finds her responsiveness impaired. Finally she tells him what is wrong, and he immediately wants her help in changing the ways he uses his body. Although the first few times he blunders and reverts to old rhythms, she corrects him and soon he improves. The intimate mood is never shattered. Navigating these tricky emotional currents requires that each partner be constantly aware of the other's efforts.

This can be seen more clearly by contrast with other possible responses. The wife might have been condescendingly patient ("Well, dear, I'll be glad to show you once more") or discouraged ("Oh, not again!"). The husband might have been angry ("Don't tell *me* what to do!") or critical ("You don't know what you're talking about"). Or each might have remained silent, and each could have assumed the worst—the husband that nothing he could do would ever satisfy his wife; the wife that her husband cared only about his own pleasure.

Variations on the script are almost limitless, but the underlying point is that a successful approach is a creative act, and the credit belongs to both partners. Conversely, any failure would be a joint failure. Each would have failed to meet the other's needs in the most painful of all circumstances: when each feels himself or herself to be alone, uncertain and exposed—and desperately in need of help and reassurance. (This may cast some light on the reason why an effective sexual relationship contributes so much strength to a marriage. It is not simply because of the physical pleasure the husband and wife experience, important though that is. It is because of the powerful sense of emotional well-being that comes when each knows that at times of greatest vulnerability the other can be relied on to provide warmth, comfort and protection.)

One cautionary note: An individual's level of sexual tension—the power of the sex drive—is not easily changed by conscious decision, and it is important to take this into account. To a large extent, the strength of the sex drive is influenced both by cultural values and by the individual's unique experience growing up in that culture. But apart from these influences, there seems to be an innate level of sexual drive that varies from person to person.

Very few couples start out perfectly matched. The question is whether a husband and wife can learn to respect and accommodate themselves to differences in sexual desires. Suppose, for example, that a woman with a comparatively mild sex drive marries a man whose enjoyment of sex depends to some degree on the intensity of his partner's enjoyment. In the beginning, his pleasure inevitably will be tempered by his wife's low-key responsiveness.

If these two are to achieve a compatible sexual

relationship, they must reach a mutual understanding of their individual natures. They must accept the fact that variations in sexual drive do exist, that neither should apologize to the other for having more or less sexual energy, that one is not "better" or "worse" than the other. The husband must make his wife feel that he accepts her nature and that any regret he may have about her inability to experience intense sexual pleasure is genuine regret, not dissatisfaction. The wife must make her husband feel that her muted response is not a reflection on his skill as a lover or a personal rejection but her natural expression of sexual fulfillment. Thus, instead of acting as two separate individuals with contrasting—or even conflicting—standards of sexual behavior, they become a couple who honor the sexuality of their marriage.

Limited sexual responsiveness is, of course, often true of the male. The same principle applies—an acceptance of variations in sexual natures. This means rejecting the idea that the husband is any less a man because his sexual needs are less urgent than his wife expected, and it also means rejecting the idea that the wife is at fault because she fails to stimulate her husband to greater activity.

The strength of the sexual drive can change over a period of time. It is not fixed at a permanent level. A woman—and of course a man—may become more responsive; physical needs may surface more frequently and with greater intensity. If this happens, it doesn't mean that there was anything wrong with that person before the change occurred. It simply indicates that the sex drives of this particular individual were stabilized at a lower level as a result of any number of factors, such as limited experience, personal problems, family demands and social pressures. As these things change, so does sexual behavior.

In trying to resolve sexual conflicts by changing their ways of interacting, a man and woman must take into account · the fact that both are not only fallible but temperamental, that they cannot and do not always act as they would like to, and that apologies are acceptable after something has gone wrong.

This is an act of faith and it is crucial to sexual conciliation. To expect or want or need something of another person, and to let that person know it, is to be open to disappointment or denial. But as long as the denial is not a deliberate act on the part of the trusted person, as long as it can be seen as a reflection of such factors as forgetfulness, impatience, lethargy or unhappiness, the hurt can be accepted or at least put in perspective. And when forgiveness is later asked for—and given—sharing has taken place. Trust has been reaffirmed, and the process of sexual accommodation can continue.

There is no formula for success. Nor are there any shortcuts to achieving genuine intimacy. But if the principles of neutrality and mutuality are used as guidelines in the negotiation of sexual differences, there is every reason to be optimistic about the outcome.

And this much is certain: All experience gained in resolving conflicts creates the facility for dealing constructively with future conflicts—which are inevitable. Conciliation is another word for marriage.

'Old'
is not a four-letter word

A report on those who are euphemistically called "senior citizens." The topic is especially pertinent because of the aging of the American population and because of the extension of the mandatory retirement age from 65 to 70.

Alan Anderson, Jr.

Alan Anderson, Jr. is a writer living in Springfield, Illinois.

Meet Jim and Mary Johnson, Americans. Both are 65 years old, married to each other and about to embark on the perilous adventure of old age. This is a crucial year for them, and their success in getting through it—especially for Jim, who has just retired—will have a lot to do with how many more years they live, and how they feel about living. The year is crucial not because they are 65—a number more or less picked out of a hat by the Social Security Administration in the 1930s—but because the bureaucrats who set that benchmark had no idea how important it would become psychologically. Nor had they any idea how many people would be flooding past it today along the poorly marked paths of aging.

This country, with much the rest of the world soon to follow, is in the midst of a demographic upheaval unprecedented in history—a gray revolution, if you will. Today there are 21.8 million Americans 65 and older, nearly seven times as many as there were in 1900. Each day some 4,000 persons turn 65 and 3,000 in that category die, for a net gain of about 1,000 a day. By the year 2000 one out of five Americans will be over 65.

And we don't know what to do with them. They tend to be retired from work, ostracized socially, displaced from their traditional position as society's "elders." We don't yet understand them physically or psychologically, and we don't know how to make best use of their own desires and abilities to remain active. "The question of what to do with old people is a new one," says Chauncey Leake, a pharmacologist and student of aging at the University of California, San Francisco. "Over all the millennia of human existence, it could not have arisen until some 50 years ago. There simply weren't enough old people."

There are enough now, and modern America is baffled. A pension system carefully set up by Franklin Roosevelt is in trouble; within a few years, more people will be drawing from Social Security than are paying into it. We are trying (late, as usual) to stave off bankruptcy of the system. First, as everyone who works knows, Social Security taxes are zooming. Second, legislation has gone through Congress to extend the mandatory retirement age, generally 65, to 70; if the employee chooses to work until the age of 70, obviously there is no Social Security payout until that birthday. But there are more fundamental questions. How long *should* workers stay on the job—a particularly pertinent question in view of the change in mandatory retirement. What kind of job? Do they feel like working, and are they effective? Can families return to the custom of honoring the elderly? And what do Jim and Mary feel like, and how can they be most productive and happy?

The study of old people is a new pursuit—so much so that even the vocabulary is strange. Geriatrics, for example, is the study not of aging but of the aged and their diseases. The science of the processes of aging is gerontology; the first important work in this field was done as recently as the 1950s. There is also confusion between life expectancy (the expected length of a life) and life span (the theoretical limit of a lifetime). The average human life expectancy has stretched from about 22 years in the time of ancient Greece to 47 years in turn-of-the-century America to 71 years now. The maximum life span, about 110 to 115 years, has not increased at all.

Another new vocabulary word is ageism—like "sexism," one of the uglier terms of tin-ear wordsmiths—the prejudice against the old that Jim and Mary have begun to encounter. Old people face a painful wall of discrimination that they are often too polite or too timid to attack. Elders are not hired for new jobs, and are eased out of old ones (they are considered rigid or feebleminded); they are shunned socially (they are thought "senile" or boring); they are edged out of family life (children often regard them as sickly or ugly or parasitic); they are equated with children (common adjectives are "cute" and "adorable"). In sum, elders are treated by many as though they were no longer people. A typical study at a California nursing home showed that staff members judged the residents less interested and able to take advantage of activities than did the residents themselves. Our humor about old people implies wickedness of sex in men (old goat, dirty old man) and ugliness in women (biddy, hag, crock). Women after menopause and men after retirement lose social status rapidly. They are considered incapable of thinking clearly, learning new things, enjoying sex, contributing to the community, holding responsible jobs; in short, incapable of living.

Can this be true? How, then, was it possible for Picasso to paint masterworks until a few months before his death at 91? Michelangelo was still sculpting a few weeks before he died at 90. Verdi wrote *Falstaff* at 80; Tolstoy wrote *What Is Art* at 88. Even Freud, who was pessimistic about the minds of old people, did not begin his best work until his forties and wrote *The Ego and the Id* at 67. Titian did his finest paintings just before he died at 100, Pablo Casals was still playing the cello in his nineties, Winston Churchill was Prime Minister at 81 and Georgia O'Keefe starred in her first television special at 90.

What, then, does life have in store for Jim and Mary Johnson? Though the science of gerontology is still in its adolescence, we can at least erase some old myths and make some predictions. In general, the needs of older persons are not much different from those of younger persons: They do best when they can enjoy friendships and social contacts, keep busy with work and leisure activities and maintain reasonably good health. True, they are more vulnerable to stresses. Physically they have less resistance to shock and disease; psychologically they are prone to loneliness, dependence, the effects of family conflicts, loss of status. But there is good evidence that failure is not inevitable. Instead it seems that the health and happiness of old people decline because we expect them to—and old people believe us.

As a married couple of 65, the Johnsons are typical in some ways and unusual in others. The marriage itself is unusual and important: Married elders live on the average five years longer than unmarrieds. Most older women (69 percent) are not married, most older men (79 percent) are. This is both because women live longer than men (75 versus 68 years) and because women tend to marry older men (by an average of three years). Although more boys are born than girls, women outnumber men by 130 to 100 in the 65–74 category; by 74+ they're ahead by 169 to 100, and by 85+ by two to one. The U.S. Bureau of the Census predicts 1,000 women to 675 men by the year 2000, with widows outnumbering widowers four to one. It's not only a gray revolution; it's a gray female revolution.

The Johnsons are typical in that they live in their community. Until a decade ago, it was widely assumed that most of our elders lived in nursing homes or other institutions. In fact, only about 5 percent do, though the number is rising. And though the Johnsons have a few chronic problems (Jim has arthritis and Mary has high blood pressure), they are freely mobile (as are about 81 percent of elders in the community). Both wear eyeglasses (90 percent do); have no hearing aids (about 5 percent do); will spend $791 each on health care this year (more than three times that spent by people under 65; about two-thirds of the bill will be paid by the government); will take in $3,540 in Social Security for the two of them; completed eight years of school each; are white (fewer blacks live to this age); and have no jobs (only 22 percent of men over 65 and 8 percent of women do). Oh, and they always vote: 51 percent of our elders do, and they are becoming an ever-stronger bloc.

Physically, Jim and Mary have aged in similar fashion. Both have slowed: Their base metabolic rate has dropped about 20 percent since they were 30. This means they need slightly less to eat and the effects of drugs and alcohol last longer. (Dr. Robert Butler, director of the two-year-old National Institute on Aging, recommends no more than one-and-a-half ounces of hard liquor a day or two six-ounce glasses of wine.) Their body temperature has declined to as low as 90°F.; the aging King David tried to prolong his life by lying against the bodies of warm young virgins.

Perhaps the most significant change is that the entire circulatory machinery is less efficient. There is less elastin, the molecules responsible for the elasticity of heart and blood vessels, and more collagen, the stiff protein that makes up about one-third of the body's protein. The heart rate does not rise as well in response to stress, the heart muscle cannot contract and relax as fast and the arteries are more resistant to the flow of blood. Heart output—about five quarts a minute at age 50—has been dropping at about 1 percent a year. With the heart muscle less efficient and the vessels more resistant, heart rate and blood pressure both rise—and are both related to heart disease. Jim's blood pressure was 100/75 when he was 25; now it is 160/90. His blood carries less oxygen to the brain and lungs. If he rises too suddenly from a chair he gets dizzy. Likewise, if Mary climbs the stairs too fast she must stop to catch her breath.

Both are slightly shorter than they used to be, and have a tendency to stoop. This is due both to muscle wastage (less skeletal muscle to hold the skeleton upright) and to loss of bone tissue. The individual vertebrae settle closer together as the discs that separate them flatten and collapse. Mary's bones began a steady loss when she was about 40; by the time she is 80 her skeleton will weigh 25 to 40 percent less. Jim's bone loss, unsuspected until two decades ago, began just a few years ago and will be less severe. Gerontologists do not understand the mechanism or cause of bone loss, though there is some evidence that a good diet (containing adequate calcium, in particular) and regular exercise can slow it.

Both Johnsons are in less direct communication with the world around them. Each is slightly nearsighted and slightly farsighted; to focus near or far the lens of the eye must flex, and their lenses are more rigid; the ciliary muscles that control the flexing are also weaker. But neither condition will get much worse and both can be corrected by bifocals. Eye pressure increases (which may lead to glaucoma) and the lens may become more opaque, leading to cataracts; the latter can now be corrected by surgery. The Johnsons cannot smell as well. Both optic and olfactory nerve fibers will eventually dwindle to about 25 percent of the number present at birth, and they are irreplaceable. Elsewhere in the body the sense of touch has begun to dull, faster in the feet than in the hands, and the pain threshold has risen, creating a greater danger from hot or sharp objects. The taste dims; the number of taste buds will have decreased by a third by age 75.

The nerve cells people worry about most are those of the central nervous system—principally the spinal cord and the brain. Studies as early as the 1920s indicated that brain cells begin to die off around age 30 and in 1958 one researcher estimated the loss rate at 100,000 a day. Unlike skin, blood, liver and other regenerative cells, neurons cannot be produced after maturity. It is now known that the brain of an aged person weighs about 7 percent less than it did at maturity. But there is no direct correlation between brain size and intelligence, and there is still no evidence that loss of brain cells means loss of intelligence.

There are, of course, other changes in the brain more worrisome—changes that seem to impair mental function. These changes are all microscopic, and involve the proliferation of abnormal blobs, tangles and intracellular "garbage." The blobs are plaques containing an abnormal protein called amyloid. By now both Jim and Mary are almost certain to have some plaques, but their role in the aging process is unknown. The tangles—called neurofibrillary—are inside nerve cells (and others) and just as poorly understood. They resemble old, snarled fishing line. The "garbage" is a mysterious brown pigment called lipofuscin, or age pigment. The accumulation of lipofuscin among cells is thought always to accompany aging, but it is not known whether the pigment is simply a by-product of cellular activity or is harmful. Pellets of lipofuscin form an outer coat by the same process oil-based paints harden, and are resistant to normal "garbage-removal" enzymes.

These mysterious blobs, tangles and pigments are linked to one of the least understood and most abused terms in the lexicon of aging: senility. The word is frequently used to apply to any act or gesture by an "old" person—forgetfulness, selfishness, a desire for a nap and so on. Health care professionals now seldom use it except to indicate senile brain disease, sometimes called chronic brain syndrome. Even these terms are vague; Robert Butler calls them "wastebasket diagnoses." Their greatest weakness is that they fail to separate those who are "senile" from those who are "normal." One expert, Adrian Ostfeld of the Yale University School of Medicine, decides it this way: "If a person knows when to get out of bed, wash, dress, eat and pay his bills, he is not a case."

Nor is there any certainty about whether dementia (the commonest designation is Alzheimer's disease) is really a disease or simply a normal part of the aging process. One reason for this confusion is that the primary indicators of dementia (plaques, tangles, lipofuscin) are also present in "normal" older people like Jim and Mary. Most cases of Alzheimer's disease show no simple pattern of inheritance, and no evidence that they are contagious. What is certain is that they are rare—more so than commonly supposed. Because diagnosis is so uncertain, the true incidence is not known. But it is known that only about 5 percent of elders live in institutions, and only a very small percentage of them can truly be called senile. In one study of 3,141 low-income persons between 65 and 74, only 12 could be identified as cases of senile brain disease. Most of the institutionalized elderly are victims of stroke, injury, arthritis, chronic respiratory diseases, alcoholism and other nonsenile conditions.

Physically, then, the elders have slowed somewhat, but they are by no means incapacitated. There is no physiological watershed at age 65 that should prevent people from working if they want to. Their strength is down slightly, their wind reduced; but neither condition is crippling and certainly not serious enough to disqualify them from most activities of "normal" life. But what of behavior? Is there something different about the workings of an older mind?

I have mentioned the irony of Sigmund Freud: At the same time he mistrusted elders (he seldom took them as patients), he himself did his best work after the age of 40. Freud referred to a "rigid ego" in old age and an "inverted Oedipal complex"—an exaggerated attachment to a child figure rather than a parent figure of the opposite sex. Jung, unlike Freud, refused to lump older people in such psychic ignominy, treating each as a unique individual.

In fact, there are signs of subtle, broad psychic changes in old age, but nothing to deserve Freud's prejudice. These are tough to test because old people are slightly less motivated than the young to take tests. A University of

Why do we have to die?

By nature's rules, death is as much a part of the game as life. Shortly after puberty (in humans as in other animals), the first signs of aging begin—a steady loss of irreplaceable cells, an accumulation of "wear-and-tear" mistakes, a slowing of metabolic rate. Eventually the accumulation of these changes and mistakes becomes fatal in one way or another.

But the death that comes to us all is not really so simple as this organic falling-apart. Otherwise we might be able to stave it off through care, just as we prolong the life of a well-loved automobile by proper maintenance and garaging. The hard truth is that humans and other animals have a maximum life expectancy that is rarely, if ever, exceeded. No matter how well sheltered from predation, disease and other "natural" causes of death, the Norway rat does not live past the age of four years, the gray squirrel past 15, the black bear past 35, the Asiatic elephant past 70 or *Homo sapiens* past 110. If death were the random result of accident and rusting away, we would expect to encounter wide variations in nature—the occasional octogenarian squirrel or, at the opposite extreme, the elephant that ages quickly and dies at 14. It is clear that a program for death is written in our genes.

The location and trigger of that program constitute the most hotly debated questions in gerontology today. By one theory, championed by Leonard Hayflick of Stanford, a clock of aging lies in each of our cells, where DNA molecules bear a gene or genes for their own destruction. Hayflick bases his thinking on his discovery less than two decades ago that even cells carefully nourished outside the body in tissue culture are programmed to die. Previous to that time, cells in tissue culture were thought to be immortal. But in the chick embryo cells he uses, Hayflick has shown that cell division ceases after about 50 generations—a seemingly clear case of genetic self-destruction. Similarly, he believes that cells in a whole-body context give orders, by some mysterious timing, for a progressive disruption of protein assembly lines and eventually their own death.

A more popular, though not incompatible, theory is that death is controlled by the endocrine system through some unidentified "death hormones." W. Donner Denckla of the Roche Institute of Molecular Biology in New Jersey is a leader in testing this hormonal clock theory. "I don't care what happens to cells in tissue culture," says Denckla. "What is important is what people die of." Denckla's clock, controlled by the brain and mediated by the thyroid gland, would, like Hayflick's, have genetic gearworks. The mechanism for either is not yet clear.

Why should we die at all? That is an evolutionary question, but one which gerontologists must consider. Presumably, the reasons humans live as long as they do is that the species is well served by a hierarchy of elders who are able to think, be wise and pass on their wisdom to younger generations. Why not let old humans do this to the age of 200, getting ever wiser? The most reasonable explanation is that more frequent death—and new life—among individuals is necessary to the survival of the species. Evolution by means of natural selection is based upon the selection of "favorable" genes and their passage to successive generations. This genetic turnover must be rapid if we are to keep up with environmental changes.

Ah, you say—but that's old-fashioned! We are seizing control of our evolution now; we'll soon be able to engineer our genes to fit the environment of our choice. That may indeed be true, and if it is we'll also be able to correct the genes that bring death. We might learn how to live in good health and sound mind to the age of 200 or 500; perhaps there will be no limit. But we can only begin to guess at the social tumult that would accompany this sudden excess of new old people. Many of us would probably prefer the stance of Lewis Thomas, president of Memorial Sloan-Kettering Cancer Center in New York and author of *The Lives of a Cell*. "At a certain age," says Thomas, "it is in our nature to wear out, to come unhinged and to die, and that is that."

—A.A. Jr.

Chicago report on interviews with schoolteachers indicates a general laying back with age: "One of the things they talked about is that they had come to deal with professional interests with less intensity in middle age. A high school principal said: 'When I started out, each disciplinary problem in the school was a special problem for me. I intervened; I went all out for it. Now I withdraw a little more and let the teacher handle it until I can see what is going on.' "

Jim and Mary find that they move more slowly now,

mentally as well as physically. Instead of making a quick response to a question, then tend to ponder it for a moment before answering. Their reaction time has slowed; in a simple response test requiring them to push a button as soon as a red light came on, both Jim and Mary took .212 seconds to react when they were in their fifties, .217 seconds now. In 10 years it will take them .245 seconds to push the button. To some people, this is evidence that older people should take driving tests periodically.

The breadth of their interests has narrowed a good deal; this seems to peak around the age of *nine*, when children respond to almost anything. They watch about the same amount of television they did when they were younger, though they prefer variety and talent shows to serious dramas or mysteries. They have adopted more solitary pursuits, especially reading, going to art galleries and spending evenings at home with each other. Both have less interest in driving automobiles, in sports and in exploring.

According to one psychologist, there is more concrete behavior after age 60, less conceptualizing. Jim and Mary are more likely to think there is only one answer to a question, or one meaning to a situation, than they used to. In one thinking test reported in the *Journal of Gerontology*, involving subjects aged 12 to 80, the older people tended to rely more on past experience for answers rather than on analytical thinking. Other intelligence tests indicate a decrease in short-term memory, more difficulty putting three random words in a sentence, poorer word association, less facile picture composition.

In other areas, the Johnsons have experienced no such decline. Their vocabulary, for example, has nearly doubled since their twenties. Definitions, verbal understanding, naming countries, counting pennies all stand up well with age. Worker studies have indicated that individual speed and efficiency do drop with age, but older people tend to take care of their age-associated handicaps better than young people take care of their deficiencies. "Considering total job behavior," writes Harold Geist, a clinical psychologist and professor at San Francisco State College, "the older worker is found to be more efficient than the younger—especially when considering accuracy, absenteeism and motivation." Other studies have revealed little or no truth in the myth that most jobs are too strenuous or dangerous for elders. The U.S. Department of Labor has found that only 14 percent of jobs in industry require much physical strength, and many surveys have shown that older workers have fewer accidents than younger workers.

Much of the pressure to retire, it seems, comes not from an inability to perform but from the negative attitude of younger people. The University of Maryland's Center on Aging has found that children typically view elderly people as "sick, sad, tired, dirty and ugly" and insist that they themselves would never be old. And the most damaging aspect of such attitudes is that old people themselves come to believe them. "They are being told it's all downhill financially, it's all downhill sexually, it's all downhill intellectually," says Edward Ansello of the Maryland group.

New research, however, is revealing no evidence that life has to be significantly downhill for the old. Duke University's Center for the Study of Aging and Human Development has been keeping tabs on more than 200 elders for the last 20 years, and the group's conclusion so far is that most old people remain sound of body and mind until the final weeks of life. "The characteristic they seem to suffer most from," says George Maddox, head of the Duke Center, "is the tendency of society to treat them as though they are all alike."

Take sex, for example. NIA president Robert Butler has written a book called *Sex After Sixty* in which he says that this is one area where all people over a certain age are—wrongly—thought to be alike. "Many persons—not only the young and the middle-aged but older people themselves—simply assume that [sex] is over. This is nonsense. Our own clinical and research work, the work of other gerontologists, the research of Kinsey and the clinical discoveries of Masters and Johnson all demonstrate that relatively healthy older people who enjoy sex are capable of experiencing it often until very late in life."

Butler and other gerontologists argue that the myth of the sexless old is one of the most insidious symptoms of "ageism." He condemns the "aesthetic narrowness" by which we think of only the young as beautiful, and which makes it so difficult for grown children to deal with their parents' sexuality. Indeed, single or widowed parents who live with younger relatives are often made to feel guilty or indecent for wanting to date.

The field is riddled with additional myths. One of the most anxiety-producing is the fear of many men that they will have heart attacks during intercourse. It is, of course, possible, but fewer than 1 percent of all coronary deaths occur then, and 70 percent of those are during extramarital sex, which tends to feature nonphysical stresses like guilt or lack of time.

Another myth is the fear among women that a hysterectomy means the end of sex. In fact there is no evidence that removal of the womb produces any change in sexual desire or performance.

Then there are the false aphrodisiacs tried by many older people: alcohol (especially wine), Spanish fly, Cayenne pepper, black snakeroot, bloodroot, vitamin E, marijuana. Sometimes alcohol has benefit as a social icebreaker, but there the benefits end. Any stimulant works more on the mind than the body, and the effects lessen with use. The only true aphrodisiacs are good diet and good exercise.

Menopause in women, which typically occurs between 45 and 50, is a rich source of both myth and misunderstanding. Physiologically it is fairly straightforward, characterized by the ending of menstruation and a sharp decline in the output of hormones—chiefly the estrogen group. Some women, however, use menopause as an excuse, for themselves or others, to slow or even halt their sexual activity. Actually, about two-thirds of women experience no dramatic changes or discomfort with menopause. With a positive attitude, there is no reason that sex cannot remain a source of pleasure long after menopause. It is even common for sex to improve with the freedom from anxieties about becoming pregnant.

Jim, like Mary, can look forward to years of enjoyable sex. Both his fertility (the ability to have children) and potency (the ability to have intercourse) should last one or two decades, possibly even longer. Havelock Ellis, the renowned British psychologist and sexologist, overcame a lifetime of impotence when he reached old age. Jim will not have to go through the broad hormonal changes experienced by Mary; there is no menopause in men (though some experience a similar psychological shock) but rather a gradual decline in the output of testosterone, the male hormone.

If we make the assumption that old age is not a curse—and it now seems clear it should not be—can and should we prolong it? Here we come upon a stumbling block: It is assumed that aging is an inexorable part of life, programmed somehow in our genes, yet some scientists think that the wear-and-tear disease of aging might be "cured" by clever manipulation of body machinery. It seems, in any event, that for the foreseeable future our time on earth is limited to about 71 years. (See box on A/E page 128.

Even the conquest of common diseases would not lead us to immortality. If all cardiovascular diseases—now causing more than half of all deaths—were eliminated, the average lifetime would increase only about ten years. If cancer were no longer a killer we would gain another two years. Wipe out all infectious and parasitic diseases and we'd last another year; hold all accidents, suicides and homicides and that's two more years—still far short of immortality. In fact, despite all the medical gains documented since 1900, most of which lessened the threats of infant death and childhood diseases, Jim and Mary at 65 stand to live only about two years longer than they might have in 1900.

Despite an immense amount of research, the only known ways to extend a human lifetime (not a human life span) are to have long-lived parents, to eat properly and to get regular exercise. The first possibility, of course, is beyond our control. The last two are matters of will. Most gerontologists agree that Americans are eating themselves into early graves. We eat too much fat, too much sugar, too much protein, too much refined carbohydrate and not enough fresh vegetables, whole grains or other roughage. Take calories alone: Male Americans aged 55–64 now get about 2,422 a day, and most nutritionists believe this is too much. The world's longest-lived people thrive on far less. The same age group of men in Hunza, in West Pakistan, get about 1,925 calories a day; the men of the Caucasus in southern Russia about 1,800. Life insurance actuaries judge that being overweight subtracts from three to 10 or more years from a lifetime. So does

Prejudiced Shakespeare?

The sixth age shifts
Into the lean and slipper'd pantaloon,
With spectacles on nose and pouch on side,
His youthful hose, well sav'd, a world too wide
For his shrunk shank; and his big manly voice,
Turning again toward childish treble, pipes
And whistles in his sound. Last scene of all,
That ends this strange eventful history,
Is second childishness, and mere oblivion,
Sans teeth, sans eyes, sans taste, sans everything.

As You Like It, Act II

cigarette smoking: for one pack a day figure seven years; for two packs, 12 years. High blood pressure, high cholesterol level, a tense disposition, and a high pulse all shorten the average lifetime as well.

Exercise is increasingly acknowledged to be an effective ingredient in building a long lifetime. But it is important that it be an endurance building kind—not intermittent bursts of youthful enthusiasm followed by weeks of spectatorship—and it must be continued into old age. The point of exercise is to strengthen the heart, and the best kinds for doing that are jogging, cross-country skiing, swimming, rowing, cycling, long walks—anything that gets the heart pumping and keeps it pumping for 20 minutes or more. It has even been demonstrated that the much-maligned weekend athlete, if he or she is vigorous enough, gains some protection against heart ailments. A recent study of 17,000 Harvard alumni has shown "strenuous leisure time exercise" to be valuable even if there are other negative factors, like cigarette smoking. And, of course, those long-lived folks from Hunza and the Caucasus get plenty of outdoor exercise all their lives.

Typically, we slow-to-arouse Americans do not yet realize the urgency of the gray revolution. Before 1950 little thought was given to systems for the elderly—easier-to-use mass transit, housing situated near vital services, a health system that has the patience to diagnose and cure old people's chronic diseases. Only now, with the emergency upon us, are we beginning to think about how to live with our elders. An important first step must be an attack on "ageism" and an acceptance of the old people who will be a larger and larger component of modern society. More and more it will have to be "in" to be old.

FACING UP TO DEATH

ELISABETH KUBLER ROSS, M.D.

ELISABETH KUBLER ROSS, M.D., *medical director, South Cook County Mental Health and Family Services, Chicago Heights, Illinois.*

□ **People used to be born at home and die at home.** In the old days, children were familiar with birth and death as part of life. This is perhaps the first generation of American youngsters who have never been close by during the birth of a baby and have never experienced the death of a beloved family member.

Nowadays when people grow old, we often send them to nursing homes. When they get sick, we transfer them to a hospital, where children are usually unwelcome and are forbidden to visit terminally ill patients—even when those patients are their parents. This deprives the dying patient of significant family members during the last few days of his life and it deprives the children of an experience of death, which is an important learning experience.

At the University of Chicago's Billings Hospital, some of my colleagues and I interviewed and followed approximately 500 terminally ill patients in order to find out what they could teach us and how we could be of more benefit, not just to them but to the members of their families as well. We were most impressed by the fact that even those patients who were not told of their serious illness were quite aware of its potential outcome. They were not only able to say that they were close to dying, but many were able to predict the approximate time of their death.

It is important for next of kin and members of the helping professions to understand these patients' communications in order to truly understand their needs, fears, and fantasies. Most of our patients welcomed another human being with whom they could talk openly, honestly, and frankly about their predicament. Many of them shared with us their tremendous need to be informed, to be kept up-to-date on their medical condition, and to be told when the end was near. We found out that patients who had been dealt with openly and frankly were better able to cope with the imminence of death and finally to reach a true stage of acceptance prior to death.

Two things seem to determine the ultimate adjustment to a terminal illness. When patients were allowed hope at the beginning of a fatal illness and when they were informed that they would not be deserted "no matter what," they were able to drop their initial shock and denial rather quickly and could arrive at a peaceful acceptance of their finiteness.

Most patients respond to the awareness that they have a terminal illness with the statement, "Oh no, this can't happen to me." After the first shock, numbness, and need to deny the reality of the situation, the patient begins to send out cues that he is ready to "talk about it." If *we*, at that point, need to deny the reality of the situation, the patient will often feel deserted, isolated, and lonely and unable to communicate with another human being what he needs so desperately to share.

When, on the other hand, the patient has one person with whom he can talk freely, he will be able to talk (often for only a few minutes at a time) about his illness and about the consequences of his deteriorating health, and he will be able to ask for help. Sometimes, he'll need to talk about financial matters; and, toward the end of the life, he will frequently ask for some spiritual help.

Most patients who have passed the stage of denial will become angry as they ask the question, "Why me?" Many look at others in their environment and express envy, jealousy, anger, and rage toward those who are young, healthy, and full of life. These are the patients who make life difficult for nurses, physicians, social workers, clergymen, and members of their families. Without justification they criticize everyone.

What we have to learn is that the stage of anger in terminal illness is a blessing, not a curse. These patients are not angry at their families or at the members of the helping professions. Rather, they are angry at what these people represent: health, pep, energy.

Without being judgmental, we must allow these patients to express their anger and dismay. We must try to understand that the patients have to ask, "Why me?" and that there is no need on our part to answer this question concretely. Once a patient has ventilated his rage and his envy, then he can arrive at the bargaining stage. During this time, he's usually able to say, "Yes, it is happening to me—*but*." The *but* usually includes a prayer to God: "If you give me one more year to live, I will be a good Christian (or I'll go to the synagogue every day)."

4. PROBLEMS INFLUENCING PERSONAL GROWTH

Most patients promise something in exchange for prolongation of life. Many a patient wants to live just long enough for the children to get out of school. The moment they have completed high school, he may ask to live until the son gets married. And the moment the wedding is over, he hopes to live until the grandchild arrives. These kinds of bargains are compromises, the patient's beginning acknowledgement that his time is limited, and an expression of finiteness, all necessary in reaching a stage of acceptance. When a patient drops the *but*, then he is able to say, "Yes, me." At this point, he usually becomes very depressed. And here again we have to allow him to express his grief and his mourning.

If we stop and think how much we would grieve if we lost a beloved spouse, it will make us realize what courage it takes for a man to face his own impending death, which involves the loss of everyone and everything he has ever loved. This is a thousand times more crushing than to become a widow or a widower.

To such patients, we should never say, "Come on now, cheer up." We should allow them to grieve, to cry. And we should even convey to them that "it takes a brave person to cry," meaning that it takes courage to face death. If the patient expresses his grief, he will feel more comfortable, and he will usually go through the stage of depression much more rapidly than he will if he has to suppress it or hide his tears.

Only through this kind of behavior on our part are our patients able to reach the stage of acceptance. Here, they begin to separate themselves from the interpersonal relationships in their environment. Here, they begin to ask for fewer and fewer visitors. Finally, they will require only one beloved person who can sit quietly and comfortably near.

This is the time when a touch becomes more important than words, the time when a patient may simply say one day, "My time is very close now, and it's all right." It is not necessarily a happy stage, but the patient now shows no more fear, bitterness, anguish, or concern over unfinished business. People who have been able to sit through this stage with patients and who have experienced the beautiful feeling of inner and outer peace that they show will soon appreciate that working with terminally ill patients is not a morbid, depressing job but can be an inspiring experience.

The tragedy is that in our death-denying society, people grow up uncomfortable in the presence of a dying patient, unable to talk to the terminally ill and lost for words when they face a grieving person.

We tried to use dying patients as teachers. We talked with these patients so they could teach our young medical students, social work students, nurses, and members of the clergy about one part of life that all of us eventually have to face. When we interviewed them, we had a screened window setup in which we were able to talk with them in privacy while our students observed and listened. Needless to say this observation was done with the knowledge and agreement of our patients.

This teaching by dying patients who volunteered this service to us enabled them to share some of their turmoil and some of their needs with us. But perhaps more important than that, they were able to help our own young students to face the reality of death, to identify at times with our dying patients, and to become aware of their own finiteness.

Many of our young students who originally were petrified at the thought of facing dying patients were eventually able to express to us their own concerns, their own fears, and their own fantasies about dying. Most of our students who have been able to attend one quarter or perhaps a semester of these weekly death-and-dying seminars have learned to come to grips with their own fears of death and have ultimately become good counselors to terminally ill patients.

One thing this teaches us is that it would be helpful if we could rear our children with the awareness of death and of their own finiteness. Even in a death-denying society, this can be and has been done.

In our hospital we saw a small child with acute leukemia. She made the rounds and asked the adults, "What is it going to be like when I die?" The grown-ups responded in a variety of ways, most of them unhelpful or even harmful for this little girl who was searching for an answer. The only message she really received through the grown-ups' response was that they had a lot of fear when it came to talking about dying.

When the child confronted the hospital chaplain with the same question, he turned to her and asked, "What do you think it's going to be like?" She looked at him and said, "One of these days I'm going to fall asleep and when I wake up I'm going to be with Jesus and my little sister." He then said something like "That should be very beautiful." The child nodded and happily returned to play. Perhaps this is an exaggerated example, but I think it conveys how children face the reality even of their own death if the adults in their environment don't make it a frightening, horrible experience to be avoided at all costs.

The most forgotten people in the environment of the dying patient are the brothers and sisters of dying children. We have seen rather tragic examples of siblings who were terribly neglected during the terminal illness of a brother or a sister. Very often those children are left alone with many unanswered questions while the mother attends the dying child in the hospital and the father doesn't come home from work because he wants to visit the hospital in the evening.

The tragedy is that these children at home not only are anxious, lonely, and frightened at the thought of their sibling's death, but they also feel that somehow their wish for a sibling to "drop dead" (which all children have at times) is being fulfilled. When such a sibling actually dies, they feel responsible for the death, just as they do when they lose a parent during the preschool years. If these children receive no help prior to, and especially immediately after, the death of a parent or a sibling, they are likely to grow up with abnormal fears of death and a lot of unresolved conflicts that often result in emotional illness later on in life.

We hope that teachers are aware of the needs of these children and can make themselves available to them in order to elicit expression of their fears, their fantasies, their needs. If they're allowed to express their anger for being neglected and their shame for having "committed a crime," then these children can be helped before they develop permanent emotional conflict.

A beautiful example of death education in an in-direct way is expressed in a letter I received from a man who became aware of my work and felt the need to convey some of his life experiences to me. I will quote his letter verbatim because it shows what an early childhood memory can do for a man when he's faced with the imminent death of his own father.

Dear Dr. Ross: May I commend you and your colleagues who took part in the Conference on "death. . . ."

I am a production-line brewery worker here in Milwaukee who feels strongly on this subject. Because of your efforts, maybe one day we can all look death in the eye. . . . In reading and rereading the enclosed account of your meeting, I found myself with the urge to relate to you a personal experience of my own.

About six years ago, my dad was a victim of terminal cancer. He was a tough, life-loving 73-year-old father of 10 with 10 grandchildren who kept him aglow and always on the go. It just couldn't be that his time had come. The last time I saw him alive was the result of an urgent phone call from my sister. "You'd better come home as soon as possible; it's Pa."

The 500-mile drive to northern Minnesota wasn't the enjoyable trip that so many others had been. I learned after I arrived that he wasn't in the hospital, but at home. I also learned that "he didn't know." The doctor told the family that it was up to us to tell him or not tell him. My brother and sisters who live in the area thought it best "not to" and so advised me.

When I walked in on him, we embraced as we always did when we'd visit about twice or so each year. But this time it was different—sort of restrained and lacking the spirit of earlier get-togethers; and each of us, I know, sensed this difference.

Then, some hours later, after the usual kinds of questions and answers and talk, it was plain to me that he appeared so alone and withdrawn, almost moody or sulking. It was scary to see him just sitting there, head in hand, covering his eyes. I didn't know what to say or do. I asked if he'd care for a drink—no response. Something had to give. It all seemed so cruel. So I stepped into the kitchen and poured me a good one—and another. This was it, and if he didn't "know," he would now.

I went over and sat down beside and sort of facing him, and I was scared. I was always scared of my father, but it was a good kind of fear, the respectful kind. I put one hand on his shoulder and the other on his knee. I said, "Pa, you know why I came home, don't you? This is the last time we will be together." The dam burst. He threw his arms around me, and just hung on.

And here's the part I'll never forget and yet always cherish. I remember when our tears met, I recalled, in a sort of vivid flashback, a time 30 years before when I was five or six and he took me out into the woods to pick hazelnuts. My very first big adventure! I remembered being afraid of the woods. Afraid of bears or monsters or something that would eat me up. But even though I was afraid, I at the same time was brave, because my big strong daddy was with me.

Needless to say, thanks to that hazelnut hunt, I knew how my dad was feeling at that moment. And I could only hope that I gave him some small measure of courage; the kind he had given me. I do know he was grateful and appreciated my understanding. As I remember, he regained his composure and authority enough to scold *me* for crying. It was at the kitchen table, after a couple or three fingers of brandy, that we talked and reminisced and planned. I would even guess he was eager to start a long search for his wife, who also had known how to die. . . .

What I am trying to convey is that everything de-pends on the way we rear our children. If we help them to face fear and show them that through strength and sharing we can overcome even the fear of dying, then they will be better prepared to face any kind of crisis that might confront them, including the ultimate reality of death.

LIVING LONGER

RICHARD CONNIFF

The subject, a healthy white male, is 29 years old, an age he would like to maintain more or less forever. At the moment, he is sitting in front of a computer terminal in a private office in Corona del Mar, California, about an hour south of Los Angeles. He is about to learn electronically, on the basis of key physical indicators, whether he is still in his prime or if his body is already slipping into the long decline to senescence. Forget what the mind feels, or what the calendar and a searching look into a mirror might suggest; this machine aims to tell how much the body has actually aged—and therefore how long the subject is likely to live.

The test takes 45 minutes. It requires no syringes, blood pressure belts or strapped-on electrodes. In fact, the whole experience is less like a medical examination than a stint at a computerized arcade game. Not quite Space Invaders, but then, the subject doesn't want to be Luke Skywalker. He's just a guy who'd like to live to 120, and never feel older than 29.

In all, there are more than a dozen tests. They measure such indicators as the highest pitch the subject can hear (known to decline significantly with age), the ease with which the eye adjusts its focus between near and far objects (lens and supporting structure become less elastic over the years) and the subject's ability to identify incomplete pictures of common objects (perceptual organization begins to fall off at about age 30).

Then comes a brief whirring of electronic thought and, ladies and gentlemen, the computer's analysis: The subject has the hearing of a 21-year-old, skin as sensitive as a child's and, overall, a body that just barely passes for 32. So much for the sweet bird of youth.

But not so fast. It turns out that there may be loopholes in the standard existential contract of birth, aging and death. Even people now approaching middle age can expect a bonus of perhaps several years of extra living, thanks to continuing medical progress against cancer, heart disease, stroke and other killers.

At the same time, gerontologists—specialists in the science of aging—are piecing together the details of diet, exercise, personality and behavior that make it practical to shoot for 80, or even 114—the longest human life span reliably recorded.

Finding the Fountain of Youth

There is hope even for people who fear diet and exercise almost as much as an early death. At the most minute level, scientists are now deciphering the basic biologic mechanisms of aging and of rejuvenation. Gerontologists are so confident about fulfilling the promise of their discoveries that a healthy young man aiming to live 120 years begins to appear reasonable. Writing in The American Journal of Clinical Pathology, one researcher recently predicted: "The discipline of gerontology is now advancing at such a rapid rate, with so much overflow from other fields ... that I rather confidently expect a significant advance in maximum

life-span potential to be achieved for the human species during what is left of the present century...." One probable means of life extension is already available, in a tentative form, and it suggests that a 16th-century Italian named Luigi Cornaro was far closer than Ponce de Leon to the fountain of youth. More about him later.

The so-called life-extension revolution couldn't come at a stranger time. American society is already on the brink of startling change. It is growing up. Whether longevity improves by only a few more years, as some expect, or by whole decades, mature people will for the first time predominate. Between 1970 and 2025, the median age in the United States will have risen almost 10 years, from 27.9 to 37.6—as substantial an age difference for a nation as for an individual. The number of people 65 and over will double, from 25 million now to 51 million in 2025, and there will be 85 million people over the age of 55. All without major new increases in longevity. In earlier societies, so few people managed to reach old age that they were deemed special, endowed with magical powers to ward off the demons of aging. In the United States over the coming decades, the elderly will be commonplace, and possibly more: a powerful, organized political and economic force.

Elderly Astronauts

What will it mean to live longer in such a society? One public-relations man, a product of the post-World War II baby boom, finds himself caught up in his generation's frantic competition for good homes and the best jobs. He suffers nightmares of an old age in which winning admission to a nursing home will prove harder than getting into Stanford or Yale. Cemeteries will be standing room only. Others worry that an increase in longevity will merely mean an increase in the time they'll spend bedridden, senile, catheterized.

Not so, say the gerontologists. They argue that even if there is no significant medical breakthrough, today's young and middle-aged can still look forward to a more youthful old age than their parents or grandparents. Instead of applying for early admission to the local nursing home, these future elderly may acknowledge their dotage merely by switching from downhill to cross-country skiing, or from running to jogging. Rather than worrying about death or about overcrowding at Heavenly Rest Cemetery, they may instead be considering the personal implications of a study, recently begun by the National Aeronautics and Space Administration, to determine how well 55- to 65-year-

---

LINUS PAULING
Scientist
Born: 1901

"I think people should try to keep healthy. I'm especially interested in vitamin C. I continue to recommend that everyone get a good supply. I take 10 grams a day."

---

old women withstand the stress of spaceflight. K. Warner Schaie, research director of the Andrus Gerontology Center at the University of Southern California, cites three well-known but rarely noted reasons for optimism about future old age:

• **The control of childhood disease.** Aging is cumulative. Instead of simply healing and going away, the minor assaults suffered by the body from disease, abuse and neglect can have "sleeper" effects. Chicken pox in a child, for example, can lead much later in life to the hideous itching affliction known as shingles. But vaccines and other wonders of modern medicine have largely eliminated such time bombs. Says Schaie, who is 53 and has lived through whooping cough, measles and mumps: "Most people who will become old 30 or 40 years from now will not have had childhood diseases. Most people who are now old have had them all. That's an important difference."

• **Better education.** Where a grade-school background was typical for the older generation, more than half of all

Americans now 30 or 40 years old have completed at least high school, and studies show that people with more education live longer. They get better jobs, suffer less economic stress and tend to be more engaged with life and more receptive to new ideas, which may help explain the third factor.

• **The fitness revolution.** "We really have changed our habits with respect to diet and exercise and self-care," says Schaie. Per capita consumption of tobacco has dropped 26 percent over the past 15 years, and the drop is accelerating, promising a decrease in chronic obstructive pulmonary disease and lung cancer. Life-style changes and improved treatment of hypertension have already produced a dramatic national decrease in cerebrovascular disease, one of the major chronic problems of old age.

Gerontologists say that these same future elderly will also benefit from the increasingly accepted idea that aging is partly a matter of choice. Speaking before a recent meeting of the American Academy of Family Physicians, Dr. Alex Comfort, the author and eminent gerontologist, argued that 75 percent of so-called aging results from a kind of self-fulfilling prophecy. "If we insist that there is a group of people who, on a fixed calendar basis, cease to be people and become unintelligent, asexual, unemployable and crazy," said Comfort, "the people so designated will be under pressure to be unintelligent, asexual, unemployable and crazy." Changing the image of the elderly may change the way the elderly behave.

Just as important as the image itself is the way individuals react to it. Performance declines on average with age, but individuals can practice not to be average. A 75-year-old man whose joints should be stiffening into immobility can run the marathon. An 80-year-old woman whose capacity for work is undiminished can model herself after Sir Robert Mayer, who declared at age 100: "Retire? Never! I intend to die in harness." (Now 101, Mayer is still arranging concerts, and recently remarried).

STROM THURMOND
United States Senator
Born: 1902

"I think the advantage of my age is the wisdom and knowledge that comes with experience. For those looking ahead to a long life, I offer this advice: Read the Constitution and demand that public officials, legislators and judges abide by it."

GEORGE GALLUP
Pollster
Born: 1901

"There's no substitute for experience. As I look back on my life, I wonder how I could have been so stupid.

"Intellectual curiosity is important, too. A lot of people die just from boredom. I have a whole program that will keep me going until age 100, at least. Incidentally, some years ago we did a study of people over the age of 95. We interviewed over 450 individuals; 150 of them were older than 100. What we found was that those who live a long time *want* to live a long time. They are full of curiosity, alert and take life as it comes."

This reliance on choice and something more—spunk, exuberance, a positive mental attitude—may sound romantic, and is, admittedly, an exotic notion in some of its permutations. At the State University College in Geneseo, New York, for example, Lawrence Casler, a psychologist, is convinced that aging is entirely psychosomatic. In 1970, to break through "brainwashing" about life span, he gave "an extremely powerful hypnotic suggestion" to 150 young volunteers that they will live at least to 120. "We're planning a big gala champagne party for the year 2070," says Casler. "I'm looking forward to it." He also gave a hypnotic suggestion for long life to residents of a nursing home who were already 80 or older. Casler says that the suggestion appears to have reduced serious illness and added two years to life span in the experimental group.

But even medical specialists in aging take the role of choice seriously. Dr. James F. Fries of the Stanford University Medical Center writes in The New England Journal of Medicine that "personal choice is important—*one can choose not to age rapidly in certain faculties....*" The italics are added, but Fries himself writes that the biologic limits are "surprisingly broad." With training, experimental subjects have repeatedly reversed the pattern of decline in testing for intelligence, social interaction, health after exercise, and memory—even after age 70. Fries, Schaie and every other gerontologist interviewed for this article reached the same conclusion: To stay younger for longer, you must stay physically and mentally active. As Fries put it, "The body, to an increasing degree, is now felt to rust out rather than to wear out." What you don't use, you lose.

The Gray Revolution

A society dominated by old people will inevitably look different. Without a medical breakthrough, even vigorous old people cannot avoid slowing down. Schaie's interpretation is positive: "Young people . . . make many more errors of commission than omission, but the reverse is true for the elderly." Caution. The wisdom of the aged. To accommodate it, traffic lights, elevators, the bus at the corner will also have to slow down and become more patient.

Housing will be redesigned. But that doesn't necessarily mean handrails in the bathroom, wheelchair lifts on the stairway or any of the other depressing impedimenta of old age. "You're thinking of facilities for the ill elderly," says Schaie. Instead, redesign may mean more one-story garden apartments (stairs waste human energy). Homes will be smaller and require less care. House cleaning, home maintenance, dial-a-meal and dial-a-bus services will proliferate. Condominiums for the elderly will be built not near hospitals—an outdated idea, according to Schaie—but near libraries, colleges and shopping and athletic facilities.

The work place will also change, because more old people will stay on the job. As early as 1990, the baby bust of the past two decades will yield a shortage of young workers. Older workers will gain as a result, and there are few things better for an older person's spunk, exuberance or positive mental attitude than a sense of continuing worth in the marketplace and the paycheck that goes with it. The change is already beginning. The personnel department of one high-technology company, unable to find enough job candidates under 30, recently hired Schaie to convince its own top management that gray-haired engineers are just as able to keep the company on the cutting edge of innovation. Schaie says that it will pay to update and retrain older workers, not just for their expertise, but because they are less prone to accidents and absenteeism than their younger counterparts. In the Information Society, automation and robotics will make youth and strength less significant; the premium will be on knowledge and experience.

Indeed, James E. Birren, who runs the Andrus Gerontology Center in Los Angeles, predicts an era of "the experimental aged." A 75-year-old female lawyer came out of the audience once when he was explaining this idea, took his chalk away and told him in detail, with notes, why he was being too re-strained. At 62, it seems, Birren still suffered the inhibitions of the conservative young. By contrast, he says, the elderly are past child-rearing and mortgage-paying, and they are also often beyond worrying about what the boss or the family thinks. But they have a much better sense of what they themselves

---

MILLICENT FENWICK
United States Congresswoman
Born: 1910

"Life gets better and better. You know why? You can help someone, and they aren't afraid of you. No one thinks that you're going to seduce them, or breach a promise or be a menace in any way. Here in Washington, your colleagues know that you are not going to interfere with them when they want to run for the Presidency.

"You are free. You aren't a young person, struggling to pay the mortgage and the children's dentist bills, with endless opportunities opening before you. When someone says that youth is the easiest time of life, that person has forgotten the terrible strain of choice."

---

think, and it is often surprising. In a 1971 Gallup poll, for example, substantially more older people thought that the Vietnam War was a mistake than did those in the 21- to 29-year-old group. If they did not do much about it, perhaps it was because they accepted the youth culture's image of old people as doddering and ineffective. But given respect, independence, a steady paycheck, the prospect of continued vigor and the knowledge of their own numbers, the old may replace the young, says Birren, as the experimenters, innovators and all-around hell-raisers of the world.

Which brings us to the question of sex and the elderly. Future elderly will enjoy, and perhaps enforce, a more tolerant public attitude toward their romantic activities. Dr. Leslie Libow, medical director at the Jewish Institute for Geriatric Care in New Hyde Park, New York, blames decreasing sexual interest among older men and women at least partly on the traditional popular expectation that interest ought to decrease. But that expectation shows signs of changing. One company not long ago introduced a line of cosmetics specially designed for older women and met with 400 times the response it had predicted. And a New York-area motel offering X-rated movies recently began advertising a senior-citizens discount. Future elderly will also benefit from subtler changes. Bernice L. Neugarten, a psychologist at the University

---

LATE, GREAT ACHIEVERS

Herein, proof that life begins—or at least continues—after 70.

Konrad Adenauer (1876-1967) 73 when he became the first Chancellor of the Federal Republic of Germany. Resigned 14 years later.
Walter Hoving (b. 1897) Chairman of Tiffany & Company for 25 years; recently left to start his own design-consulting firm at 84.
Pope John XXIII (1881-1963) Chosen Pope at 77; brought the Catholic Church into the 20th century.
Jomo Kenyatta (c. 1894-1978) Elected Kenya's first President at 70. Led the country for 14 years.
Henri Matisse (1869-1954) In his 70's did a series of sprightly paper cutouts that were exhibited at New York's Museum of Modern Art.
Golda Meir (1898-1978) Named Prime Minister of Israel at 71; held the job for five years.
Cathleen Nesbitt (b. 1889) At 92, revived the role she created on Broadway 25 years ago: Professor Higgins's mother in "My Fair Lady."
Pablo Picasso (1881-1973) Complet-ed his portraits of "Sylvette" at 73, married for the second time at 77, then executed three series of drawings between 85 and 90.
Anna Mary Robertson Moses (1860-1961) Was 76 when she took up painting as a hobby; as Grandma Moses won international fame and staged 15 one-woman shows throughout Europe.
Dr. John Rock (b. 1890) At 70 he introduced the Pill; spent the next 20 years as its champion.
Artur Rubinstein (b. 1887) Was 89 when he gave one of his greatest performances at New York's Carnegie Hall.
Sophocles (c. 496-406 B.C.) Wrote "Electra" and "Oedipus at Colonus" after 70, held office in Athens at 83.
Giuseppe Verdi (1813-1901) Was 74 when "Otello" added to his fame; "Falstaff" followed four years later.
Frank Lloyd Wright (1869-1959) Completed New York's Guggenheim Museum at 89; continued teaching until his death.
Adolph Zukor (1873-1976) At 91, chairman of Paramount Pictures.

of Chicago, suggests that as they put anxiety-producing family and career decisions behind them, men and women are likely to relax more with one another. Sex stereotypes and the arguments they provoke will decline in importance as the years go by. As for male impotence, Libow notes that 20 percent to 40 percent of men continue to have active sex lives well into their 70's even now.

Finally, what about the specter of a long and vigorous life ending wretchedly in a nursing home? The average admission age today is 80, and only 5 percent of the elderly now endure such institutions. Even so, at current rates, the number of nursing-home residents will increase by 57 percent, from 1.3 million now to 2.1 million in 2003. But there are alternatives to terminal "convalescence." Most people now die without what Neugarten calls "a final deterioration that erases individuality." Birren believes that even more people will die "in harness" in the future. Instead of dwindling away, they will remain vigorous longer, then drop away quickly. Temporary "respite care"—an innovation now being imported from Scandinavia—will be available, say, for an octogenarian down with a bad cold. Schaie suggests that old people who are burdened with large homes may also invite friends to come live with them for mutual support. Such communes will give them independence they could never hope for in a nursing home.

Supergenes

So far, all of this assumes that there will be no breakthrough in human longevity, no anti-aging pill or fountain of youth. People will become wrinkled and gray and die at roughly the biblical threescore and ten or fourscore years. But that is no longer a safe assumption.

Dr. Roy Walford is one of the leading gurus of the life-extension move-

ment, and he looks the part. His head is hairless, except for a gray moustache that thickens down past the corners of his mouth. He can seem ferocious on film, but in person he is benign, almost shy. When he tours his complex of laboratories at the School of Medicine of the University of California at Los Angeles, he keeps his elbows close by his sides, and his hands in front of him, tucked like a monk's into the sleeves of his white lab jacket. His colleagues around the country tell you first that he is odd, and second that they respect him more than any other researcher in the field.

Walford believes that he has identified a single supergene that controls much of the aging process. Since 1970, he has been studying a small segment of the sixth chromosome in humans called the major histocompatibility complex. This is the master genetic control center for the body's immune system, and it is a logical suspect in the aging process. The ability to fight off disease peaks in most people during adolescence, and then falls off to as little as 10 percent of its former strength in old age. At the same time, a kind of perversion of the immune system occurs, in which the workhorses of self-defense lose some of their ability to distinguish between friendly and foreign cells. They attack the body's own organs, leading to such characteristic diseases of old age as diabetes and atherosclerosis. The phenomenon is called autoimmunity, and it means that the body is making war on itself.

Walford established the supergene's additional role in aging by comparing 14 strains of mice. The study (conducted by his associate, Kathy Hall) demonstrated significant differences in life span among mice that were genetically identical *except* at key locations in the major histocompatibility complex. Additional study by Walford, Hall and others tied that single genetic variable to two of the most important factors in the aging process as it is now understood. The long-lived mice had improved DNA-repair rates and increased protection against cellular damage from bodily substances known as free radicals. But the most profound idea, first suggested by Richard Cutler of the National Institute for Aging and substantiated by Walford, was simply that genes control longevity. Mice with "good" genes lived longer; the strains with "bad" genes had lives that were nasty, brutish and, above all, short.

Walford points out that there may be other genes controlling longevity. But none has been located so far, and separate studies on the nature of hu-

man evolution suggest that there may be, at most, only a few such supergenes. All of which makes Walford's discovery about the major histocompatability complex more important. What to do about it? Altering the genetic information in the nucleus of every cell of an adult animal is, at least for now, impossible. Instead, scientists are trying to find other supergenes and identify the mechanisms by which they work. If these supergenes have some regulatory mechanism in common, it may then be possible to manipulate the mechanism rather than the gene.

One promising school of thought theorizes that aging results mainly from accumulating errors in the complex, tightly coiled strands of DNA that are each cell's blueprint for accurately reproducing itself. The damage comes from many sources: ultraviolet radiation, viruses, free radicals, toxic chemicals, even the body's own heat. Repair enzymes correct some damage, but some persists. Over the years, tiny breaks and infinitesimal wart-like bulges accumulate, the DNA coils loosen and the cell begins to malfunction.

The theory suggests that those animals most efficient at DNA repair will live longest and age least. And so it happens in nature. The white lip monkey has a low rate of DNA repair, and lives to be only 12 or so years old. Humans have a very high rate of DNA repair, and live longer than any other primate. Differences in the DNA repair rate appear even among members of the same species, along with corresponding differences in longevity. Walford and Hall's long-lived mice displayed a higher rate of DNA repair than their short-lived counterparts. Walford himself has an unusually high rate of DNA repair. This may be why at 56, he still has pink unwrinkled skin, and looks 45.

What if science could boost other people's DNA-repair rates to the same level as Walford's—or perhaps triple them? The theory is that enhanced repair, probably in tandem with other therapies, would slow the accumulation of errors, slow the aging process and extend human life span. It might even be possible to correct old errors, patching breaks that had become a part of the genetic blueprint, excising bulges, retightening the coils of DNA. In a word, rejuvenation.

MOTHER TERESA
Missionary
Born: 1910

"At the hour of death, when we come face to face with God, we are going to be judged on love—not how much we have done, but how much love we have put into our actions."

Keeping Paramecia Young

Researchers may already have achieved just that in lower animals. Joan Smith-Sonneborn, a professor of zoology and physiology at the University of Wyoming, chose to work with paramecia because the microorganism's single cell in many ways resembles the cells of more complex animals. In an experiment first reported in 1979, she damaged the DNA of paramecia with ultraviolet radiation—the same light waves that cause human skin to tan or burn and, eventually, to age. The damaged animals died sooner than the untreated ones, presumably because they could not repair all the breaks or bumps in their DNA. Damage. Malfunctioning. Old age. Death.

With another group of paramecia, Smith-Sonneborn first induced DNA damage, and immediately stimulated, or "photoreactivated," a repair enzyme known to respond to a particular wavelength of visible light. To her surprise, the photoreactivated paramecia lived not merely as long as untreated counterparts, but substantially longer. They were already at midlife, but somehow achieved a 296 percent increase in their remaining life span, and a 27 percent increase in overall life span. In gerontology, the so-called Hayflick limit represents the maximum life span of each species. It has to do with how many times the animal's cells can divide before they die. There is a Hayflick limit for paramecia and another for humans,

both supposedly inescapable, unmovable. The ultimate deadline. "What we did," says Smith-Sonneborn, "was break through the Hayflick limit for paramecia."

To explain how this happens, Smith-Sonneborn uses the analogy of a sinking ship. When the damage occurs, an S O S goes out. But by the time outside help arrives on the scene, the ship's own crew has plugged the leak and pumped out the bilges. Having no emergency repair to do, the outside help goes to work anyway, overhauling engines and tightening rivets, and may even stay on the scene long afterwards for maintenance. By analogy, the photoreactivated enzymes leave the paramecium more youthful—and youthful for longer—than it was before the damage occurred.

It is, of course, a huge leap from paramecia to human beings. But other scientists have already demonstrated photoreactivation of repair enzymes in human skin. Smith-Sonneborn quickly adds a caveat: No one knows how much ultraviolet damage must be induced in human skin, or with what consequences, before photoreactivation will work as a rejuvenating treatment. So it does not make sense to sit for hours under a light bulb in the hope of unwrinkling or rejuvenating the skin. Then what does any of this matter? The photoreactivation work is important because it demonstrates the possibility of enhancing other DNA-repair mechanisms and other longevity-determining processes elsewhere in the human body. The enhancement may slow aging. And if it is possible to break through the Hayflick limit for paramecia, why not also for people?

MARGARET HICKEY
Public affairs editor
Ladies' Home Journal
Born: 1902

"With age comes serenity, the feeling of being satisfied with what you have done while still looking forward to what you can do. You begin to like yourself."

The Anti-Aging Diet

Another method of enhancement—the only one that is practical now—takes the life-extension story back to the 16th century and to Luigi Cornaro. Cornaro, a Paduan, led such a profligate youth that by the time he was 40, he found his constitution "utterly ruined

by a disorderly way of life and by frequent overindulgence in sensual pleasures." Told to reform, he entered upon the *vita sobria*, a life of moderation in all things. He restricted himself in particular to just 12 ounces of food daily and lived in robust health until he was 98. Since then, scientists have repeatedly demonstrated that undernutrition—as distinguished from malnutrition—extends the lives of experimental animals. But they mistakenly thought that undernutrition had to start at weaning, when it's riskiest. As Walford puts it, "You can't starve babies and you can't have 10 percent mortality rates in order to have a few people live to be 180." When the underfeeding was delayed until midlife, the experimental animals often died prematurely, Luigi Cornaro to the contrary.

I.F. STONE
Author
Born: 1907

"There are great joys in one's later years—as many as there are in one's youth. One of them is learning and studying. The things you study have much more significance; you understand them more fully. I'm studying ancient Greek language and civilization. It's difficult work, but very rewarding.

"My advice is to persist. The mind is like a muscle—you must exercise it."

But by refining the technique of previous researchers, Walford and Richard Weindruch, a co-worker, recently achieved a 30 percent increase in maximum life span for test animals whose diet was restricted after they became adults. The crucial refinement seems to have been moderation. Where other experimenters began adult underfeeding abruptly, Walford and Weindruch gradually reduced the intake of their animals, down to about 60 percent of their normal diet. In humans, Walford says, it would work out to a loss of a quarter to a third of body weight over a six-year period—a big loss, but a slow one.

Walford has not yet developed the optimal human diet for longevity through underfeeding, but says he intends to over the next year or so. For himself, he now fasts two days a week and has shed five or six pounds from his already spare frame. But because undernutrition can easily turn to malnutrition, especially outside a doctor's care, he doesn't recommend that people follow his example. In any case, would such a diet be worth the sacrifice? Walford evidently thinks so. One reason is that experimental underfeeding did not merely delay death, it delayed aging. The lack of extra calories forestalled the development, and hence the decay, of the immune system. Autoimmunity, the body's war on itself, actually decreased. And in other underfeeding experiments, the cancer rate dropped markedly.

As for the sacrifice, it may eventually prove unnecessary. At Temple University Medical School in Philadelphia, Arthur Schwartz is working with an adrenal-gland product called dehydroepiandrosterone, or DHEA. His experiments "suggest that DHEA treatment may duplicate the anti-aging and anti-cancer effects of caloric restriction."

140 and Still Kicking

It is just this piling on of discoveries and developments in all areas of life-extension research that causes Walford, Cutler, Smith-Sonneborn and others to predict a dramatic increase in human longevity. Walford, in fact, believes that it will become possible within this decade to extend maximum human life span to somewhere between 130 or 140 years.

What such a life will be like is anybody's guess. George Bernard Shaw imagined that extraordinarily long-lived people would quickly abandon mating for more mature pursuits, such as higher mathematics. Aldous Huxley wrote of a brave new world in which old men spend their time "safe on the solid ground of daily labor and distraction, scampering from feely to feely, from girl to pneumatic girl."

The possibilities raised by extreme longevity are as numerous as the additional days people will supposedly live. Walford argues that the very vastness of the change is one reason conservative experts on aging prefer to deny the likelihood of significant life extension. "It blows the data base on which they make their projections," he says. A doubling of human life span would, of course, blow anybody's data base. To cite a single example, a young couple starting out with two children, and passing on their belief in zero population growth to their offspring, could wind up at the healthy middle age of 90 with 44 direct descendants and descendant-spouses, and at age 150, with six or seven living generations in the family. Alternately, if women were to age much more slowly and reach menopause much later, it might be possible for some future generation to put off parenthood and the whole career-family dilemma until age 50.

Whole new sets of questions arise, and at first they seem to have an absurd Woody Allen quality: If you're going to live to be 150, who's going to pay the rent? But if life extension is as near as

---

MICKEY ROONEY
Actor
Born: 1920

"A long time ago I looked around and saw the apathy that the elderly had fallen into. They had nowhere to go, no one to turn to. They were eliminating themselves from the atmosphere of potential. This became a deep concern of mine. So I started a project called Fun Filled Family for people over 45. We have trips, discounts, life insurance policies and gathering places. We have no political or religious ties. We don't use the word age at all, but talk only in terms of experience."

---

gerontologists suggest, perhaps it is time to begin thinking seriously about seemingly absurd possibilities. Does it make sense, for example, to buy life insurance at 30 if you will be living to 150 and if, barring accidents, medicine makes the time of death ever more predictable? Should you plan now for a second career? (Walford intends to be a researcher in artificial intelligence.) Will longer life encourage a flowering of abilities? Is marriage "till death do us part" practical when there is a good chance that you'll see your 100th anniversary? What if the husband pursues the life-extension therapy and the wife rejects it? What will it mean if marriages and generations become asynchronous? What will happen—in fact, is already happening—to the drilled-in timetables of schooling, mating, child-rearing, income-producing, retirement and death?

To many people, the promise and the possibilities suggested by life extension are truly wonderful. "I see humanity as a fragile organism that has been evolving all along into a more complex, autonomous, intelligent species," says F. M. Esfandiary, an author who lectures at the University of California at Los Angeles, "and I believe that in our time this ascent will rapidly accelerate, propelling us into entirely new dimensions. I also believe that our mortality, the very fragility of life, has for eons drastically impaired the quality of life. It is not just the imminence of one's own death that is so cruel, it is the ever-present fear of losing all the people one loves. In the future, people will not be as programmed to finitude and mortality. Instead, they will see a whole avalanche of new options...."

On the other hand, it may be worth remembering that Moses lived to be 120, and still never entered the promised land.

Relating to Others

The need to form relationships with others is part of the human condition. Experience is often more meaningful when it is shared, and shared experiences serve to define a relationship. Among the most significant and enduring connections an individual will forge during his or her lifetime are those with mate and child.

Judging from the proliferation of "how-to" parenting books around these days one might infer that if parents aren't more confused than ever, they are certainly more concerned. They have good reason to be confused, if only because of the very real lack of consensus about what constitutes a good parent—or a good child, for that matter. The American parent today faces a host of social and economic forces that undermine the enjoyment and purpose of having children. And in the face of overwhelming evidence of the interrelationship of early childhood experiences and later development, it is no wonder parents are increasingly concerned about the role they play.

The situation is not all negative, of course. Many parents have responded to the challenges with flexibility and determination. More mothers are working outside the home than ever before, with no apparent damage to the children. Fathers are accepting in-creased responsibility in the upbringing of their children, to the benefit of both.

Economic and social pressures have also influenced a shift toward equality in male-female relationships. This does not mean that the traditional male-dominant patterns have disappeared. Rather, it implies a viable alternative in the kind of relationship open to a man and a woman.

The key to success in these redefined relationships is communication. Interpersonal relations seldom exist without conflicts both big and small, personal and interpersonal. Effective communication is critical in keeping the conflict in perspective and in finding a satisfactory resolution. Compromises that result from arguments make it less likely that the same argument will recur. Nonverbal as well as verbal communication works at all levels to keep a relationship up-to-date, growing.

This section is concerned with some of the problems and trends in relating to others. How are shifting male-female roles affecting families and couples? What are some of the consequences when a relationship goes bad? What role does power play in interpersonal relations? What damage is done to the individual by societal stereotypes?

When Mommy Goes to Work...

What happens to her kids' emotional development... her husband's ego... her own self-esteem?

SALLY WENDKOS OLDS

Sally Olds has three daughters, aged 15, 18 and 20, and has worked part time or free lance in public relations and journalism ever since her youngest was a year old.

It used to be easy to diagnose the problems of children whose mothers worked outside the home—a group of youngsters that today totals more than 27 million in this country alone. Is Mary overly dependent and whiny? That's because she doesn't see enough of her Mommy. Does Billy do badly at school? Poor thing, he doesn't have the loving attention of a mother who could help him with his homework. Is Freddy stealing candy bars from the corner store? He wouldn't if he had Mom's guidance at home!

Such assumptions may seem logical, but they just don't hold up when scrutinized under the research microscope. As social scientists delve more deeply into the effects on children of their mothers' working, their findings are turning out to be quite different from long-accepted beliefs.

Let's take a moment for a brief history lesson. Twenty-five years ago, only 1.5 million mothers were in the labor force. Today, 14 million are. As late as 1940, only one female parent in ten worked outside the home. Today, four in ten do. Before 1969, most women with children between the ages of 6 and 17 spent their days at home. Today, the United States Department of Labor reports that a record nine million women with children 6 to 17 years old are working. In fact, nearly three million have little ones aged three to five, and over two and half million have babies under three!

With employment patterns shifting so dramatically, it's only logical that we reevaluate our long-held beliefs about child care and babies' needs in general—beliefs that for years have kept mothers tied to their babies' cribs for fear of sparking emotional and psychological traumas later on. Most of our baby-care gospel (example: "children need a loving mother at home") is based on studies of hospitalized youngsters conducted during the 1940's and 50's. Not surprisingly, researchers found that infants in understaffed institutions, who were cut off from familiar people and places and who were cared for by a bewildering succession of hospital nurses, eventually suffered severe emotional problems. Valid as these studies may be, they tell us nothing about babies who, though looked after by competent baby-sitters or day-care workers during the day, are reunited with their own loving parents come evening. Fortunately, studies of the last decade have sharpened and reinforced this distinction.

In 1973, for example, Harvard University pediatrician Dr. Mary C. Howell surveyed the voluminous literature on children of working mothers. After poring over nearly 300 studies involving thousands of youngsters, she concluded: "Almost every childhood behavior characteristic, and its opposite, can be found among the children of employed mothers. Put another way, there are almost no constant differences found between the children of employed and nonemployed mothers." To wit: Researchers found both groups equally likely to make friends easily or to have trouble getting along with their peers, to excel at their studies or to fail, to get into trouble or to exhibit model behavior, to be well adjusted and independent or to be emotionally tied to the apron strings, to love and feel loved by their parents or to reject them.

Just recently, Harvard psychologist Jerome Kagan and two researchers from the Tufts New England Medical Center, Phillip Zelazo and Richard Kearsley, zeroed in on the possible effects of day care on the emotional and developmental progress of infants whose mothers worked, as compared to children raised by their mothers at home. As the yardstick for his evaluation, Kagan used three characteristics considered "most desirable" by parents: intellectual growth, social development and ability to achieve a close relationship with the mother. His results? Provided the center was well staffed and well equipped, Kagan and his colleagues were unable to find *any* significant differences between the two groups of children.

Since a mother's working per se is no longer considered a crucial factor in a child's development, what factors *are* important? To find out, let's examine the problem from a different perspective. Instead of thinking in terms of working and stay-at-home mothers, we'll divide women according to whether or not they *enjoy* whatever it is they are doing, and here we can see the differences emerge.

Back in 1956, psychologist Jack Rouman traced the progress of 400 California school children and found that the emotional problems they suffered were related not to their mothers' employment status but, rather, to the state of their mothers' emotions. He concluded: "As long as the child is made to feel secure and happy, the mother's full-time employment away from the home does not become a serious problem."

Take Linda Farber, a Philadelphia city clerk who hates her job, is bitter at her ex-husband for leaving her, making it necessary for her to work, and who feels tied down by her six-year-old son, Greg. He, in turn, is wetting his bed again, gets stomachaches every morning before school and is withdrawing from other children. On the other hand, Marjorie Gorman would love to return to the personnel office where she worked before her kids were born, but her husband insists, "It's your duty to stay home with the children."

*According to anthropologist Margaret Mead, who has
examined child-rearing patterns around the world, the notion
that a baby must not be separated from its mother is absurd.*

Marjorie is bored and restless. Annie, her oldest daughter, has run away from home three times, has thrown a kitchen knife at her parents and is habitually truant.

Of course, these children's problems are not triggered simply by their mothers' attitudes about work. But maternal unhappiness and resentment is easily communicated to other members of the family, and can, indeed, influence the quality of home life.

Studies undertaken by University of Michigan psychologist Lois Wladis Hoffman bear this out. She found that employed women who enjoy their jobs are more affectionate with their children and less likely to lose their tempers than mothers who are dis enchanted with their daily work. Furthermore, those who are content with their situations are more likely to have sons and daughters who think well of themselves, as measured on tests of self-esteem, than are resentful workers or unhappy homemakers. Following a 1974 review of 122 research papers on working mothers and their children, Dr. Hoffman concluded, "The dissatisfied mother, whether employed or not and whether lower class or middle class, is less likely to be an adequate mother." Norwegian psychologist Aase Gruda Skard agrees: "Children develop best and most harmoniously when the mother herself is happy and gay. For some women the best thing is to go out to work, for others it is best to stay in the home."

For Ellen Anthony, staying at home to care for her small baby was stifling. "I need to work," she insists. "Without some outside stimulation and a way to discharge pent-up energy, I become bored and aggressive. Now that I'm back at my public relations post, I don't overpower my daughter and husband so much and we're all happier." Carol Brunetti, on the other hand, left a good job as a department store buyer to devote full attention to her infant son. "I haven't missed my job for a minute," she says. "I love the flexibility of making my own hours. And whenever I want to go somewhere, I just take Jason along with me."

But Mom's attitude is not the only one that must be taken into consideration. No one will argue the fact that the happiness of both mother and chil-

dren also depends on the father: How a husband feels about his wife's working is crucial to the emotional climate within the home. And his attitude is a distillation of many things—whether he considers himself a success or a failure at his own profession, what the basic marital relationship is like and how willing he is to assume a fair share of the management of the household and the children if his wife takes a job.

Obviously, the woman whose husband approves of her working is lucky: Balancing job and family is never easy, but when a wife has to do the juggling herself, as well as contend with a husband's opposition, it's twice as difficult.

Happily, many a man who was originally opposed to his wife's working has discovered that he likes spending more time getting to know his children, that money problems have lessened and that he and his wife have more to talk about now that she's also exposed to new people and situations.

Although many psychoanalysts continue to stress the need for an exclusive relationship between mother and baby, recent research has shown that such relationships are probably the exception rather than the rule, even in families where the female parent does not go out to work. For one thing, most fathers today are vital figures in their children's lives. A 1974 study by Milton Kotelchuck of Harvard University found that one- and two-year-olds are just as attached to their fathers as to their mothers. And for another, the typical baby in our society is cared for by several other people in addition to its parents.

According to anthropologist Margaret Mead, who has examined childrearing patterns in societies around the world, the notion that a baby must not be separated from its mother is absurd. Babies are most likely to develop into well-adjusted human beings, she says, when they are cared for "by many warm, friendly people"—as long as most of the loved ones maintain a stable place in the infants' lives.

There's the rub. For many working mothers, finding these "warm, friendly people" to care for their children on a long-term basis is often a frustrating and expensive proposition. Experts agree that the following scenarios are probably the most stable (and, in turn,

most successful), especially for babies and toddlers:

• A father who is able to dovetail his work schedule with his wife's so that their child can be looked after by one parent or the other.
• A grandmother, other relative, friend or neighbor who cares for a child in his or her own home.
• Family day care—an arrangement similar to the one above but between people who have not previously met, often arranged by a public agency.
• A full-time babysitter who comes to the house five days a week and may perform housekeeping chores, too.
• A well-run, well-staffed day-care center.

But once the parents have made the decision that Mommy should work, what about the kids? How will *they* take to their mother's new role—and if they don't, what can you do to make them understand?

Most likely, children will have mixed feelings about Mommy's new job. David, nine, whose mother is the only working mother on the block, sometimes asks her, "Why can't you be home when I get home from school like Mark's mother? She always gives us milk and cookies." But the day David's class visited the dress factory where his mother works, he proudly explained her role in designing the clothes they saw being produced.

One woman met her child's resentment head-on. After ten-year-old Lisa had asked for the umpteenth time, "Oh, why do you have to work, anyway?" her mother stopped what she was doing, sat down with her daughter and explained just how important her job was to her. She let Lisa know that she understood the child's annoyance but she made it clear—without getting angry—how unhappy, bored and restless she would be staying home.

A group of 11-year-olds told an investigator that they loved the responsibility of using their own keys to let themselves in and out and they relished the privilege of having the house to themselves for a few hours after school.

What can both parents do to help children more readily accept their mother's employment? Child-care experts suggest that you:

• Plan your schedules so that at least

one parent is with the baby for half his or her waking hours during the first three years of life.

• Institute new child-care arrangements a week or so before you start a job, so that your child has a chance to get used to the new set-up.

• Don't take a full-time job for the first time or make a big change in child-care arrangements when your baby is between six months and a year old, or between one-and-a-half and two-and-a-half. Try to wait a couple of months after any major upheaval—such as a move to a new home, a long

illness or the break-up of a marriage.

• Keep in close touch with whoever is caring for your child and consider her or him a partner in nurturing.

• Plan "child time" into your schedule when your youngsters can depend on having some uninterrupted time with you. It need not be long, but it should be regular.

• Let your children know how much they mean to you, and that they mean more to you than your job.

"The mother who obtains satisfaction from her work, who has adequate arrangements so that her dual role does

not involve undue strain, and who does not feel so guilty that she overcompensates, is likely to do quite well and, under certain conditions, better than the nonworking mother," insists Dr. Hoffman.

In other words, it's not a matter of "whether" or "where"—but of "how" the woman who works balances the seemingly conflicting elements in her life. As one magazine editor explains, "I feel I have the best of both worlds— I love my family and I love my work, and every day in every way I feel a little better about being me."

We want your advice.

Any anthology can be improved. This one will be— annually. But we need your help.

Annual Editions revisions depend on two major opinion sources: one is the academic advisers who work with us in scanning the thousands of articles published in the public press each year; the other is you—the person actually using the book.

Please help us and the users of the next edition by completing the prepaid article rating form on the last page of this book and returning it to us. Thank you.

The Father of the Child

Fathers are taking a more active role in caring for their newborn babies

Ross D. Parke

Ross D. Parke is professor of psychology at the University of Illinois at Champaign-Urbana. He is the editor of RECENT TRENDS IN SOCIAL LEARNING THEORY *(Academic Press, 1972),* READINGS IN SOCIAL DEVELOPMENT *(Holt, Rinehart & Winston, 1969), and co-author with Mavis E. Hetherington, of* CHILD PSYCHOLOGY: A CONTEMPORARY VIEWPOINT *(McGraw-Hill, 1975, 1979).*

The days when fathers were only permitted a glance at their new offspring through the nursery window are past. Hospital practices are changing and many more fathers are now permitted to have direct contact with their babies in the hospital rather than waiting until they go home. Now that fathers and newborns are getting together more frequently, researchers are watching more often. The aim is to determine how fathers and mothers differ in their early interactions with young infants. Our own observations, which began in 1970, revealed that fathers were just as involved with their newborn infants as mothers. They looked at the infants, touched and rocked them and vocalized to them just as often as mothers. Fathers were just as active when they were alone with the babies as when their wives were present. Mothers surpassed fathers in only one way—smiling. However, the reason for the higher rate of mothers' smiling may be that females simply smile more than males—not just at babies, but at all kinds of people.

One of my students, David Phillips, has recently taken a closer look at one part of the early parent-infant exchange—the types of speech that mothers and fathers use in talking to their newborns. Fathers, as well as mothers, change their styles of speech when addressing their new offspring. They speak in shorter phrases—about half as long as the phrases used when speaking with adults. They repeat their messages much more often and slow their rate of talking. All of these changes in the style of speaking are likely to increase the extent to which the baby pays attention or looks at the parent. In turn, the changes may make it easier for the infant to learn to recognize his caregivers.

The social setting makes a difference in the behavior of fathers. When we observe fathers and mothers together, fathers smile and explore (count fingers and toes, check eyes and ears, etc.) more than when they are alone with the baby. Mothers show a similar pattern of increased interest when their husbands are present.

Fathers are active and involved, but are they involved in all aspects of early newborn care? Apparently not. Our studies indicate that fathers' involvement is selective even in the earliest interactions. Consistent with our cultural stereotypes, fathers are less likely than mothers to be actively involved in caretaking activities such as feeding or changing diapers. Fathers are more likely to play with a baby (vocalize, touch, imitate) than to feed it. These findings suggest that parental roles as caretaker or playmate begin to emerge even in the earliest days of the infant's life. This pattern may be part of a general shift toward a more traditional division of responsibilities that occurs in most families after the birth of a baby. Even in families where there is an egalitarian sharing of household tasks before a child arrives, this shift toward traditionally defined roles seems to occur, according to a recent study by Carolyn Cowan and her co-workers at Berkeley.

Are fathers less competent to care for infants? If so, this would easily explain their limited involvement in caretaking. This hypothesis, however, is wrong. Fathers are just as competent and capable of taking care of infants, according to our research. We define competence as the parent's ability to correctly "read," interpret and respond to the infant's cues or signals. To assess fathers' feeding skills, we determined how sensitively fathers reacted to infant distress signals, such as spitting up, sneezing and coughing. Fathers reacted just as quickly and appropriately as mothers did. Fathers, like mothers, adjusted their behavior by momentarily ceasing feeding the infant, looking more closely to check on the infant, and vocalizing to the infant. Moreover, babies drank about the same amount of milk from their fathers and mothers.

Play

Nearly all fathers play regularly with their infants and spend four to five times as much time playing as they spend in caretaking.

Fathers not only play more, they play differently than mothers. Based on home observations, fathers play more physically stimulating games, such as rough and tumble play and other types of unpredictable or idiosyncratic play. Mothers stimulate their infants verbally, rather than physically, use toys in their infant play, and choose conventional games such as peek-a-boo and pat-a-cake.

5. RELATING TO OTHERS

To examine fathers' play more closely, Harvard pediatricians Michael Yogman and T. Berry Brazelton and their colleagues videotaped playful interchanges between infants and their mother, father, and a strange adult in a laboratory setting. By slow motion analyses of the videotapes, Yogman found a number of differences in the patterns of infant play with different partners. Mothers spoke in a soft, repetitive and imitative fashion more often than fathers, while fathers did so more than strangers. Fathers poked and touched with rhythmic tapping patterns more often than mothers. The temporal pattern differed as well. Father-infant play shifted more rapidly from accentuated peaks of maximal infant visual attention and excitement to valleys of minimal attention. Mother-infant play had a less jagged and sawtooth quality; it was characterized by more gradual and modulated shifts.

Play patterns of fathers are, however, influenced by the amount of time that they spend with their infants. In a recent study, Tiffany Field of the University of Miami compared the play of fathers who served as primary caretakers for their infants to that of fathers who were secondary caretakers—the traditional father role. The primary caretaker fathers smiled more often, imitated their infants' facial expressions and their high-pitched vocalizations. These play patterns were similar to those of mothers who are primary caretakers. Probably mothers and fathers who spend a good deal of time with their infants recognize that infants of this age (four months) enjoy being imitated.

One important implication of the finding that primary caretakers—whether male or female—are similar, is that father-mother differences are not necessarily biologically fixed. Instead, these differences might be due to cultural factors such as the amount of experience males and females typically have with their infants. Biological sex of the caretaker may be a less important determinant of caretaker behavior than experience with infants.

Fathers and Sons

Although it is a common cultural stereotype that fathers want a boy, there is considerable truth to this view. Not only in our own culture, but in a wide variety of other cultures, fathers have a three-to-one preference for a boy over a girl—at least for their first-born. These preferences affect reproduction patterns. According to psychologist Lois Hoffman of Rutgers University: "Couples are more likely to continue to have children if they have only girls. They will have more children than they originally planned to try for a boy."

After the birth of their infant, parents, especially fathers, have clear stereotypes concerning the particular type of behavior that they expect of boy and girl babies. Even before the opportunity to hold their infants, fathers rated their sons as firmer, larger featured, better co-ordinated, more alert, and stronger, while they rated their daughters as softer, finer featured, weaker, and more delicate.

Not only do men prefer to have sons and expect them to be different, fathers treat them differently as well—even in the newborn period. In our own hospital-based observations of father-infant interaction, we found that fathers touched first-born boys more than either later-born boys or girls of either ordinal position. Fathers vocalize more to first-born boys than first-born girls. Nor are the differences in fathers' behavior with boy and girl infants restricted to the newborn period. Various investigators report that fathers look at their year-old male infants more, vocalize more to their sons, and play more with their sons than their daughters, particularly their first-born sons. Mothers, on the other hand, do not show as strong preferences, but if they do discriminate, they show heightened involvement with girls. Cross-cultural and comparative data tell a similar story. In studies of the Israeli kibbutzim, fathers were found to visit for longer periods in the children's house with their four-month-old sons than with their infant daughters. Even adult male rhesus monkeys play with male infants more than female infants while female adult monkeys interact more with female infants. Whether this pattern of heightened involvement of fathers with sons reflects what the sociobiologists, such as E.O. Wilson and Robert L. Trivers of Harvard University, call gene investment, or whether it is an outcome of cultural shaping, is still an open question.

Fathers' Effects on Infants and Mothers

Even though fathers spend less time with their infants than mothers, the quality rather than the quantity of parent-infant interaction is the important predictor of infant development. Not surprisingly, then, variations in father-infant interaction patterns do affect the infant's social and cognitive development. However, boys are generally affected more than girls.

The majority of infants develop a positive social relationship or "attachment" (a preference or desire to be close to a specific person) to both their fathers and their mothers by the end of the first year. This is an important finding which directly challenges the popular assumption of the influential British ethologist, John Bowlby, that infants should prefer or even be uniquely attached to their mothers. Clearly both fathers and mothers are important "attachment" objects for infants. As we have already seen, the roles that father and mother play in the infant's social world may be different. What behavior affects the strength of the father-infant relationship?

According to one study, the strength of the father-infant relationship—assessed by the infant's responsiveness to his father—is related to the degree of the father's involvement in routine caretaking and the stimulation level of paternal play. This relation was especially true for boys in this study of eight-month-old infants. Confirming this relationship are studies which show that social responsiveness of five-month-old male infants is lower where the father is absent than in homes where he is present. Not only is high involvement related to a stronger father-infant bond, but a high degree of father-infant interaction helps a child cope more adequately in other social situations as well. Children react to the stress of being left alone with a stranger better if their fathers are active and involved caretakers. Children who are not cared for by their fathers show extensive distress in the laboratory situation when left alone.

Cognitive progress is affected by the father-infant relationship as well. Scores on standard tests of infant mental development were positively related to the amount of contact with the father in five-to-six-month-old lower class black infants. However, variations in father interaction were unrelated to cognitive development of female infants. Similarly, infants from homes where fathers were absent performed less well on the tests of cognitive development. Other studies with older infants suggest that fathers and mothers contribute to their infants' cognitive development in different ways. While the quality of father-infant play patterns was related to higher cognitive progress, for mothers it was verbal stimulation that was the best predictor of infant cognitive status. In short, both parents may contribute, but in unique ways, to their developing infant.

The father's involvement, however, cannot be adequately understood independently of his role as part of the family. Fathers affect infants not only in the direct ways that we have described, but in a variety of indirect ways as well. For example, a father may affect his child by modifying his wife's attitudes and behaviors toward the child. Recent studies by Frank A. Pedersen and his colleagues at the National Institute of Child Health and Development in Washington, D.C. have shown that the adequacy of a mother's feeding skill was related to the degree of emotional support provided by her husband.

Cultural Supports for Father

Just as mothers can benefit from opportunities to learn and practice caretaking skills, in a time when fathers are increasingly being expected to share caretaking responsibilities, these learning opportunities need to be available for fathers as well.

Supportive intervention for fathers might assume a variety of forms. First, an increase in opportunities for learning caretaking skills is needed. Such opportunities might be provided through pre- and post-partum training programs for fathers. Second, fathers need increased opportunities to practice and implement these skills. Paternity leaves would help provide these opportunities. Opportunities for contact with the infant in the early post-partum period could alter subsequent parent-infant interaction patterns. Preliminary evidence from recent studies suggests that father-infant interaction patterns can be modified by hospital-based interventions. John Lind, a Swedish obstetrician, found that fathers who were provided the opportunity to learn and practice caretaking skills during the post-partum hospital period were more involved in the care of the infant three months later at home.

My colleagues Shelley Hymel, Thomas Power and Barbara Tinsley and I recently presented to American fathers a videotape of father-infant interaction during the early post-partum hospital period. The videotape provided information concerning the newborn infant's perceptual and social competence, play techniques and caretaking skills. Fathers were observed during feeding and play. Fathers who viewed the film were better able to maintain infant feeding and vocalized more to their infants—especially their first-born sons—during play. In addition, the fathers who saw the film in the hospital participated in feeding and diapering activities at home when their infants were three months old. However, the film increased the amount of caretaking only for fathers of boys; fathers of girls were unaffected by the film intervention. This selective effect of our intervention for boys is similar to earlier findings that fathers are more involved with sons than daughters.

Considerable care must be taken in the implementation of these support systems. One must consider parents' rights. The aim is not to impose on all families an implicit scenario of the liberated family and an endorsement of egalitarian family organization. Too often "more" is equated with "improvement." However, in many families, increased participation by the father may cause conflict and disruption as a result of the threat to well-established and satisfying role definitions. Intervention, therefore, should be sensitively geared to the needs of individual families, and the dynamics and beliefs of the couple should be recognized at the outset.

Fathers play a unique and important role in infancy. As social standards continue to change it is likely that fathers will be assuming an increasingly larger role in the care and feeding of infants and young children. Our evidence suggests that not only can they assume these responsibilities competently, but that the result is likely to be beneficial for all—infants, mothers and fathers.

Disclosing Oneself to Others

Zick Rubin

What is the purpose of wearing a mask? Is it easier for a woman to disclose something personal about herself than for a man to do so? What happens to a relationship when you share some intimate bit of information about yourself? Dr. Zick Rubin attempts to answer these and other questions in the following article. His unique research demonstrates what happens to strangers when one discloses something personal about himself to the other. His conclusion, based on his research, shows the close relationship between personal disclosure and trust.

The most literal meaning of "intimate" is to get into another person—to really know another. Yet there often is considerable reluctance among people to be known. Self-disclosure invariably entails a risk, and the greater the disclosure, the greater the risk. When we reveal to another person something of our "true self," we must be prepared for the possibility that he will examine what we have revealed and find it wanting. Or he may use the information to take advantage of us. In courtship, for example, one partner's revelation of some blemish in his background may prompt the other to abandon him. Or one partner's disclosure of the depth of his affection for the other may enable the other to exploit him by making large and unreasonable demands. In light of these risks, it is no wonder that many of us learn early in life to be wary of revealing ourselves. "We conceal and camouflage our true being before others," psychologist Sidney Jourard writes, "to foster a sense of safety, to protect ourselves against unwanted but expected criticism, hurt, or rejection." But this protection, Jourard goes on to argue, is purchased at a steep price: "When we are not truly known by other people in our lives, we are misunderstood. . . . Worse, when we succeed too well in hiding our being from others, we tend to lose touch with our real selves, and this loss of self contributes to illness in its myriad forms." Thus, disclosing ourselves to others may be necessary not only for the establishment of close relationships, but also to permit us to keep in touch with ourselves. "A friend is a person with whom I may be sincere," Emerson wrote. "Before him, I may think aloud."

Although self-disclosure is often difficult for men and women alike, it seems to be especially difficult for men in our society. Women surveyed by Jourard typically report that they have revealed more information about their feelings and experiences to family members, friends, and lovers than men do. As Jourard suggests. "The male role, as personally and socially defined, requires men to appear tough, objective, striving, achieving, unsentimental, and emotionally unexpressive. . . . If a man *is* tender, . . . if he weeps, if he shows weakness, he will likely be viewed as unmanly by others, and he will probably regard himself as inferior to other men." During the first of the 1972 Democratic Presidential primaries, Senator Edmund Muskie, at that time the leading candidate for the nomination, expressed his displeasure with a New Hampshire newspaper publisher in an outburst that was simultaneously indignant and tearful. The incident was widely reported to have seriously weakened his drive for the nomination. It was not his indignation that hurt the senator, for this is an expression that men are generally permitted, but rather his tears. Muskie's genuine expression of feelings was considered a sign of unmanliness and weakness.

The rise of women's consciousness-raising groups has served to emphasize the relative inability of men to reveal themselves—especially to other men. Marc Festeau writes:

> Can you imagine men talking to each other saying: "Are you sure you're not angry at me?" . . . "I'm not as assertive as I would like to be." . . . "I feel so competitive that I can't get close to anyone." . . . "I just learned something important about myself that I've got to tell you." . . . "I don't have the self-confidence to do what I really want to do." . . . "I feel nervous talking to you like this."
> It just doesn't happen. . . .
> As a man, my conditioning and problems are not only different, but virtually the inverse of those of most women. We've been taught that "real men" are never passive or dependent, always dominant in relationships with women or other men, and don't talk about or directly express feelings; especially feelings that don't contribute to dominance.

In Jourard's view, men's inability to disclose themselves to others is a literally lethal aspect of the male role, contributing to the shorter life expectancy of males. "Men keep their selves to themselves and impose an added burden of stress beyond that imposed by the exigencies of everyday life. . . . The time is not far off when it will be possible to demonstrate with adequately controlled experiments the nature and degree of correlation between level and amounts of self-disclosure, proneness to illness and/or death at an early stage." I frankly cannot imagine what sort of "controlled experiments" Jourard has in mind—all of the possibilities that occur to me are rather macabre. Nevertheless, the point that openness is likely to be related to psychological and perhaps even physical health is well taken. People of either sex who are totally unable to reveal their feelings to others are likely to be labeled as poorly functioning or, in extreme cases, as autistic or schizophrenic. One recent study of Peace Corps trainees documented the link between self-disclosure and psychological adjustment by showing that those trainees who were most willing to reveal personal information about themselves to others also tended to be the most cognitively complex, adaptable, flexible, and popular.

It would be highly misleading to equate the ability to disclose oneself with positive mental health, however. People who disclose *too much* are apt to be considered as sick or sicker than those who disclose too little. To be a hallmark of psychological health or interpersonal competence, a person's disclosure must be appropriate to the particular situation and relationship in which it occurs. The appropriateness of disclosures is important in fleeting encounters between strangers as well as in the development of intimate relationships over longer periods of time. In the next section I will describe one of my own studies of encounters among strangers. The study will hopefully be of interest in its own right. But my main reason for introducing it at this point is my belief that these fleeting encounters illustrate certain mechanisms that are central to the development of intimate relationships.

Notes from the Departure Lounge

Several recent laboratory experiments have been concerned with the exchange of self-disclosure among unacquainted pairs of subjects. Their general finding is that, as one would expect, self-disclosure tends to be reciprocal. The more Person A reveals about himself to Person B, the more Person B is likely to reveal to Person A in return. My own experiment also concerned the exchange of self-disclosure among pairs of strangers, but it was conducted in a real-life setting—departure lounges at Boston's Logan Airport—rather than in the laboratory. Its central goal was to go beyond another demonstration of the "reciprocity effect" toward a better understanding of the mechanisms that underlie it.

The reciprocity effect may in fact be ascribed to at least two different mechanisms. One mechanism is that of *modeling*. Especially when norms of appropriate behavior are not completely clear, people look to one another for cues as to what sort of response is called for. If a person sitting next to you on a train talks about the weather, you are likely to respond in kind. If he proceeds to discuss his recent illness—and at the same time seems to be in command of the situation—then you may well infer that disclosing personal matters is the proper thing to do under the circumstances. Such modeling phenomena can also be observed in the initiation of new recruits to sensitivity training or encounter groups. At first unsure about how they should behave, the new members observe their fellows disclosing themselves intimately and as a result conclude that they too are expected to reveal personal information.

A second mechanism that may underlie the reciprocity effect goes beyond modeling, however, and may be called *trust*. When another person reveals himself to you, you are likely to conclude that he likes and trusts you. He has, after all, made himself vulnerable to you, entrusting you with personal information that he would not ordinarily reveal to others. A common motivation in such a situation is to demonstrate to the other person that his affection and trust are well placed. One effective way to do this is to disclose yourself to him in return. It is by means of such reciprocal displays of trust and affection that people are most likely to move from acquaintanceship to friendship.

In many instances the two mechanisms operate simultaneously and lead to essentially the same end-state. In the encounter group, for example, members not only model one another's levels of disclosure, but also demonstrate their increasing trust for one another by means of reciprocal disclosure. There are instances, however, in which the two mechanisms should lead to rather different results. These are the cases in which the first person reveals *too* much, going beyond the level of intimacy with which the second person feels comfortable. To the extent that reciprocal disclosure is dictated by modeling, even extremely intimate revelations may lead to intimate disclosures in return.[1] But excessively intimate disclosures will often breed suspicion rather than trust. If, for example, a person reveals the details of his sex life to a co-worker on their first day at the job, the second person may have reason to suspect the first's motives or discretion. Instead of being motivated to reveal the details of his own sex life in return, he will be likely to clam up.

In the experiment that I conducted at the airport, the experimenter, either a male or a female college student, began by approaching a prospective subject, an adult man or woman sitting alone in the departure lounge, and asking him if he would write a sentence or two about himself to be used as part of a class project on "handwriting analysis." There is, to be sure, a deception involved here that I wish we could avoid. In a previous experiment my students and I found, however, that when we asked people to write something about themselves as part of a study of "the way people describe themselves"—which is of course the true purpose—several problems emerge. Foremost among these was that over half of the male subjects approached by male experimenters refused to take part. As we have already noted, men find it particularly difficult to express themselves to other men. In the all-male context, "self-description" seemed to be a threatening word. When we represented the study as concerned with handwriting analysis, on the other hand, we were able to reduce male refusal rates substan-

tially. In addition, by obtaining "handwriting samples" rather than "self-descriptions" I hoped to minimize the subjects' self-consciousness about the content of their messages. As far as the subjects knew, only their handwriting, and not their personal disclosures, would later be evaluated for research purposes.

After the subject had agreed to participate, the experimenter explained that the class would be comparing the class members' own handwriting with the handwriting of other people. Therefore, the experimenter would write a few sentences about himself or herself in the top box of the response form, labeled "Class Member's Sample." The subject was invited to look at the experimenter's sample and then to write a sentence or two about himself or herself in the bottom box. The "Class Member's Sample" was the device by which I was able to vary the intimacy of the experimenter's self-disclosure to the subject. The "sample" provided by the experimenter was either a non-intimate, moderately intimate, or extremely intimate statement about himself. In all cases the experimenter began by writing his or her name and the fact that he was a junior or senior in college. In the "low intimacy" condition, he proceeded to write:

> . . . right now I'm in the process of collecting handwriting samples for a school project. I think I will stay here for a while longer, and then call it a day.

In the "medium intimacy" condition he wrote:

> . . . Lately I've been thinking about my relationships with other people. I've made several good friends during the past couple of years, but I still feel lonely a lot of the time.

And in the "high intimacy"—or, if you will, "excessively high intimacy"—condition the experimenter wrote:

> . . . Lately I've been thinking about how I really feel about myself. I think that I'm pretty well adjusted, but I occasionally have some questions about my sexual adequacy.

The experiment included a further variation. In half the cases within each of the intimacy conditions, the experimenter simply *copied* the message from a card in front of him. It was obvious to the subject that the experimenter was not directing the message to him personally, but rather was working from a prepared script. In the other half of the cases the experimenter pretended to *create* the message especially for the subject. He did not have a cue card in front of him, and he occasionally glanced up at the subject thoughtfully as he wrote. My purpose in setting up this variation was to establish conditions in which the two mechanisms of modeling and of trust would be differentially salient.

When the experimenter copied his message, it presumably furnished the subject with a cue as to what sort of statement would be appropriate to the situation. Since the experimenter was not singling the subject out for his revelation, however, there was little reason for the subject to interpret the experimenter's disclosure as a demonstration of any particular affection or trust. Under these circumstances the subject was relatively unlikely to react suspiciously or defensively to the "extremely high" message. The experimenter was not being excessively forward or indiscreet; he was merely doing his job. Following this reasoning, I predicted that as the intimacy of the experimenter's message varied from "low" to "medium" to "high," the intimacy and length of the subject's own message would correspondingly increase.

When the experimenter seemed to create a unique message for the subject, on the other hand, considerations of trust inevitably entered the picture, supplementing the modeling mechanism. Up to a point the subject might be expected to respond positively to the experimenter's apparent demonstration of affection and trust and, as a result, to disclose himself in return. Thus the reciprocity effect, considering only the low-intimacy and medium-intimacy messages, was expected to be stronger in the "create" than in the "copy" condition. But the high-intimacy message, when delivered in a personal way, might indeed be going too far and consequently should arouse sentiments of mistrust and defensiveness. "After all," a typical subject might think, "it's nice to have a young person confide in you, but this bit on 'sexual adequacy' is really going too far. I wonder what his *real* problem is. I had better

---

1. This modeling effect may explain in large measure why laboratory experiments have failed to find withdrawal as a common response to excessively intimate disclosures. In the laboratory context, the subject typically experiences considerable pressure to determine and accede to the "demand characteristics" of the experiment, those subtle cues that define the experimental situation for the subject and suggest to him how a "good subject" should behave. Thus, he utilizes his partner's disclosure as a cue to what sort of behavior is appropriate to the situation and responds in kind. As a result, laboratory studies of disclosure tend to overemphasize those aspects of encounters that evoke modeling and to underemphasize those that are relevant to trust.

write something short and be done with it."

Before revealing the results of the study, let me present a few of the "handwriting samples" provided by subjects, to give you a sense of the ways in which airport passengers responded to the request to write a sentence or two about themselves. Some of the responses were not intimate at all. They were personally uninformative or even evasive:

005[2]   Today is the 29th of October and this is Logan Airport. It is very warm for this time of year especially when waiting for a late airplane.

031   This is the start of a trip to Atlanta and other states in the adjacent area.

047   I've got to go.

Other subjects provided factual information about themselves but did not get into highly intimate revelations:

028   My name is Frank Peterson and I'm a retired police officer. I served for 30 years on the Boston Police department.

133   My name is Bertha Schwartz. I am a housewife and very happy.

236   My name is Ronnie, live in Boston—like art, studied at B.U., think handwriting analysis is a great hobby.

Still other subjects did reveal what seemed to be much more personal and private thoughts and feelings:

144   My name is Gloria Baker. I'm a grandmother but I too have been thinking of myself—where I've been—what to do—I too question my identity.

089   I've just been attending Alumna Council at Cooper College—looking ahead to my 40th Reunion. I still feel sexually adequate—never felt otherwise.

197   My name is Thomas O'Day. I'm a 3rd year medical student. Recently I haven't been getting much sleep and have been under extreme pressure; Thus, my handwriting is terrible. Generally I am well-adjusted, but 3rd year students have many adjustments to make, and I often question my ability to function under pressure.

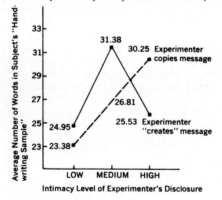

FIGURE 1   Length of subjects' messages in departure lounge experiment. Each point represents about 40 subjects. The statistical interaction between the two experimental factors is significant at the .014 level.

It is possible to have raters code the intimacy of these samples with quite good reliability. In some cases, however, interesting patterns emerge quite as clearly, or even more so, simply by using the number of words in the subject's sample as a measure of his or her self-disclosure. This is the measure employed in Figure 1. As the graph indicates, the predictions outlined above were very neatly confirmed. In the impersonal, "copy" condition, the length of the subject's statement increased steadily as the intimacy level of the experimenter's statement increased from low to medium to high. The modeling mechanism apparently operated across the entire range of the experimenter's disclosures. In the personal, "create" condition, on the other hand, the length of the subject's statement increased sharply as intimacy of the experimenter's message increased from low to medium, but it dropped off just as sharply as the intimacy of the experimenter's message increased from medium to high.

Lovers and Other Strangers

Although the airport study involved encounters between strangers, I believe that the results contain several lessons about the development of intimate relationships. In every sort of interpersonal relationship, from business partnerships to love affairs, the exchange of self-disclosure plays an important role. In some respects this exchange closely resembles other transactions on the interpersonal marketplace. . . . Just as people may exchange such commodities as approval, assistance, and status, they also exchange information about their experiences and feelings. But the exchange of self-disclosure is governed by several additional motives and mechanisms. In some cases, it is not really an exchange at all, even though the two people are sequentially emitting similar behaviors to one another. In fact they are not exchanging anything, but instead are imitating or modeling one another's behavior. Such modeling is an important aspect of the development of relationships, especially in their early stages. At such times, when people are tentatively exploring each other's potential as a friend or lover, they are especially concerned about responding in ways that are appropriate to the situation, and they frequently do so by picking up and modeling one another's cues.

At a deeper level, the exchange of personal disclosures is in fact an exchange of trust. The discloser shows that he likes and trusts the person to whom he discloses, thereby implying that he might value the establishment of a relationship with him. The person disclosed to must decide how to respond to this "move" on the part of the discloser. If he is disposed to keep relations cool, and at the same time to retain a position of relative power, he may disclose little in return. Knowing more about another person than he knows about you is a way to remain "one-up" in interpersonal relationships.

LONELINESS

Almost everyone is lonely sometimes,
but this common feeling arises not from a person's circumstance,
but from how he decides to interpret his situation.

CARIN RUBINSTEIN, PHILLIP SHAVER,
AND
LETITIA ANNE PEPLAU

Carin Rubenstein *is completing her dissertation for her Ph.D. in social psychology at New York University.* **Phillip Shaver** *is chairman of the doctoral program in personality and social psychology at NYU. Rubenstein and Shaver are writing a book based on their work, tentatively titled* What It Means To Be Lonely, *to be published by Delacorte Press.* **Letitia Anne Peplau** *is an assistant professor of psychology at the University of California at Los Angeles.*

God says in the Book of Genesis, "It is not good that man should be alone," and decides to make a fitting companion for him. The Old Testament discourses at length about the benefits of fruitful multiplying, and about the intricate attachments and intrigues between men and women, parents and children, friends and kin.

Modern evolutionary biologists, who have developed their own creation story, also emphasize the need for human beings to be together. They offer evidence for the genetic advantages of sexual reproduction, the adaptive benefits of prolonged attachment to parents in childhood, and the survival benefits of belonging to complex groups. The human ability to form strong emotional attachments has a long evolutionary history, which is why people can be seriously hurt if their attachments are disrupted by rejection, separation, or death.

The Bible and biologists share a major premise: It isn't good for people to be alone. This evaluation bodes ill for modern industrial societies, especially the United States, where the divorce rate is soaring, geographic and social mobility are high, and an unprecedented number of adults of all ages are choosing or being forced by events to live by themselves.

Many social commentators and popular writers have inferred from these statistics that *alone* means *lonely* and use the terms interchangeably. In *The Broken Heart: The Medical Consequences of Loneliness,* psychologist James Lynch argued that people who live alone (and are, he assumed, lonely) are especially susceptible to serious illnesses and may even die prematurely. Sociologist Philip Slater's *The Pursuit of Loneliness,* based primarily on armchair analysis, denounced the American commitment to individualism and competition, which, he said, frustrate the basic human desires for community, engagement, and dependence. "The competitive life is a lonely one," Slater concluded.

Like these writers, many social scientists arrive at conclusions without putting much stock in people's own interpretations of their feelings or actions. Once researchers begin talking to individuals, however, they quickly learn that "alone" is an objective term—indicating whether a person lives with someone else, how many friends he or she has, and so on—but that "lonely" is subjective, a matter of what goes on in a person's head. As we have learned, the two experiences occasionally but by no means always overlap. Feelings of loneliness do not inevitably follow from solitude or circumstance; they depend on how people view their experiences and whether they decide to call themselves lonely.

Among us, we have conducted two independent programs of research on loneliness, one at New York University (Rubenstein and Shaver) and one at the University of California at Los Angeles (Peplau). The NYU research was based on a carefully pretested questionnaire that was published in the Sunday magazine sections of several East Coast newspapers in the spring of 1978. More than 25,000 people responded, a large sample of adults of all ages, races, and income levels. The research at UCLA by Peplau and her co-workers is developing a model of loneliness that emphasizes the thought processes of lonely people. This work is based primarily on college students, who answer questions

5. RELATING TO OTHERS

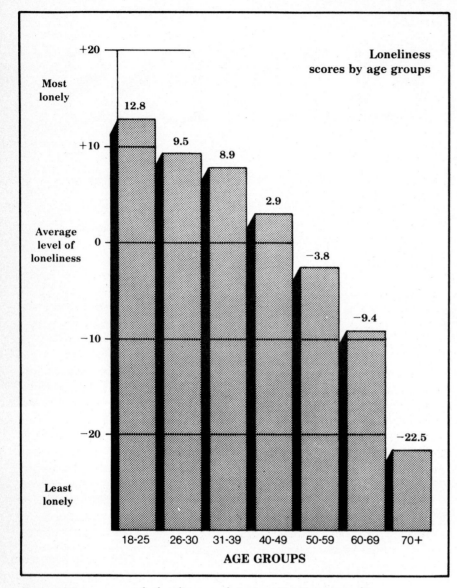

Loneliness scores by age groups

Score	Age Group
12.8	18-25
9.5	26-30
8.9	31-39
2.9	40-49
−3.8	50-59
−9.4	60-69
−22.5	70+

Most lonely / Average level of loneliness / Least lonely

AGE GROUPS

Senior citizens are not the loneliest people in America: Young people are. NYU surveys found a steady decline in loneliness as people get older. The researchers believe that young adults sense an impossible gap between romantic expectations and reality; older people interpret things more realistically.

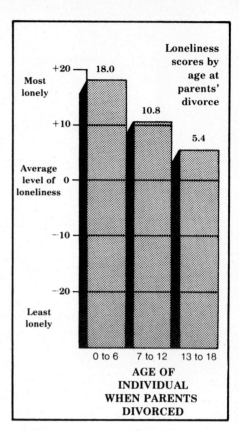

Loneliness scores by age at parents' divorce

Score	Age when parents divorced
18.0	0 to 6
10.8	7 to 12
5.4	13 to 18

Most lonely / Average level of loneliness / Least lonely

AGE OF INDIVIDUAL WHEN PARENTS DIVORCED

The older a child is when his or her parents divorce, the less lonely he is likely to be as an adult. In an NYU survey, people who were younger than six years of age when their parents separated got the highest scores on the loneliness scale; people who were in middle childhood got lower scores; but people who were adolescent or older were the least lonely as adults.

about their own experiences with loneliness and their impressions of lonely people. So far, nearly 1,000 undergraduates have participated. These different methods and the diversity of people interviewed offer the first coherent picture of adult loneliness based on data rather than on speculation.

Although newspaper surveys are subject to the bias of people who choose to fill out the questionnaire, we believe that the results are valid and representative of most of the population. Regardless of city size and location (for example, small town or metropolis, northern or southern city), the findings

within each sample remained virtually the same. And although a few people noted that "only a lonely person would bother to fill this out," we received thousands of questionnaires from people who said they were not lonely. Only 15 percent of those who replied said they felt lonely most or all of the time, and only 6 percent said they never felt lonely. The majority, as one would expect, felt lonely on occasion.

The survey results dispelled many of the popular assumptions about loneliness and confirmed others. One common prediction favored by sociologists turned out *not* to be true. The American

fondness for moving—for changing jobs, partners, cities, and social networks—has long been considered a cause of psychological distress. In *A Nation of Strangers*, Vance Packard described the chronic rootlessness of Americans, which he believed to be at the heart of the country's social problems. The NYU surveys included a number of questions to test Packard's claims, such as how often people had moved during childhood and adulthood, the length of time they have lived at their present locations, and whether, if they were lonely, moving too often was responsible.

But none of these questions was connected with current feelings of loneliness; people who had moved frequently and those who had never

Old people are less lonely, on the average, than young adults; they even complain less about physical and psychological symptoms.

strayed from their birthplace had equal chances of feeling lonely. People who change cities often have just as many friends and are just as satisfied with their friendships as people who remain rooted in one spot. We recognize, of course, that moving is often fraught with difficulty; separation from friends often causes bouts of loneliness. But the NYU data suggest that such feelings, for most people, are temporary reactions during the adjustment phase. People who move frequently, it seems, learn quickly how to make friends and put down roots in a new community.

The sociologists turned out to be correct in predicting that the loneliest people are likely to be poor, uneducated, and of minority groups; we found too that an even stronger companion of loneliness is unemployment. But none of these conditions, however adverse, was as strongly related to feelings of loneliness as a person's perception of reality—to feeling a painful mismatch between *actual* life and *desired* life.

A good example of this comes from the surprising but reliable finding that old people are less lonely, on the average, than young adults. This pattern has turned up in other large surveys as well as the NYU study, and directly counters the cliché of the lonely senior citizen. Although more old people than young live alone, and although older people see their friends less often than young adults do, the elderly are more satisfied with their friendships, have higher self-esteem, and feel more independent. They join social and civic groups more often, and get drunk far less often than the young. Old people even complain less than young folks do about physical and psychological symptoms—such as headaches, poor appetite, depression, irritability, and poor concentration.

We think that young people are so susceptible to loneliness because they feel most sharply the discrepancy between the search for intimacy and the failure to find it. Young people are romantic and idealistic; they think it is more important to find a "romantic or sexual partner" than older people do.

Because loneliness is more in one's mind than one's circumstances, living alone does not by itself foster the feeling. The NYU researchers tested the notion that living alone produces serious medical problems, but found no differences in the mental and physical health of people who live alone and those who live with others. Lonely people do have more medical and psychological problems than their less lonely peers, even though the lonely are as likely to be living with roommates, or spouses, or families, or on their own.

The NYU questionnaire included a number of items about a person's social life, which showed that although lonely people do have fewer friends and contacts, on the average, than less lonely people, their dissatisfaction with the ties they have is what makes them feel lonely. Lonely people are dissatisfied with everything about their lives: their living arrangements (whether solo or with others), the number of friends they have, the quality of those friendships, their marriages or love affairs, the number of conversations they have each day, and their sex lives.

We cannot say for sure, yet, whether dissatisfactions create feelings of separation and loneliness, or whether loneliness turns the whole world sour. But we did glean evidence that some causes of adult loneliness have their origin in childhood. Psychiatrist John Bowlby has argued persuasively that separation from parents can have lasting detrimental effects on children, and Bowlby's thesis was supported in the survey. Lonely people tended to remember their parents as being disagreeable, remote, and untrustworthy; individuals who said they were not lonely described their parents as close, helpful, and warm. (Current feelings of loneliness, though, may color one's memory of events.) But the loneliest people of all were those whose parents had divorced. As one man commented, "My mom was married twice and my father and stepfather have been nothing but pure hell for me. I have lost all of my confidence and feel not worth anything to anyone."

If their parents did divorce, people fared better the later the separation occurred. People who were less than six years old when their parents split up were by far the loneliest as adults; people who were older than six were lonelier than those who were adolescents; and so on. This is disturbing, for the Census Bureau predicts that 45 percent of all children born in 1977 will spend a significant period of their lives with only one parent.

The loss of either parent by divorce is more detrimental, in terms of later loneliness, than loss by death. Whether a parent dies when a person is a child, a teenager, or an adult has no effect on later feelings of loneliness. It is as if children regard divorced parents as having *chosen* to reject them and are tormented by the parent's inaccessibility. But most children come to understand that a parent's death is not their responsibility. It is thus not the event of parental separation itself but *how children perceive it* that will affect their later adjustment.

People who have had unhappy childhood experiences, who feel that their parents neglected or rejected them,

Lonely people remember their parents as being disagreeable, remote, and untrustworthy; the loneliest people of all were those whose parents had divorced.

may grow up with fragile self-esteem. Psychological research has shown that people who dislike themselves also tend to dislike or be less tolerant of others, possibly because a hostile stance protects a vulnerable person from the risk of rejection. We suspected that this defensiveness is part of a self-fulfilling prophesy: A guarded lonely person is hard to get to know and is therefore likely to remain isolated.

Recent experiments by Warren Jones at the University of Tulsa find that lonely students do tend to be self-focused and difficult to talk to. Jones observed college students who said they were lonely conversing with students who were not. Lonely people, he noted, talked more about themselves, asked fewer questions of their partners, and changed the topic more frequently than their socially adept peers did. Jones concluded that many lonely students simply do not know how to behave in social situations, so their encounters tend to be superficial and emotionally unsatisfying to them.

In the NYU surveys, too, lonely people had lower self-esteem than people who were not lonely. They also tended to dislike others more readily, to have fewer friends, to be less busy during the week and on weekends, to join social groups less frequently, and to say they feel bored.

Loneliness does not feel the same to everyone. The NYU surveys asked people how they usually feel when they are lonely, and found four different sets of feelings. For some people, the largest group, loneliness feels like desperation; words they use to describe the sensation include "desperate," "panic," "helpless," and "afraid." Such individuals feel cut off from others when they are lonely—abandoned and frightened.

Another cluster of feelings, which we label "impatient boredom," represents a milder loneliness, the kind that people may feel when they are unexpectedly left alone on a Saturday night, or when they are stuck in a boring hotel room on a business trip. This temporary feeling of loneliness includes such emotions as "bored," "uneasy," and "desire to be elsewhere."

The last two factors, self-deprecation and depression, are common reactions to prolonged feelings of loneliness. Self-deprecation is anger at oneself: "I am alone, unattractive, and stupid; I deserve to be lonely." Depression is a more resigned and passive state marked by self-pity: "I am isolated, cut off, sorry for myself."

The four meanings of loneliness suggest a progression from occasional dissatisfaction with one's social situation, to chronic and more intense dissatisfaction, and finally, if things do not get better, to self-hatred and self-pity.

The NYU surveys were deliberately broad and exploratory, making up in coverage of many issues what they lost in clinical detail. The UCLA studies aimed at constructing a theoretical model of the conditions and interpretations that go into the self-label "lonely." Researchers at UCLA have worked primarily with college students, and this is one topic for which it makes good sense to use them. As we mentioned earlier, the young are far more likely than the old to report feeling lonely—college students and high-school seniors most of all. (In one UCLA study, more than 70 percent of all undergraduates thought loneliness was an important problem.)

The UCLA research started off with the importance of the explanations people give for being lonely—in social-psychological terms, their causal attri-

butions. One young woman blamed her environment, for example, noting that "UCLA is such a big impersonal factory that it's hard to meet people." But another student blamed himself: "I'm just too shy to get to know people or ask a girl for a date." Many previous studies of the attribution process had suggested that people would ask themselves three basic questions about why they are lonely: Who's to blame? Can it change? What control do I have over my feelings?

In a series of five studies, the UCLA researchers found that the answers to these questions can be arranged along three dimensions: *locus of causality* ("Am I to blame for my loneliness, or is it something in my environment?"); *stability* over time ("Is my loneliness transitory, or is it likely to be permanent?"); and *controllability* ("Is there anything I can do about being lonely, or is it out of my hands?").

Some students blamed external causes, emphasizing elements of the university situation that led to loneliness (the immense size of the university, the impersonal classes, the lack of opportunities to meet people, or the existence of social cliques). Others gave internal attributions, focusing on lack of social skills, shyness, physical unattractiveness, or fear of trying. One student wrote, "The fault, I believe, always lies in the individual who is lonely. If a person is lonely it is because he or she has not taken the initiative in attempting to meet people."

The students regarded some causes of loneliness as more stable than others. They thought shyness was a temporary quality that could change with effort, but they regarded unattractiveness or an unpleasant personality as causes that would be very hard to change. Students felt that they had the most control over causes that were internal

Attributions for loneliness are important because they determine how a person will feel and how he or she will behave in the future.

(such as lack of effort) and unstable (such as being shy). UCLA undergraduates are, by and large, an optimisitc group. They were reluctant to blame loneliness on looks or personality; the single most common explanation for loneliness was that a person was not trying hard enough, a matter relatively easy to remedy, in their view. Many students, of course, recognized the complexity of the problem, assuming some personal responsibility for feeling lonely but also noting the difficulties imposed by the large university.

Attributions for loneliness determine how a person will feel (depressed, accepting, optimistic, angry), and how he or she will behave in the future. The man whose attributions are internal and stable is saying, in effect, "The fault is in me, and I am unlikely to change." The woman whose attributions are internal and unstable is saying, "The fault was in me, but next time I will try harder and make it work."

The attribution process is linked to self-blame or blame of others. The NYU surveys found that lonely people are less friendly to others, which understandably would exacerbate their social isolation. But on closer inspection of the UCLA studies, it appears that hostility and anger are marks only of people who believe they are lonely for external reasons—such as being excluded by ingroups. Several of the NYU interviewees expressed hostility toward people for rejecting or ignoring them. "You can't do anything for people," a middle-aged woman said. "Everyone is ungrateful." (In a study by Bernard Weiner of reactions to success and failure, people who felt they failed

because of other people's efforts or motives tended to feel "revengeful," "furious," "bitter," and "fuming.")

When people aim attributions at themselves, the resulting emotion is not usually anger, but disappointment, shame, or embarrassment ("Why didn't I try harder?" "How could I have been such a stupid clod?"). Their behavior in turn depends on whether they view the problem as unchangeable or fixable. Attributions are of pivotal importance in explaining why some lonely people become depressed and withdraw socially, and others ward off depression and actively work to improve their social lives. Depression occurs primarily when people account for loneliness in stable, internal terms ("I am hopelessly fat, ugly, and unlovable; there's nothing I can do about it"); other attributions may galvanize them into effective action ("I won't find fellow skiers in a place this big unless I advertise in the school newspaper"). The longer a spell of loneliness lasts, the more likely a person is to think the reasons are permanent rather than temporary, to lose the hope that life will improve.

Of course, the particular precipitating causes of loneliness that are relevant to a college student undoubtedly differ from the explanations that a recently divorced 35-year-old, an unemployed factory worker, or a disabled 80-year-old might have, but their attributions still fall along the same three dimensions of internality, stability, and control. In the NYU studies, young single people and the recently divorced were most likely to say they are lonely because they are unattached, longing for "one special person." Young adults also linked loneliness to alienation—

not being understood, not having close friends, not being needed. Among older people who felt lonely, the main reason was forced isolation (being housebound or handicapped), not the lack of friends or lovers.

Another key influence on a person's experience of loneliness is expectations: People want to know when their feelings of loneliness are "normal," and typically decide by watching how other people react in the same situation. If everyone else seems to be suffering, one's own problems are tolerable. But if everyone else seems to be happy, one's own suffering becomes unbearable. One of the NYU researchers (Rubenstein) interviewed a young black woman who expressed this sentiment well: "When I'm lonely, I don't know what to do for myself . . . I just sit in the house with my two kids and look out the window and see everybody else going by and having a good time." As social psychologist Stanley Schachter put it, "Misery doesn't just love company. It loves *miserable* company."

Past experiences also shape expectations. As psychologist Marjorie Lowenthal showed, elderly people who have lived most of their lives with minimal social contact are content with few friends and do not feel deprived or especially lonely. But elderly people who suddenly face a change in the number of friends and activities they are used to *do* feel lonely. Likewise, a person who has had an unusually good relationship may feel lonely if he or she cannot duplicate it. A woman wrote the NYU researchers: "It is possible to be alone and never be lonely. It is also possible to be lonely and never be alone. Since the death of my first hus-

Young single people and the recently divorced were most likely to say they are lonely because they are unattached, longing for "one special person."

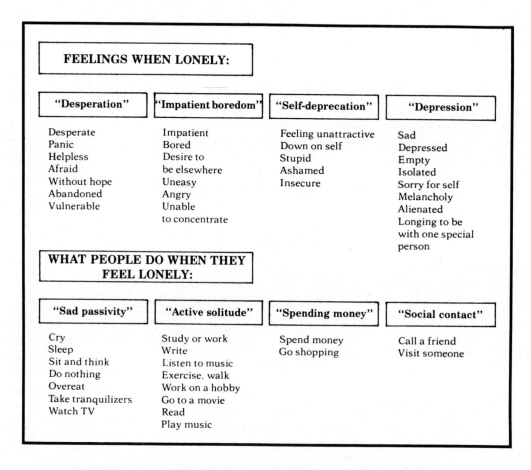

FEELINGS WHEN LONELY:

"Desperation"	"Impatient boredom"	"Self-deprecation"	"Depression"
Desperate	Impatient	Feeling unattractive	Sad
Panic	Bored	Down on self	Depressed
Helpless	Desire to	Stupid	Empty
Afraid	be elsewhere	Ashamed	Isolated
Without hope	Uneasy	Insecure	Sorry for self
Abandoned	Angry		Melancholy
Vulnerable	Unable		Alienated
	to concentrate		Longing to be with one special person

WHAT PEOPLE DO WHEN THEY FEEL LONELY:

"Sad passivity"	"Active solitude"	"Spending money"	"Social contact"
Cry	Study or work	Spend money	Call a friend
Sleep	Write	Go shopping	Visit someone
Sit and think	Listen to music		
Do nothing	Exercise, walk		
Overeat	Work on a hobby		
Take tranquilizers	Go to a movie		
Watch TV	Read		
	Play music		

NYU studies uncovered four clusters of feelings that people have when they say they feel lonely. Some people associate the experience of loneliness with desperation and abandonment; others feel bored; others sink into self-deprecation or depression. What people do when they are lonely depends on how they feel about their loneliness. The severely depressed and most lonely individuals fall into "sad passivity." People who are only mildly or rarely lonely prefer to attack the mood with vigorous strategies: They work, exercise, write letters, read books, or call or visit a friend.

band, there has been a core of loneliness within me, a void that is never filled, despite the fact that I remarried less than a year after his death."

Our studies suggest that people can benefit from understanding the multi-ple causes of loneliness, and from recognizing their own role in perpetuating or extinguishing it. Research has long demonstrated that people tend to underestimate the effects of situations on their behavior; they overemphasize personality factors. The trick is to understand which causes of loneliness are under one's control, and which are not; which events *precipitated* the lonely feelings (such as the death of a spouse, forced retirement) and which ones *maintain* it (refusal to find new friends or interests, shyness).

People want to know when their feelings of loneliness are "normal," and typically decide by watching how other people react in the same situation.

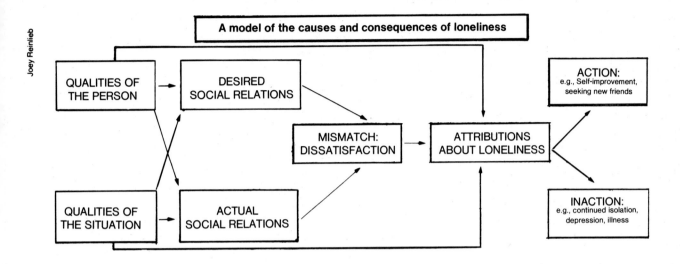

A model of the causes and consequences of loneliness

Feeling lonely has its origins both in qualities of the individual (sensitivity to rejection, shyness, physical appearance) and in qualities of the situation (unemployment, recent divorce or loss, large lecture classes, moving to a new city). The intersection of these two factors in turn affect a person's desired and actual social life—whether the person expects to have many friends, finds them, is satisfied with them. When a gap occurs between expectation and reality, the individual feels unhappy and frustrated, and is motivated to account for the discrepancy. Depending on the explanation (attribution) he makes, he will take action to overcome loneliness, or become depressed, ill, bitter, and further isolated.

The phenomenon of loneliness is both a personal and a social one. Therapy may be appropriate for people whose parents rejected them (or who feel rejected by their parents), and for lonely souls whose self-esteem is low. Therapy usually won't help people made lonely by loss of work, racial discrimination, or competition.

While collaborating coast-to-coast on this article, we discovered that we had unintentionally developed different opinions about the prospects for treating loneliness. Rubenstein and Shaver, after surveying thousands of adults of all ages and occupations (residing mostly in gray northeastern cities) and interviewing middle-aged people who have been lonely for years, felt pessimistic about reversing many of the social and personal forces that cause loneliness. Peplau and her colleagues, working with college students (in sunny California), were much more optimistic. By nipping negative attributions in the bud, she argues, severe loneliness and depression can be prevented or overturned. The three of us agree on one thing: The earlier loneliness is dealt with the more likely it is to be dispelled.

For further information:

Gordon, Suzanne. *Lonely in America.* Simon and Schuster, 1976.

Peplau, L., D. Russell, and M. Heim. "An Attributional Analysis of Loneliness." *Attribution Theory: Applications to Social Problems,* ed. by I. Frieze, D. Bar-Tal, and J. Carroll. Jossey-Bass, forthcoming.

Rubenstein, C., and P. Shaver. "Loneliness in Two Northeastern Cities." *The Anatomy of Loneliness,* ed. by J. Hartog and J. Ralph Audy. International Universities Press, 1979.

Weiss, Robert S. *Loneliness* M.I.T. Press, 1974.

COUPLING, MARRIAGE, AND GROWTH

What are the secret contracts and hidden conspiracies
that prevent us from being happy with a mate?
Why do we often cling to singleness out of the fear
that we will be somehow swamped by a love
union? Here, from an important new book, thoughtful
answers to these and other vital questions . . .

Roger Gould, M.D.

☐ Whether heterosexual, gay, or bisexual, we all feel an
increasing desire to have someone special and to be special
to someone else. By our late twenties, as our friends couple
off and spend time with other couples, if we *don't* have
someone special we feel left out.

Those of us who couple early sometimes feel superior to
our single friends. We have demonstrated our ability to be
intimate, yet in the back of our minds we wonder if we
would have the guts to bear the loneliness and rejection of
life without a partner. And that is why we stay married.

Those of us who remain single sometimes feel superior to
couples because we feel more self-reliant and independent,
but in the back of our minds we wonder whether we are just
too frightened of intimacy and dependency to find a
partner.

What's the right formula? Twenty-five years ago, the only
right way to live was as a heterosexual married couple planning to have children. All other life styles were deviant;
bachelorhood was a disease to be cured; most people cured
themselves by marrying in their early twenties. In 1978, our
society not only has a great deal of tolerance for bachelorhood but also tolerates homosexual bachelorhood and
nonpermanent couplings. Some even say marriage is bad for
human growth.

In this heyday of life-style variations and experimentation, a successful couple knows that when love is good, it is
addictive. The world looks and feels different. A walk in the
park with someone special is no longer just a walk in the
park. Our shared secrets become love-bonds, and we feel
confirmed as loving, lovable, worthwhile, and wanted.

As a couple, we *strive* for the ideal of two healthy, self-
reliant, clear-thinking people sharing a life enriched by each
person's contribution. We want to believe we are two independent people forming an interdependent unit. But alongside this hope is a fear—the fear that the other person will
siphon off our life energies and crowd out our sunlight. The
challenge of coupling, then, is how to have an intense relationship without losing our *self* in the other person.

But the truth is that we can lose our self only if that self
is already confined by our *own* rigid internal prohibitions—
as we all are to some degree—and if we go on to *confuse*
the location of that internal constraint. This can be formulated as a rule: *The only way a mutual relationship can
cause us to lose our self is when we blame our partner for
our own internal prohibitions*—that is, when we begin to
believe that he or she *could* make us feel more confident as
lovers, parents, men, women, social beings but, instead, *willfully* and *stubbornly* refuses to give us that confidence.
Once that mistake has been made—attributing to loved

ones the authority we should keep for ourselves—we feel
trapped and *controlled* by our partner; we must then
persuade, manipulate, or cajole him/her to gain permission
to grow.

Let's put this yet another way. The fears underlying our
particular lack of confidence—fears that we do not want to
face—tempt us to believe in an old false assumption left
over from childhood: *My loved ones are able to do for me
what I haven't been able to do for myself.*

The Cure of Love and the Conspiracy of Coupling

How does it happen that we tell ourselves that we lack the
capacity to remedy our inadequacies and that only a special
loved one can do this?

All of us occasionally feel inadequate in some area of our
life. "I have no talent" or, "I'm not strong enough, loving
enough, smart enough, masculine enough, or feminine
enough" are typical feelings we all share. Mostly, these feelings of self-doubt are what I have called "internal prohibitions." We are divided against ourselves and are afraid to
acknowledge our capacities and talents. They are not realistic
feelings, but feelings that express internal subjective fears.
Thus, we feel inadequate in the midst of success, or incon-
sistently attach obscure feelings of inadequacy to our body,
thinking it is ugly at one time and beautiful the next.

The loved one enters into these dynamics when we try to
get rid of the feelings of inadequacy by the "cure" of love
and the devotion of a loved one. It is quite true that being
told we are respected and important and cared for can wash
away our feelings of inadequacy—temporarily. The problem
is, it prevents us from confronting the feelings that we must
learn to outgrow—the fears that underlie our feeling of
inadequacy. And this is the danger: that too great a reliance
on the "cure" of love arrests our growth too much.

Now, this "cure" is in fact an unhealthy conspiracy with
those who have a special relationship to us. And the more
special the relationship, the more likely we are to depend on
the other person to help us. In this conspiracy—to avoid the
sources of our inadequacy—we don't have to do anything;
they, our loved ones, will do all that we can't do for
ourselves.

The problem is that such a relationship must eventually
become hostile because of its built-in dependency. Although
I no longer feel as inadequate, I still feel inferior to my
partner because he or she is able to do for me what I can't
do for myself.

The conspiracy is a no-win situation. Eventually, I feel
either hostile or dependent, and often both. In any case, my
simple pact with my loved one becomes a destructive
conspiracy that prevents my developing a fuller, more independent adult consciousness.

It is in this way, then, that we can "lose our self" when we
couple with another person. For the most part, only a small
portion of each relationship is based on the cure-by-love
conspiracy, though that part is where the problems are.

Conspiracy as an Interference With Coupling

There are many good practical reasons to remain uncou-
pled during one's twenties. There's complete freedom to

come and go as one pleases. It's so much easier to keep our own self-image in mind when it's not being blurred by someone else's constant presence. Being involved with many different people highlights different parts of us. We can make commitments to low-paying public-service or political jobs more easily if only our own living standard is being sacrificed. Jobs requiring extensive traveling and frequent dislocations can be taken. There's no reason to restrict whom we meet for lunch and no reason not to strike up a friendship when there's no potentially jealous partner waiting for a report. Love affairs, which are usually profound learning experiences, can be entered into fully without guilt or a makeshift schedule or a premature ending.

Single life clearly has advantages. Still, there are many in their twenties who don't want to remain single, yet are unable to couple. The problem is the conspiratorial relationships they stimulate. If we cannot let new relationships evolve naturally, but immediately insist that a new partner become a coconspirator with us in a script meant to cover up our inadequacies and fears, this demand interferes with intimacy and prevents coupling.

Joan, a beautician, was always abandoned early in a new relationship because she unilaterally decided the man was hers for the asking; she became petulant when the man continued to date other women.

Robin, a tall, slim beauty constantly wearing Daisy Mae shorts and revealing a bare midriff, couldn't understand why men didn't want to be just friends. Why did they always make a pass at her? It always ended her interest in them.

The common imperative buried in these patterns of behavior is: "Those who want me, I don't want. Those who don't want me, I do want, but only until it seems I can have them." The patterns are all organized by the old false assumption: "My loved ones can do for me what I can't do for myself."

Like the people in the examples above, we are all waiting for our special demands to be met. We demand a partner with traits that complement our special configuration of traits like a lock and a key. We run prospective partners through an obstacle course; we withdraw love for missteps. Partners looking to be loved by us end up feeling controlled, criticized, and guilty for not being what we decided they should be. Then they leave; or, if they stay, they come to resent us.

Though many people live out their love lives confined to these neurotic patterns, most of us learn not to place unrealistic expectations and dependence on our loved ones. We begin to have open, evolving relationships that can grow deeper because we are living in the present, not the past.

Marilyn. We all have patterns that continue to interfere with our intimacy, and living with someone brings them out more clearly than just dating. *When we believe that our loved ones can do for us what we are unable to do for ourselves, even a temporary partner has the power to hurt or help our self-image temporarily.*

Marilyn's relationships with the many men she lived with were all characterized by her proclamation: "I am a crushed little girl who can't bear pain and must be protected from the world by a big strong man." Her soft voice and kittenish ways softened her demanding look: "I am hurt; what are you doing just standing there?" But she was determined enough to leave each man after a year or so because he didn't take good enough care of her.

What's more, by the time she left, each man had her up on a pedestal, which made her feel quite powerful and superior. At one and the same time, she felt contemptuous of the men for letting her get away with her childish demands and felt resentful of anyone who didn't let her get away with it. After many such episodes, she knew she

couldn't grow up unless she learned to relate in a new way, but she couldn't bring herself to give up the indulgences she won by being a "crushed little girl."

Marilyn feels that someone special has to come along and forcibly take away her privileges. So far, no such man has appeared, so she moves from one man to the next when it's convenient for her, and despite the impact on the man she is leaving. She always considers marriage, then leaves just as the next affair begins. It's while making the decision about marrying Alan that Marilyn finally conquers the assumption that someone special will do for her what she can't do for herself. Marilyn knows she isn't going to marry Alan. However, she prefers to stay with him until a new man comes along. But she also knows that Alan couldn't stand to lose her to another man.

It's a conflict she has managed to avoid with all the previous men in her life—her need for a painless, free-floating life versus a friend's right not to be hurt needlessly by her. Her wish to be the powerful baby who is spared pain through the sacrifices made by indulgent parents (Alan is just a substitute) must be reconciled with the fact that she's a twenty-seven-year-old adult who is consciously choosing to badly hurt a trusting human being.

Is she going to wait for someone to discipline her, or is she going to discipline herself? "I know I should, but I don't want to" is her first response. She can't convince herself that her intuition is wrong about not marrying him, nor can she pretend that he won't be hurt unnecessarily if she leaves for another man. She can't ignore the contradiction. She must decide whether she will remain a spoiled, indulged child or whether she will become an adult who accepts her own mind, whether it causes her pain or not.

Marilyn chose to leave Alan as her conscience dictated, and after a year of living alone and enjoying her independence, she met a man who cared for her deeply but wouldn't respond to her demands. "I'm a real danger to you," he said, "because you can't control me; you're going to hate me for being strong, but then you'll love me." And so it was.

For many singles who begin to couple, power and control are the issues. No matter how we disguise it, when we're relating with the assumption that someone special owes us a special feat of magic, we're exercising our childhood desire for omnipotence. We are treating our partner as an actor in our personal drama. Anyone who won't play out the assigned script, we stay away from. Anyone who goes along with us, we feel in control of, even while we're bitterly complaining about being controlled or misused. These dramas are multilayered sadistic-masochistic games reflecting a basic fear of and anger toward the opposite sex.

We escape these self-imposed traps through the same sequence Marilyn went through in her decision to leave Alan: We must first recognize the pattern, then remain scrupulously honest at a critical decision-point, and then have the good fortune or good sense to choose someone who is not vulnerable to our controlling ways.

Laura. There's more to learn from living together than just the important lessons of how we interfere with intimacy. When we live with someone, our defenses are penetrated every day and our deepest personality secrets are exposed. Our lack of confidence comes out through our bravado; our timidity shows through our intimidating postures; our ignorance shows despite our know-it-all attitude; and our dependence pokes through our self-reliance.

If we're lucky, our nakedness will not hurt us badly but will teach us a beautiful lesson. Laura was such a person—lucky, and willing to accept it and learn from it.

After John returned to his wife, Laura reviewed what living with him had taught her during their six months together. Laura learned that pretending to know all of the answers didn't work and wasn't necessary. John could see when she was bluffing and called her on it and convinced her he didn't think she was stupid if she didn't have an encyclopedic knowledge or a well-thought-out opinion on every subject. When she shared her personal feelings, he listened and understood instead of telling her she was "crazy" for not being more conventional.

But it could also have turned out badly. John could have made Laura feel she was odd for having her own views, or crazy and stupid for pretending to know it all. She was quite vulnerable and instead of promoting her self-confidence, he could have worked her over viciously.

Had that happened, Laura would have learned a bitter lesson in life—that people can work you over for their own purposes and that people have blind spots that don't allow them to understand you or tolerate your individuality. Laura could have left that six-month relationship wondering for years what was wrong with her before she finally came to see clearly that it was not her, but him. By allowing John into her special space, Laura gives him some of the same enormous power that our parents had—to determine what's "real" about us. That John did not misuse that power is Laura's great fortune.

From Coupling to Marriage

As stated earlier, the more special the relationship, the more we expect from the other person. Also, the more intimate the form of the relationship, the greater our fear of it. For example, we are less afraid to date than we are to live together, and less afraid to marry than to have children.

Each form of relationship carries its own advantages and disadvantages, its own degree of intimacy or specialness. From single life up to marriage with children, the more intimate or special the form of the relationship, the greater the threat—and the greater our opportunity for happiness.

What are the threats associated with marriage? When a relationship deepens and marriage is considered, we're afraid of being trapped by greater commitment, and the latent fears about our partner's long-run potential reach center stage. Is he or she a loser, someone who will be too dependent or too overpowering; or someone who will falter under the pressures of family responsibility?

Having lived together is not a reliable guide to future behavior because that kind of impermanence has differing effects on people. It makes some of us miserable. We can't enjoy the relationship even when it's good because we're worrying about when it's going to end. We're afraid to put too much into it, for fear we'll end up with nothing. On the other hand, that same impermanence is what allows others of us to join the relationship more fully, for we have an easy escape to allay our fears of being trapped. The partner who is most pained by the impermanence is more likely to flourish in the marriage; the one who feels most relieved by the impermanence is most likely to feel trapped in marriage.

"I don't understand it; we lived together for two years, but after we married he turned into a stranger. He's become bossy and picky." "Before, she was industrious and optimistic; since we've been married, she's become morose and lazy; the only time she became her old self again was when I hurt my back and she had to work and take care of things."

So marriage is quite different from living together. But many of us don't have negative reactions to marrying; we luxuriate in the advantages. There is a great release of energy from the worries of impermanence. Competition is markedly reduced. We're not on the make, looking for a better fit. Fidelity becomes a background concern. There is a calm sense of direction; we can invest in the future by working out our problems in a new way—with the door to escape closed. We face our more intense problems with the understanding that they have to be resolved. With this commitment, we feel more solid in our everyday life.

Now, whether we can work out our problems—escape the trap of conspiracy and grow—depends in part on our conception of marriage.

If we see marriage as a static arrangement between two unchanging people, any substantial change in either of those people must initially be perceived as a violation of the unspoken contract on which the marriage is based. Change sets off guilt in one partner and envy in the other because it's not "supposed" to happen.

In a really happy, really adult marriage, change in one partner is met gladly by the other partner, who is not afraid of the growth, but welcomes it, intellectually, at least, as an interesting improvement in the relationship—and also sees it as the beginning of his or her next induced growth step. Then, when envy occurs—and it is bound to—it is not cause for righteous indignation; instead, it is the sign that a personal inadequacy has been exposed; it is a source of information to the individual who feels envious.

The static concept of marriage fosters the conspiracies of marriage that warehouse and slow down growth; the growth concept of marriage encourages empathic separateness and a continuous, flowing rhythm of change. In a growth marriage, we are married and divorced many times in the sense that we are continually divorced from old arrangements and married to new ones. We negotiate from the present only. "But you were that way before" is irrelevant. No guilt about our new self surfacing. No responsibility to remain as we were. Only a responsibility to handle change with integrity and sensitivity to our partner.

What are our chances of forming a growth marriage? If we look at this question sociologically, we can see that our chances are good. The static and growth concepts of marriage co-exist right now in our society. If one partner embraces the ideology of growth while the other tries to stop the change because of the belief that marriage should be static, then divorce is inevitable. But as society creates more partners who believe in the growth concept of marriage, we may see not only a new stabilization of marriage, but also a new form of the institution. Living through the rhythms of one's own growth against the pushes and pulls of the changes of a beloved partner over a lifetime creates a dynamic relationship. Society may come to view marriage not so much as a fixed economic unit, but as potentially the best route to the highest level of personal unfolding.

On the other hand, we may be witnessing the beginning of a new form of married family-life where we exchange partners whenever a new part of ourselves requires confirmation. All children will be members of extended families; everyone will have half brothers, half sisters, half mothers, half fathers, and dozens of grandparents.

The cement of static marriages was loosened forever when we became a sexually permissive society. Once children have grown up believing in their right to be sensuous and sexually free, they're never going to buy the same principle of fidelity that all of us bought when we were young. Once any of us discovers our mate does not have to be our only sexual resource, the power of the sex-drive will no longer serve as the cement it used to be during the rough times.

Perhaps as a society we're conducting a grand experiment by forcing this next generation of adults to do battle with sexual jealousy directly. On the one hand, if each partner sees his or her own sexual freedom as an inalienable right, battles over jealousy/possessiveness issues are inevitable. On the other hand, if they succeed in resolving these issues constructively, the present painful aspects of living within a growth ideology will be greatly diminished. If monogamy and fidelity prevail, it could be at a higher level of maturity: "I choose this because it's the best way, not because I'm told it's the only way."

The Sexual Balance of POWER

Letitia Anne Peplau, Zick Rubin, and Charles T. Hill

Letitia Anne Peplau received her Ph.D. in social psychology from Harvard in 1973, and is now an assistant professor of psychology at the University of California, Los Angeles. Her interest in the development of close love relationships is currently focused on lesbian couples. Zick Rubin taught at Harvard for seven years before assuming a position as professor of social psychology at Brandeis University. This year he is a visiting fellow at the Institute of Human Development at the University of California, Berkeley, to study children's social development. He received the 1969 Socio-Psychological Prize of the American Association for the Advancement of Science. Charles T. Hill, an assistant professor in the Department of Sociology at the University of Washington, received his Ph.D. in social psychology from Harvard in 1975. His research interests include how interpersonal relationships develop, how individuals perceive themselves and others, and how they interact with and try to influence one another.

WOMEN'S PUSH FOR EQUALITY with men extends to all areas. The traditional patterns of male dominance in marriage and close relationships are being re-examined. One young man described this shift toward egalitarian relationships: "When I was growing up, my father was the Supreme Court in our family. He ran the show. My relationship with Betsy is very different, very egalitarian. We try to discuss things until we reach a consensus. And that's the way I think it should be."

We wondered how these changing attitudes have affected young couples. As part of a two-year study of dating relationships, we examined the balance of power among 231 dating couples (see box).

These young people overwhelmingly favored equality. Ninety-five percent of the women and 87 percent of the men said boyfriends and girlfriends should have "exactly equal say" about their relationship.

The reality, they admitted, was different. When we asked, "Who do you think has more say about what you and your partner do together?" only 49 percent of the women and 42 percent of the men felt both were equal. Among the rest, two thirds of the women and three quarters of the men thought the man had more of a say.

We wondered if this general pattern held in all areas of the couples' relationships. To find out, we asked who had more say in five important areas: recreation, conversation, sexual activity, amount of time spent together, and activities with other people.

Here again, in each area fewer than half the students reported equal power. Equality was greatest in the area of conversation: "what you talk about and don't talk about when you are together." Men were most likely to control the area of recreation: "how you spend your free time together, where you go and what you do together." None of the five areas was seen as a domain for female power by a majority of students.

When we compared answers about these five areas with answers to our first question—who usually has more say—they were closely related. The more powerful person tended to have more say in each of the five areas.

Further probing showed that the balance of power is often complex. For example, fewer than half the students reported equal power in the area of sex. When decisionmaking wasn't mutual, students reported two to one that the man had more say about the type and frequency of sexual activity. Yet when it came to contraception, the woman usually had more say than the man.

Lysistrata strikes again. Couples considered many specific issues such as these in judging the overall balance of power. Making decisions about contraception was not related to the general balance of power, probably because most students see it as a legitimate area for female control. Decisions about intercourse, however, were more important. In response to our general-power question—who usually has more say—women refraining from intercourse were twice as likely as other women to report having more say than their boyfriends.

Approaching power from another standpoint, we asked the couples to imagine themselves in several hypothetical situations that called for a choice. For instance, both want to go to a movie, but disagree about which picture. Or, the couple has a serious argument. Who is the first to make up?

Many students told us that the alternatives offered were too simple to capture what actually happened. In real life, they said, they would often compromise, going to one partner's movie one week, the other's the next week. Their decisionmaking extended over a period of weeks and months; no one decision told the whole story.

This was undoubtedly true. Yet when we compared the answers about these hypothetical conflicts with answers to our first question—who usually has more say—they tended to go together. The more powerful person was likely to win in most cases.

The next question we asked was whether boyfriends and girlfriends agreed who held the balance of power. We found that half the couples agreed perfectly. Only two percent disagreed completely about who had more power, with one saying it was the man and the other the woman. Among the rest of the couples, one partner reported equal power, the other said one of them had more say.

When couples disagreed about power,

the difference was often a matter of what decisions each felt were important. Tom and Sandy, a couple who got married during our study, illustrate this point. Sandy felt she had more say because she selected their apartment, decided how it would be decorated, and generally determined the couple's lifestyle. To Tom, these were minor decisions he gladly turned over to his wife. The decisions he considered important, such as not having children and selecting a new car, were shared. As far as Tom was concerned, he and Sandy had equal power.

Disagreements about power also reflected different styles of influence. Traditionally, women use subtle ways to get what they want, while men are more direct and assertive. An article by Paula Johnson and Jacqueline Goodchilds in last month's PT ["How Women Get Their Way"] discussed this idea, and concluded that the stereotype still holds in many cases. A person unaware of subtle influence tactics may tend to overestimate his or her own power and disagree with the partner's assessment of the situation.

In addition, dating partners may have different definitions of what "having a say" really means. Imagine for instance, a man saying to his girlfriend, "Let's go to a movie. You decide which one." She picks an old Bogart film and they start off. Who exercised more power—the woman, who made the final decision, or the man, who delegated decision-making to her? The tricky task of defining power can perplex couples as well as researchers. Men and women often perceive events in a relationship differently. Although they know each other well and love each other deeply, the reality they experience may be quite different.

Tipping the balance. Even though our couples staunchly supported equality, fewer than half felt they achieved it. We explored three factors that work against achieving equal power. One was the couples' beliefs about how men and women should act. We had them answer a sex-role attitude questionnaire, which asked them to agree or disagree with 10 statements, such as: "It's just as appropriate for a woman to open a door for a man as vice versa" and "When a couple is going somewhere by car, it's better for the man to do the driving."

Dating partners tended to give similar answers. Sex-role traditionalists were likely to date other traditionalists; liberals dated liberals. We averaged the partners' scores to create a joint traditionalism score for each couple, and then used the scores to divide couples into traditional, moderate, and liberal groups.

As you might expect, men were more powerful among traditional couples. Forty-three percent of the men and 59 percent of the women said he had more power. Among liberal couples, only about 25 percent of both sexes believed the man had more say.

Yet there were important exceptions to this rule. Ten percent of traditionalists said the woman had more power, and nearly 40 percent reported equal power. Paul and Peggy are a good example. Peggy was the expert on cooking and social etiquette; Paul decided which restaurant they'd go to and what they'd do on a date. They divided responsibility in a traditional way, but they believed each had equal power overall.

Nor were all the liberal couples egalitarian, as Jim and Judy illustrate. From the beginning of their relationship, he set out to change her. Jim felt he was a Pygmalion, the skilled teacher of a naive but promising student. He encouraged Judy to join a women's consciousness-raising group and pressured her to be less feminine in traditional ways.

For her part, Judy largely accepted Jim's influence. She wanted to change and looked up to him as an intellectual leader. Yet she sometimes resented his domination and detected hints of chauvinism. For instance, he chided her for not doing more of the driving, but then criticized her performance when she got behind the wheel. Jim dominated Judy in order to liberate her, and Judy's eagerness to become liberated led her to accept his domination.

A second factor that worked against equal power was the relative involvement or dependency of the boyfriend and girlfriend. When we asked, "Who do you think is more involved in your relationship, your partner or you?" only half the couples reported equal involvement. Jill, for example, told us that "Warren would do anything I want ... I come first, he's a distant second as far as he's concerned." She was less strongly attracted to him.

Some 40 years ago, sociologist Willard Waller predicted that an imbalance of involvement would lead to an imbalance of power. "That person is best able to dictate the condition of an association," he wrote, "whose interest in the continuation of the affair is least." Our data provide strong support for this "principle of least interest." The less-involved partner has greater say than the partner who is more involved, presumably because the person who cares more defers to the wishes of the other.

Unequal involvement is costly for both partners, however. The less-involved partner may become bored or feel like an exploiter. The more-involved person may get frustrated or feel used. Not surprisingly, 54 percent of couples with unequal involvement broke up during our study, compared to only

---

How the Couples Were Recruited

In the spring of 1972 we wrote to a random sample of 5,000 sophomores and juniors, 2,500 men and 2,500 women, at four colleges in the Boston area. We asked if they would be interested in participating in a study of "college students and their opposite-sex relationships." We invited those who said they were going with someone to attend a questionnaire session with their boyfriend or girlfriend. The 202 couples who showed up, plus 29 others recruited by advertising at one of the four schools, made up our sample.

Ninety-five percent of the men and women were or had been college students, typically a sophomore woman dating a junior man. Nearly all were white; 44 percent were Catholic, 26 percent were Protestant, and 25 percent were Jewish. At the beginning of the study, a third of the couples had been going together for less than five months; a third, for from five to 10 months; and a third, for longer. The median period was eight months. Four fifths of the couples had had sexual intercourse and one fifth lived together all or most of the time.

In addition to an initial 40-page questionnaire, the couples answered follow-up questionnaires six months, one year, and two years later. We didn't lose many people along the way; 80 percent or more of the original group answered every questionnaire. To get the personal details and feelings missing from questionnaires, we also interviewed a number of couples several times during the two years.

23 percent of couples with equal involvement.

A woman's educational and career goals were a third major factor in the balance of power. Higher education and work make women more equal to men by providing special skills and expertise, additional resources such as income or prestige, and sources of satisfaction outside a relationship. Our data indicate clearly that as a woman's educational plans increased, male power decreased (see table). No such relationship was found between the man's educational aspirations and power in the relationship.

My husband, the genius. Leonard and Karen are an example, extreme in some ways, of how education can affect power. After college, Karen took a job as a high school art teacher to put her husband, whom both considered an artistic genius, through graduate school. She saw her job as a necessity, not a source of enjoyment or the start of a career. Karen's primary involvement was in her marriage.

Leonard's attitude was completely different. "For him," Karen admitted, "painting and sculpture come first and I'm second. If he had to move to New York to be famous and I wouldn't go, he'd leave me." His lesser involvement in the marriage gave Leonard the upper hand. He determined where they lived and Karen felt she had to tolerate his infidelities.

Partly because of their strained relationship, Karen took a summer-school course in a new method of teaching art. She found it exciting, became seriously interested in teaching as a career, and decided to apply to graduate school. In long talks with other women, she reexamined her ideas about marriage, sex roles, and her career.

Karen feels these changes helped her marriage and altered the balance of power. "If I'd gone on working to support him," she told us, "he'd be the more dominant. If I hadn't decided to go to school, he'd still be taking the money

and running the show." She hopes that as she gains more respect for her abilities, Leonard will, too.

As we've seen, power among these couples was influenced by three factors: attitudes toward appropriate sex roles, the balance of involvement in the relationship, and the woman's educational plans. For women, these three factors were closely related and cumulative in effect. Women who planned on graduate school had more liberal sex-role attitudes and usually dated men who were more liberal. They often planned on a full-time career as well as marriage. This made them less dependent on men in general and decreased their relative involvement in dating relationships. For men, these factors were not interrelated.

Although many women were interested in a career, they didn't see it as a substitute for marriage. Nearly all the men and women (96 percent) expected to marry, although not necessarily each other, and more than 90 percent said they wanted one or more children. What distinguished the liberal women from the traditionalists wasn't marriage, but their plans for a career.

We don't know, of course, whether the women will follow through on their plans for advanced education and full-time careers. Our results suggest, however, that their decisions will strongly affect how much power they have in personal relationships with men.

Men and women have traditionally exercised power in different ways. Men are expected to be direct, even bold in their leadership; women, to be subtle, even sneaky. These different styles often mask where the real power lies, as sociologist Jessie Bernard explained in her book The Future of Marriage: "...from time immemorial, despite the institutional pattern conferring authority on husbands, whichever spouse had the talent for running the show did so. If the wife was the power in the mar-

riage she exerted her power in a way that did not show...."

Psychologist Susan Kaplan asked 59 of our couples to participate in a study of how men and women make decisions. In one part of her study, couples read case histories of hypothetical couples who had a disagreement. To stimulate discussion, the man and woman read slightly different versions of the case history, one more favorable to the man's position; the other, to the woman's. They were asked to discuss the case and reach a joint decision about who was right.

Pretty please. The couples' discussions were tape-recorded and analyzed for 12 different power strategies people use to win arguments. Some are traditionally feminine, such as making an emotional appeal or asking for information. Others, such as taking charge of the discussion or voicing a strong opinion, are stereotypically masculine. When Kaplan analyzed the tapes to see which strategies were used most by men and by women, she found no sex differences in 10 of the 12 strategies. Men were as likely as women to use emotional appeals, for example, or ask questions.

Sex differences appeared in two of the strategies. Men gave information much more often than women did. And women were more likely to disagree with an idea or contradict information given by their boyfriends.

Because we contacted couples several times over a two-year period, we had an opportunity to see whether power shifted as relationships developed. We found no link between the balance of power and how long couples had been going together. We might expect male power to be strongest when a couple first starts to go out, and to diminish over time. This didn't happen. New couples were no more likely to be male-dominated, or egalitarian, than couples who had been going together for several months or years.

Given our students' strong preference for equality, you might think that couples with liberal sex-role attitudes and an egalitarian relationship would stay together longer and be happier. This was not the case among the 103 couples who broke up and the 128 who remained together during the two-year study. There was no relationship between who held the power and whether a couple split or stayed together. Sex-

If the Woman Planned to Get:	The Woman Reported That			The Man Reported That		
	Man Had More Power	Equal Power	Woman Had More Power	Man Had More Power	Equal Power	Woman Had More Power
Less Than B.A. Degree	87%	13%	0%	87%	13%	0%
College Degree	38%	45%	17%	47%	45%	8%
Graduate Degree	21%	60%	19%	39%	42%	18%

role liberals and traditionalists were also equally likely to stay together.

Further, both liberal and traditional couples rated themselves as equally satisfied and felt equally close. They didn't differ in their estimates of the likelihood of eventually marrying their partner, love for the partner, or the number of problems in their relationship.

Shared happiness. It's important to remember that our couples had already survived the early stages of a relationship, perhaps because they had similar attitudes—on sex roles and other issues—or had managed to reconcile their differences. The fact that a couple shares values and beliefs may be more significant to happiness than what the beliefs are.

Although female-dominated, male-dominated, and egalitarian relationships sailed along or sank in equal numbers, there was a difference in satisfaction. Both men and women were significantly less satisfied when the woman held the upper hand than when they were equal or the man was in charge. It is apparently easier for couples to follow the traditional male-dominant pattern or the currently accepted egalitarian pattern than to violate convention by female domination.

We hear a lot of talk about how men and women should act, whether it's best to adopt traditional attitudes, modify them, or reject them outright. Our data indicate that egalitarian and male-dominated couples have an equal chance for happiness. No particular pattern of power can assure a couple of a long-lasting relationship. We found a wide gap between the egalitarian ideal endorsed by the large majority of couples and the actual balance of power that couples achieved. Equality is obviously a difficult and elusive goal.

For more information, read:

Bernard, Jessie. The Future of Marriage. Bantam, 1973. paper, $1.95.

Hill, C.T., Z. Rubin and L.A. Peplau. "Breakups Before Marriage: The End of 103 Affairs" in Journal of Social Issues. Vol. 32, 1976, pp 147-168.

Johnson, Paula and Jacqueline Goodchilds. "How Women Get Their Way" in Psychology Today. Vol 10, No 5, Oct 1976, pp 69-70.

Rubin, Zick and C. Mitchell. "Couples Research as Couples Counseling: Some Unintended Effects of Studying Close Relationships" in American Psychologist. Vol 31, 1976, pp 17-25.

Rubin, Zick, L.A. Peplau and C.T. Hill. Becoming Intimate: The Development of Male-Female Relationships. forthcoming

the Masked Generation

On The Trail Toward A Sense Of Community

Hugh Drummond, M.D.

Commercials may turn out to be the major artifacts of our age. My candidate for the one to go down in history as the purest and cruelest statement of irony is Ma Bell's current shtick: "Reach out and touch someone." This is quite apart from the fact that AT&T's example of warmth, charm and romance are unlike any phone conversation I have ever had or heard of. I don't know about your last long-distance call, but mine was as much like a Reach-out chat as Hieronymus Bosch is like Norman Rockwell.

No, it would take poor, dead Lenny Bruce to do a parody of Reach-out. I can only tell you about our mad agony of loneliness, which makes the telephone company's kitsch so cruel.

Twice in my life I have seen the expression on the face of a person who was soon to die by suicide. It was not the look of depression or despair. It was more the look of a person watching life from a great distance. It was an absorbed attention, as if the person were reviewing an elaborate show, of which he or she had once been the star. I hope I never see it again.

Connectedness, which is the only alternative to suicide, can exist even in isolation. Sometimes, utterly alone, I will have a thought or experience that takes hold of me in some profound way. As I work it over in my mind I find that I am doing so as if I were explaining it to somebody. I suppose this is also what Martin Buber meant by the I-Thou as opposed to the I-It, a conception of one's experience that cannot be conceived of without the other.

This business of how we relate to one another is not just a matter of philosophy. It is the rock-bottom issue for both politics and health and may ultimately be their common ground.

The culture-makers of America have worked hard and long to create a single totem for our supposedly pluralistic society. The central feature of every movie, TV story or pop novel is the Lone Ranger. Western-cowboy, urban-cop, New York-Jew-writer: each stands alone to confront *his* destiny, to carve out (from the mushy matrix of aggression, ambition and sex around him) *his* unique identity. That the *him* is sometimes a *her* does not detract from the basic paradigm of individuality, which is characteristically male and essentially cut off from any group identity. The Bionic Woman has more than a price tag in common with her Six Million Dollar boyfriend.

Medicine too is poured in the mold of Lone Rangers. Cotton Mather, considered the colonial father of American medicine, once asked the nameless boy he had just purchased if he had ever had the pox. The slave thought for a moment and then answered, "Yes and no." Mather was about to throttle the kid for gaming him when the boy explained that his tribe in Africa had the custom of scratching each child with material from a pustule and that no one ever died from it. Mather seized the idea as his own and today is credited with stopping an epidemic and introducing inoculation to the New World.

The constant re-creation of the lone cultural hero is no accident. It is important for the survival of a capitalist society that children be trained to be competitive rather than cooperative, individualistic rather than communal, aggressive rather than contemplative. An alienated industrial worker may pour some ground glass into a cylinder block, but a collective and critical work force can take over the factory.

American education, which is only a slight refinement of pop-culture heroism, focuses on great men and their achievements. The mystique of the Lone Ranger begins in nursery school. A child's first drawings are given stars: gold ones for excellence, silver ones for competence and dreaded red ones for mediocrity. The creative experience becomes an opportunity for isolating, grading and ranking individuals. Cooperative work is considered cheating.

The same children are taught to put on their coats by stretching them out on the floor, sticking their arms into the sleeves and flinging the coats over their heads. Mothers are delighted with their children's mastery of this. In China, however, nursery school children are taught a different lesson. Their coats button up the back, and the only way to get them on is for the children to help one another.

But what does it matter? What's so hot about group identification anyway?

"The Masked Generation—On the Trail Toward a Sense of Community," Hugh Drummond, M.D., *Mother Jones,* May 1981. Reprinted by permission.

165

5. RELATING TO OTHERS

Well, for one thing, it's an issue of health. A growing body of research is supporting the conclusion that social solidarity is a protection against stress-induced illness. A number of animal studies have demonstrated that electric shocks, territorial confusion or monotonous conditioning can induce peptic ulcers, high blood pressure or disturbed behavior when animals are in isolation—but not when kept with their littermates. Less-humane studies of humans during World War II demonstrated that battle stress and all its attendant health consequences were minimized by maintaining strong identification and bonding among bomber crews.

Pregnant women with few sources of social support are found to have significantly more complications than matched controls. Rates of tuberculosis among men in the same social class are found to be higher among socially isolated samples (even though the disease is contagious). And alcoholics who try to quit drinking on their own are far more likely to be institutionalized than those who quit with the help of Alcoholics Anonymous.

I once described to you the devastating health consequences of unemployment. A study by University of Massachusetts sociologist Susan Gore determined that when men, jobless for several weeks, were in a socially supportive environment they had fewer symptoms of illness, lower cholesterol levels and a lesser tendency to blame themselves for their work loss than men who were less socially connected.

In comparison to matched controls, surgical patients for whom the hospital experience was a lonely and anomic affair required more pain medication and an average of three days more post-operative hospitalization.

Asthmatics with high rates of stressful life-changes usually need steroids to control their symptoms. But in asthmatics with strong social support, even intense stress did not create a requirement for steroids.

As you might expect, people's emotional lives are sensitively influenced by their social connectedness. In his classic study of suicide, published in 1897, Émile Durkheim concluded that "the suicide rate varies inversely with the integration of social groups of which the individual forms a part."

Alienation kills. Despite our differences, despite the whole panorama of human behavior, what emerges as characteristically human is our need to stay involved with one another. Like dogs who will snooze while angels pass but become electrically alive at the barest scent of another canine, we are, when biologically truest to ourselves, a social form of life.

That is why the propagandists of capitalism have had to work so hard and long to convince us that we are just individuals, winners or losers in the Big Game—the world of power and property. And they have succeeded. Even more effectively than feudal lords convinced their serfs that aristocracy was divinely ordained, corporate lords have convinced us (and themselves) that survival is a function of individual merit—and that group identification is a certain kind of evil.

There is a book of pop sociology that nicely sums up the fallout from all this. Vance Packard's 1972 book, *A Nation of Strangers*, is a sketch of our rootless, fragmented style of life. Actually it is you, the average *Mother Jones* reader, who is described as among the most unconnected of Americans. College-educated, between 25 and 34 and geared to a managerial, technical or professional life career, you will probably be making a long-distance move within the next year. It is tempting to call you a population of middle-class migrant workers, but the term is misleading. Migrant farm workers actually have a more settled lifestyle because they travel their perennial routes in established community and kinship patterns and characteristically return to a home base each year. You, on the other hand, are more likely to travel a different route every few years and stay connected only to your spouse and children.

If them! There tends to be an unhappy correlation between mobility and divorce. Packard points out that corporate managers are so universally expected to move every two years (out of loyalty to the sovereignty of the company rather than to the community or nation) that spouses are routinely evaluated by supervisors on the basis of whether or not they will give any lip to their peripatetic mates.

But, of course, divorce is in. It is almost sacred. In fact, to the hucksters

of consumerism, it *is* sacred. Every family break-up means a doubling of the purchases of TV sets, washing machines, sofas, etc., etc. It is no accident that movies and television sit-coms now celebrate the recently divorced or single parent as they used to celebrate the nuclear family. Divorce sells.

Is it possible that while people think they divorce because of complaints about their spouses, they really divorce because network sponsors think they should? One would have to be very paranoid to think so.

I am very paranoid. Mobility and divorce are growth industries. The long-range planners for AT&T and its brethren see bonanzas of corporate profit in each percentage increase of broken families. And if a corporation is inclined to topple a government or start a war for profit, why wouldn't it employ its own brand of social forethought to help manipulate a video-conditioned nation?

The fact that our current turn to a heartless and mindless fascism comes with familial overtones does not detract from a corporate investment in the destruction of the family. There may be some working-class Catholic and Baptist foot soldiers at the passionate fringes of the Right. As Deirdre English pointed out recently in her *Mother Jones* article on abortion, they lend a moral fervor and patina it otherwise lacks. At heart, however, right-wing sentiments are antifamily, antilife, antihealth and antispiritual: attitudes characteristic of the stupid and selfish men who dominate our institutions.

But as Engels said, dehumanization affects victims and victimizers alike. So corporate managers themselves wind up being moved, getting divorced, becoming alcoholic and committing suicide. Their own understanding of these events is clouded by the mythology they themselves created. With their therapists and divorce lawyers (thank God I don't have to talk to you about lawyers), they engage in an endless, obsessional analysis of the "reasons" for deciding to do one thing or another. The reasons are each different and all the same. They no longer "love" Exhibit A and have "fallen in love" with Exhibit B. Feelings have become the final arbiter, the universal lodestone, the Delphic oracle for a whole society.

The legal and psychotherapeutic enterprises are, of course, delighted with this mad scramble. They make hay out of "getting in touch with one's feelings." But the big picture suggests that the whole preoccupation with emotions is just one more expression of a crumbling social structure. When nothing works, when institutions fail, when nothing can be predicted, all we have to go on is how we feel.

The problem is that feelings are malleable and evanescent things. Building a life upon them is like trying to nail a chiffon pie to the wall. In order to avoid or respond to stress, humans need information of a more substantial nature, a consistent source of feedback about our behavior. Waiting for a Type-A person to drop from a heart attack, or a depressed one from a suicide, is too little and too late.

There have to be people around who care enough to say, "You don't look well." It may be that, at its existential core, *health is the result of a social feedback system that allows us to either avoid or accommodate to stress.*

What happens when a constant hunger for social engagement is frustrated by a constantly increasing alienation? Well, for one thing, we make more phone calls. The Reachout campaign deepens the illusion that we can be apart and still stay connected. Electronic intimacy; three-minute bursts of companionship; a community of dollar-a-minute gossip; sterile, staccato, disembodied items of talk: all is surrounded by an endless night of lonely silence. Each day some 20 million interstate calls are made, and every day an additional 110,000 telephones are installed. Somebody is making a lot of money off loneliness.

Telephone calls do not satisfy tribal yearnings. We turn with increased urgency in any direction where there is some promise of it. Work and sex are the two areas of life that have become the arenas in which our frustrated needs for companionship and community are played out.

People like to say they *have* to work in order to make money. In fact, more people really *want* to work to fulfill their needs for creative stimulation, a sense of self-esteem and a semblance of community in their lives. One of the problems is that the capitalist mind and the managers who minister to it (I include labor union officials) do not

believe this and therefore do not concern themselves with satisfying those needs. Another problem is that those needs are at crossed purposes with the American workplace.

Back when work took place in small, integrated situations, it was relatively easy for each individual to know that he or she belonged and counted. Today, it seems that every company that isn't actually failing is swallowed up by a larger company, which in turn is taken over by a multinational conglomerate, so that every job is embedded in layers of bureaucracy. The larger and more impersonal the organization, the greater the individual's needs for a sense of community, for self-esteem and for stimulation—and the less likely he or she is to find them.

Take the example of a clerk whose job is to stamp vouchers to be processed when they come into his department. We'll call him Joe. His company has become so large that Joe spends all of his time stamping vouchers, only one of 12 different steps a voucher has to pass through before it can be paid. The payment of the voucher is one of a hundred procedures involved in his division's purchase of chemicals to be mixed with the ink used to print the words *Enriched White Bread* on a brand of bread manufactured by an international communications company. Joe has never found out what purpose the chemicals serve. What they do is simulate the smell of freshly baked bread, so that when shoppers walk by the bakery shelf in the supermarket they can say, "*Mmmm, that smells good,*" even though the bread is packed in airtight plastic packages for long-distance shipping. In other words, Joe will spend his working life in a process that has no manifest purpose. He will never have the satisfaction of looking at a finished product and saying, "There! Me and my pals made that."

But Joe, like everyone else, wants to feel that he belongs and counts. He finds, however, that when he works quickly and efficiently in stamping vouchers he is practically invisible. But when he is slow in stamping vouchers, somebody is likely to come around and say, "Hey, Joe! Where is voucher No. 62783?" Then Joe says, "I'll have it for you in a week." He then feels he is part of a work force. And a very necessary part of it at that.

What this means is that people are

more likely to feel that they belong and count in such a work environment by exerting a negative influence than by exerting a positive one. When you have increasing numbers and levels of middle managers whose jobs are more and more vaguely defined, you have a whole ecology of people saying no instead of yes, because otherwise they would not know if they exist. So there you have it—Drummond's Laws:

1. The larger and more impersonal the organization, the greater the individual's need for stimulation, self-esteem and community.

2. The only way those needs can be met in such an organization is for the individual to exert a negative influence on its purposes.

It's amazing that those organizations accomplish anything at all. On the other hand, considering what most of them set out to do, maybe the reason we're still walking around is because of Drummond's Second Law.

The other human enterprise in which our frustrated need for community is expressed is sex. I know this is important to a lot of you, so I do not want to be too glib about it, but what goes by the name of sex is not always sex. Let me explain what I mean.

I once had a 40-year-old patient who was about to break up his second marriage because of a compulsive need to screw other women. Or at least it seemed so until we had a conversation that went like this:

HE: I'm constantly looking for new women. I was in a department store today looking at some socks. I glanced up and saw a pretty young girl watching me. I smiled and she smiled back. Something as stupid as that will stick in my mind for a week. . . . I love the seduction. I like having that first drink when we start sounding each other out. I like to see myself through her eyes. It's like a little minuet, a little dance, very proper and charming, but under it is the electricity. . . . You know, I think I'm a little disappointed when it finally happens. The payoff, I mean. That's nice too, of course, but something is lost.

ME: You like the courtship more than the sex.

HE: Sometimes I think so. With sex you have to perform. There's the adequacy thing. But when we're looking each other over there's a kind of discovery, of myself as well as of her.

ME: Maybe you want friendship.

HE: I have male friends, but it's not the same thing. I can't talk to them like I talk to a woman. I can't look at myself through their eyes. Maybe it's the competition or the fear they'll think I'm gay, but I can't even look at them directly in the eyes.

One of the reasons there is so much impotence is because sex is made to do too much work for men. Not only is it their only real hobby but it also must serve to bolster their egos *and* it is the only means most men have to experience companionship. Sexual pleasure is a plant that requires a more lighthearted kind of cultivation. Its stem cannot bear the weight our heavyhanded culture leans on it.

If the absence of a sense of connectedness wreaks such havoc on work and love, imagine what it does to the community. The Golden West seems on paper to be the most alienated area of the country. AT&T data shows California to have a mobility rate higher than the rest of the nation, and the U.S. Office of Vital Statistics finds the divorce rate there four times as high as in any other state. One study of alienation in large universities concluded that 36 percent of senior men at the University of California at Berkeley did not have a single close friend of the same sex. Despite all this, however, New York City has to rank as the most anomic, alienated, lonely, community-less community in the world.

I know this sounds like *Broadway Is My Beat*, but it is my home town and as much as I would like to be sentimental about it, it is just too unhappy a place. Every time I see one of those "I Love New York" bumperstickers, I feel like running over and drawing a pacemaker on the heart.

As one illustration of why the Emmy of anomie belongs to New York, I offer the famous wrecked-car study of psychologist Philip Zimbardo. He picked comparable social and ethnic neighborhoods in New York and Palo Alto and left an old car with its hood up in public places. In California the car was left alone by all except for a passerby who shut the hood when it began to rain. In the Big Apple the car was systematically stripped, dismantled and vandalized within hours.

Now that's one hell of a home town.

But it is not due to an accident of demographics or climate that New York is as it is. No less is it accidental that working-class whites, blacks and Hispanics kill each other for bottom-rung jobs, public housing, welfare benefits and the other crumbs of the American economy. Union-busting has been refined to a high art by the corporations and their agents in government. They live so much in terror of America's masses responding to a common rhythm that they must destroy any movement they themselves have not engineered. Seeded clouds at mass meetings, provocateurs in radical organizations, racial murders in poor neighborhoods: there is no limit to the disruptive capacities of those who fear communism.

But I do not want to close on a depressive or paranoid note. The dark view is not the one from which a revolution will spring. We need a politics of hope, one which does not wait for some distant gratification of ambiguous desires nor one which makes too much of conflict and pain. Long-awaited victories have a strange, unhappy way of being marked by triumphal arches . . . and the gallows.

Radical politics should be more warm-hearted: a matter of consistent means as well as ultimate ends. It has more to do with companionship than class hatred. The essential feature of any revolutionary process is that it brings people together. It struggles toward an inclusive rather than exclusive sense of identity, toward the blurring rather than the drawing of lines. In its purest form it has no enemies, only dilatory compatriots. And if there are times when one hand must be clenched in a fist, then the other hand, at least, should be reaching out.

The good a good friend can do

RESEARCH SAYS the song was right: We really do get by with a little help from our friends.

The need for friendship is particularly strong at two stages of our lives. In adolescence, the reassurance of being accepted by a group of friends helps give us courage to strike out on our own and assert our individuality. In old age, having at least one close friend seems to protect us against the insults of aging.

Researchers in one study asked people over 60 whether there was anyone they confided in about themselves or their problems. Those with at least one such confidant seemed to have a buffer against loss of a spouse, loss of a job through retirement and loss of social contacts and functions because of aging. In terms of morale and mental health, they had a significant advantage over similar older people who lacked a confidant.

Dr. Marjorie Fiske, the University of California social psychologist who headed the study, believes the advantage extends even to weathering such chronic illnesses of the elderly as arthritis. Without a doubt, she says, "people who have a confidant cope better."

Although adolescents and old people have an especially pressing need for friendship, giving and receiving social support seem to lessen the impact of stress for all of us.

Dr. Robert L. Kahn and Dr. Toni C. Antonucci of the University of Michigan's Institute for Social Research say that each of us moves through life surrounded by a protective escort, or "convoy," of people we rely on and those who rely on us—for admiration, liking, love and respect, for confirmation of the appropriateness or rightness of what we do and say, and for direct aid in the form of things, money, information, time and the right to ask for such help.

Some studies suggest that when our convoy of coworkers, supervisors, family and friends works well, we have a better chance of sailing through stressful situations that can make less protected individuals literally sick: for instance, the onset of high blood pressure or ulcers associated with job pressure.

Men friends, women friends

Evidence is mounting that on the friendship flank, men are relatively unprotected. According to Dr. Daniel J. Levinson, a Yale psychologist who has studied the stages of men's lives (*The Seasons of a Man's Life,* Ballantine; $6.75 paperback), "Close friendship with a man or woman is rarely experienced by American men." Though it's true that many men are sociable and have a wide circle of business acquaintances, golf partners and the like, "Friendship in the most personal sense is a sharing of self, not just a sharing of activity." And there is more than one reason why, after adolescence, American men have traditionally shied away from the kind of one-to-one friendship in which they voice and share their deepest concerns.

▶ *Competition.* A man has trouble trusting another man. He senses that his admission of shortcomings may be used against him. Dr. Joel D. Block, a Long Island clinical psychologist and author of *Friendship* (Macmillan; $10.95), writes that the experiences of the men he surveyed were "filled with incidents of rivalry and betrayal."

▶ *Group orientation.* Many men find one-to-one intimacy awkward but are comfortable and productive as part of some collective effort. They are most at ease with groups of other men. Anthropologist Lionel Tiger views this kind of male fellowship as an evolutionary heritage from the times when men had to cooperate to hunt together in groups.

▶ *Fear of presenting an unmanly image.* Men are traditionally expected to be tough, self-sufficient, unemotional and close-mouthed, traits that don't necessarily reinforce close friendships. Some men fear that the affectionate intimacy of friendship will turn into or be misinterpreted as homosexuality.

The American taboo on demonstrations of affection between men is lifted for athletes. In fact, such demonstrations are turned into a ritual. "Athletes can hug each other after a home run or a touchdown and that's just normal male exuberance," Levinson says. Closeness is also condoned for men involved in dangerous undertakings. But though the bonds between combat buddies are often intense, they may not last.

In his survey of friendships among middle-class women, Block found more evidence of support and sympathy than of jealousy and mistrust, although female friends may play second fiddle to romantic attachments in the lives of some young women. According to Block, establishing friendships with other women takes on more importance in the thirties and beyond, after career and family are on track. As one woman in her early forties said recently, "When I was young, I sought the company of men because it seemed to me that only men did interesting things. Now it's the women who seem interesting."

A number of studies indicate that women's friendships tend to be deeper and emotionally richer than men's because women are willing to disclose more about themselves and to talk about feelings and matters of deep concern. The level of emotional intimacy is so much greater with women that "men's friends equal women's acquaintances," says Dr. Sandra Gibbs Candy, a University of Kentucky psychologist and researcher. On the job, she warns, this craving for emotional depth can be a problem, for if a professional woman tries to establish close friendships, she may be viewed as excessively vulnerable, unable to handle her career or even seductive. She may be better off if the bonds she forms at work are team relationships.

In old age a woman's adeptness at making and keeping friends is an unmixed blessing. "There is a strong hypothesis that friends help women survive," says Dr. Beth B. Hess of the County College of Morris, in Dover, N.J. "Part of women's ability to sustain themselves in their older years depends on their capacity for constructing a network of friends." On the other hand, a widower who depended on his wife as his sole confidant and source of emotional intimacy, as many men do, may be left in painful isolation.

So, although being your spouse's best friend is an admirable idea and all good marriages contain an element of friendship, there's a case to be made for both partners' maintaining other friendships as well. Tremendous pressure is placed on a couple when they try to be everything to each other, or even when they limit their social contacts to family. "We cannot gain all of our gratifications from our relationships with lovers, spouses, parents or children," Myron Brenton points out in *Friendship* (Stein & Day; $2.45 paperback). "Our friendships both enhance and offer relief from the other emotional roles we play."

New circumstances, new friends

It's not unusual for people to feel that true friends are hard to come by these days and that people used to take more time for each other.

Levinson, for one, is inclined to doubt that the good old days were any friendlier, but individuals who express this kind of nostalgia may be saying, "Ten or twenty years ago *in my life,* when I was in school or in the military or some other situation where people had more time and less responsibility, things were better." But later, during the years when they were struggling with family and job responsibilities or trying to build a financial base for retirement, it may have become difficult to spare time and energy for friends. This friendship deprivation becomes more telling after 40, says the Yale psychologist. As a result, "many people in their forties and fifties feel alone and empty."

Although society is probably no less friendly than it used to be, it is more mobile, and mobility can be hard on friend-

ship. Moving every three or four years is still a fact of corporate life, although more young executives are resisting routine relocation and many major companies are worrying about the dollar cost of it. Academics and military personnel also experience frequent uprootings.

Mobility doesn't have to be geographic to be a problem. It's difficult to sustain a close friendship with someone who has prospered much more or much less than you or who has been promoted over you or left behind.

Though there are exceptions, it is no illusion that friendships with other couples tend to disappear when a marriage breaks up because of divorce or death. Numerous researchers say a single person is at least a symbolic threat to the sexual intimacy of a couple, so couples generally befriend other couples.

A law of similarity seems to operate in our choice of friends. Out of the pool of 500 to 2,500 people we meet in life, we tend to befriend those who are much like us without being directly competitive. Families with children gravitate toward similar families. Men and women tend to choose friends of the same gender. Cross-gender friendships may be very rewarding, but they are rare because of the difficulty of handling any latent sexual attraction.

As Hess puts it, we seek others who "read the world the same way." If you don't find such people in the normal course of events, one alternative is to join a group where everyone is in your boat, such as a newcomers' club, a widows' group or a Parents Without Partners chapter. Such groups may have a certain artificiality, says Dr. Robert S. Weiss, a University of Massachusetts sociologist, in *Loneliness* (MIT Press; $6.95 paperback). Nevertheless, they have helped to tide many people over difficult transitions and lonely times.

Another approach to friend-making is to join a mutual interest group and let the common interest of skiing or politics or lapidary work take you where it may. This tactic also has a limitation: It may bring you in touch with people who share only that interest. But as the philosopher George Santayana wrote, "People are friends in spots."

The truth is that "friend" is an elastic word. Many of the people we give that name to are "friends of the road" rather than "friends of the heart," a distinction made by an African tribe studied by anthropologist Robert Brain, who has looked into friendship customs around the world.

Among your friends of the road may be any number of coworkers, neighbors, and business or organizational acquaintances with whom you share at least a fleeting sociability. You may have coffee-break and football-postmortem companions; "activity" friends, with whom you play tennis, circulate a petition or frequent a bar; "favor" friends, who will lend you a hedge clipper or keep an eye on your house and for whom you will do the same. Such friends may never be very close and you may replace them often as your circumstances change, but your life would be poorer without them.

What are friends for?

Without such a social network, Weiss writes, daily life is more difficult. "The socially isolated have no one to consult about the merits of one or another grocery or film or pediatrician. . . . In consequence, they are less able to deal effectively with their world. They are likely to have failed to learn that there is a dog down the street that has already bitten a neighborhood child or that the local school has a mixed reputation."

In addition to seeking friends for such information, you may be drawn to them for status, hoping that some of their higher prestige will rub off on you and that you'll learn to be more like them. Then, too, friends are for fun and companionship. As Weiss puts it, they "make things happen." Friends are also for help in time of trouble, particularly in the absence of family. There's nothing wrong with using friends for any of these things as long as the friends don't feel used. In comfortable friendships, giving and getting tend to balance out over the life of the relationship.

Of all the things that friends are for, nothing is more valued or difficult to achieve than emotional intimacy. To a close and trusted friend you may speak with candor of your dearest wish or your most dreaded fear, confident that you will be accepted and understood. To paraphrase Emerson, the only way to have such a friend is to be such a friend. The heart of being a friend is accepting the other person as is, listening, trying to understand and then keeping the confidence. Nothing is more destructive of friendship than any action that can be regarded as a betrayal of trust. The fear of hearing what you told in confidence making the rounds is what keeps many people from ever making close friends.

A troubling aspect of close friendship, Levinson observes, is that as the positive ties get stronger, ambivalent feelings come in—including envy and jealousy. And yet "intense relationships are what makes life richer."

According to Block, you can tell the difference between a "nourishing" friendship and a "toxic" contact: The first leaves you feeling "energized and enriched"; the second, "tense, irritable and drained." To build up the nourishing side of friendship, he suggests cultivating authenticity (stop pretending to be what you're not), acceptance (stop trying to make your friend over) and direct expression (if you want an invitation, stop hinting and say so).

Yet even with the best intentions, friendship may not be forever. The parties to a friendship may grow and change in ways that make the relationship unsatisfying to one or both. They may no longer reinforce each other's values and beliefs, an important function in many friendships. Sometimes, unhappily, this happens with a friend who has shared an important part of your life.

"We had nothing to talk about," one woman recalls of a weekend reunion with a college roommate who had been her best friend. "She has turned into the total young suburban matron and I could tell that she does not understand my love of the city or my decision not to have children. When we said good-by at the train, I said we must see each other again soon, but I know we won't."

Sometimes it's best to let an old friendship rest in peace and accept the loss as gracefully as possible. As hard as it may be, we need to make new connections, even if they are temporary and imperfect. For, as you can tell by the void in your life when you don't have it, friendship is no frill.

Dynamics of Maladjustment: The Individual and Society

Information regarding the nature and origin of psychological disturbance is incomplete and inconclusive. Historically it has been explained variously in terms of demonic possession, moral degeneracy, organic disorder, and social problems. One school of thought goes so far as to contend there is actually no such thing as mental illness—there is only the inability or unwillingness to adjust to the demands of socialization.

It is a fact that the problem of defining what is normal has long concerned psychologists. Society undoubtedly contributes to most concepts of normal behavior. Those characteristics that generally conform to the rules and expectations of society are classed as normal, while those that deviate are abnormal.

There are several problems with this view of normalcy. When social environment changes, the concept of maladjustment must change accordingly. What is normal behavior among Australian aborigines is not necessarily normal in Boston. Moreover, the same behavior may be viewed differently depending on its social context: killing in combat is "normal," killing a neighbor during a party is not.

Even when a definition is agreed upon, determining who fits the standard and who doesn't is another problem. A major obstacle to diagnosing what is normal is perception, which is not only predicated on personal bias but which is also likely to be incomplete. Studies documenting massive errors of diagnosing sane patients as insane and insane as sane reflect badly on the reliability of the diagnostic process as currently practiced.

Problems that incapacitate an individual, however, are very different from problems of defining social deviance. Maladjustment may be defined as the degree to which functioning is impaired. Many of the problems of maladjustment may be the result of ineffective coping mechanisms. Individuals under extreme stress will react differently than usual. When stress doesn't ease or if the coping response is inappropriate, psychological disturbance may follow. For example, Jane has an important exam tomorrow. She can respond to her anxiety tonight by studying, sleeping, or drinking a bottle of tequila. Obviously some coping responses will work better than others.

When self-defeating coping responses become characteristic patterns of dealing with reality, the ability to function becomes impaired. What symptoms signal the onset of depression? In what way does labeling contribute to the failure of diagnostic procedure? What roles do environment, genetics, and geography play in schizophrenia?

R. D. Laing:
The Politics of Madness

Edgar Z. Friedenberg

Edgar Z. Friedenberg is author of Coming of Age in America *and is working on a book called* Privilege, Bigotry, and Freedom. *He now lives in Canada and teaches at Dalhousie University in Halifax, Nova Scotia.*

"We are all murderers and prostitutes—no matter to what culture, society, class, nation, we belong, no matter how normal, moral, or mature, we take ourselves to be." This Ronald D. Laing observes early in his introduction to *The Politics of Experience,* published in 1967, when presumably he had filled both these roles to the degree appropriate to the circumstances of his life for just 40

years. Laing was born in Glasgow in 1927 and educated in the schools and University of that city, receiving his degree as medical doctor in 1951. "From 1951 to 1953," according to the information provided by the publisher of the 1970 reprinting of his first and most conventional book, *The Divided Self,* "he was a psychiatrist in the British Army, and then worked at the Glasgow Royal Mental Hospital in 1955: The Department of Psychological Medicine at the University of Glasgow in 1956; and the Tavistock Clinic 1957-61. He was director of the Langham Clinic, London, 1962-65. From 1961 until 1967 he did research into families with the Tavistock Institute of Human Relations, as Fellow of the Foundations Fund for Research in Psychiatry."

If, then, by 1967 Dr. Laing had come to regard himself, along with the rest of mankind, as prostitute and murderer, he had surely become an exceptionally well-informed one; and one whose information included a thorough and conventional psychiatric training and 16 years of experience as a practitioner. In the course of this time he had become, along with—though on somewhat different grounds from—Dr. Thomas Szasz, one of the two leading psychiatrists to base their work on a conviction that there was, in fact, no such clinical entity as mental illness.

To be told, as R. D. Laing and his co-author and fellow

Reprinted from *Ramparts* Magazine, April 1974. Copyright © 1974 by Edgar Z. Friedenberg. Reprinted by permission of the author.

psychiatrists and Glaswegian Aaron Esterson assert in their rather truculent Preface to the second edition of *Sanity, Madness and the Family* that:

> We do not accept "schizophrenia" as being a biochemical, neurophysiological, psychological fact, and we regard it as palpable error, in the present state of the evidence, to take it to be a fact. Nor do we assume its existence. Nor do we adopt it as a hypothesis. We propose no model for it.

is more threatening to the practice of psychiatry than classifying psychiatrists among all the other murderers and prostitutes of the world. There really are murderers; and these might even be ranked and accorded respectful recognition according to observable variations in professional competence. The task would not be simple. Is a mother who, with no tools except wit, ingenuity, and the psychic heritage left her by her own family, drives a son or daughter to suicide to be accorded more or less distinction than a President of the United States who encompasses the violent death of hundreds of thousands of persons he has never even seen? The judgment is in principle possible, however difficult it might prove in practice.

Laing, in the statement from which I have just quoted and elsewhere, makes it quite clear that he is not denying the possibility of mental illness—even schizophrenia. What he denies is its relevance as either a characterization of life or a therapeutic tool; while the dangers attending the abuse of the concept are manifest. The noun "psychotic" possesses the same kind of meaning that the word "felon" does; persons so classified certainly come to have a great deal in common after the classification has been applied, thus setting in motion the social processes that attack and confine them. It can even be shown that felons, or psychotics, as groups possessed certain features in common—such as wretched families or a proneness to behave extravagantly by the standards of their society—long before they were so classified; while subsequently they display other characteristics such as anxiety, confusion, alterations in blood chemistry associated with protracted intense emotion, to a degree that serves to distinguish them from persons not so classified. All these are common enough among people who have been driven to the threshold of the insane asylum, and are probably significantly more common than among the general population—though this is a datum with which Laing has, rather curiously, refused to concern himself.

What Laing insists as the essence of his position is that the statements and behavior of those deemed mentally ill are by no means irrational, but sensible when viewed from the position of the person the patient has been. What the patient does and is makes sense from his point of view; even his nonsense serves a sensible strategic purpose of counter-mystifying the parents and hospital authorities who have devoted *his* life to mystifying *him*. All human beings are sensible; if what they do and say is not intelligible, it is because the observer has failed to comprehend the existential position from which they speak and act. That position, for a helpless infant and dependent child in the hands of adults who are, in their turn, confused, anxious, and unscrupulous, may be desperate indeed, and evoke behavior that is grotesque in its desperation. But, however grotesque it may be, it is never inappropriate or, once the relation of the patient to other persons in his world has been understood, incomprehensible. Indeed, once the pressure on the patient is lightened, much that is grotesque simply vanishes.

[A STRATEGY FOR SURVIVAL]

That two of Laing's more important statements, *The Politics of Experience* and *The Politics of the Family*, should both refer to politics in their titles, and consider the political aspects of contexts not usually seen as essentially political, is an emphatic indication of the direction his thought has been taking. His work has tended toward a major conclusion that accounts for much of the influence of his work; and it is a conclusion well suited to the spirit of our age, though perhaps equally true of all ages.

This principle is never formally stated in Laing's work; but since he applied it repeatedly in his discussion of the

"THE CRIB," NEW YORK INSTITUTION, 1882

situations that interest him, we may infer and state it for ourselves. It is something like this: Human personality develops in each of us as we respond to the particular power situations in which we find ourselves; our personality comes to be largely defined by our customary ways of coping with the demands that impinge on us, and with the anxiety those demands, and our anticipation of possible failure or punishment, arouse. This is true not only because personality and especially the complex idiosyncratic pattern of defenses that Harry Stack Sullivan called "the self-system" tend to be quite stable. It is true also because, as Laing has come to see it, personality so rarely gets a chance to manifest itself in situations that do not involve a power struggle. There are few of these in life; and none in relationships that have become institutionalized; indeed, social institutions develop primarily in order to impose the constraints required by those relatively more powerful upon those relatively weaker. And there is no institution of which this is truer than the family.

In *The Divided Self*, then, Laing perceived schizophrenia as intelligible and even as functional to the schizophrenic, but still as a distinctive clinical entity. He was already aware that only persons whose peculiar personalities threaten their families and their neighbors in certain serious ways—chiefly by undermining the repressions they depend on to keep themselves and the rest of their children in line—are likely to be classed as psychotic. But he still believed that to call these people schizophrenic conveyed some meaning about their mental state; they were people whose strategies for living did, indeed, appear bizarre until you came to understand how their weirdness served their purposes. And chief among those purposes for all schizophrenics was the need to confuse their assailants by producing a counter-mystification sufficiently obscure to throw their avid parents and guardians off the track that led to their soul, sufficiently subtle to avoid being interpreted and punished as rank insubordination.

True, psychiatry usually failed to help the schizophrenic; many psychiatrists assumed that he was beyond the posibility of help and beyond the range of human communication, except when shocked into rare intervals of lucidity by insulin or electricity. But in *The Divided Self* Laing saw this failure as innocent, or at worst as the unsought if predictable result of the way psychiatrists defined their own and their patients' roles. Having assumed that the patient spoke nonsense, they did not listen and thus failed to learn what they might otherwise have understood, while they likewise perpetuated the patient's sense of isolation and helplessness at the hands of uncomprehending forces.

[WHO ELSE *IS* THERE?]

For a young Scottish psychiatrist writing toward the close of the 1950s, this is going pretty far. Still, Laing was on the side of his own profession: a reformer, not an attacker. His real departure came as he grew to realize that psychiatry was not failing to be helpful but succeeding in being unhelpful: that the profession and its categorical

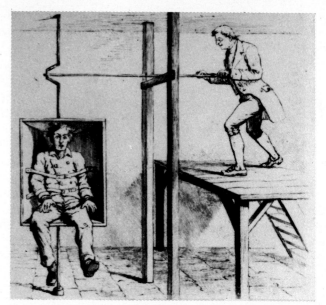

"THE CIRCULATING SWING," 1818, SUPPOSED TO BRING THE DEPRESSIVE BACK TO SOUND REASONING INSANE ASYLUM CELL, CIRCA 1880

imperatives about human behavior were explicitly, if not intentionally, a part of the patient's problem rather than its solution. This chilling insight froze Laing's attitude toward psychiatry not only as a form of medical service but, somewhat less rationally, as a research tool as well. As he became aware that psychiatry is one of the most powerful devices disposed by the forces of law and order, he seems to have lost interest in it as an instrument for investigating human character and personality.

By this time, I suspect, it would no more have occurred to Laing to look to the literature of psychiatry for information about the lives of troubled people that might be used to help them than it would have to consult the files of the CIA, if he could have gotten at them, for information useful in supporting popular revolutionary movements. And this is regrettable. In both instances, this is one place that one *should* look for pertinent information, compiled and organized at great expense of effort and money, even though it was gathered for purposes one strongly opposed. A psychiatrist who has concluded, in effect, that psychiatrists invented and maintain the category of mental illness to maximize their own status and power, must grant that they are likely to have learned a great deal about the dynamisms that make what they call mental illness possible. It is too difficult and dangerous to distort the truth if one does not know quite well what it is.

But, Laing argues, it is too late for their information to be of value. Psychiatry is compromised by the games it has been playing with—and against—its patients. It can no longer serve to distinguish the mad from the sane, for the alienist has become a part of a pervasive alienation and even the madman seems as corrupt as the neighbors and physicians who judge him. De Sade is a failed impresario; poor old Marat a friendly neighborhood revolutionary manqué:

From the alienated starting point of our pseudo-sanity, everything is equivocal. Our "sanity" is not true sanity. Their madness is not "true" madness. The madness of our patients is an artifact of the destruction wreaked on them by us and on them by themselves. Let no one suppose that we meet "true" madness any more than that we are truly sane. The madness that we encounter in "patients" is a gross travesty, a mockery, a grotesque caricature of what the natural healing of the estranged integration we call sanity might be. True sanity entails, in one way or another, the dissolution of the normal ego, that false self competently adjusted to our alienated social reality; the emergence of the "inner" archetypical mediators of divine power, and through the death a rebirth, and the eventual re-establishment of a new kind of ego-functioning, the ego now being the servant of the divine, no longer its betrayer.

This quotation is taken from "Transcendental Experience," one of the later essays, that make up *The Politics of Experience.* The man who made this statement could hardly have claimed further interest in the conventional concerns of the psychiatric profession. But his viewpoint imposes some rather stringent limitations on the range and applicability of his thought. Not that it is mistaken, or even warped—the passage quoted is convincing, if somewhat feverishly rhetorical—but it dismisses *everybody* and after all who else is there?

There is a familiar old—and by current standards, doubtless racist—joke about an indignant Southern farmer who, searching the chicken coop one dark and stormy night, elicits from one of its occupants the admonition "Boss, go away, there ain't nobody here but us chickens!" Laing's present attitude toward schizophrenia places him rather in the position of that farmer, while the disembodied voice proceeds from a suspected schizophrenic concealed among the normal occupants of the noisome and confining coop. The difference from the joke is that Laing *believes* the voice—and, in a larger sense, it may speak the truth. Chicken coops are prisons; all their occupants are in moral danger; and indeed, we are all more simply chicken than otherwise. Nevertheless, a practical problem remains. Whoever it was that spoke up like that is unlikely to get along with and be tolerated by his coopmates. He is in more immediate danger than they from the farmer as well. And he cannot be rescued by being praised for his openness and authenticity in comparison to his squawking and befeathered normal peers.

[AFTER THE FALL]

Less metaphorically, whatever degree of humanity one attributes to either mental patients or their sometimes sinister mentors and custodians, the problem of being what is called mentally ill remains an objective reality, and for most persons it is an extremely disagreeable one. They are, certainly, as Laing sees them, frightened and unskilled players who have lost their confidence in the confidence game their lives have become. But if this process is part of what is meant by the politics of experience, is it not likely that part of what they need is to become better and more effective possibly also more ruthless—politicians? This means learning to function without blowing your cool in situations in which real power is at stake; even learning, in the cliche phrase, to do unto others before they do unto you. Political skill would give them more room to manipulate in, and enable them to defend themselves better against invasion, but at the cost of enmeshing them still further in game-playing and increasing their alienation. Personal authenticity is not a political asset; and the road to effective political participation does not lead on to Nirvana. But would not most Westerners really get more satisfaction from a series of appointments in Samsara?

This Laing would apparently deny:

The others have become installed in our hearts, and we call them ourselves. Each person, not being himself to either himself or the other, just as the other is not himself to himself or to us, in being another for another neither recognizes himself in the other, nor the other in himself. Hence, being at least a double absence, haunted by the ghost of his own murdered self, no wonder modern man is addicted to other persons, and the more addicted, the less satisfied, the more lonely.

A page further on, he quotes from the *Tao Teh Ching:*

When the great Tao is lost, spring forth benevolence and righteousness. When wisdom and sagacity arise, there are great hypocrites. When family relations are no longer harmonious, we have filial children and devoted parents. When a nation is in confusion and disorder, patriots are recognized."

Laing's basic principle here is clear enough; what is still at issue is the divided self. He introduces this quotation from the *Tao Teh Ching* by observing that:

Once the fissure into self and ego, inner and outer, good and bad occur, all else is an infernal dance of false dualities. It has always been recognized that if you split Being down the middle, if you insist on grabbing this without that, if you cling to the good without the bad, denying the one for the other, what happens is that the dissociated evil impulse, now evil in a double sense, returns to permeate the good and turn it into itself.

This is surely one of the great fundamental truths on which, since the Fall if not the Creation, man has been unable to act. Indeed, the impossibility of action on this statement is built into the statement itself; to try to *use* it to build a better world or, indeed, for any practical purpose, would be grabbing *this* without *that*, clinging to the good without the bad. The difficulty is at least as old as the *Tao Teh Ching* itself, which, being filled with wisdom and sagacity, can only have been written in a time of great hypocrites, well after the great Tao had been lost. The four paradoxes from the *Book of Tao* which Laing cites— characteristic of most of its content—suggest even more about the difficulties of constructing politics of experience than he takes into consideration. The basic principle underlying all these aphorisms is that conscious virtue becomes identified as such and is deliberately put into operation only after natural wholeness has been lost; while natural wholeness knows no distinction between good and evil; it is not self-conscious enough for that; it just is, and the path away from Being is always a downward path. Had revised editions of the *Tao Teh Ching* continued to be published, the most recent edition might well have included such maxims as: "When foodstuffs are no longer wholesome and pure, science devises nutritious additives." Or, "When men become rootless and homeless, the Boeing 747 whisks them from place to place in luxury."

Whether the source be Genesis, the *Tao Teh Ching*, Norman O. Brown, or R. D. Laing the lesson is the same: self-consciousness, knowledge of good and evil, the need to live by the sweat of one's brow, the design of technology to take the drudgery out of the work—thus also fragmenting it and reducing its meaning—these are consecutive aspects of the alienation of man from his true being. Psychiatry, too, is technology—human technology—and the worst sort of meddling of all. In principle, willful intervention in destiny *cannot* improve man's lot but must create more problems or worse problems than it appears to solve.

All this may be true; indeed, it seems that it can hardly be false. But it is a truth whose implications create certain logical difficulties for its adherents. For, if "once the fissure between self and ago, inner and outer, good and bad occurs, all else is an infernal dance of false dualities," then that irrevocable and potentially fatal step has already been taken in the act of recognizing that a problem exists. This puts Laing's current position as anti-psychiatrist in a rather curious light; it does not make it logically inconsistent (unless, of course, one regards psychiatrists as a natural nuisance like mosquitoes which ought to be tolerated until it can be controlled by organic means like withholding fees), but it swamps it in a metaphysical issue so vast that Laing's meaning is easily lost.

Politics is, by definition, always concerned with action, with intervention, with the formation and execution of policy. Political action cannot even begin to be considered till after the Fall. The four aphorisms from the *Tao Teh Ching*, taken consecutively, record not merely the increasing alienation but the increasing politicization of society; politics is concerned precisely with the implementation of power and the resolution of real conflicts of interest and thus, usually, with making the best of a bad job. Lao-tze is perfectly correct in implying that politics does not become necessary until things are already badly messed up. In practice, this has not proved a difficult prerequisite to meet.

For those of us who feel that we desperately need help in dealing with our relationship to the society and the reality of which we are a part, the issues remain, I fear, much what Freud found them to be in *Civilization and Its Discontents*. The conduct of daily life in complex organized societies depends on institutions that are sustained by myths and fueled by the energies derived from the renunciation practiced by individuals who have been led to believe in

them, always at a loss to their immediate interests. What they get in return is membership, at levels providing varying degrees of satisfaction, in the social enterprise, and a variable share in what it defines as valuable. Whether their life is thereby made more worth living or less is probably impossible to answer, since only they could possibly know and they have been driven to give the answers the society demands—not as truths but as shibboleths—and to value the rewards it offers by the very processes that Laing describes. Living, in short, turns out to be in many respects a political process, in which those who still retain some access to their feelings experience moments of self-realization. Psychiatry can sometimes increase the depth and frequency of such moments; but the conditions under which it can do so are themselves politically influenced; and the experience is felt as something less than that of fully authentic personal transcendence. Dionysian exuberance may be increasingly tolerated in contemporary political life; but Promethean defiance still leads to serious trouble for the liver. So, at least, I should interpret the message of Herbert Marcuse.

[JOURNEY TO THE EAST]

In Ibsen's *Peer Gynt,* the Troll King stated that the maxim by which the complete Troll sought to perfect himself was "To thine own self be enough"; in contrast to the human injunction "To thine own self be true." It is this latter injunction which lies at the heart of Laing's teaching; but in his corrosive denigration of most relationships fostered by modern society—and, especially, of those

psychiatry offers its patients—he seems to accept the first as well. Neither, in any case, will serve very well as a guide to the conduct of political affairs. The recognition of the politicization of modern life implied in the titles of Laing's works is intended, I would judge, to convey a distaste for politics; and Laing's own political activities appear to have been minimal for a man whose writings have made him a major idol of the counterculture during a period notable for political expression.

"I was never political in an activist sense. I suppose when people think of me as political they're thinking mainly of the Dialectics of Liberation Congress." (This was a marathon symposium organized by Laing's colleagues, Leon Redler and Joseph Berke, which was held in London in July 1967. Laing participated along with Marcuse, Gregory Bateson, Lucien Goldmann, Paul Goodman, John Gerassi, Allen Ginsberg, Francis Huxley, Stokely Carmichael and others in two weeks of discussion and political analysis.) "I guess I identified myself with the Left by being there, but even at the time I made it clear that I really had no idea what could come of such an extraordinary conglomeration of people. Politically I think I'm neutral really. I engage in no strictly political actions—except in the sense of following the Tao."

To follow the Tao is to lead an essentially apolitical rather than a politically neutral life; though this, in a society dominated by liberal interventionists intent on perfecting the world if they have to destroy it in the process, may certainly, as Laing implies, be a politically momentous stance, and perhaps the only one that makes sense. Laing is surely correct in viewing his ascribed status as a Left activist ironically, as he is in recognizing his kinship to T.S. Eliot. The confusion—which he does not share—of those who lump together as left-political quasi-revolutionary compeers persons who criticize society primarily because it alienates people from themselves and their capacities for growth, and critics who complain primarily of society's gross inequities, has caused a great deal of difficulty in the past few years. It seems to be straightening out, now, with those who are most disturbed by alienation and repression being increasingly stigmatized as reactionary by political activists and self-styled revolutionaries. The extraordinarily hostile reviews which Charles Reich's *The Greening of America* received from the Left as well as the Right; the current split in the free-school movement exemplified by Jonathan Kozol's attack in *Free Schools* on rich liberals who set up schools in beautiful farmlands where privileged white children learn leather-work and grooving instead of working to overthrow oppressive urban school systems; and the current description of the counterculture as willfully self-indulgent are all examples that suggest that the polarization of dissent may finally be taking place on rational political grounds.

Those who try to follow the Tao, however, are surely more radical in their rejection of contemporary Western societies—and for reasons that would extend even to China and Japan, as highly bureaucratized, production-oriented states—than the most ardent revolutionaries bent on structural reorganization and the seizure of power in the name of greater justice and equality of opportunity, who nevertheless leave the basic values of the society intact. The cry "Power to the People" exalts power as much as any statement made by those accustomed to its exercise. In this sense, Laing is anything but politically irrelevant.

But for the time, at least, Laing's interests have apparently transcended both politics and psychiatry to include most of the great Eastern religions. A 1972 *Esquire* interview with Peter Mezan relates Laing's detailed discussion of several fundamental Buddhist and Hindu texts; a discussion that occurred when he was preparing for a journey to the East, since completed, in which he planned to examine some of the psychic phenomena associated with mystical states of awareness in the light of Western psychological thought and perhaps by techniques:

"Suppose," he muses, "we were to hook the olfactory tracts into the visual cortex. Might we then see what we now smell?" He thinks it's rather strange that we are so docile about accepting our limits, like our confinement to only five senses. . . . "Or suppose you could cut off all the input, all the activity, in all the sensory tracts and areas of the brain, leaving one area of cortex—say the optical cortex—open, and then re-route all the impulses from the other areas there. You could test one area of cortex at a time. I think that would be possible to do through meditation." It is one of the ideas he's planning to test in Ceylon—one of the reasons he's going. And, I must say, I have heard in my time more extravagant claims, met less interesting ambitions.

Laing's enthusiasm for psychological research in this context contrasts strikingly with his dismissal of controlled experimentation in investigating the possible sources of mental illness. This contrast is highly suggestive. The notion is familiar enough, and surely valid, that the institutionalization of the sciences as the dominant source of intellectual authority has tended to stultify Western thought about subjective areas of experience, especially mystical experience. But what if the stultification has been even more pervasive? Laing's comments—and there is no reason to suppose that he is unique in this—suggest that the authority of institutionalized science may even be stultifying scientific enquiry itself: by making science impervious to some of the issues with which it ought to be concerned and with which, except for its own ideological bias, it could deal quite easily; and by alienating its more imaginative practitioners, who are turned off by the uses to which science is put in society. Western thought has increasingly tended to exclude as meaningless or trivial questions that seem unamenable to empirical study and, in doing so, may have imposed limits on the scope of scientific investigation which its adversaries would have been powerless to enforce. It would surely be one of the crowning ironies of history if Laing, through his Journey to the East, should become a science-carrier, infecting its ancient monasteries and temples with the virus of empiricism in a way no less sympathetic visitor could have done. Somewhere, in a weathered pagoda lost to time in the highlands of central Ceylon, the monks may, even now, be installing an electron microscope doubtless obtainable with Ford Foundation funds and capable of minute examination of neural tissue, just in case meditation should not prove to be enough.

[IF I COULD TURN YOU ON . . . "[

One of Laing's most evocative ideas is that scarcity lies at the root of human alienation. While Laing takes the idea from Sartre, who in turn elaborated it from Marxian sources, the kind of alienation that he emphasizes is quite different from the alienation Marx saw as a central condition of capitalism. Laing is concerned with psychological alienation which deprives people of the capacity to accept or even become aware of their own feelings and respond to their own needs. Marx referred to the alienation of the worker from the fruits of his labor and the economic context in which he worked—his inability to control either his tools or his job, in neither of which he had any vested rights comparable to those of proprietorship. Both kinds of alienation proceed simultaneously in industrial societies and reinforce each other. Objective deprivation and economic insecurity create intense anxiety and lower self-esteem, making their victims unwilling or unable to take psychic risks, or tolerate their own or other persons' impulses toward growth, dissent, or rebellion. Each individual's mounting sense of existential guilt and self-betrayal makes him increasingly hostile toward signs of growth, honest feeling, and self-realization in others.

This viciously circular relationship between economic and psychic insecurity is a central social fact; it is the source of the psychological and political oppression that, like air and water pollution, we have come to accept as the emblem of life in our time, our gray badge of endurance.

What seems to me to be implied inescapably by Laing's position, though he would surely reject this conclusion himself, if possible—is that freedom and self-realization have always been, and must remain, the concerns of an elite of some kind, self-defined by its very nature as an enemy of the people. If it is not to become merely another group, obsessed and corrupted by the demands of its own defense, then clearly it must be relatively invulnerable for reasons with which it need not concern itself too much from day to day. Wealth helps, but capitalism has done a superb job of defining wealth so that nobody ever seems sure he has enough and can keep it, especially in a state made fretful by an uneasy social conscience. The national conscience has enough to be fretful about, but humaneness derived from guilt is about as trustworthy as chastity imposed by gonorrhea. Neither is evidence of a change of heart.

If my reasoning is correct, demands for a just society, as social justice is now conceived, must continue to conflict very sharply with the demand for personal self-realization. It is currently fashionable to put down the "pot left" or "freak left" as a political embarrassment to true radicals, to argue that the counterculture is a drag to the revolution; that its hair and its egotism alienate the working class; that its "free schools" delay the kind of hard-nosed educational reform needed to lift children out of the ghetto and politicize their parents. All this is true; it is not inappropriate that a counterculture be counterrevolutionary. But the counterculture, counterrevolutionary or not, is in much deeper conflict with the dominant culture of our time, whether in East or West, than any current revolutionary movement conceived in political or military form.

This conflict, though profoundly political in its implications, is really metapolitical. It transcends politics, since the countercultural position perceives political action as alienating in itself. As, in Eliot's protrayal of him, Thomas a Becket came to understand:

Those who serve the greater cause
   may make the cause serve them,
Still doing right: and striving with
   political men
May make that cause political, not
   by what they do,
But by what they are.

This is not to imply that men ought not to fight evil and social injustice. They very often must, but when they must, the price is their own objectification, their conversion—by their own consent but in ways they can seldom have anticipated or wholly accepted—into an instrument of social action.

Whatever his personal politics may be, the thrust of Laing's work, as well as much of its substance, has been the very stuff of the counterculture's vision. The old friend of Baba Ram Dass and Timothy Leary has never betrayed their joint ideal. It is finally no paradox, but a near classic example of the relationship between *yang* and *yin*, that Laing's prophetic insights into the political character of mental illness, and of experience, should have led him to a position from which politics itself can only be seen as absurd. The position is stated precisely by Laing himself, in the final paragraphs of his moving and fantastic essay *The Bird of Paradise:*

There is really nothing more to say when we come back to that beginning of all beginnings that is nothing at all. Only when you begin to lose that Alpha and Omega do you want to start to talk and to write, and then there is no end to it, words, words, words. At best and most they are perhaps in memoriam, evocations, conjurations, incantations, emanations, shimmering, irridescent flares in the sky of darkness, a just still feasible tact, indiscretions, perhaps forgivable. . . .

City lights at night, from the air, receding, like these words, atoms each containing its own world and every other world. Each a fuse to set you off. . . . If I could turn you on, if I could drive you out of your wretched mind, if I could tell you I would let you know.

ON BEING SANE IN INSANE PLACES

D. L. Rosenhan

The author is professor of psychology and law at Stanford University, Stanford, California 94305. Portions of these data were presented to colloquiums of the psychology departments at the University of California at Berkeley and at Santa Barbara; University of Arizona, Tucson; and Harvard University, Cambridge, Massachusetts.

If sanity and insanity exist, how shall we know them?

The question is neither capricious nor itself insane. However much we may be personally convinced that we can tell the normal from the abnormal, the evidence is simply not compelling. It is commonplace, for example, to read about murder trials wherein eminent psychiatrists for the defense are contradicted by equally eminent psychiatrists for the prosecution on the matter of the defendant's sanity. More generally, there are a great deal of conflicting data on the reliability, utility, and meaning of such terms as "sanity," "insanity," "mental illness," and "schizophrenia" (1). Finally, as early as 1934, Benedict suggested that normality and abnormality are not universal (2). What is viewed as normal in one culture may be seen as quite aberrant in another. Thus, notions of normality and abnormality may not be quite as accurate as people believe they are.

To raise questions regarding normality and abnormality is in no way to question the fact that some behaviors are deviant or odd. Murder is deviant. So, too, are hallucinations. Nor does raising such questions deny the existence of the personal anguish that is often associated with "mental illness." Anxiety and depression exist. Psychological suffering exists. But normality and abnormality, sanity and insanity, and the diagnoses that flow from them may be less substantive than many believe them to be.

At its heart, the question of whether the sane can be distinguished from the insane (and whether degrees of insanity can be distinguished from each other) is a simple matter: do the salient characteristics that lead to diagnoses reside in the patients themselves or in the environments and contexts in which observers find them? From Bleuler, through Kretchmer, through the formulators of the recently revised *Diagnostic and Statistical Manual* of the American Psychiatric Association, the belief has been strong that patients present symptoms, that those symptoms can be categorized, and, implicitly, that the sane are distinguishable from the insane. More recently, however, this belief has been questioned. Based in part on theoretical and anthropological considerations, but also on philosophical, legal, and therapeutic ones, the view has grown that psychological categorization of mental illness is useless at best and downright harmful, misleading, and pejorative at worst. Psychiatric diagnoses, in this view, are in the minds of the observers and are not valid summaries of characteristics displayed by the observed (3–5).

Gains can be made in deciding which of these is more nearly accurate by getting normal people (that is, people who do not have, and have never suffered, symptoms of serious psychiatric disorders) admitted to psychiatric hospitals and then determining whether they were discovered to be sane and, if so, how. If the sanity of such pseudopatients were always detected, there would be prima facie evidence that a sane individual can be distinguished from the insane context in which he is found. Normality (and presumably abnormality) is distinct enough that it can be recognized wherever it occurs, for it is carried within the person. If, on the other hand, the sanity of the pseudopatients were never discovered, serious difficulties would arise for those who support traditional modes of psychiatric diagnosis. Given that the hospital staff was not incompetent, that the pseudopatient had been behaving as sanely as he had been outside of the hospital, and that it had never been previously suggested that he belonged in a psychiatric hospital, such an unlikely outcome would support the view that psychiatric diagnosis betrays little about the patient but much about the environment in which an observer finds him.

This article describes such an experiment. Eight sane people gained secret admission to 12 different hospitals (6). Their diagnostic experiences constitute the data of the first part of this article; the remainder is devoted to a description of their experiences in psychiatric institutions. Too few psychiatrists and psychologists, even those who have worked in such hospitals, know what the experience is like. They rarely talk about it with former patients, perhaps because they distrust information coming from the previously insane. Those who have worked in psychiatric hospitals are likely to have adapted so thoroughly to the settings that they are insensitive to the impact of that experience. And while there have been occasional reports of researchers who submitted themselves to psychiatric hospitalization (7), these researchers have commonly remained in the hospitals for short periods of time, often with the knowledge of the hospital staff. It is difficult to know the extent to which they were treated like patients or like research colleagues. Nevertheless, their reports about the inside of the psychiatric hospital have been valuable. This article extends those efforts.

Pseudopatients and Their Settings

The eight pseudopatients were a

varied group. One was a psychology graduate student in his 20's. The remaining seven were older and "established." Among them were three psychologists, a pediatrician, a psychiatrist, a painter, and a housewife. Three pseudopatients were women, five were men. All of them employed pseudonyms, lest their alleged diagnoses embarrass them later. Those who were in mental health professions alleged another occupation in order to avoid the special attentions that might be accorded by staff, as a matter of courtesy or caution, to ailing colleagues (8). With the exception of myself (I was the first pseudopatient and my presence was known to the hospital administrator and chief psychologist and, so far as I can tell, to them alone), the presence of pseudopatients and the nature of the research program was not known to the hospital staffs (9).

The settings were similarly varied. In order to generalize the findings, admission into a variety of hospitals was sought. The 12 hospitals in the sample were located in five different states on the East and West coasts. Some were old and shabby, some were quite new. Some were research-oriented, others not. Some had good staff-patient ratios, others were quite understaffed. Only one was a strictly private hospital. All of the others were supported by state or federal funds or, in one instance, by university funds.

After calling the hospital for an appointment, the pseudopatient arrived at the admissions office complaining that he had been hearing voices. Asked what the voices said, he replied that they were often unclear, but as far as he could tell they said "empty," "hollow," and "thud." The voices were unfamiliar and were of the same sex as the pseudopatient. The choice of these symptoms was occasioned by their apparent similarity to existential symptoms. Such symptoms are alleged to arise from painful concerns about the perceived meaninglessness of one's life. It is as if the hallucinating person were saying, "My life is empty and hollow." The choice of these symptoms was also determined by the *absence* of a single report of existential psychoses in the literature.

Beyond alleging the symptoms and falsifying name, vocation, and employment, no further alterations of person,

history, or circumstances were made. The significant events of the pseudopatient's life history were presented as they had actually occurred. Relationships with parents and siblings, with spouse and children, with people at work and in school, consistent with the aforementioned exceptions, were described as they were or had been. Frustrations and upsets were described along with joys and satisfactions. These facts are important to remember. If anything, they strongly biased the subsequent results in favor of detecting sanity, since none of their histories or current behaviors were seriously pathological in any way.

Immediately upon admission to the psychiatric ward, the pseudopatient ceased simulating *any* symptoms of abnormality. In some cases, there was a brief period of mild nervousness and anxiety, since none of the pseudopatients really believed that they would be admitted so easily. Indeed, their shared fear was that they would be immediately exposed as frauds and greatly embarrassed. Moreover, many of them had never visited a psychiatric ward; even those who had, nevertheless had some genuine fears about what might happen to them. Their nervousness, then, was quite appropriate to the novelty of the hospital setting, and it abated rapidly.

Apart from that short-lived nervousness, the pseudopatient behaved on the ward as he "normally" behaved. The pseudopatient spoke to patients and staff as he might ordinarily. Because there is uncommonly little to do on a psychiatric ward, he attempted to engage others in conversation. When asked by staff how he was feeling, he indicated that he was fine, that he no longer experienced symptoms. He responded to instructions from attendants, to calls for medication (which was not swallowed), and to dining-hall instructions. Beyond such activities as were available to him on the admissions ward, he spent his time writing down his observations about the ward, its patients, and the staff. Initially these notes were written "secretly," but as it soon became clear that no one much cared, they were subsequently written on standard tablets of paper in such public places as the dayroom. No secret was made of these activities.

The pseudopatient, very much as a

true psychiatric patient, entered a hospital with no foreknowledge of when he would be discharged. Each was told that he would have to get out by his own devices, essentially by convincing the staff that he was sane. The psychological stresses associated with hospitalization were considerable, and all but one of the pseudopatients desired to be discharged almost immediately after being admitted. They were, therefore, motivated not only to behave sanely, but to be paragons of cooperation. That their behavior was in no way disruptive is confirmed by nursing reports, which have been obtained on most of the patients. These reports uniformly indicate that the patients were "friendly," "cooperative," and "exhibited no abnormal indications."

The Normal Are Not Detectably Sane

Despite their public "show" of sanity, the pseudopatients were never detected. Admitted, except in one case, with a diagnosis of schizophrenia (10), each was discharged with a diagnosis of schizophrenia "in remission." The label "in remission" should in no way be dismissed as a formality, for at no time during any hospitalization had any question been raised about any pseudopatient's simulation. Nor are there any indications in the hospital records that the pseudopatient's status was suspect. Rather, the evidence is strong that, once labeled schizophrenic, the pseudopatient was stuck with that label. If the pseudopatient was to be discharged, he must naturally be "in remission"; but he was not sane, nor, in the institution's view, had he ever been sane.

The uniform failure to recognize sanity cannot be attributed to the quality of the hospitals, for, although there were considerable variations among them, several are considered excellent. Nor can it be alleged that there was simply not enough time to observe the pseudopatients. Length of hospitalization ranged from 7 to 52 days, with an average of 19 days. The pseudopatients were not, in fact, carefully observed, but this failure clearly speaks more to traditions within psychiatric hospitals than to lack of opportunity.

Finally, it cannot be said that the failure to recognize the pseudopatients' sanity was due to the fact that they were not behaving sanely. While there was clearly some tension present in all of them, their daily visitors could detect no serious behavioral consequences—nor, indeed, could other patients. It was quite common for the patients to "detect" the pseudopatients' sanity. During the first three hospitalizations, when accurate counts were kept, 35 of a total of 118 patients on the admissions ward voiced their suspicions, some vigorously. "You're not crazy. You're a journalist, or a professor [referring to the continual note-taking]. You're checking up on the hospital." While most of the patients were reassured by the pseudopatient's insistence that he had been sick before he came in but was fine now, some continued to believe that the pseudopatient was sane throughout his hospitalization (11). The fact that the patients often recognized normality when staff did not raises important questions.

Failure to detect sanity during the course of hospitalization may be due to the fact that physicians operate with a strong bias toward what statisticians call the type 2 error (5). This is to say that physicians are more inclined to call a healthy person sick (a false positive, type 2) than a sick person healthy (a false negative, type 1). The reasons for this are not hard to find: it is clearly more dangerous to misdiagnose illness than health. Better to err on the side of caution, to suspect illness even among the healthy.

But what holds for medicine does not hold equally well for psychiatry. Medical illnesses, while unfortunate, are not commonly pejorative. Psychiatric diagnoses, on the contrary, carry with them personal, legal, and social stigmas (12). It was therefore important to see whether the tendency toward diagnosing the sane insane could be reversed. The following experiment was arranged at a research and teaching hospital whose staff had heard these findings but doubted that such an error could occur in their hospital. The staff was informed that at some time during the following 3 months, one or more pseudopatients would attempt to be admitted into the psychiatric hospital. Each staff member was asked to rate each patient who presented himself at admissions or on the ward according to the likelihood that the patient was a pseudopatient. A 10-point scale was used, with a 1 and 2 reflecting high confidence that the pa-

tient was a pseudopatient.

Judgments were obtained on 193 patients who were admitted for psychiatric treatment. All staff who had had sustained contact with or primary responsibility for the patient—attendants, nurses, psychiatrists, physicians, and psychologists—were asked to make judgments. Forty-one patients were alleged, with high confidence, to be pseudopatients by at least one member of the staff. Twenty-three were considered suspect by at least one psychiatrist. Nineteen were suspected by one psychiatrist *and* one other staff member. Actually, no genuine pseudopatient (at least from my group) presented himself during this period.

The experiment is instructive. It indicates that the tendency to designate sane people as insane can be reversed when the stakes (in this case, prestige and diagnostic acumen) are high. But what can be said of the 19 people who were suspected of being "sane" by one psychiatrist and another staff member? Were these people truly "sane," or was it rather the case that in the course of avoiding the type 2 error the staff tended to make more errors of the first sort—calling the crazy "sane"? There is no way of knowing. But one thing is certain: any diagnostic process that lends itself so readily to massive errors of this sort cannot be a very reliable one.

The Stickiness of Psychodiagnostic Labels

Beyond the tendency to call the healthy sick—a tendency that accounts better for diagnostic behavior on admission than it does for such behavior after a lengthy period of exposure—the data speak to the massive role of labeling in psychiatric assessment. Having once been labeled schizophrenic, there is nothing the pseudopatient can do to overcome the tag. The tag profoundly colors others' perceptions of him and his behavior.

From one viewpoint, these data are hardly surprising, for it has long been known that elements are given meaning by the context in which they occur. Gestalt psychology made this point vigorously, and Asch (13) demonstrated that there are "central" personality traits (such as "warm" versus

"cold") which are so powerful that they markedly color the meaning of other information in forming an impression of a given personality (14). "Insane," "schizophrenic," "manic-depressive," and "crazy" are probably among the most powerful of such central traits. Once a person is designated abnormal, all of his other behaviors and characteristics are colored by that label. Indeed, that label is so powerful that many of the pseudopatients' normal behaviors were overlooked entirely or profoundly misinterpreted. Some examples may clarify this issue.

Earlier I indicated that there were no changes in the pseudopatient's personal history and current status beyond those of name, employment, and, where necessary, vocation. Otherwise, a veridical description of personal history and circumstances was offered. Those circumstances were not psychotic. How were they made consonant with the diagnosis of psychosis? Or were those diagnoses modified in such a way as to bring them into accord with the circumstances of the pseudopatient's life, as described by him?

As far as I can determine, diagnoses were in no way affected by the relative health of the circumstances of a pseudopatient's life. Rather, the reverse occurred: the perception of his circumstances was shaped entirely by the diagnosis. A clear example of such translation is found in the case of a pseudopatient who had had a close relationship with his mother but was rather remote from his father during his early childhool. During adolescence and beyond, however, his father became a close friend, while his relationship with his mother cooled. His present relationship with his wife was characteristically close and warm. Apart from occasional angry exchanges, friction was minimal. The children had rarely been spanked. Surely there is nothing especially pathological about such a history. Indeed, many readers may see a similar pattern in their own experiences, with no markedly deleterious consequences. Observe, however, how such a history was translated in the psychopathological context, this from the case summary prepared after the patient was discharged.

This white 39-year-old male . . . manifests a long history of considerable ambivalence in close relationships, which begins in early childhood. A warm relationship with his mother cools during his adolescence. A distant relationship to his father is described as becoming very intense. Affective stability is absent. His attempts to control emotionality with his wife and children are punctuated by angry outbursts and, in the case of the children, spankings. And while he says that he has several good friends, one senses considerable ambivalence embedded in those relationships also. . . .

The facts of the case were unintentionally distorted by the staff to achieve consistency with a popular theory of the dynamics of a schizophrenic reaction (15). Nothing of an ambivalent nature had been described in relations with parents, spouse, or friends. To the extent that ambivalence could be inferred, it was probably not greater than is found in all human relationships. It is true the pseudopatient's relationships with his parents changed over time, but in the ordinary context that would hardly be remarkable—indeed, it might very well be expected. Clearly, the meaning ascribed to his verbalizations (that is, ambivalence, affective instability) was determined by the diagnosis: schizophrenia. An entirely different meaning would have been ascribed if it were known that the man was "normal."

All pseudopatients took extensive notes publicly. Under ordinary circumstances, such behavior would have raised questions in the minds of observers, as, in fact, it did among patients. Indeed, it seemed so certain that the notes would elicit suspicion that elaborate precautions were taken to remove them from the ward each day. But the precautions proved needless. The closest any staff member came to questioning these notes occurred when one pseudopatient asked his physician what kind of medication he was receiving and began to write down the response. "You needn't write it," he was told gently. "If you have trouble remembering, just ask me again."

If no questions were asked of the pseudopatients, how was their writing interpreted? Nursing records for three patients indicate that the writing was seen as an aspect of their pathological behavior. "Patient engages in writing behavior" was the daily nursing comment on one of the pseudopatients who was never questioned about his writing. Given that the patient is in the hospital, he must be psychologically disturbed.

And given that he is disturbed, continuous writing must be a behavioral manifestation of that disturbance, perhaps a subset of the compulsive behaviors that are sometimes correlated with schizophrenia.

One tacit characteristic of psychiatric diagnosis is that it locates the sources of aberration within the individual and only rarely within the complex of stimuli that surrounds him. Consequently, behaviors that are stimulated by the environment are commonly misattributed to the patient's disorder. For example, one kindly nurse found a pseudopatient pacing the long hospital corridors. "Nervous, Mr. X?" she asked. "No, bored," he said.

The notes kept by pseudopatients are full of patient behaviors that were misinterpreted by well-intentioned staff. Often enough, a patient would go "berserk" because he had, wittingly or unwittingly, been mistreated by, say, an attendant. A nurse coming upon the scene would rarely inquire even cursorily into the environmental stimuli of the patient's behavior. Rather, she assumed that his upset derived from his pathology, not from his present interactions with other staff members. Occasionally, the staff might assume that the patient's family (especially when they had recently visited) or other patients had stimulated the outburst. But never were the staff found to assume that one of themselves or the structure of the hospital had anything to do with a patient's behavior. One psychiatrist pointed to a group of patients who were sitting outside the cafeteria entrance half an hour before lunchtime. To a group of young residents he indicated that such behavior was characteristic of the oral-acquisitive nature of the syndrome. It seemed not to occur to him that there were very few things to anticipate in a psychiatric hospital besides eating.

A psychiatric label has a life and an influence of its own. Once the impression has been formed that the patient is schizophrenic, the expectation is that he will continue to be schizophrenic. When a sufficient amount of time has passed, during which the patient has done nothing bizarre, he is considered to be in remission and available for discharge. But the label endures beyond discharge, with the unconfirmed expectation that he will behave as a schizo-

phrenic again. Such labels, conferred by mental health professionals, are as influential on the patient as they are on his relatives and friends, and it should not surprise anyone that the diagnosis acts on all of them as a self-fulfilling prophecy. Eventually, the patient himself accepts the diagnosis, with all of its surplus meanings and expectations, and behaves accordingly (5).

The inferences to be made from these matters are quite simple. Much as Zigler and Phillips have demonstrated that there is enormous overlap in the symptoms presented by patients who have been variously diagnosed (16), so there is enormous overlap in the behaviors of the sane and the insane. The sane are not "sane" all of the time. We lose our tempers "for no good reason." We are occasionally depressed or anxious, again for no good reason. And we may find it difficult to get along with one or another person— again for no reason that we can specify. Similarly, the insane are not always insane. Indeed, it was the impression of the pseudopatients while living with them that they were sane for long periods of time—that the bizarre behaviors upon which their diagnoses were allegedly predicated constituted only a small fraction of their total behavior. If it makes no sense to label ourselves permanently depressed on the basis of an occasional depression, then it takes better evidence than is presently available to label all patients insane or schizophrenic on the basis of bizarre behaviors or cognitions. It seems more useful, as Mischel (17) has pointed out, to limit our discussions to *behaviors*, the stimuli that provoke them, and their correlates.

It is not known why powerful impressions of personality traits, such as "crazy" or "insane," arise. Conceivably, when the origins of and stimuli that give rise to a behavior are remote or unknown, or when the behavior strikes us as immutable, trait labels regarding the *behaver* arise. When, on the other hand, the origins and stimuli are known and available, discourse is limited to the behavior itself. Thus, I may hallucinate because I am sleeping, or I may hallucinate because I have ingested a peculiar drug. These are termed sleep-induced hallucinations, or dreams, and drug-induced hallucinations, respectively. But when the stimuli to my hallucinations are unknown, that is called craziness, or schizophrenia—as if that inference were somehow as illuminating as the others.

The Experience of
Psychiatric Hospitalization

The term "mental illness" is of recent origin. It was coined by people who were humane in their inclinations and who wanted very much to raise the station of (and the public's sympathies toward) the psychologically disturbed from that of witches and "crazies" to one that was akin to the physically ill. And they were at least partially successful, for the treatment of the mentally ill *has* improved considerably over the years. But while treatment has improved, it is doubtful that people really regard the mentally ill in the same way that they view the physically ill. A broken leg is something one recovers from, but mental illness allegedly endures forever (18). A broken leg does not threaten the observer, but a crazy schizophrenic? There is by now a host of evidence that attitudes toward the mentally ill are characterized by fear, hostility, aloofness, suspicion, and dread (19). The mentally ill are society's lepers.

That such attitudes infect the general population is perhaps not surprising, only upsetting. But that they affect the professionals—attendants, nurses, physicians, psychologists, and social workers—who treat and deal with the mentally ill is more disconcerting, both because such attitudes are self-evidently pernicious and because they are unwitting. Most mental health professionals would insist that they are sympathetic toward the mentally ill, that they are neither avoidant nor hostile. But it is more likely that an exquisite ambivalence characterizes their relations with psychiatric patients, such that their avowed impulses are only part of their entire attitude. Negative attitudes are there too and can easily be detected. Such attitudes should not surprise us. They are the natural offspring of the labels patients wear and the places in which they are found.

Consider the structure of the typical psychiatric hospital. Staff and patients are strictly segregated. Staff have their own living space, including their dining facilities, bathrooms, and assembly places. The glassed quarters that contain the professional staff, which the pseudopatients came to call "the cage," sit out on every dayroom. The staff emerge primarily for caretaking purposes—to give medication, to conduct a therapy or group meeting, to instruct or reprimand a patient. Otherwise, staff keep to themselves, almost as if the disorder that afflicts their charges is somehow catching.

So much is patient-staff segregation the rule that, for four public hospitals in which an attempt was made to measure the degree to which staff and patients mingle, it was necessary to use "time out of the staff cage" as the operational measure. While it was not the case that all time spent out of the cage was spent mingling with patients (attendants, for example, would occasionally emerge to watch television in the dayroom), it was the only way in which one could gather reliable data on time for measuring.

The average amount of time spent by attendants outside of the cage was 11.3 percent (range, 3 to 52 percent). This figure does not represent only time spent mingling with patients, but also includes time spent on such chores as folding laundry, supervising patients while they shave, directing ward cleanup, and sending patients to off-ward activities. It was the relatively rare attendant who spent time talking with patients or playing games with them. It proved impossible to obtain a "percent mingling time" for nurses, since the amount of time they spent out of the cage was too brief. Rather, we counted instances of emergence from the cage. On the average, daytime nurses emerged from the cage 11.5 times per shift, including instances when they left the ward entirely (range, 4 to 39 times). Late afternoon and night nurses were even less available, emerging on the average 9.4 times per shift (range, 4 to 41 times). Data on early morning nurses, who arrived usually after midnight and departed at 8 a.m., are not available because patients were asleep during most of this period.

Physicians, especially psychiatrists, were even less available. They were rarely seen on the wards. Quite commonly, they would be seen only when they arrived and departed, with the remaining time being spent in their offices or in the cage. On the average, physicians emerged on the ward 6.7 times per day (range, 1 to 17 times). It proved difficult to make an accurate estimate in this regard, since physicians often maintained hours that allowed them to come and go at different times.

The hierarchical organization of the psychiatric hospital has been commented on before (20), but the latent meaning of that kind of organization is worth noting again. Those with the most power have least to do with patients, and those with the least power are most involved with them. Recall, however, that the acquisition of role-appropriate behaviors occurs mainly through the observation of others, with the most powerful having the most influence. Consequently, it is understandable that attendants not only spend more time with patients than do any other members of the staff—that is required by their station in the hierarchy—but also, insofar as they learn from their superiors' behavior, spend as little time with patients as they can. Attendants are seen mainly in the cage, which is where the models, the action, and the power are.

I turn now to a different set of studies, these dealing with staff response to patient-initiated contact. It has long been known that the amount of time a person spends with you can be an index of your significance to him. If he initiates and maintains eye contact, there is reason to believe that he is considering your requests and needs. If he pauses to chat or actually stops and talks, there is added reason to infer that he is individuating you. In four hospitals, the pseudopatient approached the staff member with a request which took the following form: "Pardon me, Mr. [or Dr. or Mrs.] X, could you tell me when I will be eligible for grounds privileges?" (or " . . . when I will be presented at the staff meeting?" or ". . . when I am likely to be discharged?"). While the content of the question varied according to the appropriateness of the target and the pseudopatient's (apparent) current needs the form was always a courteous and relevant request for information. Care was taken never to approach a particular member of the staff more than once a day, lest the staff member become suspicious or irritated. In examining these data, remember that the behavior of the pseudopatients was neither bizarre nor

6. DYNAMICS OF MALADJUSTMENT

Table 1. Self-initiated contact by pseudopatients with psychiatrists and nurses and attendants, compared to contact with other groups.

Contact	Psychiatric hospitals		University campus (nonmedical)	University medical center		
				Physicians		
	(1) Psychiatrists	(2) Nurses and attendants	(3) Faculty	(4) "Looking for a psychiatrist"	(5) "Looking for an internist"	(6) No additional comment
Responses						
Moves on, head averted (%)	71	88	0	0	0	0
Makes eye contact (%)	23	10	0	11	0	0
Pauses and chats (%)	2	2	0	11	0	10
Stops and talks (%)	4	0.5	100	78	100	90
Mean number of questions answered (out of 6)	*	*	6	3.8	4.8	4.5
Respondents (No.)	13	47	14	18	15	10
Attempts (No.)	185	1283	14	18	15	10

* Not applicable.

disruptive. One could indeed engage in good conversation with them.

The data for these experiments are shown in Table 1, separately for physicians (column 1) and for nurses and attendants (column 2). Minor differences between these four institutions were overwhelmed by the degree to which staff avoided continuing contacts that patients had initiated. By far, their most common response consisted of either a brief response to the question, offered while they were "on the move" and with head averted, or no response at all.

The encounter frequently took the following bizarre form: (pseudopatient) "Pardon me, Dr. X. Could you tell me when I am eligible for grounds privileges?" (physician) "Good morning, Dave. How are you today?" (Moves off without waiting for a response.)

It is instructive to compare these data with data recently obtained at Stanford University. It has been alleged that large and eminent universities are characterized by faculty who are so busy that they have no time for students. For this comparison, a young lady approached individual faculty members who seemed to be walking purposefully to some meeting or teaching engagement and asked them the following six questions.

1) "Pardon me, could you direct me to Encina Hall?" (at the medical school: ". . . to the Clinical Research Center?").

2) "Do you know where Fish Annex is?" (there is no Fish Annex at Stanford).

3) "Do you teach here?"

4) "How does one apply for admission to the college?" (at the medical school: ". . . to the medical school?").

5) "Is it difficult to get in?"

6) "Is there financial aid?"

Without exception, as can be seen in Table 1 (column 3), all of the questions were answered. No matter how rushed they were, all respondents not only maintained eye contact, but stopped to talk. Indeed, many of the respondents went out of their way to direct or take the questioner to the office she was seeking, to try to locate "Fish Annex," or to discuss with her the possibilities of being admitted to the university.

Similar data, also shown in Table 1 (columns 4, 5, and 6), were obtained in the hospital. Here too, the young lady came prepared with six questions. After the first question, however, she remarked to 18 of her respondents (column 4), "I'm looking for a psychiatrist," and to 15 others (column 5), "I'm looking for an internist." Ten other respondents received no inserted comment (column 6). The general degree of cooperative responses is considerably higher for these university groups than it was for pseudopatients in psychiatric hospitals. Even so, differences are apparent within the medical school setting. Once having indicated that she was looking for a psychiatrist, the degree of cooperation elicited was less than when she sought an internist.

Powerlessness and Depersonalization

Eye contact and verbal contact reflect concern and individuation; their absence, avoidance and depersonalization. The data I have presented do not do justice to the rich daily encounters that grew up around matters of deper-

sonalization and avoidance. I have records of patients who were beaten by staff for the sin of having initiated verbal contact. During my own experience, for example, one patient was beaten in the presence of other patients for having approached an attendant and told him, "I like you." Occasionally, punishment meted out to patients for misdemeanors seemed so excessive that it could not be justified by the most radical interpretations of psychiatric canon. Nevertheless, they appeared to go unquestioned. Tempers were often short. A patient who had not heard a call for medication would be roundly excoriated, and the morning attendants would often wake patients with. "Come on, you m-----f-----s, out of bed!"

Neither anecdotal nor "hard" data can convey the overwhelming sense of powerlessness which invades the individual as he is continually exposed to the depersonalization of the psychiatric hospital. It hardly matters *which* psychiatric hospital—the excellent public ones and the very plush private hospital were better than the rural and shabby ones in this regard, but, again, the features that psychiatric hospitals had in common overwhelmed by far their apparent differences.

Powerlessness was evident everywhere. The patient is deprived of many of his legal rights by dint of his psychiatric commitment (21). He is shorn of credibility by virtue of his psychiatric label. His freedom of movement is restricted. He cannot initiate contact with the staff, but may only respond to such overtures as they make. Personal privacy is minimal. Patient quarters and possessions can be entered and examined by any staff member, for whatever reason. His personal history and anguish is available to any staff member (often including the "grey lady" and "candy striper" volunteer) who chooses to read his folder, regardless of their therapeutic relationship to him. His personal hygiene and waste evacuation are often monitored. The water closets may have no doors.

At times, depersonalization reached such proportions that pseudopatients had the sense that they were invisible, or at least unworthy of account. Upon being admitted, I and other pseudopatients took the initial physical examinations in a semipublic room, where staff members went about their own business as if we were not there.

On the ward, attendants delivered verbal and occasionally serious physical abuse to patients in the presence of other observing patients, some of whom (the pseudopatients) were writing it all down. Abusive behavior, on the other hand, terminated quite abruptly when other staff members were known to be coming. Staff are credible witnesses. Patients are not.

A nurse unbuttoned her uniform to adjust her brassiere in the presence of an entire ward of viewing men. One did not have the sense that she was being seductive. Rather, she didn't notice us. A group of staff persons might point to a patient in the dayroom and discuss him animatedly, as if he were not there.

One illuminating instance of depersonalization and invisibility occurred with regard to medications. All told, the pseudopatients were administered nearly 2100 pills, including Elavil, Stelazine, Compazine, and Thorazine, to name but a few. (That such a variety of medications should have been administered to patients presenting identical symptoms is itself worthy of note.) Only two were swallowed. The rest were either pocketed or deposited in the toilet. The pseudopatients were not alone in this. Although I have no precise records on how many patients rejected their medications, the pseudopatients frequently found the medications of other patients in the toilet before they deposited their own. As long as they were cooperative, their behavior and the pseudopatients' own in this matter, as in other important matters, went unnoticed throughout.

Reactions to such depersonalization among pseudopatients were intense. Although they had come to the hospital as participant observers and were fully aware that they did not "belong," they nevertheless found themselves caught up in and fighting the process of depersonalization. Some examples: a graduate student in psychology asked his wife to bring his textbooks to the hospital so he could "catch up on his homework"—this despite the elaborate precautions taken to conceal his professional association. The same student, who had trained for quite some time to get into the hospital, and who had looked forward to the experience, "remembered" some drag races that he had wanted to see on the weekend and insisted that he be discharged by that time. Another pseudopatient attempted a romance with a nurse. Subsequently, he informed the staff that he was applying for admission to graduate school in psychology and was very likely to be admitted, since a graduate professor was one of his regular hospital visitors. The same person began to engage in psychotherapy with other patients—all of this as a way of becoming a person in an impersonal environment.

The Sources of Depersonalization

What are the origins of depersonalization? I have already mentioned two. First are attitudes held by all of us toward the mentally ill—including those who treat them—attitudes characterized by fear, distrust, and horrible expectations on the one hand, and benevolent intentions on the other. Our ambivalence leads, in this instance as in others, to avoidance.

Second, and not entirely separate, the hierarchical structure of the psychiatric hospital facilitates depersonalization. Those who are at the top have least to do with patients, and their behavior inspires the rest of the staff. Average daily contact with psychiatrists, psychologists, residents, and physicians combined ranged from 3.9 to 25.1 minutes, with an overall mean of 6.8 (six pseudopatients over a total of 129 days of hospitalization). Included in this average is time spent in the admissions interview, ward meetings in the presence of a senior staff member, group and individual psychotherapy contacts, case presentation conferences, and discharge meetings.

Clearly, patients do not spend much time in interpersonal contact with doctoral staff. And doctoral staff serve as models for nurses and attendants.

There are probably other sources. Psychiatric installations are presently in serious financial straits. Staff shortages are pervasive, staff time at a premium. Something has to give, and that something is patient contact. Yet, while financial stresses are realities, too much can be made of them. I have the impression that the psychological forces that result in depersonalization are much stronger than the fiscal ones and that the addition of more staff would not correspondingly improve patient care in this regard. The incidence of staff meetings and the enormous amount of record-keeping on patients, for example, have not been as substantially reduced as has patient contact. Priorities exist, even during hard times. Patient contact is not a significant priority in the traditional psychiatric hospital, and fiscal pressures do not account for this. Avoidance and depersonalization may.

Heavy reliance upon psychotropic medication tacitly contributes to depersonalization by convincing staff that treatment is indeed being conducted and that further patient contact may not be necessary. Even here, however, caution needs to be exercised in understanding the role of psychotropic drugs. If patients were powerful rather than powerless, if they were viewed as interesting individuals rather than diagnostic entities, if they were socially significant rather than social lepers, if their anguish truly and wholly compelled our sympathies and concerns, would we not *seek* contact with them, despite the availability of medications? Perhaps for the pleasure of it all?

The Consequences of Labeling and Depersonalization

Whenever the ratio of what is known to what needs to be known approaches zero, we tend to invent "knowledge" and assume that we understand more than we actually do. We seem unable to acknowledge that we simply don't know. The needs for diagnosis and remediation of behavioral and emotional problems are enormous. But rather than acknowledge that we are just embarking on understanding, we continue to label patients "schizophrenic," "manic-depressive," and "insane," as if in those words we had captured the essence of understanding. The facts of the matter are that we have known for a long time that diagnoses are often not useful or reliable, but we have nevertheless continued to use them. We now know that we cannot distinguish insanity from sanity. It is depressing to consider how that information will be used.

Not merely depressing, but frightening. How many people, one wonders, are sane but not recognized as such in our psychiatric institutions? How many have been needlessly stripped of their privileges of citizenship, from the right to vote and drive to that of handling their own accounts? How many have feigned insanity in order to avoid the criminal consequences of their behavior, and, conversely, how many would rather stand trial than live interminably in a psychiatric hospital—but are wrongly thought to be mentally ill? How many have been stigmatized by well-intentioned, but nevertheless erroneous, diagnoses? On the last point, recall again that a "type 2 error" in psychiatric diagnosis does not have the same consequences it does in medical diagnosis. A diagnosis of cancer that has been found to be in error is cause for celebration. But psychiatric diagnoses are rarely found to be in error. The label sticks, a mark of inadequacy forever.

Finally, how many patients might be "sane" outside the psychiatric hospital but seem insane in it—not because craziness resides in them, as it were, but because they are responding to a bizarre setting, one that may be unique to institutions which harbor nether people? Goffman (4) calls the process of socialization to such institutions "mortification"—an apt metaphor that includes the processes of depersonalization that have been described here. And while it is impossible to know whether the pseudopatients' responses to these processes are characteristic of all inmates—they were, after all, not real patients—it is difficult to believe that these processes of socialization to a psychiatric hospital provide useful attitudes or habits of response for living in the "real world."

Summary and Conclusions

It is clear that we cannot distinguish the sane from the insane in psychiatric hospitals. The hospital itself imposes a special environment in which the meanings of behavior can easily be misunderstood. The consequences to patients hospitalized in such an environment—the powerlessness, depersonalization, segregation, mortification, and self-labeling—seem undoubtedly countertherapeutic.

I do not, even now, understand this problem well enough to perceive solutions. But two matters seem to have some promise. The first concerns the proliferation of community mental health facilities, of crisis intervention centers, of the human potential movement, and of behavior therapies that, for all of their own problems, tend to avoid psychiatric labels, to focus on specific problems and behaviors, and to retain the individual in a relatively nonpejorative environment. Clearly, to the extent that we refrain from sending the distressed to insane places, our impressions of them are less likely to be distorted. (The risk of distorted perceptions, it seems to me, is always present, since we are much more sensitive to an individual's behaviors and verbalizations than we are to the subtle contextual stimuli that often promote them. At issue here is a matter of magnitude. And, as I have shown, the magnitude of distortion is exceedingly high in the extreme context that is a psychiatric hospital.)

The second matter that might prove promising speaks to the need to increase the sensitivity of mental health workers and researchers to the *Catch 22* position of psychiatric patients. Simply reading materials in this area will be of help to some such workers and researchers. For others, directly experiencing the impact of psychiatric hospitalization will be of enormous use. Clearly, further research into the social psychology of such total institutions will both facilitate treatment and deepen understanding.

I and the other pseudopatients in the psychiatric setting had distinctly negative reactions. We do not pretend to describe the subjective experiences of true patients. Theirs may be different from ours, particularly with the passage of time and the necessary process of adaptation to one's environment. But we can and do speak to the relatively more objective indices of treatment within the hospital. It could be a mistake, and a very unfortunate one, to consider that what happened to us derived from malice or stupidity on the part of the staff. Quite the contrary, our overwhelming impression of them was of people who really cared, who were committed and who were uncommonly intelligent. Where they failed, as they sometimes did painfully, it would be more accurate to attribute those failures to the environment in which they, too, found themselves than to personal callousness. Their perceptions and behavior were controlled by the situation, rather than being motivated by a malicious disposition. In a more benign environment, one that was less attached to global diagnosis, their behaviors and judgments might have been more benign and effective.

References and Notes

1. P. Ash, *J. Abnorm. Soc. Psychol.* **44**, 272 (1949); A. T. Beck, *Amer. J. Psychiat.* **119**, 210 (1962); A. T. Boisen, *Psychiatry* **2**, 233 (1938); N. Kreitman, *J. Ment. Sci.* **107**, 876 (1961); N. Kreitman, P. Sainsbury, J. Morrisey, J. Towers, J. Scrivener, *ibid.*, p. 887; H. O. Schmitt and C. P. Fonda, *J. Abnorm. Soc. Psychol.* **52**, 262 (1956); W. Seeman, *J. Nerv. Ment. Dis.* **118**, 541 (1953). For an analysis of these artifacts and summaries of the disputes, see J. Zubin, *Annu. Rev. Psychol.* **18**, 373 (1967); L. Phillips and J. G. Draguns, *ibid.* **22**, 447 (1971).

2. R. Benedict, *J. Gen. Psychol.* **10**, 59 (1934).

3. See in this regard H. Becker, *Outsiders: Studies in the Sociology of Deviance* (Free Press, New York, 1963); B. M. Braginsky, D. D. Braginsky, K. Ring, *Methods of Madness: The Mental Hospital as a Last Resort* (Holt, Rinehart & Winston, New York, 1969); G. M. Crocetti and P. V. Lemkau, *Amer. Sociol. Rev.* **30**, 577 (1965); E. Goffman, *Behavior in Public Places* (Free Press, New York, 1964); R. D. Laing, *The Divided Self: A Study of Sanity and Madness* (Quadrangle, Chicago, 1960); D. L. Phillips, *Amer. Sociol. Rev.* **28**, 963 (1963); T. R. Sarbin, *Psychol. Today* **6**, 18 (1972); E. Schur, *Amer. J. Sociol.* **75**, 309 (1969); T. Szasz, *Law, Liberty and Psychiatry* (Macmillan, New York, 1963); *The Myth of Mental Illness: Foundations of a Theory of Mental Illness* (Hoeber-Harper, New York, 1963). For a critique of some of these views, see W. R. Gove, *Amer. Sociol. Rev.* **35**, 873 (1970).

4. E. Goffman, *Asylums* (Doubleday, Garden City, N.Y., 1961).

5. T. J. Scheff, *Being Mentally Ill: A Sociological Theory* (Aldine, Chicago, 1966).

6. Data from a ninth pseudopatient are not incorporated in this report because, although his sanity went undetected, he falsified aspects of his personal history, including his marital status and parental relationships. His experimental behaviors therefore were not identical to those of the other pseudopatients.

7. A. Barry, *Bellevue Is a State of Mind* (Harcourt Brace Jovanovich, New York, 1971); I. Belknap, *Human Problems of a State Mental Hospital* (McGraw-Hill, New York, 1956); W. Caudill, F. C. Redlich, H. R. Gilmore, E. B. Brody, *Amer. J. Orthopsychiat.* **22**, 314 (1952); A. R. Goldman, R. H. Bohr, T. A. Steinberg, *Prof. Psychol.* **1**, 427 (1970); unauthored, *Roche Report* **1** (No. 13), 8 (1971).

8. Beyond the personal difficulties that the pseudopatient is likely to experience in the hospital, there are legal and social ones that, combined, require considerable attention before entry. For example, once admitted to a psychiatric institution, it is difficult, if not impossible, to be discharged on short notice, state law to the contrary notwithstanding. I was not sensitive to these difficulties at the outset of the project, nor to the personal and situational emergencies that can arise, but later a writ of habeas corpus was prepared for each of the entering pseudopatients and an attorney was kept "on call" during every hospitalization. I am grateful to John Kaplan and Robert Bartels for legal advice and assistance in these matters.

9. However distasteful such concealment is, it was a necessary first step to examining these questions. Without concealment, there would have been no way to know how valid these experiences were; nor was there any way of knowing whether whatever detections occurred were a tribute to the diagnostic acumen of the staff or to the hospital's rumor network. Obviously, since my concerns are general ones that cut across individual hospitals and staffs, I have respected their anonymity and have eliminated clues that might lead to their identification.

10. Interestingly, of the 12 admissions, 11 were diagnosed as schizophrenic and one, with the identical symptomatology, as manic-depressive psychosis. This diagnosis has a more favorable prognosis, and it was given by the only private hospital in our sample. On the relations between social class and psychiatric diagnosis, see A. deB. Hollingshead and F. C. Redlich, *Social Class and Mental Illness: A Community Study* (Wiley, New York, 1958).

11. It is possible, of course, that patients have quite broad latitudes in diagnosis and therefore are inclined to call many people sane, even those whose behavior is patently aberrant. However, although we have no hard data on this matter, it was our distinct impression that this was not the case. In many instances, patients not only singled us out for attention, but came to imitate our behaviors and styles.

12. J. Cumming and E. Cumming, *Community Ment. Health* **1**, 135 (1965); A. Farina and K. Ring, *J. Abnorm. Psychol.* **70**, 47 (1965); H. E. Freeman and O. G. Simmons, *The Mental Patient Comes Home* (Wiley, New York, 1963); W. J. Johannsen, *Ment. Hygiene* **53**, 218 (1969); A. S. Linsky, *Soc. Psychiat.* **5**, 166 (1970).

13. S. E. Asch, *J. Abnorm. Soc. Psychol.* **41**, 258 (1946); *Social Psychology* (Prentice-Hall, New York, 1952).

14. See also I. N. Mensh and J. Wishner, *J. Personality* **16**, 188 (1947); J. Wishner, *Psychol. Rev.* **67**, 96 (1960); J. S. Bruner and R. Tagiuri, in *Handbook of Social Psychology*, G. Lindzey, Ed. (Addison-Wesley, Cambridge, Mass., 1954), vol. 2, pp. 634–654; J. S. Bruner, D. Shapiro, R. Tagiuri, in *Person Perception and Interpersonal Behavior*, R. Tagiuri and L. Petrullo, Eds. (Stanford Univ. Press, Stanford, Calif., 1958), pp. 277–288.

15. For an example of a similar self fulfilling prophecy, in this instance dealing with the "central" trait of intelligence, see R. Rosenthal and L. Jacobson, *Pygmalion in the Classroom* (Holt, Rinehart & Winston, New York, 1968).

16. E. Zigler and L. Phillips, *J. Abnorm. Soc. Psychol.* **63**, 69 (1961). See also R. K. Freudenberg and J. P. Robertson, *A.M.A. Arch. Neurol. Psychiatr.* **76**, 14 (1956).

17. W. Mischel, *Personality and Assessment* (Wiley, New York, 1968).

18. The most recent and unfortunate instance of this tenet is that of Senator Thomas Eagleton.

19. T. R. Sarbin and J. C. Mancuso, *J. Clin. Consult. Psychol.* **35**, 159 (1970); T. R. Sarbin, *ibid.* **31**, 447 (1967); J. C. Nunnally, Jr., *Popular Conceptions of Mental Health* (Holt, Rinehart & Winston, New York, 1961).

20. A. H. Stanton and M. S. Schwartz, *The Mental Hospital: A Study of Institutional Participation in Psychiatric Illness and Treatment* (Basic, New York, 1954).

21. D. B. Wexler and S. E. Scoville, *Ariz. Law Rev.* **13**, 1 (1971).

22. I thank W. Mischel, E. Orne, and M. S. Rosenhan for comments on an earlier draft of this manuscript.

A DARKNESS AT NOON

Although no less a man than Nietzsche thought it to be ultimately soul-strengthening depression is anything but beneficial to those who suffer from it. Now, medical evidence supports the theory that some forms of the disease arise from altered body chemistry

Carl Edgar Law

"I have of late, — but wherefore I know not — lost all my mirth, forgone all custom of exercises; and — indeed — it goes so heavily with my disposition that this goodly frame, the earth, seems to me a sterile promontory."

That's how Hamlet saw things in Act II, Scene II; and, say Canadian psychiatrists, that's how 15 to 20 per cent of Canadians see things at some time in their lives — seriously enough to require at least one contact with a hospital.

In fact, 50 per cent or more of Canadians may experience depression at least once in their lives. While many will simply not contact professional help despite the severity, others will find the episode sufficiently mild or short in duration to cope using their own mental resources.

Fortunately, says Dr. Sarwer-Foner, director of psychiatry for the Ottawa General Hospital and the elder statesman of psychiatry in Canada, most depression is self-limiting, with almost 90 per cent of depressions remitting within 30 days to six months. Some cases may persist up to two years and about 15 per cent tend to become resistant to treatment. The pattern may continue throughout life but even stubbornly-resistant depressions tend to mitigate with advancing age unless there are underlying organic problems.

Patients whose depressions are punctuated by periods of euphoria, often leading to extreme feelings of energy and omnipotence, as well as loss of judgment and hyper-sensitivity to criticism, are characterized as "manic-depressives" and form a relatively small subgroup.

To the layman — aided by the popular press — depression is often seen as a byproduct of an industrial, rootless age in which the increasing stress of burgeoning technology and possible breakdowns in the social and moral order constitute insidious assaults on sanity. History, however, does not bear this thesis out.

The Babylonian King Nebuchadnezzar is reputed to have suffered intensely from insomnia, with wildly erratic mood swings, corresponding to a possible diagnosis of manic depression (it is rarer in men than in women). Chroniclers also describe the biblical Kings Saul and Herod as less-than-happy men.

Homer and Plutarch made *their* contributions to the literature on depression, joining a trend that has continued among philosophers and writers to the present day. The evidence is convincing then, that depression has been an unrelenting feature of human existence throughout Mankind's history.

Throughout history, the major technique for treating depression has remained largely the same.

"Psychotherapy continues as the treatment of choice for depression," Dr. Sarwer-Foner says, although he includes a number of important qualifications.

Psychotherapy, which has become very sophisticated in recent times, had its beginnings in the practices of witch-doctors, magicians, elders of the tribe, even family members; in fact, therapeutic help could be provided by anyone whom the depressive trusted and respected. And, if one word is vital in treating depression, it is "hope". The loss of hope (a state of despair) is a prominent feature in depression. The glimmerings of renewed hope are important indicators in the cure.

EVENT-RELATED DEPRESSION

In the vast majority of cases depression is a response to a real or perceived object loss: the loss of a wife, husband, lover, mother, father, a cherished pet — in fact, any object or relationship the subject holds dearly as central to his or her happiness.

What happens frequently in the beginnings of depression is the onset of a sense of inferiority, says Dr. Sarwer-Foner who also teaches at the Ottawa University Faculty of Medicine, acts as a consultant, and has contributed prolifically to the literature since the 1950's.

"There is a shattering of the concept of the person, a sense of not being good enough. Depressed people haven't got the strength to live and they may exhibit passive dependency."

What they need is to be valued as a person, to have a place in life, to have people care for them, to be respected and to feel that they can get what they deserve

 Reprinted from *SCIENCE FORUM Magazine*, July/August 1978, pp. 32-38, with the permission of the publisher.

from life without superhuman or abnormal effort — such as that exhibited by the "workaholic" who withdraws from social contact because he is "too busy". ("Normal" people believe that they are deserving just by virtue of existing, without having to solicit outside approval excessively, or do anything specifically "good" to feel whole and well.).

These depressions are known as "reactive" depressions because they involve a reaction to a tangible loss. They are "event-related", and range from the normal grief reaction to an extreme withdrawal syndrome that precludes the maintaining of normal responsibilities and behavior.

The clinical signs psychiatrists and physicians look for in depression include: mood change; psychomotor retardation and anxiety; loss of self-esteem; delusions and hallucinations, sleep disturbance; loss of energy; change in appetite and change in sexual drive. But not all signs and symptoms will be present in individual cases. Mood changes may include an active descent into gloom and misery, or a less-pronounced loss of well-being. Psychomotor retardation means a slowing down of the mental and physical faculties. In many cases the subject's life simply grinds to a halt.

"A depression starts with a feeling of general tiredness which does not respond favorably to resting or sleeping," recounts one patient.

"Within a few days a bitter taste develops in my mouth and I lose my appetite. At night I have difficulty in sleeping.

"Within a week to 10 days an intense feeling of depression sets in, creating the impression that I am quite incapable of doing my job; unable to drive my car and, in fact, afraid to do anything involving any skill or responsibility.

"This deepens my feeling of depression and soon brings me to contemplating suicide."

Not all depressives contemplate suicide, but when depressions are put together with other mental illnesses predisposing to suicide, the figures become startling. Suicide is the leading cause of death in certain young age groups and a major cause of death in most others, tapering off at the extreme ends of the scale (childhood and old age).

Surprisingly, many elderly patients develop a condition known as organic brain syndrome, which often makes them too confused to commit suicide even when they contemplate the act. Thus, lowered suicide deaths in the elderly may indicate a lack of skill at consummating the act rather than a diminished incidence of suicidally-depressive thinking.

DEPRESSION FROM WITHIN

The second major group of depressions is classified as "endogenous" (coming from within). In these cases there is no obvious precipitating event.

In fact, though, says Dr. Sarwer-Foner, "good clinical studies show that there usually is a precipitating factor, but the patient can't talk about it while still ill."

The psychiatrist can usually distinguish between these two types of depressions by symptoms. Both types share many common symptoms, but in endogenous depression symptoms may be more severe and greater in number. Delusions and visual or auditory hallucinations are more common in this group.

For Dr. Sarwer-Foner, a primary question to ask is: "Can the patient relate — that is, communicate with — the psychiatrist or therapist?"

If the patient can communicate it is important to establish at the outset whether suicidal or homicidal tendencies are present. These questions can be answered from the patient's history and from the comments of family and friends or whoever accompanies the patient to treatment.

Such questions are vital because these tendencies suggest a crisis that must be treated immediately, in a hospital setting. The patient may be quieted with drugs. A violent episode may be halted by the use of ECT — electro-convulsive therapy — which Dr. Sarwer-Foner calls "life-saving", even though it fell into some disrepute in the late sixties and early seventies.

"When the patient is severely disturbed and pre-disposed to violence against himself and others this treatment can be life-saving." says Dr. Sarwer-Foner. It is not a punishment — although public critics may sometimes term it that — and it has few if any lasting side effects.

It is also safe. The primary side effect is short-term memory loss. The patient may not remember what happened during the day or two preceding treatment and for a time may have marked memory loss of past events, but these memories usually return over a period of days or weeks.

Six to eight shock treatments are commonly given in depression and they may be combined with antidepressant drugs. ECT has proved particularly useful in the "endogenous" depressions. If the patient does not appear suicidal or homicidal but cannot communicate, hospitalization is still generally necessary. Either ECT, anti-depressant drug therapy, or a combination of the two will frequently alleviate the worst symptoms within a period of weeks. Only then can meaningful psychotherapy begin. Neither drugs nor ECT are panaceas, but they can help restore contact with reality.

Thus, drugs and ECT are common treatments in the primary or crisis stage. In the secondary stage when psychotherapy has begun, drugs are frequently valuable adjuncts. Should the depression prove refractory (that is, long-term or chronic) drug treatment may continue for many years.

DRUGS, DRUGS... AND DRUGS

The hierarchy of drugs is fairly straightforward in psychiatry and although new derivatives of old drugs are being synthesized, the classic preparations have been used for two decades or more. While this suggests no great improvements in drug therapy, clinicians have nonetheless built up vast experience in their use. To the patient that means more likelihood of getting the "right" drug first time round, and less likelihood of severe side effects from the "wrong" prescription.

The heavyweight drugs in depression are the "neuroleptics". The most popular of these is chlorpromazine, marketed under such names as Largactil (Canada) and Thorizaine (United States). Neuroleptics may also be called "major tranquilizers" or, simply, antipsychotic drugs. In the psychotic depressions (and in schizophrenia) they reduce hallucinations, delusions, combativeness, tension, restlessness and social withdrawal. Over-all there is an emotional quieting effect. Some of these drugs have sedative effects, useful in the therapy of some patients, but considered an undesirable side effect in others.

A major feature of neuroleptics is that, though they are antipsychotic in appropriate dosage, they can be used to treat lesser disorders simply by reducing the amount administered.

"They are very effective in the treatment of anxiety in all psychiatric disorders," say Drs. E.L. Bassuk and S.C. Schoonover, in their book, The Practicioner's Guide to Psychoactive Drugs.

Patients who are not severely disturbed may often be prescribed anti-depressants. The two major families are known as "tricyclics" (because of their molecular structure) and "monoamine oxidase inhibitors' or MAOIs, (because they inhibit the destruction of certain nerve transmission substances (neurotransmitters). Both of these drugs affect neurotransmitters without specifically sedating the patient or producing unmanageable side effects.

To understand what a neurotransmitter substance is, one needs an idea of how nerve transmission works. Nerve cells or neurons in the body and brain never quite meet. There is a narrow gap between each neuron. When a single nerve fires, a current sweeps along the neuron to its end, where it stimulates the production of neurotransmitter chemicals which cross the narrow gap to receptor sites on the surface of the next nerve cell; this causes it to fire in turn. Thus, these substances are vital to the healthy operation of the nervous system.

When the nerve transmission is finished, the neurotransmitter is destroyed by other chemicals and recycled metabolically to be stored and re-used for future nerve transmissions.

Some anti-depressants simply block the chemicals that destroy these neurotransmitters, causing a higher rate of nervous activity, while others increase the overall availability of neurotransmitters in the brain. In either case, the heightened nerve activity seems to improve mood and make the patient feel more energetic and motivated.

The patient who is depressed will often be started on a tricyclic. It takes two to four weeks for such drugs to exert their full effect, at which point the physician may try another tricyclic if the first hasn't produced good results, or vary the dose according to the side effects.

When tricyclics don't work, monoamine oxidase inhibitors or MAOIs are often prescribed, but because of their potentially severe side effects (including coma and death), they are generally given in hospital where the patient can be monitored closely. These drugs produce the well-known "cheese" effect. Certain cheeses, (as well as Chianti wine and other foods), contain byproducts of fermentation called "tyramines", which can react violently with monoamine oxidase inhibitors; the effect can often be reversed however by the neuroleptic chlorpromazine.

That's why out-patients taking MAOIs are sometimes prescribed a neuroleptic drug to carry as an emergency kit in case they inadvertently (or intentionally in the case of wine and beer lovers) eat or drink anything that causes a violent reaction.

If anti-depressant effects are not produced in the patient even with MAOIs, the physician or psychiatrist may prescribe a combination of tricyclics and MAOIs, but this requires in-depth clinical experience. Each drug is administered in half its usual dose (if used alone) and the diet is carefully controlled to avoid the adverse reactions previously noted.

In depressions with anxiety as an important component, "anxiolytics" may be prescribed. The trade names Librium and Valium are virtually household words in North America and may be the most widely-prescribed drugs in the western world. Their chemical names are, respectively, chlordiazepoxide and diazepam.

These anxiolytics are widely abused by large numbers of people to relieve normal day-to-day stress. However, the word "abused" in a clinical sense does not necessarily imply over-dosing or extremely irresponsible use; rather it refers to their use for purposes other than that indicated by strict medical considerations — as a crutch to "get through a rough day at the office", for example. Fortunately, anxiolytic drugs have few side effects and even massive over-doses generally produce few, if any, long-term side-effects. Thus, unlike neuroleptics, tricyclics and MAOIs, they are relatively safe for the user who may be a potential suicide risk.

While anti-anxiety drugs may be safe in moderation, the dangers doctors watch for are gradual increase in dose by the patient, or steady long-term use for frivolous or less-than-medical reasons. With burgeoning research, more cases of long-term side-effects are being noted in users.

For example, certain patients will experience "paradoxical reactions" on anti-anxiety drugs. That is, they may become restless, agitated, aggressive, even violent — just the opposite of the drug's intended effect. It may be that anxiety is an external manifestation of bottled-up rage, anger, or frustration in such patients, the anxiety keeping a lid on "acting-out" this rage in terms of verbal and physical violence. If this theory holds, remove the anxiety and the anger surges to the surface. As one Ottawa psychiatrist put it, tongue-in-cheek, "the chap may take a swing at you but he certainly won't feel anxious about it."

Since alcohol may increase the effects of anti-anxiety drugs (as well as other psychiatric drugs) it is especially undesirable in these "paradoxical" patients. A binge on Valium and scotch, for instance, can produce a very dangerous individual. On the other hand, patients who are quieted by anti-anxiety preparations may find that mixing them with alcohol makes them drowsy or produces varying degrees of euphoria. The medical opinion on this combination: generally risky.

RARE TREATMENTS AND BREAKTHROUGHS

Four types of treatment are of special interest, and point out some directions in current research and the prospects of better cures in the future.

Insulin sub-coma treatment is not well-known but as Dr. Sarwer-Foner points out, "it is useful in patients with passive dependency needs." These are patients who feel so low that they really require "lots of tender loving care". In such cases closely-monitored doses of insulin can be extremely useful.

Too much insulin produces classic "insulin coma" because the hormone depletes the blood sugar, thereby starving the brain of this vital nutrient. This is not a desirable goal, although it was a popular treatment some years ago with certain psychiatrists. Insulin sub-coma (that is, sugar depletion, but not enough to knock the patient out) is induced in closely-monitored treatment units that feature highly-trained nurses and individualized care. This provides the patient with tangible evidence of caring people. It may also have a quieting effect, making the patient drowsy and helping him sleep when insomnia is a problem. It also increases appetite, an important feature in patients whose depression includes loss of interest in eating.

Megavitamin therapy is widely-touted by believers, but very few of these are physicians. That's why the medical literature generally dismisses megavitamin therapy in a few terse paragraphs. High doses of many vitamins, particularly B and C, have been recommended in many psychiatric illnesses by theorists who believe that some patients have physiological systems that prevent them from absorbing, storing or using these vitamins properly.

A feature of megavitamin therapy is that there is relatively little evidence of any toxicity in large doses of vitamins B, C or E. (The evidence to the contrary is generally based on extremely high doses). Vitamins A and D are very toxic in overdoses, but are not a primary focus of interest in psychiatry.

Lithium carbonate (a salt of the metal lithium) is used to treat the manic stage of manic-depression. This phase of manic-depression may begin with increased energy on the part of the victim. He may hatch grandiose plans and become impatient of criticism. This is the "workaholic" syndrome taken to extremes. His agitation may become so intense that he will go long periods without sleep and make errors in judgment, perhaps indulging in spending sprees or unwise investments that he would not normally contemplate.

Then comes the crash into depression and withdrawal, perhaps with an interim — a period of normality. In certain cases, depression is the first clinical sign, with the mania coming later. Some patients may only experience one such cycle during their lives and thus may not be considered "classical" manic-depressives, while others become chronic with the cycle repeating itself.

Lithium carbonate has been found very effective in controlling and limiting the "manic" phase of the illness, its effect in many patients also being beneficial during the depressive phase, when anti-depressants are normally prescribed

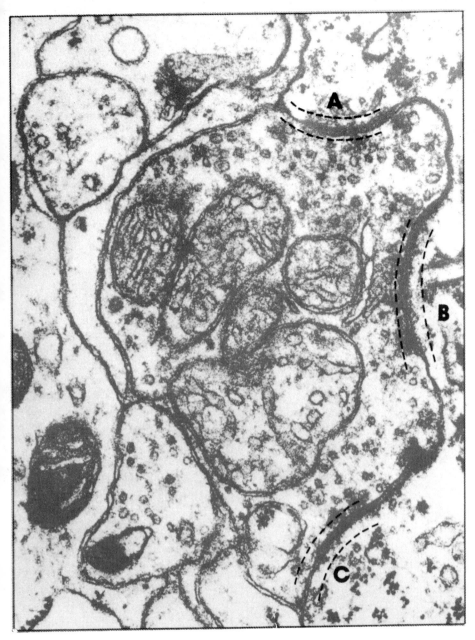

The A,B,C arrows indicate gaps between neurons (known as synaptic clefts). The small round dots clustered behind the dark-shaded gaps, contain neurotransmitter substances which flow across these gaps to conduct the impulse when the neuron fires.

There is some evidence that lithium carbonate may be effective in illnesses involving depression alone, but it is not strong. There is also suggestive evidence that the drug can be extremely useful in the "pre-menstrual" syndrome in women. That would be good news for certain women who experience pre-menstrual distress as a real and powerful illness.

Dr. Brent Waters, a Royal Ottawa Hospital psychiatrist with experience in manic depression, says that while lithium carbonate has been considered a relatively "safe" drug, recent evidence shows that "it has to be watched for toxic effects. Lithium carbonate should be treated as conservatively as many other psychotropic (mood-altering) drugs and this finding is relatively new."

Dr. Waters' comment illustrates a central issue in psychiatry. While many promising drugs appear periodically in the field, it is only after years of follow-up that long-term effects become matters of record. The other point to be made about drug therapy is that the psychiatrist does not want simply to remove all pain and anxiety from the patient in psychotherapy. An important treatment goal is to bring the patient face to face with grief, pain and anxiety and focus on mechanisms for coping with it. In fact, many psychiatrists believe much depression is a mental "re-organizing and strengthening" process that provides important experiences in growing and maturing.

Nietzsche stated, bluntly, that everything that doesn't destroy one makes one stronger and, further, there is no sun without shadow; it is essential to know the night. It is easy to see why librarians used to classify philosophy and psychotherapy under the same catalogue numbers. Both the philosopher and the psychotherapist are intimately involved with "the dark night of the soul". It can be debated, constructively, that the psychotherapist includes the role of "philosopher-mentor" among his many treatment strategies.

THE FUTURE:

The newest frontiers of psychiatry are often anything but philosophic — they are biochemical; the primary focus is on chemicals produced by the body itself, particularly the brain. Of course, there are philosophic frontiers, too, as new schools of psychotherapy evolve and older ones are refined and synthesized with others. But biochemistry and molecular biology are in the forefront of psychiatric research more intensively than ever before. While not all this research is aimed strictly at depression (schizophrenia and major psychoses are prime targets) it should have important benefits for depressive illness too.

A key area of the brain involved in the body's "chemical control" system is the hypothalamus. It produces many "releasing factors" that stimulate the nearby pituitary gland to produce a range of hormones, many of which affect mood. But there is a heated controversy between theorists who believe that hormones affect mood in complex ways. This area of study is called psychoendocrinology (endocrinology is the medical term for the study of the hormonal system).

Psychoendocrinology has addressed itself to depression more than to other psychiatric illnesses because there are sexual differences in the incidence of depression (women are more prone than men to many types) and hormones have a direct effect on sexual psychology and physiology. Indeed, some theorists see the menstrual cycle as a model-in-miniature of clinical depression because the changing hormonal balances during this cycle are closely mirrored by mood swings. This should not be interpreted as sexism since theorists suggest that men may have analogous hormonal cycles too, albeit less evident and harder to study. By comparison, menstrual mood swings in women have been recorded for thousands of years.

The "biogenic amine" theory of psychoendocrinology may not be a household word, but is one of the new buzzwords in the psychiatric lexicon. Biogenic amines (literally, body-produced amine compounds) are organic substances like adrenalin, noradrenalin, dopamine, tryptophan and serotonin that can act as neurotransmitters. Adrenalin is contained in a major, well-known drug used for asthma and other allergy treatments (generally in spray form) because it dilates the airway (bronchodilation) permitting easier breathing. It is also used in emergency treatment of allergy shock (such as that caused by bee stings) and is a powerful stimulant to the heart in emergency treatment of cardiac arrest.

The biogenic amine theory states that these substances, when acting as neurotransmitters, have important effects on emotion, states of consciousness, responses to stress and related behaviors. But they may act abnormally in certain psychiatric illnesses. In particular, the increased activity of noradrenalin in the brain has been suggested as a cause for mania while decreased activity of this neurotransmitter has been suggested as a cause of endogenous depression. Overactivity of dopamine has been suggested as contributing to schizophrenia and hyperactivity in children.

According to the biogenic amine theory, the activity of anti-depressant and anti-psychotic drugs seems best explained by their ability to increase, or to block, the actions of these amines in the brain.

But one should not be overly seduced by biological theories of depression as the prime hope for the future. For the moderately-depressed and anxious patient, such simple treatments as change to a pleasanter environment, contact with loving, caring people, social counselling leading to better management of personal affairs and involvement in new and rewarding activities, work wonders. Team counselling including psychiatrists, nurses, social workers and other professionals is expanding and changing. Preventive psychiatry in the form of social facilities, sports activities, better working environments and "amateur" or "volunteer" crisis centres also have an ever-growing role, providing a less obvious but very real hope for the future.

In 1973, depression accounted for six per cent of patient hospital days in Canada, making it the fifth largest reason for hospital admission (the third largest in the 15-65 year group). Many other depressions go unrecognized because the patient does not seek help — often because of innate societal prejudice, oftimes manifest in the phrase "lack of moral fibre".

Depression is a real illness and it is pandemic. The direct cost to the health care system, as well as the immense social cost, make it a major focus for research. The director of the United States National Institute of Mental Health, Dr. Bertram S. Brown, says three million Americans will seek help from a mental health professional annually to the end of the decade — assuming current episode rates remain constant. United Kingdom and Western European figures emphasize the point, although there are differences between the various countries.

Although biochemical and biomolecular research are exciting leads for the future, there still is a major role to be played by families and communities and by mental health workers other than physicians and psychiatrists. Depression will always be with us, but in future more cures will be effected in severe depressions, while many other types will be shortened due to newer treatments. The majority of sufferers — those with self-limiting reactive depressions — probably have the least to gain from chemical research, but new programs of short-term psychotherapy are helping them, too, to adjust more quickly and effectively to these painful episodes.

BOREDOM—NEW DISEASE OF THE TECHNETRONIC ERA

Helen Colton

Helen Colton is a writer and the director of Family Forum, family-relations consultants in Los Angeles. She is the author of Beyond the Sexual Revolution.

In the 1020s, Dr. René Spitz, in a study that is a classic in child-rearing annals, found that infants at a New York hospital, who were well fed and kept in sterile conditions, suffered a higher death rate than infants kept in far less sanitary conditions in a Mexican orphanage. The difference, Spitz learned, lay in the fact that the New York infants were left alone a great deal, while the Mexican infants were fondled, caressed, and played with by women from the village. Deprived of stimulation of their senses, the New York babies suffered an infant disease known as marasmus—a Greek word meaning "wasting away."

They were, in fact, suffering the infant version of a rapidly spreading social disease known as boredom. Increasing numbers of us, like the infants, deprived of the variety of constantly changing stimuli we desperately need in order to achieve feelings of mental and physical well-being, are experiencing an adult form of marasmus—a kind of wasting away of the psyche—manifested in apathy, hopelessness, despair, passivity, depression, and sadness.

I call boredom a social disease because it has serious social consequences. Social scientists believe it is the root cause of a good deal of drug addiction, juvenile delinquency, vandalism, and other acts of crime and violence. Youthful gangs hanging around on corners looking for something to do to relieve the pain of monotony are prone to roam the streets attacking hapless victims or breaking into buildings and wrecking equipment, as much for the excitement of feeling the adrenalin flowing and the heart racing as for the small gain from stealing a purse or wallet. Dr. Roger J. Williams, in his book *You Are Extraordinary,* said, "Many of the activities of the juvenile delinquent seem to stem from boredom, from a desire for stimulation." Erich Fromm, calling boredom "the illness of the age," wrote, "There are good reasons to assume that the increase in boredom is one of the factors responsible for the increase in aggression." Any one of us is a potential victim of another's boredom.

Just as society is becoming aware of a new physical impairment, jet lag, resulting from bodily dissonances as we rapidly go through different time zones, we need to recognize that boredom should now be added to the lexicon of human ailments resulting from the mechanization of industrial progress. As such, boredom should be given serious study as a neurological disease that will proliferate as we go ever more deeply into the unstructured timestyles of the leisured or underemployed life in this technetronic age.

Because it has not been acknowledged as a disease, boredom has not yet been the subject of much scientific investigation. A pioneering study, "The Pathology of Boredom" (*Scientific American,* January 1957), was made in the 1950s by psychologists at McGill University. Subjects lay on comfortable beds in lighted cubicles twenty-four hours a day. They wore cotton gloves and cardboard cuffs extending beyond their fingertips, which restricted their perception of touch; translucent plastic visors transmitted diffused light but prevented pattern vision, thus restricting their visual perception; and they lay with their heads on U-shaped foam pillows, which limited auditory perception. The results showed that in a remarkably short time—only a matter of hours for some subjects—they were unable to think clearly about anything for any length of time; their thoughts became disjointed and incoherent.

This and other studies have indicated that normal functioning of the brain depends on continuing arousal reaction generated in the reticular formation of the brain, which in turn depends on ever changing sensory bombardment. Deprived of a variety of stimuli, a person's reaction time, sensory acuity, power of abstract reasoning, verbal ability, spatial and visual perception, and desire to take actions decrease. Brain-wave patterns change; many research subjects have reported LSD-like hallucinations. In some, monotony quickly produced emotional disturbances verging on the violent. One can understand the housewife, who spends much time in monotonous, repetitive menial tasks, suddenly going berserk and screaming, "I can't stand these four walls." Or why assembly-line workers performing the same task over and over develop a constant "free-floating hostility," according to Dr. Estelle Ramey, biophysicist at Georgetown School of Medicine.

This article first appeared in *The Humanist,* November/December 1975 and is reprinted by permission.

6. DYNAMICS OF MALADJUSTMENT

The origins of boredom, I believe, lie in both our anthropology and our culture. Physical and mental passivity is the breeding ground for boredom. Anthropologically we are habituated and conditioned into passivity in our first months of life by the helplessness of infancy.

Imagine yourself an infant. You are hungry, but you are physically powerless to get food for yourself. You are wet and cold, but you are physically powerless to get warmth and dryness for yourself. You may feel the sharp pain of a pin sticking into your skin, but you are physically powerless to remove it. You may be too warm from too many clothes or blankets, or your skin may be pinched from the binding of a too-tight bonnet-ribbon under your chin, or you may be chafed from the binding of a diaper around your thighs or the itch of a sweater around your neck.

You are physically powerless to do anything about any of these discomforts. You are forced to wait, a helpless victim, for someone in your environment to come along and ease the pain of hunger or the sensory discomfort of cold, wetness, heat, pinching, chafing. It is during these early experiences that we are conditioned in our responses to life. We are thus strongly habituated into waiting for some larger figure—an authority figure—to come along and relieve our distress.

It does not take many such experiences for us to be conditioned to spontaneously react throughout our lives, out of our autonomic nervous systems, as though we were still powerless infants. And so the conditions for boredom—waiting for some outside force or agency to *act upon us* rather than our acting upon the environment—are set up.

As we get older, our powerlessness is no longer factual, because we now have physical skills to help ourselves to do something about a stressful situation, to initiate changes, which we did not have as an infant or small child. Now we have mental skills, reasoning ability, and knowledge, or the ability to get the knowledge that we need to affect the situation. Now we have verbal skills with which to express our discomfort or distress and to ask for what we want in life. But many of us go through life acting out our infant helplessness by taking the very real fact of our physical powerlessness in infancy and converting it into the imagined fact of our psychological powerlessness in adulthood.

Nature, in the area of prolonged human-infant helplessness, as in other areas, has designed badly, I think. Why could not Nature have made us mobile and thus more self-sufficient at birth—do*ers* rather than do*ees*—just as the colt can run, the duck can swim, and the bird can fly, soon after emerging from their places of gestation. Thus, we could not so easily have been habituated to passivity.

Compounding this anthropological conditioning, we are further acculturated to boredom by the mechanization of our push-button lives. It becomes ever easier to sit back and be acted upon by the appurtenances of affluence, to be spectators rather than participants, to be sitters and not walkers, to exercise our fingers but not our minds or bodies. As input into our nervous systems becomes less energetic, more repetitive and monotonous, output becomes equally so. In the words of Dr. Ramey: "Nothing in, nothing out is apparently the credo of the human nervous system."

Moreover, our educational system, which demands that we sit in classrooms for many tedious years reading dull, jargon-filled textbooks, when our physiology cries out to be in motion, to be active and energetic and to experience sensorily, so benumbs our creativity and curiosity—with which we are all born—that it further reinforces our conditioning to be passive and bored.

Still another cultural conditioning has come from our potent touch taboo, deriving from religion and puritanism, which has given sexual and salacious meaning to casual touch, thereby starving our senses even more. Individuals and groups within the human-potential movement who run sensory seminars, practice massage on each other, and otherwise free up their sensory selves are still looked upon derisively by most of society as "far out," "bizarre," "licentious," or "touchy-feelies."

So what can we do about this modern malaise called boredom? It will take a cultural and economic revolution to initiate and carry out therapeutic change. For a start I see the need to change our childrearing and educational philosophies so that the earliest input into our nervous systems encourages and gives permission to experience sensorily, to explore life with as few constraints for safety's sake as possible. This means, for example, fewer or no playpens (which are, in fact, *anti*play pens) in which to imprison exploring bodies and minds of small children, and fewer expensive possessions in our homes to inhibit exploring youngsters. (Already, good sensory conditioning means less spending of money. You can guess how the profit motivationers will react to that!) Preparation for parenthood will teach us that it is an antisocial act to become a parent unless we are willing to put in the tremendous time and effort of providing enriched sensory conditioning for children during their early years.

Our educational philosophy would call for students at every level, beginning with nursery school, to be taught almost entirely out of the classroom and in the community, with students physically doing, wherever appropriate, whatever they are learning about, in order to have the experience recorded on their autonomic nervous systems as part of their sensory input. This is already happening experimentally in the community of State College, Pennsylvania.

Finally, we need to have an entirely new cultural value in which it is desirable to be sensory humans. To do this, we need to accept and laud the ism of hedonism—the doctrine that the ethical goal of life is to bring about the maximum pleasure and happiness for all. It is significant that one medical term for lack of sensory stimulation is *anhedonia*, derived from the word *hedonism*. I would like to make it clear, as I often do, that I am talking about reciprocal or cooperative hedonism. Accepting reciprocal hedonism as an ethic, we would become comfortable with the enrichment of our senses in any and all ways possible: touching and hugging, even of those we know casually; having nude beaches everywhere so we can feel the delicious sensation of the sun on our bare bodies; having rooms in large office buildings for sensory breaks in which one can move to rhythm, an atavistic need of the human organism related to the fact that we originated in the sea eons ago and moved to the rhythm of the tides, caressing each other's faces as hello and goodbye gestures. I find the possibilities of living in a world of sensory humans to be enchanting.

But enriching our senses is only part of polishing up our psyches. To make the whole process as joyful as it can be, we need also to have a purpose, a life theme, to what we are about. Dr. William Menninger once wrote his prescription for the good life: "Find a mission in life and take it seriously." That is the crux of our malaise: few of us have a mission to make us feel that our lives have purpose, that someone out there—perhaps lots of someones—cares that we exist.

For the past dozen years my own mission has been to bring sex education to America's parents and thus to change how they give sex education to their children. At present my "sub" mission, part of that larger campaign, is to get parents to be comfortable about masturbation, by their children and also by themselves, and to accept young people's having sex in their own room at home, rather than having to sneak it when parents are out, or having to scout around for homes of friends whose parents are at work or away (as so many teen-agers are doing today).

It is always with delight that I read of people who have missionary zeal about something. Mildred Dickinson, of River Bend, Illinois, who is in her late seventies, has an entrancing mission: creating dances for people who are confined to wheelchairs. I can just see people wheeling, whirling, to-and-fro-ing, back-and-forthing, grapevining, and do-si-do-ing in their wheelchairs. Ned Coll, a humanist in his mid-thirties, has a mission: organizing landings by boat, bus, ladder, and once even by parachute, of minority people, mostly women and children, on private beaches to protest laws that give private individuals legal rights to what should be publicly owned beachfront.

Bernice Lewis of Maryland has a really fun mission: creating new words that more aptly describe our behavior and feelings than existing words do, such as *infernalize*, to boil and seethe inside. A short piece she wrote for the *National Observer* (May 10, 1975) has inspired a delicious dictionary of new words subsequently sent in by readers of that newspaper. To quote a few of the etymological delights: *musicaphony,* sound emitted by a rock band; *excraminating,* the act of cramming for an exam; *multiguous,* ambiguous, only more so—having many different feelings and ideas on a subject; *dietribe,* an entire family watching its calories; *senadent,* a senator who aspires to be president; *shownanigans,* shocking statements or bizarre behavior by publicity-seeking persons; *sexclusive,* sex chauvinism; *obsexed,* obsessed with sex. I would like to add the word *timestyles,* to describe people's patterns of structuring their time.

I adore people whose mission in life is to keep reminding us that the emperor is, indeed, naked; such as the Iowa clergyman who reminded the political emperors in his state legislature of their nakedness with this satirical opening prayer one morning: "We pray that You spare the legislators from the embarrassment of being victimized by unscrupulous lobbyists who would like to wine and dine them beyond the stipulated amount."

If I had the time, there are several missions I would mount national campaigns for: periodic vacations for poverty-level mothers, in which the whole community is involved in child-sitting while these overworked, harassed women get off to a camp or hotel where they, for a change, are served and waited on and get some much-needed nurturing. I would gladly volunteer, as I know many others would, to wait on tables for such "Mommy vacations." A variation of this would be vacations for poverty-level couples, who rarely if ever experience the pleasure of a weekend by themselves away from the children, which many of the more affluent so casually take for granted. Still another mission would be to have longer-lived persons (the phrase "senior citizen" has a negative connotation in our culture) live permanently in college dorms with students. All my missions are on behalf of bettering family life and rapport between the generations. Obviously I am *sympecunious,* in sympathy with the poverty-stricken and the stroke-deprived, to quote another word sent to the *National Observer.*

If I had no mission, but were seeking one, I would start by asking myself this question: "What do I feel either very loving or very hating about?" Something I loved I'd try to interest other people in loving too. Something I hated, I would try to get others to join me in hating and taking action against. The value in having a mission is, for me, summed up in these poetic words in Ignazio Silone's novel *Bread and Wine*: "In all times, in all societies, the supreme act is to give oneself to find oneself. One has only what one gives."

Ultimately, I believe, the boredom so endemic in our technetronic age could help elevate us to the next higher phase of evolution. Irving Laucks, a scientist/philosopher associated with the Center for the Study of Democratic Institutions, says we are in transition from the second to the third major phase of evolution. The three phases, as he describes them, are: primitive human, acquiring human, and cooperative human. Scientist Jonas Salk has said much the same thing: "Mankind is in the midst of a transition from an epoch of competition to an epoch of cooperation."

It has been predicted that, by the year 2000, 2 percent of the population will be producing 100 percent of the goods and food we need. As more people rebel against the dehumanization and mechanization of living in such a society, a major way, perhaps even *the* major way, in which we will achieve a higher quality of life—which really means having more good feelings about ourselves—is to be socially contributive. Avoiding the terrible pain of boredom, we may well find ourselves becoming the cooperative human of the future, our good feelings about ourselves deriving mostly from what we do for others. I believe altruism is an innate trait in human personality; physiologically and sensorily we have peak feelings of well-being when we have done something for others and like ourselves for it.

Meanwhile, we will have to wait for the age of the cooperative human, and for the happy day when you and I can comfortably be sensory humans who can caress each other's faces in greeting without being called dirty old men and women.

Naturalist Louis Agassiz was once asked how he was going to spend his summer. "Crawling across the backyard on my stomach and observing insect life, blades of grass, the pebbles, and the earth," he replied. "And what will you do for the rest of the summer?" his questioner continued. "Why, it will take me the whole summer to get halfway across the yard," Agassiz exclaimed.

And so my prescription for the social disease of boredom is this: Let's start crawling on our stomachs through the garden of life. Get excited about something—about anything: sex; touching and being touched; bringing new information to someone who needs it; nurturing someone hungering for it; saying "I love you" to one who would like to hear it and to whom you have not said it for a long time; exploring inward to learn what your "script of life" is; fantasizing about how you would be spending your day if you were already living in the time of cooperative humans.

As Hugh Prather suggests in his little book *Notes to Myself,* "boredom acts as an initiator of originality by pushing me into new activities or new thoughts."

Prisoners of Fear

August Gribbin

We start with a state of terror.... At times [it] remains diffused... in intensity running the whole scale from vague anxiety to intensest feel of impending death.... The agonized mind stands balked of any explanation whatever.... The bottom is knocked out of all security, as when in an earthquake chasms suddenly open all about.... And so friendly counselors ask, 'What is there to be afraid of?'—and add to the grievous burden of laughter.

—A phobia victim's statement from Varieties of Psychopathological Experience.

It was a golden autumn day in a Washington, D.C., suburb. A mother in her 30s sat in her magazine-modern kitchen in her magazine-modern house, sipping Sanka and relating how her life had turned to dross, her future grotesque. She was telling how, until some months before, she had been possessed by phobia—one of the most bizarre of all maladies. Her words:

"Suddenly some horrible thing happened inside me, and I had to change my whole life. I had been really active in social, synogogue, and civic affairs. I was always going out. But after the change the very worst thing I could think of was having to leave the house. The idea *panicked* me.

"At those times I felt that something was oppressing me and that the air was being sucked from my lungs. It terrified me. My eyes watered. My hands grew clammy. I felt physically weak and nauseous. I was helpless, inept, and *trapped*. I cried. Finally I resolved I'd never go out again."

It took all her courage to break that resolution, to defy the subconscious emotional forces that were warping her existence and her family's. Now Phyllis—a pseudonym—says she is cured.

Phyllis' story is not as unusual as it might seem, because phobias and the incapacitating fear they bring are not as rare as most people might think. In fact, specialists say that phobias are inhabiting an increasing number of people and that they're sometimes exorcised in ways that are ineffectual or dangerous. To Phyllis, any information is important if if helps unaffected people realize that phobics aren't kooks when they cringe at dogs, blood, or crowds; when they trudge up and down several flights of stairs because they fear elevators; or when they ride trains because airplanes terrify them.

Phyllis' case is almost classic. She's a woman, and more women than men have phobias. She had agoraphobia, or fear of open spaces, and that's the most common phobia. And her phobic symptoms matched those most cited by behaviorists.

The American Psychological Association's diagnostic manual defines phobia as "a condition characterized by intense fear of an object or situation which the patient consciously recognizes as no real danger. His apprehension may be experienced as fantasies, fatigue, palpitations, perspiration, nausea, tremor, and even panic. Phobia is generally attributed to fears displaced to the phobic object or situation from some other object of which the patient is unconscious. A wide range of phobias has been described."

Some 180 disorders, cloaked in Greek or Latin medical terms, compose an ancient cadre of phobias. Among them are acrophobia (fear of heights), anthropophobia (of people), claustrophobia (of closed spaces), mysophobia (of dirt, germs, or contamination of mind or body), and numerophobia (of a particular number or numbers).

Other phobias have been more recently described. School phobia is a fairly common reason why some kids skip school. Shyness is considered a phobia. So are intense fears of noise, of sleep (or, more precisely, of nightmares), of speaking before groups, of taking tests, and the more exotic fears of not urinating or of using public rest rooms. Other phobias are even more bizarre. A highly competitive college professor, for example, suffered from a "back" or "buttocks" phobia; he writhed internally when he thought anyone, including students in class, was watching him from behind.

The Quest for Help

Phyllis began her ordeal one Sunday 2 1/2 years ago while dining at her uncle's. Without warning she felt nauseous. She relates: "I got up from the dinner table, went to the couch, and started crying, saying I was going to faint. I did. Everyone was alarmed; the rescue squad came, but I wouldn't go to the hospital, and that night I was okay."

Next day, in the course of an exercise class, the "anxiety attack" struck again. Again she experienced oppressive terror. She fled the class. The following night, while riding with a friend to a mahjong game, she had another attack. "The spells kept creeping up on me and I dreaded having people notice me in this state," she explains.

Finally she began a long round of visits

to physicians. She took numerous brain tests, "hoping they'd find something to explain what was happening," she says. Then a gynecologist told her she should see a psychiatrist.

By now she had to sedate herself before venturing outside. At that she went out only when necessary, and preferably with her husband. She was so determined to avoid stirring from home that, she says, "I accepted the fact I might never take my three children to movies or anywhere again."

Sleep-Wrecking Nightmares

During psychotherapy Phyllis fought the doctor's insistence that she force herself to leave the house. Nonetheless, she tried. She recalls: "I'd drive to the nearby supermarket, force myself out of the car, take a few steps, and leap back in. Then I'd start over again."

She also goaded herself to go to restaurants with her husband. But she refused to enter until he had obtained the table nearest the exit so she could escape quickly if her discomfort became unendurable. All the while she routinely had sleep-wrecking nightmares about having to leave the house.

Phyllis confides that she thinks her problems started in childhood. "I was a good little girl, always did what my parents expected, accepted what they said, and didn't think for myself. I was taught to wear a uniform that didn't fit—I didn't develop into *me*. I built a life-style around doing what others wanted. And I thought I was very, very happy, although I unconsciously harbored unresolved feelings about my compliance.

"Well, I'm much happier now that I no longer do what people wish unless I want to do it. I'm no longer trapped by conflicting feelings. I no longer automatically do everything connected with the kids and the house. Now my husband and I talk things over, share chores, and as a result I think our marriage is better. We're closer."

Overprotected as Children

The personality that therapy revealed to Phyllis closely resembles the typical phobic as characterized by psychologist Barry Wolfe of the National Institute of Mental Health (NIMH). He reports that phobics' parents characteristically overprotected them.

Consequently, he says, phobics tend to be dependent, submissive, and passive. They shy from difficult situations and risks, and normally experience conflict over being aggressive and independent.

Still, phobics needn't appear outwardly meek and hapless. They're often efficient and competent people and hold down important jobs. Many famous persons were phobic. Darwin was terrorized by social gatherings; Freud, by riding trains. But theory has it that continual phobia is the price such untreated persons pay for the conflict their assertiveness or other unresolved, opposing feelings cause them.

No one really knows how many phobia victims there are. The common guess: millions. Whatever the number, some behaviorists insist the phobias are becoming commoner, if only because unprecedented numbers of women are experiencing serious internal conflict in trying to adopt to women's liberationist standards that value the self-reliant, adventurous, and independent woman more than the compliant one.

One Form of Therapy

Partly as a result, there has been increased attention to finding phobia cures. Phyllis received traditional psychotherapy based on the predominant "developmental" psychological theory. Psychologist Allan M. Leventhal, director of the Counseling Center at American University, in Washington, D.C., explains such treatment:

"It involves weekly or twice-weekly talk sessions between therapist and patient. Both try to ferret out the basis of the current problem, which presumably originated in childhood. They work through [talk about and relive] the emotions created by the past incidents or situations and try to achieve insight into the true nature of the problem. This clears the way for behavioral change. Then, because the patient develops a dependency on the therapist during treatment, the dependency—called 'transference'—has to be eliminated. The course of therapy takes time—usually years."

Leventhal is one of a growing number of therapists who lament the time such therapy takes and now incorporate into their practices faster treatments based on behavioral theory, or behavioral modification. He's utilizing an increasingly common technique called "systematic desensitization" (SD). Although he says that the treatment may be based on "errant theory" and it treats symptoms rather than root causes, he adds, "It works well, and that's the proof of the pudding."

He explains that SD requires discovering in exact detail the client's phobia, (Behavior-modification therapists call patients "clients," not patients.) In two or three sessions the therapist teaches the client to locate, tense, and relax muscle groups until at will he can relax completely.

Then the therapist creates for the individual client a series of 10 to 15 "scenes" depicting the feared object or situation. The therapist arranges them in a sequential "anxiety hierarchy," ranging from least to most terror-producing.

In a typical treatment, the therapist describes the scenes so the client can imagine them. More rarely they're taped or depicted graphically. The person who fears crowds, for example, might be confronted in imagination with a hardly discernible group in the distance. And in separate, subsequent scenes, the crowd might be depicted as becoming larger, advancing toward the client, and, in the last scene, engulfing him.

During each scene confrontation the client attempts to relax physically. He continues to confront the scene until he can do so without anxiety. He then moves on to confront the next scenario.

The treatment, including maybe 15 or 20 therapy sessions, takes weeks instead of years.

Leventhal says he has a "good" success rate with the method, as do others. Cure rates as high as 85 per cent aren't uncommon in medical literature, although they've been challenged. Yet Leventhal sees flaws in the method. He says it takes almost too much therapist time to plan and assess treatment sessions. Besides, he says: "Although in some cases I can see the logic of applying behavioral theory and can predict it will work, in others I'm not clever enough to apply it even when I'd like to."

Most traditional therapists contend that treating symptoms can't work completely and that if the behaviorist clears up one phobia, "another will pop out some other time," as one psychiatrist puts it. Still other therapists warn that since phobias are, in effect, a patient's *defense* against conflict, removing that defense without quieting the root conflict exposes him to the threat of total personality disintegration.

Leventhal, in reply, says he rarely sees recurrent symptoms, yet he sees clients a year after treatment stops just to ascertain if they have been cured. He contends that if symptoms return after more than a year, the therapist can't tell whether the therapy failed or the client's phobia is a new one fostered by fresh traumas.

'No Psychotherapy Is Perfect'

Hans Strupp, chairman of Vanderbilt University's psychology department and of the American Psychological Association's clinical division, comments: "No psychotherapy is perfect. Yet we who are doing it are expected to cure something forever. That's not expected in medicine. If a physician treats and cures a strep infection, he isn't blamed if six months later the patient has another infection. My own view is that with phobias we're not dealing with meaningless or fortuitous symptoms; they're part and parcel of an individual, and treating symptoms is not doing anything about a person's basic problems.

"A colleague of mine was treating a person with behavior therapy. The client—a pianist—feared sitting at the piano. What the therapist came to see was that there were marital problems and that dealing with an isolated phobia wasn't doing much for the total person even though it might enable her to return to the piano. My point is that in certain limited ways and at certain times, desensitization can be effective, depending on the nature of the problem."

Strupp's view seems to prevail at the moment. As Wolfe of NIMH says: "The trend is for behavioral people to be more modest. They're revising extravagant claims of effectiveness. That's good, because we still really need to know what works on whom and under what situations."

Other Forms of Therapy

Wolfe points out that systematic desensitization is just one of a host of relatively recent therapies behavioral modification theory has engendered. Others include:

Implosion Therapy (IT). It's somewhat like systematic desensitization, but, says Wolfe: "In SD the assumption is that the client will gradually master his anxiety. In this therapy the client must master the fearful object. And at one sitting a person fearing insects, say, would be asked to imagine, in sequence, a horde of bugs coming toward him, crawling on him, beginning to devour him—horrible scenes, producing maximum reaction. The therapist encourages the client to continue imagining and being fearful until—from sheer exhaustion, presumably—the client no longer fears."

In Vivo Flooding: This method is similar to implosion, but instead of imagining the phobic situation or object, the client is actually placed in the feared situation and the therapist helps him confront it. There are obvious limits to its use. To illustrate: A young woman with an incapacitating dread of worms and snakes who had been ineffectively treated in psychoanalysis and by desensitization was placed in the presence of a snake and worms during six treatment sessions totaling 10 hours. She improved significantly, according to a report in the Journal of Behavior Therapy and Experimental Psychiatry.

Modeling. The treatment derives from social-learning theories, which in essence say that we learn much from watching others, especially others we respect. Thus in treatment the therapist might, for instance, handle a live snake in a snake-phobic client's presence and so demonstrate the inappropriateness of the victim's fears.

Paradoxical Intention. This therapy calls for having the anxious person intentionally generate as much anxiety and fear as he can when facing the thing terrorizing him. Wolfe says: "The result is that sometimes as the therapist encourages him to fear, the victim sees the humor or foolishness of his situation and his phobia and the fear drops out. This is tricky. The therapy carries an implied message of disrespect for the victim and may seem to mock him."

Cognitive Therapy. The method rests on the theory that the phobic disorder originates in the patient's habit of thought rather than in mood. Change the thoughts and the person changes, the theory goes. The therapist uses discussion and argument to bring about change.

Besides these methods, phobics are being treated with drugs and even by surgery at times. Hypnotherapy, once a fad, is staging a minor comeback—accompanied with the criticism that it's inherently ineffective because it makes passive, dependence-prone individuals unusually dependent on the therapist-hypnotist.

The list could go on. Clearly there's no panacea for phobia, simply a diversity of curative attempts. Yet some see the diversity itself as a hopeful sign. At the very least it illustrates the ingenuity of the human mind—just as phobias do.

NEW LIGHT ON SCHIZOPHRENIA

THE GENETIC LINK

Strong evidence
that this debilitating mental disease
can be inherited
is emerging from studies of the family.
Despite problems of identifying schizophrenia
its shadowy borders are being defined.

Ben Rose

Current research in many fields on schizophrenia has fostered a mood of optimism among scientists. The shrouds around the disease appear to be lifting, and on CBC radio last February, Dr. David Suzuki foresaw a test as simple as blood typing to detect a potential schizophrenic.

At a recent conference of psychopathologists, Dr. Seymour S. Kety, professor of psychiatry, Harvard Medical School, stated: "I have the feeling, which I have never had before, that we are beginning to see the light at the end of the tunnel. Never has the time been more propitious or progress more promising."

About 250 000 Canadians now suffer from schizophrenia; that is one in every 100, and they fill about half the mental hospital beds in the country.

The word itself is enough to start the old "nature or nurture" debate again. Is it a result of heredity, environment or a combination of both? Or is this disease with its shadowy borders really only a myth as some investigators have suggested?

"If schizophrenia is a myth, it is a myth with a substantial genetic component," responds Dr. Kety.

As Kety infers, geneticists in recent years have piled up impressive evidence that schizophrenia is heritable and to some extent they have mollified critics who charged bias in some of the earlier studies.

Even so, as the mode of inheritance transmission slowly becomes clearer, research on the biochemical side is sharpening the focus on how closely environmental factors are also linked to its development.

The disease itself is so hard to define that terms such as "schizophrenia spectrum" and "schizoid personalities" pop up in the literature to describe patients without true schizophrenia, but with symptoms that resemble it. The oft-heard description, "He's a schiz!" is about as revealing as "He's a cancer!" would be, according to Dr. W.O. McCormick, associate professor of psychiatry at the University of Toronto.

What is true schizophrenia then? Is it a case of two minds in one body, a split personality, as so many people believe? No, say scientists, it is a condition in which the patient loses touch with reality, hears voices, suffers delusions, and suffers a loss of the ability to relate the right emotion to the right action. In the movie, The Three Faces of Eve, the title chararter was *not* a schizophrenic, but a woman suffering from hysteria.

"Only a small minority of schizophrenics are ever violent and even these will respond to treatment," says Dr. McCormick. "They come quickly under control, and at our hospital no mechanical restraints are needed."

Some famous figures in history are thought to have been schizophrenic: Joan of Arc, with her voices and visions, is one, while Louis Riel has been so described by Dr. S.K. Littman of the Clarke Institute, Toronto.

Among the most persuasive genetic studies in the field are five dealing with twins, and in all of them concordance of schizophrenia was higher in identical twins than in the fraternal (non-identical) twins. For example, in one study where one of the identical twins developed the disease, it also developed in the other twin in about 45 percent of cases, while in non-identical twins the rate of concordance was only that of siblings in the general population — about 8 percent. (Incidentally, there is no higher incidence of schizophrenia in twins than in the general population.)

Strong evidence of hereditary factors comes from a study of 47 children of schizophrenic mothers, all of whom were placed in foster or adoptive homes at an early age. As they grew up, five of these children developed schizophrenia. But among 50 children of normal parents also adopted or fostered at an early age and matched with the others for sex, age and race, no cases of schizophrenia occurred. This research, directed by Dr. Leonard L. Heston, professor of psychiatry, University of Minnesota Medical School, also revealed that the group with schizophrenic mothers scored higher on every index of mental disorder. For example, 11 of this group eventually spent more than one year in a penal or psychiatric hospital, compared with only two in the control group.

Another pioneering study was that directed by Dr. Laurette Bender, onetime professor of psychiatry at Columbia University, New York. It compared the family history of 59 schizophrenic children observed at Bellevue Hospital from 1935 to 1952 with that of 50 nonschizophrenic children observed for other problems at the same time. The first group had 39 schizophrenic relatives, while the control

Reprinted from *SCIENCE FORUM Magazine*, May/June 1978, pp. 11-13 with the permission of the publisher.

group had none, and there were no correlations with socio-economic groups.

DANISH STUDY OF ADOPTED CHILDREN REVEALS TREND

One method of trying to separate hereditary and environmental factors is to study adopted children and their natural and adoptive families. This is the object of a remarkable continuing cross-Atlantic project and its reports have stimulated wide discussion. The team is headed by Dr. Kety and includes Dr. David Rosenthal and Dr. Paul H. Wender of the U.S. National Institute of Mental Health, and Dr. Fini Schulsinger and Dr. Bjorn Jacobsen of the Psychological Institute, Kommunehospitalet, Copenhagen.

Its aim is to compare mental illness in the natural and adoptive families of adopted children who are schizophrenic with that of relatives of a control group of adopted non-schizophrenic children.

Denmark was chosen because of the compactness of its population, its excellent adoption records and its Folkeregister, which permits one to trace a person's address, household, family and children.

The team took elaborate precautions to eliminate bias of any kind. Any reference that might indicate whether the relative was a natural or adoptive kin, or related to an index or control case was edited out of the transcripts. Each of the team worked "blind", unaware of the diagnosis of others.

The records of 5481 children adopted between 1924 and 1947 were examined and revealed that 507 of them were at one time or another admitted to a mental institution. Of this group, 33 who were diagnosed as schizophrenic were chosen as the "index" cases. A control group of 34 nonschizophrenic children was selected by matching the index cases for age, sex, length of time with the natural family and so on.

After two years and amazing patience, Dr. Jacobsen traced and interviewed 341 relatives (parents, siblings and half-siblings) from the natural and adoptive families of these children. He found them in Denmark, Norway and Sweden and they represented 94 per cent of the relatives who were alive, had not disappeared or become institutionalized and had not emigrated beyond Scandinavia. He encountered the usual number of uncooperative people but this tactful and persuasive Dane did not give up easily. In the end, only 23 refused to supply enough information, and they were randomly distributed.

Dr. Jacobsen's interviews with the relatives were exhaustive and included a 35-page questionnaire, check lists, narrative material, and covered the major aspects of the life experience: sociological, educational, marital, occupational and peer relationship history from birth, medical background, and a careful mental status examination.

In their desire to keep the research "clean," the team even asked Jacobsen to list the hunches he had about whether the person being interviewed was a relative of an index or control case. Even when these "hunch" cases were eliminated, the results stayed the same.

A diagnosis of schizophrenia was made in 13.9 percent of the natural relatives of the index cases, and only in 3.4 percent of the natural relatives of the controls, the non-schizophrenic children. A similar low percentage was found in both groups of adoptive relatives.

In a previous report based only on institutional records, they found 21 people in the schizophrenia spectrum, while in the larger study they found 67, a three-fold increase. This confirmed a previous indication that there is considerably more schizophrenia-related illness in the population than reaches the doors of psychiatric hospitals.

EVIDENCE OF ENVIRONMENTAL FACTORS

The actual mode of inheritance of the disease is not yet well established. Rather than being passed on by a single recessive or dominant gene, investigators believe there may be several genes involved. Says one geneticist of this "polygenic model": "It's a complicated picture, something like diabetes."

The spurt in genetic research has served to increase interest in environmental factors, as the best studies in twins and adoptees show that the disease needs a trigger of some kind, one that is thought to be rooted in the environment (which, of course, includes the schizophrenic's family).

One indication in this environmental research is that poverty very likely does not produce the disease. After a series of studies in downtown and suburban areas of Detroit, one team reported that it is schizophrenia that results in an individual's social class rather than the other way around. "Environmental influences are nothing so simple and obvious as membership in a particular culture, subculture, or social class," reported Dr. E. Warren Dunham, professor of psychiatry at State University of New York in Stony Brook, N.Y.

The family of the schizophrenic continues to be the key area of research into the disease, both for its effect on the patient, and vice versa. One recent study proposes that the way to prevent relapse is to keep the patient on maintenance doses of phenothiazines while at the same time drastically reducing the face-to-face contact between the patient and relative, if the relative interacts with a high degree of expressed emotion.

The nine-month relapse rate in a group of 125 patients was only 12 percent if the patient stayed on drugs and had contact with a relative who interacted with little overt emotion. On the other hand, it rose to 55 percent if the drugs continued, but the patient had more than 35 hours a week contact with a highly emotional relative. In this last group, when the patients were not on drugs, the relapse rate zoomed to 92 percent.

The new genetic studies have built a stronger base on which to counsel couples on the possibility of their children being affected by the disease.

"It's very rare for a couple to come to a genetic counsellor about schizophrenia, but we should give the facts to anyone who asks," says Dr. McCormick, who is also director of psychiatric education at the Queen St. Mental Health Centre in Toronto.

According to Dr. Heston, physicians who are confronted with the question, explicit or implicit, from the family of a schizophrenic patient, "What did we do wrong?" should answer "Nothing that medical science can yet identify."

A normal individual with a schizophrenic parent or sibling, married to a normal person with a nonschizophrenic pedigree will almost certainly produce a normal child, says University of Minnesota's Leonard Heston, the risk not being significantly greater than in the normal population. But for two people with schizophrenic pedigrees, the risk is significantly greater, he added.

CHEMICAL ROOTS OF THE DISEASE

Research on the disease has now moved into an unexpected and exciting phase, with significant potential benefits to the public. Some of the excitement flows from the recent discovery that an excess of the chemical dopamine in the brain produces schizophrenic-like actions. A clue to this finding came from studies of amphetamine overdoses, which stimulate dopamine production and result in bizarre behavior.

If the genetic mechanism can be traced, it may be possible to identify persons with genetic predisposition to schizophrenia, affirming David Suzuki's prediction about a simple diagnostic test.

So, willy nilly, the geneticists and environmentalists are coming to sup at the same table, as guests of the biochemists. This could be a harbinger of more effective treatments for this crippling disease.

THE
BIOCHEMICAL BLUEPRINT

**Perception and behavior
are ultimately rooted in nerve cell chemistry
and biochemists are now discovering the nature
of the underlying chemical disorders
in mental disease.**

Joan Hollobon

Is the schizophrenic mind the result of disordered chemistry or of faulty emotional development early in life?

Abnormal brain chemistry does not in itself prove anything: brain chemistry could become abnormal *in reponse* to emotional stress. Emotions indeed express themselves biochemically: adrenalin secretion in response to anger, fear or other strong emotion is a well-documented stress response.

Until the new and exciting discoveries of the past three years, the search for abnormalities in brain structure or chemistry affecting perception and behavior were disappointing. Researchers reported pink spots and mauve spots in urine and abnormal chemicals in the blood of schizophrenic patients, only to have later researchers report that they were unable to duplicate the findings or show them to be a product of the research method.

Over the years there have been many theories advanced on the cause of schizophrenia: vitamin deficiency, slow viruses, allergies, autoimmune reactions, gluten in wheat, the hormone serotonin and a host of chemicals. All remained just that: theories. It was never possible to go that essential next step to show how these agents caused the brains of schizophrenic patients to see, hear and feel so realistically the unrealities of their delusions and hallucinations.

Despite disappointments, three research areas have kept scientists plowing on: genetic studies, transmission of nerve impulses, and psychoactive drugs. All have to do with biochemistry.

Genes write their blueprints of heredity in chemicals, so evidence of a genetic component is a strong indication of altered biochemistry. As to impulses carried from one nerve cell to another, recent research has· shown this to be largely through chemicals. Finally there is the demonstrable effect of psychoactive drugs in allaying psychotic behavior.

DRUGS THAT MODIFY THE MIND

If chemicals in drugs can affect behavior, they must do it by some effect on the brain cells that control emotions, perception, moods. That was the starting point for Dr. Philip Seeman of Toronto: how do the major tranquilizers affect the mind?

His research showed for the first time that they work by quite specifically inactivating what are called dopamine receptors. Dopamine, with other brain amines, had been suspect for some time, partly because certain patients given L-dopa to treat their Parkinson's disease developed psychotic symptoms similar to those of schizophrenia. And L-dopa is the substance from which the brain manufactures dopamine.

But while scientists had suspected dopamine metabolism might play some role, they did not know what that role was: Dr. Seeman's work was the first indication of a mechanism of action for psychoactive drugs.

Dopamine is one of several chemicals the brain uses to transmit "on-off" messages from cell to cell. One cell releases dopamine which the next cell "catches" in receptors specifically designed to recognize and bind dopamine molecules.

Dr. Seeman, in collaboration with U.S., Britist and Austrian scientists, subsequently showed that the brains of people who had suffered from schizophrenia contained too many dopamine receptors, particularly in regions governing emotional expression and modulating body motion.

Seeman postulated that too many receptors would make schizophrenics super-sensitive to their own dopamine, causing the flooding of hallucinations, delusions and tangential ideas so typical of the condition, as well as the clumsy physical movements often also seen.

This was the first hard, consistently reproducible evidence for an organic abnormality that could have a bearing on the development of this tragic disorder. Much work remains to be done, but it opens the way to possible chemical intervention based on understanding of the chemical processes involved, instead of relying on cook-book empirical observations that some drugs simply "work".

CHEMICAL TOXINS
AND MENTAL DISEASE

In mulling over the results of a Danish study on adopted children, Dr. James Cade, a University of Florida kidney specialist, wondered if the chemical abnormality in schizophrenia might be a missing enzyme that allows a build-up of a toxic chemical.

Many well-known inherited diseases, such as phenylketonuria, are caused by the lack of a catalyst that helps convert body chemicals to substances the body can eliminate.

Both Dr. Cade and Dr. Herbert Wagemaker of the University of Louisville found that putting schizophrenic patients on artificial kidney machines improved their mental states, the implication being that the machine cleared some harmful substance(s) from the body. But the treatments met skepticism and criticism. Harvard University's Dr. Seymour Kety was quoted by *Medical World News* as expressing doubt because no hard evidence exists of any circulating poison. More pilot studies are needed "to relieve Dr. Cade and Dr. Wagemaker of the criticism they may be victims of their own enthusiasm." Critics also noted that the experiment had not been double-blind (where doctors and patients do not know who is getting the real treatment and who is getting a similar sham treatment, thus eliminating the possible effect of expectations).

Discovery of endorphin and its breakdown products (enkephalins) within the past three years marks a dramatic advance in brain research, providing the most powerful clues yet to the physiological mechanisms of the emotions, pain and pleasure perception, drug addiction and, possibly, mental illness.

6. DYNAMICS OF MALADJUSTMENT

NARCOTICS RESEARCH PRODUCES SURPRISES

In other work involving the action of narcotic drugs, addiction researchers deduced the existence of specific opiate receptor sites in the brain, and more particularly, from the ability of narcotic antagonists to "switch off" the effects of narcotics. (A dose of the drug naloxone can rapidly reverse the effects of a narcotic, such as heroin or morphine).

As one scientist said, human beings are not born containing morphine, so the only explanation is that the brain contains its own opiate-like substances. The first clues from a California group that this might be so were followed up by scientists at the University of Aberdeen, Scotland, who identified just such a substance in December 1975. They called it "enkephalin" from the Greek, meaning "in the head".

Enkephalin is a short-chain peptide containing five amino acids. Subsequently, U.S. scientists found a longer chain peptide with morphine-like activity from which enkephalin is very likely derived. They called it "endorphin", meaning "morphine within".

These materials have powerful pain-relieving properties, and are short-lived due to rapid enzyme degradation. Those in the brain are found particularly in the area that regulates the emotions. Enkephalins also exist in the small intestine. Scientists do not know the exact function of endorphin (more specifically, beta-endorphin), produced by the pituitary gland, but they think it may play a role in regulating hormone secretion (morphine is known to affect the secretion of hormones).

Two well-known psychiatrists reported at an international symposium on endorphins last December in San Juan, Puerto Rico, that some of the depressed and schizophrenic patients to whom they administered beta-endorphin showed dramatic improvement. Patients whose major symptoms were anger or hostility failed to respond, however. The one normal control, Dr. Edward Laski, a psychiatrist at Albert Einstein School of Medicine, New York City, said he experienced a "spaced out, floating feeling," which went away after five hours as suddenly as "flipping an on-off switch".

The psychiatrists, Dr Nathan Kline of the Rockland Research Institute, Orange-burg, N.Y., and Dr Heinz Lehmann, professor and former head of psychiatry at McGill University, were criticized for raising public hopes without sound evidence. The experiment was uncontrolled, leading one critic to suggest the patients who did well may have simply responded to their own expectations. Negativistic, hostile people invariably resist this "placebo effect," the critics noted.

Indeed, these particular experiments prove little, but discovery of the new chemicals and their complex inter-relationships with hormones and other chemicals offers real hope for the future. Clarification of the chemical picture may even tie together many of the past theories that died aborning for lack of sufficient basic knowledge. For instance, a biochemist at the U.S. National Institute of Mental Health has detected a peptide in wheat gluten "that proves to be an enkephalin-like opioid."

Medical World News reported that Dr. Candace Pert, of the National Institute of Mental Health, "a founding mother of endorphin-enkephalin science," predicted that within 10 years there will be "at least one fantastic new drug for mental health acting by a totally new mechanism".

TRACKING THE CAUSES OF MADNESS

Why is schizophrenia four times as likely to strike a resident of
the West of Ireland as an American or a Japanese?
Why are people born in winter months more susceptible?
Worldwide studies of the incidence of disease
are turning up challenging new data.

E. Fuller Torrey

*E. Fuller Torrey is a clinical and research
psychiatrist in Washington, D.C. He is
the author and editor of six books. This
article is adapted from his* Schizophrenia
and Civilization, *to be published by
Jason Aronson.*

For a young man growing up in the
West of Ireland, the expectation that
he will be hospitalized for schizophrenia sometime during his lifetime
is one in 25. If he were growing up in
England, Germany, Japan, or the
United States, his chance of hospitalization would be about one in
100, only one-fourth the Irish rate.
This difference illustrates some
dramatic new findings in schizophrenia research that may help point the
way toward unraveling the causes of
this disease.

For years, the schizophrenia hospitalization statistics in Ireland were
dismissed as artificial. Some researchers said the Irish were just calling
more people schizophrenic. Others
speculated that schizophrenic individuals were hospitalized more readily there. In Ireland, many believed
that the healthier people migrated to
America and left the sick behind—a
theory put to rest when a high schizophrenia rate was found among Irish
immigrants in America. Thanks to
extensive epidemiological studies by
English and Irish mental-health professionals led by Dermot Walsh and
Aileen O'Hare of the Medico-Social

Research Board in Dublin, the other
simple explanations are now known
to be inadequate as well. Ireland,
especially the West of Ireland, really
does have a very high rate of schizophrenia and this has probably been
true for at least 100 years.

It is not only the professionals who
are aware of the prevalence of schizophrenia in the West of Ireland. Conversations with many people there,
most recently in August of 1978, convinced me that the man in the street
also knows of the problem. A bartender in the picturesque village of
Ballyvaughn, County Clare, made it
quite clear: "Oh, yes," he said. "That
madness is a big problem here, all
right. Last winter some of the boys
here were sitting around the fire dis-
cussing it, and counting all the folks
who have had to go down to the county asylum. It's a bad problem, all
right, and the boys figure it's getting
worse." When asked what "the boys"
think causes it, the bartender said
they blamed everything from the
weather to alcohol intake; as among
professionals, there was a clear consensus on the problem, but not on its
causes.

The "madness" to which the bartender referred is mostly schizophrenia, a term undoubtedly covering several diseases of brain dysfunction.
The predominant symptoms are disorders of perception (the person may
hear voices, or smell poison gas in his
room), disorders of emotion (the person may laugh or cry completely in-
appropriately), and disorders of think-

ing, such as loose associations and delusions (the person may pick up a
rubber band and tell you that it is a
musical instrument because it is a
"band"—that in turn may remind
him of the instruments used in the
hospital emergency room where the
FBI planted electrodes in his brain).
True schizophrenia usually begins in
the late teens or 20s and runs a variable course: some people have only a
single attack; some have recurrent attacks; others stay continuously sick.

Schizophrenics all over the world
show these symptoms, and look remarkably alike. Although the content
of their delusions may differ (the
paranoid schizophrenic in Ireland
may feel persecuted by the IRA rather
than the CIA), their shape is basically
the same. In the United States, unfortunately, the term "schizophrenia" is
used more broadly and often impre-
cisely. Schizophrenia is not, for
example, a "split personality" like
that of the main character in *Sybil* or
The Three Faces of Eve; these are examples of a rare psychiatric condition
called a dissociative reaction.

The treatment for schizophrenia all
over the world is antipsychotic drugs
whose effectiveness ranges from
complete to nonexistent. In the
United States, many psychiatrists
still treat schizophrenia with psychotherapy and psychoanalysis, although
those treatments have been largely
discredited in the rest of the world.

As a *disease*, rather than a psychiatric catchall term, schizophrenia
would be strange indeed if it did not

show marked geographical differences. Virtually every major disease known, including diabetes, the cancers, hypertension, and heart disease, has variations in prevalence in different areas and among different groups.

But the fact that schizophrenia varies in frequency around the world conflicts with what virtually all mental-health professionals have been taught; textbooks of psychiatry and psychology all say that schizophrenia is found everywhere in the world in about the same prevalence. It is now known that this teaching was not based on any research, but rather was simply an early impression passed on from textbook to textbook. All the recent research refutes it.

In addition to the West of Ireland, there are other areas of the world where schizophrenia seems to be especially common. The Istrian Peninsula on the northwestern coast of Yugoslavia is one of them; 10 years of research by a team from Zagreb and Baltimore have confirmed that schizophrenia is about three times more common there than it is in the rest of Yugoslavia. As in Ireland, local lore suggests that the high prevalence dates back at least 100 years.

Another very high prevalence area is a small part of northern Sweden where a team of researchers has studied the problem during a 26-year period. There are also suggestions that parts of Eastern Europe, especially Poland and the Ukraine, may have an abundance of schizophrenia, but it is unlikely that their regimes will permit that to be confirmed.

Much less work on regional variations of prevalence has been done in the United States. In 1903, psychiatrist William A. White, in "The Geographical Distribution of Insanity in the United States," concluded: "We are at once confronted with a condition of affairs which is so well marked that when I first saw it I was very much surprised. The greatest proportion of insanity is in the Northeast, in the New England and middle states, of which New Hampshire, Vermont, Massachusetts, Connecticut, and New York all have one insane person to less than 400 of the population. If from this center of greatest prevalence of insanity we draw a line in any direction—west, south, or southwest—we see that no

matter which way we go we find a steady decrease until we strike the Pacific slope."

Psychiatric-hospital admission statistics since White's time tend to bear out his impressions. For example, between 1922 and 1960, the average schizophrenia first-admission rate in Massachusetts, Connecticut, and New York was two and a half times the rate for Kansas, Idaho, and South Dakota; some people in the Northeast still refer to schizophrenia as the "New England disease." But systematic prevalence surveys are needed to back up the hospital figures.

"Causes of schizophrenia might include toxins, viruses, or nutritional deficiencies—all could be linked to geography."

On the other end of the prevalence spectrum, there are areas of the world where schizophrenia appears to be distinctly uncommon. Many impressions to this effect can be found in psychiatric and anthropological literature on rural and developing nations, especially tropical ones; but vast methodological problems have precluded definitive studies. The best research project on this question was done 25 years ago by Tsung-yi Lin and Hsien Rin on Taiwan. They found a relatively low rate of schizophrenia among Chinese immigrants to Taiwan, and a rate half again lower among the aboriginal Formosans who live in rural mountain villages. Less precise studies of Papua New Guinea and several African countries have also reported very low prevalence rates, even taking into account such possibilities as patients' being hidden in the villages or not surviving.

Anthropologist and psychologist Meyer Fortes reported a particularly interesting finding. From 1934 to 1937, he studied intensively the Tallensi people in northern Ghana and found only one schizophrenic in a population of approximately 5,000. In a population that size in Europe or the

United States, one would expect to find 10 to 25 schizophrenics. In 1963, Fortes returned to the area with his wife, who is a psychiatrist. In the same villages where 27 years earlier there had been a single schizophrenic, there were now 13. The research team was convinced that the dramatic rise in schizophrenia in the 27-year period was real, and that it could not be explained by population growth: "What was quite startling, from my point of view," wrote Fortes, "is that several of these cases occurred in families which were specially well known to me in 1934-37 and which were basically the same in structure in 1963 as in the early period. I knew some of the patients as young wives or youths or children. These were the families of my best friends and informants, some of whom are still living. Had such cases occurred among them in 1934-37 I could not have missed them."

In India, six separate studies since 1930 have all found a higher prevalence of schizophrenia among members of the most highly educated, and most Westernized, castes. This contrasts with the United States, England, Japan, Norway, Ireland, and Iceland, where more schizophrenia has been reported among lower socio-economic and the least educated groups. Whether schizophrenia-prone individuals "drift" downwards to these lower classes is hotly debated.

Even more intriguing than the geographical data are figures that have emerged over the past 10 years showing that individuals who later in life become schizophrenic are born disproportionately more often in the late-winter and spring months. Studies of over 125,000 schizophrenic patients have shown this to be true in nine northern hemisphere countries: England and Wales, Ireland, Sweden, Norway, Denmark, Germany, Japan, the Philippines, and the United States. Studies of South Africa, Australia, New Zealand, and Tasmania, southern hemisphere nations with reversed seasons, have tended to confirm that more schizophrenic patients are born in the cooler months.

Other aspects of the seasonality of schizophrenic births have recently come to light. Studies in Japan and England suggest that the peak months for schizophrenic births may have shifted over time from winter toward spring. In Missouri, this shift was confirmed, showing that in the 1920s, the peak month was February; in the 1930s, March and April; and in the 1940s, April and May. The change was highly significant statistically.

All of this information raises many more questions than it answers. But they are important questions, for hiding among them are almost certainly clues to the ultimate question: what are the causes of this disease? Prevalence studies of lung cancer, hypertension, and heart disease have yielded much guidance in the study of those diseases, and it is reasonable to expect the same for schizophrenia.

What have we learned to date from those studies? First, the overall data derived from them are compatible with thinking of schizophrenia as a series of diseases rather than as a single disease. In other words, schizophrenia may simply be a final common pathway of abnormal brain dysfunction, no more specific than the term "mental retardation."

Second, the data appear to provide no support for psychoanalytic theories of schizophrenia (which say, for example, that it is caused by bad mothering), and little support for sociocultural theories, which hold that it is caused by cultural stress. Sociocultural theorists might cite the data from Ghana and India in support of such ideas, but other data directly contradict them. In Ireland, for example, the schizophrenia rate is much higher in the rural, relatively peaceful, western section than in the turbulent, warring north, where the stress is very high—and this difference has been present for many years. Genetic theories of the disease appear to be supported by some of the findings (for example, the northern Swedish high-prevalence area is marked by inbreeding), but not by others.

The emerging epidemiological data would appear to be most compatible with biological theories of schizophrenia: they reinforce other evidence that shows schizophrenia to be a series of brain disorders. Neurophysiological studies have shown, for example, that schizophrenic patients have certain anatomical anomalies that can be picked up on computerized brain X rays; they also demonstrate "soft" neurological signs, such as the inability to identify, without looking, a number traced on their palms. Laboratory studies have revealed a low level of monoamine oxidase in the blood platelets of some patients, setting them apart, again, as somehow biologically different. The search for the precise causes of schizophrenia—there are probably several of them—is likely to be the most exciting development in the mental-health field in the next decade. Possible causes of schizophrenia might include such things as environmental toxins, viruses with long latency periods, heavy metals, or nu-tritional deficiencies—all of which could be linked to geographical areas, helping to explain the differing rates.

Finally, the seasonality of schizophrenic births strongly implies that, for at least one subgroup of schizophrenic patients, the original damage to the brain occurred either *in utero* or shortly after birth. (Such fetal injuries cause rubella heart damage, cleft lip, and stillbirth, all of which show marked seasonality.) This theory dovetails with what we know of the development of the brain, which shows it to be very susceptible to injury from the time of conception until the child is a year old. It is also compatible with emerging knowledge of other brain diseases, such as multiple sclerosis, which is probably contracted in the first few years of life, but doesn't show symptoms until 20 to 30 years later.

In short, the distribution of schizophrenia has emerged as a respectable and potentially valuable area for research. By looking beyond our traditional research frontiers, we may extend the horizon of our knowledge immeasurably.

For further information, read:
Torrey, E. Fuller and M.R. Peterson, "The Viral Hypothesis of Schizophrenia." *Schizophrenia Bulletin*, Vol. 2, No. 1, 1976.

Torrey, E. Fuller, B.B. Torrey, and M.R. Peterson "Seasonality of Schizophrenic Births in the United States." *Archives of General Psychiatry*, Vol. 34, No. 9, 1977.

Enhancing Human Adjustment: Learning to Cope Effectively

Behavioral psychologists view mental health as that state in which the individual copes effectively with his or her environment. It is defined by the ability to competently master the process of adjustment to daily challenges. Humanists, on the other hand, regard other criteria such as adequacy, competency, and coping as inadequate to describe the health of the whole individual. Their emphasis is on forming an awareness of psychological experience and values.

From whatever source, problems and conflicts are part of human life. The manner in which an individual copes with stress can promote or inhibit growth and can also affect relationships with others. Some recent studies show that there are stress-resistant people who because of their open attitude and feeling of involvement, are seemingly immune to stress. Attitudes can have a significant effect on human adjustment and ones ability to cope. At some point the individual who cannot cope may decide help is needed to regain that condition, whatever it is, of mental health.

Psychotherapists are concerned with the treatment of maladjustment. This treatment may take a variety of forms, from classic psychoanalysis to behavior modification.

Until recently, psychiatric help was generally viewed primarily as a "cure" for the person who had ex-

perienced some catastrophic blow to his or her emotional well-being, or who exhibited symptoms of mental disorder. Today many psychologists are focusing attention on individuals with less severe problems—those who can still function with some degree of effectiveness but who seek enhancement of their personal identities and abilities.

Behavior therapy has been effective in treating a variety of conditions, from the smoker who wants to quit to the person who wants to make major changes in his or her personality. Through the application of learning principles, specific target behaviors are increased or eliminated.

Psychologists and others have generated a variety of techniques designed to help the individual to cope with problems or to enhance the quality of his or her life experiences. These techniques fall into four broad categories of therapy: analytical, behavioral, humanistic, and transpersonal.

The essays contained in this section raise a number of questions readers might consider. How well can individuals learn to cope with their personal problems? How important is the element of communication to a person's well being? What kind of social elements determine the personal growth and behavior of an individual? What kind of interactions with one's surroundings can improve the quality of an individual's emotional well being?

HEALTH AS TRANSCENDENCE OF ENVIRONMENT

Abraham H. Maslow

My purpose is to save one point that may get lost in the current wave of discussion of mental health. The danger that I see is the resurgence, in new and more sophisticated forms, of the old identification of psychological health with adjustment, adjustment to reality, adjustment to society, adjustment to other people. That is, the authentic or healthy person is being defined not in his own right, not in his autonomy, not by his own intra-psychic and non-environmental laws, not as *different* from the environment, independent of it or opposed to it, but rather in environment-centered terms; e.g., of ability to master the environment, to be capable, adequate, effective, competent in relation to *it*, to do a good job, to perceive *it* well, to be in good relations to *it*, to be successful in *its* terms. To say it in another way, the job-analysis, the requirements of the task, should not be the major criterion of worth or health of the individual. There is not only an orientation to the outer but also to the inner. An extra-psychic centering point cannot be used for the theoretical task of defining the healthy psyche. We must not fall into the trap of defining the good organism in terms of what he is "good for," as if he were an instrument rather than something in himself, as if he were only a means to some extrinsic purpose. (As I understand Marxist psychology, it also is a very blunt and unmistakable expression of the view that the psyche is a mirror to reality.)

I am thinking especially of Robert White's recent paper in the *Psychological Review*, "Motivation Reconsidered,"[1] and Robert Woodworth's book, *Dynamics of Behavior*. I have chosen these because they are excellent jobs, highly sophisticated, and because they have carried motivation theory forward in a huge leap. As far as they go, I agree with them. But I feel they don't go far enough. I feel also that they contain in a hidden form the danger that I have referred to, that the mastery, effectance and competence may be active rather than passive styles of adjustment to reality, but that they are *still* variations of adjustment theory. I feel we must leap beyond these statements, admirable though they may be, to the clear recognition of transcendence[2] of the environment, independent of it, able to stand against it, to fight it, to neglect it, or to turn one's back on it, to refuse it or adapt to it. (I pass by the temptation to discuss the masculine Western and American character of these themes. Would a woman, a

Hindu, or even a Frenchman, think primarily in terms of mastery or competence?) My point is that, for a theory of mental health, extra-psychic success is not enough; we must also include intra-psychic health.

Another example, which I wouldn't take seriously were it not that so many others *do* take it seriously, is the Harry Stack Sullivan type of effort to define a Self simply in terms of what other people think of him, an extreme cultural relativity in which a healthy individuality gets lost altogether. Not that this isn't true for the immature personality. It is. But we are talking about the healthy, fully grown person. And *he* certainly is characterized by his transcendence of other people's opinions.

To substantiate my conviction that we must save the differentiation between self and not-self in order to understand the fully matured person (authentic, self-actualizing, individuated, productive, healthy), I call your attention to the following considerations.

1. First I mention some data I presented in a 1951 paper called "Resistance to Acculturation." I reported my healthy subjects to be superficially accepting of conventions, but privately to be casual, perfunctory, and detached about them. That is, they could take them or leave them. In practically all of them, I found a rather calm, good-humored rejection of the stupidities and imperfections of the culture with greater or lesser effort at improving it. They definitely showed an ability to fight it vigorously when they thought it necessary. To quote from this paper: "The mixture of varying proportions of affection or approval, and hostility and criticism indicated that they select from American culture what is good in it by their lights and reject what they think bad in it. In a word, they weigh it, and judge it (by their own inner criteria), and then make their own decisions."

They also showed a surprising amount of detachment from people in general and a strong liking for privacy, even a need for it.

"For these and other reasons they may be called autonomous; i.e., ruled by the laws of their own character rather than by the rules of society (insofar as these are different). It is in this sense that they are not only or merely Americans but also members at large of the human species." I then hypothesized that "these people should have less 'national character,' and that they should be

From *Journal of Humanistic Psychology*, Spring 1961. Reprinted by permission of Bertha G. Maslow.

more like each other across cultural lines than they are like the less-developed members of their own culture."[3]

The point I wish to stress here is the detachment, the independence, the self-governing character of these people, the tendency to look within for the guiding values and rules to live by.

2. Furthermore, only by such a differentiation can we leave a theoretical place for meditation, contemplation and for all other forms of going into the Self, of turning away from the outer world in order to listen to the inner voices. This includes all the processes of all insight therapies, in which turning away from the world in a *sine qua non,* in which the path to health is via turning into the fantasies, the dreams, the preconscious and conscious, the archaic, the unrealistic, the primary processes; that is, the recovery of the intra-psychic in general. The psychoanalytic couch is outside the culture to the extent that this is possible. (In any fuller discussion, I would certainly argue the case for an enjoyment of consciousness itself and for experience-values.)

3. The recent interest in health, creativeness, art, play, and love has taught us much, I think, about *general* psychology. From among the various consequences of these explorations, I would pick out one to emphasize for our present purposes, and that is the change in attitude toward the depths of human nature, the unconscious, the primary processes, the archaic, the mythological and the poetic. Because the roots of ill health were found in the unconscious, it has been our tendency to think of the unconscious as bad, evil, crazy, dirty or dangerous, and to think of the primary processes as *distorting* the truth. But now that we have found these depths to be also the source of creativeness, of art, of love, of humor and play, and even of certain kinds of truth and knowledge, we can begin to speak of a healthy unconscious, of healthy regressions. And especially we can begin to value primary process cognition and archaic or mythological thinking instead of considering them to be pathological. We can now go into primary process cognitions for certain kinds of knowledge, not only about the self but also about the world, to which secondary processes are blind. These primary processes are part of normal or healthy human nature and must be included in any comprehensive theory of healthy human nature.

If you agree with this, then you must wrestle with the fact that they are intra-psychic and have their own autochthonous laws and rules, that they are not adapted to external reality or shaped by it or equipped to cope with it. More superficial layers of the personality differentiate out to take care of this job. To identify the whole psyche with these tools for coping with the environment is to lose something which we no longer dare to lose. Adequacy, adjustment, adaptation, competence, mastery, coping, these are all environment-oriented words and are therefore inadequate to describe the *whole* psyche, part of which has nothing to do with the environment.

4. The distinction between the coping aspect of behavior and the expressive aspect is also important here. On various grounds I have challenged the axiom that all behavior is motivated. Here I would stress the fact that expressive behavior is either unmotivated or, anyway, less motivated than coping behavior (depending on what you mean by 'motivated'). In their purer form, expressive behaviors have little to do with environment and do not have the purpose of changing it or adapting to it. The words adaptation, adequacy, competence, or mastery do not apply to expressive behaviors but only to coping behaviors. A reality-centered theory of full human nature cannot manage or incorporate expression, unless with great difficulty. The natural and easy centering point from which to understand expressive behavior is intra-psychic.

5. Being focused on a task produces organization for efficiency both within the organism and in the environment. What is irrelevant is pushed aside and not noticed. The various relevant capacities and information arrange themselves under the hegemony of a goal, a purpose, which means that importance becomes defined in terms of that which helps to solve the problem; i.e. in terms of usefulness. What doesn't help to solve the problem becomes unimportant. Selection becomes necessary. So does abstraction, which means also blindness to some things, inattention, exclusion.

But we have learned that motivated perception, task-orientation, cognition in terms of usefulness, which are all involved in effectance and in competence (which White defines as "an organism's capacity to interact effectively with its environment") leaves out something, and therefore is a partial blindness. For cognition to be complete, I have shown that it must be detached, disinterested, desireless, unmotivated. Only thus are we able to perceive the object in its own nature with its own objective, intrinsic characteristics, rather than abstracting it down to "what is useful," "what is threatening," etc.

My point is that, to the extent that we try to master the environment or be effective with it, to that extent do we cut the possibility of full, objective, detached, noninterfering cognition. Only if we let it be, can we perceive fully. Again, to cite psychotherapeutic experience, the more eager we are to make a diagnosis and a plan of action, the *less* helpful do we become. The more eager we are to cure, the longer it takes. Every psychiatric researcher has to learn not to *try* to cure, *not* to be impatient. In this and in many other situations, to give in is to overcome, to be humble is to succeed. The Taoists and Zen Buddhists taking this path were able a thousand years ago to see what we psychologists are only beginning to be aware of.

But most important is my preliminary finding that this kind of cognition of the Being (B-cognition) of the world is found more often in healthy people and may even turn out to be one of the defining characteristics of health. I have also found it is the peak-experience (transient self-actualizing). This implies that even with regard to healthy relations with the environment the words mastery, competence, effectiveness suggests far more active purposefulness than is wise for a concept of health.

As a single example of the consequence of this change in attitude toward unconscious processes, I hypothesized that sensory deprivation, instead of being frightening, should for very healthy people be pleasing. That is, since cutting off the outer world seems to permit the inner world to come to consciousness, and since the inner world is more accepted and enjoyed by healthier people, then they should enjoy sensory deprivation. (I have recently heard of one experiment in which highly creative people reacted in just this way, but I don't have the details.)

---

[1] Read before Symposium on Research Implications of Positive Mental Health, Eastern Psychological Association, April 15, 1960. This paper was stimulated into existence by a series of discussions with Mr. Stephen Cohen.

[2] The word "transcendence" is used for lack of a better one. "Independence of" implies too simple a dichotomizing of self and of environment, and therefore is incorrect. "Transcendence" unfortunately implies for some a "higher" which spurns and repudiates the "lower," i.e., again a false dichotomizing. In other contexts I have used it as a contrast with "dichotomous way of thinking." The hierarchical-integrative way of thinking, which implies simply that the higher is built upon, rests upon, but includes the lower. For instance, the central nervous system or the hierarchy of basic needs or an army is hierarchically integrated. I use the word "transcendence" here in the hierarchical-integrative sense, rather than in the dichotomous sense.

[3] Examples of this kind of transcendence are Walt Whitman or William James, who were profoundly American, most *purely* American, and yet were also very purely supracultural, internationalist members of the whole human species. They were universal men not in *spite* of their being Americans, but just *because* they were such good Americans.

PSYCHOLOGICAL HARDINESS

The Role of Challenge in Health

MAYA PINES

Maya Pines writes regularly about behavior and is a contributing editor of *Psychology Today*. Her 1973 book. *The Brain Changers: Scientists and the New Mind Control* (Harcourt Brace Jovanovich) won the National Media Award of the American Psychological Foundation.

It's true, stress researchers will tell you, that tax accountants become particularly susceptible to heart attacks around April 15th—the deadline for tax returns. It is also true that air-traffic controllers, who have to make split-second decisions affecting many lives, develop hypertension with four times the frequency of people in other occupations. And it's true that the death of a close relative statistically increases one's own chances of becoming ill or dying soon afterward; in England, for instance, some 5,000 widowers who were studied for six months after the death of their wives had a mortality rate 40 percent higher than the average for men of their age.

Dozens of studies in the past two decades have shown that people who are in high-stress occupations or who have suffered a major setback in their lives run an unusually high risk of disease. Despite the increased risk, however, such disease is not inevitable. As a small group of researchers is now emphasizing, large numbers of people do not fall sick under stress.

Thus, many people work night and day at high-powered jobs without becoming ill, even while others who have seemingly easier occupations de-

velop ulcers, colitis, hypertension, or heart disease. Some people survive even the horrors of a concentration camp, while others cannot cope with everyday problems without falling apart, mentally or physically.

What distinguishes the people who stay healthy? This is one of the most absorbing questions in medical science today. A good heredity surely helps. But investigators in the field of behavioral medicine are only starting to learn how various kinds of behavior, such as the restless striving and impatience of so-called Type A's, are related to such illnesses as hypertension or coronary disease. Though the research is in its infancy, we now have a few clues to the psychological qualities and social circumstances that may account for resilience to stress.

At the University of Chicago, Suzanne C. Kobasa and Salvatore R. Maddi have defined some of the characteristics of what they call "hardiness." Stress-resistant people, they say, have a specific set of attitudes toward life—an openness to change, a feeling of involvement in whatever they are doing, and a sense of control over events. In the jargon of psychological research, they score high on "challenge" (viewing change as a challenge rather than a threat), "commitment" (the opposite of alienation), and "control" (the opposite of powerlessness). These attitudes have a profound effect on health, according to the two psychologists, who have been studying the incidence of life stresses and illnesses among hundreds of business executives, lawyers, army officers, and retired people.

Unlike researchers in psychosomatic medicine in the 1950s, who attributed much illness to patients' inner conflicts, Kobasa and Maddi have been looking at how people interact with specific aspects of their environment. In this sense, they follow in the footsteps of Richard S. Lazarus of the University of California at Berkeley, the psychologist whose 1966 book, *Psychological Stress and the Coping Process*, emphasized that stress resides neither in the person nor in the situation alone, but depends on how the person appraises particular events. (See "Positive Denial: The Case for Not Facing Reality," *Psychology Today*, November 1979.) Kobasa and Maddi have been trying to find out what determines such appraisals—as well as the consequences of these appraisals. Interestingly, their subjects' answers vary somewhat according to the unwritten rules of behavior within different occupations.

Kobasa's work began with a study of 670 middle- and upper-level managers at an Illinois public utility—all of them white Protestant males, college graduates, between 40 and 49 years old, married, with two children. As part of her doctoral dissertation, Kobasa first asked them to describe on checklists all of the stressful life events and illnesses they had experienced in the previous three years. Next she picked out two groups for comparison: 200 executives who scored above average both on stress and on illness, and another 126 with equally high total stress scores who had scored below average on illness. Members of both groups filled out detailed personality questionnaires.

Kobasa had defined the three criteria of hardiness in advance as a working hypothesis; her premises were drawn from existential psychology, whose principal exponents in the United States include Maddi, Rollo May, and Viktor Frankl. Existential psychology postulates that a feeling of engagement and of control over one's life is essential to mental health. Both Maddi and Kobasa practice a form of psychotherapy based on it.

When Kobasa analyzed the Illinois utility managers' answers in 1977, she found that the high-stress/low-illness men stood out in all three categories of hardiness: they were much more actively involved in their work and social lives than those who became sick under stress; they were more oriented to challenge; and they felt more in control of events. Those were exciting findings. As Kobasa explained, "The mechanism whereby stressful life events produce illness is presumably physiological. Yet whatever this physiological response is, the personality characteristics of hardiness may cut into it, decreasing the likelihood of breakdown into illness."

Nevertheless, this study was open to question. Might not the executives' negative view of themselves and their lives be a *result* rather than the *cause* of the illness? "What we were seeing was just the tip of the iceberg," recalls Maddi, who was Kobasa's thesis adviser. To get more reliable answers, various groups of persons would have to be studied *before* they became ill and then followed for a few years to see what happened to them.

Maddi joined forces with Kobasa in a longitudinal project of this sort. He was deeply interested in the problem because he felt that much of the advice being given to people on the basis of existing stress research was misleading. He had been particularly upset by an article appearing in a women's magazine in 1972 that reported on the widely used stress scale developed by psychiatrists Thomas Holmes and Richard Rahe called the Schedule of Recent Life Events. Used with their Social Readjustment Rating Scale, the Holmes-Rahe test measures and gives specific weight to all the recent changes in a person's life—and as-

sumes that any major change is stressful. Marriage, for example, rates 50 points on their scale, halfway up the scale from 0 to 100. The most severe stress of all, the death of a spouse, rates 100. The magazine published a checklist with which readers could add up their own stress scores. What incensed Maddi was the advice that came with it.

"It said that if your stress score is above 200, you have a 60 percent probability of being ill within the following year," Maddi recalls angrily. "And if your score is above 300, you have an 80 percent chance of falling sick. So if you want to stay healthy, avoid further stress. Don't even drive on the Los Angeles freeways, and don't have a confrontation with your spouse, because it might kill you!"

This baleful view of change contradicted some of Maddi's own research, which focused on the beneficial effects of novelty and surprise. He had not studied extreme circumstances, such as a death in the family or being sent to a concentration camp. But he had evidence that minor changes in people's routines were stimulating and led to growth. Maddi continues to believe that whether novelty is good or bad for a person depends on how it is experienced. He remains adamantly opposed to the theory that stress should be avoided whenever possible.

In this view, he would be supported by the father of stress research, Hans Selye, who has argued that certain kinds of stress—which he calls "eustress"—are good for people. Selye, who practically invented the concept of stress about 40 years ago, has described the body's physical response to it in numerous experiments. But since then, he has pointed out that the racing pulse, the quickened breathing, and the accelerated heart rate that betray stress also occur during times of great joy. A certain amount of stress is essential to well-being, though people's requirements will vary, Selye argues. In a 1978 interview ("On the Real Benefits of Eustress," *Psychology Today*, March 1978), Selye suggested that there are two main types of human beings: "race horses," who are only happy with a vigorous, fast-paced lifestyle, and "turtles," who need peace, quiet, and a tranquil environment. The trick is to find the level of stress that suits one best, he said.

Longitudinal studies of stress and disease are very rare. Most studies rely almost entirely on subjects' recollections of events and illnesses that occurred in the past. The few studies that look forward generally focus on college students and follow up on them for only a few weeks—hardly enough time to allow much stress to develop, let alone a related illness (according to Kobasa and Maddi, such illnesses often follow stress after a six-month lag). Furthermore, these studies seldom try to relate personality traits to the stress and disease, as Kobasa and Maddi did.

In their longitudinal study, Kobasa and Maddi collected information on 259 executives at three different times over a period of two years. They first analyzed the men's personalities and hardiness, based on questionnaires that pulled together a number of items which they had developed, plus some items from other scales relating to challenge, commitment, and control. They then asked the men to fill out a version of the Holmes-Rahe test and another questionnaire that asked for information on serious illnesses. To score high on the illness survey, a person would have to report far more serious illnesses than headaches or colds. A cold rated only 20 points, and even six colds a year would add up to only 120 points. By contrast, an ulcer rated 500 points, and a heart attack 855 points.

The results at the end of two years showed clearly that people whose attitudes toward life could be rated high on challenge, commitment, and control remained healthier than the others. Despite a high score on stressful life events, they had a total illness rating of only 510 for two years, compared with an illness rating of 1,080 for men who scored low on hardiness. "You see the striking degree to which a personality of the hardy type protects people who are under stress," says Maddi. "It could decrease your chance of being ill by 50 percent."

The healthier group's attitude towards change (challenge) appeared to be their most important protective factor, closely followed by commitment. When a man loses his job, for example, he can see it either as a catastrophe—an irreplaceable loss that shows he is unworthy and predicts his downfall—or as an experience that falls within the range of risks he accepted when he took the job. In some cases, he may even view it as an opportunity to find a new career that is better suited to his abilities. Similarly, when an elderly couple is forced to sell their home because it has become too expensive and too difficult to keep, they can view the change either as a tragedy or as a chance to find housing that is safer and perhaps closer to their children.

To rate people on challenge, Kobasa and Maddi asked them to what extent they agreed with statements such as, "Boredom is fatal," "A satisfying life is a series of problems; when one is solved, one moves on to the next problem," or, "I would be willing to give up some financial security to be able to change from one job to another if something interesting came along." People who strongly agreed with those statements would rate high on the challenge scale. However, those who agreed with the following statements would rate low:"I don't believe in sticking to something when there is little chance of success," or, "If a job is dangerous, that makes it all the better." The first of these two statements reflects a lack of persistence in the face of challenge. The second represents what Kobasa calls "adventurousness," a form of excessive risk-taking that is typical of people who cannot feel really involved in anything unless it is extreme—for example, a fascist movement. Those who score high on challenge are willing to take some risks, but not excessive risks, she explains.

Kobasa points out that such differences in cognitive appraisal can make an enormous difference in how people respond to events. Those who score high on challenge are much more likely to transform events to their advantage and thus reduce their level of stress. In contrast, people who are low in hardiness may try avoidance tactics—for example, distracting themselves by watching more TV, drinking too much, taking tranquilizers or other drugs, or sleeping more. These are self-defeating tactics, since the real source of stress does not go away. Instead, says Kobasa, "it remains in the mind unassimilated and unaltered, a likely subject matter for endless rumination and subconscious preoccu-

pation"—and it continues to exert its debilitating effects.

The healthy group also rated high on commitment, meaning—as Kobasa and Maddi define the word—that they *engaged* life rather than hanging back on the fringes of it. On Kobasa's tests, the hardy men strongly disagreed with statements such as, "Most of life is wasted in meaningless activity," or, "I am better off when I keep to myself." They took an active role in their work and family lives and believed that their activities were both interesting and important. The executives in the healthy group also believed they could have a real impact on their surroundings. They disagreed with such statements as, "No matter how hard you work, you never really seem to reach your goals," or, "This world is run by a few people in power, and there's not much the little guy can do about it." This gave the healthy executives a high score on control, the third aspect of hardiness.

In order to see whether the same psychological characteristics are equally protective for other kinds of people, Kobasa has also conducted similar studies of 157 lawyers and 75 army captains—all white Protestant males, college graduates, and married with two children, just like the business executives. She is now following up on 2,000 women patients reached through their gynecologists, as well as a group of men who are early retirees.

To her surprise, in the sample of lawyers there was no relationship whatever between stressful events and physical illness. The men who fell sick were often those who had scored lowest on stress, and vice versa. Some of the lawyers did show a relationship between high stress and a variety of psychiatric symptoms: they had trouble sleeping, suffered anxiety, or became severely depressed. Nevertheless, out of the 157 lawyers who had stress scores above 300 (which Holmes and Rahe would call evidence of a major life crisis), 24 reported no psychiatric illness. In line with Kobasa's previous findings, these 24 lawyers were distinguished by higher scores on the commitment scale.

In trying to explain why the lawyers did not become physically ill under stress while the business executives did, Kobasa examined the two groups'

contrasting views of stress. Lawyers tend to believe that they perform best under pressure. Their whole training—as advocates, adversaries, and cross-examiners—conditions them to produce, confront, and deal with stress. And despite all the stresses they are exposed to, they are reputed to lead very long, productive lives. The myth that lawyers thrive under stress seems to become a self-fulfilling prophecy.

Business executives, on the other hand, are constantly told that stress can kill them. As Kobasa puts it, the up-and-coming executive who is felled by a heart attack before the age of 50 is described as "the classical stress victim." Unfortunately, she says, "many business corporations, in their eagerness to set up stress-management programs, gyms on their top floors, and cardiac units in the medical department, seem to be buying into this negative, narrow view of stress. The executive is told that stress is harmful and that attempts will be made to reduce it; but in the meantime, use biofeedback or the exercise machine to ready your body for the assault." According to Kobasa, the executive's social group thus provides little support for a view of stress as positive or controllable. While a lawyer handling a difficult case might be congratulated for it by colleagues ("Gee, it must be really exciting to work on; it'll move you up in the firm"), a business executive who feels under pressure may receive only sympathy or be advised to work out frustrations in the gym.

Another professional difference came to light in Kobasa's study of army officers. In response to stress, these officers fell ill, mentally or physically, far more frequently than the business executives. Kobasa speculates that this might be because the army is a total institution, from which there is little escape; for military officers, the stresses that occur at work cannot easily be isolated from the rest of their lives. She also found that the army officers scored lower on commitment than either the business executives or the lawyers.

One aspect of hardiness that had proved particularly protective for the business executives—openness to change and challenge—actually led to more physical illness among the army officers. Again, Kobasa can only speculate on the reason. In the post-Vietnam army, she suggests, there is no room for people who have a taste for novelty or challenge. "It may be that to want interesting experiences is to want what the peacetime army is not providing right now," she adds. In this environment, those who seek only security appear to be healthier.

Such differences suggest complexities in the question of what produces stress resistance. As Hans Selye was the first to point out, many factors affect one's reaction to stress: physiological predispositions, early childhood experiences, personality, and social resources. Kobasa's findings imply that specific aspects of personality interact with specific aspects of the social environment in many ways, leading to more or less resilience. For that reason, researchers need to know a great deal more about the expectations and social pressures within different groups.

Meanwhile, other investigators have been studying the role of social supports such as family, friends, colleagues, and wider networks in protecting people from illness. The strength of these supports is closely tied in with one's personality and commitment. According to some studies, the most potent protection of all may be the closeness of a spouse.

Recently 10,000 married men who were 40 years of age or older were followed for five years in Israel. The researchers, Jack H. Medalie and Uri Goldbourt, wanted to find out how new cases of angina pectoris—a form of heart attack—develop. They assessed each man's medical risk factors for heart disease and then asked, among other items on a questionnaire, "Does your wife show you her love?" The answer turned out to have enormous predictive power. Among high-risk men—men who showed elevated blood cholesterol, electrocardiographic abnormalities, and high levels of anxiety—fewer of those who had loving and supportive wives developed angina pectoris than did those whose wives were colder (52 per 1,000 versus 93 per 1,000). It remains unclear, however, to what extent such love and support depend on the husband's personality characteristics.

Another Israeli researcher, Brooklyn-born Aaron Antonovsky, a professor of medical sociology at Ben-Gurion University of the Negev, became interested in resistance to disease as a result of his work with survivors of Nazi concentration camps. Originally, he was only trying to find out how 1,150 women of different ethnic origins had adapted to menopause. In the course of this study, he happened to include the following question: "During World War II, were you in a concentration camp?" Of the 287 Central European women who participated in the study, 77 said yes. This presented Antonovsky with an unusual, randomly selected subgroup of women whom he could compare with controls.

Not surprisingly, he found that the concentration-camp survivors, as a group, were more poorly adapted than the others on all his measures of physical and emotional health. What struck him, however, was another observation: a number of women among the concentration-camp survivors were well adapted by any standard, even though their proportion was relatively small. "Despite having lived through the most inconceivably inhuman experience," Antonovsky wrote, "some women were reasonably healthy and happy, had raised families, worked, had friends, and were involved in community activities."

Whence their strength? he asked. And what about the countless members of minorities or immigrants who have survived atrocious conditions in many countries? What about the poor everywhere? "Despite the fact that the poor are screwed at every step of the way, they are not all sick and dying," he noted. In fact, the human condition is inherently stressful. Stress cannot be avoided by human beings ("the bugs are smarter," he comments). Then how do any of us manage to stay healthy?

To answer this question, Antonovsky shifted his research focus from specific stressors to what he called "generalized resistance resources"—characteristics of the person, the group, or the environment that can encourage more effective tension management. Knowledge and intelligence offer such a resource, he be-

lieves, for they allow people to see many ways of dealing with their difficulties—and to choose, when possible, the most effective means. A strong ego identity is another vital resource, he postulates. And so is commitment to a stable and continuing social network.

Antonovsky cites a nine-year study of 7,000 persons in Alameda County, California, which showed that people with many social ties—such as marriage, close friends and relatives, church membership, and other group associations—have far lower mortality rates than others. The study, by Lisa Berkman, an epidemiologist now at Yale University, found that even men in their fifties who seemed to be at high risk because of a very low socioeconomic status, but who scored high on an index of social networks, lived far longer than high-status men with low social-network scores.

Similarly, the social support provided by life in a kibbutz seems to protect children against the anxiety that one would expect as a result of prolonged bombardment. In 1975, at a time of heavy Arab shelling in certain parts of the country, an Israeli researcher compared the anxiety levels of children in several kibbutz and urban communities, in both bombed and tranquil areas. Although urban children who had lived through prolonged bombardment had higher anxiety levels than those from urban areas who had been spared, the kibbutz children did not show any such difference: their anxiety levels were low whether or not their kibbutz had been shelled. The researchers reported that at times of shelling, the kibbutz children were calmly led to shelters that were familiar to them, where educational programs and social life went on pretty much as usual. On the other hand, the urban children, accustomed to living in family units, were suddenly taken to alien and somewhat disordered community shelters; their daily routine was upset. Their higher anxiety level could be explained by the disruption of their normal social network.

In extreme cases, the loss of one's social ties can kill, Antonovsky points out. The phenomenon of voodoo death among tribes in Australia, Central Africa, and the Caribbean is probably the best illustration. When the tribe decides to punish one of its members for breaking a taboo, a witch doctor points a magic bone at him and recites some incantations which place him under a spell of death. "The man who discovers that he is being 'boned' is a pitiable sight," wrote an explorer in Australia, as quoted by the Harvard physiologist Walter Cannon. "He sways backwards and falls to the ground . . . he writhes as if in mortal agony and, covering his face with his hands, begins to moan. After a while he becomes very composed and crawls to his wurley [hut]. From this time onward he sickens and frets . . . his death is only a matter of a comparatively short time."

In Cannon's view, the primary factor in the victim's disintegration is the withdrawal of tribal support. Once the bone is pointed, his fellow tribesmen give him up for dead—and in his isolation, he has no alternative but to die. His heart becomes exhausted by overstimulation, his blood pressure drops calamitously, and his vital functions cease. Much the same appears to happen to some old people in this country when they are consigned to dismal nursing homes or back wards of hospitals, abandoned by the rest of the members of their "tribe."

A different approach to social ties, stress, and personality comes from the eminent Harvard psychologist David C. McClelland. People establish social ties for a variety of reasons, McClelland points out. Some are driven by a deep need for friendship, while others want prestige and power. McClelland and his associates have been studying the need for power for the past 30 years. Recently, they have examined its links to various kinds of stress and to illness.

The people who are most vulnerable to illness under stress, McClelland has found, are those who have a strong drive for power coupled with a high degree of inhibition about expressing it. Such persons "control their assertiveness in a socialized way and make good managers of people," McClelland says. But when they encounter difficulties, they become good candidates for hypertension and heart attacks. McClelland compares them to monkeys that were both enraged and restrained in an experiment by two British researchers; the monkeys developed heart disease as a result. "The equivalent at the personality level would appear to be a strong disposition to act assertively which is simultaneously checked by an inner desire for control and restraint," McClelland writes.

Last year, McClelland and John B. Jemmott III, compared the effects of various types of stress on 82 male and female college students who were rated according to their need for power, their degree of inhibition in expressing this need openly, their need for friendship (called "affiliation"), and their need for achievement. First, the students were given projective tests in which they wrote stories about six pictures that were presented to them (one shows a ship captain explaining something to someone, another a man and a woman seated at a table in a nightclub). These stories were then coded, according to criteria developed by McClelland, for the frequency with which they contained "power thoughts" (of having impact on others through aggression, persuasion, or helping, or of seeking prestige and recognition); "achievement thoughts" (of performing better or of unique accomplishments); "affiliative thoughts" (of establishing, maintaining, or repairing friendly relations with others); or evidence of inhibition, such as the frequency of the word "not," which McClelland has found to be a powerful indicator of restraint. (He believes his scoring methods are statistically reliable and permit him to measure such characteristics "objectively, much as one would identify leukocytes in a blood sample, to avoid the self-serving biases that distort the self-reports of motivations obtained from questionnaires.")

Next, the students filled out a Schedule of Life Change Events for the previous six months, a checklist of mood states, and an illness inventory. The researchers then classified the life-change events according to the type of stress they represented: power/achievement stress (events that challenged or threatened the student's ability to perform powerfully or to impress others), affiliative stress (such as loss of a loved one), or other changes (such as a change in residence).

When all the information was analyzed, it turned out that the students' health or illness depended largely on whether the kinds of stress they had been exposed to impinged on their basic motivations. For example, a high degree of power/achievement stress had disastrous effects on students who scored high both in need for power and in inhibition. When students were motivated more by a need for affiliation, however, the same high degree of power/achievement stress was not associated with severe illness. "Generally speaking, when the stress is related to the dominant motive disposition in the individual, it is more likely to be associated with illness," McClelland concluded. He also found that students who were high in need for power but not too inhibited about expressing it seemed relatively protected against power/achievement stress: their illness score was less than half that of students who could not express their power urge openly. The less-inhibited students may have been much like the business tycoon who said, "I don't get ulcers; I give them."

According to McClelland, men who have a strong need for power are generally "more argumentative and aggressive; they engage more often in competitive sports; they are sexually more active; they accumulate prestige supplies, like fancy clothes and cars; and they tend to join organizations and ally themselves with others who have influence." This sounds suspiciously like the hard-driving, hostile, and aggressive Type A's who began to make headlines a few years ago. The Type-A pattern was popularized by cardiologists Meyer Friedman, and Ray H. Rosenman. In their 1974 book, *Type-A Behavior and Your Heart*, they reported on an eight-year study which showed that men with a Type-A pattern were twice as likely as the less-aggressive Type B's to develop coronary heart disease. McClelland has concluded that "the kind of behavior that has been described as Type A looks very much like that of persons who are high in the need for power, whose power motivation is inhibited, and who are also under power stress" —in other words, those he has found to be at greatest risk of stress-related illnesses.

McClelland is now running several experiments to find out how these men differ physiologically in their reaction to stress. One indication may come from an increase in the level of catecholamines and other hormones released by the sympathetic nervous system of Type A's under stress. Another clue may be that some of McClelland's subjects have smaller numbers of certain white cells in their blood—the NK (natural killer) cells that are part of the immune system—and therefore may be more prone to infections and tumors.

Meanwhile, Kobasa and Maddi have started to analyze the actual health records of the executives in their study, so they need not rely entirely on self-reports of illness. The public utility involved gives its managers a free medical exam every year, including some 40 lab tests, and the two psychologists are now working with physicians from the University of Chicago Medical School and the company's medical department to sort out this treasure trove of records.

As behavioral scientists begin to ally themselves with physicians, both groups are becoming more aware of the intricacy of the processes that lead to health or disease. Much of the information about the effects of stress in the existing research literature is still fragmentary—or even contradictory. Depending on circumstances, for example, fear can make one's heart beat either faster or slower (as when the heart "stands still"). Even more surprisingly, some kinds of stress will make breast cancers grow in mice, but the same stresses will slow down or actually prevent the growth of breast cancers in rats.

Eventually, with more research, we may be able to mitigate some of the dangerous effects of stress. Meditation techniques and biofeedback appear to help some people. Behavioral methods can, within limits, assist in breaking certain habits that lead to stress. For instance, Type-A individuals have been taught to allot more time to each activity in their lives, thus slowing down their pace and reducing tension. But these approaches are palliatives that do not deal with the basic causes of stress—or with the way stress is appraised by different people.

More fundamental kinds of reeducation are also possible, Maddi and Kobasa believe. They place their confidence in existential psychotherapy. Whether this form of therapy, however sophisticated, can give people the sense of challenge, commitment, and control that they may need in order to maintain their physical and mental health remains to be proved. It is obviously far more difficult to change one's underlying character structure than to learn a few behavioral techniques. Nevertheless, Maddi remains optimistic. He hopes to show that people of all ages can be taught hardiness. "People's attitudes and outlooks are largely learned from experience," he maintains, and "therefore, they can be altered."

Shopping for the Right Therapy

The four main schools of psychotherapy are split into more than 130 sub-schools. Choosing the "best" one can be tricky.

Morris B. Parloff

Morris B. Parloff, a clinical psychologist, is chief of the Psychotherapy and Behavioral Intervention Section, Clinical Research Branch, National Institute of Mental Health.

There is nothing absolute about the aims of psychotherapy. They are, rather, tied closely to current standards of well-being and social effectiveness. In the past, these social standards have seemed relatively fixed and stable. Today, however, our society changes its standards with ever-increasing speed, while the sciences keep fashioning new mirrors to reflect the new images of man. As a result, innumerable images are now simultaneously extant; which image we see depends on where we look.

At the same time, we make increasing demands on psychotherapy. In the past, religion and science were the main ways of achieving our aspirations. More recently, to the consternation of some and the satisfaction of others, the license for ensuring our well-being has apparently been transferred to psychotherapy! The boundaries of the treatment, never firm, have become increasingly ambiguous and provisional; in fact, they now seem to be infinitely expansible. Within the past decade the role of the psychotherapist has been greatly extended. Not only is he expected to help the patient achieve relief from psychologically induced discomfort and social ineffectuality—that is, to treat "mental disorders"; he is also expected to help the client achieve positive mental health, a state presumably defined by the extent to which the patient experiences "self-actualization," growth, even spiritual oneness with the universe. Thus, some therapists have moved away from the earlier aim of "head-shrinking" to the loftier goal of "mind-expanding."

The range of problems brought to the psychotherapist has broadened to include not only the major mental disorders—the psychoses and neuroses—but also the celebrated problems of aliena- tion and the meaninglessness of life. The conception of "pathology"—that is, what needs changing—has been modified. Where formerly the internal and unconscious conflicts of the *individual* were treated, the targets of change now encompass the interpersonal relationship, the family system, and, more recently, even society and its institutions.

CREDENTIALS for practicing psychotherapy have been broadened and, by some standards, lowered. What was initially almost the exclusive domain of the medical profession—of the psychoanalyst and psychiatrist—has slowly been opened up to include the related professions of clinical psychology, psychiatric social work, and psychiatric nursing. Among those more recently invited to provide some psychiatric services are the "paraprofessional," the nonprofessional, and even the former patient. The belief that "it takes [a former] one to treat one" has gained popularity, particularly in the treatment of drug abusers, alcoholics, criminals, and delinquents.

The number of "therapeutic techniques" also continues to grow. More than 130 different approaches are now being purveyed in the marketplace of psychosocial therapies.

New schools emerge constantly, heralded by claims that they provide better treatment, amelioration, or management of the problems and neuroses of the day. No school has ever withdrawn from the field for failure to live up to its claims, and as a consequence all continue to co-exist. This remarkable state of affairs is explained in part by the fact that each school seems to be striving for different goals—goals reflecting different views of the "nature of man" and his potential. All approaches to treatment are sustained by their appeals to different constituencies in our pluralistic society.

BY WAY OF general introduction, I shall briefly review the four self-proclaimed major schools of psychotherapy. Then I'll describe several other forms of treatment that are difficult to categorize but that currently also enjoy special popularity.

The four major schools of therapy are (1) analytically oriented therapy, (2) behavior therapy, (3) humanistic therapy, and (4) transpersonal therapy.

Analytically Oriented Therapy

The analytic (or psychodynamic, or depth) forms of therapy have evolved in a more or less direct line from classical psychoanalysis. While still flourishing, and perhaps the most frequently encountered form of treatment, this school appears—like unemployment and inflation—to be growing at a declining rate.

These psychodynamic therapies assume that people have innate and acquired drives which conflict with both the "external" requirements of society and the "internal" needs and "internalized" standards of the individual. Unacceptable drives are forced out of the conscious awareness—that is, repressed—but they continue, unconsciously or subconsciously, to press for expression.

A person's normal development may be interrupted by early-life experiences that either do not satisfy innate drives sufficiently or gratify them excessively.

In either event, the child's development may be blocked. The emotions and fantasies derived from these unacceptable drives may be allowed partial expression in a disguised and compromised form. In some instances these emotions are "sublimated" into creative, socially beneficial channels. In other cases they "surface" as undesirable physical symptoms, or as socially unacceptable character traits and behavior patterns. The psychodynamic approach postulates that socialization is required in order for the person to become human.

Psychoanalytic treatment tries to unravel internal problems by bringing the unconscious neurotic conflicts into the patient's consciousness. The direct target of treatment is not the patient's *symptoms*, but rather the forces that are believed to generate these symptoms.

The formula for bringing this repressed material squarely into the patient's awareness is: clarify, confront, interpret. Understanding and insight of this kind are presumed to be in themselves "curative," provided that they evoke emotional experiences of a compelling nature.

Typically, psychoanalytic approaches involve analysis of the relationship that the patient attempts to establish with the therapist. This relationship is presumed to mirror the patient's unresolved pathological childhood conflicts.

More recently, the analytically oriented therapist has begun taking into account the social and cultural context in which the patient lives. The classical patient-therapist pairing has been widened to permit treatment in groups as well. Some psychodynamic therapies

ity development, or internal underlying conflict. The problem is defined in terms of specific behavior that the patient or society considers to be maladaptive. The aim of treatment is to change behavior—to change, specifically, its frequency, intensity, and appropriateness.

The behavior therapist does not consider maladaptive forms of behavior as evidence of "pathology" but rather as ways in which people have learned to interact with their environment. He believes that behavior disorders develop according to the same principles of learning evident in so-called normal learning.

"Behavioral" treatment begins with detailed study of the events that precede and follow occurrences of a particular behavior problem—phobic avoidances, compulsions, temper tantrums, sexual dysfunctions, and so on.

One major form of behavior therapy consists in changing environmental conditions that stimulate or maintain the unwanted behavior; this therapeutic technique is known as "operant conditioning." Behavior therapy now includes a broad spectrum of techniques, known by such names as systematic desensitization, assertiveness training, aversive conditioning, token economy, and modeling. These procedures are offered by psychologists, psychiatrists, educators, social workers, speech therapists, and others concerned with modifying behavior.

The procedure popularly labeled as *biofeedback* is used as a potential treatment for a variety of psychosomatic disorders, such as headaches, insomnia, high blood pressure, asthma, circulatory problems, and backache. The primary principle in biofeedback* is that if some-

---

"The psychotherapist's role has been greatly extended. Some therapists have moved away from 'head-shrinking' to the loftier goal of 'mind-expanding.'"

---

have moved from long-term to brief, time-limited courses of treatment. Though many of the classic procedures have been revised and relaxed, the basic assumption that dynamic forces underlie symptomatic behavior remains unchanged.

Behavior Therapy

Most behavior therapy derives from laboratory studies of learning processes. The therapist does not postulate the existence of any disease, aberrant personal-

one is provided with information about certain changes occurring in his body, that person can "learn" to: (1) increase awareness of his or her bodily processes, and (2) bring these processes under conscious control. This control should then permit the patient to change the autonomic processes in a more benign or healthful direction. Awareness of events within the body is achieved by

*See "Biofeedback: An Exercise in 'Self-Control' " by Barbara Brown, *SR*, Feb. 22, 1975.

means of monitoring instruments, which detect the relevant internal physiological change, amplify it, and translate it into a visual or auditory display.

Humanistic Therapy

This umbrella term shelters a wide range of therapies and techniques. Perhaps the most important factor uniting them is their strong reaction against what they view as limited conceptions of human nature offered by the analytic and behavioristic therapies.

Humanists postulate that man is driven by an overarching need for self-actualization. Man's needs are, they assert, "higher" than simply mindless pleasure-seeking or avoidance of pain. Goodness, truth, beauty, justice, and order are not to be explained away as byproducts of man's efforts to sublimate, divert, or block the direct expression of the baser drives that lurk within—an explanation sometimes attributed to analytically oriented therapy. Humanists believe that the failure to express and to realize the potential of higher human needs, motives, and capacities is the cause of emotional distress.

The goals of humanistic therapy are self-actualization and the enrichment and fuller enjoyment of life, not the cure of "disease" or "disorders." To realize your potential, you must develop increasing sensitivity to your own—and others'—feelings. Such heightened awareness will help establish warm relationships and improve your ability to perceive, intuit, sense, create, fantasize, and imagine.

The humanists stress that the only reality that merits concern is one's own emotional experience—in contrast to what they view as the unwarranted faith that other therapists have placed in thought, insight, and understanding.

The analytic view holds that man's impulses must be frustrated and redirected in order that he be more fully human. But humanists argue that direct gratification of needs is ennobling and good.

Humanists such as the late Abraham Maslow hold that each individual has a biological essence, or self, that he must discover and develop, but that external influences are more powerful than biologically given characteristics and may distort or block our personal awareness and development.

The panoply of self-actualizing techniques ranges from nondirective counseling and gestalt therapy to the multiple and ever-evolving variants of "growth" groups: the encounter group, the T-group, sensory-awareness training, and so on.

Transpersonal Therapy

Unlike the humanists, the transpersonalists are not content with the aim of integrating one's energies and expanding the awareness of oneself as an entity separate from the rest of the universe. Instead, the transpersonalists' goal is to help the individual transcend the limits of ordinary waking consciousness and to become at one with the universe. The various levels and dimensions of awareness are as follows: "intuitive" states, in which vague, fleeting experiences of trans-sensory perception begin to enter waking awareness; the "psychical," in which the individual transcends sensory awareness and experiences integration with humanity; and the "mystical," representing a union of enlightenment in which the self transcends duality and merges with "all there is." Finally, there may be yet a further level of potential development—personal/transpersonal integrative—in which all dimensions are experienced simultaneously.

Transpersonalists do not share an organized theory or a clearly defined set of concepts, but, like the humanists, they assume that we all have large pools of untapped abilities, along with a drive toward spiritual growth.

One may achieve these levels by means of various techniques, including Arica training, the Gurdjieff method, Zen, psychosynthesis, yoga, Sufism, Buddhism, and transcendental meditation.

THREE TRANSPERSONAL approaches have achieved considerable popularity: psychosynthesis, Arica training, and transcendental meditation.

Psychosynthesis was developed by a Florentine psychiatrist, Roberto Assagioli. As a form of therapy, it tries to help people develop "the will" as a constructive force guiding all psychological functions—emotion-feeling, imagination, impulse-desire, thought, and intuition. Treatment aims at enabling the patient to achieve harmony within himself and with the world as a path to attaining the higher self. It consists of techniques for training the will in order that one can master life and merge with "the universal will."

Arica training is an eclectic system, devised by Oscar Ichazo in Chile. It has incorporated many of the teachings of the Middle East and the Orient, including yoga, Zen, Sufism, Kabbala, and the martial arts. The branches of the Arica Institute now established in some major American cities stress these features: special diet, sensory awareness, energy-generating exercises, techniques for analysis in personality, interpersonal and group exercises, and various forms of meditation.

Transcendental meditation (TM), a variant of Raja yoga, has become extraordinarily popular in the United States and Europe. This form of meditation has been adapted to the habits of Westerners and does not require special postures, forced concentration, lengthy or arduous training, or religious belief. Each person is assigned a mantra—a special incantatory catch-phrase—which he is to keep secret and meditate on twice a day for about 20 minutes. This meditation helps people attain deep states of relaxation that are said to release creative energies. The advocates of TM hold that if 1 percent of the population in a given area meditate properly, the energies generated will benefit the rest of the population.

Special Treatment Forms

Most techniques of psychotherapy can be included under one or another of these four rubrics—analytic, behavioral, humanistic, and transpersonal—but there remain a number of approaches that do not claim allegiance to any school and are not claimed by any. Some of these special approaches may be termed "pantheoretical"; others have evolved self-consciously "novel" techniques and procedures. The broad class of group psychotherapies and the many community-oriented therapies illustrate "pantheoretical" approaches; the "novel" therapies will be illustrated here by perhaps the best known—primal therapy.

"Group psychotherapy" does not represent any particular set of techniques or common philosophy of treatment. It refers to the *setting* in which the particular views and techniques of the analytic, behavioral, humanistic, and transpersonal schools have been implemented. In addition to having a knowledge of his own school, the practitioner of group psychotherapy must understand the dynamics and processes of small groups.

Of the many forms of group therapy, one of the best known is *transactional analysis* (TA), of *I'm OK, You're OK* fame. TA was developed by Eric Berne and represents an adaptation and extension of the psychodynamic orientation. The treatment attempts to identify covert gratifications—the "payoffs" of the "games" that people play with one another. The tasks of both the therapists and the group patients include identifying the moment-to-moment ego states (parent, child, adult) that characterize each participant's interactions. A further step is to name the "game" that the individual is playing and, finally, to identify the "unconscious" life plan that the patient appears to have selected for himself during early childhood. The life plan involves the relatively enduring position of whether the self and others are "okay" or "not okay." The dynamics of change are believed to consist in the patient's learning to shift his "real self" from one ego state to another by an act of will.

Family therapy involves the collective treatment of members of the same family in a group by one or more psychotherapists. This approach treats not merely the individual but the family unit. The individual "patient" is viewed as but a symptom of a dysfunctional family system—a system that has produced and now maintains the problems manifested in a given family member.

The pan-theoretical approaches include those therapies which extend the therapeutic focus to the community and society. The premise that environmental influences may interfere with a person's development has been taken up by a variety of therapists loosely associated with humanistic psychology. Perhaps the most extreme position is that taken by the group espousing *radical therapy*, which holds that society is responsible for most mental and emotional ills, and that, therefore, society rather than the patient is sick. People in psychological distress are considered oppressed rather than ill, and traditional psychotherapy is "part of the problem rather than part of the solution to human misery." The therapist attempts to help the patient recognize not merely his own problems but also the realities of his life situation and the role played by society in generating and perpetuating emotional problems.

Like radical therapy, *feminist therapy* believes that the root of emotional problems may be found in society rather than in the individual. Feminist therapy emphasizes that all psychotherapy must be freed of its traditional sex-role biases. Sexism is viewed as a major force impeding the "growth" of both men and

women. This approach is not characterized by any particular techniques, but rather by a shared ideology. Consciousness-raising groups, too, which were initially politically motivated, have recently become oriented toward providing women with help for their personal problems.

Primal therapy is viewed by its inventor, Arthur Janov, as unique in both its effects and its techniques, and as the "only cure of the neuroses." According to Janov, a neurosis occurs when the unexpressed physical and psychological pains experienced in childhood accumulate to the point where they are unbearable and can no longer be simply suppressed. The awareness of these feelings and needs is then "split off" when the child interprets the parents' behavior as meaning that they hate him. This formulation may occur at about the age of five or six and represents to Janov the "primal scene" that precipitates the neurosis.

In Janov's theory the pain of unmet needs is stored away somewhere in the brain and produces tension, which the patient may deal with by developing a variety of tension-relieving symptoms. Treatment requires the release and full expression of the underlying pain, by restoring physical access to the stored memories. Cure occurs only when each old painful feeling is linked to its origins. The living and reliving of the primal scene is accompanied by a "tower of terror" usually associated with screaming, violent thrashing about, pounding, and even convulsions. The screaming may go on for hours and may be repeated periodically over a period of many months as one event after another is recalled.

According to Janov, the cured individual should ideally have no psychological defenses, nor need any, since all pain and its associated tensions have been dispelled. The recovered patient thus becomes a "natural man," who is "non-industrial, non-compulsive, and non-driving," and finds much less need for sex; women experience sexual interest no more than twice a month.

therapies. Clearly, the basic conceptions differ as to who and what needs treating. It is not easy to prove that changes observed in patients and clients are due to the specific techniques and interventions. The therapist may wittingly or unwittingly provide the patient with experiences other than those assumed to be critical. It cannot be assumed that the same therapist will behave similarly with each of his patients—much less that different therapists espousing the same theory will behave similarly with all patients. The problems of research on the outcome of psychotherapy are further compounded by the concurrent impact of other events in the patient's life.

In terms of consumer guidance, then, I shall report only the most consistent trends that emerge from a review of a large number of studies:

• Most forms of psychotherapy are effective with about two-thirds of their non-psychotic patients.

• Treated patients show significantly more improvement in thought, mood, personality, and behavior than do comparable samples of untreated patients.

• Behavior modification appears to be particularly useful in some specific classes of phobias, some forms of compulsive or ritual behavior, and some sexual dysfunctions. Although behavior-therapy techniques appear to produce rapid improvement in the addictive disorders, such as alcoholism, drug abuse, obesity, and smoking, these changes are usually not maintained and relapse occurs in most cases.

• Biofeedback has been applied to tension headaches, migraine, hypertension, epilepsy, some irregularities of heartbeat. The evidence, while encouraging, has not yet established such treatment as being clinically significant.

• Meditation techniques of a wide variety all produce comparable degrees of relaxation, with associated physiological and metabolic changes. Currently, "noncultist" adaptations of meditative procedures are being applied with some

---

"It is wise for the patient to select carefully from among an array of qualified therapists the one whose style of relating is acceptable to him."

Even this truncated review of the major schools and techniques indicates the enormous complexity of any serious research effort that undertakes to compare the relative effectiveness of available

success in the treatment of anxiety, hypertension, and cardiac arrythmias. Again, findings must be viewed as tentative pending further research.

• The criteria of "growth," "self-actualization," and the attainment of transpersonal levels of consciousness remain ambiguous, and it is therefore difficult to measure them objectively.

• Apparent differences in the relative effectiveness of different psychotherapies gradually disappear with time.

• Although most studies report that similar proportions of patients benefit from all tested forms of therapy, the possibility remains open that different therapies may effect different kinds of change.

All forms of psychotherapy tend to be reasonably useful for patients who are highly motivated, experience acute discomfort, show a high degree of personality organization, are reasonably well educated, have had some history of social success and recognition, are reflective, and can experience and express emotion.

Jerome D. Frank has proposed that all therapies may incorporate the same common (non-specific) elements, although in differing degrees: an emotionally charged relationship with a helping person; a plausible explanation of the causes of distress; provision of some experiences of success; and use of the therapist's personal qualities to strengthen the patient's expectation of help.

This statement in no way endorses tactlessness, insensitivity, or psychological assault. The therapist has no license to humiliate—or to thrill. A large-scale, careful study of participants who suffered psychological injury during encounter groups (led by acknowledged experts) revealed that the incidence of such casualties was disproportionately high among clients of so-called charismatic therapists, with their often aggressive, impatient, and challenging confrontation techniques.

No matter how specific the theory, no matter how clearly prescribed the techniques for a given therapy, treatment is far from standardized. Psychotherapy is mediated by the individual therapist and further modified by the nature of the interaction with the particular patient.

When the patient is "therapist-shopping," it is wise for him to select carefully from among an array of qualified therapists the one whose style of relating is acceptable to him—and preferably from a school whose philosophy, values, and goals are most congenial to his own.

YOU ARE WHAT YOU DO

CAROL TAVRIS

Carol Tavris, Ph.D., is a social psychologist who writes frequently on adult development and social change. She is co-author of The Longest War—Sex Differences in Perspective, *and is currently working on a book about anger.*

STEP RIGHT UP, folks, step right up and choose your medicine for what ails you. We've got therapies, we've got pills, we've got religion, we've got the package that's just right for *you*. Let us calm your anxieties, pump up your self-esteem, doctor your dilemmas! Don't rush, don't crowd. First we want you to take this little test, so we'll know what you think about your prospects for improvement (choose one):

A. Adult change is parallel to child development—it proceeds in a series of biologically programmed stages. An internal clock, a rise and fall of hormones, directs the passages of adulthood.

B. Adult change can be difficult, but it is attainable through intensive therapies, individually or in groups, that liberate the real self, shucking off the outer layers like corn husks.

C. Adults don't change. The personality is formed in childhood, and although you can tinker with the blueprint, you cannot ever make major alterations.

Okay, all you A's kindly step to the left and start your end-of-decade warm-up exercises. (If the second digit of your age is 3 to 7, you'll have to wait.) B's, while you are getting ready for the soul-searching marathon, chant "FOOOOM" softly to your navels. C's! Stop that whine of despair! In 10 or 12 years of intensive work, we'll turn you around! Oh yes.

● Mrs. E. is a 53-year-old suburban housewife. In recent years, her personality has begun to change. She has become grouchy and irritable. She finds herself crying for no apparent reason. She goes to the doctor often, complaining about insomnia, nervousness, and heart palpitations. She is making life hell for her husband, who is baffled and angry.

● Mr. Q. is a business executive who has been working for his company for nearly 25 years. The presidency is so close he can smell it. His obsession with the job has intensified, and his family and friends worry that his health will suffer. He has become authoritarian in the management of his subordinates. He is aloof from his wife. He feels encased in a shell.

● Dr. S., who is 47, is a dentist. He is a very good dentist and makes over $100,000 a year. He has three houses, two cars, one wife, one mistress, a yacht, and the blues. Sometimes he feels so depressed he can barely drag himself to work. The thought of another 13 to 15 years until retirement fills him with dread.

To change themselves, willing to try anything to feel better, these people are likely to do something like this:

● Mrs. E starts going to therapy twice a week. After a few months with no improvement, she goes to a nutritionist who prescribes vitamin supplements. Now she is full of energy and miserable.

● Mr. Q. spends two weeks at an "executive seminar" encounter group, courtesy of his company. There he opens up for the first time in years. He confesses his need for intimacy. He cries when he realizes that his wife might leave him if his workaholism persists. He basks in the warmth of the group. By the time he has been home three weeks, he is back to his old obsessive patterns. With a vengeance: after all, he lost precious time at that silly program.

• Dr. S. goes into psychoanalysis. Psychoanalysis teaches him that his "burn-out" is a result of the inadequacy he always felt for not getting into medical school. While he is waiting for this understanding to take effect, he decides that if he can't enjoy his work, at least it can make him richer. Maybe that way he can retire sooner. He crowds more patients into his already crowded schedule. His wife complains that he is never home any more. He resents her.

The housewife's husband is running out of patience. "She has everything she could want and still nothing makes her happy," he says. "She's just a neurotic bitch."

The executive's wife is running out of patience. "He's a self-destructive egomaniac," she concludes. "An uptight S.O.B."

The dentist is running out of patients. They are getting tired of waiting in his cramped office and of his listless, if not downright condescending, treatment of them.

Are any of these people familiar to you? Perhaps too familiar? Hold on. They will return shortly.

THOSE WHO WISH to change some aspect of themselves have a cornucopia of choices. As diverse as these choices are, many of them share an unspoken assumption that virtually assures their failure: that there is a coherent thing called "self" that determines what we do, feel, believe, eat, or suffer; and that the self can be studied in isolation and doctored like a kidney. Whether the self is viewed as a straitjacket acquired in childhood or as a loose garment that can take alteration, it is still the focal point of change. Before we can get better, we are supposed to understand the self's motives, drives, and complexes. Root them out, and the self will flourish.

The idea that self-conversion is the prerequisite of social change is also deeply embedded in our culture. The conversion may be religious ("if everybody became a member of religion X, the social ills of mankind would vanish") or "humanistic," the secular religion of psychology ("if everybody became liberated, androgynous, sexually free, dis-uptight, etc., the social ills of mankind would vanish"). Fortunately for those who favor legal and social justice, the government has passed some laws to tide us over while we wait for the universal wave of kindness to wash over the faithful.

We each have a "self," or "ego," if by that we mean an inner eye that observes and reacts to experience. As evidence for the self, we cite the intimate, private thoughts that no one else can know. What we overlook in such a formulation is that other people have access to aspects of our "selves" that we do not. We may know our private thoughts, but they know our public behavior, including the wordless messages we convey without knowing it. In these intrapsychic days, many people dismiss the public self as being of no account; at best, they say, it is the result of what the private self decides to do.

To this belief an enormous body of research in social psychology responds with a clarion call: "Horsefeathers!" Sometimes, certainly, we believe, therefore we act. But equally often we act, and that action changes our beliefs. And sometimes the belief and the action have no connection at all. For example, consider the difference between prejudice (an attitude) and discrimination (prejudiced behavior). The self-change contingent would say that people who are prejudiced against blacks, say, or women, must reform, that the psychological reason for their prejudice must be overcome. Further, they assume that all racists and sexists actively discriminate against the objects of their dislike, and anyone who discriminates against blacks or women is, therefore, a racist or sexist. These assumptions are not always true. Many "nice" people discriminate—perhaps by not hiring or promoting a minority person—when habit, custom, or their job requirements cause them to do so. And many bigots do *not* discriminate when the law, job requirements, and economic need prevail.

To understand the mechanisms of change, the social context of the self must be entered into the equation. Trying to fix one human being apart from his or her habitat is like trying to analyze the behavior of one termite. Human beings are a lot smarter and cuter than termites, but they are no less dependent on others of their species in the determination of their character and action.

"A man has as many social selves as there are individuals who recognize him and carry an image of him in their mind," wrote William James in 1890. ". . . we may practically say that he has as many different social selves as there are distinct *groups* of persons about whose opinions he cares. He generally shows a different side of himself to each of these different groups . . . . [Division into several selves] may be a discordant splitting, as where one is afraid to let one set of his acquaintances know him as he is elsewhere; or it may be a perfectly harmonious division of labor, as where one tender to his children is stern to the soldiers or prisoners under his command."

James's observation has been amply demonstrated thousands of times, but the psychoanalytic movement that followed him tended to obscure the idea of "many social selves." Psychoanalysts, concentrating on internal desires and conflicts, typically ignored it or treated it as a pathological condition. They would later use the terrifying Nazi phenomenon as an example of national pathology, wondering what horrible flaw in the Nazi "personality" allowed those who ran concentration camps by day to cuddle their children affectionately at night. Yet, as Stanley Milgram's classic experiments showed, most normal, healthy Americans—of any age, sex, or status—obey the dictates of an authority, even when that authority instructed them to inflict what they believed was a dangerous amount of electric shock to another person.

We are, in large measure, what our environment demands that we be. The illusion of a consistent self is so strong, however, that we usually do not observe our inconsistencies. The woman who says she is timid may be thinking of how she feels in groups of men, perhaps at school or in business where she has had little experience in articulating her views. But she is probably not timid with other women, with the butcher who shortchanges her, with her children. And she will be surprised how quickly her timidity vanishes should she get a job that allots her a measure of power. Is timidity, then, a part of her "personality"?

Many traits and feelings usually assumed to be permanent fixtures of personality can be observed through the looking glass: as *results* of one's circumstances, not as causes. Sociologists have demonstrated that countless qualities—such as self-esteem, assertiveness, obedience, happiness, morality, kindness, ability to love, workaholism, authoritarianism, ambition—change remarkably easily when the structure of a person's life changes, and change hardly at all when that structure remains constant. No matter how much talking and chanting one does to break out of it.

By way of illustration, think for a moment of all the theories you have heard in the last ten years about sex differences. Some said that women aren't fit for professional and public office because they are too soft, sweet, dumb, or swayed by biological imperatives. Others said those biological imperatives were precisely the reason for getting women into corporations and governments; they'd humanize the place with their warm maternal urges. Still others, such as psychologist David Gutmann, suggested that sex differences shift at middle age: men start out aggressive and productive and end up nurturant and receptive, whereas women start out nurturant and receptive, and end up more assertive and independent. And liberationists of both sexes argued that men and women should share the same desirable qualities of personality, a condition called androgyny. (Theoretically, androgyny could also refer to the *worst* qualities of both sexes, but it rarely does.)

Well, which theory wins? The answer is all of them do, under some conditions. A woman may well want to be soft and maternal until she sets foot into the corporate or political world, at which point all that kitchy-koo stuff *stops*. (Indira Gandhi, Golda Meir, and Margaret Thatcher have been no more maternal in the governance of their respective nations than any man might be.) A man can't afford to be nurturant and androgynous if his job pays him to be ruthless, ambitious, and cold. Gutmann's ideas are very nice, and undoubtedly accurate for the four traditional agricultural societies that he studied, but they can't be extrapolated to complex industrialized societies. Cultural variation usually drowns nature when she tries to get a word in edgewise. Nature has never been very natural.

The way men and women spend their time—at work, with families, at leisure—and the structure of their social environment determine their characters and their lives far more than any dictates of biology or personality, as the predicaments of Mrs. E., Mr. Q., and Dr. S. testify.

MRS. E. AND THE WILTED-WIFE SYNDROME

Imagine a company—call it IPD—that employs most of the men in the New Jersey town where it is situated. The men respect this company and can't wait to work for it. But after a few years on the job, many of the employees show distressing symptoms. They have physical ailments. Absenteeism increases sharply. Production slows down. Some employees give up altogether.

Most observers of IPD's plight would wonder what is wrong with a company that produces a demoralized, depressed staff out of once-enthusiastic bright young men.

Chemicals they are accidentally inhaling on the job? Environmental hazards? Wretched working conditions?

Now rerun the scenario, replacing "marriage" for IPD and "wives" for employees. Most women marry. They respect the institution of marriage and can't wait to join it. But after a few years on the job, many housewives show distressing symptoms. They have physical ailments. Their happiness declines sharply. Some of them give up altogether.

So prevalent is the pattern of psychosomatic illness, depression, apathy, and dependence on drugs among housewives that the problem has been called housewife's syndrome. Yet most observers of the problem—including many of the doctors who treat it—do not wonder what is wrong with marriage that so many women cannot adjust to it, or that it causes once-enthusiastic bright young women to become depressed and demoralized. They assume that something is wrong with women if they cannot adjust to the natural role and challenge of marriage.

It is easier for people to accept the idea that bad working conditions on a job can affect happiness, personality, and health than to accept the same idea applied to the working conditions of marriage. But in recent years, researchers have identified some of those working conditions that make wives droop.

Sociologist Myra Marx Ferree interviewed 135 women from the Boston area, about half of whom were employed outside the home. Women in this group were much happier, had higher self-esteem, and were more satisfied with their lives than were the full-time housewives—and not because their jobs were so glamorous, either. Most of them were typists, clerks, waitresses, and other nonmanagerial workers. But their jobs provided two significant bolsters to self-esteem and a sense of accomplishment: social contact with customers and co-workers, and a regular paycheck.

Next Ferree wanted to see what factors distinguished the happy full-time housewives from the unhappy ones. It turned out that those in the former group, like the employed wives, had lots of people around them and got continuing support and encouragement for their activities. These housewives came from old-fashioned, close-knit neighborhoods—the kind where relatives and neighbors drop in all the time to share chores and coffee—and said that their husbands and family valued their work and gave them continuing praise for it. Ferree observes that high job mobility and the exodus to the suburbs after the war broke up these close ethnic neighborhoods, making the housewife's job a lonely one.

Perhaps you will argue that there must be something about the personalities of the unhappy housewives that makes them unhappy, whereas the satisfied ones just get on with it. If you think so, you are committing what social psychologist Richard Nisbett calls the fundamental attribution error: You are attributing a person's behavior to personality flaws and permanent qualities, when that behavior is actually produced by the constraints of the situation. When a person suffering from illness snaps angrily at you, you are likely to assume it is the illness speaking. When a person suffering from boredom and self-loathing snaps at you, you are likely to say, "What a bitch."

One way to test the cause and effect of personality and "housewife syndrome" is to follow a group of women graduating from college, women who are comparably high in self-esteem, intelligence, and ability. Get them 15 to 25 years later and compare the housewife-mothers with those who sought careers (married and single). You are likely to find, as Judith Birnbaum did, that the home-makers have the lowest self-esteem and feel the worst about their competence, even at childcare and getting along with people. They will feel the least attractive, most worried about their identities, and the most lonely. Saddest of all, they will even be less happy with their marriages than are employed wives.

The good news comes from the second way to test the cause-and-effect question: to observe what happens to women like Mrs. E. when they go back to work or find an occupation that provides a feeling of satisfaction and community. They leave the housewife syndrome behind.

MR. Q. AND THE AGGRESSIVE-EXECUTIVE SYNDROME

The encounter-group movement of the 1960s offered as good a deal as does born-again Christianity: Spend some time with us, convert to the faith, and your world will be transformed. A lot of transforming went on in those groups. Stuffy businessmen were induced to cry, ventilate hostilities, and reveal private worries. Styles of management based on fear, cutthroat competition, and authoritarianism were lacerated. The businessmen repented of their evil ways.

The postscript to the encounter sessions, however, was usually a letdown, not just for the participants, but for the researchers who hoped that these liberated businessmen would go home and humanize their corporations. Efforts to demonstrate the continued effectiveness of encounter groups usually fail. Berkeley Rice, a journalist who attended a recent seminar for business executives at the Menninger Foundation in Topeka, Kansas (many encounter groups are now called "seminars"), had this to say about the after-effects:

"I, too, left Topeka on a high, convinced I had somehow been through an important and powerfully moving experience. But when I returned to my home and my office, I had difficulty explaining what I had learned. I felt I had gained some insights into human behavior, but when I tried to explain them, I often ended up copping out: 'You just had to be there.'"

By the time Rice called his fellow participants a month after they had gotten home, the high had completely worn off. None of them felt that they had changed in any appreciable way, not with their families, not with their colleagues.

The lesson to be inferred from the experience of seminars and encounters is not that they aren't worthwhile, interesting, or correct in their analyses—or that businessmen are hopelessly rigid and competitive. The lesson is that inner conversion doesn't stand a chance in the face of corporate structure. By "structure," I mean those aspects of the work environment that reward certain "personality" traits over others, that foster insecurity and individualism. Most organizational psychologists and some companies understand this, which is why there have been many efforts to institutionalize the humanistic goals of the encounter groups. Unfortunately, it is often the case that humanistic goals are the first to go when they clutter up those numbers on the bottom line.

For much of the past decade, sociologists Melvin Kohn and Carmi Schooler have been following a random sample of American workers to find out just how jobs affect personality. Using complex statistics and comparing questions from the first interview with another after time has elapsed, they found, in essence that "job affects man more than man affects job." Aspects of the work—fringe benefits, complexity of tasks, pace, pressures, routinization—significantly changed the workers' self-esteem, anxiety, job commitment, intellectual flexibility, even their moral standards. The degree of complexity to a job was especially important, the researchers found: Constant challenges to the employee increased intellectual flexibility and self-esteem.

Sociologist Arthur Cohen demonstrated the power of job structure even more directly. He gathered a group of people, all relatively equal in ability and intelligence, and divided them into two committees, each with the same task. But he gave one group's members a high probability of promotion and individual credit, and no probability of promotion to the other. Right there in his laboratory he produced some supposedly stable personality traits. The first group got on with the task at hand. They dropped idle chit-chat and irrelevant conversation. They reported later that they liked their supervisors more than their co-workers. The second group, with the same task to do, chattered and gossiped more, practically ignoring the supervisors. Why not? They had nothing to gain from them anyway. They subsequently reported that they were critical and resentful of people with power.

You may notice that the difference between group #1 and group #2 is the stereotypical difference between men and women at work. But as sociologist Rosabeth Moss Kanter has demonstrated, those sex differences vanish when conditions of power, representation, and opportunity for advancement are equal. The participants in Cohen's two groups were men, and by the end of the study one group was behaving "like women."

What all this means for poor Mr. Q. and his worried family is probably not that Mr. Q. is a workaholic or a "naturally" cold-blooded competitor. It means that most of his behavior is an adaptive response to the demands of his company: to his worry that he may not get the presidency, that junior men are climbing up too fast; to his fear that if he doesn't keep moving up, he'll be moving out. These are extremely realistic concerns that derive almost entirely from the corporate system he is in, not from his "personality." If Mr. Q. wants to change his behavior, whether for his own or his marriage's sake, Band-Aid therapies will not be of much help. He will need to change the conditions of his job, and possibly, if his company disagrees with that effort, the job itself.

DR. S. AND THE "BURN-OUT" SYNDROME

The professional equivalent of the housewife syndrome has recently been named "burn-out," and some of the symptoms are similar. Burn-out, which is not the same thing as job tedium or plain old boredom, often afflicts people who, like housewives, feel they "shouldn't" be complaining—nurses, teachers, dentists, social workers. They have good jobs that are socially valuable and that offer plenty of challenge and complexity. Yet they run out of steam. They look at their colleagues who are working so hard and seem so satisfied, and then they feel guilty as well as depressed. They begin to retreat from work and place more emphasis on family life. When their families don't understand their anguish about work, they feel aloof even from them.

What is going on here? Social psychologists Ayala Pines and Elliot Aronson of the University of California have been working with groups of people who are suffering from this malaise. (Their book, *Burn Out: From Tedium to Personal Growth*, was published this fall by The Free Press.) The causes of burn-out, they find, typically originate in the structure of their occupations, not in some personality flaw. When burn-outs get together and talk about their needs, the following points emerge:

They lack the kind of intimate exchanges with co-workers that would help them realize that *they are not alone*. When the idealism that brought them to the career in the first place starts to fade, they fail to realize that this reaction is very common, if not inevitable, and so they doubt their commitment and their abilities. As far as they can tell, everyone but them is working at an energetic rate. Solution: to set up regular discussion groups that deal with these concerns, to establish regular lines of communication that solve practical problems and end each worker's social isolation.

Burn-outs lack a feeling of accomplishment, and they lack intellectual feedback and debate. They are rarely praised or supported for a job well done, nor are they criticized and evaluated by someone whose judgment they respect. Dentists are a good example. The typical dentist's office consists of the dentist, a hygienist (who is not at his level of expertise or training), a receptionist (ditto), and a terrified patient (ditto). There is no one around, in short, to say to the dentist, "Oh I say, what a splendid filling! What stunning root canal work! What artistry! What style!"—even if it *is* a splendid, difficult filling and stunning root canal work. (For many years my dentists have been oohing and aahing over some inlays I had done in California 15 years ago. *They* know a clever inlay when they see one.) The patient, who would be profoundly grateful to and appreciative of a surgeon who had performed a delicate operation and left no scar, just wants to go home.

The burn-out's social world, then, slowly constricts. Unconsciously, he or she begins to place all of his intellectual and emotional needs on a close friend or spouse, who usually sags under the burden. A spouse who is not in the burn-out's profession is not in a position to be mentor, adviser, evaluator, or problem-solver. The spouse can be supportive—"you're so marvelous, dear"—but a burn-

out knows the spouse *doesn't really know*. Having placed the burden of support on the spouse, the burn-out then blames the spouse for not being able to carry it.

The solution, say Pines and Aronson, begins with a re-arrangement of working conditions. For dentists like Dr. S., they recommend, first, reducing the number of patients crammed into a day. This gives the dentist more time with each; time to talk to the person, describe procedures, be reassuring, get to know the individual as something more than another mouth. This step, in turn, makes patients more responsive, less frightened, which makes the dentist's job more pleasant. Second, Pines and Aronson recommend that dentists stop trying to get their patients and wives to evaluate their work, and look to other dentists to peform this role. For each career Pines and Aronson studied, they found predictable changes in the working environment that soothe burn-out sufferers like honey on a raw throat.

THE FOREGOING ARGUMENTS suggest some conclusions that may be unpopular among the professional change-mongers of our society: 1) If so many aspects of our moods and personalities are keyed to what we do, rather than to idealistic notions of what we are or what we would like to be, it follows that if work and family circumstances change, so will we—and if they remain constant, so will we. The traditional stages of adult life—job, marriage, child, child leaves home, retirement, grandchildren—are no longer as predictable for most adults. Biological stages no longer guide us, and neither do social ones. New categories of change and new "stage theories" of adult development will not make sense unless they consider what adults have the opportunity, the desire, and the need to do. Adults grow and change, all right, but not at predictable intervals.

"The world is much more chancy than psychoanalytic theory would have us believe," says Nisbett. "Situations that people get into quite by accident have enormous impact on them, and that continues to be true throughout life. The dice just keep on rolling."

2) What does *not* cause change is any two-day or two-week program that takes you away from your everyday life and promises conversion, insight, or radical restructuring of your personality. Whether the program is sex therapy, est, an encounter group, or a weight-control clinic, the chances are very good that you will have a very nice two-day or two-week vacation and promptly return to your old habits and problems when the vacation is over. You might just as well have had a real vacation.

3) What does *not* cause change is any form of talk therapy designed to fix the self and the self only. Talk therapies may make you temporarily feel better, give you understanding of your problems, provide moral support from a wise expert. It's just that they won't help you change. Talk therapies may identify what you *want* to change, but that is not the same thing.

Many years ago, Hans Eysenck published a study showing that the cure rates for Freudian psychotherapy were no different from the rates of spontaneous remission. Most of our everyday psychological problems, like our medical ones, eventually go away by themselves (unless you happen on a psychologist who convinces you that you have a problem). Since that time, hundreds of studies have attempted to demonstrate the effectiveness of psychotherapy, all kinds of psychotherapy. Joel Fischer, a professor of social work, has recently summarized them, finding, all told, that Eysenck's conclusions "have been updated and seconded, particularly with regard to traditional, psychodynamically oriented therapies."

"The problem seems to be," Fischer comments wryly, "that many professionals fail to recognize the difference between *assertions* of effectiveness and *evidence* of effectiveness." They assert all the time, but the evidence is murky. Psychotherapy can be helpful, especially if the therapist is warm and empathic, but sometimes it slows down a person's natural rate of improvement. In a small but significant number of cases, psychotherapy can be harmful and downright dangerous to a client. Most of the time it doesn't accomplish much of anything.

I can hear the protesters already: "But it helped *me*! I would never have (taken that job) (divorced that bastard) (moved to Cincinnati) if it hadn't been for Doctor Blitznik!" Alas, you cannot be your own control group. What the studies with control groups show is that you probably would have taken that job, divorced that bastard, and moved to Cincinnati anyway, or taken other drastic action. Doctor Blitznik, like any good friend or your mother, just let you talk yourself into it. What the studies with control groups also show is that a hell of a lot of people end up talking to Doctor Blitznik for years . . . making no change whatsoever.

4) Well then, what does help a person change? Any therapy or action that intervenes in the social web that keeps him stuck. Anything that counteracts the bolsters of sameness. The therapy that is most specifically oriented to this is "behavior modification," which, for all its clumsy, big-brotherly label, has the best success record of any form of therapy. The label is a misnomer, actually, for it implies that a person's feelings and beliefs are of no account in the process of change. Behaviorists argue that if you want to feel better and change your beliefs about yourself, your behavior must change first. So they help their clients to identify the *specific* things that irritate or worry them and then to establish a program of action to accomplish the changes they want.

The research supports their approach. "There are over 200 controlled studies showing effective results using behavior modification," reports Fischer, "studies spanning the areas of psychotherapy and counseling, corrections, psychiatric hospitalization, and education." Some of these studies used a design that contrasted "be-mod" with other therapies or techniques, so that they could iso-late the most effective aspects. Be-mod helps, Fischer observes, because it is applied "in the situations where the problems actually occur."

But far and away the best therapy still is new experience. A good friend of mine—I'll call him Mike—had been in therapy, on and off, for about eight years, fighting his chronically low feelings of self-esteem. He wasn't much good at anything, he felt, and he didn't like himself besides. The arguments of his friends had no effect. Neither did therapy, although he allowed that he understood how his parents had created his sense of worthlessness.

Then Mike lost his job, a so-so job that nevertheless had been his anchor and security. His self-esteem, hovering at −3, plummeted to −27. But he had to eat, and so he joined the job circuit. One day he had lunch with some friends, who mentioned that their company was looking for someone to head a new department. The job had one of those awful descriptive labels, they apologized, "creative projects" or something, but it might be fun for Mike to try his hand at developing new ideas in his field. Was Mike interested? He hesitated. The word "creative" made his stomach sink to the floor. "I'm about as creative as a hedgehog," he said to his friends. They prevailed. He decided to try for the job, and he got it.

The effect, I have to say, was like sticking a live wire into an electric outlet. Mike lit up. The job was exactly right for him. His friends had to hold on to his leg to keep him from soaring. His self-esteem leaped to +32, and why not? He was doing beautiful work. Creative.

One day I said to Mike that his new career seemed to have done what years of therapy could not. "Oh, no," he protested. "Without therapy, I would never have had the guts to take the new job." But why, with therapy, did he not have the guts to leave a stultifying job?

The sociological view of the self and of personal change seems, to some, callous and anti-humanistic. It seems to imply that we are controlled by an invisible network of social constraints and that we never can master our own lives. I disagree. Rather than limiting our freedom, this approach expands it—far more than all the well-meaning, ego-massaging theories that surround us these days. By identifying the real causes of change and stability, the social perspective allows us to choose the productive steps to reach a goal, whether the goal is androgyny, sexual equality, self-fulfillment, or a good night's sleep.

Efforts to improve the self by introspection are doomed because the self is infinitely expandable and voracious. The irony is that self-improvement, like happiness, usually is found when you are looking for something else.

Examine Yourself and Find Your Future

AT THE HEIGHT of his fame, Albert Einstein was asked by a reporter: "How do you feel, knowing that so many people are trying to prove that you are not right?"

"I have no interest in being right," replied the great scientist. "I'm only concerned with discovering whether I am or not."

Too often we set out to prove ourselves right, not to evaluate a situation honestly. Too often we bring to our assessment a cloud of preconceived notions. Too often we see people—our boss, ourselves, whoever—the way we want them to be, the way we think they should be, or the way we fear they might be. We don't always see them the way they really are. We are blinded by our past experiences.

The price we pay for this blindness is incalculable. When truth is distorted for the sake of psychological comfort, it's impossible to take constructive action.

Learn to distinguish between what I call value-judging and evaluation. You are value-judging when you attach your own values, needs or beliefs to an appraisal and allow past experiences and prejudices to blind you. Evaluation is what Einstein had in mind—seeing reality for what it is, even if doing so proves your original assumptions wrong. Honest evaluation is liberating and always in your best interest.

One familiar form of value-judging

Managing your boss means knowing your boss and managing yourself. A most common failure in managing any kind of boss is failing to communicate—to not show clearly what you expect, to not find out what the boss wants. This is an excerpt from the book How to Manage Your Boss, *written by one of this country's top management consultants, Christopher Hegarty, with Philip Goldberg.*

is based on self-defense. We make ourselves feel tall by cutting off the heads of others. When, for example, did you last willingly accept the blame when something went wrong, instead of finding someone else to blame? If we are unhappy or frustrated, we tend to use people in higher positions as scapegoats. Bosses are one of our favorite targets. It is easy to feel resentful, easy to expect more of them than we have a right to, easy to blame them for our troubles. The problem is, sometimes they deserve it and sometimes they don't. The only way to know is to engage in objective evaluation.

Here are some examples of the difference between evaluation and value-judging. Suppose you are not getting along with your boss. A statement based on value judgment would be: "My boss is a real idiot. He can't understand me and he never will." Another example: You are frustrated over a lack of communication, and you say, "My boss doesn't know how to communicate with me."

Look at the difference between those

value judgments and these evaluations: "My boss and I are not getting along as well as we should. What can I do to improve the situation?" Or: "My boss and I are not communicating effectively. What can I do to make it better?"

Though subtle, such changes in perception hold tremendous value for you. The first style— the value judgment—will lead to more problems. The second style— evaluation—will lead to solutions. Evaluation is a major step toward higher awareness and effective action.

ANOTHER CATEGORY of value-judging involves self-blame instead of scapegoating. Just as destructive, it derives from the same source— low self-esteem. Some people have a need to put themselves down so that no one, least of all themselves, will expect much from them. A value judgment from such a person might take this form: "I'm such a jerk, it's no wonder my boss hates me." Or: "I'll never amount to anything. I can't even communicate with my boss." Value judgments distort the truth, and the truth is the first step toward making work really work. Look to your state of awareness (the sum total of everything you've learned and the values you hold); then you will know who you are and how to deal better with your boss.

The first thing we must establish is that you are where you are because of choices you have made. People who are

"Examine Yourself and Find Your Future," *Nations Business*, January 1981. Excerpt from the book HOW TO MANAGE YOUR BOSS by Christopher Hegarty with Philip Goldberg. ®1980 Christopher Hegarty. Lancaster-Miller Publishers.

having problems with their bosses have a tendency to feel victimized. "I can't stand my boss, but I'm locked into this position." . . . "I'd love to tell my boss where to get off, but I can't afford to lose this job." . . . "I'm trapped. My boss makes the rules and I can't do anything about it."

You always have a choice. To believe otherwise is to refuse responsibility for your life. Granted, it sometimes seems all the alternatives are dismal. But there are always alternatives, nonetheless. If you think of yourself as a choiceless victim, you will be weakened, if not paralyzed. If you are helpless in your mind, you are helpless in fact.

The person who accepts full responsibility for his or her reactions to events is more free than the person who sees himself or herself as a victim. If you adopt a positive attitude, you will be more alert to opportunities to change. If you pretend you have no choices, you will have none. The next time you feel trapped or victimized, realize the only place to look is at yourself—you choose your reaction.

You WORK where you work for whom you work by choice. Realizing that you chose to be where you are does two things: It creates a sense of freedom and responsibility; and it allows you to evaluate creatively whether or not to make new choices.

You are choosing to be treated the way you are at work. Even the most tyrannical boss cannot mistreat someone who chooses not to accept it. Your failure to take steps to change the situation is a signal to your boss that he or she can continue to treat you that way. By the mere fact that you did not speak up or quit when you were mistreated, you said in effect: "It's okay to do that to me."

Sometimes your situation may appear to be out of your control. But there is one thing over which you always have control: your reaction to your environment. While you may not be in control of a specific event, you're always in control of how you react.

Certainly, some bosses and some job situations are either beyond your ability to change or not worth the sustained and arduous effort. There may be irreconcilable differences between

you and your boss. Your boss may be 100 percent to blame for the conditions under which you struggle. But you are 100 percent responsible for how you react to them, and for where you go from here. No matter who put you where you are, it is up to you to do something about it. You can stay or leave—that is, and always will be, your choice.

If you are to understand your boss as much as possible, you should first learn to distinguish between him and the job itself. Many of the problems people attribute to their bosses have little to do with the boss' management style, his personality, his demands or anything else about him. The problems may be built into the career you have chosen, the company you work for or the nature of your assignment.

The key to biological survival is the ability to adapt to the occupied niche. The same can be said of work. How well do you fit your job niche? Or perhaps it would be better to ask: How well does your job fit you? Are you miscast in your work role?

THE BEST of bosses cannot make up for an inappropriate job. Be sure that your evaluation of your boss is not in fact an evaluation of your job. Keep in mind that working for an ideal boss in the wrong job is not paradise. In the long run, you are often better off choosing the right job with the wrong boss than the opposite, assuming the boss is tolerable and you will be able to move up and away from him quickly.

Bear in mind, also, that it is possible to obtain satisfaction from your work even with the wrong boss, as long as he or she doesn't prevent you from doing your job well.

Even if you have an unsolvable conflict with your boss, you may decide to stick it out.

Perhaps you don't want to handle the loss of income at this time. Perhaps you can benefit from more experience or some new contacts before looking for a new job. Perhaps you want to wait and see if things change—upper management may reorganize the company, the industry may shift gears or your boss may leave. Accept the fact that you have chosen to stay, and you will not be miserable like the person who spends his

days moaning in self-pity, believing he has no choice in the matter.

Until recently it was assumed that success meant choosing one's career early in life, joining a company and climbing the ladder in that firm until retirement. Moving from one profession, one career or one company to another was considered a sign of instability, even failure. According to Eugene Jennings, professor of management at Michigan State University, changing jobs "used to be abnormal, pathological, bordering on mental disturbance because of the disruption of a person's life."

THAT IS no longer true. A growing number of people believe that job security is not worth day after day of misery. No longer is it considered a sign of merit to do something you don't like until it's time to collect your gold watch. Changing jobs, or even careers, in the name of self-fulfillment is fast becoming socially acceptable, and in some cases admirable. Indeed, a 1978 study by the National College Board indicated that as many as 40 million people were at that time in the midst of career transition. It is estimated that the average American changes jobs once every three to four years.

In many cases, of course, staying where you are is the wise and pragmatic thing to do. You may be gaining valuable experience and connections; or other attractive jobs may be scarce. Family responsibilities may also cause you to choose to play it safe. But some people have such strong security needs, and the onus of unemployment weighs so heavily on their minds, that they would endure anything to keep their jobs— even a demeaning environment or a troublesome boss.

The option to change is available, and it might be the best choice. Although chronic or perpetual job switching will brand you as a bad risk, most employers are not as wary of moderate job changing as they once were. It is often seen as a sign of versatility.

If you are getting older, you may feel locked in because of your age. Many people think that once they turn 50, no one will want them. They may also feel stuck because of their company's pension or retirement plan. Those are legitimate concerns, but there is some good news. For one thing, there is increasing support for making retirement funds transferable to the new company after a person switches jobs. Second, more and more employers are beginning to realize that older people have much to offer. A study by Banker's Life and Casualty Company found that the productivity and reliability of workers over 65 was equal to, and sometimes better than, that of younger workers. People over 65, it turns out, are absent less often than younger people; their mental abilities are equal or superior; their health interferes with

their work no more often, and their health benefit claims are no more costly. Many people past age 50 have "started over." You can, too.

If you are highly self-directed, consider the possibility that you should not be working under any other person. If you have had a history of boss problems, that might well be the reason. Some people are better cut out for self-employment, or for independent positions, such as sales; but they delude themselves into thinking they can't make it except in a job where they are managed by someone else.

They might earn more money and be happier on their own.

A LARGE percentage of problems between bosses and subordinates stem from insecurities. One common problem is created by the need to be liked. Thousands of people who gripe about the way their boss treats them would discover—if they looked really closely at their feelings—that they are really asking to be loved. Their egos crave acceptance, often unconditional acceptance. To some, that means having the boss treat them as a

Your Ego: Primitive or Highly

Many intelligent and competent people have serious difficulty working with others because of what I call a primitive ego.

Their existence revolves around an attempt to guard the identity they project to the world. They spend a major portion of their energy defending themselves and their ideas—both to other people and to themselves. Because they have a strong, often overpowering need to prove themselves, these people often pile up notable achievements.

But the primitive ego acts as a barrier to compatibility. People with highly primitive egos often leave a trail of ruptured relationships behind them and are seldom invited to rejoin a group once they have left.

By contrast, people with evolved egos can deal with themselves and others in a straightforward way. Acknowledging freely that they don't have the final answer to every question, they ask others for help and are open to ideas.

Within their groups, they create trust, and they enhance the self-esteem of the members. They inspire compatibility because they don't need to prove themselves superior or to get credit for every achievement.

Sometimes popular, always respected, they strive for neither popularity nor agreement.

The following quiz will help you to evaluate how you relate to yourself and others. If you would like an assessment of your ego state, evaluate yourself as you are, not as you think you should be or would like to be.

Scoring

Never = 0
Sometimes = 1
Often = 2
Almost Always = 3

_____ 1. Is it frustrating when you cannot get people to do things your way?

_____ 2. Do you often find it difficult to stay with arrangements you have made after the people involved seem less important to you?

_____ 3. Do you enjoy being "center stage" (the center of attention)?

_____ 4. Do you pride yourself on being able to outfox others?

_____ 5. Are you someone who cannot be trusted?

_____ 6. Do you feel rage when be-

ing ignored or not receiving first-class treatment?

_____ 7. Do you put people down behind their backs?

_____ 8. Do you have difficulty enjoying your leisure?

_____ 9. Would you be embarrassed to be caught shopping in a store noted for low prices by someone you are trying to impress?

_____ 10. Do you drive a fancy car if it strains your budget?

_____ 11. Are you afraid to admit to others that you are sometimes scared?

_____ 12. Do you have to look your very best when seen by other people?

_____ 13. Are you seduced by praise even when you sense it may be somewhat insincere?

_____ 14. If unable to express felt anger at someone because of his or her rank or position, will you explode at an innocent person?

_____ 15. Do you feel uneasy when someone is receiving what you consider to be undue praise?

pal or a buddy. To others, it translates as a pseudo-parent relationship. You must distinguish between having a good working relationship with your boss and being liked or loved. Remember that trust is more important than affection, and that the latter is not necessary in a professional relationship.

A good relationship between boss and subordinate requires trust, honesty, mutual support and respect. It does not have to be friendly or intimate. The measure is not whether you invite each other to your homes. In fact, a lot of good working relationships deterio-

rate as soon as they turn into friendships, when the dynamics of personal involvement get muddled with the dynamics of work. It takes exceptional self-esteem to manage both sets of roles and expectations successfully.

BECAUSE OF dependency needs, we often want the boss to take care of us. We expect perfection of him, not just professionally but personally as well. As psychologist James P. Smith of Temple University put it, we ask the boss to be "reinforcing, nice, permissive, understanding and to think of all our needs even when we don't tell

him what we need. We feel he has nothing to do but worry about us."

Remember that no one—not your boss, not even your spouse—can have all your interests at heart at all times. They might not even know what your needs are unless you clearly communicate them. And in your boss' case, he might not care what your emotional needs are. Certainly, you should be treated with respect, but you were hired to perform specific tasks. The relationship is not meant to equal that of spouse or parent or friend.

Many of us are caught in a classic bind—it is difficult to live with the fact

Evolved ? Find Out

____ 16. Do you find it hard to pay a sincere compliment to someone who is doing better than you at your line of work?

____ 17. Do you often view people you meet as adversaries?

____ 18. Do you feel superior or inferior to certain people?

____ 19. Do you use people for your own advancement even if it damages them?

____ 20. Do you demand to be treated fairly (even in unimportant matters)?

____ 21. Do you mind other people talking a lot about themselves?

____ 22. Do you talk about yourself, your contacts, your accomplishments, etc.?

____ 23. Will you cover up something you have done poorly if you get the chance?

____ 24. Do you enjoy knowing that someone you dislike is having problems?

____ 25. Is it difficult for you to be gentle? Do you see it as a weakness?

____ 26. Do you make yourself a target of other people's anger?

____ 27. After scoring this questionnaire, will you discount the evaluation if you do poorly?

____ 28. Do you feel people are to be taken advantage of?

____ 29. Would you risk your life and perhaps the lives of your loved ones to prove your "courage", e.g., pursue a car recklessly on the freeway after it cut you off, to get even?

____ 30. Do you have a compelling need to prove yourself?

____ 31. Are you affected by other people's opinions of you in relationship to their importance and status?

____ 32. Do you believe that winning is the only thing, no matter what the consequences?

____ 33. Must you win even when enjoying your leisure time (golf, tennis, etc.)?

____ 34. Do you "validate" yourself even when your actions are not "valid", e.g., make lots of phone calls that are unnecessary?

____ 35. Are you attracted to people who constantly reaf-

firm how important you are?

____ 36. Are you overly sensitive when hearing unflattering comments about yourself?

____ TOTAL SCORE—To determine your ego quotient, add up the numbers.

(1) 0–25 You have reached a highly evolved ego.
(2) 26–50 You have a reasonably evolved ego.
(3) 51–75 Your ego is in a primitive state.
(4) Over 75 Your ego is in a highly primitive state.

Your total score is your "ego handicap." If your score is in categories (2), (3), or (4), you will benefit from implementing ideas to help lower your "ego handicap." In doing so, you will become more competent and creative in dealing with yourself and others. If you have done poorly and are upset by the results, recognize this not as something good or bad, but rather something that is, and that you can change.

7. ENHANCING HUMAN ADJUSTMENT

that bosses have more power than we do. Because we tend to respond to their personalities instead of their positions, it's easy to believe they don't deserve superior status. In order to accept their authority, we have to rationalize. The need to elevate the boss can conflict with a psychological block against accepting authority.

Whether ego needs are manifested as an excessive need for acceptance or a need to deflate authority figures, they can be a major obstacle to effective working relationships. Become aware of any conflicting feelings you have about your boss. Recognize that it's normal and even healthy to experience such feelings. Be certain you balance them and act in a constructive fashion toward your boss.

Fired!

Interview by Margaret S. Simmons

By year's end the U.S. unemployment rate may reach nine or 10 percent, the worst level since the Depression. Unemployment has replaced inflation as the country's top political issue. Widespread layoffs, firings, slow hirings, business failures—these signs of deep recession have left more and more Americans feeling insecure about their jobs. Quest/80 is particularly concerned about the consequent fear that may be corroding many lives. What if you suddenly lose your job: How can you avoid panic and take charge of your own destiny? How can you conduct an effective job search? How can you seize the initiative and begin a new career altogether?

To answer these timely questions, we recently interviewed Richard Bolles, a leading expert in job hunting and career counseling. Trained as an Episcopal priest, Bolles was fired from his last church during a budgetary cutback (see box, page 239). He promptly launched a new career of helping others to cope with the confusions of hiring and firing. Bolles is the author of the longtime best-seller What Color Is Your Parachute? A Practical Manual for Job Hunters and Career Changers, *and of a companion volume,* The Three Boxes of Life and How to Get Out of Them. *He is coauthor with John C. Crystal of* Where Do I Go From Here With My Life? *All are published by Ten Speed Press (Box 7123, Berkeley, Calif. 94707). For the past six years Bolles has served as director of the National Career Development Project of the United Ministries in Education.*

How can I tell when my job situation is deteriorating?

Often you can't, because terminations can occur for the most irrational reasons. Think of the president of CBS, fired at the height of his success. But in almost every office there is an invisible communication network—secretaries, etc.—who know what's going on. They get the signals before anyone else, and if they're friends of yours, they'll surely tell you if your job is in jeopardy. Workers on your own level will be the last to tell you what's going on, especially if they stand to profit by your departure.

What can I do to prepare myself before the ax falls?

My friend John Crystal, who has taught career planning for years, says that when you've finally landed a job, even if you're ecstatically happy in it, that's the time to start your next job hunt. Every job—no matter how secure it seems—is tenuous. A survey by a past president of the American Management Associations showed that the average worker goes job hunting every three years. Having options eliminates the quiet desperation that so many people feel about their work because they think there's nowhere else to go.

How should I go about planning for another job?

Every job hunt can be broken down into three parts: you have to know first what skills you have and enjoy using; second, where you want to use those skills; and third, how to locate and get hired by the organization that's right for you. You can figure out the answers to the first two questions while you're still in your present job. For example, if you have ability in graphics, would you rather work in a print shop or design a book jacket? Once you've answered these questions, you're ready, should the need arise, for the third part—the actual job hunt.

What does the actual job hunt involve?

The whole job hunt is a search for information. Let's assume you've already decided on the "what" and "where" of the job. You must now identify the kind of organization that has that sort of job (in your chosen geographical area), and how to get hired there.

Are people usually fired for professional or for personal reasons?

The reasons usually have less to do with professional incompetence than with poor self-management skills: the ability to get to work on time, to operate constructively under authority, to relate well to co-workers, etc. Often these traits are not evident until a person is on the job. And they're the hardest for an employer to level about.

How can I prepare my family for the likelihood—or certainty—of my being fired?

First, I would educate my family about the realities of the workplace—that people are fired for the most whimsical reasons—and I would do this before the eventuality of a firing is even on the horizon. Second, I would not try to hide the news from my family. You can't terminate communication in any key area of your life and expect your marriage to hold together. You have to involve your spouse, even your kids, in your decisions, your progress, your setbacks.

How closely related is being fired to other life crises, especially divorce?

One major job-counseling firm found that 75 percent of its clients had recently been involved in a separation or divorce proceeding. Hopelessness, depression, and idleness are consequences of joblessness, and they can cause you to find new comfort and strength in your marriage. But they can tear a relationship apart. Such a crisis reveals a marriage for what it is. It will survive to the extent that sharing and talking about feelings are already part of the fabric of the relationship.

Besides my family, where else can I turn for support when I've been terminated?

The best support you can get is from other people in the same situation as you, so that job hunting becomes a group effort. Nathan Azrin, who developed the concept of the job-hunting club, has produced a manual that tells you how to set one up in your own community. Essentially, his philosophy is that job hunting is a full-time job in itself, and that if we identify those factors that impede the

---

20,000 Hours at Stake

When you sit down and try to identify what it is that you want to do for your life ahead, you are planning an awful lot of time. A 40-hour-a-week job done for 50 weeks a year adds up to 2,000 hours per year. How long are you going to be doing it? Ten years? Twenty thousand hours. Fifteen years? Thirty thousand hours. It is worth spending two weeks of your life, or two months, or whatever it takes to plan well—so that what you do in those 20,000 or 30,000 hours is something you enjoy and something you do well and something that fits in with your sense of a life mission. Never mind being "realistic." For every person who "overdreams"—of doing more than his or her merits would justify—there are four people who "underdream," and sell themselves short. According to experts, 80 percent of the workers in this country are "underemployed."

---

search—loneliness, family undermining, etc.—then we can take steps to remove these obstacles. Often the person out of work is expected to do odd household chores and errands that consume valuable job-hunting time. To prevent this, a contract is drawn up that involves the family in aiding rather than impeding the search. And it works. These clubs have a higher rate of success than almost any other job-hunting method.

What about getting professional help?

I would urge everyone to first try to make it on his own, or with the support of other job hunters. But if that doesn't work out, the alternative is to find a counselor. The National Career Development Project publishes a referral list of about 300 people we have trained across the country.

But what if I find myself desperate, financially, when I lose my job?

If you're in desperate circumstances, try to find a stopgap job—one whose only purpose is to get you by when your savings are down to zero. The alternative is food stamps and welfare—a route that completely undermines the urgency of the job hunt. It fosters a slow erosion of self-esteem until you find yourself becoming more and more lethargic about looking for work. The stopgap job gives you the satisfaction of a real exchange of skills and time for money. And since it's often work that the person can't stand, it supplies additional motivation to find a meaningful job.

What are the psychological effects of being fired?

When your job dissolves out from under you—especially if you're unprepared for it—then you undergo a process analogous to the stages of grief that Elisabeth Kübler-Ross associates with death. We know that if a person suppresses his feelings (for convenience I hope you'll excuse my using the masculine pronoun for both men and women)—if he refuses to talk about his firing to anyone—then he's probably condemning himself to a long recovery during which his emotions will erupt in various strange ways and undermine his efforts to find a new job.

How long does that "recovery" period usually last?

It depends. One of the four stages of grief is anger, and that can be absolutely immobilizing. An employee can be so furious about his firing that his whole purpose in life is to prove that his ex-boss has permanently damaged his future. The world of work is strewn with people who have let themselves slide downhill for the rest of their lives after a firing. So your recovery will be shortest in proportion to your ability to deal constructively with your feelings.

How long should I expect it to take me to find another job once I've been fired?

That depends in part on how much time you devote to it. A study by an independent research bureau found that the average job hunter spends only five hours a week looking for work, so it may take him four or five months to find a new position. Most job-hunting clubs require members to spend every day, nine to five, looking for work. Some 80

He or she who gets hired is not necessarily the one who can do that job best, but the one who knows the most about how to get hired.

---

percent of these people find a job within a month, many within two weeks. But it also depends on how you go about the search and whether you do the necessary preliminary work. That means analyzing what your skills are and where you can best use them.

How many others will also be out there looking for a job in this recession?

In ordinary times, the government admits to about six million people out of work. But the government has a very limited view (to put it charitably) of what constitutes an unemployed person. For instance, if you're out of a job but did *any* part-time work recently, you're no longer regarded as unemployed. You're also off the list if you got "discouraged" and didn't look for a job during the last four weeks. Nor does the official estimate include those whom the government counts as "dropped out of the labor force" (students, the ill, disabled, etc.) even though they may still want a job. So a more realistic figure, some say, would be three times the official count in "good times." During a recession unemployment has traditionally risen three points, which means another three million out of work.

With so many unemployed, shouldn't I settle for any job I can get?

That's a common fallacy, and a lot of desperate people cling to it, especially during a recession. Compromising on what you'll accept leads to discontent, and often to another firing or quitting. So you're back to square one.

Claiming higher-level skills, then, can actually benefit me when I'm looking for a job?

Yes. With each increasingly specialized skill, there are fewer able to perform that function. So the higher the skill you can name, the less competition you'll find for the job that requires it.

How can I benefit from the experience of being fired? Is there a bright side?

Absolutely. First of all, if it makes you do a thorough inventory of your real skills, you're already ahead. Second, if it forces you to sit down and talk with your loved ones about what's going on in your life, it may strengthen your family life enormously. And if you've always been able to spend money rather freely and suddenly you have to tighten your belt and evaluate what you can buy, then you have to rethink your whole value system—something we do all too rarely. But beyond all this, there are some really essential truths to be gained about the world of work. Most of us operate on the assumption that if we do a good job, we'll be rewarded, promoted—in a word, secure. I think it's much more sensible to say, "The world of work is a pretty strange place, and I can never predict what's going to happen, and therefore I must have options and alternatives." This realization will make you much better prepared for what might lie ahead. So you needn't view a firing during a recession as an unmitigated disaster; it can be a time of opportunity leading to something much better than you've experienced before.

How do most people go about finding a job?

The traditional method depends on classified ads, employment agencies, recruiters, résumés, etc. It rests on two assumptions, both false. The first—and most fatal—is that someone else knows where the jobs are, whereas in reality, four out of five vacancies are not known to anyone but the employer, who fills them by word of mouth. A recent study conducted in San Francisco and Salt Lake City revealed that 75 to 85 percent of *all* employers in those cities did not hire *anyone* through want ads during the entire year. The second

assumption is that one should be looking for vacancies to begin with. When you go the traditional route you automatically give up control over the job search. The employer becomes the screener and you the "screenee."

How effective are the various traditional methods?

Several years ago the Census Bureau conducted a survey of 10 million job seekers. It revealed that none of these methods had a higher success rate than 24 percent. Of every 100 workers who used classified ads in daily or weekly papers, 24 found a job. The same percentage of those using employment agencies found work. For those working through the federal or state employment service, the percentage was 14; for college placement offices, 22.

As discouraging as these estimates sound, some think that even they are optimistic. Take private employment agencies, which exist theoretically to help the job hunter. The FTC has said that their success rate is only about five percent, if you count everyone who walks through the door looking for help. But the agencies are able to quote a much higher success rate, since they base their figures on a tally of actual clients—the much smaller number of "marketable" applicants they accept. And of course there's no guarantee that those who do land a job will be happy. While employers do their screening before hiring, most job hunters postpone theirs until after they've found work ("This is a lousy job; I think I'll quit").

What is the "numbers game" in the traditional job search?

It has to do with résumés—people in the form of paper—and what the odds are that yours will actually lead to a job. In one study of those who send out résumés, it was found that employers made one offer to a job hunter for every 1,470 résumés they received, on the average. That means that 1,469 out of 1,470 resumes do not result in a job.

Is there a better method of finding a job?

Yes. I call it the "creative minority" or "self-directed" approach. It assumes that nobody else really knows where the jobs are and that you should not really look for vacancies anyway, but for the places that please *you*. As soon as you make this decision, you open up the possibility of 14 million employers across the country. Now it's up to you—not someone else—to do the choosing. Of course, the more you cut down the territory, the easier it'll be to focus your energies. That is why it is so important to do your homework first—to identify your skills and where you want to use them. Then you can begin researching specific organizations.

Once I've identified the organizations that interest me, should I then apply to the personnel department, if one exists?

Only to find out more about the particular company, *not* to apply for a job. For the job hunter they mean one more screening step introduced into the job-hunting process. Unless it's an entry-level job you're after, the sole function of personnel is to pass you on to someone else who has the power to hire you.

How important are contacts?

They're crucial, first to the success of your research and ultimately to your job hunt. Most people think of contacts in too limited a sense. Anyone—whether you know him through business, church, college, even your gym—can be a contact. He may know the organization that interests you, the man or woman who has the power to hire you, his opposite number in a similar organization, or your predecessor. Or he may introduce you to someone who knows this person.

Who is the best person to see for an interview?

Very simply, the person who has the power to hire you. If you've done your research, you'll know exactly who that person is. At that point, one of your contacts might write you a letter of introduction or make a phone call to prepare the way so that you don't have to go through personnel.

How can I be hired if there are no vacancies?

Because in your research you've also unearthed the employer's problems and by now you know how you can help solve them, so he may be perfectly willing to create a new job just because he'll save money by doing so. (Problems always cost a lot.) There is usually a lapse between the time a boss first conceives the idea that he could use a person with certain skills and the time he gets around to implementing it. That's where you come in—with the answers. Contrary to widespread belief, it isn't experience or credentials that will get you a job, but your problem-solving ability. Now you are in the enviable position of being able to demonstrate your value—and with no competition, since you're virtually the sole applicant.

But won't the prospective employer see from my résumé that I've been fired, and hold that against me?

That depends on what you include in it. If it is the usual chronological résumé, there will be a noticeable gap to be explained. But what I advocate is a functional résumé, one that lists what you can do rather than where you have done it. It would say that by virtue of training, experience, or aptitude, you can perform the following kinds of functions in the following kinds of settings. It focuses on you as a worker rather than you as a job holder. It minimizes titles, which can be interpreted in many ways and often fail to reveal a worker's real skills and capabilities.

Do you have any other résumé-writing pointers?

Yes. If your résumé is to be effective, you must know why you are writing it (to create a lasting impression), to whom you're writing it (the person with the power to hire you), what you want him to know about you, how you can help him and his organization, and how you can support your claim so he'll reach a positive decision. Another piece of advice: never put in anything that would cause your résumé to be screened out. Never lie, but do select your truths carefully. Don't volunteer something that can be

The Creative Minority's Prescription

Once you have said that the fatal assumptions of the present job-hunting system are that the job hunter should stay vague, that employers decide where a job hunter works, and that employers see only people who write well, the prescription for the new system almost writes itself. Here are the few assumptions that are the key to success:

Key No. 1: You must decide just exactly what you want to do.

Key No. 2: You must decide just exactly where you want to do it, through your own research and personal survey.

Key No. 3: You must research the organizations that interest you at great length, and then approach the one individual in each organization who has the power to hire you for the job that you have decided you want to do.

construed as negative, such as having been fired or even divorced. While you're at it, you might figure out why you want a résumé in the first place. You should be out seeing people directly instead of inserting a piece of paper between you and them.

What is the key to a successful interview?

First, you must remember that you're talking to a particular person who has special enthusiasms and problems, and if you've done your homework, you'll know what they are and direct your conversation toward them. It may be up to you to take some subtle charge of the interview. An MIT study of job hunters showed a high correlation between those who got hired and those who during the interview spent about half their time asking intelligent questions about the organization and about half talking about themselves. They demonstrated an impressive knowledge of the company, but also revealed enough of themselves to be memorable.

In any interview there are four questions a prospective employer probably wants to know the answers to. Try to work them into the conversation. First: *Why are you here?* Second: *What can you do for me?* Third: *What kind of person are you?* (Remember to look professional. The man behind the desk takes in everything from dirty fingernails to chain-smoking.) Fourth: *How much are you going to cost me?*

Can you give me some tips on salary negotiation?

Find out before the interview what the salary level is for the kind of position you're shooting for or asking your prospective employer to create. He probably has in mind a range, usually $2,000 or $3,000 above or below that level, and it's worth bargaining for. If you don't bargain, he'll consider you naive, if not stupid.

Routes to Jobs

False Starts

Richard Bolles spent four years as canon pastor at Grace Cathedral, a large Episcopal church in San Francisco. In 1968 he was fired during a budget crisis. With only $800 in severance pay and a wife and four children to support, Bolles began a frustrating job hunt that lasted six months. Interested in pursuing a secular career, he first sought the help of an executive search firm. On the basis of an interview and various tests, the firm wrote up a résumé and mailed out over 600 copies. When these produced no responses, another 300 were sent out, again to no avail. Nonetheless, in keeping with standard practice, Bolles was out his initial fee of $800.

Bolles searched the classified ads daily, also without luck. He tried private employment agencies, which concluded that his "unusual background" made him a poor prospect for placement. (Most agencies don't understand "transferable skills" and are reluctant to take on a career changer for whom they can specify no previous experience in his chosen field.) Following up another lead, Bolles applied to an electronics firm but was turned down there as well.

About this time a placement director friend took a look at the résumé prepared for Bolles by the search firm. He found it misleading and unfocused—a catalogue of Bolles's past work experience, with no indication of his special abilities or possible areas in which he might use them. Eventually Bolles heard through another friend about a job in campus ministry—back with the church, but not quite. He was accepted for the position, which he still holds today. In his travels to various campuses, Bolles discovered that a number of campus clergy were also being laid off. They sought his counsel; his interest in the problem deepened. His subsequent research into job hunting and career planning served as the basis of his best-seller *What Color Is Your Parachute?*

A Letter That Worked

Midway through a master's program in health-care administration, Jane Proctor launched her first professional job hunt, using the self-directed method outlined in *What Color Is Your Parachute?* After deciding to focus on mental health administration, she wrote a basic letter that covered the following points, each in a paragraph: (1) a description of her target job; (2) an explanation of why she was writing to each individual recipient; (3) a brief outline of her work experience; (4) an indication of how she could help solve his problems; and (5) a request for an interview. With the help of her faculty adviser, Proctor pinpointed areas with expanding mental health facilities, together with key people to whom she then sent 107 letters and résumés.

Over 60 percent responded, nine of them with interview invitations and four others with application forms. After picking six facilities that interested her, she arranged for interviews, preparing herself beforehand by rehearsing her answers to the most commonly asked interview questions. She also equipped herself with illustrative posters and samples of written work that further substantiated her image as a competent and knowledgeable candidate. Offered several jobs, Proctor chose one as unit manager in a mental health facility in Ohio. After 13 months of valuable experience in line management and patient care, she began planning her next step upward.

Right Place, Right Time

Bob Wagner lived in Miami, where he had gained some experience in college administration. When he decided to change careers, he consulted an executive counselor, who helped him identify a new field—college career counseling—and where he'd most like to practice it, which turned out to be Washington, D.C.

Instead of depending on others to tell him about vacancies, Wagner took full charge of his job hunt. He flew up from Miami to research the campuses in the Washington area. When he was unable to find a counseling position with any of them, he decided to focus on the university that he liked best and to inquire there about its openings in other fields. At the very moment Wagner was being considered for a deanship, the career counselor at the same university announced his retirement. Wagner immediately shifted his application. Not only was he familiar with the university by now, but he could sell his own special skills to help solve the department's problems. Although he had never had a day's experience in career counseling, he landed the job—beating out more than 50 other candidates, all with Ph.D.'s and some with considerable background in the field.

The Phoenix Strategy

Howard Smith was earning over $25,000 in a manufacturing company when he was laid off during a severe recessionary period. A reputable career counselor helped him draw up a list of his skills by analyzing his experience both in and outside of the world of work. When Smith had completed his list, the counselor suggested that he show it to his former employer for verification. The feedback might be helpful to Smith in applying for his next job. When his ex-boss read over the list, he was staggered to discover the range of his own vice-president's abilities. About this time the president decided to reopen a plant that had been closed for two years. He put Smith in charge. Smith wound up with a better job from the very company that had fired him. And, together with Smith, about 100 other fired employees returned to work.

7. ENHANCING HUMAN ADJUSTMENT

How important is the discussion of fringe benefits to the negotiations?

Quite important. Things like health benefits, life insurance, vacation plans, retirement programs, and stock options may add up to as much as 25 percent of your pay. They are part of the package you're negotiating for.

Is it premature to discuss raises and promotions during the hiring interview?

Not at all, if you do so toward the end of the interview. You should not only ask under what circumstances you can expect an increase but, if you're hired, get it in writing. All too often verbal promises are conveniently forgotten once you're in the job. Suppose, too, that your employer leaves. His successor is under no obligation to you unless you can prove that he is. You should ask about promotion, too, since that means the possibility of more responsibility and more money. Given the current rate of inflation, a raise is necessary just in order to stand still.

How about references?

You should go to the interview with the names of five people who will attest to your personal and professional qualifications. They should be substantial citizens, successful, and respected in their own fields.

Should there be any follow-up to the interview?

It's rare that one is offered a job on the spot, even if the interview has been successful. It's to the advantage of both parties to think it over. But one thing you can do right away: send a thank-you note that very night.

How successful at landing a job is the approach you're recommending?

For 13 years John Crystal kept records of the people who have used this method, and he found that 86 out of 100 people found a job within three months or less as a result—and not just any job, but the one they wanted. Other people have found a similar rate of success with this approach—close to 90 percent.

There seems to be a growing trend among companies to use outplacement counseling. Just what services do these firms provide, and how useful are they?

When a firm fires someone of importance—usually an executive—it may bring in specialists to help that person find another job. How effective it is depends on the people running the program and the method they're using. In theory there is no difference between outplacement and executive counseling firms, except for one crucial fact—who pays for the services. But in many cases an executive search firm will simply do your résumé and help prepare you for the interview and that's it. You pay through the nose—often as much as $3,000—whether you find a job or not. The corporation, on the other hand, represents repeat business, so the outplacement firm will do the best possible job for them. Their future depends on it, so their track record is usually better.

How feasible is it to request a transfer into another department when I've been fired?

In general it's best to clear out and look elsewhere. But there are cases of employees who have done the kind of self-assessment we've been talking about while in their present job, and are therefore prepared when the boss starts cutting back, because of the recession or whatever, to go into his office with a list of their skills that so impresses him that he finds another position for them. So one minute you're in a job with a limit of X weeks and the next you have a whole new future ahead of you. The point is that the employer may actually have little comprehension of his own workers' capabilities.

Under what circumstances would you advise someone to fight a firing, even proceed with a lawsuit?

Of course there are cases of blatant discrimination when it's almost the worker's duty to contest the termination.

> **Always have your parachute prepared, for you never know when you will need it. Your own personal future planning, continuously, should be your firmest principle.** —John C. Crystal

But in most cases, it's senseless. You may succeed, but I'm not sure what you really achieve. It seems to me it's a Pyrrhic victory. All jobs depend on a rapport between workers and employer, which will have been seriously damaged. The way to deal with being fired is to look ahead, not backward. Remember that when Lot's wife looked back, she was turned into a pillar of salt.

If "last hired, first fired" holds true, would you caution against changing jobs or careers during a recession?

I think that maxim has only limited application. Of every 100 new jobs created in the last decade, something like 85 of them were created by government or small businesses and only 15 by large companies. Many large companies do indeed have set policies about firing during recessions. But they account for only about 15 percent of the job market. The majority of organizations are not that ironclad in their rules.

What is the "hidden job market" and how useful is it to someone interested in a new career?

The hidden job market refers to the creation of new jobs. And for the creative minority it is the key to the professional job market. One-third of today's jobs didn't exist 10 years ago. This is especially true whenever the economy is going through some kind of paroxysm like the energy crisis of 1974. New positions *must* be created.

Can I hope to land a good job or launch a new career if I'm over 50?

With the traditional job-hunting method, age works against you. But for those who take the more self-directed, creative route, age need not be a barrier.

How do I go about choosing a new career?

A new career is often the result of the kind of job search I've been advocating. If you do a careful analysis of your skills and think freshly and creatively about how you'd like to use them, you may very well find yourself in a field you've never even considered before.

How often does the average person switch careers?

An average person will undertake three careers during his lifetime. A woman who is a housewife and a mother already has two careers and embarks on a third the minute she enters the world of work. Some people have five or six careers, others even more.

If I'm embarking on a new career, is self-employment a good option?

Self-employment offers a faster route to bankruptcy than working for someone else. Even in good times, one out of every two businesses fails within five years and some a lot faster. If you do decide to go this route, be certain that you've chosen a business that you know a lot about. Make sure to do your homework, including interviews with people in a similar line of work. Learn what mistakes they've made. The most common pitfall is assuming you've invented the wheel, when some research might have tempered your zeal and saved your pocketbook.

How important is risk taking to the job search?

I think that risk taking is important to being alive. Harvard psychologist David McClelland has devised a clever test. He asks the subject to toss a set of ring quoits at a stake from whatever distance he likes. He finds that people fall into three predictable categories. Those in the first group stand directly over the stake and drop the rings right onto it—hence, no risk. Those in the second group stand so far away that they haven't one chance in 1,000 of hitting the stake—the denial of risk. Those in the third group stand at a reasonable distance, where there's still a challenge, but also the possibility of looping the stake. McClelland says that only the third group are achievement-oriented, not because they seek any risks, but because they choose *manageable* risks. So the job hunter must first define what are the manageable risks before he launches out into a new area. That's why an honest assessment of one's skills and capabilities is so crucial.

Do you have any last words of advice for the person out of a job?

Yes. What you think is going to happen to you probably will. If you believe that you're going to make it through the experience, hold your family together, and find a satisfying new job or career, then you'll do what's necessary to make that happen. If, on the other hand, you view this as the worst time of your life, if you fear that it'll break up your family, that you'll not find fulfilling work, then you very likely won't. So independent of what methodology you use in your search is the consideration of what you *think* is in store for you. A good motto for the job hunter is an ancient dictum from the church: "Pray as though everything depended on God. Work as though everything depended on you."

Further Resources

The Complete Job Search Handbook: All the Skills You Need to Get Any Job and Have a Good Time Doing It, by Howard E. Figler. Holt, Rinehart & Winston, $5.95, paperback.

Job Club Counselor's Manual: A Behavioral Approach to Vocational Counseling, by Nathan H. Azrin and Victoria A. Besalel. University Park Press, Baltimore, $14.95, paperback.

Who's Hiring Who, by Richard Lathrop. Ten Speed Press, $5.95, paperback.

The Truth About You: Discover What You Should Be Doing With Your Life, by Arthur Miller and Ralph Mattson. Fleming H. Revell Company, Old Tappan, N.J., $7.95, hardcover.

Job-Hunting Secrets & Tactics, by Kirby W. Stanat with Patrick Reardon. Westwind Press/Follett, $4.95, paperback.

Bernard Haldane Associates' Job and Career Building, by Richard Germann and Peter Arnold. Harper & Row, $10.95, hardcover.

Guerrilla Tactics in the Job Market, by Tom Jackson. Bantam Books, $2.50, paperback.

Sweaty Palms: The Neglected Art of Being Interviewed. Lifetime Learning Publications, 10 David Drive, Belmont, Calif., $14.95, paperback.

What to Do With the Rest of Your Life, by the staff of Catalyst. Simon & Schuster, $16.95, hardcover.

The John C. Crystal Center, Inc. 894 Plandome Rd., Manhasset, N.Y. 11030. (Tel. 516-627-8802.) Workshops and courses for job hunters and career changers.

The National Career Development Project. Box 379, Walnut Creek, Calif. 94596. Send an addressed, stamped business-size envelope for a free brochure.

WHO'S WRITING AND WRITTEN ABOUT

INDEX

Credits/Acknowledgments

Cover design by Charles Vitelli.

1. Becoming a Person
Facing overview—EPA Documerica. 15—Clemens Kalischer/Image Photos.
2. Sex Roles and Sex Differences
Facing overview—Photo by WHO/E. Mendelmann.
3. Determinants of Behavior
Facing overview—WHO photo by Jean Mohr. 94-95—Graphs by Nicholas Fasciano.
4. Problems Influencing Personal Growth
Facing overview—WHO photo by Jean Mohr. 106—Dr. Bruce Livett, from the British Medical Bulletin May 1973, modified from Ungerstedt, 1971. 108-109—Charts by Joey Reinlieb from Human Nature, July 1978.
5. Relating to Others
Facing overview—WHO photo by Jean Mohr. 152, 156, 157—Charts by Joey Reinlieb from Human Nature, February 1979.
6. Dynamics of Maladjustment
Facing overview—EPA Documerica. 174-176, 178—The Atlanta Journal and Constitution Magazine. 193—Dr. Leonard Maler; Dept. of Anatomy, University of Ottawa.
7. Enhancing Human Adjustment
Facing overview—Dover Publications/*Pictorial Archive Series*.

WE WANT YOUR ADVICE

ANNUAL EDITIONS: PERSONAL GROWTH AND BEHAVIOR 82/83

Article Rating Form

Here is an opportunity for you to have direct input into the next revision of this reader. We would like you to rate each of the 46 articles listed below, using the following scale:

1. **Excellent: should definitely be retained**
2. **Above average: should probably be retained**
3. **Below average: should probably be deleted**
4. **Poor: should definitely be deleted**

Your ratings will play a vital part in the next revision. So please mail this prepaid form to us just as soon as you complete it.
Thanks for your help!

Rating	Article	Rating	Article
	1. What It Means to Become a Person		23. "Old" Is Not a Four-Letter Word
	2. Erik Erikson's Eight Ages of Man		24. Facing Up to Death
	3. Adolescent Americans		25. Living Longer
	4. Does Personality Really Change After 20?		26. When Mommy Goes to Work . . .
	5. Becoming One's Own Man		27. The Father of the Child
	6. What We Know and Don't Know About Sex Differences		28. Disclosing Oneself to Others
	7. The Brain: His and Hers		29. Loneliness
	8. How Nursery Schools Teach Girls to Shut Up		30. Coupling, Marriage and Growth
	9. The More Sorrowful Sex		31. The Sexual Balance of Power
	10. The Psychological Pressures on the American Male		32. The Masked Generation—On the Trail Toward a Sense of Community
	11. Androgyny		33. The Good a Good Friend Can Do
	12. Breaking Out of the Lockstep		34. R.D. Laing: The Politics of Madness
	13. New Psychology: New Image of Man		35. On Being Sane in Insane Places
	14. The American Compulsion to Win		36. A Darkness at Noon
	15. Changing Channels: How TV Shapes American Minds		37. Boredom—New Disease of the Technetronic Era
	16. The Promise of Biological Psychiatry		38. Prisoners of Fear
	17. The Puzzle of Obesity		39. New Light on Schizophrenia
	18. Mental Patterns of Disease		40. Tracking the Causes of Madness
	19. Anxiety		41. Health as Transcendence of Environment
	20. That Helpless Feeling: The Dangers of Stress		42. Psychological Hardiness
	21. The Age of Melancholy		43. Shopping for the Right Therapy
	22. When Husband and Wife Disagree About Sex		44. You Are What You Do
			45. Examine Yourself, and Find Your Future
			46. Fired

(continued on back)

About you

Name _____ Date _____

Address _____

City _____ State _____ Zip _____

Telephone _____

---

1. What do you think of the Annual Editions concept?

2. Have you read any articles lately that you think should be included in the next edition?

3. Which articles do you feel should be replaced in the next edition? Why?

4. In what other areas would you like to see an Annual Edition? Why?

PERSONAL GROWTH AND BEHAVIOR 82/83

BUSINESS REPLY MAIL

First Class   Permit No. 84   Guilford, Ct.

Postage Will Be Paid by Addressee

Attention: Annual Editions Service
The Dushkin Publishing Group, Inc.
Sluice Dock
Guilford, Connecticut 06437

NO POSTAGE
NECESSARY
IF MAILED
IN THE
UNITED STATES